COMMUNISM IN KERALA

The Royal Institute of International Affairs is an unofficial body which promotes the scientific study of international questions and does not express opinions of its own. The opinions expressed in this publication are the responsibility of the author.

The Institute and its Research Committee are grateful for the comments and suggestions made by Dr David Taylor and Dr Maurice Zinkin, who were asked to review the manuscript of this book.

COMMUNISM IN KERALA

A Study in Political Adaptation

by

T. J. NOSSITER

UNIVERSITY OF CALIFORNIA PRESS
BERKELEY AND LOS ANGELES
for the Royal Institute of International Affairs, London
1982

University of California Press,
Berkeley and Los Angeles
©Royal Institute of International Affairs 1982
ISBN 0-520-04667-6
Library of Congress Catalog Card No. 81-71762
Printed in India

To the memory of
Professor A. H. Hanson 1913–1971

CONTENTS

vii

ANALYTICAL MAPS

Maps 1 and 2 and the outlines of all other maps used in this work are reproduced by permission of the Surveyor General of India, © Government of India copyright 1982. The territorial waters of India extend into the sea to a distance of twelve nautical miles measured from the appropriate base line.

DIAGRAMS

TABLES

PREFACE AND ACKNOWLEDGEMENTS

THIS book was originally intended as a joint work with Professor A.H. Hanson whose premature death in 1971 was a great loss to Indian studies. I am grateful to the Royal Institute of International Affairs for asking me to continue alone. With grants from the Institute, the Hayter Trust, and the Conference Fund of the London School of Economics I visited Kerala four times between 1970 and 1977, spending a total of one year in the state. Besides using sources not available in England I was able to interview most prominent communist leaders and a sample of second-line cadres, many non-communist politicians, and a cross-section of caste and communal office-bearers, plantation owners, farmers, businessmen, trade union officials, civil servants, journalists, and others in public life. I am indebted to all of them—and also to members of the public who volunteered their knowledge and opinions. The interviews were held, partly or wholly, on an 'off-the-record' basis and with two exceptions were conducted in English. Among those interviewees whom I can acknowledge by name are the late R. Sankar, E.M.S. Namboodiripad, kind enough to grant three interviews, Achutha Menon and A.K. Antony, Chief Ministers during the period under review, K.C. George, the late A.K. Gopalan, Smt. K.R. Gouri, Baby John, M.N. Govindan Nair, N. Sreekantan Nair, and the late T.V. Thomas. Dr R. Prasannan, Secretary to the Legislative Assembly, explained the workings of the Assembly with enthusiasm. Benedict Mar Gregorios, Archbishop of Trivandrum, offered a refreshingly practical insight into developmental issues. My thanks also go to several journalists, notably the Trivandrum political correspondents K.C. John of *The Times of India*, T.V. Krishnan of *Link*, S. Rajendran of *Kerala Kaumudi*, and K. Sampath of *The Hindu*, for their assistance. None is responsible for my interpretations.

Non-attributable material presents two problems for the author: checking its reliability; and its presentation as a source. In the first case I have endeavoured, wherever possible, to appraise contentious statements in the light of other interviews and documentary evidence. In the second I have indicated in the relevant footnote the party affiliation of the source, his or her status (for example, minister, party organizer), and the month and place of interview, but have withheld status and place when their specification could identify the person concerned. The footnotes also show whether there are other interviews or material against which the statement has been tested.

In assessing the social basis of communist support I used outline maps to illustrate party support by constituency, certain census information prior to 1971 by taluk, and census data for 1971 by constituency — and also used these last-mentioned data in a multiple regression analysis of the 1967 and 1970 Assembly election results. An adult opinion survey proved impracticable but Dr B. Dharmangadan of the Department of Psychology, University of Kerala, and I conducted a survey of teenage political opinion in 1974 in Trivandrum District, drawn on in part here.

The author does not speak Malayalam, the language of Kerala. However, English is in widespread use in the state. All government documents are printed in English; there is a valuable English synopsis of Assembly proceedings; and the more important communist literature is also generally available in English. The same considerations apply to academic work. Some biographies and autobiographies are available only in Malayalam, although the communist parties normally publish in both languages. Probably the greatest problem is the press. Of sixty-five daily newspapers circulating in Kerala in 1977 only two were in English and three were bi-lingual. I am therefore most grateful to Shri Sampath of *The Hindu* for access to his translations of the local language press, to the Public Relations Department of the state government for access to its English language digest, and to members of the Department of Politics, University of Kerala, for translating certain Malayalam material.

In view of the time-lag in the publication of certain types of government documents, the retrospective character of Legislative Assembly committee scrutiny (the results of which may be published as much as five years in arrears), and the special difficulties of attesting facts for the Emergency of 1975-7, I have judged it premature to consider communism in Kerala politics in depth beyond the mid-1970s. Nevertheless, where possible and where appropriate I have indicated what appear to be the broad lines of development up to and including the return of the Marxist-led Left Democratic Front government as a result of the mid-term election of January 1980.

I record my thanks to the Kerala units of the Communist Party of India and the Communist Party of India (Marxist); to the University of Kerala; to the academic and library staff of the

Kariavattom Campus post-graduate Department of Politics, especially the late Professor V.K.N. Menon, Professor Sukumaran Nayar—who became Vice-Chancellor of the University of Kerala—and to the head of the department, Professor Ramakrishnan Nair; to the Centre for Development Studies, Trivandrum, led by Dr K.N. Raj; to the Communist Party of India Library, the English Archives, the University Library, the Legislative Assembly Library, and the Secretariat Library, all at Trivandrum; to the India Office Library, London, and the library of the School of Oriental and African Studies, University of London. I am grateful to colleagues at the London School of Economics: the staff of the British Library of Political and Economic Science; the Drawing Office, where Mrs Eunice Wilson, Janet Baker, Elizabeth Birkett, Barbara Glover, Anne Orchard, and Jane Shepherd converted rough drafts into maps; Dr Richard Martin for statistical advice; and Keith Taylor, Verity Burgmann, Jason Myers, Dr Philip Paur, and Deborah Woods for research assistance. I have been exceedingly fortunate in enjoying the guidance of Miss Rena Fenteman of the Royal Institute of International Affairs, who has done all that an author could wish of an editor. Finally, I warmly acknowledge the personal encouragement of Shri S. Anantakrishnan, Dr M. Balakrishnan, Dr B. Dharmangadan, Mrs Joan Hanson, Mr and Mrs Derek Holroyde, Shri Samsul Huda, Shri D. Jayaraj, Shri K.P.S. Menon, Shri K.S.S. Nambudiripad, Shri Apa Pant, Professor Ramakrishnan Nair, Shri Sony Sebastian, Shri S. Varadachary, Shri R. Veeramony, Shri George Verghese, Mr Ralph Whitling, and my wife Jean. (It is a particular sadness that Professor Ramakrishnan Nair, who, with his family, was such a dear friend to so many, should have passed on early in 1981.)

T.J.N.

The London School of Economics and Political Science
February 1980

1

Introduction

THE state of Kerala occupies a narrow strip of land on the southwest coast of India, 360 miles long and nowhere more than 70 miles in width, bounded to the west by the Arabian Sea and to the east by the Western Ghats. Formed in 1956, it is a small state by Indian standards and might have remained as neglected by the outside world as its constituent elements (Travancore, Cochin, and Malabar) but for the fact that in March 1957 Kerala became the first—and until 1977 the only—Indian state to elect a communist government. Apart from the tiny Italian principality of San Marino it was the first case of a democratically elected communist government in the world. The Communist Party of India (CPI) secured 38 per cent of the poll and one seat less than an overall majority in the Assembly. Overnight Kerala became identified with the new communist strategies of 'peaceful transition' and 'the parliamentary road to socialism'.[1]

The experiment was short-lived. The new government found office a turbulent experience. Its attack on vested interests in land and education generated powerful opposition which culminated in the so-called Liberation Struggle of 1959, aimed at persuading the central government to intervene to end 'tyranny' and 'anarchy'. Twenty-eight months after the ministry assumed office the Union cabinet under Prime Minister Nehru advised the President to exercise his powers under Article 356 of the constitution. On 31 July 1959 the ministry was dismissed, the Assembly dissolved, and President's Rule declared—and a non-elected caretaker administration under the Governor of the state was installed. Controversy increased when, in the ensuing Assembly election on 1 February 1960, the CPI increased its share of the poll on an exceptionally high turnout, only to lose 31 seats in the face of a temporarily united opposition.

The communists' chance of again winning sole power through the ballot box was diminished by the nation-wide split in its ranks in 1964. However, the break up of Congress—the movement's main rival in Kerala—in 1965, its growing unpopularity, and the general fragmentation of the Kerala party system opened the possibility of pursuing popular-front tactics. The Communist Party of India (Marxist) (CPM), which had established itself as the mass-backed

1

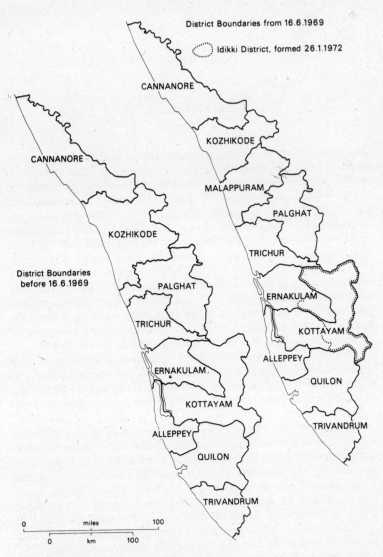

District Boundaries from 16.6.1969

Idikki District, formed 26.1.1972

CANNANORE

KOZHIKODE

MALAPPURAM

PALGHAT

TRICHUR

ERNAKULAM

KOTTAYAM

ALLEPPEY

QUILON

TRIVANDRUM

CANNANORE

KOZHIKODE

District Boundaries
before 16.6.1969

PALGHAT

TRICHUR

ERNAKULAM

KOTTAYAM

ALLEPPEY

QUILON

TRIVANDRUM

0   miles   100
0   km   100

The territorial waters of India extend into the sea to a distance
of twelve nautical miles measured from the appropriate base line.

Based upon Survey of India map with the permission
of the Surveyor General of India.

© Government of India Copyright 1982

Map 1 Kerala: District Boundaries

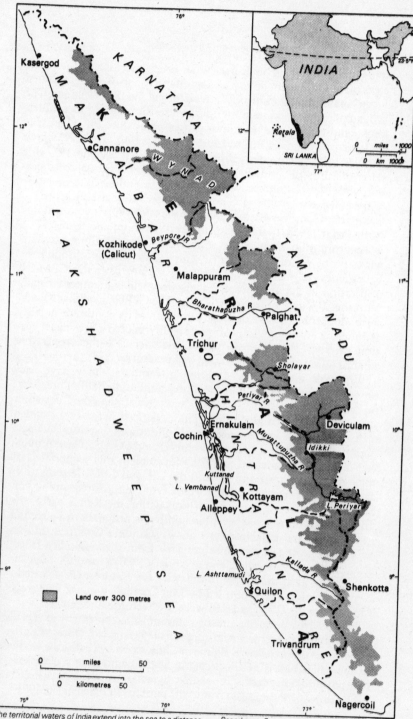

KARNATAKA

Kasergod

INDIA

23·5°N

MAHE

Kerala

SRI LANKA

miles 1000
km 1000

12°

Cannanore

WYNAD

MALABAR

L
A
K
S
H
A
D
W
E
E
P

11°

Kozhikode
(Calicut)

Beypore R

Malappuram

TAMIL NADU

Bharathapuzha R

Palghat

R

Trichur

C
O
C
H
I
N

Sholayar

Periyar R

Deviculam

Ernakulam

Muvattupuzha R

Idikki

Cochin

Kuttanad

T

L. Vembanad

R

Kottayam

A

Allepey

L. Periyar

V

Kallada R

A

N

L. Ashttamudi

C

Shenkotta

Land over 300 metres

Quilon

O

R

A

Trivandrum

miles   50

kilometres   50

Nagercoil

75°   76°   77°

The territorial waters of India extend into the sea to a distance
of twelve nautical miles measured from the appropriate base line.

Based upon Survey of India map with the permission
of the Surveyor General of India.

Note: Karnataka is the name adopted by
        Mysore State in 1973.

© Government of India Copyright 1982

Map 2 Kerala 1971

wing of the old CPI in Kerala in an otherwise inconclusive state election in 1965, went on to lead a seven-party anti-Congress United Front, including the rump CPI, to victory in the 1967 elections. The ministry lasted thirty-one months before succumbing to conflicts between the CPM and the minor parties led by the CPI.[2] Thereafter till January 1980 the CPM remained in opposition. The CPI, whose popular base was modest, if not minuscule, led (save in 1977-8) a series of ministries initially in collusion and later in formal collaboration with New Congress, which in the party's official interpretation represented the progressive section of the national bourgeoisie: a five-party Congress-backed Mini Front (1969-70); a reconstituted Mini Front (1970-1) following the 1970 election; and from 1971 a Maxi Front ministry made up of the Mini Front and Congress. This Maxi Front continued in office with minor changes through the Emergency to win an overwhelming victory over the CPM-led opposition in the only provincial election held contemporaneously with the 1977 parliamentary election. The CPI claimed that Kerala, once the 'problem state of India' by reason of its political instability as much as anything else, had successfully piloted a provincial version of the CPI's line of 'national democracy'—the progressive alliance of burgeoisie, proletariat, and peasantry.

Whatever merits these coalition governments may have had, however, there was no gainsaying the continuing hold of the CPM on the underprivileged nor the dangerous isolation of the CPI within such broadly based coalitions. The revamped Maxi Front which took office in 1977 experienced increasing strains, part local and part national in origin and skilfully exploited by the CPM. These provincial difficulties coincided in 1979 with fundamental reappraisals of their respective positions by both the CPI and CPM, leading to an agreement to forge a Left Democratic Front in the forthcoming Lok Sabha poll. Despite some opposition within the Kerala party, the CPI Chief Minister tendered his ministry's resignation, so ending nearly ten years' collaboration with Mrs Gandhi's Congress. Efforts to salvage a non-communist ministry from the Assembly failed; state elections were called; and in January 1980, a fortnight after the Lok Sabha poll, the CPM-dominated LDF handsomely defeated a United Democratic Front, led by Mrs Gandhi's wing of Congress. Once more the CPM and CPI were in government together.

If 1959 had been the end of communist involvement in Kerala government, the experiment might have been cited, along with the experience of the Allende régime in Chile, as evidence that the verdict of the ballot box is not respected in liberal democratic societies and that peaceful transition is impossible. In fact communists have been in office almost continuously from 1967 until the LDF fell in late 1981.

The CPM provided the Chief Minister from 1967 to 1969 and again in 1980, and the CPI the Chief Minister from 1969 to 1979, except for an eighteen-month interruption in 1977-8. Surprisingly, then, there has been no recent full-length treatment of the communist experience in Kerala or Kerala's experience of communism. Yet *mutatis mutandis* Kerala arguably represents the Euro-Communism of Asia. As such it deserves attention from students of comparative communism and development strategies as well as of Indian politics.

Publicly both rival communist units accepted the possibility of a peaceful transition to socialism in India. With differing emphasis they concurred in seeing the parliamentary front as one area of popular struggle. Thereafter the CPI and CPM diverged in ideological terms as a consequence of their contrasting views of the nature and role of the Indian bourgeoisie. For the CPI important sections of this class were progressive in character. Given the weakness of the organized left, it was logical to pursue the tactics of the 'united front from above'—the expedient manipulation of middle-class nationalism and democratic socialism to strengthen the party's own appeal to the people. To the extent that Mrs Gandhi's Congress was a progressive force, the CPI could and should forge alliances with it. Such deals, however, were not to preclude opposition elsewhere in India and in other arenas of political activity—the policy of 'unity and struggle'.

In contrast the CPM perceived little difference between Mrs Gandhi's New Congress and the parent body: basically both were obstacles to the march of 'people's democracy'. Mrs Gandhi's Congress was indeed the principal enemy whose destruction was the prime object of work on the parliamentary front. On the basis of 'my enemy's enemy is my friend', the CPM was prepared to ally with parties which were in some respects more reactionary than Congress itself, drawing the line only at *ad hoc* unity with communalist forces. Such tactical arrangements frequently tested the loyalty of cadres as well as the mass base. In general, however, the CPM approach approximated to the strategy of a 'united front from below', grouping small parties with a popular base together for common action on immediate popular grievances on the presumption that the superior organization and consciousness of the Marxists would secure additional recruits to their party.

At the All-India level the chance of communists even sharing in power was realistically seen as a remote possibility. Thus the debate turned on the meaning and utility of holding office at the provincial level. The CPI argued that some fundamental changes in social relations were feasible within the existing constitutional framework, especially in the light of the emergence of a progressively inclined national bourgeoisie, whereas the CPM allowed no more than 'minor' improvements—the qualification was a flexible one—in the people's condition. Such pessimism did not preclude participation in state-level ministries since office could be used to demonstrate the futility of the existing system and underline the class character of post-Independence India when just demands and progressive initiatives were obstructed by the central government or frustrated by the provincial state apparatus—the bureaucracy, judiciary, and police. Administration was to be married to agitation.

Neither the CPI nor the CPM arrived at their readings of the Indian situation entirely by the process of pure reasoning, dialectical or otherwise. It would be naive to assume that the public formulations of revolutionary parties are necessarily the same as their private objectives. However, both marxists and non-marxists alike allow that practice modifies theory. What follows is an attempt to analyse and evaluate communist parliamentary and governmental activity in Kerala in these terms, taking account of the origins and development of the party prior to the formation of the state, the unique structures and problems of Kerala, the pressures of the subcontinent's most literate and politically sophisticated electorate, the peculiar features of the Indian constitution in theory and the Indian polity in action, and national and international pressures within the communist movement.

Kerala is not a sovereign state but part of the Indian union. To that extent its significance may be somewhat restricted. The study of Kerala, it could be argued, is analogous to the analysis of the record of the Italian Communist Party in regional and municipal administration. In general such a view, however, minimizes the extent to which provincial and local patterns of politics may be reflected later at the national level, and in particular ignores the differences in constitutional arrangements between Italy and India and in the size of, say, Emilia Romagna and Kerala. Popular turnout at elections is, it may be noted, much higher in state than in Lok Sabha polls—the reverse of what might be expected.

India is neither a federal nor a unitary system, hence the common but untidy designation 'quasi-federal'.[3] Although the constitution guarantees the existence of states, the central parliament can create new ones, abolish existing ones, or alter their boundaries simply by majority vote. The constitution divides legislative powers into three groups, Union, State and Concurrent, of which the longest and most important is the Union list. Of the 66 items on the state list, 30 deal with ordinary police functions and 22 with taxation, leaving 14 items of 'development', of which the most important are education, health, agriculture, and industry. Most, however, are hedged about with qualifications; and in certain circumstances the Centre may override state powers. The concurrent list adds 'economic and social planning', trade, and repeats industry but, where there is conflict, laws passed by the central parliament prevail over those passed by the states. At the executive level there are also decided constitutional limits to provincial autonomy. The source of executive authority is the state Governor, appointed by the President. This power is normally exercised by the provincial council (cabinet) of ministers but the Governor has important discretionary functions: he initiates the process of forming a ministry and has the power to declare that no ministry is possible. Such powers give the Governor (and indirectly the governing party at the Centre) considerable influence in situations where no party has an absolute majority: he may 'reserve' bills passed by the provincial Assembly for Presidential consideration; and he has the right to advise the President to assume the government of the state. The actual administration of the state is in the hands of the All-India Services; and the Chief Secretary, the most senior administrative officer in the state, can therefore find himself subjected to a division of loyalties.

The distribution of taxation also disadvantages the states, since the Centre enjoys the most important and growing sources of revenue. The states depend on three limited sources: their own powers of taxation specified in the constitution; a share of centrally raised taxes consequential on the recommendations of the quinquennial Finance Commissions; and the Plan allocations. The main taxes available to the states are land revenue, agricultural income tax, sales and vehicle taxes, and local excise and estate duties. Historically land was the basis of state revenue. Since there is little possibility of expanding the amount of cultivable land, any increase in the offtake from land revenue is conditional on an enhancement of the rates. In turn, such increases would have to depend upon rising disposable incomes among cultivators—which have so far proved elusive. It is true that the state retains the power to levy agricultural income tax on commercial plantations and the like. However, apart from the ease with which this tax can be evaded, the potential of this source of revenue has been eroded by the diffusion of land ownership in Kerala arising from the partition of joint family properties and the impact of land reforms and their evasion. As in most Indian states, the chief source of revenue has become commodity taxation in the form of sales tax on items of mass consumption. This is regressive, politically unpopular, and, given low standards of living, finite.[4]

Under the constitution the Finance Commission, appointed every five years by the President, is a quasi-judicial body whose findings are usually accepted by the Centre. It recommends how centrally collected resources should be distributed between the Government of India and the states, how the states' share should be distributed among states, and what principles should govern the allocation of grants-in-aid to individual states. The Commission recommends how just over one-third of all the resources transferred from the Centre to the states shall be distributed, 85 per cent of this as the states' share of central taxation and 15 per cent as statutory grants-in-aid to meet the budget deficits on revenue account. In both cases the transfer is unconditional: the monthly cheque may be spent exactly as the state government thinks fit.

The Planning Commission is a non-statutory body concerned with 'plan' as opposed to 'revenue' expenditure. In practice this is an ambiguous and unreal distinction which has led to strained relations between the two commissions and much discontent in the states. The Planning Commission transfers resources to the states in two forms, Central Investment for projects of All-India significance and Central Assistance for approved local projects. Increasingly, the latter has been in the form of loans which have come to dominate the total transfer of resources from the Centre to the states. In consequence the states have run deeply into debt. In Kerala in 1968 it was costing the state Rs 160 million just to service its accumulated debt to the Centre. By the early 1970s many states were being driven to unauthorized overdrafts with the Reserve Bank to avoid 'bankruptcy'. State responsibilities have outrun income, and some would argue that central income is disproportionate to its functions.

This summary of the legislative, executive, and financial aspects of Centre-State relations, however, exaggerates the degree to which the states propose and the Centre disposes: it unduly diminishes the actual autonomy of the states. The Centre depends on the states to a large extent for the implementation of its policies as well as for the execution of those duties reserved to the states. As Morris-Jones says, the character of Centre-State relations has been one of co-operative and hard competitive bargaining.[5] Relations vary from time to time and from state to state, depending on an array of political factors including the unity and standing of the central government and the strength and determination of the state or states concerned. In cases where there have been non-Congress state governments the relationship has often been acrimonious but the victory of the Centre, either total or partial, is by no means guaranteed.[6] In normal circumstances the states' position is thus not entirely the subordinate one of constitutional theory. Six hundred and fifty million people could not be governed in a liberal democracy without a substantial measure of decentralization of power, especially when language and culture so divide them. Individual states certainly enjoy a kind of relative political autonomy but whether this extends to the transformation of social relations, notably in the field of land reforms, or the pursuit of the economic goals of growth and redistribution is a question which should be considered in the light of the evidence in subsequent chapters.

Kerala's provincial status under the Indian constitution also needs to be set in the context of its population in world terms. In 1971 its population of twenty-one million was larger than that of several European states including Czechoslovakia, East Germany, and Hungary as well as Chile, Cuba, and what was North Vietnam. More people speak Malayalam, the language of Kerala, than speak Bulgarian, Czech, Hungarian, Rumanian, or Serbo-Croat.

Within the Indian communist movement Kerala's significance is considerable. Historically communist support has been marked in only two other states, West Bengal and Andhra Pradesh, and in the city of Bombay.[7] Prior to the split, the size of the party and the quality of its leadership ensured Kerala an influential position in the formation of Indian communist party policy in so far as this was independent of Soviet guidance. After the split the CPM virtually became a two-state party based on Kerala and West Bengal. After a brief period of enthusiasm for the Chinese line the CPM became an internationally independent communist party; and the influence of the Kerala leadership, notably that of E.M.S Namboodiripad, the party's major theoretician, has been pronounced. In the case of the CPI, support has been more evenly spread over some seven states and the party has unambiguously remained within the Soviet orbit; thus the impact of the Kerala party probably owes more to its sympathy with the Soviet reading of the Indian situation and to the personal status of some of its leaders including C.Achutha Menon and M. N. Govindan Nair than to its inherent weight in party councils. Since the early 1950s the political lines first of the united CPI and then of the two wings of the movement have remained generally congruent with the lines taken by the Kerala parties. Until such time as the communist movement establishes a real base in the Hindi-speaking area of north India Kerala's influence on the communist movement in India is likely to remain strong.

Like Franda on West Bengal, the present author emphasizes the regional moorings of communism in Kerala.[8] There are, of course, important commonalities of socio-economic structure in India but the failure of communist movements thus far to strike deep roots in the country as a whole justifies close attention to the unique features of Kerala's history, geography, society, culture, and economy. These matters form the core of the next two chapters. Chapter 2 begins with a brief examination of those geographical, linguistic, and cultural factors which gave Kerala a distinct identity as a region of India. It then examines the major internal differences and their causes within the state, as constituted in 1956, in terms of its political history, agrarian relations, levels of development, and its caste and communal structure. Lastly the chapter outlines the way in which the component parts of Kerala have been integrated to give a distinctive political culture which both accommodates and transcends the continuing diversity of sub-cultures in the society. Chapter 3 outlines the economic background, including the demographic pressures on land, food, and employment.

The fourth chapter considers the development of the communist movement in Kerala up to 1950 and the fifth its emergence as an electoral force from 1951 through 1957 to the peak of its popular support in 1960, against a background of the ideological differences within the CPI over its correct tactical line. Chapter 6 reassesses the objectives, record, and demise of the first communist ministry. Chapter 7 considers the impact on the Kerala party of the 1964 split in the communist movement and evaluates the relative strengths of the CPM and the CPI as evidenced in the 1965 mid-term election in the context of the general fragmentation of Kerala's party system between 1960 and 1965.

Chapter 8 outlines the genesis of the United Front, the temporary accommodation of the rival communist parties, and explains the Front's 1967 electoral success. Chapter 9 provides the political background to the subsequent period of Front government from the perspective of the electorate's search for ministerial stability and its desire for governmental action to ameliorate Kerala's problems. Chapter 10 then analyses Front politics in relation to communist theory as adumbrated by the CPI, CPM, and the breakaway groups, including the Naxalites, who rejected parliamentarism not only as a strategy but also as a tactic. Chapter 11 discusses Front politics from a developmental perspective, assessing the reality of the structural constraints set by Centre-State relations and evaluating the ministries' performance in selected key areas.

The last substantive chapter discusses the electoral basis of party support in Kerala between 1967 and 1977 with particular reference to the communist parties, using both qualitative and quantitative methods. In that chapter, in the introductory material of chapter 2, and in the consideration of the emergence of communism as an electoral force, maps are presented to illustrate the striking political geography of the state. Finally, the epilogue summarizes the author's findings and considers the future prospects of communism in Kerala.

No attempt has been made here to discuss party organization systematically: the problems of obtaining reliable information on this issue and the need to keep the study within manageable bounds militated against the inclusion of such material.

Notes

1 See R. Ramakrishnan Nair, *How Communists Came to Power in Kerala* (1965); V.M. Fic, *Kerala: Yenan of India* (1970, title abbreviated hereafter to *Kerala*) and *Peaceful Transition to Communism in India* (1969); M. Turlach, *Kerala: Politisch-Soziale Struktur und Entwicklung eines Indischen Bundeslandes* (1970); Robert L. Hardgrave Jr, 'The Kerala Communists', in Paul Brass and Marcus Franda, eds., *Radical Politics in South Asia* (1973).

2 K.V. Varughese, 'The Seven Party United Front Government in Kerala', in Saral K. Chatterji, ed., *The Coalition Government* (1974).

3 K.V. Rao, *Parliamentary Democracy of India* (1961), ch. IX.

4 Govt of Kerala, *Report of the Taxation Enquiry Committee* (1969), pp. 123-58.

5 W.H. Morris-Jones, *The Government and Politics of India*, 3rd rev. edn (1971), p. 152.

6 A.H. Hanson and J. Douglas, *India's Democracy* (1972), pp. 118-19.

7 M. Franda, *Radical Politics in West Bengal* (1971); C.R. Irani, *Bengal: the Communist Challenge* (1971); S.S. Harrison, 'Caste and the Andhra Communists', *American Political Science R.* L (2), 1956; B. Sen Gupta, *Communism in Indian Politics* (1972), pp. 401-3; Carolyn M. Elliott, 'Decline of a Patrimonial Régime: the Telengana Rebellion in India 1946-51', *J. of Asian Studies* 34(1), 1974; Gail Omvedt, 'Non-Brahmans and Communists in Bombay', *Economic and Political Weekly*, 21 and 28 Apr. 1972.

8 Franda, *Radical Politics in West Bengal*, pp. 242-52.

2

Kerala's Identity: Unity and Diversity

The Basis of Kerala's Separate Identity

As early as 1920 the Indian National Congress committed itself to a linguistic arrangement of provinces for an independent India. Among its own re-organized units was the Kerala Pradesh (i.e. province) Congress Committee. At Independence there was no substantial realignment of boundaries but in 1955 the States Reorganization Commission recommended, *inter alia,* the creation of a united Kerala. This would be composed of the whole of the Malabar District and the Kasergod taluk of South Canara District immediately to the north (both from Madras state) and the Part B state of Travancore-Cochin less its five Tamil-speaking taluks in the south. (The taluk is the first-level administrative subdivision of the District.) Despite some opposition in Travancore to the loss of the Tamil area, the scheme secured general approval and with the passage of the States Reorganization Act Kerala came into existence on 1 November 1956 in the form recommended. Like other states, Kerala reproduced the structure and organization of the Union government in miniature: Governor, Chief Minister, Council of Ministers, and Legislative Assembly. There was, however, no second chamber.

The rationale for the new state rested in the first place on language.[1] Keralites, commonly known as Malayalis, are primarily Dravidian in stock and their language, Malayalam, is closely related to other south Indian languages, particularly Tamil. The first surviving text, the *Ramacharitam,* is dated to the early twelfth century while the distinctive modern script came into use in the fifteenth century. Just as Aryan influences are evident in the population, so the language has been more strongly marked by Sanskrit than have other south Indian languages. Malayalam has also been affected by commercial and religious contacts with the Middle East and maritime Europe. The language involves a wide range of sounds and the script can record almost any sound in the Indian languages. Malayalis in consequence acquire other languages easily, including English, which was the medium of instruction in high schools until the 1930s and remains in use in colleges. Dialects exist but the basic form of Malayalam is used and understood throughout Kerala and forms an effective means of communication in both literature and politics.

Prior to the seventeenth century such historical writing as there was in Kerala was confined to local and family chronicles but two works of the seventeenth century—the *Kerala Mahatmyam* (Sanskrit) and the *Keralolpatti* (Malayalam)— which mix history, mythology, and speculation are usually taken to indicate the birth of a 'national' or regional consciousness, directly and indirectly stemming from the contact with, and impact of European commerce.[2]

Physically and culturally Kerala is one of the most distinctive regions of India.[3] To the east it is isolated from the rest of India by the Western Ghats through which only the Palghat Gap (1,100 ft) in the north and the Shencottah Gap (1,500 ft) in the south give access to the rest of India. On the west the long, low coastline has exposed Kerala to maritime influences from the earliest times. Contact with the Arab and European world in search of pepper and spices from the interior of Kerala has materially affected its economy, society, and culture: the commercialization of agriculture; the presence of large Muslim and Christian minorities; exposure to forces destructive of traditional social structures; and the export of capital.

By virtue of a climate which is India's nearest approach to equatorial conditions, Kerala is visually distinctive (and beautiful). The characteristic scenery is a rich, green patchwork of coconut palm and paddy, laced together along the coast by backwaters and lagoons. Maximum temperatures rarely exceed 90°F or fall below 70°F. The region benefits from both northeast and southwest monsoons, and has more rainy days and a higher average rainfall than any other state. In contrast to the rest of India, historically the problem in the main paddy-growing areas has been to drain the water from the land rather than to bring it to the fields and until recently there has been no necessity for large-scale artificial irrigation works. The characteristic pre-imperialist socio-economic structure was not the 'Asiatic Mode of Production' but a modified form of feudalism very probably unique in India.[4]

Kerala's three natural divisions—coastal lowlands, midlands, and highlands—run longitudinally. In contrast the pre-independence political divisions ran latitudinally, with the result that Malabar, Cochin, and Travancore were geographical microcosms of the whole. The coast is low-lying, alluvial, and fertile. It is also the most densely populated region, rising in the south to more than 1,500 persons per square mile (see map below, p. 46). The backwaters provide an important and in some parts the only means of communication.[5] The midlands zone is made up of a 200-600 feet high lateritic plateau, heavily dissected by intensively cultivated valleys. The laterite itself has been graphically described as 'about as attractive for agriculture as railway ballast'.[6] Tapioca, introduced about 1920, will, however, tolerate the conditions and has become the staple diet of the poor.[7] The highland zone is wet, relatively cool, and naturally either forest or downland. Until the latter part of the nineteenth century it was inaccessible and virtually uninhabited. From 1877 European entrepreneurs experimented with a variety of plantation crops; rubber estates now dominate the foothills, and tea estates the higher ground. Large tracts remain under valuable hardwood forest. The heavy rainfall and the steep descent to the plains offer excellent opportunities for hydro-electric generation which has led to the opening-up of new areas in the hills, notably in the Idikki District. The region, however, still remains comparatively sparsely populated.

Like India as a whole, Kerala is overwhelmingly rural in character. Despite a generous official definition of urban settlement only 16 per cent of the state's population lived in urban areas in 1971.[8] Three centres exceeded 200,000 inhabitants: the major port of Greater Cochin (439,000), the administrative capital of Trivandrum (410,000), and the chief town of Malabar, Calicut (334,000). (For clarity in this work the town of Kozhikode is referred to by its older name, Calicut, and the District of which it is the centre as Kozhikode.) In contrast to the rest of the country, however, Kerala lacks the nucleated village which marks Indian settlement patterns. Ribbon development extends not just along the roads and tracks but through the fields as well. The village is more an administrative concept than a physical fact. In recent times this unusual pattern has been accentuated by the pressure of population on land, but the pattern itself dates from an earlier period.[9] Joan Mencher has argued that this peculiar settlement pattern facilitated the growth of feudal relationships unique to Kerala in the Indian subcontinent. However, cause and effect are difficult to distinguish.[10] A similar interaction perhaps contributed to the strain of individualism found in modern Malayali culture. The absence of nucleated villages is also a significant factor in the development of the communist movement. During the underground era party workers were better able to escape detection since police resources could not be concentrated. Conversely, the cadre has itself been stretched when operating as a legal party by reason of the dispersal of the population. The contrast with West Bengal, where the movement can capitalize on the solidary loyalties of the village community, is marked. In Kerala the one area where nucleated settlements are common is in the Muslim area of southern Malabar. Together with the distinctive role of the mosque as a communal gathering place, this has served to reinforce the hold of the Muslim League on the Moplah population.[11]

Paradoxically the absence of clearly delineated villages does not diminish the Malayali's attachment to his native place. This strong sense of territorial allegiance, found at all levels though most obvious among the more affluent, is related to the economic and symbolic significance of land holding, the manifold functions of the extended family, and the difficulty of physical communications. Politically, it is both cause and consequence of the existence of highly localized political parties, the effort to balance ministries geographically, and the importance of constituency work to the legislator's career.

Regional Diversity

Within the broad unity of Kerala society and culture there were at Independence significant social, economic, and political differences between Malabar, Cochin, and Travancore, notably in levels of development and in agrarian relations. Although the contrasts in modernization were partially associated with the distribution of the major communities between the three areas, the policies of the respective administrations were the decisive factor. Malabar was a neglected outpost of Madras, on which the British spent little beyond the requirements of law and order. In contrast the Travancore and Cochin governments actively stimulated agriculture, commerce, and industry, built roads and canals, founded schools, colleges, and hospitals, and in the 1930s jointly modernized the port of Cochin. Cochin was regarded by the British as a model state and both were exceptional among the princely states for their development policies.

On a composite index of socio-cultural indicators used in the 1961 census the three Malabar districts were the least developed of Kerala's nine districts and a similar, though less extreme, ranking emerged on a composite economic index.[12] Substantial disparities remain. In 1974 the fourteen most developed of Kerala's fifty-seven taluks as measured by an index combining levels of education, health, industrialization, and economic infrastructure were all in Travancore-Cochin and the fifteen least developed in either Malabar or the High Ranges.[13]

The most crucial area in which the component parts of Kerala diverged was in agrarian relations. As the accompanying Table shows, in Malabar three-quarters of those dependent on land were tenant cultivators. In Travancore more than half of the agricultural population were peasant proprietors. The origins of this contrast, extensively treated elsewhere,[14] lie in government policies pursued

in the period between 1792 and 1865. After the defeat of Tipu
Sultan in 1792 the new British rulers of Malabar established a land
settlement beneficial to the Hindu *jenmis* (landlords) and deleter-

Table 2.1   *Kerala 1957-8: Agrarian Structure*
            (Percentage of agricultural population)

Tenurial status	Malabar	Cochin	Travancore
Landless labourer	12	19	13
Owner cultivator	10	29	56
Tenant cultivator	75	50	25
Rentier	3	2	1
Other	—	—	5

Source: Adapted from T.C. Varghese, *Agrarian Change and Economic
Consequences*, p. 167.

ious to the cultivator. Historically, the *jenmis'* rights had been
heavily qualified by custom and the cultivators had enjoyed inalien-
able rights subject to modest obligations. Under the British system
the *jenmi* became the absolute proprietor with a contractual title and
enforceable rights in a court of law. The effects of the change were
compounded by the prevalence of intermediaries (*kanomdars*) between landlord and peasant, and it was this class that was made
responsible for the collection of land revenue. The *kanomdars'* position is fairly reflected in the fact that the peasants did not distinguish
between them and the landlords. Both were 'thampuran' (lord). The
intermediary also benefited from the change from custom to contract and the net effect was gradually to reduce the actual cultivator
(*verumpattomdar* or *kuzhikanomdar*) to the status of a tenant-at-will,
the *thampuran's* will. After meeting the charge to land revenue and
payments to landlord and intermediary, the peasant was left with
one-third or less of his net proceeds. According to the 1900 Settlement Report, South Malabar had 'earned the unenviable reputation
of being the most rack-rented country on the face of the earth.'[15] A
further feature of the Malabar settlement of political significance was
the treatment of the ownership of waste lands. The *jenmi* secured
what the *zamindar* of the north was denied, the title to extensive
tracts of uncultivated land. Potential cultivators were thus discouraged from opening up new land since the *jenmis* dictated the
terms of the lease. As late as 1951 more than one-quarter of the total
arable area of Malabar was still uncultivated. In a district where

one-quarter of the agricultural population in 1911 were landless labourers and the majority of tenants insecure and oppressed tenants-at-will, the British settlement had foreclosed one obvious outlet for agrarian discontent.

The course of events was otherwise in Travancore. Until the early eighteenth century agrarian relations were essentially the same as in pre-Mysorean Malabar. Thereafter by conquest and expropriation successive Maharajas concentrated land ownership in the hands of the government (*sircar*) until by 1812 only one-third of the cultivated area was left in private or corporate hands. The revenue assessment was comparatively light; there was security of tenure; and customary practices were undisturbed.[16] In 1865 the tenant cultivators on government land were enfranchised and a free market in land developed. Agrarian tensions were also diminished by the government's positive encouragement of the development of waste land.

Cochin, as the table suggests, was in an intermediate position.[17] Although the Rajas of Cochin had sought to subdue the feudal aristocracy, they were less sucessful than the rulers of Travancore. By 1812 some 40 per cent of the cultivated area was held by the *sircar*. Government tenants enjoyed fixity of tenure but bore the brunt of a heavy land settlement, resulting from an excessive British impost. The few thousand *jenmis* who owned the remaining 60 per cent of cultivated land were as unbridled as their counterparts in Malabar and many tenants were progressively reduced to the position of farm labourers. If Cochin suffered from this lack of regulation somewhat less than Malabar it was because of the existence of *sircar* waste land and the industrial outlet afforded by the port and its industry.

Communal Diversity

As a partial consequence of the separate histories of the three regions of Kerala, there are substantial Christian and Muslim minorities. The Hindu caste system also achieved its highest degree of elaboration here, while at the same time departing from the typical structure of Hindu ritual ranking. Until the 1920s and 1930s joint family systems predominated and matriliny prevailed in the largest high-caste group. Caste reform was an early phenomenon among both low and high castes and caste associations have played a large role in politics to the present time.

India is 83 per cent Hindu. Kerala is only 60 per cent so and apart from the Punjab the only major state where two-fifths of the population are non-Hindu. In three of the state's initial nine Districts Hindus were in a minority or constituted a bare majority of the

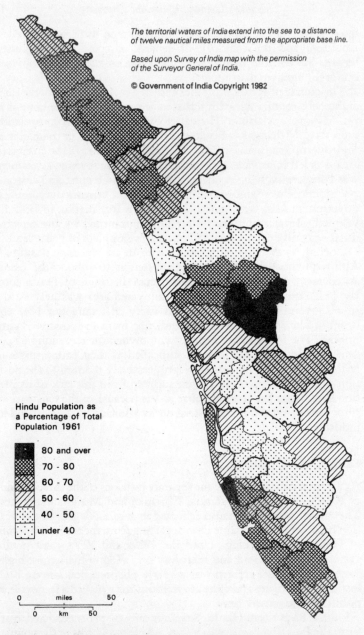

The territorial waters of India extend into the sea to a distance
of twelve nautical miles measured from the appropriate base line.

Based upon Survey of India map with the permission
of the Surveyor General of India.

© Government of India Copyright 1982

Hindu Population as
a Percentage of Total
Population 1961

███	80 and over
▓▓▓	70 - 80
▨▨▨	60 - 70
▧▧▧	50 - 60
∴∴∴	40 - 50
⋯⋯	under 40

0   miles   50

0   km   50

Source: Data from *Census of India 1961*, vol. VII: *Kerala*, pt IX, *Census Atlas*.

Map 3 Kerala 1961: Hindus as % of Total Population by Taluk

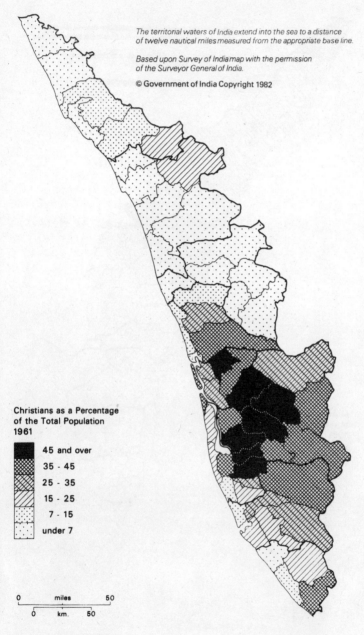

The territorial waters of India extend into the sea to a distance of twelve nautical miles measured from the appropriate base line.

Based upon Survey of India map with the permission of the Surveyor General of India.

© Government of India Copyright 1982

Christians as a Percentage of the Total Population 1961

- 45 and over
- 35 - 45
- 25 - 35
- 15 - 25
- 7 - 15
- under 7

0   miles   50
0   km.   50

Source: As Map 3 above.

Map 4 Kerala 1961: Christians as % of Total Population by Taluk

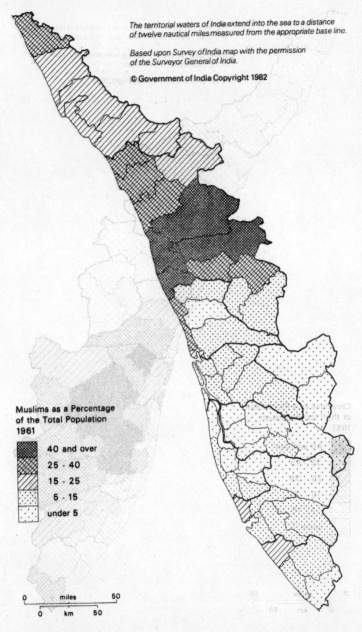

The territorial waters of India extend into the sea to a distance of twelve nautical miles measured from the appropriate base line.

Based upon Survey of India map with the permission of the Surveyor General of India.

© Government of India Copyright 1982

Muslims as a Percentage of the Total Population 1961

40 and over

25 - 40

15 - 25

5 - 15

under 5

0   miles   50

0   km   50

Source: As Map 3 above.

Map 5 Kerala 1961: Muslims as % of Total Population by Taluk

population: Ernakulam (46 per cent), Kottayam (49 per cent), and Kozhikode (53 per cent).[18] There were only three taluks where 80 per cent or more were Hindu and only seventeen at 70 per cent or more. The non-Hindu population is fairly evenly divided between Christians (21 per cent in 1961) and Muslims, locally known as Moplahs, (18 per cent, and rising through a higher birth rate).[19]

Kerala is a unique instance of communities of three major world religions living peacably within one territory. Indeed, in so far as communism makes analogous truth claims to those of religion, Malayalis have four faiths. The minority communities are concentrated in certain Districts, as the accompanying maps show, but religious enclaves are exceptional and all three groups widely distributed. Hindu, Christian, and Muslim interact daily and tolerance is the norm. In one popular manifestation of Hinduism in Kerala, the cult of Lord Ayyappan, the god is served by an Arab lieutenant for whom he has constructed a mosque.[20] Communal clashes are rare and there has been no serious bloodshed since 1921-2. The only confessional political party is the Muslim League though a minority of Muslims support Congress or CPI.

Christians

The minority communities of Kerala differ in many ways from their counterparts in the rest of India, not least in their antiquity. Christianity and Islam are as much religions of Kerala as Hinduism is. Tradition attributes Christian proselytization to St Thomas the Apostle and certainly immigrants from west Asia were making converts among the higher castes of central Kerala in the early fourth century.[21] By the fifteenth century the Syrian Christians were estimated at about 200,000. The arrival of the Portuguese disrupted the tenuous links with the west Asian patriarchates and for a time the Syrians submitted to Rome but in 1653 the majority rejected papal authority. Thereafter the Syrians have been broadly divided, despite later schisms, into Romo-Syrians, recognizing the Pope but still practising the Syrian Rite, and Jacobites who recognize only the Patriarch of Antioch. Like all other 'communities' in Kerala, the different groups of Syrians practise endogamy but they share common social characteristics, patriliny, the dowry system (now illegal), and an equivalent status to the high-caste Hindus.

Syrians make up about three-quarters of the Christian population and about 16 per cent (3.2 million in 1968) of the whole population.[22] They are concentrated in central and northern Travancore and southern Cochin, which contributes to their political influence by creating 'safe' Assembly constituencies. After the Brahmins the Syrians are the most prosperous community in Kerala. Diagram 2.1

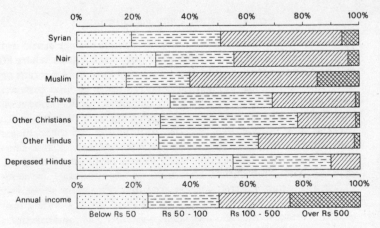

Diagram 2.1 Travancore 1931: Distribution of Annual Income per Family by Caste and Community

Source: Census of India 1931, vol. XXVIII, Travancore: pt I, Appendix IV.

shows that by 1931 in Travancore the Syrians had already overtaken the high-caste Hindu Nairs in terms of annual income per family (to some extent as a result of the partition of joint-family properties among the Nairs). In 1968 only 1.6 per cent of all Kerala households were estimated to have an annual income in excess of Rs 8,000 (about £430 at the prevailing rate of exchange); 3.1 per cent of Syrian households fell into this bracket, constituting nearly 30 per cent of all high income households.[23] The Syrians are strongly represented in most forms of business, banking, and government service but they are particularly identified with plantation agriculture.

The community's political influence is considerable. Prior to Independence Syrians had supported the Travancore State Congress though they were less closely involved with the equivalent organization in Cochin, the Praja Mandal. After Independence the identification of Syrians as well as the other major Christian grouping, the Latin (Roman) Catholics, with Congress became such that it was seen by critics as 'Christian Congress'. The central government has normally included a Syrian Christian member in recognition of the community's services to the party and against communism in Kerala. In 1964, however, the Kerala Provincial Congress Party (KPCC) split and since then Syrian political influence has been divided between the two parties. (See below, p. 195.)

The second largest group within the Christian community is the Latin Catholics who practise the Latin Rite within the Roman communion. Like the west coast Christians generally, the Latins originate in conversions during the Portuguese era (1492-1665) among the lower castes of the coastal region. Excluding a small number of

Anglo-Indians and a larger but unknown number of converts from the scheduled castes, Latin Catholics constituted 3.6 per cent of the Kerala population in 1968, still concentrated in the coastal areas. Socially and economically they are a 'backward' group, officially listed thus for purposes of education and job reservation. However, the evidence of the Backward Classes Commission indicates that their relative position has improved: in 1968 1.6 per cent of Latin Catholic households enjoyed an annual income in excess of Rs 8,000 compared to 1.1 per cent of the largest low-caste Hindu group, the Ezhavas, and a figure close to the state average.[24]

Politically the Latin Catholics have been strong supporters of Congress and vehement opponents of communism. The laity have generally followed the lead of the episcopate, headed by the Cardinal Archbishop of Ernakulam, which, though not unanimous, mainly sided with the official Congress party in the 1964 split. During the early communist period—the pontificate of Pius IX—the two branches of the Roman connection, Latins and Romo-Syrians, were fiercely anti-communist; and the disciplines of the Catholic church ensured massive demonstrations and block voting in elections. Since the mid-sixties the church has moderated its stance and an implicit concordat has emerged with the CPI and CPM.[25] There has also been a tendency for some parish priests to play a political role independent of the episcopate, articulating the social and economic concerns of their flock. Of these the best-known example is Father Vadakkan, prominent in the anti-communist Liberation Struggle, but later founder of a peasant union and a militant peasant-worker party that was subsequently allied with the CPM.[26]

A wide variety of protestant missions and evangelical sects as well as Roman Catholics have been active among the scheduled castes especially in the southernmost areas of Travancore, but scheduled converts to Christianity form only 1.5 per cent of the total population and some 16 per cent of the total scheduled castes. Some missionaries are said to have been reluctant to work among the backward and scheduled classes during the nineteenth century for fear of compromising their work among the higher castes and their relations with the Syrians.[27] Marriage between different sections of the Christian community is still unusual and considered morally wrong among the Syrians.[28]

Muslims

The Muslims of Kerala originated in the eighth and ninth centuries through the settlement of Arab converts trading with the Malabar coast; and the community has grown by extensive proselytization as well as natural increase. As Map 5 above shows, in southern Malabar

Muslims form 40 per cent or more of the population and 15 per cent or more throughout Malabar. The proportion is less in Travancore and Cochin but even here there are only 14 taluks (1961) where the Muslim percentage falls below 5 per cent.

The arrival of the Portuguese in 1498 checked the then well-established community's progress and, though during the succeeding Dutch and British periods the Moplahs increased by conversion, this was chiefly among the outcaste groups of the southern interior as Muslim traders turned inland in search of alternative occupations to commerce. By the mid-eighteenth century the majority were landless labourers, poor fishermen and petty traders, and Kerala Muslims were in psychological retreat.[29] This trend was reversed during the Mysorean invasions of the late eighteenth century when the Muslim leaders, Hyder Ali and his son, Tipu Sultan, occupied Malabar. For a little over a quarter of a century after 1766 the Moplahs were members of the dominant community.[30] The victory of the British and princely Hindu confederacy in 1792 placed the Moplahs once more in economic and cultural subjection, a condition which found expression in a recurrent form of 'pre-political protest',[31] known as the Moplah Outrages (1836-1919).

Periodically small groups of Moplahs ritually sought martyrdom in suicidal attacks on landlords, moneylenders, and officials. The essential nature of these episodes is disputed but it is clear that the attacks involved economic and cultural dimensions—agrarian disabilities and a Moplah tradition of *shahīd* or holy war.[32] Finally in 1921-2 the outrage tradition merged with the Turkophil Muslim Khilafat movement and the early freedom struggle in a large-scale rising against British authority in the southern interior of Malabar, known as the Moplah Rising or Rebellion (see below, p. 68). The localized incidence of Moplah 'fanaticism' led British officials to make and maintain a distinction between the troublesome and barbarous 'jungle Mappillas' of the southern interior of Malabar and the well-behaved and respectable traders of the coast, centred on Calicut.[33] Shorn of its pejorative overtones, the division is a politically interesting one. Such limited inroads as the communist movement has made in Muslim areas have been among the depressed landless Moplahs of the interior.

Two other regional groupings can be identified: the high-status Muslim families of Cannanore in the north; and the Muslims of Travancore and Cochin. The former are distinguished by matriliny—they are arguably converts from high-caste Hindu Nairs—and by proprietorship of land.[34] The Muslims of Travancore and Cochin do not identify closely with their Moplah co-religionists in the north, having escaped the worst attentions of the Portuguese.

A comparatively prosperous community, often shopkeepers or businessmen, they have generally lived amicably with the host Hindu or Christian communities and proved more susceptible to 'modernizing' trends including education than the Muslims of the north.[35]

The majority of Kerala Muslims belong to the *Sunni* sect of Islam, the conservative mainstream in which the *Hadith*, the authoritative tradition of the words and deeds of the Prophet, is held in almost equal regard to the *Quran* itself. A minority, estimated at a quarter, are *Mujahids (Wahabis),* moderate reformers, somewhat rationalist in outlook and critical of undue reliance on the *Hadith*. Miller notes that communism has had more impact among *Sunnis* than among *Mujahids*.[36] This may, however, be a function of the fact that *Sunnis* predominate among the backward Moplahs of interior south Malabar. Although the Muslims are far freer of caste-like distinctions than either Hindus or Christians in Kerala, worshipping in *Sunni* or *Mujahid* mosques, irrespective of status, four endogamous and heirarchically ordered groups do exist. At the top are the *Thangals* (a Malayalam term of respect), who claim descent from the Prophet. Below them are the *Arabis,* said to derive from Arab intermarriage with Malayali women. They are followed by the landed aristocracy of Muslim society, centred on Cannanore, partly matrilineal and still using pre-Muslim family surnames. Lastly, there are the converts from the backward and scheduled castes. The native tongue of all groups is Malayalam, though religious services are conducted in Arabic in *Sunni* mosques. Urdu is understood only among some of the well educated.

Politically, the Moplahs have exhibited more unanimity than any other community in Kerala. Since Independence the overwhelming majority in Malabar have supported the Muslim League (or after 1974 one or other of its rival wings). To all intents and purposes the All-India Muslim League has been synonymous with the Muslim League of Kerala. In the south of the state, the Muslims generally support Congress and in the north a small proportion, estimated by Miller at one-fifth, vote communist.[37] Since the concentration of Muslims in south Malabar yields ten to twelve 'pocket boroughs', while sizeable Moplah minorities elsewhere in Malabar strongly influence election results, the League proved a highly effective confessional party, at least until its split in 1975.

Hindus
The Hindu community of Kerala experienced the most elaborate system of caste found in India at the turn of the century. With over 500 divisions and sub-divisions and conceptions of pollution which

extended beyond untouchability to unapproachability, Kerala was
described by Vivekananda as a mad-house of caste.[38] Yet the system
was unusual in its structure. Of the four basic *varnas* or occupational
categories in the Hindu caste system—Brahmin (priest), Kshatriya
(warrior), Vaisya (businessman), and Sudra (service)—Kshatriyas
were rare and Vaisyas non-existent. In Kerala, Nairs took the place
of Kshatriyas, although they were regarded as Sudras by the
Namboodiri Brahmins. The absence of a Vaisya caste is of more than
technical significance. Muslims and Syrian Christians have to some
degree provided a trading and business community but neither has
fulfilled the role often attributed to the Vaisya. Kerala has had no
indigenous community primarily concerned with either money-
lending or entrepreneurial activity. Money-lending has been mainly
undertaken by outsiders such as the Konkani and Tamil Brahmins
and entrepreneurship by Europeans and Gujeratis.[39] In the coir
centre of Alleppey, where the daily cash flow on the eve of the
Depression was Rs 1.5 million, 35 of the 88 business houses were
non-Malayali Hindu, 7 British, and one Swiss.[40] The absence of a
Vaisya community, coupled with the deep-rooted reluctance of the
upper castes of Kerala to engage in (polluting) commercial or industrial activity, has undoubtedly limited the state's development.

At the top of the system were the Namboodiri Brahmins—and in
southern Travancore the (ritually inferior) Potti Brahmins—
numbering no more than a few thousands and often accorded ritual
superiority by Brahmins elsewhere in India. In origin Aryan, the
Namboodiris had established a chain of thirty-two settlements in
Kerala by the end of the eighth century and from then onwards there
appears to have been a steady alienation of land to individual
Brahmins or their temples.[41] Their patrilineal and primogenital
customs discouraged any fragmentation of property. Only the eldest
son married within his caste. His younger brothers were permitted a
kind of concubinage known as *Sambandham* with women from the
ritually polluting Nair community below. Any children of such
unions were, of course, Nairs, and so polluted their fathers.
Namboodiri women were generally condemned to a life of near-
purdah within the *illam* or 'palace'. As the administration of the joint
family property was the responsibility of the eldest male, the remaining males had no obligation beyond priestly duties. Different
verdicts were passed on them. O. Chandu Menon, Nair author of
the first Malayalam novel (written in 1889), refers to the 'rich,
licentious, profligate, unsteady Namboodiripad so often found in
Malabar',[42] while the *Travancore State Manual* (1906) notes their
'credulousness, simplicity and innocence'.[43] Two years after the
foundation of the *Yogakshema Mahasabha* in 1910, dedicated to re-

forming the community's customs and attitudes, a Namboodiri who dared to travel by train was required to atone.[44] Legislation to permit the break-up of joint family properties and to reform marriage customs was enacted in Malabar only in the 1930s and it was not until the 1950s that Namboodiris generally entered the ordinary schools and colleges of the district. In contrast to the alien Brahmins resident in Kerala, the Namboodiri Brahmins have taken little part in public life.[45] With the exception of the communist leader E.M.S. Namboodiripad no Namboodiri Brahmin has held ministerial office and in the two Assemblies since 1970 there were one and two Namboodiri members respectively.[46] Of 101 Indian Administrative Service officers in the state secretariat in 1974 just one came from the community.[47] Perhaps no caste in India has proved so resistant to change, preserving its ritual status in disregard of its material privileges.[48]

Among the non-Malayali Brahmins of Kerala the Tamil Brahmins, disparagingly dubbed Pattars by the Namboodiris, are the most numerous. In contrast to the Namboodiris they have proved highly adaptable to modern conditions, for to the veneration accorded Brahmins as a caste in Kerala and a favoured position at court historically (as a counter-weight to the Nair aristocracy) they add a readiness to use educational opportunities. In some key areas of government service in Travancore the Tamil Brahmins had established a virtual monopoly by the mid-nineteenth century. Political consciousness in Kerala is conventionally dated to the *Malayali Memorial* of 1891, a petition to the Maharaja by his Malayali subjects protesting against Tamil dominance in the higher reaches of the Travancore government.[49] As late as 1974 the tradition of Tamil senior civil servants had not been entirely extinguished.[50] In Trivandrum itself and in Palghat District there are a number of Tamil Brahmin families long domiciled in Kerala. No separate figures are available for either Namboodiri or Tamil Brahmin incomes but the Backward Classes Reservation Commission, which was set up in 1968, reports that 10.4 per cent of all Brahmin and related (temple servant) castes had incomes in excess of Rs 8,000—that is, over six times the state average and more than three times the Syrian Christian percentage.[51]

Below the Brahmins in ritual status are a small number of Kshatriyas and Ambalavasis; but the major high-caste group, and until the inter-war years Kerala's 'dominant caste',[52] is the Nairs (Nayars), some 15 per cent of the population.[53] Together with the Namboodiris, the Nairs have formed the land-owning class. Historically a military caste, the Nairs increasingly turned to administrative service with the development of the modern state in Travancore

and Cochin.[54] The most distinctive feature of Nair social organization was the family structure, which was hypergamous, matrilineal,
and matrilocal and so loosely arranged as to raise doubts as to
whether 'marriage' existed at all.[55] Matriliny was also found among
some Muslims and some low-caste Ezhavas but it was among Nairs
that it was universal. It has been suggested that the matrilineal
system 'tends to produce a society at once heirarchical and authoritarian in outlook', built round family pride as well as loyalty to
the *karanavar*, the eldest male who heads the joint family or *tarawad*.[56]
It was in this and other respects congruent with the role of a military
caste in a feudal society. However, the ending of the warrior role, the
abolition of agrestic slavery, the growth of a money economy, and
the impact of Western education combined to undermine the relevance of Nair traditions. The young men of the *tarawad* were condemned to idleness; the management of the estates was more difficult; the expenses of customary practices more burdensome; and
the competition of rival communities, notably the Syrian Christians
and Ezhavas, more challenging.

By the early twentieth century the Nairs had lost their pre-
eminence based on the ascriptive rights of feudalism and caste but
reforming movements were emerging. These culminated in 1914
with the foundation of the Nair Service Society (NSS) by a group of
fourteen young Nairs centred on Mannath Padmanabha Pillai (1878–
1970). Owing something by way of inspiration to both the Sree
Narayana Dharma Paripalan Yogam (SNDP), the Ezhava caste
association founded in 1903, and the Servants of India Society
(1905), the NSS aimed to liberate the community from superstition,
taboo and otiose custom, to establish a network of educational and
welfare institutions, and to defend and advance Nair interests in the
political arena. Under three lawyers, Mannath, K. Kelappan Nair
(1889–1971), and Changanacherry K. Parameswaran Pillai (1877–
1940), who mixed idealism with 'the common place devices of the
professional politicians of Europe and America',[57] the NSS became a
potent factor in Kerala politics.

The most important single achievement of the movement was the
reform of family law: the recognition of Nair liaisons as effective
marriages (Madras 1896; Travancore 1913; Cochin 1920); and the
legalization of the partition of joint family properties and therefore
of individual inheritance and alienability (Travancore 1925; Madras
and Cochin 1932). The results were complex. In many cases the
tarawad had already been weakened by economic and social change.
Many properties were fragmented into unviable holdings on the eve
of, or during the Great Depression. By sale or the foreclosure of
mortgages much land in Travancore and Cochin passed into Syrian

Christian and, to a lesser degree, Ezhava or Muslim hands. In the south particularly this division of Nair estates practically destroyed the landed aristocracy. The traditional structure of rural society collapsed, facilitating the growth of communist and socialist movements. Many younger Nairs were themselves drawn into State Congress, Congress Socialist, and Communist parties, and some have argued that a disproportionate number of the early members of the CPI were from recently partitioned Nair joint families.[58] Certainly Nairs are prominent in the leadership of all the major non-confessional parties. In Malabar the process of transition from a matrilineal to a patrilineal system was slower than in the south because of the exceptional pattern of agrarian relations (see below, p. 48). Joint families still existed in the early post-war period. Increasingly unwieldy and lethargic, most of those which remained broke up in the late 1940s and early 1950s and, as in the south, some land passed in the process to the inferior communities and the Syrians as well as to Nairs who had earlier changed to a simple patrilineal family structure.[59]

The once-dominant caste was now uncertain of its position in the social order. Unable to adjust readily to modernization and technological change, it no longer provided the political stability associated with the existence of a dominant caste. Since Independence the Nairs have not given their consistent and solid support to any political party, though Congress and Kerala Congress have drawn more votes than socialists or communists. The political focus of the community has been—at least until recently—the NSS, with more than a thousand village units and an infrastructure of schools, colleges, and hospitals concentrated in Travancore. This powerful interest group, though still important, no longer commands the unswerving political allegiance of the majority of Nairs nor the influence in government it once had. This is reflected in the fact that in 1973 it formed its own National Democratic Party, bought off by Congress with a handful of nominations to Nair-dominant constituencies in 1977.

According to the 1970 Backward Classes Reservation Commission (which stemmed from a Nair challenge in the courts to the existing system of job reservation)[60] 2.8 per cent of Nairs sampled in 1968 earned in excess of Rs 8,000 annually, a slightly lower proportion than among Syrian Christians. The size of the Nair community still meant that it included 25 per cent of all high income households in the state. Nairs continue to enjoy a disproportionate share of educational facilities and of government posts (see below, pp. 34-7). The inquiry did not give figures for low income households but it is widely conceded that some Nairs are now found among the poorest groups. The community is far more socially and economically differentiated than in the past.[61]

The major low caste is the Ezhavas (Iravas, Ilhavas), known as Chokons (Chogons) in central Travancore and as Tiyyas (Thiyas, Theeyas), who claim a higher ritual ranking, in Malabar. Though performing the tasks of Sudras the Ezhavas were defined as untouchables by the Namboodiris and denied both temple entry and temple approach. The Ezhavas, officially estimated at 22 per cent of the total population, are found throughout the state[62] but are particularly concentrated in the coastal regions and in Palghat District. Their traditional occupation is the tending and tapping of the coconut palm, though their common designation of 'toddy tappers' (toddy is a country liquor made from the sap of the palm) is misleading.[63] Most Ezhavas in fact were, and are, agricultural labourers, or, in favoured areas, small cultivators. Since the latter part of the nineteenth century Ezhavas have also been extensively employed in the manufacture of coconut matting and related products.

Marriage customs have varied considerably among the Ezhavas. In northern Malabar the Tiyyas were matrilineal (but patrilocal), in southern Malabar patrilineal and their property partible. In northern Travancore the Ezhavas were purely matrilineal, generally matrilocal but sometimes patrilocal, while in the south a mixed system of inheritance was practised. Compared to the Nairs, the Ezhava matrilineal system was less irksome and in the absence of the *tarawad* system and extensive properties, its reform (Travancore 1925; Malabar 1933) was relatively straightforward.

As low castes, the Ezhavas had little to lose and much to gain by the economic and social changes of the nineteenth and twentieth centuries. There are records of Ezhava agricultural innovation and desire for English education well before 1857 and by the 1880s a small group of prosperous and educated Ezhavas was demanding admission to colleges and government service and an end to their caste disabilities.[64] After a series of unsuccessful petitions ten wealthy Ezhavas established in 1903 the first caste association in Kerala, Sree Narayana Dharma Paripalan Yogam (SNDP), 'to promote religious and secular education and industrious habits among the Elava community.' Sree Narayana Guru (1857-1928) was an Ezhava *sanyasi* from south Travancore who had established an *ashram* in 1877 and with his unifying creed of 'one caste, one religion, one god' became an influential figure comparable locally to Swami Vivekananda.[65]

By 1928 the SNDP membership had risen to 50,000. In 1974 it was 60,000, roughly twice the total membership of the two major communist parties combined, both of which draw disproportionate support from the same caste. However, since the commitment involved in membership of the CPI or CPM is of quite a different order from that of the SNDP, no conclusions are warranted beyond indicating the continuing significance of the Ezhava communal association. Although some fraternal organizations developed in Cochin, the Tiyyas of Malabar showed little interest. Under British administration the Tiyyas of the north did not suffer the disabilities of their counterparts in Travancore in seeking admission to education or government service. Further, social and economic disadvantage did not run along caste lines to quite the same extent as in the south. Arguably these factors and the relative importance of the SNDP may help to explain the varied rate of communist progress in the different regions.

The tone of the early years of the SNDP,[66] set by Narayana Guru himself, was essentially nineteenth century but nineteenth-century India merged with nineteenth-century England—the Sanskritization of Self-Help. 'God helps those who help themselves' proclaimed the banner of the association's magazine *Vivekodayam* (Sunrise of knowledge), in English, at a time when about a thousand Ezhavas could read the language of progress. From this small class emerged a politicized leadership touched by the ferment of ideas in India in the post-First World War period. T.K. Madhavan (1885-1930),[67] founder of the influential *Deshabhimani*, had for some time been steering the association into covert political causes and had persuaded the local congress organization to take up temple access as a way of reviving Congress fortunes in South India. Although the campaign to allow *avarna* Hindus access to the roads around a famous temple at Vaikom in 1924-5 ended in defeat dressed up as a compromise, the *satyagraha* was important in disseminating a new, radical rhetoric.[68]

The gospel of self-help was from the beginning something of an irrelevance to the Ezhavas at large, dependent as it was for meaning on the circumstances and opportunities of an industrializing society such as Victorian England. The SNDP did not make capital available to individuals. Even partition of landed properties in the 1920s scarcely helped. Of the beneficiaries of 60,000 acres of Ezhava land partitioned between 1926 and 1930, 60 per cent received one acre or less. The fortunate 2 per cent who gained two acres or more took 40 per cent of all the land partitioned.[69]

From the Vaikom *satyagraha* onwards the SNDP had stirred the ordinary Ezhava without materially improving his situation. The subsequent impact of the Great Depression on the staple coir industry afforded fertile opportunities for wider politicization which were associated with the appointment of C. Kesavan (1891-1969) as Secretary of the SNDP, a man who had 'imbibed the teachings of Karl Marx, Sri Narayana Guru, and Gandhiji.'[70] The British Agent

reported in December 1930 'There has been considerable political
and social activity in Shertallay . . .for the last eight years since the
Vaikkom Temple entry Satyagraha . . .During the past 8 months,
mushroom political organisations have risen . . .the Atheistic League, Revolutionary League, Youth League, Labour Association,
etc., all sponsored by local Congress Extremists . . .'[71] Kesavan,
together with the militant and revolutionary elements of the Youth
League fought against the moderate and conservative elements to
carry the SNDP leftwards. Despite the achievement of two of the
Yogam's long-standing aims—the opening up of government service
and the Temple Entry Proclamation—the SNDP was undoubtedly
weakened by the political and personal rivalries of the 1930s.
Eventually in the 1950s under R. Sankar (1909–72) it recovered its
unity, playing a role analogous to that of the NSS as founder of
educational institutions and political pressure group.[72] Meanwhile it
had lost actual and potential members to the communist movement.

In some respects the Ezhavas have proved better able than the
Nairs to adjust to modernization, and a middle class has emerged. In
1968 just over 1 per cent cent (7,900) of Ezhava households received
annual incomes in excess of Rs 8,000.[73] The majority are, of course,
much poorer than their Nair counterparts. Since the Ezhava middle
class is proportionately tiny the Ezhava élite has not exercised the
political influence over its community that the NSS has done among
Nairs. The SNDP leadership has favoured Congress but, like the
NSS, formed its own Social Revolutionary Party (SRP) in 1972. The
Ezhavas at large have preferred the CPM and CPI, though in the
1970s Youth Congress made considerable inroads.

In 1968 the scheduled castes and tribes made up 10.7 per cent of the
total population, 8 per cent Hindu scheduled castes, 1.5 per cent
Christian converts, and 1.3 per cent scheduled tribes. The scheduled
castes are to be found concentrated in three areas, Peermade (26 per
cent of the taluk population), Palghat–Trichur (12 to 16 per cent),
and Trivandrum–Quilon (9 to 11 per cent), while the scheduled
tribes are important only in the formerly malarial taluks of North
and South Wynad in the interior of Malabar (20 to 24 per cent).
Despite the abolition of slavery in the mid-nineteenth century, the
Harijans often continued as chattels prior to Independence. Although government action has since generated a tiny élite, the
scheduled castes remain predominantly landless labourers who are
employed on the most arduous agricultural tasks and against whom
social discrimination is still practised.

Social change, legislative enactment, and executive action have
done much to reduce overt caste disabilities (see below, p. 159) but
customary disabilities remain despite the noteworthy efforts of the

first communist government. Although the 1970 Backward Classes Reservation Commission records many examples of continuing discrimination,[74] it is probably fair to claim that 'untouchability and other forms of direct oppression on the basis of caste' were less prevalent in Kerala than in perhaps any other state in the 1970s. None the less basic attitudes 'which take their origin in the circle of casteism, have their family life in it, and shape the subconscious' have changed more slowly.[75] The very structure of Malayalam, as well as its vocabulary, reflects the caste system—there are more than a dozen words for house, mainly referring to dwelling by caste—as is evident even in the work of revolutionary and socialist writers.[76]

Education and Social Mobility

Of all the changes destructive of the traditional order in Kerala education has probably been the most important. The state's addiction to education and its achievements in this sphere, most notably in literacy, have contributed to its distinctive political culture. Between 1961-2 and 1978-9 the cost of general education rose eightfold.[77] By 1971 the literacy rate had reached 60 per cent, twice the national average.[78] No other state had achieved a female literacy rate of more than half that in Kerala. Virtually all Malayali children now attend the four standards of lower primary school; most continue into the three standards of upper primary school; and one third reach the final tenth standard of high school.[79] What has distinguished the Kerala educational system is not so much the levels of initial enrolment but the lower rates of drop-out and the fact that the levels of attainment of those who do fall by the wayside are higher there than in other parts of the country.[80] Although Kerala's expenditure on higher education and its output of graduates is above the Indian average, successive governments have not given the pre-degree, degree, and postgraduate sectors the priority visible elsewhere in the country. The University of Kerala, founded in 1937, is one of the largest in India but until recently served the whole state. The emphasis has been on mass education rather than on the education of an élite.

To a greater extent than anywhere else in Asia, education in Kerala has been run by private agencies: in 1978-9 they managed 59 per cent of lower primary schools, 68 per cent of upper primary schools, and 65 per cent of high schools. At college level 57 per cent of the 47 colleges in existence in 1956-7 were privately owned and managed, rising to 81 per cent of 149 colleges in 1967-8 and falling slightly thereafter to 75 per cent of 167 colleges in 1977-8.[81] Although, compared with most of India, 'Kerala had an unusually high proportion of literate people in the traditional period'[82] with an especially

noteworthy level of literacy among women of the matrilineal castes,
foreign missionaries provided the first modern schooling in Kerala
in the early nineteenth century;[83] and during the twentieth century
the Hindu NSS and SNDP Yogam and Muslim Education Society
(MES) emulated the indigenous Christian communities in establishing a network of schools and colleges. Grants-in-aid were introduced by the government, linked to elementary forms of supervision and inspection. approved syllabi, and common examinations.
None the less the private managements successfully resisted substantive government control until the 1970s and at college level are still
adept at circumventing the supervision of appointments and admis-
sions. Despite many admirably conducted private institutions, a
significant number fell below the standards and conditions
maintained in the state sector. As early as 1939 there had been a
widespread strike of school teachers in Malabar and the radical
schoolteacher hounded by Dickensian school proprietors is a familiar figure in novel and autobiography. A.K. Gopalan, Kerala's best-
loved communist leader, and Joseph Mundassery, Education Minister in the first communist government, are well-known examples.[84]
The latter's efforts to bring private managements to heel and end
such abuses as the donations commonly required for admission to
colleges or appointments to staff contributed to the difficulties of the
1957-9 communist government (see below, p. 156). In some cases
such payments were used for legitimate purposes but in many they
went no further than the managers' own purses. Education had
become a private business enterprise. To lecture in most colleges it
was a necessary condition to belong to the right community and a
sufficient one to be able to 'donate' a large sum to the foundation.
Qualifications or ability were often minor considerations. Ezhavas
were particularly disadvantaged, with comparatively few institutions of their own and scant resources behind them. There was
widespread recognition even prior to Independence of the necessity
for reform, but every effort at realizing it from 1945 onwards has led
to serious political difficulties for whatever government has been in
power in the face of communal vested interests and the readiness of
opposition parties to exploit the situation.

Social Mobility

Evidence of the cumulative impact of education provision, reservation, and social change on the traditional caste and communal
structure is contained in the 1970 Backward Classes Reservation
Commission report.[85] The accompanying tables show the relative
educational attainments of the different communities in 1968 and the
degree to which they are represented (uncontrolled by age) in the

Table 2.2 Kerala 1968-9: Index of Educational Attainment by Caste and Community
(100 = number of enrolments exactly proportional to community's representation in population)

Group	Community*	Estimated percentage of population 1968	All standard X students	All students on graduate courses in arts and sciences	All on degree courses in engineering	All on degree courses in medicine	All on degree courses in law
IX	Brahmin	1.8	200	394	550	178	372
IV	Nair	14.5	148	181	149	128	200
III	Syrian	16.0	167	208	179	166	129
	(Brahmin, Nair, and Syrian percentage of seats)	(32.3)	(51.7)	(66.5)	(60.1)	(48.4)	(56.4)
I	Ezhava	22.2	88	60	70	49	62
II	Muslim	19.1	43	35	49	60	41
VII	Latin Catholic	3.6	69	50	86	81	50
	Scheduled castes (Hindu)	7.9	68	33	22	39	96
	Scheduled tribes	1.3	8	15	0	0	0

* The Brahmin, Nair, Syrian, Ezhava, and Latin Catholic designations relate to the predominant community in each of the Groups used in BCRC, but in each case certain other small communities are included.

Source: Based on BCRC, vol.2, Appendix 14.

Table 2.3   Kerala 1968: Index of Appointments in Government Service by Caste and Community
(100 = number of appointments exactly proportional to community's representation in population)

Group	Community*	Estimated percentage of population 1968	Services under Government & Legislature			Kerala State Electricity Board			Kerala State Road Transport Corporation			University of Kerala		
			Last Grade†	Non-Gazetted	Gazetted	Last Grade†	Non-Gazetted	Gazetted	Last Grade†	Non-Gazetted	Gazetted	Last Grade†	Non-Gazetted	Gazetted
IX	Brahmin	1.8	111	217	672	106	211	972	56	117	144	117	506	1194
IV	Nair	14.5	219	219	229	240	252	159	173	203	331	348	351	234
III	Syrian	16.0	74	114	136	111	124	164	49	88	77	111	96	143
	(Brahmin, Nair, and Syrian percentage of posts)	(32.3)	(45.6)	(54)	(67)	(54.4)	(60.1)	(66.8)	(33.9)	(45.7)	(86.3)	(70.3)	(75.3)	(81.1)
I	Ezhava	22.2	84	83	73	93	86	75	91	84	6	22	45	18
II	Muslim	19.1	45	48	33	31	25	22	77	34	14	13	15	11
VII	Latin Catholic	3.6	108	75	69	69	75	117	169	189	0	125	72	72
	Scheduled castes (Hindu)	7.9	144	70	23	82	51	18	116	53	34	80	11	16
	Scheduled tribes	1.3	62	15	0	23	8	0	15	8	0	0	0	0

*The Brahmin, Nair, Syrian, Ezhava, and Latin Catholic designations relate to the predominant community in each of the Groups used in BCRC, but in each case certain other small communities are included.

†This term is used for the bottom-most grades of government service.

Source: Based on BCRC, vol.2, Appendices 15, 16, and 17.

various grades of employment in some government-sector organizations. For clarity the results are presented in index form. If the community was represented exactly in proportion to its estimated number in the population it would score 100. Larger numbers indicate statistical over-representation and smaller numbers under-representation.

The table of educational attainments shows that although the backward classes—Ezhavas, Latin Catholics, Muslims, and Scheduled Castes and Tribes—have made progress, they are still under-represented while Brahmins, Syrians, and Nairs are over-represented. The Commission for Reservation of Seats in Educational Institutions, set up in 1965, reported that in the preceding decade, without reservation, the forward communities (Brahmin, Nair, and Syrian), would have taken 80 per cent or more of places in medical training.[86] The communal balance of appointments in government service is more uneven still and the ascendancy of Brahmins, Kshatriyas, and Amabalavasis in the gazetted grades of the Secretariat, Legislature, University, and Electricity Board is remarkable, and that of the Nairs in all grades striking. The forward communities who together form one-third of the total population held two-thirds of the gazetted posts in the Secretariat and the Electricity Board and over four-fifths in the University and Transport Corporation. How far such distributions result from the differential advantages of high-caste or communal background and how far from quasi-freemasonic bonds is impossible to say. The evidence does, however, support the Trivandrum Centre for Development Studies' conclusions to a discussion of the educated job market in Kerala: the role of education in reducing inequality is limited; and higher education is an avenue to the social status of 'white-collar' employment rather than higher income.[87]

The Integration of Kerala

Education, agitation, government action, and the mass media have in complex combination contributed to the integration of Kerala as a political system. The role of education in creating a literate public, female as well as male, and poor as well as rich, has been emphasized above. The leaders of the major political movements and major parties have tended to take Kerala as their platform from the 1930s onwards, when the first *jathas* (processions) were brought south from Malabar in support of the struggle for responsible government in Travancore. Those parties which have distinct and localized socio-economic support have been forced to seek alliances on a state-wide basis in order to secure influence in decision-making. To a greater degree than in perhaps any other Indian state, public meetings (and elections) are a living ritual of the society, a source of entertainment and prestige to the village and its leaders, as well as the arena of conflict between factions, groups, and classes. Politics is the national sport of the Malayalis and the finest orators in a language which lends itself to political rhetoric are an attraction irrespective of party affiliation. Such a politically conscious electorate in 'a problem state' has sought large-scale governmental intervention. The state has become the most important employer and the frequent transfer of officials from place to place has had some integrative effect. The articulation of political and social concern through the daily press, novels, poetry, and the prolific Malayalam film industry has also undoubtedly assisted the formation of a regional consciousness, even though at the same time the newspapers in particular have facilitated particularist expressions within it. It is noteworthy that two of Kerala's three current largest circulation newspapers— *Malayala Manorama* (1890) and *Kerala Kaumudi* (1911)— antedated the first All-Kerala Political Conference (1921). The third— *Mathrubhumi*—followed in 1923. By 1975 there were 71 Kerala dailies (1.1 million copies), of which 12 sold a total of 800,000 copies. Newspaper readership is higher in the state than anywhere else in India and the habit of reading a politically informed daily paper well enough established among the lower castes and poorer classes as to render the claim that by lunchtime every Malayali has read his morning news a pardonable exaggeration.[88]

The very concept of a regional political consciousness is open to a variety of powerful objections. Its epitomization in a particular case warrants caution. Claremont Skrine, British Agent in Travancore and Cochin illustrates this. Writing in 1939, he believed Travancoreans to be virtually ungovernable. 'Not only is communalism rampant, but discipline, *civic* sense . . .and genuine respect for authority are notably lacking in public life.'[89] It is a view which, generalized to Kerala as a whole, finds echoes among the middle classes of present-day Kerala. Gough's work, however, documents a well-developed civic sense at panchayat level in the 1960s.[90] Indeed the very emergence of a powerful, mass-based socialist and communist movement, led by the higher castes and at least relatively disciplined, must tend to vitiate such an analysis.

There is a diversity of sub-cultures within Kerala society. Nevertheless from the elements discussed in this chapter there has emerged a Malayali culture which transcends the component cultures of caste and community, region and village, class and party and renders Kerala politics distinct from the politics of other Indian states. Paradoxically the Keralite is individualistic, independent, excitable, even anarchic yet at the same time capable of intense identification with the group whether it be the extended family, the village, caste, party, or college class mates.[91] How far this identification with a group is a matter of sentiment, calculation, or ideology in a particular context need not concern us here. The fact remains that communists, consciously or subconsciously, have been bound to take account of the patterns of thought and action in the society of which they are a part and to which they appeal. The most effective leadership in Kerala may still be that of the *karanavar*—the head of the traditional joint family. In a tribute to one of the communist party's determined opponents, Pattom Thanu Pillai, on his death, the CPI Chief Minister, C.Achutha Menon, told the Legislative Assembly that 'What attracted [me] in Pattom was that he was a sort of *karanavar* who was deeply concerned with the welfare of his family. Of course, he had also the frailties and rigidities of an uncle'.[92] The 'family' was Kerala as well as the sectional interests with which Pattom was identified. The same judgement might be passed on most of the communist leaders who appear below. Party, class, and (sub-) national identities have been in tension. Whether the resultant melding of expediency, ideology, and tradition is strength or weakness for the communist movement in Kerala, it has given rise to a recognizable indigenous mutation of marxism-leninism.

Notes

1 For the language and literature see Krishna Chaitanya, *A History of Malayalam Literature* (1971).

2 K. Gough, 'Literacy in Kerala', in J. Goody, ed., *Literacy in Traditional Societies* (1968), p. 143; E.M.S. Namboodiripad, *Kerala, Yesterday, Today and Tomorrow,* 2nd edn (1968, title abbreviated hereafter to *Kerala*), pp. 66–7.

3 O.H.K. Spate, *India and Pakistan* (1954), p. 626.

4 Namboodiripad, *Kerala,* p. 52. Namboodiripad's most recent formulation is 'Castes, Classes and Parties in Modern Political Development with Special Reference to Kerala', *Social Scientist* (Tvm) 64, 1977, originally presented to the 1st World Conference on Malayalam, Kerala Culture and Development, Trivandrum, Nov.1977; Joan P. Mencher, 'Kerala and Madras: a Comparative Study of Ecology and Social Structure', *Ethnology* V (2), 1966; A. Sreedhara Menon, *A Survey of Kerala History* (1967); K.A. Wittfogel, *Oriental Despotism* (New Haven, Conn., Yale UP, 1957).

5 Nineteenth-century cuts made it possible to travel from Trivandrum to the mouth of the Periyar River by boat, a distance of some 200 miles.

6 Spate, p. 630.

7 Govt of Kerala, *Kerala 1959: an Economic Review* (1960), pp. 27–33. (Subsequently the title of this annual publication became *Economic Re-*

view, and hereafter the series will be referred to as *ER*.)

8   From 1961 a place was classified as a town if there was a minimum population of 5,000 at a density not less than 1,000 persons per square mile and of whom not less than 75 per cent were engaged in non-agricultural pursuits. *Census of India 1971*, Series 9: *Kerala*, pt X, *District Census Handbooks—Cannanore*, p. 5.

9   'Mulaybar, which is the pepper country, extends for two months' journey along the coast...there is not a foot of ground but what is cultivated. Every man has his orchard, with his house in the middle and a wooden palisade all round it.' Ibn Battuta, *Travels in Asia and Africa 1325-1354*, trans. H.A.R. Gibb (New York, McBride, 1929), pp. 231-2.

10 Mencher, *Ethnology* V (2) 1966. Dr Mencher is suitably cautious in her summary.

11 Conrad Wood, 'Historical Background of the Moplah Rebellion', *Social Scientist* (Tvm) 25, 1974, p.9.

12 *Census of India 1961*, vol. VII: *Kerala*, pt IX, *Census Atlas*, pp. 325 and 327. The twelve socio-cultural indicators used were percentage of urban population, of scheduled castes and tribes, of literates excluding age-group 0–4, of female literates excluding age-group 0–4, of school-going female children of age-group 5–14, of population at level of secondary or higher education in age-group 15–29, of teachers per 1,000 primary pupils, of teachers per 1,000 secondary pupils, of workers in educational and scientific services to all workers in services, and the numbers of medical institutions per 10,000 census houses, of hospital beds per 100,000 population, and of medical doctors per 100,000 population.

13 Kerala State Planning Board, *Fifth Five Year Plan 1974-9: a Draft Outline* (1973), pp. 40–6. (Hereafter *FFYP 1974-9.)*

14 T.C. Varghese, *Agrarian Change and Economic Consequences: Land Tenures in Kerala 1850-1960* (1970); M.A. Oommen, *Land Reforms and Socio-economic Change in Kerala* (1971).

15 M. Moberly, *The Report of the Settlement of the Malabar District* (Govt of Madras, 1900), p .10.

16 Varghese, p. 31.

17 Ibid., p. 32.

18 The new District of Malappuram, created in 1969 out of parts of Kozhikode and Palghat, is only 34 per cent Hindu (1971); Muslims at 64 per cent are the majority. The revised Districts of Palghat and Kozhikode are 76 per cent and 62 per cent Hindu respectively.

19 The communal growth rates for Kerala, 1951-61, were: Muslims, 27.5; Hindus, 23.3; Christians, 26.9; and 1961-71: Muslims, 37.5; Hindus, 23.3; Christians, 25.3. Between 1951 and 1971 the Muslim percentage of the population increased from 17.5 to 19.5. The Muslim growth rate substantially exceeds that of Muslims nationally. See Christie Davies, 'The Relative Fertility of Hindus and Muslims', *Quest* 99, 1976.

20 P.T. Thomas, *Sabarimalai and its Sastha* (1973), pp. 10–12, 32-7.

21 For the early history of the Syrian church in Kerala see E. Tissérant, *Eastern Christianity in India* (1957); L.W. Brown, *The Indian Christians of St. Thomas* (1956); and V.C. George, *Christianity in India through the Ages* (1972).

22 Govt of Kerala, *Report of the Backward Classes Reservation Commission* (1970), vol. II, Apps. XI and XII (A). Group III, the category used in the appendices, includes certain other small communities but is overwhelmingly Syrian. (This *Report* will hereafter be cited as *BCRC*.)
23 Ibid., App. XVIII.
24 Ibid.
25 Interviews E.M.S. Namboodiripad, Tvm, Aug. 1973; Joseph, Cardinal Parecattil, Archbishop of Ernakulam, Ernakulam, Sept. 1973; Benedict Mar Gregorios, Archbishop of Trivandrum, Tvm, Nov. 1970.
26 J. Vadakkan, *A Priest's Encounter with Revolution* (1974).
27 R. Jeffrey, *The Decline of Nayar Dominance* (1976), p. 25.
28 R.E. Miller, *Mappila Muslims of Kerala* (1976), p. 28. See also Ninan Koshy, *Caste in the Kerala Churches* (Bangalore, Christian Inst. for the Study of Religion and Society, 1968).
29 R.E. Miller, p. 82.
30 S.F. Dale, 'The Islamic Frontier in Southwest India: the Shahīd as a Cultural Ideal among the Mappillas of Malabar', *Modern Asian Studies* II(1), 1977; R.E. Miller, p. 94; C.K. Kareem, *Kerala Under Haider Ali and Tipu Sultan* (1973).
31 Conrad Wood, *Social Scientist* (Tvm) 25, 1974; S.F. Dale, The Mappilla Outbreaks: Ideology and Social Conflict in Nineteenth Century Kerala', *J. of Asian Studies* XXXV (1), 1975; P. Hardy, *The Muslims of British India* (1972).
32 S.F. Dale, *Modern Asian Studies* II (1) 1977, p. 47.
33 *Reports of a Joint Commission from Bengal and Bombay appointed to inspect into the state and conditions of the Province of Malabar in the years 1792 and 1793* (Madras, Courier Press, 1879); vol. I, p. 164. F.H. Buchanan, *A Journey from Madras through the countries of Mysore, Canara and Malabar* (London, Cadell & Davies, 1807), vol. II, p. 435.
34 R.E. Miller, pp. 251-2.
35 Wakkom Maulavi (1873-1902), the community's first modern reformer, came from Quilon in Travancore. R.E. Miller, p. 270, and see also p. 221.
36 Ibid., pp. 196-203.
37 Ibid., p. 203.
38 See M.S.A. Rao, *Social Change in Malabar* (1957) for an account of caste in Kerala.
39 *Report of the Travancore Banking Enquiry Committee* (1930), vol. I, p. 34; *Report of the Travancore Unemployment Enquiry Committee* (1928), pp. 33-4 (Appendix D lists the major firms then in existence); *FFYP 1974-9* p. 607; but see V.R. Pillai and P.G.K. Panikar, *Land Reclamation in Kerala* (1965), p. 16, for examples of indigenous entrepreneurial activity. Generally, see M.A. Oommen, 'Rise and Growth of Banking in Kerala', *Social Scientist (Tvm) 51, 1976.*
40 Emily G. Hatch, *Travancore: a Guide Book for the Visitor* (1933), p. 28.
41 Varghese, pp. 12-13.
42 *Indulekha, a Novel from Malabar,* trans. W. Dumergue (1890, reprinted 1965, Calicut, Mathrubhumi), p. xxiii.

43   V. Nagam Aiya, *Travancore State Manual,* vol. II (1906), p. 255.

44   The Namboodiri reform movement is discussed in Joan P. Mencher, 'Namboodiri Brahmins: an Analysis of a Traditional Elite in Kerala', *J. of Asian and African Studies* I, 1966, pp. 183-96.

45   Although young Namboodiris discontented with joint-family life are often claimed to have been prominent in the early political movements, K. Karunakaran Nair, ed., *Who is Who of Freedom Fighters in Kerala* (1975), which contains some 2,400 names, does not offer supporting evidence of a conclusive nature.

46   I am indebted to Shri D. Jayaraj formerly of the Dept of Politics, U. of Kerala, for details of the communal composition of the Kerala Legislative Assembly since 1957.

47   Information kindly supplied by an official, Trivandrum Secretariat, Nov. 1974.

48   Interview K.S.S. Nambudiripad, Kariavattom, Nov. 1970. Kattumadam Narayan (Nambudiripad), 'Nambudiris', *Illustrated Weekly of India,* 5 Mar. 1972.

49   Jeffrey, *The Decline of Nayar Dominance,* pp. 106 ff., discusses the *Memorial.*

50   On 1 July 1974 in the 101-member Kerala Cadre of the Indian Administrative Service, there were 20 Tamil Brahmins of whom 14 were from outside Kerala. The number of Tamil Brahmins has since declined.

51   *Report,* vol. II, Appendix XVIII, Group IX.

52   On the concept of the 'dominant caste' see L. Dumont, *Homo Hierarchicus* (London, Paladin Books, 1972); Peter M. Gardner, 'Dominance in India: a Reappraisal', *Contributions to Indian Sociology,* New Series, no II, Dec. 1968; F.G. Bailey, *Tribe, Caste and Nation* (Manchester, Manchester UP, 1960); T.K. Oommen, 'The Concept of Dominant Caste: Some Queries', *Contributions to India Sociology,* New Series, no. II, Dec. 1968. For its application to the Nairs, see Jeffrey, *The Decline of Nayar Dominance.*

53   *BCRC* estimated 14.47 per cent on the basis of a 1968 sample survey: vol. 2, p. 440. The *Report of the [Kerala] Commission for Reservation of Seats in Educational Institutions* (1966) estimated Nairs at 15.35 per cent by projection from the 1941 Census Reports for Travancore and Cochin and the 1921 Census Report for Madras (Malabar District). *The Kerala Mail,* 23 Aug. 1959, offered a figure of only 12.5 per cent.

54   See Jeffrey, *The Decline of Nayar Dominance,* pp. 11-32, and also C.J. Fuller, *The Nayars Today* (1976), p. 123.

55   K. Gough, 'The Nayars and the Definition of Marriage', *J. of the Royal Anthropological Inst.* LXXXIX (1 and 2), 1959. See also Fuller, ch. 5. An interesting account of Nairs generally is to be found in Usha Chettur, 'Nayars', *Illustrated Weekly of India,* 20 Dec. 1970.

56   V.K.S. Nayar, 'Kerala Politics since 1947: Community Attitudes', in I. Narain, ed., *State Politics in India* (1967).

57   O.M. Thomas, *Under the Knife,* pp. 56-67, quoted in P.K.K. Menon, *History of the Freedom Movement in Kerala* (1972), vol. 2, p. 479, n. 45.

58 R. Jeffrey, 'Matriliny, Marxism, and the Birth of the Communist Party in Kerala, 1930-1940', *J. of Asian Studies* 38 (1), 1978. For comment on Jeffrey's interpretation see below, pp. 66-7.

59 Varghese, pp. 105-7.

60 *BCRC*, vol. 2, pp. 1-31.

61 All informants concurred on this point. I was introduced to Nairs engaged in a variety of manual labour including road works and field labour.

62 *BCRC*, vol. 2, Appendix XVIII, Group I.

63 A. Aiyappan, *Social Revolution in a Kerala Village* (1965), p. 117.

64 R. Jeffrey, 'The Social Origins of a Caste Association, 1875-1905: the Founding of the S.N.D.P. Yogam', *South Asia* I (4), 1974, p. 45. See also Cyriac K. Pullapilly, 'The Izhavas of Kerala', *J. of Asian and African Studies* XI (1-2), 1976. A marxist view is F. Houtart and G. Lemercinier, 'Socio-Religious Movements in Kerala: a Reaction to the Capitalist Mode of Production', *Social Scientist* (Tvm) 71 & 72, 1978.

65 D.Thomas, *Sree Narayana Guru* (Bangalore, Christian Inst. for the Study of Religion and Society, 1965).

66 Jeffrey, *South Asia* I (4), pp. 53-4.

67 For an English profile see R. Jeffrey, 'Travancore, Status, Class and the Growth of Radical Politics', in R. Jeffrey, ed., *People, Princes and Paramount Power* (1978), p. 149.

68 Ibid., p. 154. See also Jeffrey's 'Temple-entry Movement in Travancore 1860-1940', *Social Scientist* (Tvm) 44, 1976.

69 *Census of India 1931,* vol. XXVIII: *Travancore,* pt I, Appendix IV, Economic Condition of the People.

70 K. Karunakaran Nair, *Who is Who of Freedom Fighters in Kerala*, p. 213.

71 Madras States Agency, Fortnightly Reports, 17 Dec. 1930, India Office Library (hereafter IOL).

72 Interview, R. Sankar, Quilon, Dec. 1970.

73 *BCRC*, vol. 2, Appendix XVIII.

74 Prosecutions under the 1955 Untouchability (Offences) Act continue, despite the obvious barriers of ignorance, poverty, and fear to the registration of complaints (the 1966 *Report of the* [Kerala] *Commission for Reservation of Seats in Educational Institutions*, p. 33). *BCRC*, vol. 1, pp. 69-73, quotes an advertisement from the Ezhava daily *Kerala Kaumudi* in 1970 for 'expert makers of pickles . . . Persons belonging to the Brahmin or Potti caste alone need apply.'

75 P.K. Balakrishnan, 'The Caste System in Kerala', *Quest* 100, 1976, p. 15.

76 Ibid., pp. 11-12.

77 *ER 1978*, p. 148, Appendix 9.15.

78 In 1971 district literacy rates varied from a minimum of 46.69 per cent in Palghat to a maximum of 70.44 per cent in Alleppey (both predominantly lower-class/caste areas). Male rates varied from 54.58 per cent in Palghat to 75.22 per cent in Alleppey and female rates from 39.22 per cent in Palghat to 65.69 per cent in Alleppey. The state literacy rate was 60.16 per cent (India 29.34 per cent). For the mapped distribution of

general literacy and female literacy by Assembly constituency in 1971
see below, p. 340.

79   *ER 1978,* p. 146, Appendix 9.7 shows the number of persons
matriculating in 1978 as 164,000.

80   Centre for Development Studies, *Poverty, Unemployment and Development Policy* (1975, indian edn. 1977), pp. 122-3. (Hereafter referred to as
CDS, *Poverty.*)

81   *ER 1978,* p. 147, Appendix 9.10.

82   K. Gough, in J. Goody, ed., *Literacy in Traditional Societies,* p. 151.

83   Ibid., p.155; *Kerala District Gazetteers: Kottayam* (A. Sreedhara Menon,
ed., 1975), p. 425.

84   A.K. Gopalan, *In the Cause of the People* (1973), pp. 5-15, and Joseph
Mundassery, *Professor,* a novelette in Malayalam (1948). This latter
work is briefly reviewed by Thazhaki Sivasankara Pillai, *Indian Litera-
ture* X (2), 1967. On union organization in 1939 see C.J. May, 'Some
Lesser Leaders of the Communist Movement in Kerala', in W.H.
Morris-Jones, ed., *The Making of Politicians* (1976), and Prakash Karat,
'The Peasant Movement in Malabar 1934-40', *Social Scientist* (Tvm) 50,
1976 and 'Organised Struggles of Malabar Peasantry 1934-40',
Social Scientist (Tvm) 56, 1977.

85   *BCRC,* vol. 2, Appendix XX, p. 472.

86   The Commission's *Report,* Appendices IX and X.

87   CDS, *Poverty,* p. 132.

88   Dept of Public Relations, *The Press in Kerala* (1977) is a useful summary
of the history of the newspaper industry.

89   Madras States Agency, Fortnightly Reports 1/39, 15 Jan. 1939, IOL.

90   K. Gough, 'Communist Rural Councillors in Kerala', *J. of Asian and
African Studies* III (3-4), 1968.

91   R.E. Miller, p. 7.

92   *Synopsis of the Proceedings of the Kerala Legislative Assembly* (hereafter
SPKLA), 26 Oct. 1970, p.6.

3

Economic Background

Demographic Pressures

THE demographic pressures on land, food, and employment in Kerala have been a desperate exaggeration of All-India trends. Between 1951 and 1971 Kerala's population rose from 13.5 million to 21.3 million, an annual increase of 2 per cent, and well above the national average. With a population density 2.4 times (1971) that of India as a whole, Kerala is not only the most densely populated state in India but one of the most crowded rural areas in the world. Averages conceal the enormity of the situation. In the 10 per cent of land at an elevation of less than 25 feet, the average density in 1971 was 1,385 persons per square kilometre; and, as shown in Map 6, densities above 1,500 per square kilometre are found in the coastal taluks of Travancore and Cochin.

Population increase has been a function of a high birth rate, low infant mortality, and a falling death rate. In the mid-1950s infant mortality in Kerala was 50 per thousand compared with 113 in the whole of India. As late as 1977 Kerala's death rate of 7.5 per thousand was well below India's average of 15.2. For these reasons—and probably also the impact of high levels of female literacy and education—Kerala's birth rate is now declining. The estimates for 1977 show 27.0 births per thousand in Kerala compared with 34.8 in India.[1] This decline, however, can affect the rate of population increase only in the longer term, since the population profile is skewed towards the young. In 1961 15 per cent of Malayalis were below 5 years of age, 43 per cent below 15, and 51 per cent below 19, a distribution which strains resources in education,[2] health,[3] and above all employment.

Unemployment figures are indicative rather than exact. The 1954 Survey of Unemployment (Travancore-Cochin) suggested that 10 per cent of adult and able-bodied adult males were seeking employment, of whom 16 per cent had achieved at least the Secondary School Leaving Certificate (SSLC). As many as 23 per cent were classified as 'casually employed', working on average 3.6 days per week at low rates of pay.[4] The *Economic Review 1959* noted that if 'unemployment is a serious and growing problem everywhere in

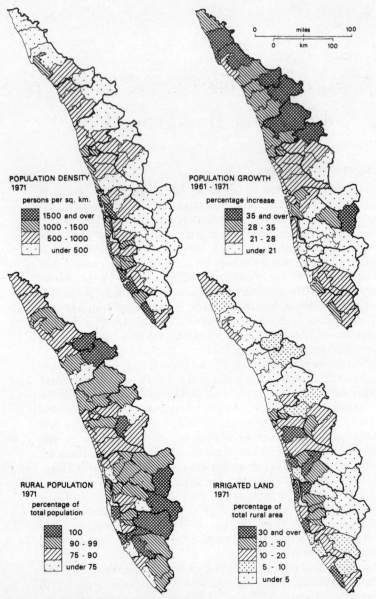

POPULATION DENSITY
1971

persons per sq. km.

1500 and over
1000 - 1500
500 - 1000
under 500

POPULATION GROWTH
1961 - 1971

percentage increase

35 and over
28 - 35
21 - 28
under 21

RURAL POPULATION
1971

percentage of
total population

100
90 - 99
75 - 90
under 75

IRRIGATED LAND
1971

percentage of
total rural area

30 and over
20 - 30
10 - 20
5 - 10
under 5

The territorial waters of India extend into the sea to a distance
of twelve nautical miles measured from the appropriate base line.

Based upon Survey of India map with the permission
of the Surveyor General of India.

© Government of India Copyright 1982

Source: Data from *Census of India 1971*, Series 9: *Kerala*, pt X, *District Census
Handbooks*.

Map 6 Kerala: Population Density 1971; Population Growth 1961–71;
Rural Population as % of Total Population 1971; Irrigated Land
as % of Total Rural Area 1971. All by Taluk

India . . .it has reached menacing proportions' in Kerala.[5] The 1971 Committee on Unemployment in Kerala estimated total unemployment at 900,000, of which one-quarter consisted of 'educated unemployed'. Underemployment had risen to an estimated 1.8 million.[6] A national sample survey suggests that Kerala's share of All-India under- and unemployment may be as high as 10 per cent. By 1972 the number of educated work-seekers registered with employment exchanges had reached 258,000, the total for all work-seekers in the 1954 survey; and at the end of 1978 the figure had risen to 558,000, representing 53 per cent of those seeking work through the employment exchanges.[7] The youthful structure of the population and lack of employment opportunities affect the dependency ratio. In the 1950s there were 200 non-earning dependents for every 100 economically active persons, a heavier burden than in any other state, a ratio that has since deteriorated further.[8]

Rising population cut the *per capita* availability of cultivable land from 53 cents (0.53 acres) in 1921 to 38 cents in 1956-7 (All-India average 1.09 acres) and 27 cents in 1974. It has sunk no lower because cultivation has been extended into areas of extreme marginality and into 'reserved' forests.[9]

In Kerala two acres of standard fertility is taken as the minimum requirement for family subsistence. By 1931 virtually the whole of the available land in the lowlands and midlands of Travancore and Cochin had been brought under cultivation. Thereafter land hunger could be sated only by migration to the hills or to the cultivable wastes of interior Malabar, where as late as 1951 land was still available. In both cases Christians were prominent. Total landlessness was more acute in Kerala than in any other state. In 1962 31 per cent of all households owned no land whatsoever in Kerala, compared with 12 per cent in all India.[10] The impact of land reforms is a complex issue (see below, p. 300) but it is not in dispute that there has been very little transfer of 'surplus land' to the landless—by the end of 1978 an official 45,000 acres. The percentage of agricultural labourers is again the highest in India, rising from 39 per cent in 1951 to 63 per cent in 1971 (India 38 per cent), and reaching more than 70 per cent in coastal areas and in Palghat.[11] The general problem of land scarcity is compounded by the extreme fragmentation of holdings, their uneven distribution between classes in rural society, tenurial arrangements, the progressive shift on larger holdings from food to cash crops, and the low levels of capital formation and agricultural technology.

Sub-division of holdings is most acute in Travancore-Cochin. According to official returns in the early 1950s two-thirds of the holdings were less than one acre and 96 per cent less than 2.5 acres in extent. The comparable figures in Malabar were 29 and 52 per cent respectively.[12] Above 2.5 acres the fragmentation of individual holdings assumes importance. Holdings between 2.5 and 5 acres average three portions, and above 10 acres the figure rises to five or six fragments.[13]

The proportion of land cultivated by different classes in rural society has remained extremely unequal. In 1966-7 the 60 per cent of land-holding households with plots of less than one acre in size owned only 10 per cent of the total area. The 0.9 per cent of households with 20 acres or more held 32 per cent of the total cultivated area. It is doubtful whether later land reforms have fundamentally altered this pattern of inequality since there were many ways in which the intentions of the legislature could be evaded (see below, p. 297).[14] Detailed analysis of the District figures shown in Maps 7 and 8 indicates no major variation from the basic pattern anywhere, but the biggest landholders—usually commercial farmers—are most prominent in Cannanore, Kottayam, and Alleppey Districts and insignificant in the two southernmost Travancore Districts of Quilon and Trivandrum. These variations may, however, in part be artifacts of the evasion of ceilings on land holding.

No comparable information is available for the present distribution of land by caste and community. Such statistical evidence as there is suggests that land ownership is still preponderantly high caste, overwhelmingly so in Malabar and Cochin, but that in Travancore the process of diffusion of ownership which had been taking place from at least the 1850s has continued. In Malabar, according to Varghese, the extreme concentration of land in Namboodiri (south Malabar) and Nair (north Malabar) hands, recorded by Logan in 1881, did not begin to change until after 1940. In Varghese's own 1958 sample 90 per cent of the non-corporate landlords were drawn from the superior castes, 31 per cent Namboodiri and 32 per cent Nair.[15] In Cochin the same survey indicates that Namboodiris (mainly resident in Trichur District) and *devaswoms* (temples) dominated land ownership to an even greater degree than in Malabar.[16] In Travancore the 1931 economic census gives the pre-war distribution in detail for 'wet' (paddy) and 'dry' lands and by size of unit (see Diagram 3.1). The Brahmins dominated ownership above five acres, especially in the case of 'wet' land, but lower castes did own land, particularly dry land. Varghese's 1958 study suggests that the process of diffusion continued although substantial inequalities remained. The 20 per cent of his sample who belonged to the superior castes owned 46 per cent of the total and farmed 38 per cent. Ezhavas, who formed 28 per cent of the sample owned 22 per cent and cultivated 24 per cent.[17]

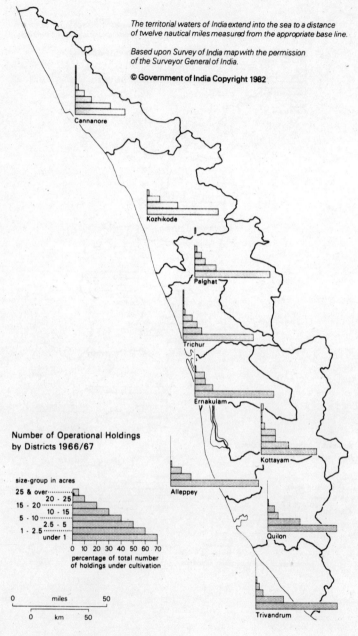

The territorial waters of India extend into the sea to a distance
of twelve nautical miles measured from the appropriate base line.

Based upon Survey of India map with the permission
of the Surveyor General of India.

© Government of India Copyright 1982

Cannanore

Kozhikode

Palghat

Trichur

Ernakulam

Number of Operational Holdings
by Districts 1966/67

size-group in acres
25 & over
        20 - 25
15 - 20
        10 - 15
5 - 10
        2.5 - 5
1 - 2.5
        under 1

0 10 20 30 40 50 60 70
percentage of total number
of holdings under cultivation

Kottayam

Alleppey

Quilon

0   miles   50

0   km   50

Trivandrum

Source: Data from LRSK, Table 8.3, p. 53.

Map 7 Kerala 1966-7: Distribution of Numbers of Operational Holdings
          by Size-group and District

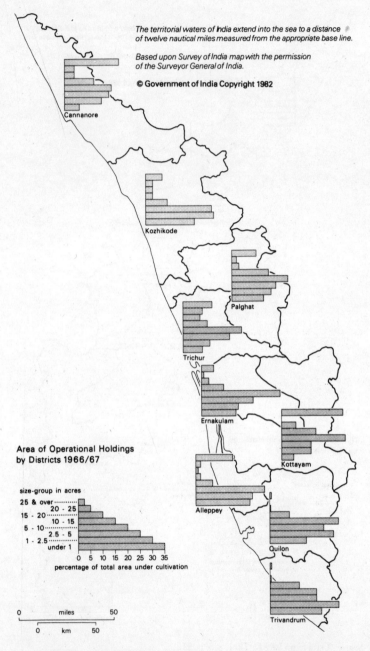

The territorial waters of India extend into the sea to a distance of twelve nautical miles measured from the appropriate base line.

Based upon Survey of India map with the permission of the Surveyor General of India.

© Government of India Copyright 1982

Area of Operational Holdings by Districts 1966/67

size-group in acres

25 & over ....
　　　　　20 - 25
15 - 20 ....
　　　　　10 - 15
5 - 10 ....
　　　　　2.5 - 5
1 - 2.5 ....
under 1

0 5 10 15 20 25 30 35
percentage of total area under cultivation

0 ____ miles ____ 50
0 ____ km ____ 50

Source: Data from *LRSK*, Table 8.4, p. 54

Map 8 Kerala 1966-7: Distribution of Area of Operational Holdings by
　　　　Size-group and District

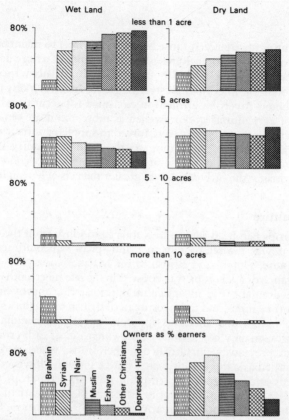

Diagram 3.1 Travancore 1931: Percentage of Wet and Dry Land Owned
within Each Community by Acreage; Landowners of Wet
and Dry Land as Percentage of Earners by Community

Source: *Census of India 1931*, vol. XXVIII: *Travancore*, pt I, Appendix IV.

Tenurial arrangements exacerbated the effects of population
growth in three major ways: their sheer complexity; the existence of
intermediaries between landlords and cultivators in the form of
kanomdars; and the crowding of interests on any given piece of land.
It has been estimated that there were nearly 500 different forms of
tenure in the state. The system was a 'maze of intermediary rights,
esoteric usufructuary mortgage tenures [and] complex sub-
infeudation'.[18] Neither the operation of the free market nor intervention by the state could readily simplify the structure. The intermediary class constituted a second layer of unproductive interests
to be carried by the tenant-at-will. In turn the agricultural labourer
bore landlord, intermediary, and tenant cultivator on his back. The

higher interests squeezed those below in an effort to maintain their own economic position. Rents rose; the security of tenure declined; the opportunities for casual labour contracted and daily wages fell in real terms as the inferior interests struggled to survive. Many labourers accepted covert enserfment in exchange for security while the ranks of agricultural labour swelled as more and more tenants-at-will and owner cultivators were forced to supplement their income with casual labour. According to the Second Enquiry on Agricultural Labour the deterioration of the labourer's condition in Kerala during the early 1950s was greater than elsewhere in India.[19]

Agriculture

Cash crops had been central to Kerala's economy from the earliest times: it was the region's pepper and spices which attracted the Portuguese, Dutch, and British to the Malabar coast. The relative importance of cash crops was boosted in the late nineteenth century by the dramatic rise in agricultural prices, the improvement in transport facilities, and the investment of British capital on a significant scale, first in plantations and subsequently in manufacturing industries, mainly coir. Much of the extension of cash crops took place in previously uncultivated higher lands, where paddy and pulses, the basic food crops, could not be grown. However, in the lowlands and midlands the tempting prices of cash crops and the limited irrigation facilities for rice discouraged the growth of the area under food crops commensurate with the rise in population. By 1956 only 44 per cent of the cultivated area was under food crops with a further 14 per cent under food-cum-cash crops. Kerala was then producing just over half of its rice consumption, but by 1978 the proportion had fallen to little more than two-fifths.[20] When 1956-7 is taken as a baseline the area under paddy had increased by 15 per cent by 1970-1 whereas the area under rubber and coffee had risen by 117 per cent, arecanut by 81 per cent, cashew by 76 per cent, and coconut by 48 per cent.[21] During the 1970s the area under rice fell slightly—the proportion of high-yielding varieties sown doubled, from 18 to 33 (1978) per cent—while the area under commercial crops continued to increase.[22] Productivity showed a similar pattern. With 1959-60 as the base year, the productivity of cereals (rice, jowar, and ragi) was 10.9 per cent better in the Fourth Plan period (1969-70 to 1973-4) and 13.6 per cent better in 1977-8 (provisional), of non-grain food crops (banana, tapioca, pepper, ginger, arecanut, cardamom, and cashewnut) 45 per cent better in the Fourth Plan period and 39 per cent in 1977-8, and of plantation crops (tea, coffee, and rubber) 56 per cent better in the Fourth Plan period and 91 per cent better in

1977-8. Agricultural production overall in 1977-8 had not yet reached the average level of the Fourth Plan period despite progress in the case of some plantation and commercial crops.[23]

Outside the commercial sector the effective adoption of new agricultural technologies has been constrained by absence of capital and shortage of credit as much as by conservatism. Although there was a remarkable extension in banking facilities in Travancore and Cochin from the 1920s onwards, agricultural loans were sought primarily for the development of the more profitable cash crop activities. Furthermore, the majority of these enterprises were in Christian hands and tended to benefit that community. Much of the paddy land was owned by Brahmins and Nairs and although some of the latter, particularly in the Kuttanad, showed outstanding enterprise, the majority did not. Cultivating tenants-at-will had little incentive to invest without security of tenure and found it difficult to raise loans except at punitive rates of interest. The small owner-cultivators of Travancore were scarcely better placed. For the small man the main lines of credit were the *chitty* (a savings-cum-credit club in which loans were given either by lot or auction), the co-operative, or the village money-lender. For the most part such small credit as they provided was used for urgent necessity rather than investment. According to the Travancore Banking Enquiry (1930) the average debt of a rural family was Rs 380. The majority of new debts incurred were simply to clear past debts, often from previous generations. Land, the report observed, had become unremunerative in consequence of existing methods of cultivation; and the backwardness of agriculture was as much a consequence of chronic indebtedness as its cause.[24] In these conditions the green revolution is very much a high-cost, high-risk technology (see below, p. 303).

The plantation crops—rubber, tea, coffee, and cardamom—are of great national as well as local importance, nationally as foreign exchange earners, or in the case of rubber as an essential raw material for domestic use. Ninety-two per cent of the Indian-produced rubber is tapped in Kerala. In 1956-7 of 340,000 acres under plantation crops, 200,000 acres was under rubber and 100,000 under tea, employing a total of 175,000 persons. By 1975-6 the plantation acreage had grown to more than 800,000 acres, more than half under rubber with the tea acreage unaltered.[25]

Twenty-eight of the 35 tea estates in Kerala are owned by the British company of James Finlay and Co., which, as Finlay Muir and Co., had been responsible for the development of tea planting in the Kanan Devan Hills from 6,000 acres in 1895 to 30,000 acres in 1956. Tea estates require a regular and experienced labour force, plucking being a delicate task suited to female labour. One person per acre is

employed as a daily average. Much of the labour force is Tamil, since
Malayalis are reluctant to work in the cool, damp conditions and
employers prefer a Tamil workforce.[26] Whereas tea is organized in
large estates and production dominated by one company, rubber can
be grown efficiently on relatively small plantations and three-
quarters are small holdings averaging 3 acres. The estates are entirely
in local ownership, with Syrian Christians prominent. The doubling
of the area under rubber is not entirely a function of its profitability
for the small farmer: it lends itself to tax evasion and affords a means
of circumventing land-ceiling legislation, since rubber estates are
exempt. The characteristics of the cardamom and coffee growing
industries are similar to those of rubber.[27] Daily wage rates on
plantations compare unfavourably with industrial wage rates but the
regularity of work, and, in the tea industry, security of employment
compare favourably with field labour. Historically, pepper has been
Kerala's most important commercial crop; and 90 per cent of Indian
pepper is grown in the state. Although pepper gardens are organized
on a plantation scale, their cultivation requires a modest input of
labour. The acreage under pepper has risen modestly from 220,000
acres in 1958 to 272,000 acres in 1977-8, of which 40 to 50 per cent is
located in the northernmost District of Cannanore.[28]

Food Supply
The combination of demographic pressures, the steady shift to cash
crops, the slow rise in productivity in the food grain sector, and
post-Independence restrictions on the interstate movements of rice
produced an era of acute shortage of the major cereal in the Kerala
diet. Rice became in the 1960s a luxury item and its *per capita*
availability declined, while in the early 1970s when the monsoons
'failed' rice was at times unobtainable in Kerala. Until 1977 the 'food
problem' was invariably an issue in elections; and studies appeared to
show that 'the scale of mass poverty in Kerala' was 'not only higher
than in other states in India but among the highest in the world' as
measured by undernourishment.[29] Subsequent reviews of the evidence have revised the estimates of calorie intake upwards to the
point at which the average intake does not appear to be lower than
the national average,[30] while the smaller consumption of protein is
partially compensated for by the greater share of animal protein.
Even so the relative infrequency of cases of food deficiency diseases
and the low levels of infant mortality and high levels of life ex-
pectancy are remarkable enough in an Indian context to require
explanation. Five factors may be isolated: the increased availability
of tapioca—1.6m tons were produced in Kerala in 1961-2 but 5.7m
tons in 1974; a free school meals programme originating in

Travancore and Cochin in the mid-1940s and now covering three-quarters of primary school children; the provision of a comprehensive network of fair-price shops, which accounted for some 13 per cent of cereals consumed in Kerala in 1961-2 and over 37 per cent by 1971-2; the impact of improved levels of education among the poor; and the extensive network of medical care. Possibly, also, land reforms may have helped to equalize food consumption.

Exports

The share of India's export earnings actually originating in Kerala is subject to some margin of error. Most estimates are based on exports passing through the ports of Kerala—chiefly Cochin, which serves a wider hinterland than Kerala alone. In some cases such as the spice trade it is safe to assume that virtually all such exports emanate from the state, but in the case of tea and coffee, for example, the proportion grown in other southern states and exported through Kerala is uncertain. In the mid-1950s Kerala's exports were estimated to earn Rs 500 million in foreign exchange, and in 1975-6 Rs 3,000 million.[31] It has been a persistent complaint of Kerala politicians of all parties that its unusually high contribution to foreign exchange earnings—conventionally set at 10 per cent of India's total and 'roughly of the order of 8 to 10 per cent' according to a 1972 sample survey[32]—has gone unrecognized either in plan allocations or in making good the state's food deficit (see below, p. 265).

Since the mid-1950s the pattern and direction of exports from Kerala (subject to the margin of error mentioned above) have changed significantly.[33] In 1956-7 tea (37 per cent by value), cashew (21 per cent), and coir (16 per cent) headed the list of exports. By the later 1970s marine products (18 per cent in 1977-8), cashew (18 per cent), and coffee (13 per cent) were of considerable importance. Tea after several years of difficult trading conditions had recovered its former primacy (29 per cent) but coir had sunk to a mere 5 per cent of exports by value. Pepper, after declining as an export crop in the face of Indonesian competition from 1952 onwards, has begun to recover its lost share of the world market.[34] The varying performance of different sectors has impinged on the fortunes of the political parties and on the agenda of politics. The state of the cashew industry, concentrated in Quilon, has a bearing on the position of both the CPI and the Revolutionary Socialist Party (RSP). The RSP is also a beneficiary of the growth of the fishing and fish-processing industry as is Kerala Congress, a rebel Congress grouping dating from 1964, of the burgeoning plantation economy; while the CPM has sought to mobilize—with mixed success—the depressed workers of the coir sector and—with more success—farmers and workers in Cannanore where the markets for pepper, coconut (coir), and beedis (the cigarette of the poor) were long depressed.

Equally interesting is the shift in the direction of Kerala's exports. In 1956-7 35 per cent of Kerala's estimated exports went to the United Kingdom, 30 per cent to the United States, and only 4 per cent to the Soviet Union. By 1969-70 Kerala exports to the Soviet Union had risen to 31 per cent (39 per cent to the Communist bloc), exports to the UK had fallen to 7 per cent, while the United States figure remained steady at 32 per cent.[33] Table 3.1 shows the value of Kerala's exports to the USSR and the USA from 1951-2 to 1969-70 with All-India comparisons.

Table 3.1 *Kerala and All-India 1951/2 — 1969/70:*
Exports to USSR and USA
Rs lakh (100,000)

	Kerala			All-India	
Year	USSR	USA	Year	USSR	USA
1951-2	214	1,911	1951	·647	13,606
1952-3	20	2,293	1952	174	11,637
1953-4	155	1,701	1953	36	9,540
1954-5	51	1,730	1954	251	8,548
1955-6	178	1,669	1955	247	9,117
1956-7	209	1,531	1956	1,232	8,482
1957-8	306	1,640	1957	n.a	n.a
1958-9	660	1,501	1958-9	2,591	8,602
1959-60	792	1,951	1959-60	3,038	9,613
1960-1	650	1,734	1960-1	2,881	10,293
1961-2	523	1,810	1961-2	3,220	11,574
1962-3	695	1,918	1962-3	3,825	11,433
1963-4	1,067	1,931	1963-4	5,210	12,989
1964-5	1,652	2,391	1964-5	7,792	14,689
1965-6	1,666	2,585	1965-6	9,299	14,775
1966-7	2,226	4,001	1966-7	10,151	17,947
1967-8	3,303	4,317	1967-8	12,179	20,743
1968-9	3,349	4,514	1968-9	14,831	23,436
1969-70	4,212	4,390	1969-70	17,637	23,797

Sources: SFP, 10 : *Export and Import Statistics;* Govt of India, *Statistical Handbook of the Indian Union 1951-1956* (1957); *Reserve Bank of India Bulletin.*

Soviet trade with India had grown rapidly from the mid-fifties but it is clear that exports from Kerala to the USSR had increased relative to those to the USA far more than from the rest of India. By 1967-8 exports to the Soviet Union from Kerala were 70 per cent of those to the USA but in India as a whole (excluding Kerala) only 55 per cent.

Trade is a well-known strategy for the exercise of political influence at the level of the nation state. The figures given above suggest that the Soviet Union may have sought to influence developments in a province. Prior to the creation of Kerala State, Soviet purchases peaked in election years (1951-2 and 1953-4), quadrupled between the beginning and end of the first communist ministry, tailed off in the early 1960s to climb again during the CPI split and the 1965 election, and grew steadily through the United Front Ministry of 1967-9 to reach their highest level in the first year of the CPI-led Mini Front Ministry in 1969-70. No coherent political pattern is evident in US imports. It is, however, now on record that the United States did use CIA funds in the hope of averting communist election success in two Indian state elections, one of which was almost certainly the Kerala contest of 1960.[36]

The sceptic might object that the apparent correlation between Soviet imports and the needs of the Communist Party could well be spurious: Soviet trade with India was growing; Kerala happens to be the state which produces what the USSR wants; and the course of the annual figures merely reflects market conditions, the state of the Soviet economy, and perhaps a distaste for trade with certain régimes. It is more difficult to account for the balance of commodities purchased. In 1967-8 Kerala's main exports were cashew (40 per cent of major commodities), tea (26 per cent), fish and prawns (13 per cent), pepper (10 per cent), and coffee (8 per cent). Almost as much tea went to the USSR as to the UK and we know that before 1956 the Soviet Union had bought its tea elsewhere in India. It is commonly alleged in Cochin that the Soviet Union's abrupt switch to Kerala sources in 1956-7 was politically motivated.[37] Soviet purchases of pepper are also interesting. In the fifties and sixties Kerala's share of the world market shrank to one-third as Indonesian advantages both in terms of price and quality made their impact. The Soviet Union purchased more than one-third of the Kerala crop, almost half of it grown in the communist stronghold—albeit marxist—of Cannanore. While the massacre of the Indonesian communists in 1965 might explain the pattern of Soviet pepper procurement in recent years, the fact that Soviet purchases in Kerala were at a high level prior to 1965 suggests a political element in Soviet imports here also. Finally cashew is the USSR's chief import from Kerala, which may help the CPI, which is relatively strong in the processing district. Overall the evidence suggests political investment through trade but is not conclusive.

Industry

In both Travancore and Cochin pressure on the land had become so acute by the 1920s that the percentage of the population engaged in agriculture had begun to fall. By 1951 only 51 per cent of the total Kerala workforce was in the agricultural sector, compared with 70 per cent in the whole of India. That the proportion of workers (22 per cent) engaged in non-agricultural production was double the Indian figure (11.7 per cent) did not imply advanced industrialization. Information is sketchy but it is unlikely that more than 164,000 workers were employed in what were classified as factories in 1958 (the generosity of the definition is reflected in the fact that only half the number of such establishments employed as many as 100 workers). In contrast to India as a whole, factories in Kerala are mainly found in agricultural and forest-based industries. Forty-six per cent of factory labour in Kerala was employed in food processing, compared with 13 per cent in India.[38] The only industry averaging more than 100 workers per factory was cashew processing (67,000) at nearly 400 per factory, almost all within 25 miles of the town of Quilon. Small-scale and cottage industries accounted for the remaining 80 per cent of the industrial workforce, of which the biggest component was the coir workers.

In India coir manufacture (the processing of the fibres of the coconut husk) is virtually confined to Kerala and presents a unique problem. In 1953 it was estimated that 200,000 were directly engaged in coir work. In the mid-1970s it was estimated that 450,000 people were directly employed in coir-making and 1 million indirectly.[39] Coir, which had prospered in the late nineteenth and early twentieth century on the basis of Western demand for cheap floor covering, suffered badly during the Depression. War contracts revived it during the 1940s but the development of synthetic floor coverings, rising Western standards of living, and the disruption of markets during the war had a disastrous effect thereafter. In the mid-1950s the wholesale price per quintal of coir yarn was hardly more than its price in the late 1920s.[40] A 1969 report described conditions in the industry as 'pitiable'.[41] In Shertallai, a leading coir taluk, 36 per cent of the establishments were closed or closing; of 117 working units, only two were registered under the Factories Act; 60 per cent employed five workers or less; 56 per cent paid their workers less than Rs 2 per day; and 75 per cent worked no more than 200 days per year. 'Expenditure was always found to be higher than income ... The calorific value of the food was ... far below standard', and the children stunted and thin. The majority 'purchase cloth once in a year...Most of the workers were illiterate or semi-literate' and among the children 'college education was almost nil and technical education...unheard of.'[42] A recent study of coir indicates a further decline in the industry's viability resulting from low demand and the dual price structure (in export and domestic markets); and further decline also in the condition of the workforce, subject to acute unemployment and under-employment and increasingly deprived of the minimal protection of executive regulation or unionization as the industry reverts to handloom operations.[43] The daily wage rates in coir—Rs 3 to 6 per day when work is available—were typical of the entire industrial sector with the exception of a few modern industries such as rayon, fertilizers, and cement. The worst rates of all were in the cashew factories, on a par with those of agricultural labour in most of the period.

The overall industrial situation had changed modestly for the better by 1977.[44] Of the average daily employment of 286,000 in registered factories, 134,000 were in cashew processing. Only cotton textiles (22,000), tiles (11,000), plywood (10,000) and chemicals (10,000) employed some 10,000 workers or more daily. Just 12 per cent of the identifiable factories were not based on agricultural or forest products. One important growth area is the fish-canning and freezing industry, centred on Quilon. Almost all the advanced chemical and manufacturing industries are found in the public sector: the Central sector Fertilizers and Chemicals Travancore (FACT) Ltd, Indian Rare Earths, Cochin Refineries, and Hindustan Machine Tools; and in the State sector: Travancore Cochin Chemicals, Transformers and Electricals, and Travancore Titanium Products. Two— FACT (7,000) and Hindustan Machine Tools (2,500)—employ more than 2,000 people. By District, factory employment remains heavily concentrated in Quilon (44 per cent), which is also the area of RSP and major CPI political influence.[45] (A fuller discussion of industrial development can be found in chapter 11 below.)

Trade Unionism

By Indian standards Kerala has a significant trade union movement.[46] In 1961-2 reported union membership in India was 2 per cent of the total workforce but in Kerala 5 per cent.[47] *Actual* membership may have been double. In the same year 7 per cent of reported union membership in India was from Kerala.[48] Unions in Kerala are also comparatively militant, industrial disputes in the state accounting for 8, 17, and 9 per cent of all disputes in 1961, 1966, and 1969 respectively.[49] As in India as a whole, Kerala unions are generally attached to one or other of the trade union federations: the communist (later CPI)-led All-India Trade Union Congress

(AITUC); the CPM-led Centre of Indian Trade Unions (CITU)—formed in 1970—the Congress-led Indian National Trade Union Congress (INTUC), or the Revolutionary Socialist United Trade Union Congress (UTUC). The socialist centre, Hind Mazdoor Sabha (HMS), is of little importance in the state.

The union movement in Kerala began among coir workers before 1925. In 1938 the Travancore Coir Workers Association was strong enough to lead a general strike in the Alleppey coir district and by 1945 had a membership of 20,000. Other unions were founded during the 1930s, especially in 1936-8, but the emergence of a widespread movement dates from 1945-6. Between 1950-1 and 1956-7 reported union membership increased more than six-fold to 41,000, far in excess of the growth in All-India membership. The first communist ministry of 1957-9 occasioned a huge upsurge, the CPI extending its work on the labour front in the changed climate while Congress and Revolutionary Socialists struggled to counter its ascendancy. Many of these unions were evanescent, and exaggerated claims were made for their membership but it is clear that the movement was extended during this period into previously little-organized sectors. The three main federations claimed by 1959-60 a combined membership of 319,000, organized in 425 unions, of which 250 unions with 78,000 members were verified by the Registrar. In the first year of the ministry 80 per cent of union members (claimed or verified) belonged to AITUC, compared with about 30 per cent nationally but this had fallen by 1959-60 to 66 per cent (claimed) and 55 per cent (verified).[50] Loss of office handicapped the CPI unions and in 1960-1 AITUC membership was 38 per cent of the total, INTUC 19 per cent, and UTUC 16 per cent, virtually all the rest belonging to non-aligned unions.[51] Membership declined to an all-time low of 50,000 reported members in 1967, quickly rising under the United Front ministry to 280,000 in 1968.

Figures are not available to show the degree of unionization in different sectors but it is clear from the incidence of disputes and man-days lost that cashew, plantations, advanced manufacturing, mill textiles, brick and tile, government service, and teaching are highly organized. Union organization is also relatively well developed in the Kuttanad rice belt where there is a high concentration of agricultural labour, a critically timed agricultural cycle, and acute contrasts of wealth and poverty.[52] Coir is a far less important union sector than in the past, a fact that reflects the weakness of the workers' situation. Increasingly the union movement has become dominated by government-sector workers, among whom the highly skilled and technically trained, for example the State Electricity Board engineers, have wielded most industrial power. It should be noted that students are highly organized also under party political affiliations—not strictly trade unions—in which the conflict has been mainly between the Kerala Student Congress and the CPM-led Kerala Students' Federation. The constant turnover of the student body ensures volatility and the shifting patterns of voting in college elections often anticipate trends in public opinion generally in the state.

Unions are typically small and localized, with some notable exceptions such as the Non-Gazetted Officers Union. Averaging 300 to 400 members, many are transient. Few have a highly developed organization and most depend on the charisma of local leaders for their continued existence. Although there have been some first-rank organizers, the quality of full-time officers is low, as is evidenced in the management of trade union finances. Too often they are an aristocracy of labour in a very different sense from the normal meaning of that phrase.[53] Only latterly has the movement generated leaders from below. The majority of state legislators hold several functional or honorific posts in unions, one Revolutionary Socialist member claiming in 1971 to be an office-bearer in 'about 21 trade unions'.[54] Class consciousness has been the casualty of political divisions within the marxist left as much as between the communist and Congress parties, and efforts to create unity such as the T.V. Thomas (CPI)/Sreekantan Nair (RSP) formula (see below, p. 161) have quickly foundered.

Notes

1 *ER 1978*, p. 12, Table 2.4. Demographic trends are discussed in CDS, *Poverty*, ch. X.
2 *ER 1976*, pp. 83–5. In 1955–6 41 per cent of the 5–16 age group in Kerala did not attend school. *ER 1959*, p. 15.
3 *ER 1976*, pp. 86–8. In 1955–6 there were 38 hospitals and dispensaries and 726 hospital beds per million population (India 26 and 320 resp.). *ER 1959*, p. 15. In Sept. 1978 the bed/population ratio varied from 37 (Idikki) to 215 (Trivandrum). *ER 1978*, p. 9.
4 Quoted in *ER 1959*, pp. 33–4.
5 Ibid., p.33.
6 *FFYP 1974-9*, pp. 601-2; *Report of the Committee on Unemployment* (1971), pp. 13–14. One distinctive feature of unemployment in Kerala is the high proportion of female unemployment. In a 1965 survey conducted by the Bureau of Economics and Statistics, Govt of Kerala, 14 per cent of the female labour force was reported as unemployed (of whom 40 per cent were actually seeking employment) whereas only 1.1 per cent of the male labour force was reported as unemployed. Ibid., p.10; National Sample Survey, 27th Round (1972-3), quoted in *ER 1978*, p. 13.

7   *ER 1978*, p. 14, Table 2.9. Unemployment and population growth are discussed in CDS, *Poverty,* ch. VI.

8   *ER 1959*, pp. 3–4; cf. CDS, *Poverty,* p. 75.

9   Interview, Chief Forest Officer, Tvm, Sept. 1973. This offical estimated that one-quarter of Kerala's forests had been illegally occupied since 1945.

10 M.A Oommen, *Land Reforms and Socio-economic Change in Kerala,* p. 64.

11 For the 1951 figures see India, Ministry of Labour and Employment, Labour Bureau, *Report of Second Enquiry on Agricultural Labour in India,* vol. VII: *Kerala* (1961), p. 9. For the 1971 figures see below, Map. 27.

12 *ER 1959*, p. 5, Table 1.6.

13 Kerala Bureau of Economics and Statistics, *Land Reforms Survey in Kerala 1966-7* (1968, mimeo), pp. 57–8 and 60. (Hereafter *LRSK*.)

14 Ibid., p. 62, Table 8.12. The authors of CDS, *Poverty* are more sanguine in relation to the northern Districts of Kerala although their grounds are also inferential: see p. 69. *The Reserve Bank of India Bulletin* (Oct. 1966), in an article 'Distribution of Value of Total Assets among Households Resident in the Rural Sector of India', suggests that the distribution of such assets is more unequal than in any other Indian state except Andhra Pradesh.

15 Varghese, pp. 192–8. Malabar Special Commissioner [W. Logan], *Report on Malabar Land Tenures* (1882), vol. 1, p. 1vi.

16 Varghese, p. 195.

17 Ibid., pp. 190–1, 195.

18 R.J. Herring, 'Redistributive Agrarian Policy: Land and Credit in South Asia, (1976), pp. 248 and 255. Dr Herring's work on land reform is pending publication by Yale UP.

19 As n. 11 above, pp. 55–6.

20 *ER 1959*, pp. 6–7 and 35–6; *ER 1978*, p. 20. The distinction between food and cash crops is somewhat artificial but conventionally the major crops are assigned as follows: *food*, rice, pulses, sugar cane, pepper, ginger turmeric, cardamom, betel nuts, bananas and other plantains, cashewnut, tapioca; *cash*, coconut, tea, coffee, rubber.

21 Calculations based on Kerala State Planning Board and Bureau of Economics and Statistics, *Statistics for Planning,* 5: *Prices* (1972), p. 228, Table X, Index of Area, Production and Productivity. (Hereafter, *SFP*.)

22 *ER 1972*, p. 32, Table 3.3; *ER 1976*, p.21, Table 4,4; *ER 1978*, p. 25, Table 4.5. For High Yielding Varieties of rice see *ER 1959*, p. 5, Table 1.5; *ER 1972*, p. 35, Table 3.6; and *ER 1978*, p. 27, Table 4.8.

23 *ER 1978*, p. 23, Table 4.1.

24 *Report of the Travancore Banking Enquiry Committee,* vol.1, pp. 52–4.

25 *ER 1959*, pp. 20–1, Tables 1.19, 1.20, 1.21. *ER 1976*, p. 22, Tables 4.6, 4.7.

26 Interview, Mr M.R. Lappin, General Manager, Kanan Devan Estate, James Finlay & Co., Munnar, Aug. 1973.

27 For details see *Kerala District Gazetteers: Kottayam*, pp. 114–30.

28 *ER 1959*, p. 7, Table 1.7. *ER 1976*, p. 22, Table 4.6, 4.7. For regional

distribution see *Census of India 1961*, vol. VII: *Kerala*, pt IX, *Census Atlas*, pp. 106–7, Map 49.

29 CDS, *Poverty*, p. 7.
30 Ibid., p. 24.
31 *ER 1959*, p. 53, Table 4.1, and p. 54, Table 4.2; *ER 1976*, p. 76, Table 8.4.
32 *ER 1978*, p. 83.
33 SFP, 10: *Export and Import Statistics* (1972), pp. 22–44, Tables 11–20.
34 *ER 1978*, ch. 8.
35 As n. 33 above, p. 45, Table 22.
36 D.P. Moynihan with Suzanne Weaver, *A Dangerous Place* (1979), p. 41. Moynihan states that after an inquiry within the US Embassy in Delhi 'to establish what we had been up to . . .I was satisfied we had been up to very little. We had twice, but only twice, interfered in Indian politics to the extent of providing money to a political party . . .in the face of a prospective Communist victory in a state election, once in Kerala and once in West Bengal . . .Both times the money was given to the Congress Party, which had asked for it. Once it was given to Mrs. Gandhi herself, who was then a party official.' For Mrs Gandhi's denial and other comments see *Hindustan Times*, 15 Apr. 1979 and Kuldip Nayar, 'Funding the Elections', *Indian Express* (hereafter *IE*), 18 Apr. 1979. Bernard D. Nossiter, *Soft State: a Newspaperman's Chronicle of India* (1970), pp. 115–17, reports an approach from a Samyukta Socialist Party minister in Kerala during the 1967–9 ministry which the US Embassy rejected.
37 Interview, retired planter, London, Mar. 1976. A communist (CPI) view is found in Sadhan Mukherjee, *Who Really Aids India, USA or USSR?* (1972), pp. 54–7.
38 *ER 1959*, pp. 22–3.
39 Ibid., p. 22; M.V. Pylee, *A Study of the Coir Industry in India* (Cochin, Coir Board, 1976), p.22.
40 SFP, 5: *Prices*, p. 148, Table IV, Coir Prices; *Kerala District Gazetteers: Kottayam*, p. 288.
41 Coir Board, Cochin, *Report on Labour Conditions in the Coir Manufacturing Industry* (1969), p. 35.
42 Ibid., also pp. 4–12.
43 B.A Prakash, 'Coir Manufacture in the Doldrums', *Social Scientist* (Tvm) 61, 1977.
44 *ER 1978*, p. 127, Appendix 6.1
45 Ibid., pp. 128–31 Appendix 6.2–6.6.
46 A good general survey is H. Crouch, *Trade Unions and Politics in India* (1966). On Kerala see also V.B. Karnik, *Communist Ministry and Trade Unions in Kerala* (1959); K. Ramachandran Nair, *Industrial Relations in Kerala* (1973).
47 C.K. Joshi, *Unionism in a Developing Economy* (London, Asia Publishing House, 1967), pp. 36–7.
48 Ibid.
49 SFP, 4: *Industries and Infrastructure*, p. 4, Table 1.10; ibid., 3: *Labour and*

Labour Force, p. 23, Table 8.5.

50   Karnik, *Communist Ministry and Trade Unions in Kerala*, p. 15.
51   *SFP*, 3: *Labour and Labour Force*, p. 17, Table 5.4.
52   T.K. Oomen, 'Agrarian Tension in a Kerala District', *Indian J. of Industrial Relations* 7(2), 1971; Govt of Kerala, *Kuttanad Enquiry Commission* (1971), pp. 22–4 and 33–9; Joan P. Mencher, 'Agrarian Relations in Two Rice Regions of Kerala,' *Economic and Political Weekly*, Annual no. Feb. 1978.
53   Interview, CPM trade union leader, Tvm, Sept. 1973.
54   Kerala Legislative Assembly, *Who's Who 1971* (1972), p. 225, entry under R.S. Unni.

4

The Communist Movement in
Kerala to 1950

COMMUNISM came late to Kerala, a fact which contributed to its subsequent success in acquiring a mass following. The local movement was little affected by the *laager* mentality associated with the sectarian line of non-participation in the wider Freedom Struggle pursued by the CPI in the late 1920s and early 1930s. The Communist Party of India dates from the early 1920s but apart from the publication in Trivandrum of a short, factual biography of Marx in 1912 and a sympathetic obituary of Lenin (1924) marxism attracted little interest in any part of Kerala until the 1930s.[1] The first proto-marxist organization was the tiny Trivandrum-based Communist League of 1931 and it was not until 1939 that a state unit of the party was secretly established. Those who were to become the core of the Kerala CPI participated first as Gandhians and then as Congress Socialists in the indigenous political movements of the time. By the mid-1930s some leaders of the socialist wing of Congress in Kerala, as elsewhere, were marxists and in contact with the CPI nationally, usually on a clandestine basis, but any conflict of loyalties was minimized by the contemporaneous shift in Comintern policy towards Congress from an 'ultra left' sectarian rejection to co-operation (and penetration) by means of the 'united front'. A party fraction was formed in 1937 but it was through Congress Socialism—a very broad church of the left—that communism gained its mass base in Kerala by 1939-40. Few of those present at the inaugural meeting of the party in late 1939 claimed a sophisticated theoretical knowledge of marxism. The ninety leaders enjoyed a more valuable asset: a decade's immersion in the political and social movements of Malabar, Cochin, and Travancore. It was this, above all else, which enabled the party to tread water in face of the nationalist tide of the 1940s and to survive the externally dictated conversion of the Imperialist War into a People's War when Hitler invaded the Soviet Union in 1941.

Even if the fortunate coincidence of interest in marxism, the burgeoning of socio-political movements in the 1930s, and the shift in international communist strategy is recognized, one is still left with the problem of why marxism should have proved so attractive to the Malayalis, and in particular to the educated middle class, in contradistinction to the situation prevailing in most other parts of India. While most commentators agree on the factors to be included in an explanation, there is considerable divergence in emphasis: Selig Harrison's emphasis on caste; Kathleen Gough's on agrarian relations and class divisions; Zagoria's on the interaction of landlessness and literacy; and, most recently, Jeffrey's on the breakdown of a social system in which matrilineal joint families were of crucial importance.[2] Only a comprehensive study, which is outside the author's present remit, is likely to afford a convincing account. By way of preface to the author's own treatment of the rise of communism in Kerala, however, three general considerations should be taken into account. First it may be wise to distinguish explanations of the different stages of the development of the movement: the genesis in the 1930s; the survival in the war years; and the expansion in the early 1950s. Second it should be emphasized that Kerala is not a self-evident unit of explanation in the 1930s. If there was a potential for the emergence of a state-wide consciousness, it needed to be forged. In searching for socio-economic determinants we should not neglect the skill with which the leadership of the embryonic communist movement exploited the potential of the place and time. On the evidence of party support even in the 1970s the political system remains far from (sub)nationalized. It follows that particular attention should be paid to the special features of areas of early or above-average support for the communist movement. Third one should beware of the historical equivalent of the ecological fallacy. Because Kerala is highly distinctive in certain respects, there is no necessary simple causal connection with communist support. This appears to apply to the relationship of literacy and communism (see below, p. 339) and may apply to Jeffrey's stimulating discussion of the significance of matriliny.[3] It is not disputed that the break-up of the joint family system was certainly a factor in the social experience of that generation of young men who provided the leadership of the emergent communist movement in the 1930s. However, to speak of caste Hindus as *déracinés* may exaggerate the degree to which the traditional family system changed. Arguably a more flexible form of traditional family ties arose, rather than a truly nuclear family system. More important, Jeffrey does not clearly establish that the *déracinés* were disproportionately attracted to communism. In his analysis of the social composition of candidates contesting the 1940 Kerala Pradesh Central Committee elections he shows that 21 successful Gandhian candidates (60 per cent) were identifiably Nair as compared to 27 (44 per cent) of the successful Congress Socialist candidates. On the unlikely assumption that all Nairs elected were *déracinés* this would show that Gandhianism also had considerable appeal. A few instances are given (p. 81 and p.82, n.13) of communist cadres who came from disintegrating joint families, but no evidence is offered that they were necessarily typical (or that the phenomenon did not occur among Gandhians) beyond the note that it 'became a common pattern for Kerala Communists to remain bachelors or to marry only in their 40s, partly because the marriage system had been in such flux in their youth that they had no guardians to arrange their marriages' (p. 81, n. 11). Communists whom I interviewed attributed their bachelorhood or late marriage to the nature of their political life. Gandhians in other parts of India often either did not marry or married late. The difficulties of gathering evidence probably render a resolution of this issue just about impossible.

Landlordism, Congress, and the Raj in Malabar

In Malabar the development of the Congress movement was intimately connected with the agrarian question. A district Congress committee had been formed in 1908 but the first district conference was not held until 1916, stimulated partly by the founding of the All-India Home Rule League and partly by the formation in the previous year of the Malabar Tenancy Association with branches throughout Malabar.[4] Although the Nair leadership of the Tenancy and Congress organizations overlapped—drawn mainly from the professional sons of the wealthier *kanomdar* families—efforts to use the district Congress conference as a platform for pro-tenant resolutions were unsuccessful until the fifth conference in 1920, when, after the passage of a resolution in favour of full and immediate self-government which precipitated the withdrawal of the landlord moderates, the motion for tenancy reforms was carried. For the next decade the organization was run by Nair *vakils* (lawyers) from the *kanomdar* class. Through the District conferences of Congress and the Tenancy Association the pressure for tenancy reform was stepped up, helped by an impressive showing in the elections for two General Constituencies of the 1923 Madras Legislative Council, and by 1928 the movement was strong enough to hold an All-Kerala Tenants Conference to establish a state-wide organization.

The attitude of the authorities was essentially pragmatic: the *jenmis* were a powerful political force on the government side; only if the tenants exerted irresistible pressure would the British modify their policy. 'As education spreads, the labouring cultivator may wake up to the fact that he is being ruthlessly exploited by the *ryotwari*

landlord and may demand a longer (*sic*) share of the fruits of his
labour. But at present this has not occurred . . .it is not our business
to arouse agrarian discontent.'[5] By 1929 the *kanomdars* could no
longer be ignored and a government-sponsored compromise, the
Malabar Tenancy Act 1929—neatly reconciling the *de jure* rights of
the *jenmis* and the *de facto* power of the intermediaries—laid the
century-old power struggle between the two to rest.

The Act did not, however, deal adequately with the problem of
the tenant-at-will, with whose fate neither Congress nor the Tenancy Association was much concerned.[6] It has been forcibly argued
that it was this deficiency which accounted for the success of the
Congress Socialists and later the CPI who integrated the question of
exploitation by landlords into the struggle against imperialism.[7] A
further factor was the impact of the Depression on a district heavily
dependent on cash crops, in particular coconut. Leadership was
often supplied by young, educated, and politically conscious members of upper-caste joint family systems under increasing stress. The
early strength of the Congress Socialist movement in northern
Malabar was probably related not only to the degree and character of
landlordism locally but also to the fact that as a 'dry' area, deficient in
rice, northern Malabar suffered the effects of the Depression more
than the south and also to the predominance of Nairs among the
landed families in the north whose politically conscious members
were working in the area they knew best. In contrast the rice-
growing Brahmin-dominated Palghat area, where feudal relations
persisted, became a communist stronghold *after* the war. During the
pre-war period there appears to have been relatively little political
activity.[8]

The Moplah Rising and its Consequences

For different reasons the Moplah region was also comparatively
politically inert in the 1930s: in this case the reason is to be found in
the consequences of earlier political activities of the Khilafat movement and the Moplah Rising. Until 1920 Congress, nationally and
locally, had been predominantly a Hindu organization. Gandhi's
decision to support the Muslim Khilafat movement was designed to
rectify this and to gain reciprocal support from the Muslim leaders
for his Non-cooperation movement. The Khilafat agitation aimed at
the restoration of the Turkish Caliphate and the Ottoman Empire,
dismembered by the 1919 Treaty of Sèvres, and had a powerful
symbolic appeal among Indian Muslims. Among resolutions passed
at the 1920 district Congress conference was one of support for the
Khilafat movement 'and Khilafat committees were established
alongside existing tenancy and non-cooperation committees. In Au-

gust 1920 Gandhi and the Khilafat leader, Shaukat Ali, jointly addressed a meeting at Calicut. In a community with traditions of *Shahīd* and long-standing agrarian grievances, where many young Muslims had recently been demobilized from the army to lead a precarious existence with little chance of work, the effect was inflammatory.[9]

At first, in line with All-India policy, the Collector of Malabar adopted a cautious policy of non-intervention and remonstrance. As the movement gathered weight the authorities became increasingly nervous and clumsy. Finally on the night of 20 August 1921 the British raided Tirurangadi, searching the mosque. The fact that the soldiers left their shoes at the door did not save the situation. A crowd of 3,000 gathered rapidly, shots were fired and the rising, once begun, swept south Malabar, though it did not spread to Calicut or northern Malabar. It was not until November that the authorities recovered control of the rural area and martial law was not lifted until 25 February 1922.[10]

Initially the rebellion was directed primarily against the symbols of British authority, but the Moplah leaders' orders prohibiting the molestation of Hindus testified to their apprehension. The local Congress leadership appeared to have been taken unawares by the Moplah recourse to violence, and hastily withdrew its support. As the rebels broke up into small bands under military pressure, and the Hindu population—voluntarily or involuntarily—was persuaded to co-operate with the authorities, Moplah discipline broke down and the rising degenerated into dacoity and communalism. No reliable figure of Hindus killed is available (or of Moplahs by Hindus) but the numbers were clearly large; it seems likely that few were *jenmis* since the wealthy had either fled the area or taken refuge in British camps.[11] More than 200 villages were affected over a wide area of southern Malabar and as much as two-fifths of the district was under the control of Moplah peasant bands. Not less than 46 soldiers, 500 to 600 civilians, and 2,000 to 3,000 Moplah insurgents were killed, including those suffocated in the notorious waggon tragedy. Thousands received jail sentences, and because of overcrowding in the prisons, many were transported to the Andaman Islands for imprisonment there. Hindu communalist organizations from the north worked among the refugees while the Moplah community, judging itself betrayed, nurtured a sullen resentment against its erstwhile Congress allies. A solid wedge had been driven between the two communities at all levels. When political organization was gradually rebuilt, Congress in Malabar was divided into Hindu and Muslim Congresses, centred on two newspapers *Mathrubhumi* (Motherland) and *al-Ameen* (One who is honest). Growing Muslim consciousness was reflected in the formation of the Young Muslims Association (1926), which influenced many later leaders, and the Muslim Majlis (1930), the establishment of a Muslim Club (about 1933) in Tellicherry, and the foundation of the daily newspaper *Chandrika* (1934). Nationalist Muslims tended to side with the more aggressive Congress Socialist Party, formed in 1934, but already the Muslim League was emerging as a distinct force. In the same year a League candidate, Abdul Sattar Sait, narrowly defeated the nationalist Muslim leader, Muhammad Abdurrahiman, in an election for the Central Legislative Assembly. In 1945 the League swept the Muslim seats in Malabar in the election to the Central Legislative Assembly and by 1947 League leaders were proposing a separate province for south Malabar (to be known as Moplastan) where Muslims would be in a majority.[12] Ironically, the British failure to match their military resources to the potential threat in August 1921 divided the political movement along communal lines and temporarily arrested its progress.[13]

Political activity began to revive in Malabar in 1928. The fourth All-Kerala Political Conference in May was presided over by Nehru himself, who adopted a distinctly socialist line of argument in his address.[14] During the first Civil Disobedience Movement in 1930 the campaign against the salt tax, foreign cloth, and country liquor was firmly under the direction of the gentry and urban middle class. In Calicut crowds were large for the salt march but notwithstanding the presence of some younger militants the overall tenor was Gandhian. The agitation did not elicit much enthusiasm among peasants, labourers, or (for self-interested reasons) among merchants and small shopkeepers and it secured little support from the low castes except among handloom weavers.[15]

Unfavourable comparisons were drawn between British and caste-Hindu attitudes to the lower castes. Leaders of the backward classes argued that the Congress movement was really an instrument for the perpetuation of caste-Hindu domination. Where there was low-caste support it was sometimes as much an expression of a feudal obligation to local magnates as of political belief.[16] The younger and more impatient volunteers at the forefront of the one-sided battle between *khadi* and *khaki*, increasingly disillusioned with Gandhian methods, were advancing their political education in jail through informal classes run by prisoners from the north. P. Krishna Pillai (1906–48), future CPI leader in Kerala, and K.P. Gopalan formed a branch of the Bengal terrorist organization *Anuseelan Samiti* after their release, and Krishna Pillai was already distinguishing between a 'Congress of the poor' and a 'Congress of the Rich' in late 1930.[17]

One common denominator between Gandhians and militants

which could provide a focus for common action was caste discrimination, and when negotiations between the national Congress leaders and the British government were resumed Malabar leaders
turned their attention to the position of the depressed classes. While
it was the untouchables who suffered the assaults and the low castes
the indignities, caste disabilities extended to a majority of the population. In September 1931 Congress determined to picket the most
famous temple in Malabar, at Guruvayoor, to which four-fifths of
the Hindu community were denied admission. The decision split the
movement: the old guard resigned from the Working Committee
virtually *en bloc* leaving the Gandhians, led by K. Kelappan Nair
(1889-1971)[18] and Manjeri Rama Iyer (1877-1958),[19] and the Young
Turks in control. The Zamorin of Calicut, the temple trustee, and
one of the two biggest landowners in Malabar, backed by the social
and sacerdotal powers of the orthodox Hindu community, eventually drove the *satyagrahis* into emulating Gandhi's tactic of fasting.
However, after twelve days Kelappan Nair's fast was withdrawn at
Gandhi's insistence in exchange for an implicit understanding that
the temple would be opened after a decent interval.

It was a victory of sorts but the longer-term impact was more
important. Either voluntarily, or under social pressures, some of
the higher-caste Congressmen faded from view and the flow of
funds to the organization was checked. For others Guruvayoor
confirmed the growing disenchantment with Gandhian methods:
the temple guards had been brutal and their masters obdurate while
Gandhi appeared pusillanimous. The second Civil Disobedience
Campaign in 1932 was a shadow of the first in Malabar. Congress
was an empty shell, a table, chair and almirah in the corner of the
Mathrubhumi office, and serviced by a staff of 'Sunday Congressmen', drawn chiefly from the legal community of Calicut.[20] It was
ripe for a take-over.

Similar developments at the All-India level led to the founding
conference of the Congress Socialist Pary (CSP) at Bombay in April
1934 as a left-wing pressure group within Congress.[21] Among those
who attended was P. Krishna Pillai. Two other future Kerala communist leaders, E.M.S. Namboodiripad and A.K. Gopalan, were
also active in the formation of a Kerala unit of the CSP in 1934. The
socialist leaders received support from a minority of moderates in
the parent body including Kelappan Nair, C.K. Govindan Nair, the
Kerala CSP's first secretary, and K.A. Damodara Menon, later
editor of *Mathrubhumi*, and established a working alliance with the
nationalist Muslims. The CSP was now the dominant force within
the Kerala Congress organization, having won six out of nine places
on the provincial committee and five out of the eight Kerala seats on

the All-India Congress Committee (AICC) and pushed through a series of left-wing resolutions, including an explicit rejection of Gandhian methods at the Kerala Provincial Congress Committee (KPCC) meeting in October 1934. In December E.M.S. Namboodiripad became joint national secretary of the CSP, an early recognition of his stature and a reflection of the progress made by the Kerala unit of the CSP; it was a position which Namboodiripad used to effect as the CPI sought to penetrate the CSP after 1936.

The initial expansion of the CSP in Malabar was perfervid and conducted on all fronts of mass activity. Conditions were favourable. The economy was slowly beginning to improve, making agitation a viable proposition. During the Depression the *jenmi-kanomdar* class had continued to require its feudal dues and the limited protection afforded by the 1929 Tenancy Act had become clear. The educated young men had their paper qualifications but little prospect of employment. The moderates did not at first perceive the danger to their position and allowed the young militants to work from within. When at the end of 1934 an *ad hoc* committee was formed to resuscitate Congress organization, its joint secretaries were A.K. Gopalan, close to Krishna Pillai and Namboodiripad as well as to Kelappan Nair, and the amiable anti-socialist Kunjissankara Menon.

Inside a year the CSP activists had established a 'Congress' committee in almost every village in Malabar outside the Moplah zone, backed by reading rooms where local activists taught the illiterate to read socialist books and pamphlets and conducted study classes. Special attention was paid to attracting the young by means of youth work, generously interpreted to include football matches and competitions. Peripatetic groups put on performances of socialist dramas, including K. Damodaran's highly successful *Rent Arrears*. On the labour front the CSP activists joined forces with existing union leaders, notably the Labour Brotherhood, whose leaders had joined the CSP. Some eighty local trade unions, two district union centres, and an All-Kerala Trade Union Committee were formed in the following three years.

A successful movement, however, rested on the peasantry. Despite the surge of discontent triggered by the fall of agricultural prices during the Depression the Congress attitude towards the peasant movement was lukewarm at most. Krishna Pillai, one of the few leaders with personal experience of the peasant's condition, had written a postcard in 1930 with the cryptic advice to work among the peasants if the recipient was with the Congress of the poor,[22] and he was the main organizer behind the launching of agitation against feudal exaction in Cannanore and Kasergod in 1934-5. The creation of a *kisan* movement was altogether more difficult than work on the labour front. No unions existed here and the CSP faced the whole edifice of the rural power structure in a feudal situation. The leaders perforce led the processions to prominent landowners with varying numbers of peasants behind them. Since they were from ancient landed families the *jenmis* could not easily resort to *goonda* violence to disperse the crowd. It was only in 1936 that a *kisan* unit—in Chirakkal—was strong enough to exist independently of such backing[23] and not until December 1938 did the work on the peasant front reach the stage where *jathas* consisted of regular peasant activists elected by local *kisan* units.[24] As the Kerala CSP became actively involved in strikes and peasant movements and made its scepticism of constitutional or Gandhian methods more explicit, the moderate patrons began to drift away so that by early 1935 only one right winger was left on the local Congress Working Committee. However, the prospect of office under the 1935 constitutional reforms revived their interest, and, taking advantage of the new Congress constitution, the right recovered control of the higher units of the party in 1935 though the lower units remained largely in the hands of the left.

In 1936 a last compromise was patched up whereby membership of the Working Committee was split equally between left and right, the post of president was (temporarily) abolished, the Calicut barrister Raman Menon (1896-1939), leader of the right, became general secretary,[25] and the socialists were allowed a free hand on the labour front. In August 1936, with the provincial elections in the offing, the right attacked through the disciplinary procedures of the party. The KPCC, on which the moderates had a majority by virtue of the Travancore and Cochin delegates, dissolved a number of left-dominated local committees, including that of Malabar district, and suspended several known socialist members. However, the probable effects on the mobilization of Congress votes in the forthcoming election campaign led the Working Committee to revoke this action.

Nationally the CSP had been hostile to the 1935 Government of India Act from the beginning. Congress, while condemning the new constitution did not ban its members from standing for election or taking up membership of the legislatures and avoided the question of whether it would accept office. The CSP acquiesced in the decision to contest the election but bitterly opposed 'office acceptance' when Congress won an absolute majority in six of the eleven provinces. In Madras the scale of victory initially strengthened the right and the local CSP unit's opposition to forming a ministry was defeated. Raman Menon became Malabar's representative in the Congress movement as Minister for Courts and Prisons.

The resurgence of the right proved temporary. In January 1938 the CSP recovered control of the KPCC; and Namboodiripad was elected general secretary by one vote. The CSP's final victory stemmed from five causes: the disillusionment which followed the mass upsurge of 1936-7 as it became obvious that the new Congress ministry was pursuing much the same policies as the previous administrations, notably in its attitude to the peasantry; the growing co-operation with the nationalist Muslims in Malabar against the caste-Hindu right; the loss of moderate interest in controlling the organization once the elections were over, which led the right to agree to Namboodiripad's appointment in 1937 as full-time Congress secretary for 'mass contact';[26] a dramatic improvement in the quality of the CSP's own organization in the course of 1937; and, finally, the success of the mobilization of the peasantry against the *jenmis* and *kanomdars* in northern Malabar, symbolized in the formation of the All-Malabar Peasants' Union in May 1938 which by the end of 1938 enjoyed a paid-up membership of some 30,000.

In 1934-5 the CSP had relied on enthusiasm as much as systematic organization. In the absence of serious opposition the fact that the CSP shared many of the weaknesses of the parent body—disorganization, personal ambition, and ideological confusion—had not mattered unduly. By 1936, however, the CSP had lost momentum and direction as the right reasserted itself. 'On the whole', Gopalan records, 'there was organisational chaos everywhere. Apart from an annual conference and a few committee meetings . . . there was no forethought, no system of follow up.' The party executive met before KPCC meetings: 'Comrade Krishna Pillai would speak about some temporary activities. Some others would be busy thinking about how to get funds to return home. Each would go his own way . . . There was no secretariat to frame a programme on the basis of the reports from lower units . . . Except for busybodies who shuttled through the country without any political ideology or programme at all, there were not proper party organisers or agitators . . . It was a loose and disorganised movement', with 'neither political policy nor plan', brilliant at seizing opportunities but hopeless at consolidating them. The leaders 'Managed to get things done sometimes by being very rude, sometimes by getting angry with the party workers and sometimes by just patting them on their backs.' Consciousness was raised through speeches, spot agitations, processions, and plays but then allowed to dissipate. The education of cadres 'was simply non-existent'. Even the party paper *Prabhatham*, founded in early 1935, so crucial to the nascent organization, was run in amateurish fashion: the manager was never there;

there was no clear schedule of work; the agents spent the proceeds when they ran short of money; and the editorial staff decamped whenever there was an agitation, leaving no one behind to get the paper out.[27] The improvement in 1937-8 was dramatic, even allowing for a measure of exaggeration in the accounts. From a few thousand in 1936 Congress membership in Kozhikode was said to have risen to 70,000 in 1938. Some were recruited by the Kerala Congress *Gandhi Sangh*, organized by Kelappan Nair and K.A. Damodara Menon[28] as a counterweight to the socialists, but more were recruited by the CSP now coming under the influence of the disciplined organization of the communist party after the formation of a party fraction at Calicut in 1937.

There was in fact little to differentiate the CSP from the CPI at the ideological level. The high-caste detainees in Nasik Jail, near Bombay, who had conceived the plan for a socialist ginger group within Congress in 1933 had readily avowed marxism at the time. The second CSP conference in January 1936 had not only endorsed the proposition that Marxism alone can guide the anti-imperial forces to their ultimate destiny but had also agreed to admit communists as members in recognition of the CPI's switch to the united front line.[29] Between 1934 and 1935 the real difference between the two parties had been tactical. The CSP recognized the need to use the national movement to advance socialism, not in the expectation of converting Congress but of splitting it into progressive and reactionary wings. The CPI still regarded Congress as the organ of bourgeois nationalism and a counter-revolutionary force with which no alliance was possible. During the course of 1935 the Soviet Union and also the banned CPI changed to a united front line, and in the second half of the year Krishna Pillai and Namboodiripad had a detailed exchange of views with Sundarayya, the Andhra CPI leader. By early 1937 it was difficult to distinguish between the CSP and the CPI in Kerala.[30]

The speed with which individuals moved from Gandhianism through Congress Socialism to communism varied considerably. As early as 1934 Krishna Pillai and Communist League workers from Trivandrum met in order to concert activities. However, his disdain for Gandhianism and his admiration for the Soviet Union were more obvious than his marxism.[31] The same was true of Namboodiripad at this time. In 1935 Krishna Pillai was distributing clandestine communist literature at the Lucknow session of the Congress party; the CPI journal *National Front* was in circulation; and during the CSP's first major venture into mass struggle—the forty-day strike of tile workers at Feroke—the Communist leaders, Dange and Sundarayya, visited Calicut to offer advice on tactics.[32] In February

1937 communist literature was seized from Namboodiripad's house; and in April Krishna Pillai personally raised the hammer and sickle over the All-Kerala Labour Conference held in Trichur (Cochin).

By 1937, if not earlier, the CPI was systematically working towards the transformation of the CSP in Kerala, as elsewhere, into an undeclared unit of the party. In 1937 S.V. Ghate formed a five-man party fraction in Calicut, with Krishna Pillai as its secretary, to match the work of the Communist League cell in Trivandrum.[33] Party discipline required fractions to accept directions from higher organs and that they should work to advance the party's policies through mass organizations.[34] CPI documents explicitly outlining its intention to capture the CSP by stealth had reached the CSP Executive in 1937 and 1938. The second of these, published by M.R. Masani in September 1938, gave CSP membership as 200 'entirely under our influence' with very widespread agitational influence on all fronts. The 'Congress majority in P.C.C. peasant and T.U. movements entirely under their influence.' It commented adversely on the quality of CSP organization—'comrades had failed to give up Congress methods . . . . Individuals function as units'—though it commended the recent foundation of a weekly newspaper.[35] Despite such compromising revelations and the consequential resignation of some senior figures, the CSP did not break with the CPI. (One-third of the CSP National Executive were members of the CPI.) In the end it was the CPI which withdrew from the CSP after the latter's failure to oppose the 'imperialist war' as wholeheartedly as the CPI wished.

The CSP's success in winning control of the Kerala provincial Congress organization raised the problem of the party's attitude to participation in representative institutions, anticipating the arguments of the 1950s. Although there had been some disagreements in 1936–7 over the new provincial legislature, and Namboodiripad had stood for and been elected to the Madras legislature at a by-election in 1939 in order to influence discussion on the tenancy question,[36] the issue became pressing only in late 1939 when the election to the Malabar District Board fell due. The district boards which had been revamped in 1930, exercised important responsibilities including the administration of schools and hospitals, the control of charitable endowments, and the construction and maintenance of roads; they also dispensed a considerable amount of patronage, both in their own right and through the lower taluk boards.[37] The boards were an important influence on the rural power structure against which the CSP and the *kisan* organizations had been inveighing.

The qualification to vote was fixed at the payment of Rs 10 in rent or land revenue per year and lease and sub-lease-holders were qualified for local elections. Since there were no government records of lessees there was scope for the manufacture of electors by the *jenmis*. On the other hand partition of joint family properties had swelled the potential electorate to which the CSP might appeal. The party could not escape involvement in the Malabar District Board election, particularly since the right was determined to retain its control. The CSP-CPI in alliance with the nationalist Muslims won, but their Muslim nominee for the presidentship lost. 'The logical course for the party' was to propose K.P.R. Gopalan but this was rejected because 'accepting office would mean taking responsibilities without objective conditions to discharge them.' Nevertheless 'the lure of office' turned 'many heads, even the best, among party comrades'.[38]

Caste, Community, and Responsible Government in the Princely States

In Malabar socialism developed within the organizational framework of the Freedom Struggle, in Travancore and Cochin within the framework of the struggle for responsible government. In Malabar the key issue was the extreme concentration of rights over land in the hands of a few, even among caste Hindus. Organized political parties—Congress, Congress Socialist, and finally Communist—developed in the context of feudal landlordism. The un- or under-employed 'landlords' boys' provided the officers, and the peasants the troops of the people's army. In the princely states on the other hand land was a less important issue to the degree that rights on land were diffused—more in Travancore and less in Cochin. The central question was the democratic control of the executive, but since communalism ran deep and governments had manipulated it to buttress their authority this was readily transformed into the issue of communal control of the executive. Did citizenship extend to low-caste helots or to non-Hindus in a state dedicated to a Hindu God? The answers had very practical consequences for the distribution of patronage and recruitment to government service.

In Travancore although the Congress Socialists were active in the State Congress organization and the Youth League as well as in the communal associations they were unable to win control of the political movement, which remained under the direction of an uneasy alliance of the bourgeoisie of the three major communities, Nair, Syrian and Ezhava, a middle and upper middle class which had developed further than in Malabar. The communist appeal was directed towards the dwarf landholder, normally secure in his tenure but with insufficient land to support his family, the hutment-dwelling landless labourer, and the coir worker. (There is here some measure of contrast to the situation in Malabar, where the communists' most responsive audience was an exploited peasantry whose problem lay not so much in the size of holdings as in insecurity of tenure and the expropriation of much of their product.) In Travancore the communist task was facilitated by the higher levels of literacy, the greater caste oppression, the existence of some tradition of unionization, and the impact of the Depression on a coastal area heavily dependent on the export market in coconut products for its prosperity. That the majority in these areas were Ezhavas was, at least initially, co-incidental. Here, as in the north, the leadership was provided by young men from high-caste Hindu families—the exceptions, such as the Syrian Christian K.C. George, are remarkably few—moved by the ferment of ideas in schools and colleges, the disorienting effects of the break-up of the joint family system, and in many cases by the lack of employment opportunities. In Cochin also the middle classes dominated the political movement but the greater readiness of the government to grant some measure of responsible government in the second half of the 1930s limited the nascent communist party's chances of working from within. In northern Cochin the CSP was able to exploit agrarian discontent; in southern Cochin the party made some headway among such groups as the toddy tappers of Anthikkad and the working class of Cranganore; but its progress was circumscribed by the past Christian penetration of the lowest Hindu castes, the greater resilience of an urban and commercial economy compared to the agriculturally based cottage industry of the coast of Travancore or the cash crop economy of Malabar, and the more flexible character of the Cochin administration.

Travancore

Although Travancore in 1888 had been the first princely state to establish a legislative council, little progress had been made towards responsible government by the early 1930s. Politics was largely the politics of the Maharaja's court. Congress's policy of non-intervention in the affairs of the princely states discouraged political activity and apart from the Vaikom temple *satyagraha* in 1924 there was no significant agitation before 1931. By 1928, however, the Unemployment Enquiry Committee—primarily concerned to investigate the problem of the educated jobless—was prophesying that the burgeoning intellectual proletariat seeking white collar posts constituted a 'menace to good Government . . . . whatever form the Government may assume' and noting 'the growing fascination which socialistic and communistic ideas . . . . exercise upon the minds of the young men educated in our colleges.'[39]

The initial phase of the agitation for responsible government from 1931 to 1936 was precipitated by the power struggle attending the young Maharaja's coming of age in 1931. The Christian-backed Senior Maharani, who had acted as Regent during the heir's minority, sought to perpetuate her influence by securing the appointment of a new Dewan (Chief Minister) in the last months of the Regency. The new ruler's mother, the Junior Maharani, backed by the Nairs, countered by persuading her son to accept a personal adviser, Sir C.P. Ramaswami Aiyar, a choice which was to shape Travancore politics up to Independence, and arguably beyond.

Chetpat Pattabhirama Ramaswami Aiyar (1879—1966), generally known as 'C.P.', was to become the last of the modernizing Dewans of Travancore. A towering, at times arrogant figure, with a formidable intellect,[40] C.P.'s economic achievements were legendary: major public sector enterprises in aluminium, fertilizer and titanium, the modernization of the port of Cochin in collaboration with the neighbouring state, and an airport at Trivandrum built in a matter of months. He was also instrumental in the decision to open the temples of Travancore to all castes in 1936 and in the creation of the University of Kerala in 1937. There were, it was said, few fields open to an upper-class Victorian Indian in which he did not distinguish himself.[41] Born into one of the two leading families of Mylapore (Madras) and the son of a judge, C.P. became a leading civil lawyer and the lynch pin of the Mylapore set, an extraordinarily influential group of Madras lawyers and administrators.[42] All-India Congress secretary in 1917-18 during its home rule period, he turned from Congress to become Advocate General of Madras in 1920, the first in a dazzling list of official appointments culminating in a brief membership of the Viceroy's wartime Executive Council in 1942, a post from which he resigned in protest at the arrest of Gandhi. From 1936, with this short interruption, he was Dewan of Travancore until 1947 when in the course of an obstinate attempt to establish an independent state of Travancore an attempt on his life led to his retirement from politics. He was one of the earliest to perceive the possibility of a communist Travancore—at times his concern with the communist 'threat' to India bordered on the obsessional—but by his antipathy to the movement for responsible government and his skilful exploitation of communal conflict C.P. did much to make his fears a reality. Like other eminent Victorians he failed to comprehend the passion of lesser intellects for self-government even if it entailed bad government. With the more vulgar marxists he shared the illusion that political aspirations were a mere reflection of economic forces. Kerala's problem was economic imbalance: correct that, and communism would wither away.[43] Fittingly, C.P. died in London's National Liberal Club.

Aiyar's hand was first seen in Travancore politics with the constitutional reforms of 1932.[44] Cautiously these offered responsive government not responsible government. Opposition, however, focused on the defects of the proposed electoral system. Of twenty-three elected members in the existing Legislative Council fifteen were Nairs, only four Christians, and not one an Ezhava or Muslim.[45] Sixty-two per cent of government servants were Nairs and at least 75 per cent were high-caste Hindus of one sort or another.[46] The government's refusal to depart from the payment of land (and municipal) tax as the basis of the franchise or to consider communal electorates was bound to perpetuate this Nair ascendancy. The Christian, Ezhava, and Muslim communities therefore formed the Joint Political Congress (JPC) to boycott the ensuing elections, the *Nivarthanam* or Abstention Movement. Neither the appointment of a Muslim Dewan nor the announcement of a one-man commission to advise on the reform of recruitment to public service assuaged the opposition, and early in 1935 the Ezhava SNDP Yogam gave notice that, unless its demands were met, this, the biggest Hindu caste, would sidestep its disabilities by embracing Christianity. Faced with such a threat, C.P. advised removal of all religious and civil disabilities by means of the (1937) Temple Entry proclamation. The effects of this bold move were, however, mitigated by the simultaneous arrest of Kesavan, the SNDP leader, on charges of sedition. Under pressure from the suzerain power, the government conceded the principle of communal representation in August 1937. Meanwhile, however, C.P. had been confirmed as Dewan by the British.

The second phase of the struggle for responsible government began with the victory of the JPC in the April 1937 elections and lasted till October 1938. T.M. Varghese, the Syrian Christian leader, was then elected Deputy President of the Assembly (the Dewan was President *ex-officio*) but early in 1938 he was ousted from his post on the grounds that he had compromised his neutrality as an officer of the Assembly by presiding over a public meeting to felicitate Kesavan on his release from prison. The move was widely attributed to the anti-Christian machinations of the Dewan though he continued to deny it even after his withdrawal from public life.[47] The Dewan did not attempt to save Varghese and, in a welter of communal rivalry and personal intrigue, the JPC collapsed. C.P. likewise declined to use the official bloc of votes to support the bid of the Trivandrum Nair leader, Pattom Thanu Pillai, for the Deputy Presidency. Pattom had been the founder of the first Travancore State

Congress in 1931.[48] In place of the JPC there now emerged a far more dangerous opponent, the (second) Travancore State Congress (TSC) which brought together Nairs, Ezhavas, and Christians on a common platform whose minimum demand was the resignation of the Dewan and whose central objective of responsible government received a filip from the decision of Congress nationally to support popular movements in the princely states. On 30 May the TSC sent the Maharaja a memorial requesting responsible government and a memorandum detailing the Dewan's unfitness for office on the grounds of his alleged corruption, nepotism, and brutality. Encouraged by Gandhi's intervention in the affairs of Mysore, another south Indian princely state, the TSC then launched a civil disobedience campaign on 26 August in collaboration with the Travancore Youth League, the Kerala Provincial Congress and the Travancore Struggle Aid Committee, all three organizations closely connected to the Malabar Congress Socialist group. The Dewan's uncompromising response—the proscription of the TSC and the League and the arrest of Pattom and other leaders—proved ineffectual. Those arrested tended to be the moderate elements, men of substance and influence, leaving the less known and younger militants, linked to a communist party centre operating from just over the Cochin border in Ernakulam, to make the running. Even among his own supporters the Dewan was not a popular figure, and the heavy-handed repression—the police opened fire twelve times in two months—spread sympathy for the agitation rather than contained it.

C.P.'s difficulties were increased by a strike of 40,000 workers in the coir district of Alleppey. Labour disputes had erupted throughout the year, and led by Krishna Pillai the CSP-marxists formed an Alleppey group which met the union leaders and converted a proposed industrial stoppage into a general strike in which political demands were mixed with arguments about wages and conditions.[49] C.P. was forced to divert police and troops to the north. Meanwhile in the south the TSC was threatening a mass demonstration in Trivandrum on the occasion of the Maharaja's birthday. At this point Gandhi intervened, advising a delegation to withdraw the memorial. The government responded by lifting the ban on the TSC and Youth League and releasing the detainees. The employers were persuaded to grant a wage rise, labour to accept an inquiry into conditions in the coir industry, and both to agree to a conciliation board. The office-bearers of the union, newly released from prison, publicly called for a return to work, a step somewhat reluctantly endorsed by the CSP-led strike committee. C.P., the British Agent reported, had weathered the severest storm in the memory of Travancoreans.[50]

Travancore politics settled back into communal channels whose banks were reinforced by the institution of communal reservation in government service and a communally based electoral system. The Nairs, whose position was already threatened, were further alarmed by the Dewan's hints that future constitutional change would lead to Syrian ascendancy. The Syrians suspected that the Dewan's policies were anti-Christian: they were certainly received warmly by the high-caste Hindus, who were their economic rivals. The Ezhavas, for their part, were alienated by the Nairs' enthusiasm for Gandhi's prohibition campaign. Once it was clear that C.P. could not be moved, the growing army of brief-less lawyers who had hoped to gain from a TSC victory melted away.

The Youth League, successor to the 1931 Trivandrum Communist League, stood in much the same relationship—though a weaker one—to the TSC as that of the Congress Socialists to the KPCC. Unlike the CSP the Youth League was led by marxist sympathizers from its inception and the authorities regarded it as 'a much more dangerous organisation than the State Congress.'[51] Among its members were most of the future figures of the Travancore wing of the CPI and the Kerala unit of the Revolutionary Socialist Party (RSP). Lastly, the CSP-marxists had taken their opportunity in the Alleppey strike to radicalize the major working-class district of the state and it was on this foundation in 1946 that the CPI built its rising in Punnapra—Vayalar (see below, pp. 89-92).

Cochin

In contrast to Travancore, Cochin experienced little political disturbance during the 1930s.[52] According to V.K.S. Nayar the character of the ruling family ensured a greater responsiveness to public opinion than in most princely states. The Maharaja typically succeeded to the throne in old age, with the consequence that there were frequent changes in ruler and so in ministers. The royal family itself exceeded 500 members which in a small state meant that 'practically all' its members 'lived a middle class life in close touch with the people.' The system of succession involved a diffusion of power and influence among the elite of the state.[53] Public opinion itself was characteristically moderate as a result of the large Christian population and the importance within the Nair community of the Menon caste, a group which shone in administration and practical politics. The appointment of Sir R.K. Shanmughom Chetty as Dewan in 1935 was a fortunate one. A wealthy businessman and industrialist from Coimbatore, he had extensive political experience in Madras and Delhi and greater sympathy with the movement for responsible government than Ramaswami Aiyar.[54] Finally, Cochin had a progressive record in land reform; and in 1943 the Verumpattomdars Act gave security to virtually all tenants.

Cochin had no Legislative Council until 1925 but thereafter it advanced rapidly to diarchy in 1938, becoming the first princely state to concede a measure of responsible government. The elected members of the Council chose a Minister to be responsible for Agriculture, Industries and Rural Development.[55] Both parties contesting the election, Cochin Congress and Cochin State Congress, were essentially moderate but in January 1941, after continuous agitation in the council for an extension of its powers, a new and more militant party, the Praja Mandal, led by Panampilly Govinda Menon and K.P. Madhavan Nair, was formed to demand responsible government.[56]

Although a communist cell operated in Ernakulam from at least 1938 onwards, the party seems to have been content to confine its operations to the labour front through the Labour Brotherhood centred on Trichur. A unit of the CSP existed, which, like the Malabar branch, went over to the CPI in 1939 but it was not until the formation of the Praja Mandal that communist party workers began to participate on a significant scale in Cochin politics. For the communists Cochin was a small prize, its main significance being that it was a base from which to attack Travancore. Chetty had no particular regard for Ramaswami Aiyar, did not share C.P.'s obsession with communism, and, despite repeated remonstrances, took no action against the cell until the war was well under way.[57]

The Communist Party 1940–1945

By 1939 communist cells existed in Calicut, Ernakulam, and Trivandrum and the party was in many parts of Malabar co-extensive with the local Congress organization. The party members led the peasant union in Malabar and had penetrated a number of other organizations, including the SNDP *yogam*. The actual creation of a Kerala Unit of the CPI, however, was precipitated by All-India developments and was, arguably, premature.

Faced with the reality of war, Congress modified its earlier hostility. The CSP also reacted cautiously, merely asking its members to despatch postcards of protest to the authorities. Apart from Bose's Forward Bloc only the CPI, anxious to give what comfort it could to the Soviet Union in the period of the Nazi-Soviet Pact, maintained a militantly anti-war stance with the slogan of 'the revolutionary utilisation of the war crisis for achievement of National Freedom'.[58] In south India where the CPI had generally operated through the CSP grouping within Congress, a distinct organization now became necessary. Thus, immediately after the Wardha session of the AICC, ninety Malayali CSP members met secretly at a village near Tellicherry in Malabar on or about 13 October 1939 to formalize the transformation of the Kerala CSP into the Kerala CPI. Three months later on 26 January 1940—the tenth anniversary of Congress's declaration of Independence as its goal—the party announced its existence with tarred slogans on walls, culverts, and government offices.[59]

In line with national party policy the Kerala unit continued to work through Congress as well as independently. This enabled the CPI to operate comparatively freely during early 1940, as both the president and the secretary of the KPCC were party members. In the elections to the KPCC in early 1940 only thirty-five of the ninety-seven successful candidates were classified as Gandhians, twenty-four of whom were elected from south Malabar. Congress socialists dominated northern Malabar and Calicut. Allied military reverses in April and May were followed by arrests of prominent KPCC-CPI and peasant leaders, but there were still sizeable demonstrations in Malabar in support of the CPI's Anti-Repression Day on 15 September, held in defiance of an AICC order to boycott it.[60] This could be attributed to the left's effective organization of three campaigns in 1939-40: the lobbying of the Malabar Tenancy Committee as it toured the District taking evidence on the working of the 1929 Malabar Tenancy Act; the resistance to landlords' efforts to reassert their right to a variety of fees and levies lost during 1938; and the demand for action to mitigate the economic consequences of the war. Shrewdly, the party muted its campaign against the war as such. The KPCC's indiscipline provided the Congress Working Committee with its excuse to purge the Kerala unit of its communist elements. A commission of enquiry was appointed; the Malabar District Committee disbanded; and the KPCC superseded in favour of an *ad hoc* committee with the rightist C.K. Govindan Nair as secretary. As the government's search for CPI members intensified, the cadre's inexperience in underground work began to show.[61] By mid-1941 almost all the key figures except for E.M.S. Namboodiripad had been detained.[62] including 'a Nambudri communist on whom were found papers giving details of the party's underground organisation'.[63] A further blow was the arrest of sixty *kisan* leaders and the prohibition of the All-Malabar Peasants' Union in the wake of an agrarian clash at Kayyur in the far north in March 1941. The party, however, maintained some organization by means of the Distress Relief Committees, initially formed after a cyclone had hit the area in 1940, and the Food Committees arising from the famine conditions of 1942-3.[64] On the eve of the German invasion of the Soviet Union and the transformation of the Communist conception of the war from an Imperialist War into a People's War, the Kerala party could claim to have played a difficult hand remarkably well.

As elsewhere, the majority of Kerala party leaders first heard of the attack on the USSR in jail. There is some evidence that the majority resisted the conclusion that they should now abandon their opposition to the war. According to Damodaran, for instance, many south Indian comrades supported his counter thesis that the best way to help was by stepping up anti-imperialist activity. Only when a party circular reached them did his Jail Committee accept the line of People's War and support for the war effort.[65] The CPI was thus isolated for the second time in a decade from the mainstream of the nationalist movement, it having stood aside during the Quit India agitation of 1942. According to Namboodiripad the consequences were no less disastrous in Kerala than for the party generally.[66] A new generation of anti-imperialists believed the CPI was the agent of British imperialism. Rival organizations were established on trade union, peasant, and student fronts and the efforts of party members in such associations as the SNDP Yogam were neutralized. In Cannanore (the CSP-CPI stronghold in Malabar) former CSP members joined Dr K.B. Menon[67] and Mathai Manjooran's Socialist Party of Kerala,[68] formed in 1942; and although Menon himself eventually returned to the Congress fold in 1964 the majority of these national-minded marxist socialists later found their way into Manjooran's post-war Kerala Socialist Party (KSP) or the Revolutionary Socialist Party (RSP). The failure to recruit such men as Manjooran and Sreekantan Nair, the future RSP leader, dominant figures in the labour movements of Trichur and Quilon respectively, was a serious barrier to communist ascendancy in the Kerala trade unions. After 1942 the All-Travancore TUC fell under the control of such men. Namboodiripad, however, also states that after 1943 the party made a remarkable recovery, whether measured in terms of funds, the numbers and quality of cadres, or the sale of party literature including the Party's Kerala organ *Desabhimani*. Although the party's progress did not compare with that of Congress, there is some truth in the claim. Membership had risen from some 200 in 1940-1 to 600 in 1945.[69] No major figures had defected and the new recruits were of ability and conviction. The party took advantage of its legality to build a more effective organization and, under the guise of co-operating with the authorities in anti-fascist propaganda and Grow More Food Campaigns used every opportunity to proselytize. Noting that at anti-fascist meetings the communist speakers devoted more time to the importance of establishing a national government and the necessity of guerilla training, a Madras official reported that the 'Malabar comrades were 10 per cent anti-Nazi and 90 per cent anti-British Government . . . Collectors generally find them intolerable friends of the Government.'[70]

Two factors were of particular significance in enabling the party to hold its ground in Kerala: the party's partial success in redefining the Freedom Struggle in terms of a struggle against feudalism as much as imperialism between 1938 and 1941; and by 1943 the loss of what limited local interest there had been in the war, even among the educated public, in the face of the all-absorbing problem of food supplies.[71] Only on the labour front does the party appear to have experienced some setback. Where the party enjoyed influence and the industry was directly related to the war effort, the provincial leadership exercised some restraint in leading industrial action. However, as the tide of war turned, plans were reported to have been laid at a party meeting in Alleppey at the end of 1943 to couple the deteriorating economic situation with an intensified programme of labour agitation. Intelligence reports also claimed that cells and study classes were actively discussing the possibility of planned uprisings in the event of a breakdown of law and order at the end of the war. Labour disputes multiplied in 1944-5. How far they were communist-inspired is impossible to establish. RSP sources claim there was a significant difference in levels of wages and bonus between socialist-and communist-led industries in 1945 arising from the CPI's war-time restraint.[72]

Leftist Strategies, Insurrection, and Repression 1946-50

With the end of the war, the CPI was relieved of the incubus of the People's War line, only to face the challenge of a rapid move to Indian independence without clear guidance from the Soviet party, without anything approaching consensus as to the CPI line within the country as a whole, and as a puny political force when compared to a Congress of five million members sweeping all before it.[73] Initially the party returned to its pre-war line of a united front combined with militant action on the labour and peasant fronts with the object of radicalizing the masses. Of particular concern to the Kerala unit, as to the Andhra party, was the uncertainty surrounding the future of the princely states. In Travancore the policy of the Dewan, like that of the Nizam of Hyderabad, was geared towards the proclamation of an independent state when paramountcy lapsed. The August 1946 resolution of the CPI Central Committee called for broad-based struggles to ensure the incorporation of the princely states into the Indian Union. The party's interpretation of the Mountbatten Award of June 1947 was cautious. India had not gained

full independence. Imperialism and feudalism were too well entrenched for that; and so the party would need to continue its united front
policy after the transfer of power. The bloodshed of partition appeared to reinforce the case for co-operation with Congress.

However, by late 1947, sections of the party were arguing that the
CPI was becoming an appendage of Congress, was neglecting the
opportunity to lead a mass upsurge against imperialism and feudalism, and was inviting repression by its very timidity. This leftist
faction won control of the party's higher counsels by December 1947
and in February–March 1948 the 2nd Congress, held in Calcutta,
adopted the Calcutta or Ranadive (its main protagonist) Theses as
party policy. Indian independence was dismissed as a chimera. The
earlier distinction between progressive and reactionary sections of
the bourgeoisie was rejected and with it any collaboration with
Congress. The objective now was People's Democracy—democracy
and socialism combined—to be achieved by a prolonged struggle
using politicized strikes in the urban areas leading to a general rising
in the villages. As a model of revolution it echoed Russian experience
but in the Indian situation it over-estimated the potential of the
working class and under-estimated the importance of the peasantry
and landless labour and was un-marxist in denying the national
bourgeoisie any role at all in the revolutionary process.[74] In any case
the party lacked the machinery, resources, or influence to implement
such a policy.[75] The result was a series of ill-considered and ill-co-
ordinated actions, subsequently labelled 'adventurist' by the party,
which led to deaths, detentions, the exposure of undercover comrades, loss of influence in the union movement, a split in the peasant
organization, widespread demoralization and defection, and the accelerated growth of rival Congress and socialist mass organization.

At the beginning of 1949 the party turned to terrorism, sabotage,
and jail strikes which led to still more determined measures by the
authorities. Only in the Telengana area of Andhra was there effective
organization, based on a radically different model. In the Andhra
Letter of June 1948 the Andhra leadership proposed a quasi-Maoist
strategy based on a united front of the entire peasantry and parts of
the bourgeoisie under working-class leadership which would sustain
a prolonged civil war fought from liberated areas and founded on
agrarian revolution.[76] From 1950 to 1951 the Andhra line briefly
prevailed, with Rajeshwara Rao (from Andhra) supplanting Ranadive
as general secretary until under pressure from labour leaders and a
number of provincial leaders the party sought to end its dissension
and avert imminent extinction by seeking authoritative guidance
from the Communist Party of Great Britain and the CPSU. The
resultant 1951 Draft Programme and Statement of Policy, underpin-

ned by the confidential Tactical Line, became official party policy at
the 3rd Congress at Madurai in 1953, and formed the basis of its aims
and tactics until the 4th Congress at Palghat in 1956. The franker
Tactical Line[77] followed the Andhra Thesis in many respects, but
with realistic modifications. The document endorsed the concept of
armed struggle and the complementarity of peasant partisan war and
worker uprisings, but only when the situation was ripe. Such a
maturity was to be conditional on radicalizing the masses and in this
process the 'coming [1951-2] general elections' were to form the
basis 'for the most extensive popularisation of [the CPI] programme, for mobilising and unifying the democratic forces [and] for
exposing the policies and methods of the present government'.[78]

The CPI in Kerala 1946-1950

In Kerala the CPI underwent its own convulsions. These were
occasioned not only by controversies in the party nationally but also
by particular provincial difficulties: the complexities of tackling
three distinct political situations—Malabar, Travancore and
Cochin—simultaneously; the strength of communal associations
such as the SNDP Yogam and the NSS; the competition of non-
communist marxists and left-wing socialists in the labour movement; and a low level of theoretical awareness—Stalin's official
history of the CPSU, published in Malayalam in 1941, was the
cadres' textbook and Marxist-Leninism was identified with
Stalinism.[79]

During 1946-7 the Kerala unit experienced an acute inner party
crisis about which comparatively little is known.[80] Krishna Pillai, as
party secretary, unilaterally dissolved the state party committee but
was overruled by the party centre. There were also frequent changes
in the party's office-bearers on the Malabar District Committee.[81]
All accounts are agreed that ideological differences were of little
significance. The unit's stance was largely left to Namboodiripad, a
member of the CPI's Central Committee since 1943 and then as later
very much a centrist on party policy. On the eve of the switch from
the united front strategy to the Calcutta Theses Namboodiripad was
arguing that the State Congress in Kerala was still a progressive
organization although its leaders were prone to betray the masses
and that the CPI unit was willing to build a united front on the basis
of a democratic programme in the forthcoming election in Travancore-
Cochin.[82] However, Namboodiripad accepted the change in the
party's line at the Calcutta Congress and the Ranadive line was
readily accepted by the membership. This was hardly surprising
since Namboodiripad reports that the state committee's role in

decision-making was a mere formality. 'If this had been the state of affairs at the state party level, the position in the lower level units can very well be imagined.'[83] Party conferences were held quite regularly but debate was rare and then routine. Those who stood out against the decisions of the ruling duumvirate of Namboodiripad (ideology and political issues) and Krishna Pillai (organizational and practical questions) were ordered to implement them or face party discipline.

The real nature of the crisis seems to have been organizational and personal. The local unit was broadly divided into cadres working on the mass front and those working underground, the latter led by Krishna Pillai, K.C. George, and N.C. Sekhar, 'two sets of experiences, methods of work . . .' To link them, 'shortcuts were resorted to.'[84] These organizational differences overlapped with personal conflicts of which the best known is the disquiet about Krishna Pillai's marriage.[85] His sudden death (from snake poisoning) on 19 August 1948 caused further dislocation at a time of acute pressure from the authorities, although the shock of the loss of its major mass leader healed wounds. According to Namboodiripad, 'over 3,000 party members and sympathisers' from Kerala were imprisoned during 1948-50.[86] None the less the Kerala party was, on the evidence of the election results of 1951-2 (see below p. 111), stronger than ever when it returned to legality. This can be explained by reference to five factors: the party's bold efforts to overthrow Sir C.P. Ramaswamy Aiyar in Travancore; its involvement in working class and peasant agitation; the contrast between the *sanyasi* (holy man) life-style of its workers and the bourgeois style of the local Congress leaders; the hostility generated towards Congress by the communalism, regionalism, and corruption of its provincial governments; the growing distance between the middle-class leadership of the communal associations and their humbler caste constituency; and the party's involvement with the state-wide movement for a united Kerala and the associated cultural renaissance.

The Punnapra-Vayalar Rising 1946

At the end of the war Ramaswami Aiyar was still in command of Travancore, was as opposed as ever to the grant of responsible government and was now bent on an independent state when paramountcy lapsed. In January 1946 he announced his constitutional proposals: an American-style constitution in which the position of the Dewan with respect to the legislature and judiciary would approximate to that of the President of the United States but whose authority would rest on the Maharaja's prerogative not on popular election.[87]

This manoeuvring united all shades of opinion against the Dewan, and in some quarters of the Kerala CPI it was believed that this popular upsurge could be converted into a revolutionary one by means of a general strike—even though the party's mass influence was limited to the northern part of the Alleppey coir belt. Conditions in the coir industry generally were now far worse than at the time of the first general strike in 1938. According to an internal government document wages had risen 75 per cent since 1938 but prices 200 per cent, while the proportion working in regulated factories had fallen. Famine stalked the coastal areas during the lean months of July and August.[88]

Soon after the Dewan's announcement of his proposed reforms in January 1946 the CPI, from an advanced base across the water in Ernakulam, began to prepare for an insurrection in north Travancore.[89] Camps were established on both sides of the Cochin-Travancore border and partisans trained under the supervision of Kumara Panicker, known as the Stalin of Wynad and K.C. George, one of the party's intellectuals. Active support was forthcoming from sections of the Cochin Praja Mandal and of the left-wing of the Travancore State Congress.

In mid-1946 the 17,000 strong Coir Workers' Union, led by Sreekantan Nair, a non-communist left-wing socialist, and T.V. Thomas of the CPI, struck for bonus to be granted as of right, irrespective of productivity or profitability. At this stage there were no political demands. The Dewan intervened to offer a tri-partite government, employer, and union conference, which led swiftly to the acceptance of bonus as deferred wages and the creation of an industrial relations committee for the industry. In circumstances which are unclear the communist section of the workforce then put forward a further set of claims, this time coupled with political demands for the immediate introduction of responsible government. At about this time some sources claim that K.C. George travelled to Bombay to seek permission for a Soviet-style insurrection which Ranadive, the senior party official available, granted.[90] Krishna Pillai and Namboodiripad remained in Calicut and it was from there that the final approval for the general strike was given in the light of K.C. George's reports that a reign of terror prevailed in the area.

The Dewan's response to the new demands was to declare the CPI, the Coir Workers' Union, and the Alleppey Fishermen's Union illegal organizations, to arrest three leading members of the State Congress—State Congress had in fact declined to support the call for a general strike—and to detain a large number of communist workers and youth leaders. Accounts diverge at this point but it appears that the Dewan was insufficiently apprised of the situation either through the ineptitude of his police officers or wilful withholding of intelligence.[91] No major reinforcements of the police or military establishment were made until one of the leading landlords and employers, Applon Aroj, requested protection. State Reserve Police then camped at Punnapra as tension rose.

On 24 October, the second day of the strike, after one demonstrator had been shot, 2,000 strikers attacked the temporary police station set up in Aroj's house at Punnapra. In the ensuing battle four policemen and some thirty-five of the assailants died, and a dozen rifles fell into rebel hands. Government reinforcements arrived the following day and martial law was declared in the taluks of Ambalapuzha and Shertallai. The insurgents, now out of contact with their leadership, retreated to Vayalar island, followed by large numbers of villagers. After a military helicopter dropping leaflets urging surrender had been driven off, 500 troops crossed to the island on 27 October and in the ensuing carnage communist sources claim that more than 300 were killed, mostly peasants but also 'the real comrades.'[92] By 30 October factories and mills were reopened, and on 10 November martial law was withdrawn.

The original plan is said to have been to convert the strike-bound area into a liberated zone, a not impossible objective—given the terrain of backwaters and islands and neutrality on the part of the Cochin authorities—provided there was a supportive general strike in the rest of the state and the destruction of communications.[93] However, once the State Congress declined to co-operate, the scheme was doomed to failure. According to Sreekantan Nair, the party persevered with its plans notwithstanding, because it was desperate to recover its lost hold on the coir district.[94] A communist participant attributes that decision to a combination of K.C. George's determination to stage the rising and the imperfections of the party's intelligence. It had, he alleges, trained its partisans on the assumption that they would face standard .303 calibre rifles, not machine guns. There was also some expectation that the Nair troops could be dissuaded from firing. If this view was held, it had no evidence to support it. This communist source also claims that the destruction of communications was inadequately planned and executed. Although explosives were not hard to come by, either from quarries or from military encampments in Cochin, none had been obtained. One of the two persons sent to buy explosives was caught, while the other is alleged to have disappeared to Bombay to be captured in Mysore six months later. Generally the organization suffered from inadequate leadership: the party centre remained at Calicut; and the local centre at Alleppey, twelve miles from events.[95] Woodcock concludes that the episode was a 'cold-blooded political calculation' resting on Tertullian's maxim that the 'blood of the martyrs is the seed of the Church', a view essentially shared by Sreekantan Nair.[96] On the other hand the Kerala leadership had not risked life wantonly in the past nor was it to do so in the future. Retrospectively the party claims that Sir C.P. Ramaswami Aiyar's pyrrhic victory sealed his fate.[97]

Soon afterwards Britain announced its decision to withdraw from India but without explicitly indicating what would happen to the princely states when their treaties with the paramount power lapsed.[98] Sir C.P. worked during 1946 to persuade the princely authorities to agree on a common demand for autonomy, but finding 'many of the Princes were still living in a fool's paradise'[99] he outlined a new constitution in April 1947. It was still based on the concept of a non-removable executive.[100] On 11 June he announced the intention to resume Travancore's independent sovereign status.[101]

The Dewan's proposals provoked a state-wide campaign for his resignation and the immediate grant of responsible government. Even the Nair Service Society which had consistently supported Sir C.P. Ramaswami Aiyar now abandoned him. Its powerful leader Mannath Padmanabha Pillai, was promptly arrested. An anxious Mountbatten summoned Sir C.P. to Delhi. Sardar Vallabhai Patel, who was present at the interview, warned him that 'if you return to Travancore without giving up your idea of Independence your life could be in danger', to which Sir C.P. retorted, 'I am aware that you can have me assassinated but then there will only be one left to fight Communism.'[102] On 18 July 1947 the Maharaja confirmed that Travancore would revert to sovereign status on 26 August. However, on the evening of 25 July the Dewan was attacked and seriously wounded while leaving a concert in Trivandrum. The Maharaja then telegraphed the Viceroy agreeing to join the Republic of India. On 19 August Ramaswami Aiyar formally resigned as Dewan. Neither Sardar Patel nor the CPI was responsible for the attack, which was undertaken by a Brahmin on behalf of left-wing socialists and meticulously planned and executed.[103] Three years later in 1950 the Kerala CPI did itself agree to an assassination plan during the party's brief terrorist phase, a bizarre project to bomb the entire Travancore-Cochin ministry on its way to the Assembly. The conspiracy is alleged to have leaked out via the Revolutionary Socialist Party and the ministry sent out empty cars.[104]

In Cochin the CPI was offered no equivalent opportunity to the Punnapra-Vayalar situation to stake its claim to be in the forefront of the struggle against absolutism. The diarchical system established in 1938 allowed for the possibility of constitutional obstruction from within the legislature. In August 1946 the Praja Mandal-dominated

Assembly declined to vote finance for general administration and won a vote of no confidence in the Council of Ministers. Piecemeal concessions followed until in June 1947 the office of Dewan was finally abolished.[105] The party did, however, take a prominent part in the Paliyam *satyagraha* of 1948, aimed at securing the rights of untouchables to walk past a private temple owned by the biggest landlord in Cochin.

In Malabar, where the CPI had roots that had penetrated deeper than in the princely states prior to 1945, the party continued its activity on the peasant front. Amidst the political and economic uncertainties of 1946-7 large-scale hoarding of food grains led to famine conditions in northern Malabar. In December 1946 communist-led peasants occupied 'private forest' land and in clashes at Karivalloor and Kavumbayi six peasants were killed. Despite preventive arrests and the banning of *Desabhimani* the movement spread during April and May 1947, precipitating determined action by the Madras Congress ministry. Malabar Special Police—a paramilitary force originally raised to contain the Moplahs—were stationed throughout the district and, according to a non-communist source, 'landlords encouraged to take the law into their own hands'.[106] Given that communist support was not unimpressive as measured by the party's performance in the 1946 provincial election and that it was decidedly impressive in its radicalization, such steps tended to undermine what little support Congress had among the peasants, the landless, and semi-industrial workers of the District.[107]

Throughout Kerala the communist party workers had earned a reputation even among their political enemies for their sincerity and simplicity. Membership was contingent on proof of these qualities, some degree of literacy, and evidence of a period of (what at this time was dangerous) work on behalf of the party. It was not enough to affect outward symbols—a Gandhi cap, for instance—or to pay a nominal subscription. Since there was no immediate prospect of power, there were then no bandwaggon members. In the face of repression and brutality the communists had shown the villagers the depth of their convictions. In their own way they had lived an ascetic life. Alcohol was forbidden; family life was disrupted, and the party's permission was required for marriage; personal income was remitted to the party and party workers lived on small stipends and charity; many, including Namboodiripad and Krishna Pillai, gave their share of landed property to the party; and all were expected to live the life of a political *sanyasi*. Breaches of the party's discipline occurred, especially under the pressures of 1948-50, and in 1951 a general 'amnesty' was declared, which in the view of some led to a deterioration in individual integrity.[108] None the less the party was widely perceived as a band of true believers, reluctantly admired by its political enemies, and exalted by those among whom it worked. The contrast with Congress and State Congress was all too obvious in the early years of Independence. Later it was to become less clear and older party members and sympathizers themselves emphasize the loss of innocence that followed political success.

The dismal performance of Congress after an overwhelming victory in the Travancore election of February 1948 is mirrored in the fact that there were three ministries in Travancore between March 1948 and July 1949 and three in the newly formed United State of Travancore-Cochin from July 1949 to the 1951-2 general election. The Congress parties of Travancore and Cochin lacked cohesion, unity, or discipline and were unable to manage caste and communal rivalries, or, after the integration of the two states, regional interests, including Tamil sub-nationalism in the south of Travancore.[109] Prior to 1947 Congress had been dominated by younger and more progressive elements from the major communities and in particular the Nairs. As Independence approached, the more conservative elements recognized the inevitable and joined Congress. It was at this time that first the SNDP Yogam under Sankar and then the NSS under Mannath abandoned Sir C.P., subsequently forming the Hindu Mandalam, directed against Christian economic and political influence and founding a short-lived political arm known as Democratic Congress. Disillusioned by these developments, some of the more progressive high-caste members left to join one or other socialist party[110] or the CPI.

A further important source of support for the CPI was its identification with the movement for a linguistically defined Kerala state and the associated Malayali cultural renaissance. The post-war phase of the United Kerala Movement commenced with the Maharaja of Cochin's proclamation in July 1946 of his wish to merge Cochin into a new province of Kerala. This, however, was not a linguistically defined entity but an echo of the ancient Chera empire which had stretched from Cape Comorin, the southern tip of India, to Gokarnam in South Canara. It was on this basis that the KPCC held a convention in April 1947. The political obstacles were formidable and with the formation of Travancore-Cochin state the United Kerala Committee was dissolved. The CPI and the socialist parties remained wedded to a purely Malayali Kerala, in the achievement of which the efflorescence of Malayali writing was a powerful factor. By 1947 almost every village had its reading room containing newspapers, novelettes, and copies of sacred texts and famous Malayalam literature (and the communist party benefited by its attention to recruiting party members or sympathizers to supervisory positions in these village 'libraries'). As yet the readership consisted mainly of the higher castes and communities but much of the modern literature available came from members of the Progressive Writers' Association in whose work social criticism predominated: Kesava Dev, Thakazhi Sivasankara Pillai, K. Kumara Pillai, Basheer, and the future minister of education in the 1957 communist government, Joseph Mundassery. The titles of the novels speak for themselves: Kesava Dev's *From the Gutter* (1942), and Thakazhi's *Scavenger's Son* (1947) and *Two Measures of Rice* (1948).[111] Namboodiripad estimated that in 1951 alone no fewer than 2,000 poems and short stories dealing with aspects of the struggle for a United People's Democratic Kerala were published in left-wing magazines.[112] With the continuing spread of literacy as well as the explosion of public gatherings after Independence the CPI was an important beneficiary.

Most of the party's leaders were from the higher castes or communities, and in a caste-conscious society that made their personal involvement in peasant and labourers' existence the more effective. Through study classes in the evenings and school holidays the party used teacher and college student volunteers to teach the rudiments of marxism in a manner relevant to the environment, backed up by village reading rooms and colloquial-style leaflets. The CPI treated the neglected youngsters of the economically and socially backward communities as if they mattered. These teenagers of 1947 were to be the electors of 1957.

Notes

1 The date of the foundation of the CPI is disputed: see G.K. Lieten, 'Indian Communists Look at Indian Communism.' *Economic and Political Weekly*, 10 Sept. 1977, p. 1610. The biography of Marx, the first in an Indian language, was written by K. Ramakrishna Pillai, editor and then proprietor of *Swadeshabhimani* (Tvm) until his deportation from Travancore and the confiscation of the press on 26 Sept. 1910 after a series of articles highly critical of the Dewan and the régime in Travancore. The Malayalam biography is translated in P.C. Joshi and K. Damodaran, *Marx comes to India* (Delhi, Manohar Book Service, 1975). Pillai's career is summarized in *The Press in Kerala* (Tvm, Dept of Public Relations, Kerala, 1977), pp. 13–14 and R. Ramakrishnan Nair, *K. Ramakrishna Pillai* (Tvm, Kerala Academy of Political Science, 1977). The obituary of Lenin was published in *Swadeshabhimani*, 1.3.1099 Malayalam Era (Oct. 1924) and is cited in Jeffrey, *J. of Asian Studies* XXXVIII (1), 1978. p. 87.

2 S.S. Harrison, *India: the Most Dangerous Decades* (1960), pp. 193-9;

K. Gough, 'Kerala Politics and the 1965 Elections', *International J. of Comparative Sociology* VIII (1), 1967, pp. 64–5; D.S. Zagoria, 'The Social Bases of Communism in Kerala and West Bengal', *Problems of Communism* 22 (1), 1973 and 'A Note on Landlessness, Literacy and Agrarian Communism in India', *Archives européennes de sociologie* 13 (2) 1972 and 'The Ecology of Peasant Communism in India', *American Political Science R.*, LXV (1), 1971; Jeffrey, *J. of Asian Studies* XXXVIII (1), 1978.

3	*J. of Asian Studies*, XXXVIII (1), 1978. For his analysis of the 1940 KPCC election candidacies see his Table V, p. 95; for instances of communists from a *déraciné* background see p.81 and p.82, n. 13; and for the quotation used in my own text see p. 81, n. 11.

4	*Kerala District Gazetteers: Cannanore* (A. Sreedhara Menon, ed., 1972), p. 165.

5	Madras Revenue Dept G.O. 3021, 26 Sept. 1917, quoted by K.N. Pannikar, 'Agrarian Legislation and Social Classes: a Case Study of Malabar', *Economic and Political Weekly*, 27 May 1978, p. 885.

6	Varghese, pp. 226–31.

7	K.N. Pannikar, as n. 5 above, p. 887.

8	A.V. Jose, 'The Origin of Trade Unionism Among the Agricultural Labourers in Kerala,' *Social Scientist* (Tvm) 60, 1977.

9	R.E. Miller, p. 132: 'Mappilas who were present recall the energetic exhortations to joint action in order to drive out the British within a year and the assurances... the British could easily be overcome.'

10	S.F. Dale, *J. of Asian Studies*, XXXV (1), 1975 and 'A Reply to Wood', ibid., XXXVI (2), 1977; *Modern Asian Studies*, II (1), 1977; *Islamic Society and the South Asian Frontier: the Mappilas of Malabar 1498-1922* (Oxford, Clarendon Press, 1980). D.N. Dhanagare, 'Agrarian Conflict, Religion and Politics: the Moplah Rebellions in Malabar in the Nineteenth and Early Twentieth Centuries', *Past and Present* 74, 1976, pp. 113–41; Robert L. Hardgrave Jr, 'Peasant Mobilisation in Malabar', in R.I. Crane, ed., *Aspects of Political Mobilisation in South Asia* (1976), 'The Mappilla Rebellion, 1921', *Modern Asian Studies* 11 (1), 1977. R.E. Miller, pp. 128–53; Conrad Wood, 'Historical Background of the Moplah Rebellion', *Social Scientist* (Tvm) 25, 1974, and 'The First Moplah Rebellion Against British Rule in Malabar', *Modern Asian Studies* 10 (4), 1976, and 'Peasant Revolt: an Interpretation of Moplah Violence in the Nineteenth and Twentieth Centuries', in C. Dewey and A.G. Hopkins, eds., *The Imperial Impact* (1978), and 'Moplah Outbreaks: a Discussion Contribution', *J. of Asian Studies* XXXVI (2), 1977.

11	R.E. Miller, pp. 145–6.

12	Ibid., p. 162. Jeffrey, *J. of Asian Studies*, XXXVIII (1), 1978, notes the failure of communist campaigning among the Moplahs in 1946 (p. 83, n. 2).

13	R.E. Miller, pp. 158–62. Namboodiripad, *Kerala*, p. 167.

14	As n. 4 above, p. 167; Jawaharlal Nehru, *Autobiography* (London, Wishart, 1936), p. 182. Nehru afterwards wrote pleading for a more serious Congresss organization in the district. P.K.K. Menon, vol. II, p. 146.

15   *The Hindu*, 14 Oct. 1929, gives Congress membership in Kerala as 3,265. However, crowds of from 10,000 to 20,000 watched the *satyagrahis* at Calicut in May 1930; and Malabar is said to have remained 'the most troublesome district in the Madras Presidency throughout 1930'. Jeffrey, *J. of Asian Studies*, XXXVIII (1), 1978, p. 85.

16   Gopalan, *In the Cause of the People*, pp. 22 and 62.

17   T.V. Krishnan, *Kerala's First Communist: Life of Sakhavu Krishna Pillai* (1971), p. 19.

18   K. Kelappan Nair was Kerala's Jayaprakash Narayan. An aristocratic Nair from Quilandy (Kozhikode), he was educated at Madras and Bombay but broke off his legal studies to join the 1919-20 non-cooperation movement. Kelappan worked consistently against untouchability and was a leader in both the Vaikom (1924) and Guruvayoor (1931) struggles. Initially he was secretary of the Congress Socialist Party unit in Malabar—unlike 'JP' never a marxist—withdrawing his support in 1935-6 and with Damodara Menon organized the Kerala Congress Gandhi Sangh as a countervailing force in 1939. After organizing the Kisan Mazdoor Praja Party in Malabar in 1951-2, Kelappan retired from active political life, devoting himself to Gandhian social work.

19   Manjeri Rama Iyer was a Tamil Brahmin from Manjeri (Malappuram). After a distinguished college career at Presidency College, Madras, Manjeri became a well-known criminal lawyer. He was close to Mrs Beasant and one of the founders of the Malabar Theosophical Society, and a prominent Home Rule Leaguer. Among his philanthropic gestures was the foundation of a temple open to all castes and communities. Manjeri was sometime editor of the *West Coast Spectator*.

20   Gopalan, *In the Cause of the People*, p. 59

21   Saul Rose, *Socialism in Southern Asia* (1959), ch. III; Hari Kishore Singh, *A History of the Praja Socialist Party 1934-1959* (1959), pp. 27-33.

22   Krishnan, p. 19.

23   Chirakkal was marked by a high incidence of *kuzhikanom* leases—leases of waste land conditional on improvement—direct from the *jenmis* who, led by the Chirakkal Raja, were locally extremely powerful. Sixty-one families owned more than half the land and were among the most oppressive in Malabar. Tenure was highly insecure, notwithstanding the 1930 Tenancy Act, while income was particularly unreliable owing to the cultivators' dependence on pepper and coconut which were both subject to wide price fluctuations. Adrian C. Mayer, *Land and Society in Malabar* (1952), pp. 85 and 93. At the end of 1938 the All-Malabar Peasants' Union had a paid-up (two annas per year) membership of about 30,000, of which 10,000 was from Chirakkal and 5,000 from Kasergod. Jeffrey, *J. of Asian Studies,* XXXVIII (1) 1978, p. 91.

24   Gopalan, *In the Cause of the People*, p. 96.

25 Kongattil Raman Menon (1896-1939) was a member of a prosperous
    Nair family from Chowgat (Palghat). A practising lawyer and a skilful
    political organizer, he received jail terms in 1930 and 1932 for acts of
    civil disobedience. In 1937 Menon became Minister for Courts and
    Prisons in the first Madras Congress ministry.
26 Fearing that the growing *kisan* movement would be captured by the
    left wing—which would lead to demands unacceptable to their land-
    lord supporters—Congress established a Mass Contact Committee at
    the 1936 Lucknow Congress. Though the committee did not produce
    a report, some provincial units took up the idea. The CSP leadership
    was initially sceptical but quickly realized the possibilities of using
    mass contact organizers to strengthen their influence. H.K. Singh,
    p. 38.
27 Gopalan, *In the Cause of the People,* p. 77; cf. Democratic Research
    Service (Bombay) *Indian Communist Party Documents 1930-1956* (1957),
    hereafter *ICPD,* p. 40. *Prabhatham* ceased publication in Aug. 1935
    after the Madras government demanded Rs 2,000 security; it was
    revived in 1938 and continued until 1940.
28 Krishnan, p. 66.
29 H.K. Singh, pp. 26-47; PSP (Praja Socialist Party), *PSP: a Brief Intro-
    duction* (Bombay, 1956), p. 5.
30 E.M.S. Namboodiripad, *The National Question in Kerala* (1952), pp.
    148-9.
31 Krishnan, p. 29. N.C. Sekhar recalled that his group (the Communist
    League) 'displayed towards the congress-socialism of Krishna Pillai
    the contempt typical of communist intellectuals of those days.' For
    Namboodiripad see E.M.S. Namboodiripad, 'My First Taste of
    Bolshevism', *New Age,* Nov. 1957. The history of the Trivandrum
    Communist League (Mar. 1931—?) is obscure. N.P. (sometimes gi-
    ven as N.B.) Kurukkal (1905-47) is credited with organizing the
    group. Kurukkal, though an important figure, is not apparently listed
    in K. Karunakaran Nair, ed., *Who is Who of Freedom Fighters in Kerala*
    and is elsewhere referred to only in passing. He was allegedly
    murdered by Travancore government *goondas.* Two other prominent
    figures in the League were N.C. Sekhar (1906-   ) and Ponnara G.
    Sreedhar(an). Sekhar is said to have organized the League (*Who is
    Who . . . ,* p. 563), was a leading freedom fighter and trade unionist, and
    a major link between the CSP, CPI, and Travancore Youth League. A
    full-time CPI worker, he left the CPI for the CPM at the time of the
    split and in 1968 was expelled for his 'ultra' left activities. Ponnara
    Sreedhar (1898-1966), a qualified lawyer, successfully assisted in the
    organization of the League, Travancore Youth League, and Travancore
    State Congress. Known as the bell-wether of Kerala socialism, he was
    a Praja Socialist MLA in the Assemblies of 1957 and 1960. The Com-
    munist League gained prominence by publishing in Malayalam por-
    tions of the statements filed by the accused in the Meerut Conspiracy
    dealing with what should be done in India. The group was not con-
    nected with the All-India communist party. Its contributions to politi-

cal developments included the first United Kerala Conference, a Press Workers' Union, and a Young Men's Association (1931), the basis of the Youth League (1933).

32 Gopalan, *In the Cause of the People,* p. 70.

33 Krishnan, p. 68.

34 DRS, *ICPD,* pp. 33–4.

35 Ibid., pp. 40–1. The entry is headed 'Madras' and apparently refers to Malabar. Tamil Nad (including Madras City) and Andhra are discussed under separate headings. Rose, pp. 22–3; M.R. Masani, *Communist Party of India* (1954), pp. 68–71; Jayaprakash Narayan, *Towards Struggle* (Bombay, Padma Publishers, 1946), pp. 172–3.

36 A.K. Gopalan and Sardar Chandroth Kunhiraman Nair disagreed with the official CSP attitude to accepting office and temporarily resigned from the party. Krishnan, p. 37; Gopalan, *In the Cause of the People,* pp. 79–84. For the tenancy issue see E.M.S. Namboodiripad, *Economic Problems of Kerala* (1956, Malayalam); Govt of Madras, *Report of the Malabar Tenancy Committee,* (1940), 2 vols.; Varghese, p. 231; Mayer, pp. 86–95. Consideration of the report was postponed owing to the war.

37 C.J. Baker, *Politics of South India 1920-1937* (1976), pp. 106–28.

38 Krishnan, pp. 71–2. The new district board was dissolved by the Adviser's régime in 1940. Namboodiripad, *The National Question in Kerala,* p. 141.

39 Govt of Travancore, *Report of the Unemployment Enquiry Committee* (1928), pp. 47–8.

40 No critical biography exists. See C.P. Ramaswami Iyer, *'C.P.' by his Contemporaries* (Madras, C.P.'s 81st Birthday Celebrations Cttee, 1959). Wavell noted him as 'one of the cleverest men in India, of course': *Wavell: The Viceroy's Journal* (ed. Penderel Moon, 1973), p. 241. Skrine, resident British Agent in Travancore, wrote in 1938 of 'the intense, almost hysterical, hatred shown by the educated and semi-educated classes for the Diwan' arising partly from clashes of personality and partly circumstances. Sir C.P. was a Brahmin in a state where Brahmins were few and without political power. He was incapable of suffering fools gladly, incorruptible 'by money' and hated for it. Though his ends were the peace and prosperity of Travancore 'His methods are Machiavellian; he rules by dividing, he bribes with office and other favours, he sets traps for his critics and plays on the weaknesses of his enemies. It is no wonder that the man in the street does not love him.' Skrine attributed some of Sir C.P.'s problems to the necessity of carrying out the ideas and ambitions of the Junior Maharani, 'the villain of the piece', though he did not report the allegations of a romantic relationship between them then current. ('Skrine's note to Glancy of his impressions of the present crisis in Travancore affairs, Trivandrum, 11 Oct. 1938': Political Dept, Political Branch, R/1/29/ 1849, IOL.) Madras officials were less enamoured: 'Sir C.P. . . . who quite obviously prefers to be a dictator in Travancore to one of a crowd in Delhi.' (Sir Arthur Hope, n.d. [Nov. 1942] Report no. 10, Madras

Government's Reports, L/P and J/5/205, IOL.)
41 *IE,* 27 Sept. 1966.
42 Baker, *The Politics of South India 1920-37,* p. 23.
43 Sir C.P. Ramaswami Aiyar, 'Introductory Essay', *Illustrated Weekly of India,* 12 Sept. 1965, p. 11.
44 R. Ramakrishnan Nair, *Constitutional Experiments in Kerala* (1964), pp. 12-18 and 71-84.
45 Ibid., p. 17.
46 P.K.K. Menon, vol. 2, p. 337, n. 7.
47 Private communication from Professor R. Ramakrishnan Nair based on his interview with Sir C.P. in 1954.
48 A. Pattom Thanu Pillai (1885-1970) was a leading Trivandrum Nair lawyer, a man of considerable ability, and a certain egotism. He represented Trivandrum constituencies from 1927 for thirty-five years and was the most prominent leader of the Travancore State Congress. Pattom was the first Chief Minister of Travancore in 1948 while still a Congressman. After his resignation as CM, he formed the Democratic Socialist group, though still effectively leading Congress. He was PSP Chief Minister of Travancore-Cochin in 1954-5 and again Chief Minister of Kerala in the PSP-Congress ministry of 1960-2 when he resigned to become Governor of the Punjab, and (1964) of Andhra Pradesh.
49 Krishnan, pp. 50-65.
50 Fortnightly Reports 1/39, 15 Jan. 1939, Political Dept, Political Branch, R/1/29/2025, IOL.
51 Fortnightly Reports 23/38, 16 Dec. 1938, Political Dept, Political Branch, R/1/29/1676, IOL.
52 M.J. Koshy, *Last Days of Monarchy in Kerala* (1973), ch. 11; R. Ramakrishnan Nair, *Constitutional Experiments in Kerala,* ch. III; P.K.K. Menon, vol. 2, ch. 24.
53 V.K.S. Nayar, 'Kerala Politics Since 1947: Community Attitudes', in Iqbal Narain, ed., *State Politics in India,* p. 153.
54 Baker, *The Politics of South India 1920-37,* pp. 80,241-2, and 333; *Kerala District Gazetteers: Ernakulam* (A. Sreedhara Menon, ed., 1965), p. 218.
55 *Kerala District Gazetteers: Ernakulam,* pp. 218-19.
56 Ibid., pp. 219-20.
57 Sir C.P. Ramaswamy Iyer [Aiyar] to Glancy, 23 Mar. 1940, Political Dept, Political Branch, R/1/29/2237, IOL. Fortnightly Reports 5/41, 19 Mar. 1941, IOL, quotes Sir C.P. as claiming the hatchet has finally been buried. However, the governments of the two states continued to take contrasting stands on the handling of communist agitation: 'Communist disturbances—Attitude of the Government of Cochin, 17 Jan. 1947', L/P & S/13/1285, IOL.
58 Politbureau Resolution, Oct. 1939, quoted by G.D. Overstreet and M. Windmiller, *Communism in India* (1960), p. 177.
59 Krishnan, p. 72.
60 Jeffrey, *J. of Asian Studies* XXXVIII (1), 1978, p. 94, gives details of the cross-caste character of those arrested.

61 Gopalan, *In the Cause of the People*, p. 142.
62 P. Krishna Pillai, A.K. Gopalan, and K.C. George.
63 Govt of Madras, Public (General) Dept, 4 July 1941, IOL.
64 Namboodiripad, *The National Question in Kerala*, p. 155.
65 K. Damodaran, 'Memoir of an Indian Communist', *New Left Review*, 93, 1975, pp. 39–40. Damodaran was not released till 1945, which he attributes to (justified) British doubts about the degree to which he had accepted the changed CPI line.
66 Namboodiripad, *Kerala*, p. 172.
67 Dr Konnanath Balakrishna Menon (1897-1967) is a neglected figure. Of prosperous Nair background in Cannanore, he became an academic economist in the USA and was associated with Indian revolutionary circles there before returning to India in 1936. In 1938 he was secretary to the All-India States Peoples' Conference and spent two years with Gandhi. During the early 1940s he turned to violent political action including sabotage and was arrested in 1943 in connection with the Keezhariyur Bomb Conspiracy Case. On his release in 1946 Menon joined the Socialist Party and was a member of its National Executive. Subsequently a PSP MP, he submitted a documented statement on the conduct of the first communist government in Kerala in support of a motion in the Lok Sabha to discuss the situation in the state: K.B. Menon, *Sixteen Months of Communist Rule in Kerala: a General Review*. Calicut, Amala Printing Works, 1958.
68 Mathai Manjooran (1912-70) was one of comparatively few Syrian Christians to turn to socialism. A graduate of Madras University, he was for a period the Dewan of a small north Indian princely state. Associated with Dr K.B. Menon, he was sought in connection with the Keezhariyur Bomb Conspiracy Case but remained underground till 1946. He was a member of the CSP, the Cochin Praja Mandal, and in 1947 organized the Kerala Socialist Party, a non-communist marxist party. Manjooran was a prominent trade unionist and Labour Minister in the 1967-9 United Front Ministry.
69 Figures given in interviews with senior communist leaders.
70 Madras government's Reports, Political and Judicial, Jan. —Dec. 1942, Fortnightly Reports, Second half Sept. 1942, L/P & J/5/305, IOL. For a CPI account see E.M.S. Namboodiripad, *A Short History of the Peasant Movement in Kerala* (1943), ch. IV.
71 Madras States, Fortnightly Reports, First half July 1943, 13/43, Political Dept, 'P' Branch, R/1/29/2570, IOL.
72 Interviews, T.V. Thomas (CPI), Feb. 1971 and N. Sreekantan Nair (RSP), Nov. 1977. Sreekantan Nair was arrested in Nov. 1943 after urging a 'go slow' policy at Harrisons & Crosfield, Quilon, a company extensively involved in war work. Madras States, Fortnightly Reports, First half Nov. 1943, 21/43, IOL. K.C. George, *Immortal Punnapra-Vayalar* (1975), pp. 11-26, gives an account of socio-economic conditions in the area at the end of the war.
73 G. Adhikari, *Communist Party and India's Path to National Regeneration and Socialism* (1964); Overstreet & Windmiller, *Communism*; J.H.

Kautsky, *Moscow and the Communist Party of India* (1956); and Mohan Ram, *Indian Communism, Split within a Split.* (1969).

74 Namboodiripad, *Kerala*, p. 195.
75 P.C. Joshi, *Problems of the Mass Movement. Part 2 of P.C. Joshi's Letter to Foreign Comrades entitled 'Are we only Stupid?'* (N.C. Jain, Allahabad, n.d. [*ca.* 1950]). Joshi, who had been expelled from the party at this time, was bitterly critical of the style and quality of party organization.
76 Ram, *Indian Communism*, pp. 24–6.
77 The texts are given in DRS, *ICPD*, pp. 72–85 and 86–124.
78 Ibid., p. 81.
79 Interview, K.K. Warrier (CPI), Tvm, Feb. 1971; Damodaran, *New Left R.* 93, 1975 pp. 37–8. In July 1940 Murphy, the British agent, itemized literature seized from K.C. George; a party intellectual: 'Human Values Behind War', 'Women in Russia,' 'Students and Politics in China', 'The Lamp of Poverty (Malayalam), the Feb. 1940 issue of *Labour Monthly* (CPGB), Shaw's *Intelligent Woman's Guide to Socialism,* and the *Communist Manifesto.* Isaac's *Life History of Stalin* was also in circulation. Murphy to Glancy, July 1941, Political Dept, Political Branch, IOL.
80 Krishnan, p. 106, quotes from a memorandum which Krishna Pillai was preparing at his death on the unit's inner-party difficulties. Interviews T.V. Krishnan, Tvm, Aug. 1973; E.M.S. Namboodiripad, Tvm, Sept. 1974; K.C. George, Tvm, Aug. 1973; P. Raghavan, Tvm, Nov. 1977.
81 Krishnan, p. 104; see also p. 109.
82 Namboodiripad, *People's Age*, 16 Nov. 1947, quoted by B. Sen Gupta, 'S.A. Dange, E.M.S. Namboodiripad, and Jyoti Basu', in R. Swearingen, ed., *Leaders of the Communist World* (1971), p. 564.
83 Krishnan, p. 105.
84 Ibid., p. 104.
85 Ibid., p. 108.
86 Namboodiripad, *The National Question in Kerala* p. 172.
87 R. Ramakrishnan Nair, *Constitutional Experiments in Kerala,* pp. 19–22 and 84–101.
88 Report on the Indian Coir Industry (1 July 1946). C.S. 546/46, English Archives, Secretariat, Tvm. Sreekantan Nair claims conditions were worst in the Ambalapuzha and Shertallai taluks where the CPI had organized the workforce since the late 1930s because the party's collaborationist policies had not secured bonuses for the workers. Interview, Sreekantan Nair, Tvm, Nov. 1977.
89 The Punnapra-Vayalar Rising has not yet received the scholarly attention it merits. For opposing readings by political activists see K.C. George, *Immortal Punnapra-Vayalar* and N. Sreekantan Nair, *Vanchikkappette Venadu* (Travancore Betrayed). For a recent accessible account see K.K. Kusuman, 'Punnapra-Vayalar Rising 1946', *J. of Kerala Studies* II (1), 1976. The tentative account offered here rests on interviews with both authors and with T.V. Thomas, T.K. Divakaran, V.N. Parameswaran Pillai (General Officer Commanding, Travancore, in 1946 and later *sanyasi*), and other CPI and CPM leaders as well as on the limited

documents available in the India Office Library.

90 K.C. George denied this when interviewed. A former CPI leader, no longer active in the party, offered details of the alleged visit. Interview, Tvm, Sept. 1973.

91 V.N. Parameswaran Pillai inclined to the latter view. The disagreements between the military and police commanders were connected with palace politics as well as personality clashes.

92 Interview former CPI leader, Tvm, Sept. 1973.

93 Ibid.

94 Interview, Tvm, Nov. 1977.

95 K.C. George, pp. 128-30, reports a claim that Namboodiripad addressed a Namboodiri caste reform organization at Punnapra, the day after the bloodshed, with the comment 'A small doubt raised by a comrade has become a big doubt with me ... There were so many misunderstandings about the role of individuals in the ... struggle that I decided to include this here.' *Prima facie* such an appointment might be regarded as a useful legitimation of Namboodiripad's presence in the area. The two men belong to the rival communist parties.

96 George Woodcock, *Kerala* (1967), p. 248.

97 K.C. George, pp. 169-70.

98 V.P Menon, *The Story of the Integration of the Indian States* (1956) and Urmila Phadnis, *Towards the Integration of Indian States 1919-1947* (1968) are the standard authorities.

99 Wavell, p. 266.

100 *Travancore Information and Listener,* Apr. 1947, pp. 22-33. The proposals are summarised in R. Ramakrishnan Nair, *Constitutional Experiments in Kerala*, pp. 19-22.

101 *Travancore Information and Listener,* July 1947.

102 Private communication, W.S.S. MacKay, Doune, Scotland, based on Sir C.P.'s account of the incident at Ootacamund, 1947.

103 Interviews, V.N. Parameswaran Pillai, Tvm, Nov. 1977, and a Revolutionary Socialist leader, Tvm, Nov. 1977.

104 Interview, former CPI leader, Tvm, Sept. 1973.

105 R. Ramakrishnan Nair, *Constitutional Experiments in Kerala*, pp. 28-32; *Kerala District Gazetteers: Ernakulam*, p. 221. A communist interpretation is given in Namboodiripad, *The National Question in Kerala*, p. 160.

106 Mayer, p. 93.

107 In Malabar the communists fought Congress in five General Constituencies which together accounted for two-thirds of the District, and won 25 per cent of the vote, reaching 44 per cent in Chirakkal. Namboodiripad, *The National Question in Kerala*, p. 157, describes this as 'an index of the Communist leadership in this post-war revolutionary upsurge'.

108 This view was expressed by many present and retired communist leaders interviewed.

109 Fic, *Kerala*, pp. 31-43. Ministries are listed at p. 381 below.

110 The Kerala Socialist Party, the Kerala unit of the RSP, or the PSP.

111 Varghese Ittiavira, *Social Novels in Malayalam* (1968) and R.E. Asher, 'Three Novelists of Kerala', in T.W. Clark, ed., *The Novel in India* (1970) give details.
112 Namboodiripad, *The National Question in Kerala*, p. 176.

5

The Emergence of the Kerala Communists as an Electoral Force 1951–1960

From Parliamentary Tactic to Peaceful Transition

THE period after withdrawal from the Telengana struggle in 1951 to the adoption of the parliamentary road to socialism at the Amritsar Congress in 1958 is difficult to interpret. In Bhabani Sen Gupta's view the CPI's decision to contest the first Indian general election was tactical and more an inevitable reflex after the failure of the Ranadive and Telengana lines than the product of serious deliberation on how to use parliament to further the cause of revolution.[1] As stated categorically in the 'Tactical Line', written for the Indian Politbureau in 1951 and circulated to Central Committee members in 1953, this did not mean the party had abandoned revolution. The CPI's objectives 'cannot be realised by a peaceful, parliamentary way' but 'only through a revolution, through the overthrow of the present Indian State and its replacement by a People's Democratic State.'[2] Read as a whole, however, the document clearly relegates the revolution to a distant and more propitious future. Meanwhile the party would use elections for the 'most extensive popularisation of its programme, for mobilising and unifying the democratic forces, [and] for exposing the policies and methods of the present government.'[3] During the 1950s this tactical approach to the machinery of liberal democracy was elevated to the strategic level and finally in 1958 incorporated in the CPI's constitution and programme. Most commentators explain this change as essentially a function of Soviet pressure on a weak and divided Indian party: Moscow's growing appreciation of Nehru's importance in cold war politics was crucial in pushing the CPI in the direction of constitutionalism and parliamentarism. Though the CPSU failed to persuade the CPI to adopt its preferred line of whole-hearted support for Congress in a national democratic front, it did, in this view, succeed in securing the acceptance of qualified support for Congress— 'uniting with and fighting against it'—and the adoption of the concept of peaceful transition as the Indian road to socialism in keeping with the conclusions of the CPSU's 20th Congress of 1956.[4] Sen Gupta further argues that the CPI, or at least a majority of its leaders, 'succumbed to the values and forms of the bourgeois parliament,' thus straying from the Leninist approach to the use of representative institutions, and failing to make any creative contribution in the 1950s and early 1960s to the general "pool" of applied Communism'.[5] This process of embourgeoisement, he asserts, provoked bitter inner-party controversy and thereby doubly facilitated Soviet direction of CPI strategy.

It would be idle to underestimate the importance of Soviet influence on the CPI's emerging line or to dispute that *some* party leaders succumbed to the blandishments of bourgeois parliamentarism and the temptations of office.[6] None the less both arguments can be overstated. There were indigenous roots to the new line. It had already been spelt out with some sophistication by the end of 1953 in the light of the special conditions of the Indian situation. It was the subject of varied experimentation in provincial and local government elective bodies prior to the perceptible change in CPI conduct in the Lok Sabha in 1955-6.[7] In Kerala, at least, where the two district units of Malabar and Travancore-Cochin were dominated by a leadership whose past experience generated optimism about the potentialities of the electoral path, the weakness of the party centre enabled the provincial party to pursue its own path regardless of criticism. By late 1954 'the actual day-to-day functioning of the PB [Politbureau] virtually came to a stop' but the same secret CPI report noted that E.M.S. Namboodiripad 'Remained at the Centre most of the time' and 'Was burdened with many jobs.'[8] As the only member of the Politbureau who was constantly present at the centre, Namboodiripad was organizationally well placed to play a key role in the transformation of parliamentarism from tactic to strategy. His important theoretical writings in 1953 (see below, p. 109) strongly suggest that he used his influential position to direct the party towards a two-stage model of the path to socialism in India, and one inspired by reflection on the Chinese rather than Soviet experience. It was Namboodiripad, somewhat unexpectedly, who was chosen by the Politbureau to oversee as Chief Minister of Kerala the CPI's first pilot study of government as 'an instrument of struggle'. Whatever the failings of this and subsequent communist-led governments in Kerala, it could reasonably be contended that they have made a creative contribution to the 'pool' of applied communism which goes beyond the Leninist aim of shaking the faith of the masses in reformist politics by discrediting representative institutions from within, as the Bolsheviks sought to use their handful of seats in the Duma between 1907 and 1915. In particular the Kerala communist

movement has learned how to use representative institutions within
a federal framework; to operate them within a fragmented society; to
exploit the possibilities of government and opposition to provide
'immediate relief to the people' and strengthen the party; to combine
agitation with parliamentary and administrative work; and to
pioneer the forms of transitional collaboration with other parties
without substantially impairing the organizational autonomy of the
communist parties.

The special problems and possibilities of the Indian situation for a
revolutionary party were amply demonstrated in the 1951-2 election. Though Congress emerged as the dominant party it did not
command the majority allegiance of the electorate, gaining its
ascendancy through the combined effects of the simple majority
electoral system and the disunity of the opposition. The left-wing
parties secured little representation in the Lok Sabha but polled 20
per cent of the votes. In three provincial Assemblies—those of
Madras, PEPSU,[9] and Travancore-Cochin—Congress lacked a majority; and in Madras, Hyderabad, and Travancore-Cochin the CPI
or CPI-led fronts won large numbers of seats.[10] Congress manoeuvres averted any non-Congress provincial governments but the
CPI now urgently needed to clarify its opposition tactics and its
attitude to possible future involvement in non-Congress provincial
administrations.

Although sections of the party, including members of the Malabar
District Committee,[11] maintained that the only way to weaken
Congress's hold was by class-based struggles outside the legislatures, sometimes even to the extent of eschewing the Leninist exploitation of the parliamentary arena, the debate centred on two
linked questions: the precise use to which the party could put its
membership of a variety of elective bodies from the municipality
through to the Lok Sabha; and what its relationship should be
towards other non-Congress parties. The Draft Resolution to the
1953 Madurai Congress criticized generalized denunciations and
stereotyped speeches aimed at the converted. Instead, the party
should skilfully exploit the procedures of parliament to expose concrete grievances and so win more support. Too often the CPI had
failed to make use of existing legislation to ameliorate the conditions
of the masses and to secure concessions, forgetting that much progressive legislation had been enacted only as a result of past mass
struggles. It was important to initiate legislative proposals as a
rallying point for the mass movement.[12] Although the document is
not explicit on the point, by implication if past struggles had led to
reforms, then future struggles could lead to more.[13] The resolution
noted that, while at the provincial and national levels legislative and

executive functions were separated—because the latter were 'totally
outside the pressure of the people's representatives, no positive tasks
of execution' could be done by the legislators—this was not the case
in municipal and local bodies. 'By their limited spheres of action, the
proximity to the very people who elect them, the day-to-day constant contact with the executive machinery which is not like the
hardened bureaucracy of the State machine, the municipal and local
bodies can be used for the direct benefit of the people . . .However
poor and meagre be the powers, these small centres are centres of
power, power to do good to the life of the people. Our representatives must learn the art of running them properly.[14] It was a short
step to a similar assessment of the significance of the provincial
Assembly.

From its infancy as a fraction within the CSP to its coming of age
in 1939 the Kerala party had accepted electoral competition as one
form of popular radicalization. It boycotted only one election
(Cochin 1948) during the insurrectionist period and its experience
of the rewards of both electioneering and united front tactics had
been favourable. The 1951 programme, to which Namboodiripad
(appointed to the Politbureau in 1950), contributed, was welcomed.
A.K. Gopalan, Kerala's most popular mass leader and an influential
member of the reconstituted Central Committee, came out in favour
of legal campaigning on his release from jail, led the party team
seeking to negotiate the end of the Telengana rising, and announced
its unconditional withdrawal in October 1951.[15] A tacit bargain was
struck with the Madras authorities and the remaining detainees were
freed. Some Rs 30,000 were raised in Malabar, an office opened, and
Desabhimani, the party's newspaper, revived.[16] In Travancore-
Cochin the government took a more cautious line: the CPI remained
illegal until the eve of the election and further arrests were made
during 1951. The party did, however, succeed in contesting the
election, its candidates standing as independents sponsored by the
United Front of Leftists.

On the more divisive issue of the CPI's relationship to other
non-Congress parties, the Kerala leadership pursued an essentially
pragmatic path, in theory seeking a united front of *classes* but in
practice negotiating united fronts of *parties*. K. Damodaran, then
secretary of the Malabar District Committee, perceived in this the
abandonment of the concept of the dictatorship of the proletariat and
the substitution of 'party' for 'class' as the unit of revolutionary
action.[17] As stated in the Draft Political Resolution and the Review
Report presented to the Madurai Congress in 1953, the CPI's position on united fronts was that the current situation required united
front committees made up of the various parties and organizations

representing the interests of 'all classes and elements' opposed to imperialism and feudalism. These *ad hoc* committees 'from place to place and from issue to issue' would strengthen the mass movement. However, there was a 'very strong trend'—especially in South India—favouring the surrender of party autonomy where viable united fronts could be formed on the basis of agreed minimum programmes in provincial assemblies and mass organizations. This the party opposed, though it admitted that the Central Committee and the Politbureau had 'failed to fight this trend' and 'sometimes even [given] in to it.'[18]

In 1951-2 the three marxist parties in Kerala—the CPI, RSP, and KSP—had formed the United Front of Leftists (UFL) but fought the election on their own manifestos. When Congress won only 44 of the 108 seats, the CPI sought to persuade its partners to force the Governor's hand to invite a non-Congress leader to form a ministry by agreeing to a minimum programme and adding the Socialist Party (12 seats) and the Travancore-Tamil Nad Congress (TTNC, 8 seats) to the UFL. A.K. Gopalan, Lok Sabha CPI group leader, went further and urged a meeting of all non-Kerala Congress Pradesh MLAs to arrange a coalition.[19] The CPI was understood to be ready to drop nationalization, land to the tiller, and the abolition of landlordism without compensation from its programme and to work with parties in some respects 'more reactionary' than Congress to achieve its end. 'Within the constitutional framework', K.C. George told the press in a statement anticipating the CPI's position in 1957, 'we could do ten times more good things than Congress' has done.[20] Both the RSP and the KSP insisted that the front be confined to left parties, while the KSP declined to surrender its aim of a Kerala state independent of India. Negotiations foundered. In Malabar the party centre had given permission for an understanding with the KMPP (Kisan Mazdoor Praja Party) which extended to a minimum electoral programme, but this arrangement broke down with the amalgamation of the KMPP and Socialist Party into the Praja Socialist Party.[21] When in August 1953 the ministry composed of the Travancore-Cochin Congress and the Travancore-Tamil Nad Congress collapsed and fresh elections were called, the issue of a united front again arose. After a visit from a Central Committee delegation made up of Namboodiripad, Gopalan, and Dange in November, the State Committee approved an attempt to form a United Democratic Front which would embrace the Praja Socialist Party as well as the RSP and the KSP on the basis of a minimum programme.[22]

It was at this juncture that Namboodiripad published two articles—*Stalin and Mao on the National Liberation Movement* and *Why No Socialism Now in India*—which sought to swing the CPI from a limited conception of the 'united front of leftist forces' to the broader (and more flexible) notion of the 'national democratic front' which would incorporate the national bourgeoisie.[23] Not only in Travancore-Cochin but also in Madras and Hyderabad important elements in the local units had concluded that the CPI's interests might be thus advanced. By reflecting on Chinese experience in particular, Namboodiripad provided a reasoned and respectable theoretical underpinning, The Maoist theory of a two-stage revolution—national democracy and socialism—applied, he argued, equally well to India; and though the tactics of the Chinese could not be copied mechanically, their techniques were highly relevant to the CPI. For example, the party could learn how the Chinese had deprived the national bourgeoisie of its leadership of the revolution by uniting with it when its policies were congruent with the people's interests and fighting against them when they were not. The CPI should aim to control the key organs of the state apparatus and the army and nationalize the property of foreign imperialists and 'national traitors'. Socialism could not be attained immediately. Even in the Soviet Union Stalin had emphasized how slow and complicated the process was. The soundest course was to proceed cautiously with a programme on which all progressive and patriotic forces could agree, including the national bourgeoisie. When a People's Democratic Government should emerge in India one of its major tasks would be to solve the immediate problems of the country—food, jobs, industrialisation, and the like. In this, capitalism, shorn of its political power, must fulfil its historical mission. Namboodiripad's articles were not addressed to the more immediate prospect of power at the provincial level but *mutatis mutandis* they offered an insight into the objectives of the first communist ministry in Kerala and a sketch of the framework of Kerala-style coalition politics from 1967 onwards. Further, he anticipated the CPSU's switch to the peaceful transition line in 1956.

Electoral Support for the CPI 1952-54

From a marxist-leninist perspective theory and practice should interact. As the remainder of this chapter shows, the emergence of the CPI as a powerful electoral force in Travancore-Cochin and Malabar formed the backcloth to the commitment of the Kerala party to a parliamentary strategy; and on the evidence of the votes cast in the 1960 election it was a strategy that was vindicated.

Travancore-Cochin

In February 1948 Travancore was the first Indian state to hold an election on the basis of universal suffrage. The CPI contested only 17 of the 120 seats as part of a united front with the KSP. Congress swept the board with 111 seats, but the front's 10 per cent of the votes was no mean achievement, given pro-Congress euphoria and anti-communist repression. The CPI and KSP both boycotted the Cochin election held in September but in June 1949 Gopalakrishna Menon was elected as a CPI member at a by-election in working-class Cranganore. In 1951-2 in the first election to the Assembly of the integrated Travancore-Cochin State the CPI, its candidates nominally standing as independents, won 18 per cent of the poll, and its partners in the United Front of Leftists a further 5 per cent. The CPI, fighting in 53 of the 122 constituencies, won 29 seats, and its Revolutionary Socialist and Kerala Socialist allies 7 of their 21 contests. Congress—including the Tamil Nad (Madras) Congress parties contesting the Tamil taluks of the south—fought all constituencies and won 52 seats with 43 per cent of the poll.[24]

Maps 9 and 10 show (exclusive of the Tamil taluks) the distribution of seats by party and of the communist vote.[25] Together they indicate the degree to which communist and UFL support was concentrated in the coastal lowlands and Congress support in the interior. Along the coast there were only two notable breaks in the chain of UFL support—the Congress-held urban area around Ernakulam and the Socialist-held Trivandrum. Outside the lowlands the CPI and its allies won victories in only three places: Shencottah, a strongly scheduled caste constituency in the southern foothills of the Western Ghats, and the industrial constituencies of the north, Alwaye and Perumbavoor.

The performance of the CPI and the pattern of its support may be explained by reference to several factors. Between 1948 and 1951-2 there were changes in the conditions under which the elections were held. Although the CPI had contested Travancore in 1948, it was compelled to campaign clandestinely. In 1951-2 it was tolerated though nominally illegal. Further, in 1948 the newly enfranchised poor had cast their votes as their landlords wished. In *Two Measures of Rice* (1948) Thakazhi describes the atmosphere of early election-eering: 'Kunjappi came out with his own story: "It was like a festival at my Thambran's [landlord's] house—even for a month before the voting. Meat and drinks were in plenty" . . . Samayal who was brood-ing all the time on the imminent first elections in which all were entitled to vote piped up: "Then we will also get money, won't we? . . . Then it will be wonderful!"[26] The impact of social deference and purse power declined over the next three-and-a-half years, ar-guably more than anywhere else in India and for a variety of reasons: intensified political competition; changing authority relationships

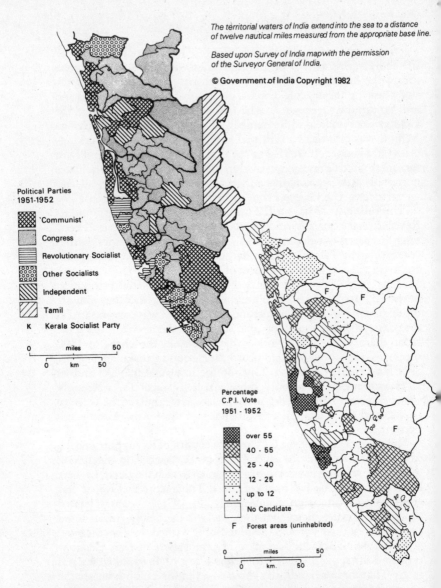

The territorial waters of India extend into the sea to a distance of twelve nautical miles measured from the appropriate base line.

Based upon Survey of India map with the permission of the Surveyor General of India.

© Government of India Copyright 1982

Political Parties 1951-1952

- 'Communist'
- Congress
- Revolutionary Socialist
- Other Socialists
- Independent
- Tamil
- K Kerala Socialist Party

```
0        miles        50
|____|____|____|
0        km           50
```

Percentage C.P.I. Vote 1951 - 1952

- over 55
- 40 - 55
- 25 - 40
- 12 - 25
- up to 12
- No Candidate
- F Forest areas (uninhabited)

```
0        miles        50
|____|____|____|
0        km.          50
```

Note: Vertical line indicates one seat in two-member constituency.

Sources: Data from Election Commission, India, *Report on the First General Elections in India 1951-2;* list of communists standing as Independents supplied by R. Ramakrishnan Nair, Dept of Politics, U. of Kerala.

Map 9 Travancore–Cochin 1951-2: Assembly Election, Seats won by Parties

Map 10 Travancore–Cochin 1951-2: Assembly Election, CPI % Vote

in the rural areas; and the communist and socialist mobilization of the poorer sections in the context of the cultural renaissance of the late 1940s and early 1950s (see above, pp. 94–5). The 1948 elections in Travancore and Cochin had been celebratory rather than competitive. In 1952 seven parties besides Congress fielded candidates, with Pattom Thanu Pillai's Socialist Party contesting 59 of the 96 seats. Including 132 (non-CPI) Independents, there were 379 candidates in all. Turnout was a remarkable 71 per cent, far in excess of that in any other state. The change in authority relationships is more elusive but no less real. As Mencher has shown, Kerala was unusual in the degree to which authority relations had in the past been individualized patron–client relationships rather than ranked caste groupings, a description which, however, applies more particularly to Hindus.[27] Joint family partition, the cash nexus, the growth in population, declining *per capita* income, and the growing inability of patrons to sustain an extensive clientage combined with the spatially diffused settlement pattern and the erosion of caste discrimination to free many electors from the necessity to follow their high-caste patron's political wishes. The cultural renaissance, growing unionization, and left-wing social, economic, and political mobilization of the lower castes accelerated the process of emancipation to make the universal franchise more of a reality in Kerala than elsewhere.[28]

A comparison of Map 11 (the distribution of caste and community in Travancore in 1941, excluding the Tamil-speaking taluks), with Maps 9 and 10 shows that there is a marked spatial association between caste and party support.[29] (Cochin figures are not available in the form required.) The CPI and the UFL did best in those areas where the low-caste Ezhavas were proportionately largest. The same was also true in 1954. Congress did well in Syrian Christian- and Christian-convert areas in the extreme south, and the Socialist Party succeeded in the Nair-dominant districts around Trivandrum. This should not be interpreted to mean that CPI support was based on caste as such but rather that most of the disadvantaged class were found in low-caste communities. The CPI did not campaign on caste, did not control the relevant caste associations, and was led primarily by high-caste Hindus. It may be appropriate at this point to note that the present writer shares Gough's view of the relative importance of class and caste in relation to politics in Kerala. Taking issue with those scholars who have interpreted Kerala politics largely, and sometimes exclusively, in terms of caste and community, Gough grants that caste has played a 'remarkable role' while she avers that it had not been of overwhelming significance for political affiliation even in the fifties and early sixties. The 'identification of caste with party' was 'always...far from complete.' It has been

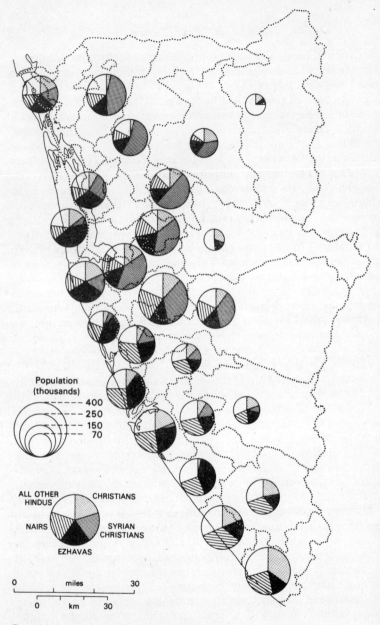

Population
(thousands)
------ 400
------ 250
------ 150
------ 70

ALL OTHER   CHRISTIANS
HINDUS

NAIRS   SYRIAN
                         CHRISTIANS

        EZHAVAS

0   miles   30

0   km   30

The territorial waters of India extend into the sea to a distance
of twelve nautical miles measured from the appropriate base line.

Based upon Survey of India map with the permission   © Government of India Copyright 1982
of the Surveyor General of India.

Source: Data from *Census of India 1941*, vol. XXV, *Travancore*, pt I, Table IX.

Map 11 Travancore 1941: Distribution of Caste and Community by
         Taluk

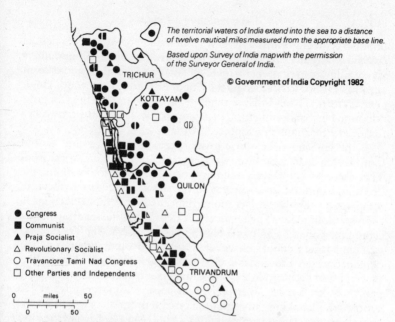

- ● Congress
- ■ Communist
- ▲ Praja Socialist
- △ Revolutionary Socialist
- ○ Travancore Tamil Nad Congress
- □ Other Parties and Independents

Note: Broken symbols indicate two-member constituencies.

Source: Redrawn from Election Commission, India, *Report on the Second General Elections to the PEPSU and Travancore-Cochin Legislative Assemblies 1954*, map between pp. 24 and 25.

Map 12 Travancore-Cochin 1954: Assembly Election, Seats won by Parties

weakening for a variety of reasons which include socio-economic differentiation within castes; and it is noteworthy that caste sentiment has played a greater role among the propertied and also the salaried than among wage workers, poorer tenants, the landless, and the unemployed. It is of course true that there is a continuing divergence between the official philosophy of the major parties, including the CPM and CPI, and their day-to-day conduct. Nevertheless the 'communal view' of Kerala politics seriously underestimates the importance of the movement's ideological and practical commitment to political mobilization along class lines.[30]

The result of the 1954 mid-term contest vindicated the broad front strategy as an electoral manouevre at the same time as it cast it in doubt as a political line. Congress, though taking 47 per cent of the poll on a 74 per cent turnout, won only 45 of the enlarged 118-member Assembly seats. The CPI, which had been over-generous in surrendering constituencies to its allies, particularly the PSP, won 23 seats, proportionately a smaller share than in the dissolved Assembly, while the PSP won 19 and the RSP 9. Twelve TTNC members and 9 independents made up the total. Congress was unable to form a ministry either alone or in coalition. Presidential rule was virtually precluded on grounds of its universal unpopularity, while an invitation to the CPI to try to build a united front administration was vetoed by the Congress High Command.[31] However, Pattom Thanu Pillai of the PSP agreed to resolve the Congress dilemma by abandoning his CPI and RSP allies in order to construct a minority PSP ministry supported by the votes of Congress.

In the ensuing post mortem the entire Politbureau and Central Committee apart from the two Central Committee members from Travancore-Cochin criticized the State Committee for including the PSP in the united front,[32] a reaction which was an important factor in the party's subsequent decision to fight the first Andhra elections in 1955 without allies. The result was a débâcle: while securing 31 per cent of the poll, the CPI won only 15 seats out of 195. The Travancore-Cochin leaders could, however, argue two other points in their defence besides the disaster in Andhra. The electoral alliance between Hindu high and low castes had further isolated Congress as the party of the Syrian Christian bourgeoisie. Congress lost in the south, while making only modest compensatory advances in Christian-dominated areas in erstwhile Cochin (Map 12). Second the local unit could claim that not only were the PSP's unprincipled tactics widely condemned but also that its eleven months in office before Congress withdrew its support severely damaged the party's standing, notably by its handling of labour disputes and the Tamil separatist agitation which led to police firing on demonstrators.[33]

Malabar

The CPI's tactics in Malabar were complicated by the existence of two important non-Congress parties in the District, the Muslim League and the KMPP. In theory any arrangement with the League was precluded by its categorization as a communal party, although Namboodiripad did not exclude the possibility in a book published shortly after the election.[34] The KMPP, a *sarvodaya* and socialist breakaway of 1951, led nationally by Acharaya Kripalani, and locally by two prominent former Congressmen, K. Kelappan Nair and K.A. Damodara Menon, could be regarded as a progressive force. The CPI had ruled out an alliance at the All-India level but gave permission for an *ad hoc* electoral arrangement in Malabar. Kelappan Nair had been associated with the CSP for a time in the mid-1930s and had been close to A.K. Gopalan, who had assumed responsibility for rebuilding the party in Malabar. Since the CPI and the KMPP drew their support from the north and south respectively, the agreement was of mutual benefit. On a smaller share of the vote the two parties won twice as many seats as Congress. Out of 32 seats Con-

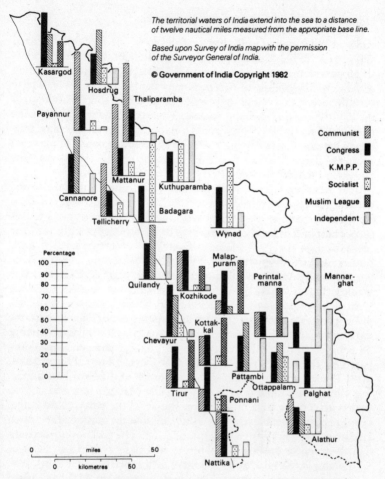

The territorial waters of India extend into the sea to a distance of twelve nautical miles measured from the appropriate base line.

Based upon Survey of India map with the permission of the Surveyor General of India.

© Government of India Copyright 1982

Communist
Congress
K.M.P.P.
Socialist
Muslim League
Independent

Percentage
100
90
80
70
60
50
40
30
20
10
0

Kasargod
Hosdrug
Thaliparamba
Payannur
Mattanur
Cannanore
Kuthuparamba
Tellicherry
Badagara
Wynad
Quilandy
Kozhikode
Malappuram
Perintalmanna
Mannarghat
Chevayur
Kottakkal
Tirur
Pattambi
Ottappalam
Palghat
Ponnani
Alathur
Nattika

miles 0 — 50
kilometres 0 — 50

Source: Data from Election Commission, India, *Report on the First General Elections in India 1951-2.*

Map 13 Malabar District, Madras State 1951-2: Assembly Election, Percentage Vote

gress won 7 (32 per cent of the poll), the CPI 6 (16 per cent), and the KMPP 7 (13 per cent). In addition the League won 5, the Socialist Party 4, and Independents 3 seats. Map 13 shows the effectiveness of the CPI-KMPP division of labour in minimizing Congress success.

In the light of the unknown extent of cross-voting, one can make only tentative statements about the distribution of support but it appears that the CPI was exceptionally strong in the north, but had not yet won a substantial following in Palghat. The emergence of the party in Palghat may indeed be a partial consequence of the electoral alliance of 1951-2. By co-operating with the CPI, the KMPP leadership conferred a certain measure of legitimacy on its partner among sections of the middle to rich peasantry (and their labourers) whose Gandhian consciousness they articulated. When shortly afterwards the KMPP merged with the Socialist Party to form the Praja Socialist Party, and Kelappan Nair retired from politics, the CPI became residuary legatee. Certainly the PSP secured far fewer votes (11 per cent) at the Malabar District Board elections of October 1954 than the combined KMPP-Socialist Party vote in 1951-2 (28 per cent).

The Malabar Communist District Committee's attitude to the contest for control of the 48-member District Board was coloured by three factors: its past history of involvement in elections to this important unit of local government; the encouragement given by the resolution of the 1953 Madurai Congress to participation in such bodies; and the disenchantment with the PSP arising from its manoeuvres in Travancore-Cochin earlier in the year. As Congress was weaker than in 1951-2 the CPI decided to fight the election in alliance with 12 progressive independents only, fielding its own candidates in the remaining 36 seats. Under the supervision of Damodaran, the party set up election committees in virtually every village, winning 38 per cent of the poll (inclusive of progressive independents) compared to the 35 per cent won by Congress.[35] The CPI and allies, with 24 seats to Congress's 15, took control of the Board, nominating Bhaskara Pannikar as President. The Malabar unit had shown that with a mass base nursed over the years the party could defeat Congress in a sizeable territorial unit and that the party could in such circumstances dispense with a united front. The CPI now undertook a pilot study for the provincial responsibilities it was to assume three years later in Kerala. Subsequently, as the party noted in its 1957 election manifesto, some of its representatives in Malabar earned awards from Nehru for their model administration.[36]

States Reorganization and the CPI

The continued separation of the administration of Malabar, Travancore, and Cochin even after the formation of the Part B State of Travancore-Cochin was one of many anomalies in political organization perpetuated after Independence. Congress had long been committed to a reconstruction of provincial boundaries that would take account of the country's linguistic and socio-cultural heterogeneity; and a Malayali-speaking Kerala was a part of this grand design (see above, p. 12). In 1946-8, however, the Congress High Command was understandably more concerned with the maintenance of unity than the fulfilment of past promises that could undermine it. The Dar Commission and the three-man Congress committee composed of Nehru, Patel, and Sitaramayya reported against linguistic reorganization in general, but by 1952 the agitation for a separate Telegu province of Andhra had become irresistible. After the new Andhra State was conceded Nehru sought to placate other regional interests with the establishment of the States Reorganisation Commission in 1953. It was on the basis of its recommendations that Kerala State came into existence in November 1956.

The CPI, which during the People's War period had swum against the tides of Indian national fervour, had been consistently sensitive to regional and linguistic movements, notably in Kerala and Andhra. After the first Indian general election in 1951 A.K. Gopalan, leader of the CPI in the Lok Sabha and himself a Malayali, asserted that 'India's most important problem, the Communists' No. 1 goal' was the formation of linguistic provinces.[37] While dissociating the CPI from the 'communal and anti-North' slogans of the Dravida Kazhagam and Dravida Munnetra Kazhagam (DMK) in Madras, the Madurai Congress backed 'wider provincial autonomy' as well as the creation of linguistic states on the Andhra model.[38] Indeed in a 1953 commentary on the CPI's approach to the nationalities question, Namboodiripad left the party's options open: 'The right of secession should not be confused with expediency of the formation of separate states.' It is for 'the working class and its allies in every nation to decide ...' In India 'the principle of self-determination means and naturally includes the right of separation' but 'it is inexpedient ... to exercise the right.'[39] While Harrison argues that it might become expedient in 'a period of political disarray in which every party in every region' was on its own, the communist movement can justifiably claim that it has not reneged even in the troubled 1970s on its primary attachment to the consolidation of the unity of India within a framework of federal democratic centralism.[40]

Three basic proposals had been put to the States Reorganization Commission (SRC, 1953-6) on Kerala: its incorporation into a large multi-lingual southern state; *Akhanda Kerala*, a greater Kerala which would include at least the existing Tamil-speaking taluks of Travancore-Cochin; and *Aikya Kerala*, basically the union of Malayalam speaking areas of Travancore-Cochin with Malabar and Kasergod taluk of South Canara.[41] The Travancore-Cochin Congress and PSP favoured *Akhanda Kerala*. Historically the Tamil taluks were part of Travancore, had been colonized by Tamil labour, and provided food (rice and salt) and revenue (plantations). Congress was also anxious to minimize the effects of Malabar communism on the balance of power in a new state. Three times the Tamil question had contributed to the fall of Travancore-Cochin ministries—1953, 1954, and finally in March 1956 when Panampilly Govinda Menon's Congress administration was ousted by the defection of six Congress MLAs, ostensibly in protest at the ministry's acquiescence in the SRC proposal for *Aikya Kerala*.[42] Hectic political activity followed. The CPI, desperate to avert President's Rule at such a juncture, approached Pattom and the PSP as well as the RSP and KSP in the hope of forming a coalition government. The communists were prepared, if need be, to support a PSP ministry from without, as Congress had done in 1953.[43] Although the allies secured the support of two rebel Congressmen to give them 59 supporters in the 116-member Assembly, the plans were thwarted when Narayanan Potti, an RSP MLA, announced he would not support a government led by Pattom and mysteriously disappeared, allegedly at the instigation of Congress.[44] The Indian President then dissolved the legislature and appointed P.S. Rao as Adviser to the Rajpramukh to administer the state since no new cabinet could be formed. Travancore-Cochin had in its last few months of existence come close to a 'national democratic government'.

The Palghat Line

After the 1953 Madurai Congress, differences within the CPI became increasingly serious, leading to the party crisis of 1954-5. Essentially these turned on the party's attitude to Congress.[45] As Congress's foreign and domestic policies moved rapidly in socialist directions, and the CPSU pressed the CPI to reassess its relationship to what—for the Soviet Union—was now a friendly régime in a strategically significant country, the CPI leadership divided into a left, right, and centre. The Left remained adamantly hostile to Congress on the grounds of its class character as manifested in its domestic policies; the Right took the Soviet part in advocating collaboration with the left wing of Congress in a 'general united front', even countenancing an 'alternative government of national unity'; while the Centrists, including Namboodiripad, argued that Congress's domestic policies exhibited progressive *and* reactionary features, and that these reflected the dialectical character of the bourgeoisie, now the leading force in the state as both a modernizing and an exploitative agent in history. It followed that the CPI should 'unite with and fight against' Congress. In practice, of course, Centrism was at once a line and an expedient compromise. As such it was adopted at the CPI's next Congress at Palghat (Malabar) in 1956. The Report of the Central Committee to the Congress, in the drafting of which Namboodiripad is said to have played a key role, was

subtle and ambiguous, urgent but ultimately pragmatic: it rejected a
united front with Congress but stressed that the continuance of the
democratic front tactic of *ad hoc* alliances with the left did not imply
anti-Congressism. If Nehru's domestic policies were criticized, the
report recognized elements in Congress as well as in the Socialist
Party and the PSP which were democratic, progressive, and honest.[46]
None the less about one-third of the delegates to the Congress voted
for the Rightist 'collaboration' line.[47]

Overshadowing the Congress was Khrushchev's denigration of
Stalin and endorsement of peaceful transition to socialism at the 20th
Congress of the CPSU. In a closed session Ajoy Ghosh mediated the
new Soviet line to the Congress. Starting from Marx's visualization
of peaceful transition in countries like Britain in his lecture at The
Hague in 1871, Ghosh argued that the same was possible in India
provided the working class remained the vanguard, the police and
the bureaucracy were curbed, and the state apparatus, including the
army, was democratized. The 'most reactionary elements' should be
removed and the battle waged for the 'extension of the rights and
powers of the people's elected organs—Panchayats, District Boards,
etc.'[48] At a Congress held in Kerala it is reasonable to suppose that
'etcetera' covered provincial assemblies.

Two months later, at the end of June 1956, the Kerala CPI held a
Provincial Conference at Trichur to prepare its own application of
the Palghat line to the Kerala situation. The resulting resolution
(Communist Proposal for Building a Democratic and Prosperous
Kerala) is significant for two reasons: its continuation of the united
front strategy, including a special appeal to the PSP to reconsider its
recent national decision to decline all alliances or adjustments with
communists as well as Congress and communal parties;[49] second,
the adoption of a minimum programme aimed at political stability,
social justice and economic reconstruction as the platform of such a
united front.[50] Further meetings in Ernakulam in October and Alwaye in January 1957 underlined the party's commitment to this
two-pronged strategy. In the event negotiations with both the PSP
and RSP failed[51] and the party ended by fighting 100 of the 125
constituencies and supporting 19 independents.

The party's election manifesto, launched in January 1957 was
certainly a new-style communist manifesto. It bore a distinct resemblance to the basic outline of the central government's Second
Five Year Plan—more Congress-socialist than communist. Alone
among the contestants, the CPI offered a detailed plan for the regeneration of Kerala, albeit one that depended on a major increase in
plan expenditure in the state. Among the key points were: a rise of
130 per cent in Kerala's plan allocation; the establishment of new

industries; the development of co-operatives in the small-scale industrial sector; wage increases and guaranteed bonuses; a house-building programme; increased domestic food production; model administration and a move towards decentralization; an impartial police policy; the reform of education; the nationalization of foreign plantations; and, above all, a comprehensive Agrarian Relations Bill prefaced by an Anti-Eviction Bill.[52] It was a logical extension of the Kerala unit's past involvement in specific popular grievances, an expression of the non-sectarian approach recommended at Madurai and Palghat, and an echo of the new Soviet line.

Assembly Elections 1957 and 1960

The CPI's victory in 1957 and its 'defeat' in 1960 have been extensively analysed elsewhere and the account here concentrates on an assessment of the widely accepted view that communal voting patterns were a key factor in the results.[53] Tables 5.1 and 5.3 show the overall results in 1957 and 1960; Table 5.2 the District figures for 1957; and Table 5.4 the CPI performance in 1957 and 1960 for those constituencies in each District contested on both occasions. The accompanying maps plot the communist vote in 1957 by constituency (Map 14); turnout in 1957 by constituency together with the increase in turnout in 1960 by constituency (Map 15); the communist vote in 1960 by constituency (Map 16); and CPI gains and losses in 1960 (Map 17).

Table 5.1 Kerala 1957: Assembly Election

Party	Seats contested*	Seats won	Votes polled†	% Vote
Congress	124	43	2,209,251	37.84
CPI	100	60	2,059,547	35.28
CPI-supported independents	19	5	318,465	5.45
PSP	62	9	628,261	10.76
RSP	28	0	188,553	3.22
Muslim League	19	8	275,623	4.72
Independents	37	1	158,077	2.70

* Of the 126 seats, 102 were in single-member constituencies and 12 in two-member constituencies.

† Total number, 5,837,777.

Source: Election Commission, India, *Report on the General Election to the Kerala Legislative Assembly 1960*, with amendments by present author.

The 1957 Election

In 1957 the CPI contested 100 of the 126 seats in the election, winning 60, which, together with 5 victories by party-supported independents, gave it an overall majority. Congress, contesting all but one seat, managed only 43. In terms of votes cast the CPI polled 35 per cent, or if party-backed independents are counted 41 per cent of the poll. Congress won 38 per cent of the votes. Only two other parties won any seats, the PSP with just 9 from 62 contests and 11 per cent of the poll, and the Muslim League with 8 seats and 5 per cent of the votes. Of the 389 candidates 107 lost their deposits and only 53 won their constituencies with an overall majority of the votes cast; of these 26 were CPI and 20 Congress. Turnout at 66 per cent was good by All-India standards; and it was higher in Travancore-Cochin (71 per cent) than in Malabar (58 per cent). The regional strength of the CPI is shown in Table 5.2. The CPI won two-thirds of the seats in all Districts except in Kottayam and Ernakulam (where there was a sizeable Christian presence) and Kozhikode (where there was an important Muslim minority).[54] Except for Kozhikode (29 per cent) the percentage vote by District varied

Table 5.2 Kerala 1957: Assembly Election Results by District*

District	No. of seats	Seats won by Cong.	Seats won by Comm.	Turn-Out %	Cong.	Comm.	Others	% Hindu 1961
Trivandrum	12	1	8	69	18.8	42.8	38.4	72
Quilon	14	4	10	77	33.9	41.2	24.9	64
Alleppey	14	4	9	74	38.2	43.4	18.4	65
Kottayam	13	9	3	73	47.5	29.2	23.3	49
Ernakulam	14	10	4	71	50.5	38.0	11.5	46
Trichur	12	3	6	72	44.0	32.1	23.9	63
Palghat	15	3	10	54	36.4	40.8	22.8	70
Kozhikode	18	6	3	62	25.9	18.1	56.0	53
Cannanore	14	3	7	63	34.1	36.4	29.5	70
Total	126	43	60	66	37.8	35.3	26.9	61

* These figures differ from those supplied by Craig Baxter, comp., *District Voting Trends in India* for Trivandrum, Kozhikode, and Cannanore Districts and are based on revised figures collected by the Department of Politics, University of Kerala.

Sources: Calculations from figures in Election Commission, India, *Report on the General Election to the Kerala Legislative Assembly 1960.* Last column, *Census of India 1961*, Vol. VII, pt IX, p. 261.

modestly around the state average from 38 per cent in Kottayam and Trichur to 49 per cent in Alleppey and 48 per cent in Cannanore. Map 14 of the CPI vote by constituency reveals a pattern concealed by the District averages. The CPI was strongest (shown by hatching) in mid-Cannanore, Palghat, the coastal belt of Travancore-Cochin, and in a contiguous belt of Quilon (except the coast) and north Travancore. A comparison with the earlier maps of communist performance in Travancore-Cochin 1951-2 (Maps 9 and 10) and 1954 (Map 12) and Malabar 1951-2 (Map 13) shows two interesting differences. In the north, Palghat had become a communist stronghold and in the south the party gained ground in Trivandrum. The CPI's performance in the Lok Sabha elections was also remarkable. Congress, which fought all but one of the 18 seats, won 6 seats with 35 per cent of the poll; the CPI, contesting 15, won 9 with 37 per cent of the poll—or, if a party-supported independent is included, 10 seats with 42 per cent of the poll.

The considerable literature seeking to explain the communist victory in 1957 is comprehensively reviewed by Ramakrishanan Nair.[55] Among the factors most often cited are: the sorry state of the provincial Congress; its widespread unpopularity because of its inability to deliver either stable or positive government; the failure of the PSP to offer an alternative; the contrast with the well-organized CPI, supported by large numbers of volunteers, and standing on a bold manifesto; the addition of communist Malabar and the transfer of the Tamil taluks of Travancore to Madras; the alignment of low- and high-caste Hindu behind the CPI; the impact of the Palghat line on the middle classes of town and countryside; and the growing cordiality between India and the Soviet Union symbolized in the exchange of official visits and the adoption by Congress in December 1954 of the Socialist Pattern of Society as its aim. In Kerala non-communists increasingly came to believe that if socialism was to be the goal prescribed by Nehru, then the CPI was more competent for the task in Kerala than the KPCC.[56]

Although the CPI was surprised by the scale of its success, most 'vote bankers' as well as the central government's Intelligence Bureau regarded a Congress defeat as a foregone conclusion.[57] Communal leaders reacted by encouraging their followers to support candidates belonging to their own community, largely irrespective of party labels. Obligingly the CPI acquiesced in this political agnosticism by its backing for progressive Independents of the dominant caste in certain constituencies and its efforts to match its own candidates to the communal as well as class bent of constituencies.[58] This however does not mean as Fic contends that 'communities vote(d) on communal lines', that politics in Kerala in 1957 was 'strictly

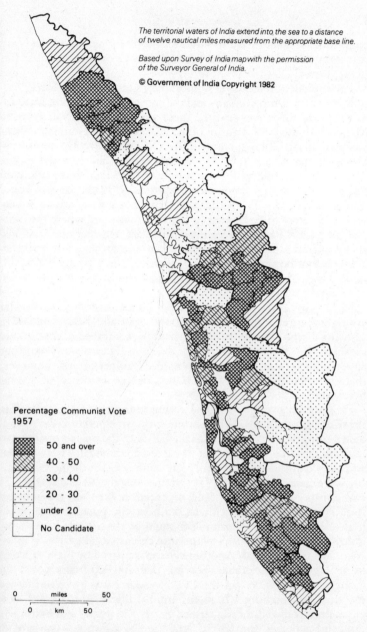

The territorial waters of India extend into the sea to a distance
of twelve nautical miles measured from the appropriate base line.

Based upon Survey of India map with the permission
of the Surveyor General of India.

© Government of India Copyright 1982

Percentage Communist Vote
1957

50 and over
40 - 50
30 - 40
20 - 30
under 20
No Candidate

0   miles   50
0   km   50

Source: Data from Election Commission, India, *Report on the General Election to the
            Kerala Legislative Assembly 1960*.

Map 14 Kerala 1957: Assembly Election, Percentage Communist Vote

communal affair' or that 'the shift in the voting pattern of the Nair
community in favour of the Communists . . . was responsible for
[their] victory.[59]

The evidence presented in support of this case takes two forms: the
influence of prominent Nairs and the comparison of voting patterns
in 1954 and 1957. At this time there were three key Nair leaders:
Mannoth of the NSS; Pattom of the PSP; and M.N Govindan Nair,
the provincial CPI secretary. The NSS was currently anti-Congress—it had some hold on the rebels who had brought down
Panampilly's ministry and was hostile to Christian 'domination' of
the party. Mannoth gave encouragement to Nairs to vote communist where suitable candidates appeared but it was advice which
was only likely to be heeded in central Travancore where the NSS
had its base.[60] Pattom, recently PSP Chief Minister and strongly
anti-communist, exercised influence in and around Trivandrum.
While his authoritarian tendencies alienated some young Nairs, the
bulk of the older Nairs accepted his *karanavar* qualities as in the order
of things.[61]

M.N. Govindan Nair, an ex-NSS leader, had appealed to the
younger section of the community, and especially the student body,
as a man who, it was believed, happily combined a charismatic
idealism with the thinking of Nair thoughts; but his was a minority
appeal. Such assessments of individual influence are, however,
matters of judgement. What is not, is the evidence of voting
behaviour.

Fic's argument for communal voting rests on the assumption that
the distribution of MLAs by community corresponds to the overall
distribution of party vote. Thus the CPI was 'the most communal in
outlook' because 90 per cent of its successful candidates were Hindu;
and as two-thirds of successful Nair candidates for the new Assembly were standing for the CPI he assumes that the Nairs gave the CPI
two-thirds of their vote.[62] Such a procedure does not recommend
itself. Further, it is difficult to see how the putative support of
high-caste Nairs for communism could be considered 'communal'
unless one credits the NSS with more extensive geographical influence than is warranted. Another version is offered by Jitendra Singh
in an 'approximate' table showing that 200,000 Nairs voted for
Congress and 200,000 for the CPI. No source was given or implied
for this information.[63] It seems improbable that it would have
emanated from CPI headquarters. As for Congress, it is extremely
doubtful whether the KPCC had the organizational capacity to
produce adequate figures. Further Singh's estimate leaves 500,000
Nairs out of account. Projections from earlier census data suggest
there were some 900,000 adult Nairs entitled to vote, who therefore

must have either abstained or mainly voted for the only other substantial party, the PSP. The PSP, though it drew disproportionate
support from the Nair community, was not simply a communal
party. It seems unlikely that up to five out of six PSP voters were
Nairs—the PSP vote was 600,000; or that, considering the total
Congress vote of 2.2 million, more than twice as many Nairs voted
for the PSP as Congress. The PSP was not expected to win many
seats, and in a state where an MLA oils a thousand wheels would so
many Nairs have backed a party with a very slender chance of
winning in so many constituencies?

For a variety of reasons some Nairs voted for a communist, a
party-sponsored independent, or abstained. The relative and in
some instances absolute poverty of a growing proportion of the Nair
community was a factor of importance in predisposing some Nairs
to vote communist. In a few instances (Changanacherry, Kottarakkara, Perumbavoor, and Tiruvalla) this cost Congress the seat and in
others (Nemom, Neyyatinkara, and Ullur) the PSP was hit but the
case for a massive and crucial switch of high-caste Hindu votes in
1957 is not proven.[64] The CPI performed best (Map 14) in Hindu-
dominant districts (Map 4). However, the fact that the party won 35
per cent of the vote in a state which (inclusive of Christian and
Muslim constituencies not fought by the CPI) was 61 per cent
Hindu, suggests that the communists had established a beach-head
among the Nairs rather than conquered them; this argument assumes
that the CPI would make most rapid headway among the underprivileged who were concentrated in the lower castes. Comparisons
with 1954 are difficult because of the different electoral alignments as
well as boundary changes. It may be significant that, overall, the
smaller the party the greater the loss in votes between 1954 and 1957:
Congress lost 18 per cent, the PSP 29 per cent, and the RSP 43 per
cent. Congress's shortfall in the Travancore-Cochin area also owes
something to the retirement of many sitting Congress MLAs. Personal influence still counted for much. Of 45 Congress MLAs from
non-Tamil Travancore-Cochin in the previous Assembly, only 18
stood in 1957, itself a comment on Congress morale. The CPI had
richly deserved a victory forged by assiduous attention to the possibilities of the particular situation in Kerala over the years but its
task was made easy by Congress's lack of stomach for the contest.

The 1960 mid-term election

By 1960 the major non-communist parties, Congress, the PSP and
the Muslim League, backed by the churches, NSS and SNDP, had
come to an anti-communist electoral understanding. In the circumstances the most striking feature of the election was not that the com-

munists lost half their 60 seats—even in 1957 they had won only 26 seats with more than 50 per cent of the votes cast—but that they improved their share of the poll. (Table 5.3): 41 per cent (including 5.45 per cent from CPI independents) in 1957 and 44 per cent (including 4.7 per cent from CPI-supported independents) in 1960. Fic in fact concludes that the party in Kerala 'commanded an ever-increasing mass base.'[65]

Comparison of the two elections is complicated by four factors. First, the Election Commission replaced the separate, party-labelled ballot boxes as previously used, with a common ballot box. It seems probable that this change would have encouraged humbler electors to cast their votes more independently of social pressures. Second, the register of electors grew by 8 per cent; third, turnout increased by 18 per cent as Malabar turnout levels rose to those of the south; and fourth, the CPI, though contesting eight more seats overall in 1960, dropped some fought in 1957 with the result that the communist vote is strictly comparable in only 87 single-member constituencies. Table 5.4 summarizing the party's performance in the constituencies shows little net change. The improvement in 31 constituencies in Malabar was virtually cancelled out by the swing against the CPI in 56 Travancore-Cochin constituencies. The change in the register varied: in the south there was an increase of some 10 per cent; and in Malabar little or no net change. How far the contrast reflected demographic differences—higher life expectancies and reproductive

Table 5.3 Kerala 1960: Assembly Election

Party	Seats contested*	Seats won	Votes polled†	% Vote
Congress	80	63	2,789,556	34.4
CPI	108	26	3,171,732	39.1
CPI-Independents	23	3	378,404	4.7
PSP	33	20	1,146,028	14.1
RSP	18	1	106,137	1.3
Muslim League	12	11	401,925	5.0
Others	21	0	32,512	0.4
Independents	17	2	77,783	1.0

* Of the 126 seats, 102 were in single-member constituencies and 12 in two-member constituencies.
†Total number, 8,104,077.

Sources: Adapted from Election Commission, India, *Report on the General Election to the Kerala Legislative Assembly 1960* and *Kerala Mail*, 14 Feb. 1960.

Table 5.4   Kerala 1957-60: Communist Electoral Performance by District

% Hindu 1961	District	CPI seats 1957-60 (N=126) Net change	% Turnout 1957	Increase in turnout 1957-60★	Mean CPI vote (N=87) 1957	1960	Net change	Total CPI vote 1960 (N=125)	No. of seats where CPI vote higher than 50% 1957	1960
72	Trivandrum	−6	69	14	42.1	44.8	+2.7	45.5	3	1
64	Quilon	−6	77	12	44.8	43.2	−1.6	42.8	5	1
65	Alleppey	−3	74	14	49.6	44.8	−4.8	39.6	6	4
49	Kottayam	−1	73	16	42.9	40.3	−2.6	40.6	2	1
46	Ernakulam	−3	71	18	43.8	42.4	−1.4	31.4	1	1
63	Trichur	−5	72	18	44.9	43.9	−1.0	43.2	1	1
70	Palghat	nil	54	25	49.8	55.5	+5.7	53.8	5	8
53	Kozhikode	−2	62	20	27.8	35.8	+8.0	30.0	0	1
70	Cannanore	−5	63	23	47.1	45.7	−1.4	39.1	3	2
61	All	−31	66	18	43.7	44.4	+0.7	39.1	26†	20†
60	Travancore-Cochin	−24	71	15	44.7	43.3	−1.4	40.6	18	7
63	Malabar	−7	58	22	41.9	46.3	+4.4	36.4	8	13

★ In percentage points.

† Hardgrave in Weiner and Field, eds., *Electoral Politics in the Indian States*, vol. 4., p. 179, gives 30 for 1957 and 22 for 1960 as the CPI totals.

Sources: first column, *Census of India 1961*, vol. VII, pt IX, p. 261. Calculations from figures in Election Commission, India, *Report on the General Election to the Kerala Legislative Assembly 1960*.

rates—in Travancore and Cochin, how far political influences on the process of registration,[66] and how far the technicalities of administration, is impossible to guess. Never the less it is probable that the main effect was to weaken the communists in the south through the addition of a generation of first-time young voters which on the evidence of college elections had turned against the CPI.[67]

The growth in turnout is shown by constituency in Map 15. It was most marked (20 per cent and over) in Cannanore, northern Kozhikode, Palghat, and the hilly interior of Kottayam. The improvement in turnout reflected intensified party competition, which was particularly visible in the substantial increase in female voting. More women went to the polls in 1960 than men. Official sources claim that, among the lower classes, women give more support to the communists (and subsequently the marxists) than their menfolk.[68] Certainly in Palghat there could be a plausible explanation for this in the extensive use of female labour in paddy cultivation. Though the area was slower to abandon semi–feudal modes of thought than the coconut gardens of Cannanore, once political consciousness developed, it proved more profound because of the collective character of field cultivation.

Neither the bigger electorate in Malabar nor the state–wide higher turnout helped the CPI in terms of seats won. In just over half the constituencies contested in both elections the party's share of the vote improved but in only three cases did the CPI gain a seat, while in twenty-nine cases it lost (Map 17). The main effect of the pro-communist swing was to extend the area covered by absolute majorities in the Palghat 'heartland' (Maps 14 and 16)

Mitra, however, notes how finely balanced the CPI and the anti-communist alliance were. A uniform swing to the left of 2 per cent would have given the communists a further 24 seats while a 2 per cent swing to the right would have reduced communist representation to 14 seats.[69] In fact there was no uniformity of swing between 1957 and 1960[70] though there was some modest evidence of an equalization of support for the communist party in the 87 constituencies compared in the above table. In 1957 half these constituencies fell within a range of 16 percentage points; in 1960 half fell within a range of only 10 points. Reference to the earlier maps of religious loyalties (see above, pp. 18, 19 and 20) suggests that this was associated with a closer identification of CPI strength with areas of Hindu predominance in 1960 than in 1957. Where Muslims or Christians were significant minorities or actual majorities an anti-communist movement was generally evident. Cutting across this communalization of the electorate, however, was a greater measure of class polarization among the Hindu community. Palghat District

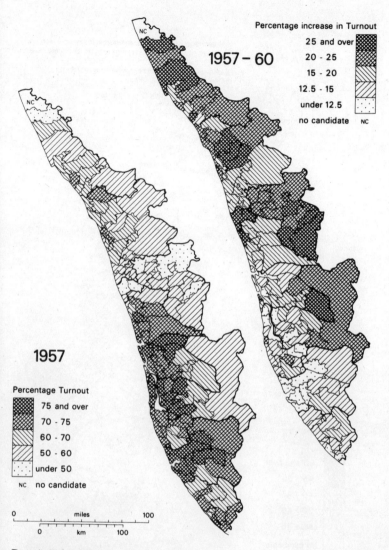

Percentage increase in Turnout

25 and over
20 - 25
15 - 20
12.5 - 15
under 12.5
no candidate   NC

1957 - 60

1957

Percentage Turnout

75 and over
70 - 75
60 - 70
50 - 60
under 50

NC   no candidate

0   miles   100

0   km   100

The territorial waters of India extend into the sea to a distance
of twelve nautical miles measured from the appropriate base line.

Based upon Survey of India map with the permission
of the Surveyor General of India.   © Government of India Copyright 1982

Source: Election Commission, India, *Report on the General Election to the Kerala
        Legislative Assembly 1960.*

Map 15 Kerala: Turnout by Constituency 1957; Percentage Point In-
        crease in Turnout 1957-60

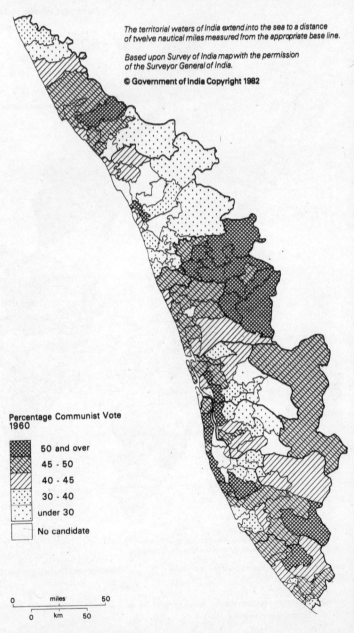

The territorial waters of India extend into the sea to a distance
of twelve nautical miles measured from the appropriate base line.

Based upon Survey of India map with the permission
of the Surveyor General of India.

© Government of India Copyright 1982

Percentage Communist Vote
1960

50 and over

45 - 50

40 - 45

30 - 40

under 30

No candidate

miles

0   50

0   km   50

Source: As Map 15 above.

Map 16 Kerala 1960: Assembly Election, Percentage Communist Vote

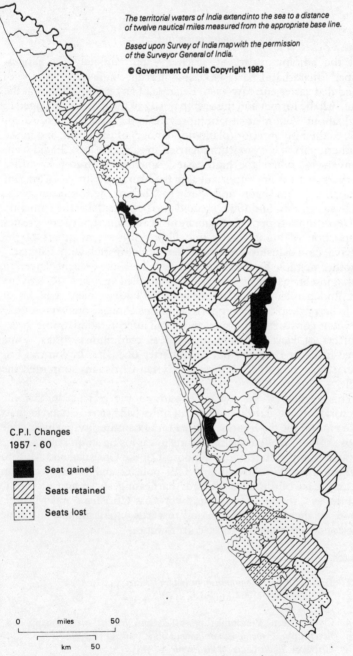

The territorial waters of India extend into the sea to a distance of twelve nautical miles measured from the appropriate base line.

Based upon Survey of India map with the permission of the Surveyor General of India.

© Government of India Copyright 1982

C.P.I. Changes
1957 - 60

■ Seat gained

▨ Seats retained

⊙ Seats lost

0 miles 50

km 50

Note: Vertical line indicates one seat in two-member constituency.

Source: As Map 15 above.

Map 17 Kerala 1957-60: Assembly Elections, Change in Communist Representation by Constituency

and the adjoining part of Trichur—approximately the funnel-shaped Bharathapuzha river basin—has the highest percentage of scheduled castes and low-caste Ezhavas of any extensive area in the state. All the former and the vast majority of the latter are engaged in field labour. A similar situation prevails in the coastal area of Alleppey, in the hilly interior (plantation labour) of the south, and in the southern part of Trivandrum District. In each case the CPI did well. Conversely, where the high castes, whether cultivators or office workers, were more important as in the Nair (and Christian) interior of northern Travancore and southern Cochin, the communist vote fell between 1957 and 1960. It could also be argued that the reduction of communist support in Cannanore was a function of the greater proportion of higher castes and higher income members of the Ezhava (and Muslim) communities as compared with Palghat.[71] Another possible explanation may have been the credence given to damaging allegations of impropriety levelled against V.R. Krishna Iyer, Independent Law Minister in the CPI government, who lost at Tellicherry despite CPI support.[72] The one contemporaneous sample survey is consistent with such an overall interpretation. Some three-quarters of Harijans were reported as communist voters, some three-fifths of Ezhavas, but one-quarter of Nairs. In contrast less than 10 per cent of Catholics and Syrian Christians supported the CPI.[73]

This review of the evidence leads to the conclusion that the electoral impact of the CPI's term of office had been to extend its mass base among the 'have-nots' of the Hindu community, including the poorer Nairs, while at the same time it was losing support among the better-off and all but the very poorest of the Christian and Muslim communities. It followed that CPI policies and tactics would in future years be directed towards harnessing social and economic change as a means of making lower-class Christians and Muslims aware of their class position and towards exploiting any available lines of cleavage within those communities.

Notes

1   B. Sen Gupta, *Communism in Indian Politics,* p. 37.
2   'Tactical Line' (1953), in DRS, *ICPD*, p. 72.
3   Ibid., p. 81.
4   Overstreet and Windmiller, pp. 481-2; Ram, *Indian Communism*, pp. 75-6.
5   Sen Gupta, *Communism in Indian Politics,* pp. 37 and 39.
6   Gopalan, *In the Cause of the People*, p. 181.
7   Overstreet and Windmiller, p. 481, note a mellowing in the attitude and behaviour of CPI members of the Lok Sabha in the year or two before the 1957 general election.

8 'Organisational Methods and Practices of Party Centre' (1956), in DRS, *ICPD*, p. 315-16.

9 Patiala and East Punjab States Union.

10 R.L. Park, 'Indian Election Results', *Far Eastern Survey* 7, May 1952; Govt of India, Election Commission, *Report on the First General Elections in India* 1951-2, vol. 2 *Statistical* (1955); Craig Baxter, comp., *District Voting Trends in India* (1969).

11 Damodaran, *New Left R.* 93, 1975, p. 45.

12 'Draft Political Resolution' (1953), in DRS, *ICPD*, pp. 114 and 120-1.

13 'Tenancy Legislation, Social Security Act, Payment of Wages Act, etc . . .these legislations have been enacted as the result of mass struggles and are a weapon in the hands of the people.' Ibid., p. 114. 'The introduction of such Bills [on the burning problems of the people] can and must become the rallying point of a wide mass movement . . .' Ibid., p. 121

14 Ibid., p. 121.

15 Gopalan, *In the Cause of the People*, p. 177.

16 Ibid., p. 178

17 Damodaran, *New Left R.* 93, 1975, p.45.

18 DRS, *ICPD*, pp. 112-13, 123-4, 140-52 especially p. 144. See also 'Report to the Party Congress' (1956), in DRS, *ICPD*, pp. 280ff. The Politbureau (1953) quotes *Ramamurthy's Letter to N.M. Jaisoorya and G.M. Shroff* (1953) approvingly as clearly setting out the party's stand: 'Communist Party's conception of united front is basically a front of classes . . .In our country today different democratic political parties or groups exist . . .It will not help us to discuss here which party represents which class most or which ideology or practice is more correct. We have to take this reality of the existence of these parties and groups. Wishing them away will not do.' DRS, *ICPD*, pp. 147-8. For the text of Ramamurthy's letter see DRS, *ICPD*, pp. 179-84.

19 *Hindu*, 2 Mar. 1952; 'A.K. Gopalan Suggests Minimum Programme for Travancore-Cochin: Non-Congress Forces Must Unite' and 'United Front Firmly Rooted in Travancore-Cochin', *Crossroads*, 7 Mar. 1952; 'Statement of Policy and Programme of the United Front of Leftists, of the People's Democratic Party, and of the Travancore-Tamilnad Congress', *Crossroads*, 28 Mar. 1952; 'Review Report of the Politbureau' (1953), in DRS, *ICPD*, pp. 150 and 154-5.

20 *Malayalarajyam* (Quilon, Malayalam), 3 Feb. 1952.

21 E.M.S. Namboodiripad, 'United Front in Malabar: People's Weapon to Oust Congress', *Crossroads*, 21 Mar. 1952, also 'Unite to Oust the Congress from Power', ibid., 14 Mar. 1952.

22 'Review Report of the Politbureau' (1953), in DRS, *ICPD*, p. 150.

23 *New Age* (monthly), Nov. 1953. Fic, *Peaceful Transition to Communism in India*, p. 77, affords an accessible summary.

24 I am indebted to the late Professor R. Ramakrishnan Nair for providing a verified list of CPI 'Independents'; Govt of Travancore-Cochin, Election Commission, *Report on the First General Elections in the Travancore-Cochin State held under the Constitution of India 1951-2* (1953).

25   No official maps of constituency boundaries are published in India. The boundaries presented in the maps in this book are approximate and based on tracing out the constituency delimitations available in the Legislative Assembly Library, Tvm, on to large-scale maps in the Drawing Office Map Collection, London School of Economics. Independently Robert L. Hardgrave Jr has produced maps of electoral support in Kerala for the period 1957-70 in 'The Communist Parties of Kerala: an Electoral Profile', in M. Weiner and J.O. Field, eds., *Electoral Politics in the Indian States,* vol. 4 (1975).

26   Thakazhi Sivasankara Pillai, *Two Measures of Rice,* trans. M.A. Shakoor (1967), p. 40.

27   Mencher, *Ethnology* V (2), 1966, p. 156.

28   Govt of Travancore-Cochin, Election Commission, *The Report on the First General Elections in the Travancore-Cochin State held under the Constitution of India 1951-2* notes that women participated as actively as men, if not more so, in some areas (p. 15). In 1960 common ballot boxes replaced separate ballot boxes for each candidate. K.P. Bhagat, *The Kerala Mid-Term Election of 1960: the Communist Party's Conquest of New Positions* (1962), p. 122.

29   *Census of India 1941,* vol. XXV: *Travancore,* pt I, Table IX. Of the Hindu population of 3,671,480, 1,062,357 were Nayars (Nairs), 1,038,494 Ilavan (Ezhavas), and 76,834 Brahmins, of whom only 4,229 were Namboodiris. Of the Christian population of 1,963,808, 560,834 were Syrian Catholics, 405,057 Jacobite Syrians, 171,962 Mar Thomites, 223,066 Latin Catholics, and 230,066 Roman Catholics. 'Syrian Christians' as mapped are the combined total of the first three groups. Although the impact of differential birth and death rates between communities and selective migration to Malabar during the decade 1941-51 was not insignificant, it seems unlikely that the communal pattern within and between taluks would have changed markedly by 1952.

30   K. Gough, *International J. of Comparative Sociology* VIII (1), 1967, pp. 63-5.

31   Fic, *Kerala,* p. 42.

32   'Organisational Methods and Practices of Party Centre' (1956), in DRS, *ICPD,* p. 309.

33   Justice K. Sankaran, *Report of the Inquiry into the Action of the Police in Having Resorted to Firing on 11 August 1954* (Tvm, Govt of Travancore-Cochin, 1955).

34   Namboodiripad, *The National Question in Kerala,* p. 174.

35   Of the 48 seats, the CPI won 24, Congress 15, the Muslim League 8, and the PSP 1. Of votes cast, the CPI received 38.3 per cent, Congress 35.4 per cent, the League 14.3 per cent, and the PSP 11.3 per cent. K. Damodaran, 'Malabar District Board Election', *New Age* (monthly), Dec. 1954, and 'What the Malabar Election Results Show: an Analysis', *New Age,* 7 Nov. 1954. See also Damodaran, 'A Programme to Meet People's Demands: Draft Programme of the Democratic Front in the Malabar District Board', *New Age,* 28 Nov. 1954.

36 R. Ramakrishnan Nair notes that in the Alleppey Municipality, the other major local body administered by the CPI, the party's popularity declined between 1952 and 1957 as measured by the Assembly voting figures. *How Communists Came to Power in Kerala*, p. 43. T.V. Thomas (CPI) won the Assembly constituency of Alleppey in 1957 with 54 per cent of the votes cast and lost in a straight fight in 1960 polling 47 per cent.

37 *Times of India*, 26 May 1952.

38 'Draft Political Resolution' (1953), in DRS, *ICPD*, pp. 107 and 109. *Minimum Programme for United Democratic Front* issued by Communist MPs and MCs, 25 Apr. 1952 (Mimeo). Chapter IV of Namboodiripad's *The National Question in Kerala* is entitled 'Birth of a Nation' and is repeated in his *Kerala*, which also includes 'Aikya Kerala—Realisation of a Dream'. Namboodiripad's thinking on provincial identity can be followed in *Problems of National Integration* (1966). While recognizing the complexity of the issue, he there traces regional rivalries to uneven development: 'Provincialism and regionalism cannot be tackled through any other means than of conscious removal of the provincial and regional disparities' (p. 55).

39 'Questions and Answers: Nationalities and the Right of Secession', *Crossroads*, 6 Sept. 1953, p. 10.

40 Selig S. Harrison, 'Communism in India: the Dilemma of the CPI', *Problems of Communism* 8 (2), 1959, p. 35; Namboodiripad, 'Class Character of the Nationalist Movement', *Social Scientist* (Tvm) 37, 1975.

41 As constituted in 1956, only 5 per cent of the Kerala population did not speak Malayalam as their mother tongue; 3.1 per cent spoke Tamil. Tamil-speakers in Kottayam (10.0 per cent) and Palghat (9.3 per cent) Districts are concentrated chiefly on the estates of the High Ranges. *Census of India 1961*, vol. VII: *Kerala*, pt IX, *Census Atlas*, pp. 262-3.

42 Disgruntlement with the Panampilly ministry's willingness to concede the Tamil-speaking southern taluks to Madras was only one factor in the manoeuvres which led to its downfall. Panampilly was unpopular with key figures in the Congress establishment since he was neither their choice as Chief Minister nor susceptible to their manipulation. Though a Nair, Panampilly was not on good terms with the NSS while the Catholic Church was apprehensive that he might reintroduce the educational reforms they had forced him to shelve in 1952.

43 *Malayala Manorama* (Malayalam), 10 Mar. 1956.

44 Ibid.

45 Extended treatments of the issues summarized here are found in Overstreet and Windmiller; Fic, *Peaceful Transition to Communism in India*; and E.M.S. Namboodiripad, *Note for the Programme of the CPI* (1964). Leading documents are found in DRS, *ICPD*. The CPI's own programme of publication of primary sources has not yet reached this period.

46 'Report to the Party Congress' (1956), in DRS, *ICPD*, pp. 297-8.

47 Namboodiripad, *Note for the Programme of the CPI*, p. 71.

48 'Report of Ajoy Ghosh to the Fourth Congress of the CPI' (1956), in DRS, *ICPD*, p. 334.

49   Resolution: 'Communist Proposal for Building a Democratic and Prosperous Kerala. Adopted by the Kerala Provincial Conference of the Communist Party, held in Trichur from June 22 to 24, 1956', *New Age*, 22 July 1956. See also 'Kerala. Communist Party's Slogan. Alternative Government of Democratic Opposition'. *New Age*, 19 Aug. 1956; 'Kerala Committee of the CPI. Unity on Programme and Formation of Alternative Government. Adopted at the Conference held in Ernakulam on October 9, 1956', *New Age*, 21 Oct. 1956.

50   The PSP's decision (Gaya Conference, Dec. 1955) was modified in Nov. 1956 (Bangalore) to permit accommodation in exceptional and extraordinary cases, which proved legion. Rose, p. 53.

51   'Communist Party Explains Why No Election Agreement in Kerala, Resolution of the Kerala Committee of the CPI, adopted at Alwaye on January 1-3, 1957', *New Age*, 20 Jan. 1957. The PSP's claim to more than half the seats in Travancore-Cochin suggests that Pattom was not seriously interested in an agreement.

52   'Communist Manifesto for Stable Government, Prosperous Kerala', *New Age*, 10 Feb. 1957. Fic notes that the full Malayalam version's 20,000 print run was sold out within days: *Kerala*, p. 75, n. 19.

53   R. Ramakrishnan Nair, *How Communists Came to Power* summarizes and reviews the literature and includes the detailed results in an appendix. For a communalist interpretation see Fic, *Kerala*, pp. 70-4; Jitendra Singh, *Communist Rule in Kerala* (1959) and 'Communism in Kerala', in B.E. Pentony, ed., *Red World in Tumult* (San Francisco, Chandler, 1962); Ashok Mitra, 'The Kerala Elections: a Statistical Analysis', *Economic Weekly* Special no. June 1960; Bhagat; Hardgrave in Weiner and Field, eds., vol. 4.

54   The Muslim League won 8 of the 18 constituencies in Kozhikode.

55   *How Communists Came to Power*, pp. 24-76.

56   Nair cites as illustrative of this trend the fact that two leading Congress dailies, *Desabandhu* and *Kerala Kaumudi* owned by a Nair businessman and a prominent Ezhava respectively, took pro-communist lines during the campaign. Ibid., pp. 72-3.

57   B.N. Mullik, *My Years with Nehru* (1972), p. 339.

58   Taya Zinkin, *Reporting India* (1962): '[Nair's] nice calculation of caste and class division constituency-wise' (p. 155).

59   *Kerala*, pp. 71-3.

60   Democratic Research Service (Bombay), *Kerala under Communism: a Report* (1959, hereafter DRS, *KUC*): 'The Nair aristocracy in central and northern Travancore made common cause with the Communist Party ostensibly because the Congress in that region was Christian-dominated but in reality to spite their Christian tenants. In Perumpavoor, Changanacherry, Tiruvalla and Kottarakkara Assembly constituencies...communist candidates were successful mainly because of the help of the Nair Service Society' (p. 67). Mannoth subsequently urged those Nairs who had voted CPI in 1957 to oust the communists. *Deepika*, 24 Dec. 1958.

61   Pattom was noted for his dictatorial approach to his party and collea-

gues. 'Shri Pattom wears Malayali dress on all occasions and is intensely nationalistic. He has a personality that is impressive and aggressive. He is reputedly known as a strong man with firm determination. He is dynamic but at times dogmatic perhaps even dictatorial. One may be tempted to call him the Bismarck of Kerala. Once he defines his goals he does not like to look back but just go ahead in spite of opposition and difficulties. He is quite competent to rule with an iron hand if necessary.' Bhagat, p. 86. For Legislative Assembly tributes to Pattom see *SPKLA*, 26 Oct. 1970, p. 6. Pattom won 52 per cent of the vote in his Nair-dominant Trivandrum II constituency in 1957 and 58 per cent in 1960.

62 *Kerala*, pp. 72-3.
63 Jitendra Singh, 'Communism in Kerala', in B.E. Pentony, ed., *Red World in Tumult*, p. 247. R. Ramakrishnan Nair, who was well acquainted with NSS and communist leaders, comments: 'The substance of [Singh's] statement is as imaginary as the figures given in his table showing the communal distribution.' *How the Communists Came to Power in Kerala*, p.40.
64 For Congress seats, see DRS, *KUC*, p. 67; for the PSP, calculations from the election results of 1954 and 1957. In no other cases was the margin between the CPI and the PSP small.
65 *Kerala*, p. 127.
66 Fr Vadakkan refers to the alliance's efforts to ensure full registration of their supporters. 'Wellington and I travelled all over Kerala organising franchise committees ... We succeeded beyond expectation.' *A Priest's Encounter with Revolution* (1974), p. 75.
67 DRS, *KUC*, p. 82.
68 Bhagat, p. 123. Interview, senior election official, Tvm, Sept. 1974.
69 Mitra, *Economic Weekly*, Special no. June 1960, p. 1002.
70 Ibid., p. 998.
71 R. Sankar, leader of the SNDP *yogam* and then President of the KPCC, contested and won Cannanore I, albeit in a constituency where the CPI had won in 1957 on a minority vote.
72 Krishna Iyer was alleged to have been instrumental in the conversion of a large part of his father's land into trusts to evade the provisions of the Agrarian Relations Bill. His reply to the charges is found in his *David Come to Judgement* (Ernakulam, Prabath Book House, 1959).
73 The survey was sponsored by the Diwan Chand Trust, New Delhi, and conducted by the Dept of Politics, U. of Kerala. I am grateful to the then Professor Sukumaran Nayar for a sight of the full results, summarized in *Times of India*, 2 Sept. 1960. See also F. Victor, 'Who voted for Communists in Kerala?', *Social Action* 10, Apr. 1960.

6

Communists in Government
1957–1959

Party Attitudes and Conflicts

THE many commentators on the events of 1957-9 are agreed that 'communist rule in Kerala was a novel experiment in the practice of communism under conditions of democracy',[1] but they disagree fundamentally on the nature of that experiment. For Karnik and Fic, when Namboodiripad assured the press on taking office that 'it will be our endeavour to see that our programme is fully implemented',[2] he really meant the secret version of the 1953 Tactical Line: 'the communists would make use of the power entrusted to them to destroy democracy and to establish a dictatorship of their own party.'[3] For H.D. Malaviya, a leftist Congressman, and press attaché to the Communist government, the programme was at once the minimum programme of the election manifesto and the Congress socialism to which the INC had recently committed itself.[4] Overstreet and Windmiller, American authors of a major study of Indian Communism published in 1958, thought Namboodiripad's outline of his goals reflected a general aim of respectability and that Kerala posed a clear challenge to Marxist-Leninist orthodoxy.[5] In their assessment of the outcome the Democratic Research Service,[6] Fic, and others claim that capitalizing on the illusions of many in Kerala and Delhi, including Nehru, who believed that communism and democracy could co-exist, the communists went far towards transforming the state into a communist dictatorship between April 1957 and June 1958. According to Fic 'it is fairly certain that had Kerala been a fully sovereign state . . .the opposition would not have been permitted to challenge the regime and stage a comeback.'[7] Malaviya, and most recently Leiten,[8] have on the contrary argued that the government achieved a great deal within a Congress–socialist and developmental framework, despite its limited powers, and that it was the opposition and the Centre which flouted democracy. Privately, party leaders are prepared to concede that there were excesses and abuses but contend that these resulted largely from a combination of inexperience with the difficulty of controlling the spontane-

ous actions of the hitherto oppressed, the self-seeking of opportunists, who had lately joined the party, and the criminality of
'anti-social elements' who used the party's name as a cover for their
malign activities.[9]

The present chapter does not attempt to review all the evidence—
which would in any case be an infructuous task since the fading
memories of the participants are coloured by the selective percep-
tions of the time. For reasons of space, only a number of central
issues are discussed here: the party's own conception of its role; the
formation of the ministry; agrarian and educational reform; law and
order; administration; and the principal mass front, labour. In the
author's view there was no single understanding in the party of its
'programme'. It was twice necessary for the national party secretary,
Ajoy Ghosh, to intervene to resolve conflict within the State Committee. None the less the dominant view remained that of the Chief
Minister and Politbureau member, Namboodiripad: for situational
reasons—the configuration of forces within the state, the powers of
the Centre, and pressures for legislative reform from organized
groups linked to the party—as well as for ideological reasons the
party should pursue a temperate and constitutionally correct
course.[10] This did not, of course preclude other tactics but these were
to be subordinate to an attempt to implement peaceful transition
policies at their face value, suitably adapted to the requirement of the
quasi-federal political system. Kerala could not become a people's
state because it was not a state in the marxist sense, but by implementing progressive policies the ministry could hasten the creation
of conditions for a people's state nationally.

The provincial decision-making centre of the party was the State
Committee. Under the discipline of democratic centralism it set the
framework within which the various wings of the party operated.
However, in practice there was more flexibility than this formal
description implies. The State Committee was a reconciliatory organ, often papering over unresolved conflict by ambiguous
formulae. It could not be summoned to decide on every issue that
arose and the office of the party secretary, held by M.N.Govindan
Nair, was of crucial significance in day-to-day interpretation of the
party line. Govindan Nair was himself sceptical of the parliamentary
road: he once quipped to a Western journalist that communism with
a democratic constitution was like capitalism without private
enterprise.[11] In the nature of the division of labour between
ministerialists and organizers, Nair's position entailed articulating
the interests of the field workers. Similar considerations applied at
the district level and on specific fronts such as labour, peasant, and
student, as well as on the new ministerial front itself. These

polycentric tendencies help to account for some of the incon-
sistencies evident in the communist record.

Dissent within the party surfaced immediately after the election
victory. Damodaran, a leading figure in the Malabar wing of the
party, later reported that he had expressed a minority view in the
State Committee that as the state remained essentially capitalist at
provincial as well as national level, the real task of the ministry was
to use the situation to strengthen the party and the mass
movement.[12] The official line was tantamount to parliamentary
cretinism. He claims that Namboodiripad argued that the combination of a majority in the Assembly with extra-parliamentary agitation and class confrontation could transform the government and the
(provincial) state from within. Ghosh on behalf of the Politbureau
sided with the majority and the minority was forced to submit.

The real issue was that the 'moderate' majority emphasized what
might be done within a bourgeois democratic framework and the
'radical' minority what could not. In fact it is doubtful whether
anyone, including Nehru, had any real idea of what room for manoeuvre a non-Congress controlled state might have. The constitution was essentially latitudinarian on this point; and there was no
'custom and practice'—if we discount the provincial administrations
under the Raj—to guide those involved. Nehru's leftward shift and
his resistance to those in Delhi anxious to perpetuate President's Rule
suggested that the CPI government would be allowed to function
relatively freely.[13] At lower levels of autonomy—district board,
municipality, and panchayat—the Kerala CPI had already experimented with some success. There was no good reason to reject
the opportunity to test how far the armour of the bourgeois democratic state might be penetrated by its own parliamentary weapons.
In the process the CPI might make modest but worthwhile improvements in the condition of peasant and worker. The pressures on the
party to attempt it were irresistible: the Soviet Union wanted it; the
Indian Politbureau willed it; and most important of all the bulk of the
state party and its supporters yearned for it. Damodaran remembers
'hearing poor, illiterate workers telling policemen on the streets:
"Now you daren't attack us because our government is in power.
Namboodiripad is our leader. We are ruling."'[14] Nevertheless the
radicals were pessimistic: some remained opposed to any acceptance
of office, while others argued that office ought to be exploited for the
benefit of the party. However, during the first year of the ministry,
Namboodiripad's conception of its role remained dominant. We
may in part attribute this to the heightened levels of Malayalee
patriotism to which the party had contributed by its role in the
campaign for a United Kerala.

In the wake of the Moscow Conference of 64 Communist Parties in November 1957, which affirmed the possibility of peaceful transition provided communist parties also launched non-parliamentary mass struggles against reactionary forces, two decisions of the CPI's Extraordinary Party Congress at Amritsar in April 1958 were to prove important for the future of the ministry: the transformation of the CPI into a mass party; and the adoption of a new constitution.

At the time of the third Kerala state conference at Trichur in June 1956, when the provincial units of Malabar and Travancore–Cochin were amalgamated, the party had 25,000 members, some of whom were candidate (and recent) members. Of these some 2,000 were members of long standing, comrades whose commitment had stood trial. The circulation of the three party dailies in April 1957 was 40,000. In 'many parts of Kerala' there were very few and even no party units in 1956.[15] At the election the party claimed to have had nearly 250,000 volunteer workers. After the CPI victory, membership began to rise: on the one hand communist *anubhavis* (supporters) and those whose own jobs or family connections had hitherto precluded open commitment tended to seek membership; on the other opportunists sought admission. The conversion of the party in April 1958 to a mass party accelerated this tendency and by 1960 party membership stood at 60,000, of whom 18,000 were candidate members. The circulation of the party daily press had not grown proportionately. Loss of office, coupled with the effects of the split, was to cut membership rapidly: to 41,000 in 1961 and some 23,000 in 1963-4.[16]

Arguably, the party's membership in 1956 outran the CPI's ability to maintain discipline and raise consciousness, while the 1957-8 membership drive undermined the party's great asset, its relatively disciplined organization. 'I have to boost the party up to 50,000 card-members,' Govindan Nair said at the time. 'They think I am a magician. I can increase the membership only at the cost of discipline.[17] If such an argument is a convenient one, there appears to be some truth in the claim that the excesses committed in the name of the party were disproportionately the work of the new comrades.[18]

The CPI's new constitution adopted the concept of a contingent peaceful transition to people's democracy in line with the 1957 Moscow Declaration, though deviating from it by specifically guaranteeing the continued existence of other parties after the CPI had captured a parliamentary majority, provided that the opposition abided by the constitution. On the key issue of what role mass struggle would play, the party's public posture was defensive rather than offensive. The Amritsar Political Resolution (in the subsection 'Kerala Shows the Way') warned members that the ballot box was not necessarily respected by vested interests and had to be 'defended by mass action'. 'This imposes heavy responsibilities on our party in Kerala—responsibilities that have to be carried out in a very difficult situation and within the framework of the present constitution.[19] Fic discerns a distinct Kerala pattern of transition: the opposition was to be pushed aside and neutralized by a combination of the direct actions of mass organizations, the neutrality of the police, and the use of the courts to legalize the results of such actions.[20] However, it seems doubtful that politicians of the sophistication of Namboodiripad and Govindan Nair imagined the church could be so easily overcome. Within a few weeks of Amritsar, Namboodiripad spoke of the danger of civil war, as in China, in a speech at Coimbatore (Madras state) on 3 June which attracted national attention.[21] In the context of the Catholic heirarchy's determination to defeat a revised Education Bill, the formation of a volunteer Christian militia,[22] and politically inspired labour troubles the Chief Minister's speech was not as out of character with his generally moderate and constitutional line as at first appears. Fic contends that Namboodiripad badly overplayed his hand and 'tragically erred in reading the then existing correlation of forces in Kerala.' It was the Coimbatore speech coupled with Govindan Nair's call for a party militia which, he believes, ultimately led to the downfall of the régime. While the threat—and in July and August the actuality—of mass action by the CPI did have serious consequences, this reading neglects the fact that the Chief Minister, an experienced politician with no weakness for rash or rhetorical utterances, had cause for concern in opposition activity. By February 1958 the Catholic community had organized what appeared to Namboodiripad to be a paramilitary organization. *Deepika,* the Catholic organ, certainly indulged in inflammatory editorials: 'the Chief Minister may not understand the real strength of the "Christophers". Five good Christians might be more than sufficient to face even five thousand Communists, since . . . for a true Christian, life on this earth is immaterial'.[23]

While Namboodiripad is alleged to have 'climbed down' when Nehru expressed strong disapproval of the alleged speech at Coimbatore[24] and took the opportunity to clarify his remarks for the press,[25] the question of how to respond to the expected opposition challenge on the streets precipitated a crisis within the party. The radicals—led by the State Committee secretary, Govindan Nair— who had instigated the formation of the party's own militia, maintained that when reactionary forces attacked a legitimate government, the party would not breach the Amritsar doctrine by counter-attacking with violence through the mass organizations.[26] The moderates, led by Namboodiripad, argued that Kerala had to be seen in a national and international perspective—undue militancy would damage the party's prospects in India and upset the Delhi-Kremlin entente. In any case in a federal system one communist state government could not be successfully defended. Namboodiripad turned for advice to the Central Secretariat, and a balanced delegation of S.A. Dange (moderate), A.K. Gopalan (radical), and Ajoy Ghosh, the party secretary, visited Moscow for consultations.[27]

Meanwhile the situation had deteriorated markedly. After the government had nationalized water transport its decision to abolish a student concessionary fare in the backwater district of the Kuttanad provoked an unexpectedly severe reaction by the students affected. There were grounds for suspicion that the student protest had been orchestrated by Christian interests. The ministry's tough attempt to suppress the agitation, in which party members as well as the police are alleged to have participated, was a miscalculation.[28] The incident tended to alienate large sectors of the student body. The mounting tension was heightened by a wave of violent clashes between the workers of communist and anti-communist parties, of which the worst involved the deaths of six Congressmen at Varandarapally (Trichur),[29] a number of police firings, and on 7 August 1958 the public intervention of Nehru. The party executive hinted that it was considering ordering the ministry to resign or to seek a coalition with the PSP and the RSP in the hope of dividing the opposition.[30] After an on-the-spot inquiry by Ranadive the CPI Central Executive Committee (which had replaced the Politbureau) met in Trivandrum on the day Nehru made his concern public.[31] Several days' discussion produced a compromise between the militant organizational wing and the more cautious ministerialists. Mass action in defence of the régime was to be abandoned. Krishna Iyer, the Independent Law Minister, announced that instructions had been given to the police to ignore pressures from local communist leaders.[32] Little more was heard of the communist militia, though the State Committee proved unable to restrain its anti-social elements entirely.

The party was thus separated from the state apparatus. The régime was henceforth to defend itself through constitutional channels alone. In exchange for accepting the party's subservience to the ministerial wing in matters of law and order, the organizational wing was to be brought more closely into the formation of policy and the supervision of executive action by means of a special joint committee and the introduction of the state party secretary, Govindan Nair, into the cabinet.[33] The joint committee seems to have stiffened the ministry's line on agrarian reform but Govindan Nair did not in fact join the government. This general understanding was confirmed by the National Council, meeting at Madras in October.[34]

The argument was renewed in November when the Kerala unit held a special conference at Alwaye.[35] The moderates suggested expanding the ministry into a united front of leftists, a move that would split the opposition. Some radicals argued for the ministry's resignation; some that the demonstrations were the work of a handful of reactionaries that could be overwhelmed by massive popular mobilization. Govindan Nair, the state party secretary, is said to have urged resignation at the first favourable opportunity; and Namboodiripad is reported to have been advised in Moscow in January 1959 to continue for the moment but to be prepared to offer the ministry's resignation if that appeared the best course.[36]

In some interpretations the party's decision not to support the militant defence of the Kerala ministry has been seen as the sacrifice of the party's national interest to the strategic requirements of the Soviet Union.[37] Such a view neglects the national consequences of the radical course and ignores the fact that it was Nambooripad, by no means subservient to Soviet direction, who led the so-called moderates.

As the law and order situation continued to deteriorate during the spring of 1959 Achutha Menon took over the portfolio from Krishna Iyer. In the light of the party's experience in July the previous year, the cadres were given only the limited task of protecting party workers and offices in the event of their being attacked. All arms licences were withdrawn in the four most sensitive districts of Trichur, Ernakulam, Kottayam, and Quilon. In a further show of strength Achutha Menon announced that the government intended to recruit 10,000 special police officers and that it would not hesitate to bring in the army to quell the disturbances. Namboodiripad— without consulting Govindan Nair—invited Nehru to visit the state in the hope that he might restrain his own Congressmen. Nehru avoided any temptation to compromise his own position. Krishna Rao, the State Governor, is reported to have complained 'If only Panditji had told me what he wants me to do!'[38] At a private meeting with the KPCC Nehru admitted he did not consider the communist ministry deserved to remain in office but averred that things had to get much worse before he could advise the President to dismiss it. He did not want the rest of India or the world to believe that Congress would not abide by the rules. 'Panditji has given us his blessing for stirring up violence,' was one gloss, 'but he has done so privately, in such a manner that he is not personally committed . . .'[39] The first question the Prime Minister put to a delegation from the CPI State Committee was 'How did you manage to so wonderfully isolate yourself from the people in such a short space of time?' He suggested that the ministry should seek a negotiated solution to controversial

provisions in the Education Bill—declined by the opposition[40]—
institute a judicial enquiry into the police firings—rejected by the
CPI—and agree to hold fresh elections in the near future—also
refused.[41] Nehru's stalling tactics, actuated by political as well as
constitutional considerations, discomfited the CPI. Govindan Nair
opined that 'the longer things drag on the more we will lose.'[42] After
an offer to negotiate with the Liberationists in June 1959 was refused
the State Committee decided on resignation, only to be overruled by
the National Council which preferred downright dismissal for its
propaganda value.[43] From 12 June the campaign against the government intensified. In its course 17 people died in police firings, some
300 were seriously injured in police *lathi* charges, and an estimated
150,000 arrested. As late as 5 July the Centre still took the view that
the ministry should be allowed to collapse 'by force of events' but the
announcement that the Liberationists intended to storm the Secretariat on 9 August finally forced a change of policy. Meanwhile the
Centre had received 'very reliable' information that Namboodiripad
wanted Central intervention.[44] The decision having been taken in
Delhi, a detailed memorandum was sent to the State Governor on 24
July listing the misdeeds of the state ministry and on 31 July
Namboodiripad finally received the long-sought Presidential dismissal of his government under Article 356 of the constitution. The
effect of the Kerala experience on CPI thinking is considered in the
next chapter.

Formation of the Ministry

The party's first task was decide on its Chief Minister. The most
obvious candidates were T.V. Thomas, a prominent trade unionist,
leader of the communist bloc in the Travancore-Cochin Assembly
and a Syrian Christian in a predominantly Hindu leadership, and
M.N. Govindan Nair, the provincial party secretary, popular
among non–communists and communists alike, and a prominent
Nair. Both were, of course, from the Travancore-Cochin area.
Against the choice of Thomas were rumours about his private life
and against Govindan Nair his allegedly exessively friendly relations
with the Nair establishment.[45] The Politbureau's choice was
Namboodiripad, something of a surprise in so far as it had been
presumed that he was indispensable at the national level. On all other
grounds he was well qualified: one of the founder members of the
Kerala unit, a Brahmin who had given his property to the party, a
man of unimpeachable integrity, and an intellectual and organizer of
All-India stature. As he had worked chiefly in Malabar his appointment was a reassurance to the north that its views and interests

would not be neglected. Finally, whether intentionally or not, the choice allayed the fears in Delhi of 'extremism'. Namboodiripad was generally regarded as being a centrist and a practical and congenial communist.

The next job was to select a ministry, a process complicated by the party's reliance on five independents for its overall majority and the need to take into account regional and communal considerations in order to protect the government from internal and external charges of sectional partiality. Communalism had played a part in the destruction of every ministry in Travancore-Cochin and it was certain that Congress would exploit any deafness to the lessons of Kerala history. Two of the Independents virtually selected themselves, Dr A.R. Menon and V.R. Krishna Iyer. Menon was a popular 71-year old Edinburgh-trained doctor from Trichur with an unimpeachable record of political activity—founder director of *Mathrubhumi,* past leader of the Cochin Congress, and former member of the KPCC and AICC.[46] By nature a blunt man, he had made a reputation as a fearsome critic of administrative incompetence and he was unique in having experience of office—as Minister for Rural Development in Cochin from 1938 to 1942. Dr Menon was an admirable choice for the Health and Welfare portfolio and hardly the kind of man to include in a cabinet if the party's declared aims were not to be taken at something like their face value.

Also obvious was the claim of Krishna Iyer, a Tamil Brahmin lawyer with a large and lucrative law practice in Malabar, whose expertise was ideal for the law portfolio. (He was later appointed to the Indian Supreme Court.) Apart from the party's own legal minds, the ministry could thus call on the advice of one of the country's front-rank lawyers.

In terms of the communal composition of the senior party leaders one might have expected a preponderantly high-caste Hindu ministry; in terms of the mass base of the party one might have expected a preponderantly low-caste ministry. The communal origins of the ministry (one Namboodiri Brahmin, one Tamil Brahmin, two Syrian Christians, one Latin Catholic, one Muslim, two Nairs, two Ezhavas, and one scheduled caste) suggest that if attention was paid to the political expediency of including in the cabinet a member of every significant community in the state, the final shape of the government was determined more by a desire to create a ministry of talent than to reflect communal proportionality. The same argument could be advanced with respect to the regional origins of the ministers—Malabar (3), Cochin (2), and Travancore (6)— which did not closely reflect either the distribution of population in the new state or the strength of the communist mass base in

Malabar. Given the background of the nine CPI ministers, it is clear that all fronts of party activity were represented: organization, trade unions, peasantry, education, women, as well as the parliamentary. Though the party men had no experience of administration above the local level, seven of the nine had legislative experience. If politicians are judged by their actions rather than their words, the party gave every intention of fulfilling its election campaign promise to create a democratic and prosperous Kerala. It had formed a ministry on paper strong, capable, and honest with only a minimal reference to communal and regional factors.

Agrarian Reform

The most important legislative reform attempted by the ministry was the Agrarian Relations Bill, which Namboodiripad regarded as the government's greatest achievement.[47] It was indeed the first comprehensive measure of its kind attempted in India; and it tackled tenurial relations of greater complexity than anywhere else in the country.

The special character of the structure of land tenure and the acute degree of landlessness has already been outlined (see above, p. 47). After Independence a variety of measures had been enacted as partial and ineffective remedies for particular problems.[48] In its election manifesto the CPI promised an Anti-Eviction Bill pending an Agrarian Relations Bill whose main aims would be to safeguard tenants' interests, introduce a ceiling on land holdings, fix fair rents, and redistribute surplus land to the landless. Within a week of assuming office the ministry proclaimed its Kerala Stay of Eviction Proceedings Ordinance to afford interim protection to both tenants and hutment dwellers (*kudikidappukarans*). Although drafting of the main measure began almost immediately the bill did not pass its third reading until 10 June 1959, only a few days before the Centre intervened to impose Presidential Rule. By the time the bill returned with the President's comments the Congress-PSP ministry was in office and the final version—which passed into law on 21 January 1961—was significantly modified to accommodate landed interests. In the event the revised bill had little real impact as crucial provisions were struck down by the Supreme Court in 1961 and the Kerala High Court in 1963. However, the measure is of vital significance for assessing communist policy and understanding the politics of 1957-60, including the polarization of rural interest groups.

Two striking features of the ministry's approach to land reform stand out: its moderation; and its effort to escape the problems of effecting significant change raised elsewhere by bureaucratic implementation and judical review.[49] The bill's provisions for compensation and its objective of creating a free peasantry were, at one level, inevitable if the party was to work within the existing constitutional framework, especially as the government's majority in the Assembly was only two. In fact the draft followed the framework suggested by the Congress Agrarian Reform Committee of 1949, as did the definitive 1969 bill of the Marxist-led United Front (see below, p. 291).

Political constraints did not, however, conflict with the party's intentions. Namboodiripad had argued—*On the Agrarian Question in India* (1952) and *The Peasant in National Economic Reconstruction* (1954)—that land reform should be directed initially to the abolition of feudalism and the generation of capitalist relations in agriculture. This, the correct tactical line for a semi-colonial, semi-feudal country, would rally all the non-feudal classes behind the reform.[50] Achutha Menon, the CPI Finance Minister, added a further justification. The inclusion as 'tillers' of those who personally supervise cultivation but do not actually engage in manual labour themselves 'we thought...was necessary in the interests of production.'[51] He also noted that since the *per capita* availability of land was only one-third of an acre, no land redistribution could materially aid the labourer. What land was available was to be allocated first to tenants whose land had been resumed by the landlord for his personal use, second to landlords with less than five acres who had lost their land to labourers' co-operatives, and only then to individual agricultural labourers. More radical solutions—state ownership or collective farms— were ruled out by Namboodiripad on the grounds that the best revolutionaries try to help the peasantry carry out those schemes they have themselves evolved, whether or not they appeal to intellectuals 'from a scientific point of view'.[52]

It would be incorrect to imply that the ministry neglected the agricultural labourer. The security of hutment sites, the work of industrial relations and minimum wages committees, the new 'neutralist' police policy (see below, p.157) and the Agricultural Debt Relief Bill were all important; and it is worth noting that the party's organizational work on this front contributed to a greater rise in the daily wage rates for casual male field labour, relative to productivity, than anywhere else in India during the late 1950s and early 1960s.[53] In December 1957 the government fixed the minimum wages of agricultural labourers and at a level higher than those in the neighbouring state of Madras.

Nevertheless the true 'tiller' of the soil did not feature largely in the land reform draft. Herring's explanation is helpful: the agricultural labourer's consciousness was quasi-proletarian; he recognized the unreality of further fragmentation of land; and, beyond the propriet-ory right to his hutment site, concentrated on demands for improved wages, working conditions, and security of employment.[54] (In that sense the CPI–Congress Agricultural Workers Act of 1974, farm labour's 'Magna Carta' (see below, p. 301), was a socialist rather than reformist solution.) However, it would be unwise to lose sight of the influence of the *All-Kerala Karshaka Sangham* (Peasant Union) as a pressure group within the CPI. The agricultural labourers' unions, substantially scheduled caste in membership and in their organiza-tional infancy, were a less effective pressure group.

The second important feature of the bill was the party's subtle approach to the problem of execution and adjudication. The rela-tionship between the courts and land reform has been a destructive one in South Asia.[55] The ministry removed most clauses of the bill from the purview of the courts and charged the Land Board and Land Tribunals—composed of officials and non-officials—with its implementation, backed by advisory People's Committees. Argu-ment quickly developed over the composition and status of these popular committees. Congress alleged they would be packed with communists and party sympathizers. If this were true it was unbe-coming of Congress to complain, since as Namboodiripad ob-served, communists had been excluded from administrative posi-tions by past governments. Gopalan cites examples to show that the opposition parties were given disproportionate representation.[56] In principle there was much to be said for democratization of local administration, and, as Gough has shown, partisan considerations can be transcended by village consciousness of natural justice.[57] One puzzling aspect of the ministry's thinking remains. It did not seek to protect the bill under the 9th Schedule of the constitution which debars judicial review of state legislation relating to land reform. No satisfactory explanation has been offered to the author for this omission.

The Agrarian Relations Bill's major provisions are easily outlined. Fixity of tenure was conferred on a wide range of tenants and quasi-tenants. To obviate recent attempts by landlords to circum-vent the imminent legislation, the fact of cultivation was deemed to prove tenancy 'irrespective of the deed or document held by the landlord'. Landlords were permitted to resume land for personal cultivation subject to a variety of conditions and the payment of compensation; but, unless the landlord was a smallholder with less than five acres, he could not resume an acreage that would leave the tenant with less than a subsistence holding. Tribunals were to ad-judicate in the grey area of competing claims. Arrears of rent were drastically reduced and machinery was outlined for determining fair rents (between one-sixth and one-twelfth of the gross produce on dry lands and one-quarter and one-sixth on wet lands). On an appointed day, all *cultivating* tenants would be deemed to have purchased their holdings. The landlords' and intermediaries' rights would be vested in the government. The state was responsible for the collection of compensation from the tenants, which was set at sixteen times the fair rent for small owners (less for large) and to be paid in instalments. The ceiling on landholdings—fifteen acres of double-crop paddy or its equivalent—was clearly consonant with capitalist farming, though still the lowest in India. In addition there were further entitlements for families of more than five persons, but no family unit was to hold more than twenty-five acres of double-crop paddy. Needless to say, there was a good deal of room for evasion by the creation of new family units. The government also aroused criticism by sticking to its position that any voluntary transfers undertaken before 18 December 1957 would be accepted as valid.[58] Exemptions from the ceiling included not only public, religious, and charitable institutions but also plantations—not, however, the *kayals* of the Kuttanad. Twenty-two of the thirty-one members of the Liberation Struggle Committee in the Kuttanad owned more than 1,000 acres of *kayal* each.[59]

The ministry was determined to produce a bill that would both be workable and would achieve the widest possible consensus among the interests affected. On the eve of the introduction of the bill the communist *Karshaka Sangham* organized a monster demonstration demanding its speedy passage. However, the government took a broader view. Before the bill reached the Assembly there had been an extensive process of consultation, including discussions with the Central Committee on Land Reform and five Central ministries. According to Chander, the final draft rested on seven or eight versions produced in the Law and Revenue Departments, and Mrs Gouri, Achutha Menon, and Krishna Iyer were all closely involved.[60] The second reading lasted 124 hours. More than 1,000 amendments were debated of which 175—mainly government sponsored—were accepted. The bill was at last referred to Select Committee on 2 April 1958. In November Govindan Nair announced that its progress had been delayed; and the bill did not reach the Report stage until March 1959.

There were two important reasons for the relatively slow progress of the bill through the Assembly: the very complexity of the issues; and divisions within the party on the detailed shape of the bill.[61] Besides Congress itself, the major opposition to the bill came from the Nair Service Society, and Syrian Christian plantation and *kayal* interests. The NSS, representing a broad spectrum of land-holding interests, was in something of a special position. It could claim that its assistance in a number of central and north Travancore constituencies had put the CPI into power.[62] Several key figures in the Travancore section of the CPI were Nairs who had maintained contacts with non-communist Nairs, partly as a function of the party's entrist policy and partly from personal and family connections. Govindan Nair had, in his early life, been an active NSS worker, and like many retained a certain respect for Mannoth. Further, the Travancore communists recognized the dangers of provoking a Nair-Christian alliance. Finally, the consequences of partition and economic change generally had created the awkward problem of small Nair landlords whose tenants—often Christian—might be more prosperous than they were themselves. Leasing out of small parcels of land had taken place on a significant scale and any blanket transfer would give from the poor to the prosperous as well as vice-versa. The Travancore party therefore had grounds for counselling moderation and concession.

The agrarian situation in Malabar was not confused by such anomalies. The Malabar party members had few if any links with the NSS, and articulated the demands of the *Karshaka Sangham*.[63] Matters came to a head—allegedly compounded by conflict between the ministerial and organizational wings and personal rivalry between Govindan Nair and Damodaran—at the Alwaye State Plenum in November 1958. Influential cadres of Nair origin, it is claimed, were briefed by Mannath, to plead elements of the NSS case.[64] Ajoy Ghosh, the party's national General Secretary, sought a rapprochement at least as a matter of expediency; however, although the NSS won delay, such non-technical changes as took place in the bill as a result of almost daily meetings of the communist MLAs appear to have been 'radical'.[65] What concessions would have been necessary to secure a compromise acceptable to the NSS are unknown—Mannath had to consider the benefits of the bill to Nair tenants. Whether a deal would have averted the later invalidation of parts of the act in the courts is doubtful, but it might have averted the Liberation Struggle which commenced two days after the bill had completed its legislative stages. Mannath concluded that since the NSS could not influence the ministry's policy, the ministry must go.

Educational Reform

Kerala's education as measured by literacy levels and school-leaving and college qualifications was the best in India. Its record could largely be attributed to the work of private, communally based institutions, led by the Catholic Church, and to the financial support

of government. On all sides it was conceded, however, that reform
was necessary to eradicate corruption, communal bias,
maladministration and malpractice, and to confer on the government (which subsidized much of the private sector) a measure of
control commensurate with its financial commitments. Successive
governments from 1946 when Sir. C.P. Ramaswami Aiyar had
sought to take over all primary schools[66] to 1955 when Panampilly
Govinda Menon had introduced a private secondary school scheme,
had all been frustrated by the opposition of the Christian managers.

By the time the communists came into power the broad shape of
reform had been outlined and its political difficulties made plain. For
the party there were three reasons for taking up the issue: its 'duty to
Toddy Tappers',[67] the educationally disadvantaged Ezhavas; the
support enjoyed by the party among teachers; and the importance of
shaping the minds of the young. The opposition also claimed that
the Education Minister, Mundassery, was motivated by personal
animus against the Catholic managements because he had been
dismissed from a Christian college after a visit to China, despite
twenty-seven years' service.

The draft bill presented to the Assembly on 13 July 1957 aimed to
provide for the better organization and development of educational
institutions in the state. For all its bitter reception by the Catholic
Church it was a modest enough set of proposals.[68] In thirty-six
clauses—prepared in the Secretariat and later approved by the
party—the government sought to regulate the appointment and
conditions of teachers, ensure proper records, establish local education authorities with official, nominated, and elected members, and
provide for temporary or permanent state takeover of managements
which failed to comply with the act where it became necessary in the
public interest to do so and in exchange for compensation. Vaguely
drafted some of the bill may have been, and though it threatened the
vested interests of college managements its general thrust need have
worried non-communists only on the improbable assumption that
the communists would govern Kerala for ever. Initially indeed the
bill was welcomed by Ezhavas, Nairs, the PSP, and the Malabar
wing of the Congress party, on which the Christians had no influence. The sectional character of the opposition to the bill is indicated
by the fact that the Select Committee, on which the communists did
not have a majority, spent its time modifying and clarifying the
clauses rather than rejecting them.[69] Only one of the four notes of
dissent attached to the report of the Select Committee emanated
from the six Congress members of the Committee. Hostility to the
bill in principle was essentially extraparliamentary and Christian.

The papacy of Pius XII was a period of conservative attitudes in the Roman Church and uncompromising attitudes towards communism, fuelled by the persecution of Christians in Eastern Europe. The complete control of children's education is, of course, jealously guarded. The Kerala church, itself highly traditionalist, faithfully reflected this outlook. Within weeks *Deepika,* the main Catholic daily, was urgently warning the ministry not to interfere with education after Mundassery had spoken of the disease found among church leaders of seeking to monopolize fundamental rights in education even by challenging the constitution.[70] On 28 May 1957 Catholic bishops met at Eranakulam to resolve to resist 'tooth and nail' any curtailment of the rights of school managements and any plan to 'nationalise education'.[71] The Vicar General of the Archdiocese of Changanacherry, Mgr Chittoor, went further. Educational institutions were as sacred to Catholics as their churches and they were prepared to lay down their lives for the cause of educational freedom.[72]

Given the entrenched attitudes of the Roman Church and the provocative tone of the minister, it was not surprising that no attempt was made to achieve a compromise. The bill's progress was rapid. The Select Committee report was presented on 24 August 1957 and the bill completed its stages on 2 September. The real struggle, however, was to take place in Delhi. The Christian contribution to the Congress party in Kerala was fully appreciated at the Centre: without the churches the KPCC would have been a sorry organization. The point was driven home in organizational elections held in 1958-9 when the Catholic Church used its influence to secure pliant local officers and (April 1959) R. Sankar, a stalwart anti-Communist, as president of the KPCC. Central intervention was facilitated by the doubts widely expressed as to whether the bill infringed the rights of minorities as enshrined in the constitution. On the advice of the Union cabinet, the President took the unusual but legitimate course of referring the bill to the Supreme Court for an Opinion. On 17 May 1958 the Court reported that some clauses were, indeed, destructive of minority rights as defined in Article 30(1) of the constitution and that others came perilously near to violating them. The President, in returning the bill, made no specific recommendations but the ministry accepted the tenour of the Supreme Court's Opinion. A revised version was passed by the Assembly in November 1958 and secured presidential assent on 19 February 1959.

A further clash in the educational sphere was provoked by the ministry's decision to take over the preparation and the publication of textbooks, a course increasingly followed by non-communist state governments in order to check profiteering and to encourage uniformity of content and standards. Critics naturally raised the danger of communist bias and cited chapter and verse from the first productions.[73] In response, the government appointed an Expert Committee under Kuruvilla Jacob in October 1958 to examine the allegations. In January 1959 the ministry published a brief summary of the Committee's report which Jacob found it necessary to 'clarify'.[74] The Committee found that, though there had been no concerted attempt to indoctrinate the pupils in anti-religious ideas or communist ideology, haste and the absence of adequate vetting had led to expression of the opinions and prejudices of individuals (especially in the area of social studies), offence to social, religious, and political sentiments, and a belittling of the achievements of India in comparison with those of China. For all the criticism, succeeding Kerala governments have persisted with offficial texts.

The Catholic Church's hostility to the educational reforms was so intense that it turned for support to its traditional rival, the NSS. Mannath, though primarily motivated by his fears of the impact of land reform on Nairs, also had grievances on education. He had understood that one concrete reward for partial Nair support for the CPI at the 1957 election would be the approval of an NSS engineering college to be sited at Palghat. Mundassery, however, on behalf of the party informed Mannath late in 1958 that the money was needed for Ezhava education and that the government would not support a Nair college.[75] Further, the effect of the revision of the Education Bill to safeguard the rights of minorities was to leave the NSS institutions as those most likely to suffer.

Faced with an alliance of Christian and Nair, the ministry now indicated its readiness to make concessions.[76] A common friend of Mundassery and the Archbishop of Changanacherry arranged a meeting in March 1959 but no compromise emerged and the Catholic Church then decided to close its schools until the Education Act and its rules were amended. The churches now prepared to defy the rule of law, the very crime of which they had accused the communists. *Deepika*, semi-official organ of the Catholics, quoted the Biblical reference from an earlier pastoral letter directed at Sir C.P.'s plan to take over primary schools: 'he that hath a purse, let him take it . . . and he that hath not, let him sell his coat and buy a sword . . .'[77] Congress kept its distance, partly because many shared Nehru's own reservations about the constitutional propriety of such agitations against a duly elected government, partly because of anxiety about aligning with communal forces, and partly because of internal party divisions. When the KPCC sought guidance from the central leadership, it was Mrs Gandhi who visited Kerala in early May and openly endorsed the demands of the private school managements and the right of the people to seek to thwart the legislation of their duly elected government.[78] This was the very stance which the communists had at least temporarily foresworn in adopting the parliamentary road.

Law and Order

One justification advanced by an opposition that wishes to flout the normal rules of democracy is that government has lost its legitimacy by acting in a flagrantly partisan and lawless way. The Liberationists alleged that this was indeed what had taken place. The detailed charges turned on two issues: the ministry's new policy of police neutrality in labour, property, and political disputes, and party interference in the normal course of justice. In its manifesto the CPI had promised far-reaching changes in the use of the police. The police, Namboodiripad declared, 'should not be used in an anti-people way' to break up strikes or agitations or to side with the propertied against the propertyless. Their main duty was to investigate 'anti-social crimes'. At the same time the Chief Minister emphasized that the toiling classes would not be allowed to go beyond a 'well-defined limit' in collective bargaining and direct action. The personal life and property of the employer or landowner was inviolable.[79] According to the opposition, the government went much further by conducting a virulent press campaign in party journals against officers of integrity and independence including the Inspector General of Police, Chandrashekhar Nair, infiltrated the force with party men and sympathizers, and generally demoralized the service by transfers and threats.[80] The second charge was neatly summarized by Panampilly Govinda Menon, the former Congress Chief Minister, in July 1958: 'If the Communists violated laws, they would not be arrested; if they were arrested, they would not be prosecuted; if they were prosecuted, the cases would be withdrawn; and if the cases ended in conviction, the sentences would be remitted ...'[81]

In private the party did not dispute the existence of so-called cell courts—summary justice meted out by party officials—and in certain communist strongholds such as Alleppey and Trichur there was some settling of scores in the class war.[82] The communists deny that revolutionary justice was ever party policy. According to M.N. Govindan Nair the excesses resulted from the party Centre's loss of control over a membership which doubled during the life of the ministry without the thorough vetting and apprenticeship required for admission in the past and the adherence of many more sympathizers who included opportunists, hooligans, and anti-social elements. 'The comrades were too impatient, too undisciplined, too stupid.'[83]

The *prima facie* evidence of a breakdown in law and order generally is set out in the State Administration Reports: in 1956 there were just under 9,000 cognizable crimes; in 1957 10,000, rising to 15,000 in 1959.[84] Murders rose from 167 in 1956 to 294 in 1959; and riots and unlawful assemblies grew from under 500 in 1956 to nearly 2,000 in 1959. No such alarming increases took place in the neighbouring states of Madras and Mysore.[85] This rise in crimes known to the police was matched by a decline in the detection rate from 41 to 27 per cent.[86] A couple of hundred 'political prisoners' were amnestied when the government took up office;[87] and up to the end of 1958 1,800 cases were withdrawn mainly—according to the Law Minister—in the wake of the settlement of industrial and other agitations.[88] Despite and because of this evidence it is doubtful whether a strong case for a communist-inspired breakdown of law and order can be sustained.

Table 6.1　 *Kerala 1956-1967:　Criminal Statistics*

Year	True cognizable crimes	No. of murders	Rioting and unlawful assemblies
1956	8,745	167	479
1957	10,461	256	870
1958	13,002	287	1,478
1959	14,741	294	1,893
1960	14,070	249	1,114
1961	14,289	261	1,181
1962	13,053	221	969
1963	13,120	204	1,002
1964	13,791	228	1,187
	14,156★		
1965	*15,383*	267	736
1966	*15,175*	247	972
1967	*17,992*★★	297	1.374

★A new categorization began in 1964, shown in italic type.
★★This marked increase is associated with the difficult economic conditions of the period.
Source: Administration Reports.

The accuracy of the statistics is a matter of surmise. Bayley's emphasis on the susceptibility of Indian criminal data to political pressures[89] might suggest that the general incidence of crime could well have been higher, though the reporting of murders is less likely to vary for these reasons. The statistics may also have been affected by the amalgamation of Malabar with Travancore-Cochin. Relatively speaking the figures do record a deterioration in law and order, though the rise in riot and unlawful assemblies was, almost by definition, the work of the opponents rather than the supporters of governments. When the statistics for the communist period are compared with those for the 1960s it is noteworthy that true cognizable crimes do not fall dramatically. What does decline is riotous assembly and murder. Even if a generous allowance is made for the probability of under-reporting of crime between 1957 and 1959 and full credence given to the qualitative evidence that party workers and their lower caste supporters took the law into their own hands the Kerala crime rate during the late 1950s of roughly one per thousand persons is scarcely an indication that law and order had broken down. In a society chronically afflicted by poverty, debt, unemployment, and landlessness it is a remarkably low figure.[90]

What excited and alarmed the higher castes was not, outside certain localities, any imminent fear of robbery or assault, but lawlessness of the mind: 'Paul [a wealthy Christian] stopped to curse, his handsome face turning a slow red. "You saw that fellow. He did not get off the path for us. Well, he is an Unseeable. Of course, we have done away with Unseeability a long time ago and that's only right. But until six months ago that fellow knew his place; when he saw me he would get off the path; today he nearly brushed me aside. That is what they call equality."'[91] This attack on caste oppression and the domination of the local *muthalalee* (rich man or boss) was an uncivil disobedience which rapidly alienated many of those among the higher castes who had supported the CPI or viewed its victory complaisantly in 1957.

The Labour Front

Although Kerala was industrially underdeveloped the working class was well organized and a growing political force. In 1956-7 there were nearly 800 registered trade unions with a claimed membership of 130,000, rising to 1,650 with a claimed membership of 320,000 in 1959-60. Three of the national union centres were represented—in ascending order of industrial militancy the Congress INTUC, the CPI AITUC, and the RSP UTUC—but of these it was the AITUC which dominated. In 1957-8 80 per cent of union members belonged to the AITUC compared with about 30 per cent nationally.[92]

During the 1950s the policy of the AITUC nationally had veered dramatically towards moderation and the encouragement of Indian economic development even at the price of the short-term interests of the working class. By 1952 the party had come round to supporting capitalist and state-sector activity as opposed to imperialist enterprise, and to general support for the Soviet-aided Second Five

Year Plan: 'while fighting for the workers' demands, we must learn to combine the demands of the worker with the demands of the employer...and defend our national interests against foreign monopoly capital.'[93] The new moderate industrial line emphasized that 'every struggle need not culminate in a strike...strikes must be peaceful in order to secure the largest measure of popular support' and that struggles should combine strikes, mass actions, including (though there was resistance to this) such non-proletarian forms as *satyagraha* and hunger strike, collective bargaining, wage boards, and parliamentary work.[94]

The formation of the communist ministry in Kerala was therefore an interesting test of the new tactics. T.V. Thomas, the state's AITUC leader, became Labour Minister and committed himself to implementing AITUC policy.[95] Namboodiripad, speaking at the silver jubilee session of the AITUC at Ernakulam in December 1957, urged the need for a long-term solution of labour-capital relations. There was no intention of 'forcefully subduing' the capitalist classes. Unless there was close co-operation of workers and owners and 'unless the resources of the State, private capitalists as well as the financial resources even of the smaller man were tapped in order that all the existing industrial units were not only maintained but further expanded ... and new industrial units were established, the working class in Kerala had no salvation.'[96] The instructions to the police to limit their intervention in labour disputes to the protection of life and property rested on an equitable view of relations between labour and capital, not a belief in industrial licence. Management was less likely to engage in realistic negotiation of disputes if it could call upon the police to intervene to disperse agitated labour. In the Congress propaganda offensive of 1957-9 it was often forgotten that perhaps the most hotly contested police firing in a labour dispute—on the European-owned Pasumala estate—in erstwhile Travancore-Cochin had involved the Congress INTUC.[97]

The CPI ministry's labour policy was essentially constructive, notwithstanding some partiality in its administration. T.V. Thomas, the Labour Minister, was not only a veteran union leader but also a well-known critic of mass militancy except as a last resort and an advocate of negotiation and conciliation.[98] In addition to granting increases in wages to all but the highest-paid government servants, the government expanded the scope of minimum wages legislation. It implemented the recommendations of the 1955 report on the coir industry produced by the G. Parameswaran Pillai Committee. The introduction of uniform wages, the elimination of middlemen, and the creation of the Coir Industrial Relations Council, coupled with the strong CPI control of the workforce, virtually eliminated strikes in the coir industry between 1957 and 1960. Tripartite consultative bodies were established or developed in all the important industries with the state-wide Industrial Relations Board, a reconstituted version of the earlier Labour Advisory Committee, at the apex. Finally on 2 April 1959 the ministry introduced its comprehensive Industrial Relations Bill, which, however, proved a casualty of the imposition of Presidential rule. Based upon a report from a subcommittee of the Industrial Relations Board, the measure was centrally concerned with the prevention, investigation, and settlement of disputes, and, according to Karnik—an anti-communist commentator—bore a close family resemblance to the 1946 Bombay Industrial Relations Act which had encouraged 're-sponsible unionism' by promoting one union in each industry.[99]

The 'one industry one union' formula had already been tried in Kerala in the form of the T.V.–Sreekantan agreement (see above, p. 61) with rather different results: a proliferation of rival unions in advance of inter-party negotiations as to which union enjoyed majority support in each industry; physical clashes between RSP and CPI supporters; the destruction of the prospects for a united front of left-wing labour against capital; and irresponsible unionism. The RSP UTUC as well as the Congress INTUC believed, on the evidence of events since the CPI had come to power, that the 1959 Bill would be used, whatever its preamble said, to further the interests of the AITUC. Whether or not all the UTUC and INTUC charges against the ministry could be sustained, there seems little doubt that the communist government—like Congress governments before it—favoured its own unions. There were indications of discrimination in the reference of disputes to adjudication, as for example in the two-month INTUC strike at the government-managed Sitaram Mills, Trichur,[100] while the police tailored their attitudes to disputes on occasion according to which party was involved.[101]

On the other hand the opposition parties inevitably sought to create embarrassment for the government by stirring up industrial discontent. Despite the dominance of the moderately inclined AITUC and the reference of a large percentage of disputes to tripartite bodies, the number of days lost through strike action remained far higher than in neighbouring Madras or Mysore.[102] No figures are available for disputes involving the different trade union federations but it is clear that, with the exception of the plantations strike of 1958, the major disputes involved either INTUC or UTUC. The plantations strike, which greatly inflated the number of days lost of 1958, involved the CPI for two reasons: the principal employer, the British–owned Kanan Devan Company, was a representative of foreign monopoly capital; and the fierce rivalry between the three union federations in the tea industry. In sum it would be fair to say that the communist ministry seriously attempted to implement current AITUC policy while none the less using, or permitting its local leaders to exploit, governmental influence to strengthen its own section of the union movement.

On one issue, however, relations between the ministerial and union wings of the CPI were seriously strained: the use of firearms and *lathis* against strikers. In July 1958 after an attack on the factory manager of a cashew canning factory by UTUC-led workers, the Revenue Divisional Officer ordered the police to fire to disperse the workers. In Indian police practice, fire is directed at individuals and to kill.[103] Two workers died. Damodaran, the Malabar party secretary later recorded, 'I remember vividly how the situation developed. We were stunned. Workers had been shot dead...while the Communists were in office. The immediate response of *all* the comrades present was to condemn the firing, institute an immediate enquiry, give compensation to the bereaved families, publicly apologise to the workers on strike and give a public assurance that such a thing would never happen again...This was our instinctive class response. But a discussion started which lasted for two hours and at the end of it the decisions taken were completely different...The logic of the comrades who advocated changing the initial position...went something like this: if we attack the police, there will be a serious decline in their morale; if there is a serious decline in their morale the anticommunist movement will be strengthened...our government will be overthrown; if our government is overthrown it will be a tremendous blow against the communist movement. The final resolution...defended the police action.'[104] On behalf of AITUC, Dange issued a statement regretting that the police had to resort to firing but pointing out that this, as the first incident in 16 months, compared favourably with the record of previous Congress and PSP ministries in Kerala.[105] Despite the closing of ranks, the death of the strikers contributed to the growing conflict between ministerial 'moderates' and organizational 'radicals'. Thereafter there were further firings and *lathi* charges. According to the government the final count (but opposition figures are higher) was eight *lathi* charges in which seventy-eight persons were injured and four firings in which four were killed and ten injured, exclusive of the deaths and casualties during the climax of the Liberation Struggle in June and July 1959.[106]

Administration and Administrative Reforms

The administration of Travancore-Cochin had been marred by communalism, nepotism, political patronage, and simple inefficiency. In its manifesto the CPI promised to restore both honesty and economy to the government by means of a substantial degree of decentralization. Despite the party's record in local administration and the Chief Minister's known integrity, popular expectations were not entirely fulfilled. According to the opposition, the CPI had placed the interests of the party before those of the state, of its own supporters before those of the citizens at large, and tolerated individual self-aggrandizement.

It would be impossible to check the many allegations of favouritism, corruption, maladministration, and incompetence levelled at the government; and, in view of the politically charged atmosphere, unwise to presume there was substance in the charges simply because they were widely credited.

However, there is evidence of the intrusion of party interest into administration. In September 1958 the Law Minister assured a conference of District Collectors and police officers that the interference by local party officials in day-to-day administration would be checked.[107] In one instance Namboodiripad himself ordered an inquiry into serious allegations of public loss and party gain in the purchase of grain from Andhra. According to *Link* (9 August 1964), the Chief Minister was lured into conceding an investigation by the skilful debating of the opposition leader P.T. Chacko. The Deputy Controller of Accounts, C.Sankara Menon, who had audited the accounts of the state government's negotiated contract with a Madras firm for the supply of 5,000 tons of rice, deposed to the Inquiry Commission that the state had incurred an avoidable loss of Rs 153,000. The Commission's report, submitted on 13 February 1959, accepted Menon's deposition and concluded that there were strong grounds for suspecting the deal was not solely dictated by considerations intrinsic to the merits of the situation. Noting that there was nothing in the antecedents of the firm in question to suggest that it was capable of undertaking such a deal and that it was unknown to the rice merchants of Kerala, the Commission observed that the agent was known to K.C. George, the CPI Food Minister, and was formerly an active member of the party. Whether the loss was due to the ineptitude of the Madras firm 'or to something worse' did 'not fall within the scope of this enquiry.[108] Much greater losses were incurred through the ministry's use of co-operative societies for the construction of public works (Labour Contract Societies) and the running of the toddy (country liquor) industry. The Public Works Department in Travancore-Cochin, as elsewhere in India, had been a by-word for corruption and inefficiency which the CPI attributed in large part to the use of private contractors. On taking

office the communists established forty-two Labour Contract
Societies and directed that government works be given to them at 50
per cent more than the estimated cost as specified by government
engineers. During 1957-8 400 items of work had been undertaken at
a cost of Rs. 2.3 million. Several societies failed, with the loss of the
sums advanced, and there was considerable obscurity about the
financial arragements in general, the opposition alleging that a
significant part of the money found its way into CPI funds.[109] Similar
efforts to eliminate middlemen in the sale of toddy led to a considerable reduction in excise revenue and an increase in illicit liquor
trafficking.[110] While the new system benefited the exploited toddy-
tappers it indicated a certain indifference to the maximization of
government revenue. According to the RSP leader, Sreekantan
Nair, Labour Contract Societies and Toddy Tappers' Societies
were sanctioned only to communists and impediments were thrown
in the path of non-communist co-operatives.[111]

Nevertheless the above evidence must be viewed in the All-India
context of the late 1950s. The senior-most administrator in the
Kerala Secretariat, the Chief Secretary, expressed a view commonly
held among senior civil servants when he said that while there had
been maladministration under the communists there had been just as
much under Congress in Travancore-Cochin. He asserted that the
communist government would, given a chance, be no better and no
worse than provincial Congress governments elsewhere in India.
The one difference, in his view, was that 'the Communists are new
to power and far more dependent than the Congress on local party
men who were often uneducated, ill-informed and vindictive.'
When a communist had a grievance he took it straight to the Minister
who often acted unwisely and without consulting his officers. The
Chief Minister, he reported, was very much against this and had
asked him to recommend reforms. The Secretariat inclined to the
view that party interest intruded into administration irrespective of
the party in power.[112]

Information on the relationship between senior officials and
ministers is limited. In general, bureaucrats in India were under
stress as a consequence of their changing responsibilities after
Independence.[113] The central role of the administrator was no longer
that of the omnipotent District Collector, primarily concerned with
law and order, and revenue, but rather the file-moving Secretary to
Government at the beck and call of elected Ministers and charged
with a growing variety of development and welfare tasks.

In Kerala this broad picture requires modification in several ways:
the Travancore-Cochin-trained officials had considerable experience of development and welfare activities albeit under autocratic

conditions; many officials, especially in Malabar, had experience of working with local democratic institutions, sometimes communist-controlled; since Independence the frequent changes of ministry had encouraged flexibility as well as a capacity to carry on the administration irrespective of political developments; and finally the Secretariat personnel were not themselves immune from the widespread disenchantment with Congress and PSP politicians. The tone of the Chief Minister's initial address to the senior Secretariat staff was a firm but sympathetic appeal for mutual co-operation. 'Our experience and approach to conducting affairs and yours are of two different types. Both of them should be combined for the good of the people and the state ... It is true that in administrative affairs, excepting one (Dr. Menon) none of us have any experience. In this we have to learn a lot from you. Similarly we have opportunities to feel the pulse of the people. You will have to learn from us ... There may by many among you who have ideas about the Communist Party. There may even be a few among you who do not like the democratic system itself. We are building a Socialist society. The old social order is changing. You must correctly understand this change ... Only if we exchange our views ... can we succeed in building a Socialist order ... let us be partners.'[114]

The CPI was officially committed to the view of senior officials as agents of the ruling class rather than servants of the people. In evidence to the Administrative Reforms Committee, the Alleppey District unit denied there was any need for IAS officers other than the Chief Secretary.[115] To protect ministers from their civil servants, the party introduced non-official personal assistants for the Chief Minister and three other ministers. At the suggestion of Achutha Menon, party cells were formed inside departments. Whether these were, as Menon said, designed to expedite the work of administration, or, as the opposition claimed, to subvert the system, there is no evidence that they significantly affected the working of the Secretariat for good or ill.

Until the latter part of 1958 relations between ministers and senior officials appear to have been generally satisfactory. One or two of the more unbending secretaries were transferred but there were no complaints from ministers of lack of co-operation from the IAS cadre as a whole. Officials found their new masters at least no worse than the old and in some cases decidedly better: full of ideas, ready to listen, and aware of administrative sensitivities to the bending of rules in the interests of party.[116] Towards the end of 1958 there were, however, signs of a deterioration in relations. In September Namboodiripad complained that Congressmen were inciting disobedience in the Secretariat, probably a reference to the so-called 'class of '57', a group of young officers close to P.T. Chacko, the (Christian) Congress opposition leader, and in September Krishna Iyer was seeking to conciliate District Collectors (see above, p. 145). There were allegations in party circles that the Chief Secretary was functioning on the orders of the Centre and not those of the Chief Minister; and according to one IAS officer by 1959 the line between pro- and anti-communists in Kerala was said to run right through the Secretariat.[117]

Nevertheless, the key figures in the party saw the problem in non-marxist terms. Govindan Nair, the party secretary, later stated that the 'main weakness' of the ministry had been its failure to improve the *efficiency* of the administrative machine. His evidence to the Administrative Reforms Committee dwelt on the absence of a sense of responsibility among government officers and employees, the duplication of work, the neglect of business-like management of men and resources, and the weakness of the accounting system.[118] This Committee, set up in August 1957, and chaired by Namboodiripad himself, was no propaganda exercise. Its members were Mundassery, the Education Minister, not usually regarded as a 'party man'; the Chief Secretary; a retired Chief Secretary, G. Parmeswaran Pillai; a former Travancore-Cochin minister, P.S. Nataraja Pillai; the founder of the Indian Institute of Public Administration, Professor V.K.N. Menon; and the left-wing Congressman, H.D. Malaviya. The terms of reference were to review the existing administrative machinery; to assess its adequacy for a democratic government in a *welfare state*; to recommend improvements in co-ordination, measures for the decentralisation of powers at various levels, and procedures for the expeditious despatch of government business; and to suggest methods for the democratisation of the organs of Government with a view to the effective participation of local self-governing institutions.[119] All interested parties were invited to submit comments. A detailed questionnaire was distributed to more than a thousand persons inside and outside the state; 158 witnesses were examined; and the committee sat for 62 days on Part I of its report alone.

The report, published in July 1958, was widely welcomed, and apart from a minor note of dissent from Menon and Nataraja Pillai effectively unanimous. On the principle that the composition of a committee reflects the intentions of those establishing it, the Chief Minister sought consensual reform, not drastic upheaval. The Committee rejected such far-reaching solutions as were demanded by Damodaran—the only witness to refer to 'the ideal of a Socialist State'—who urged that budget proposals should go from an elected District Board to the Assembly for decision and then be returned to the District Board for implementation.[120]

The basic unit of administration at village level was to be the panchayat. An elective body, it was to act both as an adviser to and an agent of government in the areas of development and welfare. These modest proposals were broadly incorporated into the ministry's Kerala Panchayats Bill, 1958, which though lapsing on the dissolution of the Assembly was resurrected in the Kerala Panchayats Act, 1960, piloted by the succeeding Congress-PSP government. Above the panchayat the Committee recommended the reconstitution of the ministry's Block Advisory Committees as indirectly elected taluk councils confined to an advisory role. At District level the Committee was divided between those who favoured District Boards with some teeth—elected bodies with both agency functions and independent powers—and those who preferred a kind of non-elected advisory council to the District Collector. The government, mindful of the record of the erstwhile Malabar District Board, based its Kerala District Councils Bill, 1959, on the former recommendation; but this, like the Panchayats Bill, lapsed on the dissolution of the Assembly. Another casualty was the Calicut City Municipal Bill, 1959.[121] Overall, then, the ministry took its twin objectives of more democratic and more efficient administration seriously even though pressures from the party organization at the local level in particular and from the opposition at the Secretariat level frustrated its intentions.

Retrospect

The central issues discussed in this chapter, as also Chander's study of the legislative process during this period, suggest that the CPI seriously addressed itself to the implementation of Congress-socialist style reforms. As governing party the CPI differed from Congress (and the PSP) by virtue of its discipline and coherence. There was of course no single understanding of the purpose of assuming office at the provincial level; the creation of a joint committee of the legislative communist group and the party organization in part reflected this;[122] but the democratic centralist structures of the party ensured that party decisions were more, rather than less, consistently applied. Like any other party which has won power through democratic elections, the CPI experienced a conflict of loyalties between the demands of its own 'constituency' and its desire to expand it on the one hand and considerations of public interest above party and group on the other. Namboodiripad in retrospect noted that several of his friends in the Congress and other Opposition parties told him that he was no more the leader of the communist party but the Chief Minister of the State and so their leader too. 'I entirely agreed. The Government... should be carried on in the interests of all parties by persons who can rise above the narrow interests of their own party ... I was, however, tempted to explain:"physician, heal thyself!" to those of my friends who belonged to the Congress Party.'[123] A similar point of view was expressed in marxist language in the July 1957 Politbureau directive to Communist legislators: 'the parliament and State legislatures have become the most important forums for fighting for the cause of the people ... for uniting the democratic masses on policy issues ... Tendencies to move in one's own narrow groove must be discarded ... Our work must reflect the mass movement and comrades must constantly develop a truly national approach on all matters. At the same time, they must take the position of the exploited classes ... This class standpoint must on no account be abandoned ...'[124]

No account of the communist ministry could avoid placing the accent on education and land reform. In the ensuing confrontation between property and poverty there were acrimonious exchanges in the Assembly, demonstrations and counter-demonstrations, growing politicization on the labour front and in government service and the settling of old scores. While some part of this deterioration in liberal democratic protocol might be put down to past precedents set by Congress, to the CPI's inexperience, and to its rapid transformation from vanguard to mass party it should be emphasized that the experience was for Kerala central to the mobilization of the poor—historically divided by caste and community—along class lines. As Rudolph and Rudolph have argued, the 'very success of the CPI in gaining power under the banner of class ideology and in governing, for the most part, in the interests of the poor and dispossessed crystallized class tendencies within the various communities and helped free their members for mobilization by party rather than by community ...'[125]

However, it would be misleading to leave the impression that the chequered history of the CPI ministry was simply a titanic battle between the forces of light and darkness. Red star-red peril polemics ignore the fact, that for the most part, life went on very much as usual in both the Assembly and the Secretariat until the last months of the ministry. Controversial bills occupied a small proportion of legislative time: there was also a great deal of routine legislation, needed to reconcile the laws of Malabar and Travancore-Cochin and to promote 'modernization'. In any case a British legal system adapted to Indian conditions—the Kerala Hackney Carriages Bill, for example—was bound to be a severe constraint on the communist transformation of society by parliamentary means. Those without previous experience as legislators discovered the utility of access to the Secretariat, directly and through party channels, in tackling the problems and grievances of constituents and constituencies. And it would be admitted inside the party, as well as alleged without, that some MLAs succumbed to the temptations of office not as party intermediaries but as individuals.[126] In background CPI MLAs shared more in common with the MLAs of other parties than with the party's workers on the organizational front. In sum the party developed an appreciation of the possibilities and techniques—as well as the limitations—of work on the parliamentary front, though uncertain or ambivalent as to its ultimate importance in Indian communist strategy.

Assembly work should not be seen in isolation from the holding of representative office in lower elective bodies or in trade unions and other mass organizations. Panchayat boards, for instance, elected by universal suffrage and with significant powers had existed in all parts of the state since 1950. They provided a training ground for the class struggle, electoral mobilization, and administrative and technical expertise and a stepping stone in a political career that could lead to the Assembly. Although candidates were officially forbidden to campaign for election under party labels, conflict in Kerala panchayats, in contrast to the situation elsewhere at the time, took place primarily between the propertied and the propertyless and the high and low castes. Gough emphasizes that, despite the intensification of the class struggle at the local level during 1957-9, it was generally contained within bounds during the 1950s and early 1960s for a number of reasons of which some are pertinent here: the dynamics of electoral politics in multi-caste panchayats requires even a revolutionary movement to compromise and manouevre; there was a scepticism of officialdom and a commitment to the well-being of the locality which often transcended party boundaries; as well as the tendency of small and exclusive groups with administrative rather than policy-making functions to seek consensual solutions. Whether they did so consciously or not, Gough states that communist members of politically mixed boards did seek to insulate their board work from the wider political battle, to keep discussions concrete, and to avoid reaching decisions by voting.[127] Local government in Kerala nourished a subtle reconciliation of revolutionary and constitutional roles which was supportive of the 'Centrism' which characterized not only the 1957-9 ministry but the Namboodiripad-led Kerala CPM after the split and the Achutha Menon-led Kerala CPI in the 1970s.

While this short review of some of the major controversies surrounding the 1957-9 ministry's record has tried to separate reality from rumour, the very currency given to the view that communist profession was at odds with communist practice has an unnoticed significance for the theory and tactics of peaceful transition. In Travancore–Cochin (see above, p. 134) the CPI lost the support or at least the benevolent neutrality of key influentials, many middle-class sympathizers, students, and such sections of the under-privileged as were organized by the Catholic Church and the SNDP *yogam*. Lenin had, of course, emphasized the importance of dispelling petty bourgeois democratic illusions as a primary aim of the parliamentary tactic. Gramsci, however, is equally relevant. Distinguishing Italy and Western Europe as a whole from Russia and Eastern Europe in terms of the degree to which civil society had become differentiated from the state, Gramsci argued that the state was only an outer ditch in advanced societies behind which there stood a powerful system of fortresses and earthworks.[128] To win power a social group must already exercise hegemony or leadership; to bring about real change, having won governmental authority, it must continue to lead.[129] The struggle was for the minds and hearts of the masses; and Gramsci's model of the sucessful deployment of such hegemony was the church.[130] Kerala, and certainly its southern part, is a complex society in which civil society is well developed. The communists had come to power in 1957 because they had established a hegemony counter to that articulated by Congress and its allied forces. However sympathetic one may be to the claim that dual standards are applied to communist as contrasted to other parties, it can be argued that the advance of the communist movement in Kerala was arrested because it permitted a precarious moral leadership to be eroded in 1957-9, in 1963-4 at the time of the split in the party, and in 1967-9 during the United Front ministry.

Notes

1   Karnik, *Communist Ministry and Trade Unions in Kerala*, p. 9.
2   *Hindu*, 6 Apr. 1957; Karnik, as n. 1, p. 9; Fic, *Kerala*, pp. 77 and 115.
3   Karnik, as n. 1, p. 9; 'Tactical Line' (1953), in DRS, *ICPD*, pp. 72-3.
4   *Kerala: a Report to the Nation* (1958). Malaviya was nephew of K.D. Malaviya, a leading Congress politician, both allegedly 'well-known fellow traveller(s)': Peter Sager, *Moscow's Hand in India: an Analysis of Soviet Propaganda* (Bombay, Lalvani Publishing House, 1967), p. 178.
5   *Communism in India*, pp. 481-2.
6   DRS, *KUC*.
7   *Kerala*, p. 115.
8   G.K. Lieten, 'Progressive State Governments: an Assessment of the

First Communist Ministry in Kerala', *Economic and Political Weekly*, 6 Jan. 1979.

9   Zinkin, p. 164; Mullik, p. 359.

10 Interviews, E.M.S. Namboodiripad, Tvm, Oct. 1970; T.V. Thomas, Alleppey, Nov. 1970; M.N. Govindan Nair, Tvm, Aug. 1973; K.C. George, Kulathoor, Aug. 1973; P. Raghavan, Tvm, Nov. 1977.

11 Zinkin, p. 154.

12 *New Left R*. 93, 1975, p. 47. Damodaran, however, was a signatory of the 'rightist' alternative resolution submitted by P.C. Joshi and others to the Palghat Congress. Fic, *Peaceful Transition to Communism in India*, p. 256.

13 Mullik, pp. 133–4 and 339–40.

14 *New Left R.* 93, 1975, p. 47.

15 C. Unniraja, 'Fifth Kerala Communist Conference', *New Age* (monthly), Jan. 1960, p.1.

16 Ibid.; *Proceedings of the Seventh Congress of the Communist Party of India, Bombay, 13-23 December 1964*, vol. 1: *Documents* (New Delhi, CPI, 1965), p. 109. See also *Our Tasks on Party Organisation. Adopted by the Central Committee of the CPI (M), Calicut, 28 October-2 November 1967* (Calcutta, CPI (M), 1968, pp. 5, 14–15, and *Times of India*, 22 Dec. 1968.

17 Zinkin, p. 155.

18 Interviews, former District Collectors, Tvm, Sept. 1974.

19 *Resolutions of the Communist Party of India. Adopted at the Extraordinary Party Congress, held in Amritsar in April 1958* (New Delhi, CPI, 1958), p. 15.

20 *Kerala*, pp. 90–6.

21 *Hindu*, 4 June 1958. Chinese experience is evident in Namboodiripad's thought at this period, reinforced by a visit to China in 1956, e.g. 'State System and the Communist Party of China', *New Age* (monthly), Dec. 1956.

22 For interesting indications of the ramifications of the Christian militia in Delhi as well as Kerala see Vadakkan, pp. 66–9.

23 Fic, *Kerala*, p. 114; *Deepika*, 18 Aug. 1958, also 9 and 14 Aug; cf. comment of *The Statesman* (Calcutta) on an interview with Fr Vadakkan: 'There must be two sides for a civil war, and Fr Vadakkan with his missionary zeal in the cause of peace, seems anxious and ready to provide one' (23 Aug. 1958).

24 Mullik, p. 344.

25 *Hindu*, 10 June 1958.

26 Fic, *Peaceful Transition to Communism in India*, pp. 380–1.

27 Ibid., p. 38.

28 Mullik, p. 343.

29 Vadakkan, p. 72. This leader of the Liberation Struggle now holds that the communists killed in self-defence after being attacked by drunken anti-social elements.

30 'Mr. Dange Disapproves of Police Firing in Kerala: Ministry May be Asked to Resign', *Times of India*, 28 July 1958; 'Leftist Coalition in Kerala Proposed: Dange's offer to PSP and RSP', *Statesman*, 5 Aug.

172   *Communism in Kerala*

1958; 'Move to Patch up Rift Among Kerala Reds', *IE*, 3 Sept. 1958.

31 'Nehru Critical of Kerala', *Statesman*, 8 Aug. 1958; 'Nehru Favours Impartial Probe into Kerala Situation', *Deccan Herald*, 11 Aug. 1958. Nehru had visited Kerala in late April at Namboodiripad's invitation when he had expressed himself glad that the CPI had veered somewhat to 'what I call a more reasonable approach in Indian terms. If they think in terms of India, they may veer more and more. In fact, if they think more and more they may cease to be a CP on international lines.' *New Age*, 4 May 1958. On his return to Delhi he was critical of the CPI as Muscovite in its 'thinking apparatus', *New Age*, 18 May 1958.

32 V.R. Krishna Iyer, *Police in a Welfare State* (New Delhi, Asian Book Centre, 1958).

33 'Central Executive Committee's Statement on Kerala', *New Age*, 24 Aug. 1958.

34 Ajoy Ghosh, *On the Decisions of the National Council* (New Delhi, People's Publishing House, 1958).

35 'Special Conference of the Kerala Communist Party', *The New Kerala*, 30 Nov. 1958; 'Disagreement on the Basic Approach: Different Trends in Communist Party', *The Weekly Kerala*, 4 Oct. 1958; 'Kerala Reds Face Grave Crisis', ibid., 1 Nov. 1958; 'New Bid for Power in the Communist Party: E.M.S. Namboodiripad Should Quit, says Ministerial Group', ibid., 8 Nov. 1958; 'Factionalism in Communist Party: Struggle for Power Takes New Form', ibid., 24 Jan. 1959.

36 *Malabar Herald*, 19 Jan. 1959; 'Namboodiripad's Mission to Moscow: Reactions in the Kerala Press', *The Weekly Kerala*, 10 Jan 1959. Namboodiripad was attending the 21st Congress of the CPSU.

37 Fic. *Kerala*, p. 110 and *Peaceful Transition to Communism in India*, p. 393.

38 Zinkin, p. 179.

39 Ibid.

40 A secret meeting was arranged by Mathew M. Kuzhiveli, the Malayalam Encyclopaedist, a friend of both Mundassery and the Archbishop of Changanacherry. Mundassery visited the Archbishop, convenor of the Bishop's Committee on Education, but no compromise emerged. *Deepika*, 10 Mar. 1959.

41 Mullik, p. 350; Zinkin, p. 179; *Deepika*, 26 June 1959; *Hindu*, 29 June 1959.

42 Zinkin, p. 181

43 Report of the Joint Session of the CPI National Council and Kerala State Committee, Trivandrum, 15 July 1959, *New Kerala*, 19 July 1959.

44 Mullik, pp. 351–7.

45 Thomas was alleged to have been directed by the State Committee to marry as a condition of ministerial office. He offended some as a non-teetotaler. Govindan Nair, a former NSS worker, had married into a prosperous Nair family, and maintained contact with the Nair establishment. Alleged party scandals are covered in K.C. John, *The Melting Pot: Kerala 1950s—1970s (1975)*. For brief biographies of Thomas and Govindan Nair see below, pp. 386 and 385.

46 See K.K. Nair, *Who is Who of Freedom Fighters*.

47 See his *Conflicts and Crisis, Political India: 1974* (1974), p. 54.

48 Varghese, pp. 234–43.

49 The author has benefited from discussions with R.J. Harring of the U. of Wisconsin, Madison, and Professor M.A. Oommen of the U. of Calicut.

50 E.M.S. Namboodiripad, *On the Agrarian Question* (1952), pp. 27, 49 and 61.

51 C. Achutha Menon, *The Kerala Agrarian Relations Bill: an Interpretation* (New Delhi, 1958), p.20.

52 *The Peasant in National Economic Reconstruction* (1954), p. 81.

53 M.A. Oommen, *Land Reforms and Socio-Economic Change in Kerala*, pp. 63–5. The average daily wage rate for male agricultural labour increased by 92 per cent during the period 1956–7 to 1964–5 in Kerala compared with 17 per cent in the Punjab, India's most prosperous agricultural state. Oommen notes elsewhere that the rise in wage rates was accompanied by a fall in days worked. 'Development of Capitalism Kerala Agriculture: Some Preliminary Observations', *Mainstream*, 19 Mar. 1977.

54 Herring, pp. 265–9.

55 Ibid., p. 275.

56 Namboodiripad, *Twenty-Eight Months in Kerala: a Retrospect* (1959), pp. 26 and 35; A.K. Gopalan, *Kerala—Past and Present* (1959), p. 114.

57 *J. of Asian and African Studies* III (3–4), 1968, p. 197.

58 It was alleged that senior members of the government had an interest in maintaining this date, and the name most frequently mentioned was Krishna Iyer, the Independent Law Minister; see ch. 5 above, n. 72.

59 *Janayugom* (Quilon, in Malayalam), 26 Sept. 1963.

60 N. Jose Chander, 'The Legislative Process in Kerala 1957–1969' (unpublished Ph.D. thesis, U. of Kerala, Tvm, 1973), pp. 188–91.

61 Ibid., pp. 220–9.

62 DRS, *KUC*, p. 67.

63 Membership in 1957 was 185,521. K.V.K. Warrier, 'Provincial Kisan Conference in Kerala', *New Age,* 27 Oct. 1957.

64 Chander, p. 207. Shortly afterwards Mannath called on Nairs in the CPI to resign and fight for the rights of the community after the ministry had declined to accept the recommendations of the Administrative Reforms Committee (1958) in favour of a gradual reduction of communal reservation in admission to government service, and a switch to an economic from a caste and communal basis in that reservation. *Malayala Manorama*, 28 Dec. 1958.

65 Chander, p. 229.

66 The CPI had supported the Catholic lobby as a result of its desire to build the widest coalition against the Dewan.

67 Zinkin, p. 158.

68 *Proceedings of the Kerala Legislative Assembly* (Malayalam, hereafter *PKLA*), I (19), p. 1643; *Towards a Better Education System: Two Years' Endeavour of Kerala Government* (Tvm, Govt of Kerala, 1959). *New*

Age, 16 Mar. 1958 quoted the London *Daily Telegraph* correspondent's interview with the Roman Catholic Archbishop, Dr Paul Varghese, in which the Archbishop said that the Education Bill 'is an instrument by which the Communists hope ultimately to strangle all religious faiths here and Roman Catholicism first,' a line claimed to have been approved in Moscow. The *Daily Telegraph's* correspondent commented: 'The truth seems to be that the Bill contains some necessary, if unpalatable medicine . . . but wrong doctors are administering it.'

69 Chander, pp. 146–7. For the ministry's account see J. Mundassery, *Kozhinja Ilakal*, vol. 2 (Trichur, 1965, in Malayalam), p. 123.
70 *Deepika*, 25 Apr. 1957.
71 Ibid., 30 May 1957.
72 Speaking at Aruvithura (Kottayam), 16 June 1957. *Deepika*, 18 June 1957.
73 DRS, *KUC*, pp. 46–9. The Bishops took particular exception to an abridged edition of Victor Hugo's *Les Misérables*, prescribed for the 9th school standard, as presenting a distorted and abusive account of convent life. *Deepika*, 19 Aug. and 10 Oct. 1958. For pro-government accounts see Malaviya, p. 40; and *Towards a Better Education System* (Tvm, Govt of Kerala, 1959).
74 DRS, *KUC*, pp. 47–9, and G.K. Lieten, 'Education, Ideology and Politics in Kerala 1957–59', *Social Scientist* (Tvm) 62, 1977, pp. 9–10.
75 Zinkin, p. 169.
76 See above, n. 00.
77 *Deepika*, 17 May 1959, quoting the Revd J. Kalacherry's Pastoral Letter no. 123 of 15 Aug. 1945 in which he quotes from St. Luke: 22: 36–8.
78 Nehru was reluctant to support the agitation, at least publicly. *Deepika*, 15 May 1959. Mullik, ch. 3. It should be noted that the KPCC was still racked with factionalism. High Command received contradictory advice from Kerala factions. For Mrs Gandhi's visit see *Deepika*, 3 May 1959.
79 E.M.S. Namboodiripad, 'Police and the People: a Basic Change in Approach is Necessary', *New Age*, 18 Aug. 1957.
80 DRS, *KUC*, pp. 73–5; Karnik, *Communist Ministry and Trade Unions in Kerala*, pp. 31–5. The *Report of the Kerala Police Reorganization Committee, 1960*, p. 12, opined that 'The greatest obstacle to efficient Police administration flows from the domination of party politics in the State administration.' As D.H. Bayley shows, Congress state governments were no less culpable than the Kerala communist ministry in this respect: *The Police and Political Development in India* (1969), pp. 374–5.
81 'Party Has Usurped Government's Functions: Panampilli Attacks Reds', *IE*, 30 July 1958.
82 *Malayala Manorama*, 30 June and 10 July 1957. *PKLA* III (5), pp. 33–4; KPCC, *Memorandum Submitted to the President, Indian Republic* (1958), pp. vi–vii; *Kerala's Answer to KPCC Charges* (CPI, 1959), pp. 42–3; K. Padmanabha Pillai, *Red Interlude in Kerala* (1959), pp. 65–8.
83 Zinkin, p. 164.

84 Govt of Kerala, *Administration Report 1957–8, 1958–59*, and 1959–60.
85 Namboodiripad noted a massive increase in crime between the period 1 Jan. to 15 Apr. in 1956 and the same period in 1957: 'Police and the People', *New Age*, 18 Aug. 1957. *The Statistical Abstract of Mysore 1959-60* (Bangalore, Govt of Mysore, 1967) shows a 60 per cent increase in cognizable crime between 1956 and 1957. However, the number of reported cases remained static in Mysore from 1957 to 1959 (*Administrative Statistics Mysore*, XXVIII: *Police*, p. 590). *Criminal Court Statistics, 1956-9* (Govt of Madras, Home Dept), shows a stable number of cognizable cases for Madras state. See also Malaviya, ch. 6.
86 Govt of Kerala, *Administration Report 1957–8*, p. 100 and *1958-9*, p.68
87 Such amnesties were not unusual in India. The 1954 PSP Travancore-Cochin ministry had amnestied prisoners serving sentences imposed after the Punnapra–Vayalar Rising of 1946. See also Namboodiripad, *Twenty-Eight Months in Kerala*, pp. 5–14. Mullik, however, reports 'much consternation in the Government of India' and that 'Prime Minister Nehru questioned the morality and the validity of this action more than once but restrained the hawks in the Government of India from interfering with the discretion of a non-Congress State Government' (pp. 339–40).
88 *PKLA* IV (13), p. 830; *PKLA* VIII (8), p. 582; *PKLA* I (2), pp. 23–6; IV (17), pp. 1244–5; VII (21), p. 1826.
89 Bayley, pp. 97–106.
90 In 1963 Kerala's crime rate (95.27 per 100,000 population) was the second lowest in India and its ratio of police to population (1960) the third highest (1: 1,263) Bayley, pp. 104 and 66. Serious crime was more than ten times greater in Britain per unit of population than in India (p. 105). Bayley does not deal in detail with the working of the CPI ministry's police policy but notes that the documentation of partiality in the administration of justice was a critical factor in turning the tide of opinion against it (p. 365). See Indian Commission of Jurists, 'Report of the Kerala Inquiry Committee', *J. of the International Commission of Jurists*, Winter 1959 and Spring-Summer 1960; *Report of the Kerala Police Reorganisation Committee 1960* (Tvm, Govt of Kerala, 1960).
91 Zinkin, p. 152.
92 H. Crouch, *Trade Unions and Politics in India* (1966), pp. 180, 184, and 293.
93 *Trade Union Record*, Aug. 1952, p. 103.
94 Overstreet and Windmiller, p. 374 and Crouch, p. 179.
95 *Trade Union Record*, 20 Jan. 1958.
96 Malaviya, pp. 39–40.
97 K. Ramachandran Nair, p. 123.
98 Ibid., p. 122; interviews, T.V. Thomas, Alleppey, Oct. 1970; N. Sreekantan Nair, Tvm, Nov. 1977; and E. Balanandan, Tvm, Aug. 1973.
99 *Report of the Sub-Committee of the Industrial Relations Board* (Govt of Kerala, 1957); *PKLA* VII (31), p. 2680; Karnik, *Communist Ministry and*

Trade Unions in Kerala, p. 14; Govt of Kerala, *Administration Report 1958-9*, p. 64. The delay in the introduction of the Industrial Relations Bill benefited the CPI AITUC position since its ascendancy was growing and might be checked by the establishment of formal machinery to establish one union per industry.

100 Jitendra Singh, pp. 70–4; Karnik, as preceding note, pp. 16–17. The dispute centred on the transfer of five INTUC members from one department to another, according to their union, to help to build up the AITUC. The communist account contends that the transfer was necessitated by the management's wish to increase production, that seven other workers not belonging to the INTUC union had agreed to the transfer, and that negotiations failed because of the recalcitrance of the Congress union leaders and lawyers. The Congress view is that the ministry declined to settle the issue through conciliation or refer it to adjudication because its objective was to oust INTUC from the department in question. After a prolonged dispute and much unfavourable publicity, the government yielded. In the subsequent adjudication, INTUC's case was substantially vindicated.

101 This does not mean there were instructions to this effect or for that matter that the ministry necessarily approved. Partiality was, however, condoned. Karnik (as n. 99 above) lists alleged instances of police intervention against non-CPI unions and neutrality where CPI workers were involved in violence (pp. 26–37).

102 K.N. Vaid, *Industrial Relations Statistical Series*, V: *Industrial Disputes in India* (New Delhi, Shri Ram Centre Press, n.d.).

103 Bayley. pp. 268-9.

104 *New Left R.* 93, 1975, p. 48. The subsequent judicial inquiry found the police action justified and deprecated the general defiance of the law which had become a feature of working-class and student agitation and was actively encouraged by the political parties. At least one instance is recorded of a police *lathi* charge against communist workers in a cashew factory dispute at Kilikolloor. After the strikers had locked up the son of the factory manager and occupied the factory compound, the police dispersed the crowd, injuring 18 workers. K. Ramachandran Nair, p. 127.

105 *Trade Union Record*, 5 Aug. 1958.

106 Karnik, *Communist Ministry and Trade Unions in Kerala*, p. 35.

107 *Times of India*, 10 Sept. 1958; see *IE*, 26 Nov. 1958 and V.R. Krishna Iyer, *Police in a Welfare State*.

108 *Report of the Rice Deal Inquiry Commission* (Tvm, Govt of Kerala, 1959), p. 63. For allegations of corruption see KPCC, *Memorandum submitted to the President, Indian Republic*, pp. 20-1.

109 *PKLA* VII, supplement, part I, p. 78 and part II, p. 306; *PKLA*, VII (2), pp. 65 and 71, (3), pp. 159, 189, and 196, (16), pp. 1319 and 1583. See also *Kerala's Answer to KPCC Charges*, p. 36; Karnik, as n. 106 above, pp. 48-9.

110 F. Moraes quotes one estimate of Rs. 2.5m. *India Today* (1960), p. 126. Both the Revenue Board and the Finance Dept opposed the abandon-

ment of the existing practice of auctioning the right to sell toddy. Karnik, as n. 106 above, p. 49.

111 Sreekantan Nair's open letter to the Prime Minister quoted in Karnik, as n. 106 above p. 48.

112 Zinkin, p. 165. Author's own interviews with civil servants who had, at the relevant time, been junior Gazetted Officers in the Trivandrum Secretariat.

113 R.P. Taub, *Bureaucrats Under Stress* (1969), pp. 191-203; A.D. Gorwala, *The Role of the Administrator: Past, Present, and Future* (Poona, Gokhale Institute, 1952), p. 36; *Report of the Administrative Reforms Committee* (Govt of Kerala, 1960-1), vol. 1, pp. 23-4 and vol. III, p. 132; E.M.S. Namboodiripad, 'Administrative Reforms', *New Age,* 24 Nov. 1957.

114 'EMS meets Secretariat Staff', *New Age,* 21 Apr. 1957. Namboodiripad expressed similar sentiments in *Twenty-Eight Months in Kerala* (p.35).

115 *Report of the Administrative Reforms Committee,* vol. III, p. 115.

116 Interviews, IAS officers who served in the Secretariat, 1957-9, and Professor V.K.N. Menon, Tvm, Dec. 1970.

117 Interview, Senior IAS officer, Tvm, Sept, 1973.

118 *Report of the Administrative Reforms Committee,* vol. III, pp. 121-2.

119 Ibid., vol. I, pp. 2-3.

120 Ibid., vol. III, p. 94.

121 The introduction of these three measures into the Assembly was given as the explanation for the postponement of panchayat and municipal elections, due in 1958-9, while the opposition claimed the government was afraid to face the electorate. D. Jayaraj, 'Democratic Governments in Kerala, 1957-1970' (unpublished Ph.D. thesis, U. of Kerala, Tvm, 1977), p. 84; for local government see N.R. Visalakshi, *Administration of Village Panchayats in Kerala* (1967).

122 *IE,* 3 Sept. 1958.

123 Namboodiripad, *Twenty-Eight Months in Kerala,* p. 36.

124 *New Age* (monthly), Sept. 1957, pp. 21-2.

125 L.I. Rudolph and S.H. Rudolph, *The Modernity of Tradition: Political Development in India* (Chicago, U. of Chicago Press, 1967), pp. 72-3.

126 Interviews, communist legislators. Some allegations were certainly unfounded. Zinkin, p. 163.

127 *J. of Asian and African Studies* III (3-4), 1968, p. 197.

128 A. Gramsci, *Selections from the Prison Notebooks,* eds. and trans. Q. Hoare and G. Nowell Smith (London, Lawrence & Wishart, 1971), p. 238.

129 Ibid., pp. 57-8.

130 A. Gramsci, *Quaderni del Carcere,* ed. V. Gerratana (Turin, Einaudi, 1975), p. 908: 'The Pope understood the mechanism of cultural reform of the popular peasant masses, much better than many elements of the left. He knew...one had to win over the natural leaders of the masses, that is, the intellectuals, or else one had to form new groups of intellectuals of the new type, thus the creation of indigenous bishops.

He knew that it was necessary to understand the thought patterns of these intellectuals in order to appreciate the organisation of intellectual and moral culture, and be able to decide whether to assimilate or destroy it...' Gramsci had studied the methods of the church in the Third World, and especially in India. I am grateful to Fr Marius Peiris for drawing my attention to this passage, and his own unpublished paper 'Formation of the Communist Mind in the Thought of Antonio Gramsci' (1979) is interesting in this context.

7

Kerala and the CPI Split 1960-1965

THE general background to the break-up of the CPI in 1964 into Right and Left parties has been extensively treated elsewhere.[1] Its course at the national level is outlined here to provide the context for an analysis of the Leftists' overwhelming victory in the Kerala mid-term Assembly election of March 1965.

Origins and Course of the Split

Although the ideological schism between the Soviet and Chinese communist parties had its repercussions on the CPI, the fundamental cleavage within the Indian party predated the Sino-Soviet rift. Namboodiripad reflected the view of all sections of the CPI in asserting that 'the internal differences within the CPI [were] as old as the decision of the British Government in 1947 to create the new independent state of India; they came up again in different forms. The leading organs of our Party . . . tried to furnish answers . . . however, it became clear that there were different trends, different approaches within the Party. This led to a continuous bitter inner-Party struggle, at first of an ideological and political character, but subsequently reflecting itself in the organisation of our Party.'[2]

Among the dimensions of conflict during the 1950s, two stand out: the differences in assessments of the role of the party in relation to the national bourgeoisie, and so to Congress and Nehru; and divergent attitudes towards the possibilities of working within the existing Indian constitution. Besides their indigenous sources, both disputes were compounded by the impact on a party that had longstanding and close links with the CPSU of changing Soviet policies: the increasingly positive attitude of the Soviet Union towards Nehru; and the adoption of peaceful transition as a path to socialism. Contrary to Soviet policy, even in 1957 a faction remained unconvinced that Nehru's domestic or foreign policies deserved CPI support. At the opposite pole a Right minority favoured closer collaboration with Congress. Likewise there were those who rejected constitutionalism as, in marxist-leninist parlance, parliamentary cretinism: and those who wholeheartedly welcomed working within a parliamentary framework reinforced by mass struggle.

The Kerala victory initially dampened the conflict though there was resentment outside the state as well as within it at the consequential curb on more militant mass activities. Subsequently the ministry's difficulties and ousting refuelled the argument. Although after the CPI's defeat in the 1960 Kerala election, Namboodiripad announced that the party would continue to function as a constructive and responsible opposition,[3] the dubious manner in which the ministry had been overthrown reinforced the Leftist arguments that Congress would never accept peaceful transition. However, since the Kerala party was able to contain its own dissensions—it was the 'radical' Govindan Nair who presented the State Committee's Politico-Organizational Report to the 5th Kerala State Conference in November 1959—[4] the CPI nationally absorbed the differences. In an article in September 1959 the editor of *New Age,* B.T. Ranadive, author of the 1948 Calcutta Thesis, and later CPM leader, wrote that 'the acceptance of ministerial responsibility ... had tremendously helped to organise and consolidate the democratic forces in India ... The masses have seen that the Party can deliver the goods ... that it is not simply a party of agitation and opposition This experience is bound to exercise influence on the politics of the country and the next general elections.'[5]

More serious problems were presented by India's deteriorating relations with China. Events in Tibet had culminated in the flight of the Dalai Lama, who entered India on 31 March 1959, and, more important, the Sino-Indian border dispute had erupted in the Chinese occupation of Longju in the North East Frontier Agency in August 1959. The resolution of the CPI Central Executive Committee (CEC) in its search for the middle ground—confidence in China's non-aggressive character but commitment to India's territorial integrity—satisfied neither the pro-Chinese internationalist Left of the party nor the nationalist Right. Party differences were fully exposed as a consequence of a further incident on 20-1 October in which nine members of an Indian police patrol were killed and ten detained in a clash with Chinese forces forty miles inside the border of Ladakh as understood by India. The CPI's formal acceptance of the McMahon Line in mid-November amounted to a victory for the Right and further alienated the internationalist Left.[6]

The long-standing internal differences within the party, the course of events in Kerala, and the Sino-Indian dispute now became enmeshed with the Sino-Soviet quarrel. In April 1960 the Peking journal *Red Flag* had published an article 'Long Live Leninism' which attacked the CPSU in ideological terms; and the conflict developed at the World Confederation of Trade Unions' conference in Peking and the 3rd Congress of the Rumanian Workers' Party, both in June. In the light of the impending World Congress of Communist Parties, to be held in Moscow in November, the CPI needed to clarify its position. The CEC's resultant resolution, based on the draft of the national party secretary, Ajoy Ghosh, and supported by Namboodiripad, is said in its unabridged version to have 'explicitly condemned the Chinese party' and endorsed the Soviet line on peaceful transition and expressed concern at the way in which differences in the world communist movement were being handled by the protagonists.[7] The published version criticized the Chinese for their 'basically wrong assessment' of the Indian situation and their failure to consult the CPI.[8] Ajoy Ghosh's speech to the World Congress was conciliatory in tone towards both the CPSU and the CCP but indicated support for the Soviet Union in the ideological quarrel and opposition to the Chinese on the Sino-Indian border dispute.

The CEC position met with strong opposition within the party, notably in West Bengal, and it was clear that the party's differences would be difficult to compose at the forthcoming 6th Party Congress at Vijayawada in April 1961. In the event, while the CPI National Council voted in February 1961 to recommend Ajoy Ghosh's draft political resolution to the Congress for approval, it agreed to circulate the Left alternative, prepared by Ranadive. A third document, written by Namboodiripad and critical of both Left and Right positions, was also circulated.[9] In essentials the Right saw the principal threat as coming from monopoly and foreign capital, which encouraged reaction and communalism. Congress represented progressive as well as reactionary elements. The CPI should therefore be prepared to work with and against Congress and be ready to extend a welcome to progressive Congressmen in a national democratic front led by the working class. The Left agreed that Congress's record was not entirely black but accused the Right of compromising with Congress and underestimating its reactionary character. The CPI should vigorously oppose Congress. The working class leadership of democratic forces was emphasized in the choice of the slogan 'People's Democracy'. Namboodiripad's draft distinguished between two sections of the bourgeoisie—foreign and Indian monopoly capital on the one hand and the anti-imperialist and anti-feudal elements on the other, and argued for efforts to win over the latter to the CPI side.

The 6th CPI Congress proved inconclusive for two reasons. First the Right had only the barest majority; and second the Soviet delegation (the first formal delgation in CPI history), led by the prominent

ideologist Mikhail Suslov, while supporting the Right counselled
against pressing matters to a split in the party. Thus the alternative
drafts of the political resolution by the Leftists and by Namboodiripad were withdrawn in tacit exchange for the amendment of the
official draft in a Leftward direction to make it more anti-Congress
and more anti-Nehru in tone. At Namboodiripad's suggestion the
revision of the long-term programme was remitted to the National
Council, with the rival drafts as a starting point. Meanwhile the
Amritsar programme of 1958 was to stand for the forthcoming 1962
Indian general election. The outcome may be seen in the perspective
of one non-party report on the strength of the three tendencies at the
time: in the newly elected and expanded 110-member National
Council, 56 were said to support the Right, 36 the Left, and 18
Namboodiripad.[10]

In January 1962 Ajoy Ghosh, the CPI secretary, died. In the
circumstances the choice of a successor (from CEC members) by the
National Council was difficult. In April a compromise was accepted
by which Namboodiripad became general secretary but Dange, the
leading Rightist, was appointed to the new position of party
chairman, an arrangement not helped by the personal antipathy
between the two men.[11]

On 20 October 1962 the Sino-Indian border dispute took a more
serious turn, creating an acute dilemma for the party. On 1
November the National Council, adopting an unequivocally
nationalist stand, condemned Chinese aggression and called on the
Indian people to unite in the defence of the motherland. This precipitated the resignation of three members of the CPI Central
Secretariat. The remainder of the Secretariat, including
Namboodiripad, then issued an explanatory letter addressed to
world communist parties.

Shortly afterwards on 22 November 1962 the central government
commenced to detain nearly 1,000 CPI Leftists under the Defence of
India Ordinance.[12] Among those arrested in Kerala were five
former CPI ministers, including the Centrist Namboodiripad who
was in custody for a week, and the Rightist Achutha Menon.
Whether or not it was true, as the Left alleged, that the Right had
supplied lists of Leftists to the Home Ministry to facilitate the
detentions, tension mounted as the Right used its opportunity to
reorganize the West Bengal and Punjab state units and to pass
Rightist and pro-Soviet resolutions in a depleted National Council
meeting in February 1963.[13] Namboodiripad's own resolution, 'Revisionism and Dogmatism in the CPI', was rejected and he tendered
his resignation as general secretary. His document criticized the
CPI's past zigzags between revisionism and dogmatism, attacked

the Right's current chauvinism, and accused it of tailing along behind the Congress government and even more reactionary forces.[14] In a further resolution Namboodiripad argued that the CPI should not take sides in the Sino-Soviet dispute till it had put its own house in order.

Meanwhile the Left—with A.K. Gopalan prominent—had been building up parallel party centres, further strengthened in late 1963 by the release of the détenus.[15] In October seventeen National Council members, including five from Kerala, submitted a document to the council on 'The Threatening Disruption and Split of the Party—How to Avert the Disaster'. Namboodiripad and Jyoti Basu were reported to have unsuccessfully sought an accommodation to maintain the unity of the party before and during the CEC meeting of January 1964.[16] The split finally came at the National Council meeting in April when the Left and some who were known as Centrists pressed for an inquiry into the authenticity of letters published in an anti-communist weekly *The Current* (7 March 1964) allegedly written by S.A. Dange from prison in 1924 offering his services to the imperial government in exchange for a pardon. When this was rejected thirty-two members of the National Council, including Namboodiripad and six others from Kerala,[17] walked out, publishing an appeal condemning 'Dange and his group', their 're-formist political line', and 'factional' organizational methods. On 15 April 1964 the National Council suspended the dissidents, who simultaneously released a draft programme, followed by a further independent draft from Namboodiripad. In July the Leftists and Namboodiripad, having campaigned vigorously at provincial level and in the mass organizations, met at Tenali (in Andhra Pradesh) to formalize the existence of the breakaway group as a new party and to make arrangements to hold their 'own' 7th CPI Congress at Calcutta in October to pre-empt the official party's 7th Congress at Bombay in December. Of 146 delegates at the Tenali Convention, 20 were from Kerala.

A comparison of the programmes which emerged from the rival CPI congresses confirms the view that the split turned essentially on the domestic issue of the character of the Indian ruling class as exemplified by the Congress party.[18] For the Right, India's Independence was a historic event and India was now on the path of independent development. For the Left, the transfer of power was a mere 'settlement' between British imperialism and Congress: subsequent economic development in India was therefore an attempt by the bourgeoisie to strengthen its position—a compromise with imperialism and feudalism at the expense of the people. The Rightist view of India's economic development was comparatively optimistic. Though growth was inadequate there was some economic progress and to that extent Independence was being realized. The Left on the other hand argued that economic development was illusory and that what passed for planning in India was subordinate to the profit motive of domestic and foreign capital. For both Right and Left the Indian state expressed the class domination of bourgeois and feudal elements; thereafter Right and Left diverged. For the Right the key group was a classic marxist national bourgoisie. For the Left the national bourgeoisie was insignificant: the key fraction of capital was the monopoly bourgeoisie in league with the forces of imperialism. The Right's central slogan was therefore the establishment of national democracy through a front of all patriotic and progressive forces, including the national bourgeoisie. From its different perspective the Left argued that there could be no national democratic road because this was barred by the big bourgeoisie's dominance and its compromises with imperialism; thus the Left's slogan was People's Democracy formed and led by the working class. Two other distinctions are discernible: the Right tended to emphasize national identity and the Left regional identity; and the Right saw the proletariat as the principal motive force of revolutionary change, while the Left relied on the peasantry.[19]

The draft programme of the Right, prepared by Dange, was adopted by the Bombay Congress without significant alterations. The Left draft, prepared by M.Basavapunniah, underwent some modification before and during the Calcutta Congress, largely in response to the Centrist reservations of Namboodiripad and Jyoti Basu. The final version fell short of committing the party to an all-out confrontation with Congress and the bourgeoisie by taking account of the contradictions within the ruling class which might lead some sections to align themselves with the People's Democratic Front.

Namboodiripad's role in the events leading up to the split can hardly be understimated. It was the Centrists under his leadership who had enabled the Left to mount an effective challenge to the Right. Namboodiripad not only had a significant political following in the party but also was recognized as one of the CPI's most able ideologists, and by virtue of long organizational experience culminating in the post of general secretary had a virtually unrivalled knowledge of the party machine and its mass base. According to J.B. Wood, Namboodiripad's resolution 'Revisionism and Dogmatism in the CPI' (presented and rejected at the National Council meeting in February 1963), established him as the principal theoretician of the 'anti-Right'.[20] His position as *de facto* spokesman of the Left was crystallized by his participation in the 7th (Calcutta) Congress, his

Note for the Programme of the CPI (1964), and the fact that Adikhari, the leading theoretician of the Right, singled him out for particular attention. Namboodiripad's moderating influence and commanding position in the communist movement ensured that the new party would be neither revolutionary nor Maoist. His position was (and is) well put in *The Economics and Politics of India's Socialist Pattern* (1966) in which he quotes the former general secretary of the party, Ajoy Ghosh: '*Either* the democratic forces unite, isolate and defeat the forces of right reaction, arrest the shift of the government to the right and bring about a shift to the left, i.e. towards democratic advance. *Or* forces of reaction, pressing on with the offensive and aided by their allies in the Congress and the government bring about an all-sided shift to the right.'[21] No less than the CPI, the CPI (Marxist)—as it became known in early 1965—accepted the constitutional path for the foreseeable future even though its revision of the Amritsar Constitution at the 1964 Congress omitted the original preamble underlining the possibility of peaceful transition in India. So long as Namboodiripad was a member, the CPM would not be an anti-system party. From a medium-term perspective, where the CPI and the CPM differed was in the tactics for the conduct of the march down the constitutional road: the People's Democratic Front was free to adopt a more militant air and to wage an uninhibited campaign against Congress whereas those in the National Democratic Front must perforce behave 'responsibly' and co-operatively for fear of impeding the nation's development.

The Left's Success in the Mid-term Election 1965

Immediately after the suspension of the thirty-two National Council Members in April 1964 the Right dispatched representatives to the states to explain their position and to try to avert any further erosion of their support. The mission of Achutha Menon and M.K. Kumaran to Kerala was, however, futile since Namboodiripad and Gopalan had not only preceded them but also established that at rank-and-file level they accurately articulated party feeling. Among party functionaries—the State Council and the MLAs—the Right commanded a majority of two to one,[22] and initially it also dominated the Kerala branch of the trade union federation AITUC. The Left, however, enjoyed an overwhelming majority among the organized peasantry and agricultural labourers; and since the rural poor was the power base of the majority of the district and constituency committees, the Left controlled most local organizations. In Malabar full-time workers and party members aligned themselves with Namboodiripad and Gopalan virtually *en bloc*. In Travancore the Quilon District Committee was under Right-wing control while Alleppey and Trivandrum were claimed by the Left; and in Cochin the Trichur Committee was reported to be inclined to the Right and Ernakulam to the Left. In the panchayat elections held in December 1963 Left-wing CPI candidates did well in Malabar.[23]

In Kerala the Congress party had also split. The Congress ministry had fallen and President's Rule been proclaimed on 10 September 1964. Politics in the state was thus geared to the forth-coming mid-term election and to the testing of the popular support of rival factions of the communist and Congress parties. National interest in the first confrontation between the CPI and CPM was further intensified by the arrest of nearly 800 CPM cadres under the Defence of India Rules on and after 29 December 1964. Of these, 130 were detained in Kerala on the eve of the pre-election CPM Polit-bureau and Central Committee meetings at Trichur. Those arrested included A.K. Gopalan but not Namboodiripad. Explaining the swoop, the Central Home Minister, G.L. Nanda, alleged that the new party had Chinese links and had rejected the parliamentary path. Nanda's evidence was, however, generally received with scepticism and gave rise to that very misunderstanding he claimed to fear, that the detentions would be interpreted as a clumsy attempt to influence the imminent election in Kerala.[24] The uncertainty sur-rounding the outcome was compounded by the failure of the merger of the PSP and SP. Many democratic socialists in Kerala remained in the newly launched Samyukta Socialist Party (SSP); others re-estab-lished the PSP; and some joined Congress on the grounds that the break-away Kerala Congress, formed largely but not exclusively out of landed Christian and Nair elements in central Kerala, had purified the parent body. The number of constituencies had increased by seven as a result of the new delimitation but the number of candi-dates rose by 80 per cent. Straight contests fell from sixty-three in 1960 to four in 1965 while five- or more-sided contests rose from five to forty-seven.[25]

In this fluid situation neither wing of the communist party was entirely clear how best to assert its claim to represent the body of the communist movement in the state and to advance it against an array of forces, including a revival of communalism, that did not fit neatly into boxes labelled People's Democracy or National Democracy. Rivalry between Christians and Nairs on the one hand and Ezhavas on the other had been one of the major dimensions of the local Congress split; and since Kamaraj, the All-India Congress Presi-dent, stuck firmly to his pro-Ezhava stance during the campaign, battle was inevitably joined between Congress and the communists for the allegiance of the lower castes or—and the two were largely coterminous—the lower classes. The Muslim League, disenchanted with the failure of its participation in the anti-communist front of 1960, remained in the wilderness.

The campaign planning of the CPI (or the Right Communists, as they were known at the time) was beset with difficulties. The evidence of its performance in the Trivandrum municipal election and in recent demonstrations against rising prices had shown that it wielded less influence at the mass level than the CPM (or the Left Communists as they were then known).[26] The local unit enjoyed rather less autonomy than the CPM unit, which was led by the dominant national figure in that party and was one of the two strongest units in the new organization. Lastly, the CPI nationally had wholly rejected any kind of deal with communal parties—which in Kerala meant not only the League but also Kerala Congress.[27] The CPM, of course, had its own problems to contend with: the detention of many of its skilled organizers; and shortage of funds., However, the CPM enjoyed the obvious advantages of tactical flexibility and the larger mass base.

From the beginning of the campaign the CPM, CPI, and RSP entered into negotiations for a united front of leftist parties, an objective approved by the CPI National Council meeting in Trivandrum on 10 November.[28] (Fic alleges that the CPI flirted with the possibility of an electoral alliance with Congress, but there is no firm evidence that any approaches were made.[29] In any case the faction, led by Damodaran, that favoured local collaboration with Congress was a minority within the CPI itself.) It is possible, of course, that the whole exercise was an elaborate charade but the manoeuvring is consistent with serious intent. Argument centred on the content of the minimum programme, the question of an explicit statement of support for India's defence effort, and the admissibility of 'some sort of understanding' with the League jointly to sponsor mutually acceptable independents, which Namboodiripad fairly claimed had been the arrangement in 1957 and 1962.[30] Such a deal obviously mattered more to the CPM, because of its power base in Malabar where marginal Muslim votes were of crucial importance, than to the CPI. Although the CPI National Council's stance was a principled rejection of the inclusion of communal forces such as the League and Kerala Congress in 'the alliance', the term alliance left room for flexibility of interpretation.

More important was the question of the fundamental principle by which front formation should be directed. For the CPI the criterion was that candidates must be progressive and democratic. Namboodiripad claims that the CPM's position was more flexibly Leninist. Well aware that Kerala Congress, for example, was in some respects more reactionary than Congress, the Leftists were prepared to heed Lenin's advice to exploit fissures among the various groups and types of the bourgeoisie 'to take advantage of every, even the smallest opportunity of gaining a mass ally, even though this ally may be temporary, vacillating, unreliable and conditional.'[31] The CPM would, and did, fight the reactionary and communal forces as represented by the League and Kerala Congress but was prepared to make arrangements to support 'independents' of a communal character if that would avoid a Congress victory.

After four months the negotiations finally broke down on 13 January 1965—less than three weeks before the closing date for nominations—ostensibly on two issues: the CPI's insistence that the United Front should declare its unequivocal opposition to the League and Kerala Congress as well as Congress; and the CPI-RSP demand that the negotiators should reopen discussion on the agreement of 8 January that the three-party UFL would support not only some SSP and KTP candidates but also a handful of (League) independents where that was critical to mobilization of the anti-Congress vote. In view of the arrests of CPM cadres a fortnight earlier and the prolonged meetings of the CPI State Committee between 8 and 13 January it seems reasonable to accept Namboodiripad's reading of the situation: that the CPI intentionally pressed the League issue so as to provide itself with a principled exit on the presumption that a beleaguered CPM would now accept the CPI's claim to an allotment of seats based on their respective support among full-time workers rather than among the membership.[32]

Confident both in the rectitude of its line and the support of the communist electorate, the CPM declined any renegotiation and quickly reached a comprehensive understanding with the SSP, local agreements with the KTP, and accommodations with the League in six constituencies. The CPI completed its arrangements with the RSP (which were of significance only in Quilon) but otherwise limited its accommodations to the support of fourteen independents—seven, despite all that had transpired, jointly with the CPM. As for Congress, it eschewed any electoral deals whatsoever, while the League and Kerala Congress agreed to exchange support in the 76 constituencies contested by one or the other.

The results of the poll on 4 March 1965 were a severe blow to the official wings of both CPI and Congress, but calamitous for the Right Communists. On a 75 per cent poll the Left Communists had emerged as the biggest single party with 40 seats, followed by Congress with 36.[33] The rebel Kerala Congress had won 24 seats and the CPI a humiliating 3 seats in a 133-member assembly. Of 40 Left Communists elected, 29 were in detention. The outcome was scarcely more comforting for the CPI in terms of votes cast. The CPM's 73 candidates took 20 per cent of the poll; the CPI's 78 just 8 per cent. In the 45 constituencies where the two parties clashed directly, the CPM won 24 and the CPI none. In addition the CPI had lost 67 deposits. The verdict of the communist section of the electorate was indisputable: the Left Communists were the true heirs of the movement in Kerala.

Tables 7.1–3 show the overall results, the party distribution of seats won by District, and the communists' percentage vote by District. Map 18 shows the distribution of the CPI and CPM vote by constituency. In percentage terms the CPI won a larger share of the vote only in Quilon and Trichur and was overwhelmed in Cannanore and Kozhikode. In all of Malabar there was just one constituency (Pattambi, 28 per cent) where the CPI managed more than 15 per cent of the poll. Even in Quilon, the one District where the CPM secured no seats, its share of the poll was 9 per cent. Its best performance was in Palghat where 41 per cent of the vote won 11 of the 14 seats. As the map indicates, there were only two areas where the CPI performed well: Quilon and the southern part of Trichur.

Two questions follow: Why did the CPI fail so badly overall? And why was Quilon the significant exception? According to Namboodiripad the Left's assessment was more in tune with popular consciousness than the Right's 'narrow sectarian approach' to other opposition parties and its Right opportunist approach to Congress.[34] He further emphasizes the CPM's success in winning the co-operation of disgruntled Catholic laity and clergy (Father Vadakkan, the KTP, and MKU), Muslims, and others. Neither argument is entirely convincing. Gough—not unsympathetic to the CPM—reports distaste among village party members and followers for deals of any kind. The SSP was seen as an opportunist clique which was even more reactionary than Congress.[35] As for the support of the disaffected elements of the erstwhile anti-Communist Front, this can have been of no more than marginal significance in 1965. The KTP, despite CPM support, secured only 77,000 votes compared to Kerala Congress's 844,000. Generally the perish clergy, influential laity, and the Catholic dailies, including *Deepika*, supported Kerala Congress. Among Catholic-read newspapers, apart from the Congress *Manorama,* only the small circulation *Thozhilali* (Vadakkan) and *Kerala Prakasam* (Mathai Manjooran) articulated a class-conscious viewpoint. As for the Moplahs there is no evidence of growing radicalization. On pragmatic grounds the League leadership exchanged Congress for CPM support while continuing to castigate communism in the mosque.[36] At 6 per cent the League's share of the poll was virtually the same as in 1957.

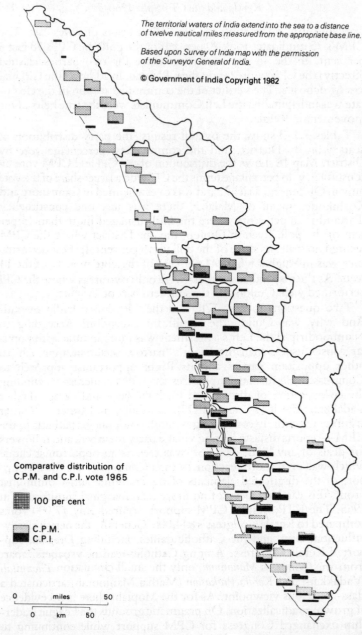

The territorial waters of India extend into the sea to a distance of twelve nautical miles measured from the appropriate base line.

Based upon Survey of India map with the permission of the Surveyor General of India.

© Government of India Copyright 1982

Comparative distribution of
C.P.M. and C.P.I. vote 1965

■ 100 per cent

C.P.M.
C.P.I.

0   miles   50

0   km   50

Source: Data from Fic, *Kerala*, Tables XVII–XXV.

Map 18 Kerala 1965: Assembly Election, Comparative Distribution of Percentage Vote for CPM and CPI

Table 7.1 Kerala 1965: Assembly Election (turnout = 75.20 %)

Party	% Vote		Number of candidates	Number of seats
CPM	19.55		73	40
CPI	8.02		78	3
Independents (CPM)	1.26		9	1
Independents (CPI)	1.41		14	0
Independents (CPM/CPI)	1.46		7	2
All Communist		31.70	181	46
SSP	8.00		29	13
RSP	1.30		13	0
KTP	1.19		10	1
CP allies		10.49	52	14
Congress	33.03		133	36
Kerala Congress	13.11		60	24
Independents (KC)	0.77		12	1
All Congress		46.91	205	61
Muslim League	3.71		16	6
Independents (ML)	0.18		1	0
Independents (ML + CPM)	2.32		6	6
All Muslim League		6.21	23	12
Others (incl. invalid votes)	4.69		87	0
Totals	100.00		562	133

Source: Adapted from Fic, *Kerala,* Table XVI, p. 499.

Two further explanations of the CPI's defeat may also be questioned: Fic's belief that the CPI was caught in the cross-fire of communal tensions and lost the support of marginal Ezhava and Nair supporters;[37] and Hardgrave's claim that the CPM's base was concentrated in areas where agricultural labourers heavily out-numbered the peasant cultivators and the CPI's in regions of predo-minantly peasant proprietorship.[38] If the CPI did suffer more than the CPM from the efforts of Congress to win over the Ezhavas, and Kerala Congress to win over the Nairs, then this was because exist-ing Ezhava and Nair communist supporters preferred the CPM on other grounds. The labourer-cultivator ratio is also dubious, first because of doubt about the reliability of the 1961 occupational categories, and second, because of the inadequate fit between either district or taluk-level figures and comparative communist perform-ance (see below, Table 7.3).

The CPM's victory over its rival is more simply explained in political terms. Namboodiripad and Gopalan stood in a symbiotic relationship with party members and sympathizers. As Kerala's most charismatic communist leaders, their influence was state-wide rather than localized but the affectionate (though not uncritical) regard in which they were held rested on the fact that for the

Table 7.2 Kerala 1965: Assembly Election Results by District

	Cong.	KC	CPM	CPI	SSP	ML	Others	Total
Trivandrum	10	—	3	—	1	—	—	14
Quilon	7	6	—	1	1	—	—	15
Alleppey	4	6	4	—	—	—	—	14
Kottayam	1	7	4	1	—	—	1	14
Ernakulam	5	4	3	—	—	—	3	15
Trichur	7	—	2	1	—	—	2	13
Palghat	1	—	11	—	2	—	—	14
Kozhikode	—	—	6	—	5	6	3	20
Cannanore	1	—	7	—	3	—	3	14
Totals	36	23	40	3	13	6	12	133

Source: Calculated from Fic, *Kerala,* Tables XVII–XXV, pp. 500–17.

ordinary communist villager they were closely identified with the unsophisticated revolutionary ideals of the propertyless. Furthermore the belief at the grass roots that the CPI was a party of revisionists, prepared to compromise with Congress, excited strong feelings at a time when the standing of Congress locally and nationally was very low. According to Gough's village studies of 1964 the more informed were certain that 'Congress is the captive of the national and imperial bourgeoisie, and cannot bring socialism to India.'[39] The overthrow of the communist ministry and the character of Congress's 1963 Agrarian Relations Act (see below, p. 292) were immediate illustrations of Congress's readiness to surrender to vested interests. Second the Sino–Indian border dispute evoked little interest, though even among some Left Communists there were anxieties about Chinese intentions.[40] The Himalayas were far away. The CPM voter was not unpatriotic, but he resented the fact that Delhi recalled his existence only when it needed his support and then proceeded to arrest Kerala heroes on trumped-up charges of subversion, whilst action on escalating food prices was markedly less urgent. The nationalism of the Right Communists had little resonance in Kerala. The degree to which Namboodiripad and Gopalan accurately reflected the hopes and fears of the poor, at least in the Hindu community, goes far to explain the contrast in organizational efficiency of the rival parties. The CPI had more of the officers, the CPM more of the non-commissioned ranks and most of the troops in the people's army.

The exceptional position of Quilon District may be explained by reference to three factors: first, the CPI's alliance with the RSP;

Table 7.3 · Kerala 1965: Assembly Election, CPI and CPM Performance

District	Seats contested CPI	Seats won CPI	Seats contested CPM	Seats won CPM	% Vote CPI (N=133)	% Vote CPM (N=133)	CPI Vote as % of CPM	% Vote CPM+CPI+CPM/CPI independents (N=133)	% net change in communist vote in core constituencies† 1960-5	Labourers as % of agricultural workers (1961)
Trivandrum	9	0	7	3	7.5	19.9	38	27.9	−6	41
Quilon	10	1	10	0	19.0	9.1	209	31.7	−7	30
Alleppey	10	0	9	4	7.0	19.9	35	29.0	−10	52
Kottayam	7	1	6	4	10.2	10.9	94	21.1	−2	43
Ernakulam	8	0	5	3	3.1	16.9	18	23.6	−2	41
Trichur	10	1	4	2	16.8	12.5	134	33.4	−7	48
Palghat	10	0	12	11	6.4 ·	41.3	15	47.7	0	61
Kozhikode	7	0	12	6	1.4	21.1	7	22.8	5	47
Cannanore	7	0	8	7	2.6	30.4	9	35.5	9	42
Totals	78	3	73	40	8.0	19.6	41	31.7	−3	45

★ These figures differ slightly from those given in Craig Baxter, comp., *District Voting Trends*. Baxter gives CPI 7.6 per cent and CPM 13.7 per cent in Kottayam.

† Core constituencies in 1960 are those previously contested in 1957 (N=87) and in 1965 those in which a CPM or CPI candidate or a CPM, CPI, or CPM/CPI-supported independent (but excluding the 6 independents jointly supported by the CPM and the Muslim League) polled more than 5,000 votes (N=84).

Sources: Calculations from Fic, *Kerala*, Tables XVII–XXV, pp. 500-17, with verification of political affiliation by Dept of Politics, U. of Kerala; last column, *Census of India 1961*, vol. 7, pt 9, p. 159.

second the influence of M.N. Govindan Nair among the Nairs—
who formed a larger proportion of the population than the Ezhavas
in the interior (see above, p. 114); and third the CPI's hold on the
heavily-unionized cashew factories of the District. Little more than a
year earlier the CPI and RSP had led the biggest strike in Kerala's
history against the 'cashew kings'.

Communist Support: a Watershed

The final and most difficult issue is the extent to which the total
communist vote had declined between 1960 and 1965. The combined party vote in 1965 was under 28 per cent. Including 30 independents supported by one or both parties, this rose to 32 per cent,
substantially below the 44 per cent of 1960. Allowance must be made
for the effect of electoral adjustments, especially the CPM's arrangement with the SSP which from a base of 13 seats in the dissolved
Assembly was allocated 35 constituencies in the 1965 election. However, even the attribution of half the SSP poll to the CPM raises the
'communist' vote only to 36 per cent. Conversely by contrast the
total Congress vote (Congress and Kerala Congress) at 45.6 per cent
compares favourably with the 37.8 per cent poll when Congress
stood alone in 1957.

This apparent decline in the total communist vote and obverse
increase in total Congress vote should not be taken at face value.
Gough correctly suggests that the gross percentages may well be
misleading and notes that this change in party fortunes was the
reverse of the results derived from her village studies conducted in
1964. She argues that the most accurate estimate of changes in
communist support should rest on a comparison of the total communist vote (inclusive of CPI-or CPM-supported independents) in
constituencies contested by the CPM in 1965 with the communist
vote in the same, or, allowing for boundary changes, similar constituencies in 1960.[41] Her conclusions are that there was at most a 2
per cent fall in communist support overall, that the communists
maintained their support in Malabar and Cochin and actually increased it in Trichur and Cannanore, but suffered serious losses in
Alleppey (5 to 6 per cent), Kottayam (9 to 10 per cent), and Quilon
(8 to 12 per cent).[42] An alternative approach is to compare the communist vote in 'core' seats, those 87 constituencies contested by the
united CPI in both 1957 and 1960 and the 84 constituencies in 1965 in
which a 'communist' candidate (including a communist-supported
independent but excluding the six independents supported jointly by
the CPM and the League) polled more than 5,000 votes. By this
method the fall in communist support in its heartland was 3 per cent

overall, which is the line with Gough's figure of 2 per cent; it also confirms Gough's general conclusions that the communists maintained or improved their position in Malabar but suffered setbacks in Travancore (see above, Table 7.3). The results differ in detail but do agree on success in Cannanore, decline in Alleppey and Quilon, and the maintenance of high levels of support in Palghat.

An explanation of the changing pattern of communist support involves three basic factors: the split in the communist movement; the revival of communalism; and the growing appeal of Congress to the middle class, irrespective of communal origin. The effects of the split are clear enough: the disillusionment which led to defections among some party members and abstentions among sympathizers, both more marked where the parties were in the most serious contention in the south; the organizational disruption compounded by the effects of the detention of CPM cadres; and the shortage of funds available to the dominant wing.

Equally there can be no doubt that Kerala Congress, aided by the NSS and sections of the Catholic Church, was highly successful in mobilizing the Nair and Catholic communities in central Kerala at a time of economic difficulties, just as the League secured an impressive response from the Muslim community in the Moplah zone. For the communists this meant the marginal loss of Nair and Muslim votes, even though it led to temporary gains of seats in Kottayam as a consequence of the division of the traditional Nair and Christian Congress vote between Congress and Kerala Congress. Most disturbing from the communist point of view in the longer term, however, was the resurgence of Congress itself in Travancore-Cochin. Despite the loss of Nair and Catholic votes to Kerala Congress, the official Congress won 34 of the 85 seats in Travancore-Cochin. If it won only two seats in the whole of Malabar, its share of the total poll improved significantly in both Cannanore and Palghat when compared with 1957. For thirty months the Sankar ministry— R. Sankar was the SNDP leader—had been dispensing favours and patronage designed to create a new basis of support for the Congress party in line with Kamaraj's policy of extending its appeal among the lower castes. Ironically, Sankar himself lost his seat to the CPM, but the erosion of communist support in Quilon and Alleppey testified to his success in consolidating Congress support among the increasing number of middle class Ezhavas and in winning over new adherents among the community at large through the expansion of educational and so occupational opportunities.

The broadening of Congress's communal base is reflected in the origins of its MLAs (and its candidates) in 1965: 2 Harijans, 2 Nadars, 7 Ezhavas, 4 Muslims, 8 Christians, 9 Nairs, and 3

Brahmins. In 1957, by contrast, 19 of its 43 MLAs had been Christians.[43] This shift reflected a growing secularization of Congress in Kerala, explanation of which is beyond the scope of this study. Clearly, however, important factors involved were the KPCC's response to the communists' own secular appeal, the national realignment of Congress policy enshrined in the Kamaraj Plan for rejuvenating Congress nationally, and the unintended consequences of the interplay of party factionalism in the years 1963-5. Struggles between the organizational and ministerial wings of the party, Malabar and Travancore activists, and groups owing allegiance to Sankar, P.T. Chacko, and C.K. Govindan Nair, as well as rivalries within and between communities were exacerbated by the so-called Chacko affair,[44] Chacko's resignation from the ministry, and his sudden death in August 1964. The resulting breakaway of the Chacko faction removed many of the Christian-Nair propertied class of central Kerala from the parent body, leaving a party where no group dominated and the process of secularizing its organization, programmatic appeal, and electoral base could further develop. The subsequent rise of radical Youth Congress was facilitated.

There can be no doubt that the 1965 election was a fundamental divide. Such was the fragmentation of parties and electoral support that neither the communists nor Congress could hope to gain a workable governing majority in the foreseeable future. Any elected government must therefore be a coalition; but, whereas in the past communist-led united fronts had been predicated on an alliance of 'left and progressive forces', no such purism was possible after 1965, as the ideological lines of both the CPI and CPM recognized. Growing economic differentiation combined with the declining ability of the Indian and Kerala economies to satisfy rising and competing aspirations by caste, class, and region found its political expression in a shattering of the party system which offered a profound challenge to the communist movement precisely at the point when its own failure to agree on the class analysis of Indian society had come to a head in the split.

Notes

1   W.E. Griffith, *The Sino-Soviet Rift* (1964) and *Sino-Soviet Relations 1964-5* (Cambridge, Mass., MIT Press, 1967); H. Gelman, 'The Communist Party of India—Sino-Soviet Battleground', in A. Doak Barnett, ed., *Communist Strategies in Asia* (1963); John B. Wood, 'Observations on the Indian Communist Party Split', *Pacific Affairs* 38 (1), 1965; J.M. Kaul, 'The Split in the CPI', *India Quarterly* 20 (4), 1964;

R. Retzlaff, 'Revision and Dogmatism in the Communist Party of India', in R.A. Scalapino, ed., *The Communist Revolution in Asia* (1965); Namboodiripad, *Note for the Programme of the CPI*; Ram, *Indian Communism*; Franda, *Radical Politics in West Bengal*.

2   Namboodiripad, *Note for the Programme of the CPI*, pp. 59-60.

3   *Hindustan Times,* 19 Feb. 1959; for reactions in West Bengal see Franda, *Radical Politics in West Bengal*, p.84.

4   C. Unniraja, *New Age* (monthly), Jan. 1960, p.2.

5   'Lessons of Kerala', *New Age* (monthly), Sept. 1959, p. 19.

6   Ram, *Indian Communism*, p.103.

7   'On India-China Relations, Resolution adopted by the National Council of the Communist Party of India, Meerut, 11-15 November 1959', in CPI, *The India-China Border Dispute and the Communist Party of India* (New Delhi, CPI, 1963), pp. 13-17; Ram, *Indian Communism*, pp. 89-91; Namboodiripad is reported to have said 'In case of agression we are one with the government. It is for the government of the day to decide whether aggression has been committed or not' (*Link*, 1 Nov. 1959). A.K. Gopalan is also identified as 'nationalist' in *Link*, 20 Sept. 1959.

8   'On Certain Questions Before the International Communist Movement', in CPI, *India-China Border Dispute and the Communist Party of India*, pp. 22-8.

9   Retzlaff, as n.1 above, p. 324. Namboodiripad's organizational report attributed the sharp fall in membership, loose discipline, and organizational weakness to the leadership's revisionist stance (*Link*, 26 Jan. 1961).

10   *Hindustan Times*, 17 Apr. 1961; for the discussions at Vijayawada see Savak Katrak, 'India Communist Party Split', *China Quarterly*, July-Sept. 1963, and Ram, *Indian Communism*, pp. 111-23.

11   The contrasting personalities and political styles of the two men are brought out in B. Sen Gupta, 'S.A. Dange, E.M.S. Namboodiripad, and Jyoti Basu', in R. Swearingen, ed., *Leaders of the Communist World*. The deterioration in relations appears to date from around 1958 at the time of Dange's comments on the performance and prospects of the Namboodiripad-led Kerala government.

12   A breakdown of arrests by states is given in *New Age*, 24 Feb. 1963.

13   Wood, p. 52; Ram, *Indian Communism*, p.139; Franda, *Radical Politics in West Bengal*, pp. 100-1; Retzlaff in Scalapino, ed., pp. 327-8.

14   Ram, *Indian Communism*, p. 145. See Namboodiripad, *Revisionism and Dogmatism in the* C.P.I. (1965).

15   Retzlaff, in Scalapino, ed., p. 330. Gopalan was censured by the CPI National Council in mid-October but was not suspended. This may have indicated the Right wing's awareness of its weakness as well as constituting an invitation to negotiate a reconciliation: *The Tribune* (Ambala), 16 Nov. 1963. The parallel party organization is described in CPI, *Resolution on Splitters* (New Delhi, CPI, 1964).

16   Retzlaff, in Scalapino, ed., p. 331.

17   The Kerala members of the '32' were Namboodiripad, A.K. Gopalan,

A.V. Kunhambu, E.K. Nayanar, Imbichi Bava, C.H. Kanaran, and V.S. Achuthanandan, 7 of the 15 representatives on the National Council.

18 *The Programme of the Communist Party of India* [Left]. *Adopted at the Seventh Congress of the Communist Party of India, Calcutta, October 31-November 7, 1964* (Calcutta, CPI, 1966); *Constitution of the Communist Party of India* [Left]. *Adopted at the Seventh Congress, October 31 to November 7, 1964* (Calcutta, CPI-M, 1965); *Draft Programme of the Communist Party of India* (New Delhi, CPI, 1964); *Proceedings of the Seventh Congress of the Communist Party of India, Bombay, December 13-23, 1964*, vol. 1: *Documents* (New Delhi, CPI, 1965); *Fight Against Revisionism. Political-Organisational Report adopted at the Seventh Congress of the Communist Party of India* [Left], *Calcutta, October 31—November 7, 1964* (Calcutta [CPI-M], 1964); E.M.S. Namboodiripad, *The Programme Explained* (Calcutta, CPI-M, 1966); B.T. Ranadive, *The Two Programmes: Marxist and Revisionist* (Calcutta, CPI (M), 1966).

19 E.M.S. Namboodiripad, *A Brief Critical Note on the Programme Drafts* (New Delhi, CPI, 1964); Wood, p. 59.

20 Wood, p. 54. For Namboodiripad's text see *Revisionism and Dogmatism in the CPI*.

21 p. 412; italic as in Namboodiripad's text.

22 Fic, *Kerala*, p. 208; Hardgrave, in Brass and Franda, eds. (pp. 129-32) discusses possible correlates of the differentiation between Left and Right among the leadership, claiming that there was a geographical basis for the distinction between a pro-CPM Malabar and a somewhat pro-CPI Travancore. He also argues that Right communist leaders were more middle class and (in terms of formal education) better educated. The latter, however, may be seen as a function of the environmental characteristics of the north and south of the state.

23 *Hindu*, 5 Apr. and 4 May 1964; the pro-Rightist *Link* noted the Leftist hold on the party machine in Cannanore, Kozhikode, and Alleppey (26 Apr. 1964). For the panchayat elections see D. Jayaraj, 'Democratic Governments in Kerala 1957-1970', pp. 164-6.

24 Fic, *Kerala*, pp. 190-211; E.M.S. Namboodiripad, *What Really Happened in Kerala* (1966), p. 37.

25 D. Jayaraj, *Majority Rule in Kerala: a study of Five Elections 1957-1970* (Tvm, D. Jayaraj, 1974), ch. V.

26 Namboodiripad, *What Really Happened in Kerala*, p. 18.

27 Ibid., pp. 25-6, Namboodiripad alleges that the CPI stand was in any case not consistent since the CPI had had an understanding with the Muslim League with respect to the Calicut Corporation election.

28 *Hindu*, 11 Nov. 1964.

29 Fic, *Kerala*, p. 213. Namboodiripad does not claim this in *What Really Happened in Kerala*. He is, however, quoted as hinting at pro-Congress attitudes in the Kerala CPI (*Times of India*, 20 Apr. 1964). See also *Hindu*, 18 Apr. 1964 for a report of the CPI State Council's unanimity in favour of a united front against Congress.

30 Namboodiripad, *What Really Happened in Kerala*, p. 21. Support for India's defence effort was categorically given by Namboodiripad in Apr.

1964 when he denied the existence of a pro–China lobby in the united CPI if that meant the sabotage of India's defence efforts or support for China's acts of aggression against India (*Times of India*, 18 Apr. 1964). A deal with the Muslim League appears to have been accepted so long as it was not widely publicized. A.K. Gopalan, however, caused some upset in both the League and the united CPI by revealing its existence. *Hindu*, 15 Apr. 1964.

31 Quoted by Namboodiripad from Lenin's *Left-wing Communism: an Infantile Disorder* in *What Really Happened in Kerala,* p. 65.

32 Ibid., pp. 44–6. The CPI version is available in *New Age,* 18 Apr. 1965. Most Kerala newspapers and *The Hindu* (Madras) support Namboodiripad's account.

33 Party affiliations are based on the verified results prepared by the Dept. of Politics, U. of Kerala.

34 Namboodiripad, *Kerala*, pp. 230–1.

35 K. Gough, 'Village Politics in Kerala-I', *Economic Weekly*, 27 Feb. 1965, p. 417; see also Gough's 'Kerala Politics and the 1965 Elections', *International J. of Comparative Sociology* VIII (1), 1967, p. 73.

36 R.E. Miller, pp. 169-70; P. Sukumara Panikkar, 'The Muslim League in Kerala' (unpublished Ph.D. thesis, U. of Kerala, Tvm, 1977), p. 111; see also Theodore P. Wright, Jr, 'The Muslim League in South India since Independence', *American Political Science R.* LX (3) 1966.

37 Fic, *Kerala*, p. 249.

38 Hardgrave, in Brass and Franda, eds., pp. 140-3, based on data in K.G. Krishna Murthy and G. Lakshmana Rao, *Political Preferences in Kerala* (1968) and G. Lakshmana Rao, and R. Seethalakshmi 'Socio-Economic Support Bases of Communists in Kerala', *Indian J. of Political Science* 29, 1968, pp. 342-3. See also D. Zagoria, 'Social Bases of Indian Communism', in R. Lowenthal, ed., *Issues in the Future of Asia* (New York, Praeger, 1969).

39 Gough, *Economic Weekly,* 20 Feb. 1965, p. 417.

40 Ibid.

41 Gough, *International J. of Comparative Sociology* VIII (1), 1967, pp. 77–81.

42 Ibid., p. 81.

43 Calculations from data supplied by Dr D. Jayaraj, Kariavattom Campus, U. of Kerala; see also B. Ahmed, 'Communist and Congress Prospects in Kerala', *Asian Survey* (VI), July 1966.

44 P.T. Chacko, while driving a car near Trichur collided with a cart, causing minor injuries to its occupants. It was alleged that he failed to stop and that this neglect was occasioned by the presence of a woman passenger in his car (*Kerala Kaumudi*, 9 Dec. 1963). On 30 Jan. 1964 P. Gopalan, a Congress MLA who was alleged to have a personal vendetta with Chacko, announced in the Assembly that he proposed to fast to death to secure Chacko's resignation. Although the fast was called off after AICC intervention the registration of a police case against the Home Minister increased the political pressures upon him and on 20 Feb. 1964 he resigned.

8

Communist Accommodation: Formation of the United Front 1965–1967

Towards CPI-CPM Accommodation

THE CPI's rout in 1965 came as a shock to the Soviet Union, which had accepted the CPI's own assessment of its prospects: the Kerala débâcle therefore proved a turning point for the CPSU as much as the CPI. Doubts began to assail the Soviet leadership that it could well have committed itself to supporting generals without troops— and its anxieties were not allayed by the relative performance of the CPI and CPM in exploiting politically the famine and civil commotion which afflicted much of India in 1965-6.

The year had begun with serious rioting throughout southern India over the language issue. The demonstrations in Madras against the adoption of Hindi as India's sole official language were the worst since the Quit India Movement of 1942; and in Kerala there was a complete *hartal* or strike in the urban areas on 18 February.[1] The CPI came on as something of an extra, whereas Namboodiripad, who had always shown a profound awareness of regional nationalism, was in the front of the fight in Kerala.[2] Similarly, it was the CPM which used the two long-running issues of the period—conflict with Pakistan and the worst food crisis since Independence—to most effect.[3]

Ironically, the CPI's line on these two issues was based on Namboodiripad's formulation of 1953, 'uniting with and fighting against Congress', which on the face of it seemed the perfect tactical line with which to build the National Democratic Front while allowing a flexible approach to events as they occurred. On the one hand the party would bolster its nationalist image by beating the patriotic drum; on the other it would growl at the government's record on food. In practice, there was more 'uniting with' than 'fighting against' in 1965: first, because that was what Dange believed the Soviet Union wanted; secondly, because the government's firm action under the State of Emergency had stifled the food agitation nationally; and thirdly, because, as a party with All-India pretensions, the CPI needed to balance the pressures of its followers in those states with rice to spare—at a price—and those in food-deficit states like Kerala.[4] The patriotic posture ensured the worst of both worlds: playing Congress at its own game, and abandoning the class war to the CPM which accused its rival both of 'tailism'—tailing on behind the class enemy—and of succumbing to chauvinism.

In contrast, the CPM line—or more accurately the Namboodiripad-Basu line, as almost all the other important figures were incarcerated—concentrated on 'fighting against', with token gestures to nationalistic 'uniting with'. While the central government's detention of many comrades as alleged fifth columnists would inevitably have alienated the CPM there were very strong ideological grounds for muting the trumpets of a war waged by the national bourgeoisie. There is, after all, no false consciousness like the hysteria of war. If the struggle was to be prolonged, there would be a war machine and a war economy that would grossly distort the social structure of both India and Pakistan.[5] It followed, then, that resistance to aggression should be combined with efforts to negotiate a peaceful settlement of the issues in dispute between India and Pakistan, a policy which had in the meanwhile become—for rather different reasons—that of the Soviet Union.

Soviet Policies

Soviet diplomacy in the subcontinent had latterly been conditioned by the growing rift with China. The assumption that the CPM was pro-Chinese had contributed to the CPSU's backing of the CPI. Now it became clear that this was not entirely an accurate reading of the CPM's position and that Namboodiripad and Jyoti Basu, who were running the party while many of their comrades were in jail, sought to maintain a critical independence of both sides in the Sino-Soviet dispute.[6] It was also clear that, except on the urban trade union front, the CPM enjoyed more mass support than the CPI.[7] Soviet analysts, thinking ahead to the 1967 All-India elections, were anxious to minimize the risk of repeating the Kerala catastrophe nationally and so recommended the construction of at least a temporary bridge between the CPI and CPM.

Indian Communist Tactics

After the shock of the 1965 Kerala election the CPI did not need much encouragement to explore the possibilities of practical cooperation without prejudice to ideology, and raised no protest when

P. Sundarayya, the CPM general secretary—fortuitously released from jail—was invited to Moscow for talks early in 1966. Exactly what transpired at this meeting is unknown but the tone of the joint communiqué on the ensuing talks between the CPI and the CPSU suggests that Sundarayya's arguments had carried weight.[8] The leaders of the CPI were left in no doubt that the USSR was far from impressed with their performance against either the Indian government or the CPM. The CPI must abandon its existing line of flirting with progressive Congress and concentrate on 'fighting against' rather than 'uniting with' the class enemy; and it should revert once more to the strategy of building up a left united front for the 1967 election, while, of course, taking what limited opportunities it could to upstage the CPM. There was a distinct irony in the CPI's situation: having, arguably, followed Soviet advice to the destruction of its own unity, it was now expected to swallow its pride and adopt what was tantamount to its rival's political line.

The new tactic was adopted at the meeting of the CPI National Council at Hyderabad in June 1966, though there was a brief period in July when it seemed the party had spoken too soon. The break-up of the West Bengal Congress party brought the number of states where Congress had split to six; and Kamaraj, Congress President, accepted an invitation to Moscow for talks on Congress-CPI co-operation.[9] Nothing, however, came of it all and the CPI was driven back into the arms of the CPM. A measure of pragmatic co-operation had already developed in the course of the previous year especially over the food crisis, largely one suspects because of pressures from the rank and file of the Communist and Socialist parties, but also in the communist case because it was of mutual benefit: the CPM had the followers but many of its organizers were in jail; and the CPI had the cadre and the cash. What was more difficult was to convert this negative unity of extra-parliamentary opposition into the positive co-ordination of a bid for parliamentary power. Who was to conduct the orchestra: the CPM or the CPI? Who would be the first violins and who second fiddles?

The question was a matter of substance in those three states—Andhra, West Bengal, Kerala—where the communists as a whole could expect to do well. In each instance the matter was resolved differently; that in itself, if the merits of the strategies are excluded, was redolent of the fact that—like Congress—the CPI and the CPM are coalitions of (state) parties with minds and traditions of their own. In Andhra there was the experience of Telengana, intense ideological feeling, and bitter personal acrimony between Rajeshwar Rao of the CPI and Sundarayya of the CPM. It is doubtful whether either party ever seriously sought accommodation except on its own inflated terms. In the event there was no agreement and the resulting fratricidal contests in 75 constituencies left the combined parties with a mere 12 seats in the 186-member Assembly.[10]

In West Bengal the outcome was curious. After the failure of negotiations for a general united front two rival fronts were formed—the People's United Left Front led by the breakaway Bangla Congress and the CPI, and the United Left Front led by the CPM. The CPI and CPM observed some of the constituency agreements arrived at earlier; and actually united in a coalition government after the election. Bengali communism had a tradition of united electoral fronts as well as of factionalism. In 1967 the readiness of Bangla Congress to treat with the Communists—the only rebel Congress party in India to do so—reinforced the former tradition while the interplay between the CPM Left and Centre, the one dominating electoral mobilization and the other the parliamentary front, contributed to the apparent inconsistency of the CPM's position. An additional dimension is possibly that Basu, the Centrist leader, had not fully reconciled himself to the permanency of the split in the CPI, whereas the Left was sensitive to pressure from Peking directed at the Soviet-oriented CPI.[11]

Creation of the United Front

The successful formation of an across-the-board anti-Congress alliance in Kerala needs little explanation. First, here the communists had already moved well down the parliamentary road, a statement only modestly qualified by the split. By definition, since the masses who had jubilantly cheered 'the people's government' in 1957 had sided with the CPM, it inherited the Malayali traditions as much as the CPI. The difference in 1967 was that the CPM had rejected the National Democratic Highway, with its capitalist toll gates to Delhi, in favour of the winding old lanes of Village India. Second, the issue which so hampered the formation of electoral fronts elsewhere—the relative following of the rivals—had been settled in Kerala in 1965. Third, the food crisis had brought the left together in bitter agitation against Delhi to a greater extent than in other states, partly because the situation was so grim, partly because it accentuated the Keralite sense of unjust neglect by Delhi—their handsome contribution to foreign exchange entitled them, it was claimed, to better treatment—and partly because, had the CPI staged its own demonstrations, they would have been outfaced by the marxist multitude. It was a choice between running a one-man *bandh* or playing the occasional solo in the Big *Bandh*. Fourth, Kerala was under Presidential Rule, a situation that enables every party—even

Congress—to agree on the lowest common denominator of political argument in Kerala: the wickedness of 'foreign', non-democratic government. In consequence opposition party co-operation took far deeper root in Kerala than in India generally. It is symptomatic of this that co-ordination of the left-wing campaign in 1965-6 took place under the umbrella of the modest-sounding Consultative Committee of the Left Opposition Parties and in Kerala of the militantly labelled Committee for Joint Struggle (*Samara Samithi*).[12] The Kerala Committee's first major venture—a plan for a state-wide stoppage on 28 September 1965 in protest against the food shortage—was overtaken by the Indo-Pakistan war; and the strike was cancelled in favour of a massive protest against Pakistan aggression in which the CPM participated. The announcement of a further reduction in the daily rice ration in January 1966 led to a new flexing of muscles, and to a highly effective Kerala *Bandh* on 28 January involving every party in the state except the rebel Kerala Congress.[13] The impetus was sustained during a number of strikes, particularly among plantation workers and government employees.[14]

It was the CPM which first appreciated the possibility of converting the joint agitations into an electoral front.[15] In Kerala there was every chance that a united front harnessing the tide of anti-Congressism and Malayali resentment of Delhi and its local fellow traveller, the KPCC, could secure a comfortable majority. Anything less than such a broad-based front would make the outcome uncertain. The key to such a front was held by the Muslim League. It was on its role that negotiations in 1965 had ostensibly broken down; and as late as April 1966 the CPI State Council was still declaring its opposition to any electoral deal with the League (or Kerala Congress), though in the muted tones of not perceiving 'the need or necessity' for such an alliance.[16] At this point the League contrived to ease the CPI's path with a resolution from its All-India Working Committee that it was ready to co-operate with all non-Congress parties, including the communists, on the basis of a minimum programme so as to create as many non-Congress governments after the elections as possible, a grander formulation of the position the League had adopted in Kerala at the 1965 election.[17] The League's position was as always in Kerala dictated by practical politics: Congress would not treat with it on the grounds that it was a communal party; younger Muslims in Malabar were proving responsive to communist influence; and the uninhibitedly bazaar approach to politics of the League's leadership in Kerala—business with anyone if the price was right.[18] And what could be a more attractive bargain than the promise of two portfolios as well as a generous allocation of seats and an implicit understanding that a UF ministry would attend to the under-representation of Muslims in government service.[19]

Assembly Election 1967

Once the League had come over, the parties, great and small, settled down to agree on the distribution of seats to be contested and a common programme. Namboodiripad played an admittedly strong electoral hand with finesse. The UF partners accepted an allocation of constituencies based on tricks won in 1965 or, where the constituency had been lost, on the best hand played at the last election. On the face of it, the CPM had dealt fairly with its allies, and in accordance with the spirit of its political line. It appropriated only 61 of the 127 constituencies contested by the front, leaving 24 to the CPI, 23 to the SSP, 15 to the League, and a total of 10 to the minor parties, the RSP, KTP, and KSP. The Marxists' conciliatory approach was not, however, devoid of calculation: the CPI's constituencies lay in the peasant owner-occupier belt, where, facing a powerful Congress opposition, it was unlikely to build a long-term political base; to its chagrin nothing was conceded in Malabar, though on the evidence of the 1965 poll it had little claim there. The SSP, weakened by factionalism[20] and ripe for plucking, was confined to the north while the minor parties were arguably well-treated so as to make them more dependent on the CPM. Further, the generous attitude of the CPM helped to minimize the impact of the minor splits which occurred—typically involving elements of anti-CPM feeling—in each of the non-communist parties in the run up to the election. The majorities in each case, tempted by government as 'a holiday for politicians',[21] had no difficulty in convincing themselves that they would be well able to look after themselves once in power, particularly as the Joint Declaration on the guidelines for a non-Congress government agreed by the seven-party front at Ernakulam on 17 July 1966 appeared decidedly moderate as an election manifesto.[22]

The document, theoretically a minimum programme, did not preclude separate party manifestos but, in practice, it constituted the maximum programme on which agreement could be reached. Eschewing ideology and embracing shibboleth, it omitted any reference to those issues which divided the parties at the national level, a relatively easy task since only the CPI and the CPM were national parties of any moment; and like the genre it was long on panaceas and short on practicalities. As a concession to the Muslim League, the preamble made no reference to socialism and justified the formation of the front as the means of defeating Congress and restoring political stability in the state. In the early paragraphs the emphasis was, understandably in view of the food crisis, on the solution of the food problem: land reform was linked to productivity as well as to social justice. In contrast, industrialization got short shrift: the Centre must do more; state corporations must be run more efficiently; and small-scale industry must be reorganized. Steps must be taken speedily to complete the Idikki and Kuttiadi (hydro-electric) projects, set up three thermal stations to avoid power-cuts, and redress the grievances of electricity workers. How it was all to be done was not indicated. Bland the document may have been, but it served its purpose well enough in emphasizing all those regional problems—food, education, unemployment, and centre-state conflict—which united the partners and tended to isolate Congress as the fifth column in Kerala.

The Results

Riding the wave of anti-Congressism in a state where Congress had never established its one-party dominance, Namboodiripad's grand design was bound to be successful. After a series of Congress mishaps, including the virtual disappearance of rice from both markets and ration shops, Congress expected defeat but the scale of the disaster came as a surprise. Congress had contested every seat but won only 9, as against 36 in 1965, and failed even to qualify as an opposition party in the Assembly. Kerala Congress, fighting in 61 constituencies, slipped from 24 to 5 MLAs. A united Congress could have won another 20 seats.[23] In contrast, the United Front, won 113 victories, to which could be added 4 of the 6 independents who later joined the front (CPM 2; CPI 1, SSP 1). All the partners did well: the CPM improved its position from 40 in 1965 to 52, which made it the dominant party but—and it had not been a party objective—without an overall majority within the front; the CPI with 19 seats (3 in 1965) was rescued from oblivion; the SSP also with 19 (13 in 1965) and the League with 14 (12 in 1965) were well placed; while the RSP with 6 seats (none in 1965) and the KTP with 3 seats had reason for self-congratulation.

How effectively the coalition had been put together is evident from the striking difference between seats won by Congress and its share of the poll. Congress had actually improved its percentage vote since 1965 from 33 per cent to 35 per cent, though this was almost certainly at the expense of Kerala Congress whose vote was virtually halved from 13 per cent to 7.6 per cent, largely as a result of changes in Nair and Christian support. Mannath, having weakened Ezhava influence in Congress by his tactics in 1965, now returned to the fold, bringing with him some of the dissident Nairs while the churches were much divided on politics.[24] Of course, part of what Congress won on the Nair swings it lost on the Ezhava roundabouts. Overall the combined support of the two Congress parties fell by some 3 per cent between 1965 and 1967, hardly in the circumstances a *poor* result.

Long-run Trends in Communist and Congress Support

It is surprising that, at a time of acute food shortage and widespread disenchantment with Congress, a united front which included every significant left-wing party in Kerala, as well as the Muslim League, still managed to secure only half the total votes cast in 1967. One assessment of this election goes further, however, in claiming that the United Front victory was 'due solely to the effectiveness of coalition', thus discounting anti-Congressism altogether.[25] The evidence adduced—a comparison of individual party votes in 1965 and 1967—is of doubtful value, as party alignments were totally different in the two elections.

A better test of the movement of opinion might be to compare Congress support in 1957 with Congress and Kerala Congress support in 1967: Congress itself contested every constituency in both elections and stood independently of all other parties. Over the decade Congress's poll in Kerala fell by 3 per cent compared with a drop of 5.5 per cent at the All-India level; but the total 'Congress' vote over the same period rose nearly 5 per cent. The broadly favourable comparison, however, needs to be qualified immediately by taking into account the virtual disappearance of the Nair-dominated Praja Socialist Party which won 10 per cent of the vote in 1957. In Malabar it seems probable that the chief beneficiary was the successor party, the SSP, whereas in Travancore and Cochin, where the PSP has been strong in Trivandrum District (25 per cent) and Trichur (15 per cent), it is reasonable to suppose Congress gained most—as the party with which Praja Socialist supporters had most affinity.

The District figures in the accompanying table clarify the question. Over the decade, save in Trivandrum and Trichur, the KPCC share of the poll fell. On the other hand the total 'Congress' vote in 1967 is higher in all but the two southernmost Districts of Malabar—Palghat and Kozhikode—partly, it seems, as a result of the emergence of Jana Sangh and Swatantra there. What cannot be gainsaid is that *total* 'Congress' support was falling in Malabar and rising in Travancore-Cochin: some 3 per cent loss in the north and 8 to 9 per cent gain in the south. Interestingly, the real gains for the combined

Table 8.1 Kerala 1957-67: Non-Communist Vote by District
(percentage)

District	PSP 1957	Congress 1957	Congress 1967	Kerala Congress 1967	Total Congress* 1967	Jana Sangh & Swatantra 1967
Trivandrum	25.2	18.8	44.8	—	44.8	0.1
Quilon	8.1	33.9	31.5	12.7	44.2	n.a.
Alleppey	8.7	38.2	36.3	13.6	49.9	0.9
Kottayam	6.3	47.5	25.3	27.3	52.6	n.a.
Ernakulam	3.8	50.5	37.6	12.1	49.7	0.6
Trichur	14.6	44.0	46.5	1.8	48.3	n.a.
Palghat	7.1	36.4	32.1	n.a	32.1	3.7
Kozhikode	9.8	25.9	34.1	0.2	34.3	3.2
Cannanore	16.1	34.1	31.6	0.9	32.5	1.0
State	10.4	37.8	35.4	7.6	43.0	1.1

* Total Congress 1967 = Congress and Kerala Congress.
Sources: Election Commission, India, *Report on the General Election to the Kerala Legislative Assembly 1960* and results of Kerala Legislative Assembly election 1967 verified by Dept of Politics, U. of Kerala.

'Congress' parties were being made in predominantly *Hindu* areas: Trivandrum (23 per cent), Quilon (10 per cent), and Alleppey (8 per cent). In the two Districts with large Christian minorities (Kottayam and Ernakulam) total 'Congress' support was maintained at its previous high level.

For the most part District boundaries are by no means perfect reflections of the social and political geography of such a complex society as that of Kerala. It may therefore be useful to refer to Map 19, which plots by constituency the two Congress parties' share of the poll in 1967. The nearer the shape of the box to a perfect square the greater is Congress support (Kerala Congress in black shading). Several conclusions can be drawn. It is clear that the boundary between Cochin and Malabar almost exactly divides Congress as the dominant party from Congress as an also-ran. Significantly, as the comparable map of communist support in 1965 shows, (see above, page 190), the converse does not hold: the CPM (and in one or two areas the CPM and CPI combined) have marked areas of strength in Cochin and Travancore. Map 19 also highlights the geographical concentration of Kerala Congress in the Christian heartland and the weakness of Congress proper in the Muslim area of southern Malabar. Finally, as a comparison with the map of Congress support in 1957 shows, the KPCC was improving its position along the coastal (and Ezhava) strip of Alleppey and Quilon Districts. The

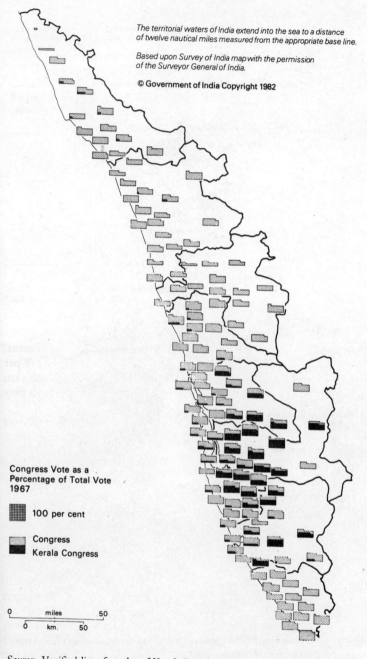

The territorial waters of India extend into the sea to a distance of twelve nautical miles measured from the appropriate base line.

Based upon Survey of India map with the permission of the Surveyor General of India.

© Government of India Copyright 1982

Congress Vote as a
Percentage of Total Vote
1967

100 per cent

Congress
Kerala Congress

0   miles   50

0   km.   50

Source: Verified list of results of Kerala Legislative Assembly election 1967 supplied by Dept of Politics, U. of Kerala.

Map 19 Kerala 1967: Assembly Election, Comparative Distribution of Percentage Vote for Congress and Kerala Congress

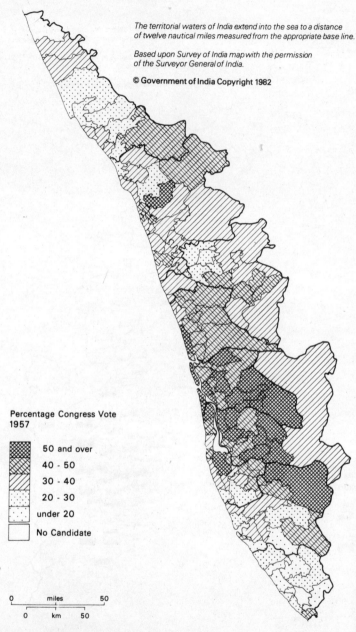

The territorial waters of India extend into the sea to a distance
of twelve nautical miles measured from the appropriate base line.

Based upon Survey of India map with the permission
of the Surveyor General of India.

© Government of India Copyright 1982

Percentage Congress Vote
1957

50 and over
40 - 50
30 - 40
20 - 30
under 20
No Candidate

0   miles   50
0   km   50

Source: Data from Election Commission, India, *Report on the General Election to the
Kerala Legislative Assembly 1960.*

Map 20 Kerala 1957: Assembly Election, Percentage Congress Vote

evidence, then, suggests that there were countervailing trends in Malabar and in Travancore-Cochin.

In the north outside the Moplah areas the Marxists had long been the dominant party; Congress organization had been weakened still further by the departure from the scene of key figures through death or disenchantment; and it was plain enough that such leverage as this most backward part of the state was likely to exercise in Trivandrum would come from the CPM or the League.

In the last resort, however, such statistical comparisons are bound to be crude because the particular circumstances of any pair of elections vary so much. Congress had, we may conclude, succeeded in minimizing its loss of votes in 1967, but to have lost ground at all was a sign of fundamental changes in the rules of the political game, as well as a reflection of shifting national and provincial opinion. The religious and communal organizations had failed to sway the vote in favour of Congress.[26] The NSS, the SNDP, and most of the bishops had cast their lot with Congress but to little avail. Political consciousness was clearly making headway against communal consciousness and Congress was not the beneficiary. That said, it followed that if the KPCC was to return to power in the future it had little option but to abandon its splendid isolation and build its own coalition of forces against the CPM, a task made very much easier than it need have been by both the internal and external politics of the Marxists.

Notes

1 *Hindu*, 19 Feb. 1965.
2 The CPI Central Executive Committee met at Trichur on 20 Feb. 1965. Its resolution on the language issue is summarized in Fic, *Kerala,* p. 290. Namboodiripad's view was that it was futile to dismiss the demand for Dravidanad, Punjabi Suba and Nagaland 'as simply separatist, disruptive, anti-national movements, as the leaders of the ruling party are, in fact, doing. True, they are all this, in a superficial sense, but the fact remains that millions are rallied behind them. Those movements give a distorted expression to some democratic urges of the people as well ... the urge of non-Hindi people for equality with Hindi, the resentment of low caste Hindus against social oppression and the aspiration of the more backward territories and regions ... A correct policy therefore demands the recognition of what is democratic in all these movements ... The nation can be united and integrated not by putting a legal ban on the demand for the separation of any State or territory, but by creating the necessary conditions for making such demagogic, separatist movement completely ineffectual.' *Economics and Politics of India's Socialist Pattern,* p. 396.

3 For a theoretical analysis of the situation by Namboodiripad see *Economics and Politics of India's Socialist Pattern*, ch. 20. Single-state food zones were introduced in Nov. 1964 in place of regional zones. Kerala's rice production fell from 11.21 lakh tons in 1964–5 to 6.97 lakh tons in 1965–6; in Jan. 1966 the Kerala rice ration was 4 oz per adult per day compared with 12 oz in Andhra Pradesh and Tamil Nadu. On 28 Jan. 1966 all parties engaged in protest demonstrations, all shops and factories closed, and in a unique gesture all daily newspapers joined the *hartal*. Thereafter Congress withdrew from the agitation which continued in the form of picketing under the umbrella of the Kerala Samara Samithi in which the CPM was the dominant force. By 25 Feb. 1966, when the agitation was withdrawn, 5,000 volunteers had been arrested. *Kerala Kaumudi* 7, 18, 22 and 30 Jan. 1966; *Arishamavum Avaganayum Pouraswathanthriya Dhwamasanavum* (Ernakulam, Kerala Samara Samithi, n.d. [1966], in Malayalam), p. 11. The rice ration was increased from 10 Mar. 1966 and virtually all cases arising from the food agitation withdrawn.

4 During 1965 growing disenchantment with the Dange line was exemplified in a memorandum by Bhupesh Gupta. Though withdrawn at the National Council meeting, 19–24 Aug. 1965, the episode cost Dange some further loss of power and prestige. Sen Gupta, *Communism in Indian Politics*, p. 89.

5 Statement issued by Namboodiripad on behalf of the CPM Central Committee, 8 Nov. 1965. *Hindu*, 9 Nov. 1965.

6 Namboodiripad's statement as acting General Secretary, 14 Aug. 1965, *People's Democracy*, 29 Aug. 1975; also, ibid., editorials 19 and 26 Sept. 1965.

7 For the situation in AITUC see Crouch, pp. 198–200.

8 'CPI–CPSU Joint Communique', *New Age* 8 May 1966. Sen Gupta, *Communism in Indian Politics*, pp. 92–5.

9 For the Congress split in West Bengal see Franda, *Radical Politics in West Bengal*, p. 141. The break-up was the more significant because the unit had been one of the most cohesive in India. For Kamaraj's visit see *Hindu*, 30 July, 1 and 3 Aug. 1966.

10 Fic, *Kerala* pp. 358–63.

11 Franda, as n.9 above, pp. 123–7 and 141–7; Fic, *Kerala*, pp. 363–77.

12 *People's Democracy*, 7 Aug. 1966 reports the agreement of the CPI, CPM, and SSP resulting from the meeting of party representatives 24–7 July 1966. Namboodiripad and Sundarayya acted for the CPM. The *Kerala Samara Samithi* had been formed on 29 Aug. 1965. Fic, *Kerala*, p. 378.

13 *Times of India*, 28, 29, and 30 Jan. 1966; also n. 3 above.

14 130,000 teachers struck work on 22 June 1966. *Kerala Kaumudi*, 23 June 1966. After some concessions by the governor, V.V. Giri, the, strike was called off on 24 June. Ibid., 25 June 1966. The Non-Gazetted Officers struck for twelve days from 5 to 17 Jan. 1967 in what had originally been intended as a one-day token strike in response to a nation-wide call by the All-India Federation of State Government Employees backed by the

Samara Samithi. The Governor, now Bhagavan Sahay, took a firm line, promulgating an Essential Service Ordinance and arresting union leaders, which precipitated the 'indefinite' strike. *Kerala Kaumudi,* 6 and 18 Jan. 1967.

15 Fic, *Kerala*, p. 380 claims this as a CPI initiative but that appears to be controverted at p. 382. Cf. Namboodiripad, *What Really Happened in Kerala*, published in Jan. 1966, p. 71.

16 'Left Unity for a Stable Government in Kerala: CPI Call', *New Age*, 15 May 1966.

17 *Kerala Kaumudi*, 20 Nov. 1964; Indian Union Muslim League, *The Indian Union Muslim League Resolutions* (Madras, 1966); Kerala State Muslim League, *Janadip Athyathinte Magna Carta* (Calicut, 1966).

18 R.E. Miller, p. 169, traces this policy to the League's post-partition manifesto which permitted it to 'combine or cooperate under any name they chose with any other parties or individuals ... whose programme was identical or approximate to the goals appropriate to Muslim interests' and notes the influence on Moplah leaders of the Tamil Muslim, Raza Khan, a proponent of the view that League politics should be about sharing power. Cf. Theodore P. Wright Jr, 'The Muslim League in South India since Independence', *American Political Science R.* LX (3), 1966. Muhammad Raza Khan, *What Price Freedom?* (Madras, 1969), p. 501.

19 In 1967 only 22 of 511 government appointments carrying a salary of Rs 80 or more per month were held by Muslims. There was no fixed quota for Muslims in the system of communal reservation for the backward classes in government service. *PKLA* VI (18), p. 1119.

20 *Hindu*, 15 Feb. 1967.

21 Interview, Congress leader, 1965, conducted by Dept of Politics, U. of Kerala.

22 *Forward to a Non-Congress Government in Kerala—Declaration of Policy of the Seven Non-Congress Parties of Kerala* (CPI, Ernakulam, n.d. [1966-7]). Also *People's Democracy*, 9 Oct. 1966.

23 Fic, *Kerala*, p. 405.

24 Cyriac Thomas, 'The Church and Politics in Kerala' (unpublished Ph.D. thesis, U. of Kerala, Tvm, 1975), pp. 319-20.

25 Fic, *Kerala*, p. 406. Fic also asserts that 'even hunger—the veritable famine which hit Kerala early in 1966 and the food riots—was only tangentially related' to the outcome.

26 Horst Hartman, 'Changing Political Behaviour in Kerala: a Preface to Elections', *Economic Weekly* Annual no., Jan. 1964, pp. 177-8.

9

Front Politics and Ministerial Stability 1966–1977

FROM 1967 onwards Kerala's politics becomes highly complex. Four features, however, stand out: it was an era of front politics; the last of four coalition ministries provided ministerial though not political stability; the pole around which coalitions were built shifted from the CPM to (Ruling) Congress; and the respective positions of the CPM and CPI were clearly distinguished. What concerns us here is the rival communist parties' response to the changed environment in which they perforce operated. However the reader may find the following summary account of Kerala politics during the period necessary background to the assessment of communist theory and communist performance in the two succeeding chapters. The course of the United Front ministry (1967–9), which is well covered in other works, is charted only in outline. The less familiar later ministries are treated somewhat more fully.

United Front Ministry 1967–1969

The UF ministry's essential problem arose from inter-party rivalries exacerbated by India's economic crisis and intra-party conflict. These factors dominated the front's history and led to its collapse in October 1969. The initial battle over the allocation of portfolios, though not unexpected, indicated the shape of things to come. The CPM as the dominant partner took the key departments—Chief Minister, Home, Revenue, and Law—as well as Transport and Harijan Welfare, while its major rival, the CPI, was given three important 'nation-building' portfolios, Agriculture, Electricity, and Industries, whose successful management largely depended on the goodwill of the Marxist–controlled central departments.

Within weeks national economic difficulties impinged on Kerala in the form of a serious food crisis. While there was general agreement on the Centre's primary responsibility for the non-availability of grains and for the steep rise of prices in the open market, the alleged failure of the Kerala CPM Food Minister to hold the Centre to its commitments, or to step up local levels of procurement, led to early clashes between the CPI and CPM. Defending the CPM in July 1967 Sundarayya, the party's national general secretary, publicly blamed the CPI for blocking CPM initiatives designed to improve the situation. In reply Govindan Nair, the CPI Agriculture Minister, accused Sundarayya of trying to destroy the Kerala front for 'political and organisational reasons', as he had 'finished' the West Bengal UF government.[1] Further clashes took place later in the year over the CPM's decision not to support the cabinet's agreed industrial policy as drafted by the CPI Industries Minister, T.V. Thomas.[2]

The growing tension was not confined to CPM-CPI relations. By September 1967 commentators reported the existence of a 'Front within the Front' or Inner Front—composed of the SSP, CPI, and Muslim League—which accused the CPM of a 'big brother' mentality in that it had demanded the redrafting of agreed policy, interfered in the administration of other parties' departments, and publicized differences for propaganda purposes.[3] The RSP independently presented a charge sheet on CPM conduct to the all-party co-ordination committee. If, the SSP, CPI, and Muslim League said, the CPM 'did not mend its ways', they were prepared to leave the ministry.[4] The CPM counter charged that its partners were thwarting the implementation of the UF programme, unfairly blackening the CPM's image, and actively conspiring to bring down the ministry. In May 1968 Namboodiripad alleged that Kerala Congress had organized a secret meeting with several members of the front to which T.V. Thomas was privy to sound out the possibility of forming a government which excluded the CPM.[5] In this atmosphere of mutual suspicion and recrimination the minor parties in the UF had little choice but to align themselves with the CPM or the Inner Front.

Besides quarrels between parties, there were serious divisions within parties. Three of the seven parties in the UF experienced defections or splits. In April 1968 the two SSP Ministers, P.K. Kunju (Finance) and P.R. Kurup (Co-operation), defied the instructions of their national headquarters to withdraw from the government and in May formed a separate Kerala SSP (KSSP), taking with them eleven of the parent party's eighteen MLAs and most of the organization.[6] Despite SSP protests, Namboodiripad declined to expel the KSSP from the ministry, though in August the UF partners agreed to admit the SSP to the co-ordination committee, this time in face of KSSP opposition. A further split in May 1969 led to the bulk of the KSSP reconstituting itself as the Indian Socialist Party (ISP). There was also dissension in the KTP and, more significantly, in the CPM (see below, p. 248). During 1967 and 1968 'left extremists', or 'ultras', as they were termed in Kerala, had fought the Namboodiripad line (see below, p. 249), and by February 1969 five of the CPM MLAs had either resigned or been expelled from the party. The combination of inter-and intra-party disputes not only impaired the government's effectiveness and undermined its public standing; it also began to threaten the ministry's survival.

The UF's growing weakness was reflected in a marked deterioration in law and order and in proliferating charges of corruption. The continuing economic crisis, party tension at local level, and the police force's uncertainty as to its role under the CPM Home Ministry contributed to a sharp rise in registered criminal cases: 46 per cent between 1966 and 1969 and 23 per cent between 1967 and 1969. Murders increased from 247 in 1966 to 297 in 1967 and to 390 in 1969. The ministers for Home and Labour (Namboodiripad, and M. Manjooran of the KSP) also adopted an equivocal attitude towards the practice of *gherao* (the encirclement of a person till the demands of his antagonists are met). Though illegal, the government took no effective steps to curb its growth even when it involved officials or ministers.[7]

As in 1957-9 there were widespread allegations that the CPM influenced the administration of law and order, and some of the charges appeared well-founded.[8] Both the Opposition and the CPM formed volunteer vigilante corps: Congress and Kerala Congress organized the *Paura Samithi*, Jana Sangh sympathizers a branch of the *Rashtriya Swayam Sevak Sangh* (RSS), and the CPM the *Gopala Sena*, named after A.K. Gopalan, its leader.[9] Finally, former CPM workers were active in Naxalite attacks in late 1968 and early 1969 and in an outbreak of intimidatory communications directed against landlords, shopkeepers, teachers, and officials. (See below, pp. 251 and 361.)

It was the issue of corruption as the focus of intra-party conflict which ultimately brought down the UF in October 1969. According to the UF election manifesto, corrupt MLAs would 'be brought to book effectively' and anti-corruption measures would be initiated on 'as extensive a scale as is possible for a State Government to do'. The ministry, however, was generally regarded as corrupt and specific allegations were made in the Assembly against every single minister.[10] Whatever the truth of charges against individuals, there was clearly no doubt that ministers by-passed normal methods of recruitment to public service of which Imbichi Bava's irregular appointment of more than 200 alleged CPM supporters to posts in the state Transport Corporation was the most widely criticized.[11]

The existing machinery for the investigation of corruption consisted of the government's Vigilance Department and the Commission of Enquiries Act. The UF manifesto had promised a new judicial body with authority to investigate alleged corruption once a *prima facie* case had been established. The parties, however, disagreed about what constituted corruption, the degree of independence to be accorded to the agency, and the exemption of the Chief Minister from the procedure. The CPI, in particular, sought to stick closely to the principles of the national inquiry by the Santhanam Committee on Corruption in Public Life (1964), while the CPM wished the Chief Minister to be exempt and to have the authority to investigate the *prima facie* case and to elect the judicial body by a two-thirds majority of the Assembly.[12] In consequence the Kerala Public Men (Inquiries) Bill, 1968 was not introduced into the Assembly until March 1969 and was still in committee when the ministry fell. As drafted, it was in any case largely irrelevant since it excluded ministers and MLAs from its provisions.[13]

In contrast to 1959 the role of external factors in the collapse of the government was minimal: the opposition in the Assembly was insignificant; there was no liberation struggle; and the Centre was only a minor irritant. The UF tore itself to pieces. In April 1969 the CPI presented the CPM with a thirteen-point ultimatum summarizing the discontents of the Inner Front: 'whatever may be the Front election programme, whatever the co-ordination committee may decide ... only the CPM rules ... all others have either to fall in line or get out.' If the CPM did not respond positively within three months, the CPI warned, it would have to reconsider its participation in the government.[14]

The CPM's moves to isolate the CPI within the front proved abortive. Indeed its efforts to reassert its hegemony, by claiming for the Chief Minister the right to establish *prima facie* cases of corruption against his colleagues, served to harden the Inner Front's solidarity, particularly after the Muslim League had secured its twin objectives of the Moplah-majority District of Malappuram and a university at Calicut.[15] The co-ordination committee had specifically given Namboodiripad the authority to investigate the *prima facie* case against the first minister charged in the Assembly, the politically friendless ISP Finance Minister, P.K. Kunju. Namboodiripad's impartiality was, however, challenged when in August 1969 he announced to the Assembly that he found no *prima facie* case against either the KTP Health Minister B. Wellingdon, or the CPM Forest Minister, M.K. Krishnan. The exoneration of Wellingdon, who had originally been accused of corruption in a CPM newspaper, aroused particular anger. The allegations were widely credited (and later largely proved) and it was claimed that the Chief Minister had been influenced in his decision by ministerial favouritism shown to his brother-in-law, an official in the Health Department.[16] All parties except the CPM, KTP, and KSP demanded an inquiry and the SSP Speaker adjourned the Assembly in uproar. The following day, 23 August, the CPM state executive issued a statement that the Chief Minister, who had been ill for some time, was departing for medical treatment in East Germany and would return in two month's time. Until then this and other disputed issues would be shelved.

During Namboodiripad's absence A.K. Gopalan, the CPM state secretary, first sought an accommodation with the CPI and the Muslim League and then counter-attacked with the preparation of charges against the CPI ministers. On 3 October the Assembly agreed to a CPI motion calling for an inquiry to be instituted into Wellingdon's conduct by 18 October, and on 11 October the Inner Front warned that it would withdraw from the ministry if the resolution was not honoured. Two days later Namboodiripad returned to Trivandrum and on 17 October announced inquiries into the allegations against Wellingdon, Kurup (ISP), and the two CPI ministers but said they would not, as was normal practice, be required to resign when the Commission was set up. Declining to order similar inquiries into the charges against the CPM ministers, he challenged the Inner Front to move a motion of no confidence. The Inner Front Ministers then resigned, together with Wellingdon, and on 24 October, after a three-day debate, a CPI resolution calling for an inquiry into the conduct of the three CPM ministers (excluding the Chief Minister) and the one other minister, Manjooran (KSP), left in post, was carried by 69 votes to 60. Namboodiripad thereupon resigned. His first ministry in 1957-9 could be said to have gone down with guns blazing in the face of the superior firepower of the Centre and provincial vested interests. His second ministry slid from view, unmourned, with a mutinous quarter-deck and its bilges full of corruption, leaving in its wake little in the way of *completed* legislation for its thirty-two months' voyage.[17] Despite its troubled course it had, to its credit, carried the Agrarian Relations bill through all its stages in the Assembly.

Mini-Front Ministry 1969-1970

According to one explanation, Namboodiripad's decision[18] to force the Inner Front to choose between accepting CPM hegemony and bringing down the ministry was based on his assumption that his defeat would entail an unpopular period of President's rule. The 1969 split in the All-India Congress party, coupled with the limited electoral strength of the CPI, League, RSP, and ISP, even in alliance, would then enable the CPM to dictate terms at the next election. The

Governor, Venkata Viswanathan, a distinguished ICS officer, had other ideas.[19] After consulting Govindan Nair (CPI), Bafaki Thangal (League), and others, Viswanathan invited Achutha Menon, Finance Minister in the 1957-9 government and then a member of the Rajya Sabha, not the Kerala Assembly, to form a new ministry. It was an initiative which was to have three far-reaching consequences: ministerial stability; the erosion of a Marxist-dominant party system; and the institutionalization of programmatic 'socialist' government.

On 1 November 1969 Menon was sworn in as Chief Minister, a post he was to hold until his retirement from active politics in March 1977. The new cabinet consisted of eight ministers drawn from four parties: the CPI, the League, the JSP, and Kerala Congress—an opposition party during 1967-9. The RSP, fourth member of the Inner Front, joined the co-ordination committee, but on instructions from the party centre in West Bengal, declined a portfolio. The Government's chances of survival were improved by the New (Indira) Congress's assurances of benevolent neutrality though the Chief Minister, publicly at least, declared that he would resign if his ministry became dependent on Congress votes.[20]

The new ministry's aims were ostensibly modest: to the irritation of the CPM it claimed to be the residuary legatee of the UF government, committed to the time-bound implementation of the 1967 minimum programme, the restoration of law and order, total abstinence from partisan interference in administration, and an end to bickering between like-minded parties. In reality the ministry's objective was more fundamental: to destroy the CPM's post-1964 hegemony in Kerala politics. Aware of the threat, the CPM threw itself wholeheartedly into the oppositional role on which all sections of the party could unite.

Belligerent CPM pronouncements were matched with action on the mass front. Not a day would pass, A.K. Gopalan warned, without the government having recourse to the *lathi* or bullet.[21] According to official figures, between 1 November 1969 and 31 August 1970 the police fired on seven occasions, killing nine persons and injuring four, though the CPM claimed that as many as forty-two died in mass struggles.[22] Namboodiripad warned the League Home Minister, C.H. Mohammed Koya, that he would meet Sir C.P. Ramaswami Aiyar's fate, and within days an attempt was made on Koya's life by a CPM worker in Tellicherry. Initially the agitation was aimed at forcing Menon to recall the Assembly, which stood adjourned until 9 January. The Chief Minister, however, appreciated that it was essential to master the CPM on the mass front first, a task made easier by the unity of the Mini Front parties, the firm backing given by Koya to his police force, and the growing popular desire for a restoration of law and order. Further, his chances of winning a vote of confidence in the fragmented Assembly would be improved if in the intervening two months he could demonstrate that his ministry meant business as *unusual*.[23] Obligingly, the Centre expedited presidential approval of the land reform bill, the one major achievement of the previous UF ministry (see below, p. 293). By 1 January 1970 the act was law, machinery had been established to implement its provisions, and Achutha Menon was claiming to be the Chief Minister who had abolished landlordism. Among other steps, Menon also ordered commissions of inquiry into the allegations against the former CPM ministers, Imbichi Bava, M.K. Krishnan, and Mrs Gouri, as well as their KSP ally, Mathai Manjooran.

The Ministry now turned to face the onslaught in the Assembly. The Governor's address outlining the government's proposals to strengthen the police force, implement the 1967 Industrial Policy statement, nationalize the private forests of Malabar, and explore the possibility of taking over the foreign plantations, was drowned in uproar. The address was, however, approved with a ministerial majority, excluding Congress votes, of nine. Tension continued, and on 29 January CPM members invaded the Speaker's dais after he had disallowed an adjournment motion. Five Marxist MLAs were suspended for the rest of the session.[24] The ministry's closest shave came at midnight on 17/18 March 1970 when five MLAs—three government supporters and two independents—requested the Speaker to allot them seats with the opposition.[25] At the same time the deputy leader of the Old (or anti-Indira) Congress group switched to the New Congress. The government was now in a minority of two, even with the support of the five New Congress members, in the middle of the debate on appropriations for the 1970-1 budget. In the small hours of the morning T.K. Divakaran, RSP Leader of the House, suggested an elementary solution to buy time and (*sic*) votes: the government would table a motion of confidence, which took precedence over all other business, courteously offer the opposition time to prepare, and allow two days for the debate. In the event only two of those who had crossed the floor voted with the opposition, while all four Old Congress members supported the ministry, giving it a clear majority of eight. After passing the Appropriation Bill, the Assembly was adjourned *sine die*. It was not to meet again.

There followed a test of public opinion in three by-elections: at Kottarakkara (Quilon), where the Chief Minister won handsomely;[26] Nilambur (Kozhikode), where the government-backed New Congress candidate won the seat from the CPM;[27] and Madai (Cannanore) where the opposition KSP's majority was slashed.[28] Menon was now confident that he could win a further term of office at a mid-term poll, given New Congress support.

The timing of the election was largely dictated by the impact on the government's majority of renewed dissension in the socialist camp.[29] After what appeared to be a routine cabinet meeting, the Chief Minister astonished the press corps by announcing that the Governor had granted a dissolution and that he would remain in office till the date of the election had been determined. The CPM protested vigorously but Achutha Menon's tactics were entirely constitutional.

The 1970 Mid-term Assembly Election

Whatever the Mini Front's standing in popular esteem, it was clear that Achutha Menon's prospects of a second term depended on the construction of a broad-ranging electoral combination. In view of the socialists' disarray and Kerala Congress's growing affinity with Old Congress, it was imperative to reach an electoral understanding with New Congress, which because of CPI and RSP party sensitivities must fall short of an outright alliance. Such an arrangement met with opposition in the KPCC on three grounds: the party, and particularly its activist Youth Congress wing, was reluctant to campaign simply to put others in office; hostility to working with a communist party; and reluctance to accord power or even recognition to the Muslim League, despite Mrs Gandhi's assertion that in Kerala it was non-communal in character. The Congress High Command, however, insisted that the need to defeat the CPM and to demonstrate the party's progressive character in the first Assembly election after the Congress split outweighed all other considerations. New Congress therefore agreed to back the CPI-led Mini Front.

The final party line-up consisted of 22 parties, loosely arranged into 3 fronts: the CPI or Mini Front composed of the CPI, Muslim League, PSP, and RSP backed by the New (sometimes called Ruling) Congress; the CPM-led People's Democratic Front (PDF), made up of the CPM, SSP, ISP, KSP, and KTP; and the right-wing Democratic Front (DF) comprising Old (sometimes called Organization) Congress, Kerala Congress, Jana Sangh, and Swatantra. To confuse matters further, the PDF and DF had agreed to avoid victory for Mini Front or New Congress candidates through a vote split between the far left and far right of Kerala politics.

The electorate, facing its fifth poll in thirteen years, appeared to have ignored the fact that its decision had a national dimension and was seen in Delhi as a crucial test of the relative standing of Old and New Congress.[30] Despite visits from the country's leading politicians and the gravity of the All-India situation, the essential question in the campaign was which of the rival fronts was most likely to deliver the state from its chronic political instability and economic difficulties. The CPM's campaign lacked its customary fire. The party failed adequately to exploit the courts' actions in maiming the Land Reform and University Acts during the run-up to the election; there was little fresh election literature—a 1967 manifesto was reprinted; and there were signs of inner-party dissension over candidacies.[31] The CPM's capacity to mobilize its grass-roots support was also adversely affected by the widespread disenchantment with its electoral tactics: the tacit understanding with the 'right reactionaries' of the Democratic Front and the gift of some safe constituencies to its inconsequential allies. Lastly, as a party of opposition, the CPM lacked a sensational issue, for example the arrests of 1965, the anti-Congressism of 1967, or, for that matter, the ousting of the CPI ministry in 1959.

In the light of all these factors the result of the election was hardly unexpected: the CPM suffered a considerable setback; New Congress, in making a good though not brilliant showing, confirmed that it was the dominant wing of Congress in Kerala; the extremists of both left and right were routed; and the Mini Front was given not so much a vote of confidence as a stay of execution. New Congress, which had contested 56 seats, and won 32, formed the biggest group in the new Assembly, followed closely by the CPM with 28 seats from 72 contests. The Mini Front won 36 seats—16 CPI and 11 League—and the Marxist People's Democratic Front 41. The rightist Democratic Front managed only 12 seats, all won by Kerala Congress, although three 'Independents', who had enjoyed Marxist support threw off their disguise when the Assembly met to reveal their allegiance as Old Congressmen. Syndicate, Jana Sangh, and Swatantra between them forfeited 34 of their 49 deposits and collected only 300,000 votes in total, on a par with the extreme left, the Communist Revolutionary Party, led by K.P.R. Gopalan.

Despite the proliferation of choice before the electorate only the CPM and New Congress really counted. The CPI, League, and Kerala Congress enjoyed localized support and nuisance value elsewhere while Old Congress and the SSP lacked even significant District followings. Fourteen parties failed to win a single seat.

In view of the complex electoral arrangements, total party votes are probably not very helpful. More interesting is the major parties' share of the poll in the constituencies actually contested—on the presumption that in most cases this was where their support was strongest.

Table 9.1 *Kerala 1970: Assembly Election*

	Candidates	Seats	% Poll
Mini Front			
CPI	31	16	9.3
RSP	14	6	4.4
PSP	7	3	2.4
ML	20	11	7.7
New Congress	56	32	18.3
Totals	128	68	42.2
People's Democratic Front			
CPM	72	28	23.4
SSP	14	6	4.1
KSP	3	2	0.7
ISP	11	3	3.3
KTP	4	2	1.2
Totals	104	41	32.6
Democratic Front			
Kerala Congress	31	12	5.9
Old Congress	39	(3)*	3.5
Jana Sangh and			
Swatantra	10	0	0.7
Totals	80	15 †	10.1

* Contested as Independents
† Including Old Congress-Independents

Source: Adapted from Election Commission, India, *Report on the General Election to the Kerala Legislative Assembly 1970.*

New Congress won 43 per cent of the vote in its 56 constituencies, a marginal increase on the 40 per cent secured in the same constituencies by the nationally undivided Congress party in 1967. If allowances are made for a modest number of votes cast in 1970 for Congressmen by Mini Front supporters, New Congress had probably lost little ground as a result of the split in Kerala. Of particular interest here is that the KPCC had maintained its standing in these 'core' constituencies while changing the composition of its candidates. Though contesting less than half the seats it had fought in 1967 the party had preferred Young Turks to the praetorian guard, so signalling a break with past factionalism and offering the prospect of a parliamentary career to young college and INTUC politicians. All the Youth Congress leaders who stood for election were successful.

The CPM's showing was generally interpreted as a setback, but

Table 9.2   Kerala 1970: Strength of Major Parties by District (percentage)

	CPM	CPI	New Congress	Old Congress	Kerala Congress	ML	SSP	Total as % of the poll
Trivandrum	43.3	20.6	25.3	5.7	—	5.1	—	69.8
Quilon	31.2	31.0	20.4	1.0	16.4	—	—	63.1
Alleppey	47.0	11.7	26.9	—	14.4	—	—	73.4
Kottayam	28.9	15.3	14.9	5.7	33.7	1.5	—	78.8
Ernakulam	47.4	8.9	29.6	2.1	9.6	2.5	—	84.4
Trichur	42.1	10.4	31.3	5.7	—	3.2	7.3	85.7
Palghat	52.9	7.2	19.0	2.9	—	14.1	4.0	87.3
Kozhikode	25.7	3.6	25.7	1.2	0.6	36.5	6.8	80.6
Cannanore	49.4	7.3	20.6	5.8	—	13.5	3.5	76.1

Note: Party percentages are calculated only for candidates securing 8 per cent or more of the vote. The final column shows the sum of the row for each District, expressed as a percentage of the total poll. The old nine-District system is used for comparability with previous elections rather than the ten adopted in 1969.

Source: Calculated from Election Commission, India, *Report on the General Election to the Kerala Legislative Assembly 1970.*

the results do not show that the party was losing its *mass* base (see below, p. 323). Contesting 72 constituencies, including some chosen to maximize the vote of the front as a whole, the CPM won 23 per cent of the total poll: certainly that did not compare with the 1967 result of 24 per cent of the vote from 59 constituencies—a misleading baseline because of the broad character of the United Front—but it was better than the 20 per cent from 73 constituencies in 1965. The CPM share of the poll fell in 21 of the 28 constituencies won in 1970, in eight cases by as much as 10 to 20 per cent, but this was to a large extent a function of the loss of League support—as well as, to a smaller degree, of Mini Front votes.

Second Mini Front Ministry 1970-1971

On 4 October 1970 Achutha Menon's second ministry was sworn in, consisting of four ministers from the CPI, two each from the Muslim League and the RSP, and one from the PSP. With only 36 MLAs, the minority ministry was dependent on the support of New Congress in the Assembly, a fact recognized by New Congress representation in the co-ordination committee. In an expanded nine-man committee, four members were nominated by New Congress and one each by the four ministerial parties, with the Chief Minister presiding *ex officio*. Menon later claimed that the narrowness of the majority enjoyed by the Mini Front and New Congress in the Assembly, coupled with the CPM's vigorous opposition, did much to ensure the comparatively smooth working of the committee.

One might expect a minority government to concentrate on survival. The Mini Front, however, reasonably confident that New Congress needed it as much as it needed New Congress, claimed to pursue a positive policy, what Achutha Menon called a 'humble attempt to reconstruct the state and make a modern Kerala'.[32] Given the CPM's capacity to mount opposition within and without the Assembly, the ministry's one real hope was to counter agitation with firm and constructive government backed by the full resources of the official and party publicity machines. As in 1969-70 Menon and Mohammed Koya, the League Home Minister, were determined to quell agitation whenever it became violent. Koya's support for police action, even when co-ordination committee parties were involved, led to heavy criticism from government supporters.

During the early months of the ministry the CPM's conduct inside and outside the chamber was above criticism. Its opponents twitted the CPM leaders for transforming themselves into a responsible opposition (see below, p. 297). However, the calm was broken on 27 December 1970 by the news from Delhi that Mrs Gandhi had asked for a dissolution of the Lok Sabha a year before its full term after the Supreme Court had upheld the princes' claim that the abolition of privy purses by presidential action was invalid. The pointers to the outcome were good: there had been a bumper harvest; the economy was showing signs of recovery; the right was in disarray; and the Naxalites were scattered or in prison.

At the national level the Prime Minister ruled out alliances of any kind but at the state level she encouraged certain understandings. Within three weeks the Mini Front, New Congress, and Kerala Congress announced an accord by which New Congress would contest seven seats, the CPI and Kerala Congress three each, the League two, and the RSP and PSP one apiece. Such a combination placed the CPM on the defensive: A.K. Gopalan switched from Kasergod to Palghat on the grounds that his health—undeniably bad—would not stand a stiff contest; Krishna Menon was offered the party's support as an independent in Trivandrum; there were to be official CPM candidates in ten constituencies; and the CPM's stance in the remaining eight seats was to be decided on the merits of party alignments.

This alliance of the Mini Front and Congress parties virtually swept the board and the CPM retained only two of its nine seats, Palghat, and, by a narrow margin, Tellicherry. Krishna Menon also won in Trivandrum, where a CPM-led agitation by government employees was one factor in the result. Despite the loss of seats at the peak of the 'Indira Wave', the CPM had once again confirmed its hold over substantial sections of the electorate. In eleven contests (including Trivandrum) it had secured 43 per cent of the poll. Though the party's own assessment of its performance in Kerala was justifiably optimistic, one feature of the election caused concern: the success of Youth Congress, which had not only been the main campaigning force against the CPM, but also was represented in the new Lok Sabha by four out of the six New Congressmen. Revolutions—peaceful or otherwise—may be made by grandfathers but they are executed by the young, a lesson lost on neither Namboodiripad nor Achutha Menon.

Maxi Front Ministry 1971–1975

The most important consequence of the Lok Sabha results was that, by strengthening Mrs Gandhi's personal position and by demonstrating New Congress support in Kerala, they opened the way for New Congress participation in the Mini Front ministry. Within a month the New Congress MLAs had passed a resolution in favour of joining the government, Youth Congress MLAs dissenting. Subsequently a joint meeting of MLAs and the KPCC, in which Youth Congress influence was strong, arrived at the compromise formula that there would be no immediate entry into the ministry but that the New Congress Party's central Parliamentary Board should be free to determine when the time was ripe to request an invitation to join the state government.[33] After yet another realignment of the socialist parties nationally had rendered the PSP's support for the ministry highly uncertain, Achutha Menon informed Mrs Gandhi that New Congress would have to join the ministry.[34] It was shortly after the conclusion of the Indo-Soviet Treaty in early August that the Mini Front formally invited Congress to join the government, a timing which was probably not fortuitous.

After three weeks' hard bargaining the size and composition of the new 'Maxi Front' ministry were agreed on 13 September: expansion of the cabinet from nine to thirteen; the CPI to concede Harijan Welfare to New Congress, thus giving it five ministries to the Mini Front's eight; the League to surrender the Home portfolio, leaving Koya with Education; and New Congress to abandon its claim to the dual headship of the ministry, implicit in its demand for the creation of a post of Deputy Chief Minister. The CPI and the League were well content. For modest concessions they had established an All-India precedent. New Congress, by sharing power with them, had signalled an end to their political untouchability. For all parties, however, one problem remained. Youth Congress (and its student wing) had reneged on its earlier commitment to join the ministry, though its leader acted as convenor of the co-ordination committee. The refusal of Youth Congress to be shackled by ministerial responsibility was to have serious consequences.

Kerala now had a government capable of surviving its full term. But ministerial stability did not prove to be synonymous with political stability, nor was it to be a simple recipe for the gradual solution of the state's problems. The CPM, as the leading opposition party, was far from dismayed by the turn of events; indeed, by sustained agitation on the mass front and pressure in the Assembly, it had sought to bring the union about, the better to discredit New Congress, the CPI, and National Democracy. 'The issue . . . today is not Government', Namboodiripad commented in early October, 'but development of the people's struggle for the problems they are facing.;[35] The CPM was not the prime mover in all the agitation which affected Kerala during the ensuing thirty-three months prior to the 1975 Emergency nor did it manufacture *hartals* and *bandhs* out of the air. However, it endeavoured to orchestrate all forms of people's struggle whatever their origins.

In its first year the Maxi Front ministry coped adequately with agitation if at some cost in terms of time, energy, and money—to finance pay settlements at the expense of job creation. More taxing, as the college teachers' disputes of September–October 1971 and June–August 1972 illustrated, were agitations jointly sponsored by the CPM and Youth Congress. A further source of difficulty was the strained relations between New Congress and the Muslim League: 'misunderstandings' at ministerial level and brawls at rank and file level, which culminated in December 1971 in the worst outbreak of communalism seen in Kerala since 1921-2. In two days 24 mosques, 50 prayer halls, and some 400 Moplah-owned shops and houses were wholly or partially destroyed in and around the Malabar town of Tellicherry.[36] Though Hindu hostility to Moplahs may have been fuelled by events in Bangladesh, a more immediate precipitant appears to have been the League's determination to celebrate the 50th anniversary of the Moplah Rebellion, still regarded by the Hindu population as a communal outrage. The alleged complicity of the CPM was dwelt upon by New Congress supporters, but the League's own reaction was to blame the recently appointed New Congress Home Minister, K. Karunakaran, whose attitude to warnings of impending trouble appeared casual, and those local officers for whom he was responsible whose conduct was at the very least pusillanimous. In an effort to repair its position the ministry announced (at Tellicherry) a new 26-point, time-bound programme on the eve of an important test of public opinion in a by-election for the CPM-held set of Trichur.[37] The outcome—a comfortable victory for the New Congress candidate—which reflected both national trends and local factors, marked the ministry's high-water mark.[38]

By the autumn of 1972 the ministry's reply to a CPM-KC motion of no confidence was decidedly defensive.[39] 1971–2 had been a bad year for the Indian economy with an erratic monsoon adding to the inflationary pressures consequent on the Bangladesh war. The increase in the cost of living had far outstripped the rise in incomes. In Kerala the problem was accentuated by the state's chronic food deficit and the fall in demand for some of its cash crops.[40] Early in 1973 the ministry's growing unpopularity was confirmed in two Assembly by-elections, at Nileswaram where the CPM increased its majority, and at Parur where the ministry lost a traditional New Congress seat.[41]

In the Assembly the Maxi Front's position now came under threat from dissensions within the PSP and the Muslim League. On the eve of the budget session in February 1973 a 'united socialist bloc' of National PSP and Congress Socialist members threatened to boycott the vote on the Governor's address. The ministry, however, was far more disturbed by signs of a crack in the monolithic Muslim League, whose support in Malabar was crucial to containing the CPM's electoral prospects. In January 1973 its unchallenged spiritual and political leader, Syed Abdur Rehman Bafaki Thangal, died. His formidable personality, together with his success since 1967 in taking the League from a reviled 'communal' party to a courted member of ruling fronts, had contained the growing contradictions in Moplah society: the conservative *Sunnis* versus the (comparatively) liberal *Wahabis;* the landed aristocracy of Cannanore and the commercial bourgeoisie of Calicut versus the labourers and coolies of Malappuram; and the traditional *Thangal* leadership versus the modernizing Muslim Education Society (founded in 1964)[42]. Bafaki Thangal had not chosen a successor but it is doubtful whether any nomination could have averted a war of succession.

From January 1973 the rival factions began to manoeuvre for control of the party organization, the main protagonists being the official group—led by Abdul Koya, backed by Mohammed Koya, lately Home and Education Minister and at this time member of the Lok Sabha for the safe League seat of Manjeri—and the dissidents led by Bafaki Thangal's son-in-law, Ummar Bafaki Thangal.[43] Personal rivalries apart, the main issue was the League's attitude to New Congress, the two Koyas wishing to continue the existing rap-

prochement with it, and Ummar Bafaki, avowedly hostile, prepared
to align the League with the CPM if need be. Throughout 1973-4 the
League's dissensions were a recurring source of alarm to the Maxi
Front and of hope to the CPM, with the New Congress's allegedly
partial conduct of the Home portfolio a constant source of tension.

However, the final confrontation was delayed until March 1975,
for three reasons: the difficulty of gauging the rivals' support; Mrs
Gandhi's shifting stance on League-Congress relations; and the dissident Leaguers' desire to strike the best political bargain by postpon-
ing definitive alignment until the eve of the scheduled 1975 Assembly election. After the official wing had demonstrated its majority in
the 200-member State Council of the League on 9 March 1975, it
commenced disciplinary action.[44] The dissidents then threatened to
withdraw their support for the ministry. On paper the government
no longer commanded a majority in the house.

In 1973, worrying though the trend of events was in League
circles, the ministry had two far more urgent problems on its
mind—the deteriorating state of the economy and the food crisis.
The previous year had been a bad one for the Indian economy, but
1973 was even worse. The general index of prices rose by almost
one-quarter. Industrial growth continued to decline and agricultural
production slumped badly, largely as a result of an adverse monsoon. In Kerala during July and August rice was not available at any
price and the coastal areas of Travancore were officially designated
famine zones.[45] By the autumn the ministry was under siege from its
own supporters as well as from the CPM and Kerala Congress
opposition. Inflation provoked a rash of strikes to maintain annual
bonuses—which had come to be regarded as equivalent to dearness
allowance and distinct from productivity or profitability. Given the
state's parlous financial position, the ministry had little choice but to
resist these demands even at the price of alienating its own union
wings. For the first time during this administration a leading cabinet
minister used the phrase 'political crisis' to describe the effect of the
state-wide transport strike, and according to one version Achutha
Menon threatened to resign unless his own CPI-led unions met the
ministry half way.[46] On this basis the AITUC and INTUC transport
workers returned to work and on 20 September the Joint Action
Council, representing the opposition-led unions, finally called off
the strike. The Maxi Front had survived its stiffest test thus far but it
had suffered an internal haemorrhage: the ministerialists no longer
controlled their colleagues on the labour and mass fronts. The Youth
Congress convenor of the co-ordination committee had resigned his
post; INTUC was preparing to censure the government; and the
CPI had picketed state offices. No less alarming was the fact that the

economic crisis had brought the CPM and Kerala Congress into alliance on the mass front. If, as was widely predicted, the League did split, the ministry's only hope of survival was a deal with Kerala Congress, and that may be one explanation of why the Prime Minister was invited to attend (and accepted) the Golden Jubilee celebrations of the Catholic Diocese of Calicut in late October.

Advance forecasts of Kerala's food situation in 1974 were as bleak as the economic prognosis and on 6 January five opposition parties— the CPM, Kerala Congress, Socialist Party (SP), KSP, and KTP— formally met at Cochin to organize 'virulent and far-reaching agitations' on food, prices, and yet another postponement of the panchayat elections. Their first public action was mass picketing of government offices on 28 January.[47] Three days later the CPM pressed matters further by an attempted *gherao* of the Governor as he tried to open the budget session of the Assembly.[48]

Despite the Maxi Front's record of reforming legislation, including the recent passage of the Agricultural Workers Bill and the Kerala University Bill, the ministry had made little progress on the basic economic issues, and was increasingly driven to heavy-handed police action to contain popular discontent. All this placed acute strains on party relations. On this bedrock the CPM launched a new 'liberation struggle' in August 1974, the leanest of lean months.[49] The phrase consciously echoed Kerala in 1959 and Gujarat and Bihar in 1974, though the CPM kept the 'JP' movement at arm's length.[50] In October the party led a march on the Assembly to demand the investigation of allegations that the police had beaten up two Marxist and two SP MLAs and of newspaper reports of ministerial corruption.[51] The ministry proved obdurate and after further exchanges of incivilities irate Marxist members hurled sandals across the chamber. On the eve of the budget session in February 1975 Namboodiripad announced that the five-party opposition front would boycott the Assembly since 'no self-respecting person can take part when four ministers charged with corruption sit on the treasury benches'.[52] The Chief Minister had in fact ordered probes into the allegations against two ministers but had not required them to resign. On this occasion the opposition undertook a hunger *satyagraha* in front of the Speaker's chair and in March, with a few exceptions, boycotted the proceedings altogether to demand the dismissal of the ministry and fresh elections, which were due in any case by September. When the Assembly met on 31 March for the last time (prior to the Emergency) to despatch eleven bills in time for morning coffee, the ministry was technically in a minority as a result of the split in the League. More disconcerting to the Maxi Front was the distinct possibility that it would lose the forthcoming election

New Congress–CPI relations, for both national and local reasons, were acrimonious; New Congress was itself torn by the conflict between Youth Congress and the party elders as well as by resurgent communal alignments;[53] and the CPI was increasingly divided on the merits of its alliance with New Congress. The opposition front was an imposing combination with a broad communal and regional basis. For all the ministry's record of reforming legislation (see below, p. 289) implementation had fallen short of expectation. Finally, after two desperate years of food shortages and rising prices, it faced an election campaign with the lean months once more at hand.

The Emergency

It was the Maxi Front's good fortune that the declaration of a national State of Emergency in June 1975 led to postponement of the election until 1977.[54] Though no threat to security existed in Kerala and the parties and organizations proscribed under the Emergency had little following in the state, some hundreds of political activists were detained, mainly from the CPM and the SP. The government was reluctant to make a martyr of Namboodiripad, who was only briefly detained, but it had no such reservations about removing the CPM's middle-level cadres from circulation, especially those working on the agrarian and labour fronts.

Initially public reaction was muted. Though heavy rain and flooding, as well as the element of surprise, handicapped the opposition, it appears that the Emergency was not unwelcome among the people at large. The middle classes, in particular, were delighted at the prospect of a respite from agitation and politics, which many believed to be the bane of Kerala's existence. In governing circles the Emergency was greeted with more mixed feelings and scepticism. Experienced Congress hands did not relish the prospect of increased Central intervention, while the junior partners, including the CPI, feared the assertion of Congress hegemony. For the Chief Minister the Emergency offered on the one hand the opportunity to speed the reconstruction of Kerala into a modern state but on the other the danger that Karunakaran, Congress's senior minister, would become *de facto* Chief Minister.

In one important sense the Emergency changed nothing in Kerala. The major problem facing the government on 26 June was exactly what it had been on 24 June: how to ensure the continuation of the ministry into and beyond the next election. The solution—winning over Kerala Congress to the ruling front—was, however, now much nearer realization. By the test of Mrs Gandhi's Twenty Point

Programme or Sanjay Gandhi's Five Point Programme, Kerala Congress was not 'reactionary'. In so far as it was backed by sections of the Christian church it might be seen as 'communal', but such considerations had not precluded alliance with the Muslim League. The real stumbling block had always been the Youth Congress wing of Congress, which steadfastly opposed any truck with the principal organ of the privately controlled colleges. Now, since the law proscribed agitation by Youth Congressmen and students as much as anyone else, this opposition was no longer an insurmountable obstacle.

Negotiations with Kerala Congress began in November 1975, apparently at Mrs Gandhi's own instigation. According to some accounts they were conducted under the barely veiled threat of detention (for economic offences) if the Kerala Congress leaders did not come to heel, but this seems at variance with the long-drawn-out character of the discussions and the outcome.[55] Kerala Congress held a dozen seats in a 133-member Assembly and would be a decisive factor, when it came to the election, in perhaps another dozen constituencies in central Kerala. Even so, it got the best of the bargaining: two ministries—Finance and Transport—plus the vacant Speakership of the house and the astonishing promise that it could take its choice of 25 seats to contest at the next Assembly election. In a typical piece of Kerala-style political bargaining no existing ministers were displaced. Congress gave up Finance and the CPI Transport, and the government was expanded from 13 to 15.

Despite the high price paid for Kerala Congress support, the deal all but foundered. Factionalism was endemic in Kerala Congress circles and by October 1976 rival groups had been allocated separate blocs on the ministerial benches. The situation deteriorated with the death of K.M. George, leader of one faction, at the end of the year and Congress High Command took the unprecedented step of imposing its own arbitration to resolve differences in an autonomous party. It was to little avail. After posing for a photograph of unity and amity at Trivandrum airport on arriving back from Delhi, Balakrishnan Pillai's faction (KC-Pillai) turned to the CPM camp.

The call for national self-discipline also went unheeded in Congress itself. Long-running conflicts between Youth Congress and the 'elders', between organization and ministerial wings, and among Nair, Ezhava, and Christian were intensified by a number of factors. The deal with Kerala Congress reduced the pool of 'safe' seats for ambitious young men waiting their chance after six arduous years of organizational work. Many elders used the Emergency as an opportunity to establish or re-establish their own fiefdoms. There was also growing resentment at the burgeoning power of Karunakaran,

well-placed as Congress Home Minister to hire and fire in the
Emergency situation. A tough political operator in normal conditions, he was the more feared under the Emergency. Nor did it help
the resolution of Congress' internal difficulties that he was a Nair
while many of his rivals were Ezhavas or Christians.

Youth Congress does not appear to have been a potent influence
during the Emergency. First, relations between its local chief, A.K.
Antony, a man of great personal integrity, and Sanjay Gandhi were
decidedly cool, and Achutha Menon and Antony between them
effectively vetoed any visit by Mrs Gandhi's son to Trivandrum.
Second, shortly before the Emergency the ministry had finally conceded most of those educational reforms which had been the central
demand of the Youth Congress movement in Kerala. Third, Youth
Congress power had been its capacity to counter marxist agitation
with equal or greater demonstrations—and now there was no need of
its services on the streets, its influence shrank. Finally, a little violence
goes a long way in Kerala; the fear of arrest kept most at home. Even
gossip, the lifeblood of local politics, was dangerous. This abrupt
curtailment of customary channels for letting off political steam—no
bandhs, no garlands, and no arguments—did, however, lead to a
frustration which was to find its outlet during the 1977 election and
in its aftermath interrupt Karunakaran's political career (see below,
p. 235).

In Kerala political manoeuvring continued throughout the
Emergency. If politics was strictly rationed the shop was generally
open to powerful customers. In party and communal terms the
ruling front was taking an unexpected opportunity to repair its
position. Shortly after Mrs Gandhi's surprise announcement to hold
a parliamentary election in March 1977, it was decided that Kerala's
Assembly election would be held at the same time and that the ruling
parties would fight as a front. This coincidence of elections enabled
the non-Congress parties to concede a preponderance of seats in the
Lok Sabha contest, which mattered most to Delhi, in exchange for a
preponderance in the Assembly contest, which was what concerned
them.

Opposing the Ruling Front was an Opposition alliance of six
parties—the CPM, Janata (in Kerala a mixture of long-time
Socialists and some Old Congressmen), the Congress Radicals (a
group expelled from New Congress in 1973), the Opposition
Muslim League, the RSP (National), and the Kerala Socialist Party.
A few days later a seventh party joined, the breakaway Kerala
Congress faction, KC (Pillai). At the beginning of the campaign the
CPM had called for a strong left front. What it had managed to piece
together was neither strong nor obviously left. Indeed the front

fought its campaign almost entirely on the issue of liberty versus dictatorship as the Opposition alliance did nationally. The alloca- tion of constituencies presented no real difficulties. The KC (Pillai) and the Opposition Muslim League were simply pitted against their parent parties, while the CPM and Janata were sufficiently removed in their geographical bases not to quarrel. The CPM stood in 68 seats, Janata in 28, and the KC (Pillai) and Opposition League in 16 seats apiece.

After so long in government, the Ruling Front inevitably campaigned primarily on the basis of its record—but a record which antedated the Emergency. Since the ministry, dominated by Con- gress from 1971, could hardly argue that it had fallen asleep at the wheel to be rudely awakened in June 1975, the benefits of the Emergency were minimized. In the manifesto the emphasis was on such achievements as land reform, housing, the Agricultural Work- ers Act, and, above all, stability and steady progress. The guidelines for the future were in many respects simply 'more of the same', though there were promises directed at key interests as well as an assurance of the fullest protection of the rights (unspecified) of minorities.[56] One (privileged) minority—the high-caste Nairs—had already been placated with the concession of half a dozen candidacies for members of the (Nair) National Democratic Party on the Ruling Front ticket.

The opposition's 'joint declaration of policy' was far stronger on what it condemned than on what it proposed to do if elected. Details of policies would 'emerge only after the Government is formed and through the new style of governmental functioning which will lead the State to a new path.'[57] Most of the statement was taken up with an attack on the Emergency in general and the pernicious ways of the ministry in Kerala in particular, mixed with allegations that the only people to profit from the so-called stability were the ruling politi- cians themselves. The problems of the farmer and the worker in traditional industries were singled out for special attention in the future, but, as for solutions, the voter was invited to sign a blank cheque: 'pragmatic programmes would be formulated with rep- resentatives of labour, peasants, Government staff and the public to save the State from the ill-effects of the enveloping economic crisis.'[58] As an appeal for a mandate to govern, which was what the electorate saw itself as deciding in the Assembly election, the hastily drafted declaration of aims inspired little confidence, whatever views the electorate might have had on the merits of the Emergency.

On the eve of the poll the general expectation of commentators and activists alike was that the Ruling Front would lose ground in the Assembly election in terms both of votes cast and seats won, and that the outcome would be a close-run affair.[59] Prophecy was confounded: the Ruling Front had won an overwhelming victory. In the Assembly contest the ministerial alliance had polled 53 per cent of the vote and taken 111 of the 140 seats, while in the Lok Sabha election it had won every single seat. The biggest surprise of all was undoubtedly the CPM's performance, a mere 17 seats in the Assembly. None the less, as its vote shows, 22 per cent from 68 Assembly contests as against Congress's 20 per cent from 54, it remained a considerable electoral force (see below, p. 326).

After such a triumph in the Assembly poll one might have expected the Ruling Front to sweep triumphantly into power but the formation of the new ministry proved far more troublesome than the election. First, the scale of the victory was such that the parties threw normal caution to the winds in bargaining for portfolios and it took a fortnight after the first appointment was made to complete the process. Achutha Menon, who might have exercised a restraining influence, had retired from politics on the eve of the election.[60] Second, the bargaining position of the non-Congress partners was strengthened by the fact that they actually held an absolute majority in the Assembly without Congress support. Finally, there was the Rajan affair. This unfortunate young student, P. Rajan, was not the only Naxalite suspect believed to have died in police custody in Kerala. Two aspects of the matter particularly scandalized the Kerala public. Karunakaran, Home Minister when Rajan disappeared and for three weeks the new Chief Minister, at first denied that Rajan had ever been detained but then claimed to have been misinformed by senior police officers. Second, rightly or wrongly, Rajan was presented as an ordinary non-political young man, whose fate came to light only through the pertinacity of his professional father. On these sensibilities Youth Congress played, partly as representative of student interests and partly out of deep-rooted antipathy to Karunakaran, the politician. In the aftermath of the Janata victory there was no possibility of the Chief Minister riding out the storm and on the advice of Congress High Command he resigned—to be replaced by A.K. Antony, perhaps the bitterest pill of all for the Congress 'elders'.[61]

In October 1978 Antony was himself to resign on the issue of principle that the official Congress party to which he belonged had compromised its integrity by declining to put up candidates in Lok Sabha by-elections against Mrs Gandhi's supporters.[62] Thereupon P.K. Vasudevan Nair of the CPI took over as Chief Minister. His ministry was also short-lived. Following conflicts, exploited by the CPM, within the Ruling Alliance (notably over the extension to Christians of certain privileges enjoyed by Hindus under land re-

Table 9.3 Kerala: 1977 Assembly Election

No. of Seats: 140   Electorate: 11,461,455
                                                     Valid votes polled: 8,777,794
                                                     Invalid votes: 301,699

Party	Seats contested	Seats won	Votes polled	Percentage
Ruling United Front				
Congress	54	38	1,755,859	20.00
CPI	27	23	862,184	9.82
Kerala Congress	22	20	754,849	8.59
Muslim League	16	13	584,198	6.65
RSP	11	9	368,642	4.19
PSP	4	3	127,096	1.43
NDP (Independents)	6	5	200,063	2.27
Opposition Alliance				
CPI-M	68	17	1,952,893	22.24
Janata	28	6	739,110	8.42
Kerala Congress (Pillai)	16	2	411,845	4.69
Muslim League (Opposition)	16	3	390,169	4.44
KSP	2	0	27,097	0.30
Congress Radicals	2	0	48,978	0.55
RSP (National)	2	0	24,034	0.27
Independents in the Opposition Alliance	6	1	156,626	1.78
Independents (289)	107	0	345,841	3.93
			Invalid	3.43

Source: Based on results reported by *Hindu*, 21 and 23 Mar. 1977.

form legislation) and against the inclination of Vasudevan Nair, the ministry resigned on 7 October 1979. Contrary to the calculations of both Namboodiripad of the CPM and M.N. Govindan Nair of the CPI, the Governor responded to Congress (I) demands that the possibility of an alternative government should be explored—which would, of course, exclude the CPM and CPI.[63] C.H. Mohammed Koya of the Muslim League then accepted the Governor's invitation to form a ministry on 12 October 1979. Only two other members (from the Nair NDP and the PSP) were however, appointed, and after hectic political manoeuvring Mohammed Koya abandoned his struggle and resigned on 1 December 1979. Kerala then came under Presidential Rule until elections for a new Assembly were held on 21 January 1980, as a result of which the CPM-led Left Democratic Front won a handsome victory with 93 of the 140 seats. At the time of writing E.K. Nayanar of the CPM leads this UDF ministry.

The sixty year-old Nayanar, the CPM state secretary from 1971, and one of the accused in the celebrated 1942 Kayyur incident, is not a well-known figure outside the party. Though his experience—as chief editor of *Deshabhimani* and as an MP as well as state secretary—is varied, he does not enjoy the stature of Namboodiripad or that of Jyoti Basu in West Bengal. It remains to be seen how effective a leader of a disparate coalition with an embarrassingly large majority he will prove to be. (In fact the LDF disintegrated in October 1981.)

Notes

1   *IE*, 11 and 12 July 1967.
2   *IE*, 15 July 1967. Thomas' industrial policy followed the guidelines of the 1966 Joint Declaration. Sundarayya's criticism turned on two questions: the alleged anti-labour implications of government support for trade unions committed to negotiation rather than strike action, and the Industries Minister's announcement of his intention to seek foreign collaboration—in Japan.
3   *IE*, 1 Oct. 1967.
4   K.V. Varughese, in Chatterji, ed., p. 65.
5   *Malayala Manorama*, 28 May, 27 and 28 June 1968; E.M.S. Namboodiripad, *Anti-Communists Gang-up in Kerala* (Calcutta, CPI (M), 1970), pp. 40-1.
6   *Kerala Kaumudi*, 16 and 20 Apr. and 18 May 1968.
7   Namboodiripad had issued a directive to the Home Secretary on 15 June 1967 indicating that the government would not tolerate industrial actions that affected employers' life and property. Manjooran, the KSP Minister, defended the *gherao* by reference to Art. 19 (b) of the constitution which guarantees citizens the right of peaceful assembly but he ignored Art. 19(d) which provides for freedom of movement. Kurup and Kunju, the SSP ministers, both experienced *gherao*, though neither made an official complaint to the police. *PKLA* XXII, part I, p. 117.
8   The Kerala Congress leader, K.M. Mani, read four letters from local CPM secretaries to senior party officials complaining that police officers had not responded according to their directions: *PKLA* XXIV (26), p. 2364. See also *PKLA* XXIV (26), p. 2365 and XXIV (24), p. 2188 for reports of judicial criticisms of the CPM's interference in the administration of justice.
9   *PKLA* XXII (2), p. 49; *PKLA* XXII (19), p. 2326; *PKLA* XXII (3), pp. 378-9; *PKLA* XXIV (21), p. 97.
10   The manifesto is quoted by Jayaraj, 'Democratic Government in Kerala', p. 269. Most of the Commissions of Inquiry on charges of misconduct against Ministers in India were set up after 1967 and Kerala's total in the years 1967-70 was the highest. Though many of the Kerala inquiries were instituted for political reasons and do not necessarily indicate that the state was worse than others, the reports reveal much about the nature of corruption and misconduct. See A.G.A.M. Noorani, *Ministers' Misconduct* (Delhi, Vikas Publishing House, 1973), ch. 7 for a summary of the findings of the inquiries. Noorani notes that Kerala inquiries adopted a distinctive and restrictive definition of

11 Noorani, as preceding note, p. 239. Interview, former Transport Corporation executive, Tvm, Sept. 1973.

12 Thelma Hunter, 'Indian Communism and the Kerala Experience of Coalition Government 1967-69', *J. of Commonwealth Political Studies* X (1), 1972, p. 56.

13 Interview, Attingal Gopala Pillai, Tvm, Nov. 1977. According to the Mini Front partners the co-ordination committee had agreed at the end of 1967 to the preparation of an anti-corruption bill by a three-man subcommittee including the Chief Minister. The subcommittee reported with a draft bill within a month, but the CPM Politbureau later repudiated the draft. *Janayugom*, 10 Sept. 1969.

14 C. Achutha Menon, *What Happened in Kerala: Review of the 30 Months of Namboodiripad Government* (1969), pp. 51-4.

15 Malappuram District was instituted on 16 June 1969, and the University of Calicut on 23 July 1968.

16 It was alleged that a post of Deputy Director had been created for Namboodiripad's brother-in-law, Dr Bhattatiripad. The Congress MLA, R. Gopalakrishnan Nair, also claimed that the Chief Minister had improperly reinstated some officials indicted for corruption. The charges were *not* referred to a Commission of Inquiry by the incoming Chief Minister, Achutha Menon.

17 The Kerala Land Reforms (Amendment) Bill, 1969, the ministry's major measure, had not received presidential assent. Namboodiripad argued that the corruption issue was only a weapon in an eighteen months' crusade by Kerala Congress, Congress, Jana Sangh, and the Mini Front parties to bring down the CPM-led ministry. *Desabhimani*, 3 Nov. 1969.

18 Interviews, CPM leader, Tvm, Sept. 1973 and political correspondent, Tvm, Sept. 1973.

19 Interview, T.K. Divakaran, Tvm, Nov. 1974.

20 *IE*, 2 Nov. 1969.

21 *Link*, 16 Nov. 1969. Namboodiripad is reported as saying that partymen would take up arms to force out the ministry: *IE*, 29 Jan. 1970. The CPM party office was alleged to have issued a secret circular on 31 Oct. 1969 to student and youth federation workers calling on them to organize chaos (*sic*) and arson on a state-wide basis as soon as the Mini Front ministry was formed. The plans included the picketing of buses as well as government buildings and 'deflation of tyres': Political file, *Hindu* office, Tvm.

22 *PKLA* XXVII (6), p. 360; *Hindu*, 2 Dec. 1969.

23 The CPI view is found in N.E. Balaram, *Kerala: Three Years of UF Government Headed by C. Achutha Menon* (New Delhi, CPI, 1973).

24 *PKLA* XXVI (13), p. 1002.

25 Interviews, T.K. Divakaran, Tvm, Nov. 1974 and T.V. Krishnan, *Link* correspondent, Tvm, Sept. 1973. Luiz, the nominated Anglo-Indian MLA, is reported to have taken a room at the Mascot Hotel, Tvm, with Rs 20,000 to tempt those in the Assembly known to be in personal difficulties. *Link*, the pro-CPI weekly, claimed that Zacharia, a CPI MLA, had been offered a one-way ticket out of the state and

generous 'travelling expenses' and was held drugged and incommunicado in case he should change his mind. Zacharia was subsequently given police protection and was absent from the vote of confidence. Luiz, under pressure from his own community, abstained.

26 Under the constitution the Chief Minister was required to secure election to the Assembly within six months of his appointment. Meanwhile he could sit in the house but not vote. The Kottarakkara constituency vacated by the sitting member to make way for Menon was one of the few safe CPI seats. Further, Kerala Congress, one of the Mini Front partners, had been runner-up in 1967 with 23,000 votes. Nevertheless the Chief Minister's winning margin over a Marxist-supported independent (26,000 votes on an 83 per cent poll) had some propaganda value.

27 The sitting CPM MLA had been killed in a clash between the supporters of rival political parties. In 1967 the CPM majority over Congress had been 10,000 votes. With the support of the Mini Front (including 10,000 Muslim votes mostly cast for the UF CPM candidate in 1967) the Congress candidate was elected by 5,500 votes from an electorate one-third larger than in 1967. See *Desabhimani* and *Chandrika* (both in Malayalam), 6 Apr. 1970.

28 The Madai by-election resulted from the death of Mathai Manjooran, the KSP leader, whose majority was nearly 20,000 in 1967. His brother John won the by-election by 4,000 votes.

29 Kunju, the former UF ISP Finance Minister, won a High Court order (on technical arguments) quashing the Namboodiripad order for a Commission of Inquiry, and the ISP requested its nominee N.K. Seshan, Finance Minister in the Mini Front, to resign. Fortified by opposition to Kunju within the ISP, Seshan declined to oblige until Achutha Menon formally requested his resignation on 2 Apr. on the grounds that it was a matter for the constituent parties to decide who their nominees to cabinet should be. Menon, however, ordered a fresh inquiry into Kunju's conduct as a minister. Three ISP MLAs then defected to the PSP, seeking admission to the front as an independent entity. The ISP informed Menon that it would secede from the ministry if the PSP was so much as represented in the co-ordination committee (*IE*, 25 Feb. and 9, 18, and 27 Apr. 1970). Kerala Congress was also increasingly restive (Robert L. Hardgrave Jr, 'Marxist Dilemma in Kerala: Administration and/or Struggle', *Asian Survey* X(11), 1970, p. 1002).

30 For a discussion of the mid-term poll see R. Ramakrishnan Nair and T.J. Nossiter, 'The Rules of the Electoral Game: Kerala 1970', *South Asian R.* IV (3), 1971.

31 Disciplinary action followed the election. 'Many' party members, according to Namboodiripad, had been affected by the bourgeois parliamentary mentality. *IE*, 12 Nov. 1970.

32 *Hindu*, 5 Oct. 1970.

33 *IE*, 25 Apr. 1971.

34 The Opposition mustered 64 votes out of 134. There were only 4 PSP MLAs, who were in any case split into two factions. It was thus unlikely that the government would fall.

35 *Hindustan Times*, 13 Oct. 1971.

36 *Mathrubhumi*, *Chandrika* (both in Malayalam), and *Hindu*, 30-1 Dec. 1971 and 2-3 Jan. 1972.

37 *IE*, 13 Jan. 1972.
38 The vacancy at Trichur resulted from the acceptance by the sitting MLA, Joseph Mundassery, of the Vice-Chancellorship of the new University of Cochin. Mundassery had aligned himself with the CPM after the split but recently emerged as one of the growing number of dissidents within the party. As an intellectual and a nominal Christian he satisfied the criteria for the appointment while at the same time offering the government the chance of a victory in the by-election: Mundassery had won the seat in 1970 by 2,000 votes over the Mini Front-Congress candidate but the Organization Congress Democratic Front candidate had polled 10,000 votes. Namboodiripad's tactic was to persuade Organization Congress to stand down in favour of an independent. This and the choice of a candidate who appeared to be a legal careerist further divided an already fragmented local party. A final local factor was that the Youth Congress candidate, P.A. Antony, was a Christian and the independent was a Hindu which led to some right-wing votes being cast on communal lines. *Link*, 6 Feb. 1972.
39 *SPKLA*, 26-7 Sept. 1972.
40 *ER 1972*, p. 75. The farmers' parity index (ratio of prices received by farmers to price paid) at 85 was the lowest since 1963–4 (p. 79).
41 *Hindu*, 24 Jan. 1973.
42 R.E. Miller, pp. 211-22, 281-8, and 302; *Hindu*, 15 Apr. 1972.
43 *IE*, 10 and 11 May 1974; 1 Apr., 16 June, and 4 July 1975.
44 *Hindu*, 10 Mar. 1975.
45 *ER 1973*, pp. 61-5.
46 Interviews, CPI trade union leader, Tvm, Sept. 1973.
47 *IE*, 7 and 29 Jan. 1974.
48 *PKLA* XXVI (1), p. 1.
49 Namboodiripad and A.K. Gopalan described the campaign as a Liberation Struggle. *IE*, 2 and 8 July 1974.
50 Interview, E.M.S. Namboodiripad, Tvm, Nov. 1974.
51 *PKLA* XXXVII (4), p. 167; *Hindu*, 15 Oct. 1974.
52 *PKLA* XXXVIII (1), p. 1.
53 K. Karunakaran, the senior Congress minister, was accused of favouring the Nair community, to which he belonged. Allegations printed in the Ezhava-owned Trivandrum daily, *Kerala Kaumudi*, against another Nair Congress minister, Dr Adiyodi (Finance and Forests), were commonly presumed to be motivated primarily by communal rivalry. Editorial staff of the newspaper denied this in interviews with the author, Tvm, Dec. 1974.
54 For a fuller account of the Emergency in Kerala see T.J. Nossiter, 'State-level Politics in India, 1975-1977: the Emergency and its Aftermath in Kerala', *J. of Commonwealth & Comparative Politics* XVI (1), 1978.
55 Kerala Congress finally joined the ministry on 26 Dec. 1975.
56 *IE*, 24 Feb. 1977.
57 Ibid., 28 Feb. 1977.
58 Ibid.

59 *Sunday Standard,* 6 Mar. 1977.
60 Menon resigned ostensibly on health grounds. For a discussion of other possible considerations see *IE,* 17 Feb. 1977.
61 On 12 Mar. 1979 after a lengthy legal process the case against Karunakaran—of filing a false affidavit to the Kerala High Court in 1977—was rejected by the Ernakulam Chief Judicial Magistrate on the grounds that the prosecution had failed to prove the charge beyond reasonable doubt. For a full account see Mukundan C. Menon, 'The Ghost of Rajan', *Economic and Political Weekly,* 14 Apr. 1979.
62 *IE,* 26 Oct. 1978.
63 Trivandrum Staff Correspondent, 'Will Antony's Strategy Succeed?', *Hindu,* 18 Oct. 1979; K.T. Zacharias, 'Divided Ruling Front', *Economic and Political Weekly,* 9 June 1979 and 'Ministry on Way Out', ibid., 8 Sept. 1979; T.C. Zacharias, 'New Alignments', ibid., 25 Aug. 1979.

10

Front Politics and Communist
Theories 1967-1977

PARTY lines are not formulated in a vacuum. They are intellectual constructions abstracted from developments in the individual states in the light of divergent readings of the marxist-leninist traditions, and, in the case of the CPI, of the geopolitical interests of the CPSU. In an effort to contain the differences generated by provincial, factional, and personal factors national lines are often ambiguous and their implementation characteristically flexible. It is difficult to make sense of the actions of either the CPM or the CPI without reference to the interaction of party ideology, state-level political problems, and the logic, if not imperative, of electoral competition. In Kerala the dilemma for both communist parties has been that the combination of their mutual competition, the limits on action imposed by federal hegemony, and the pressures of the rank and file for the fruits of office have tended to transform both from parties of principle into parties seeking power, and so to be judged (and found wanting) by the electorate on the same criteria as all others. Mathew Kurian, a key Malayali CPM theorist said to have been recruited to work in Kerala by Namboodiripad, argued that 'Any political party, however revolutionary, if it understands real politics functioning within the bourgeois system, must play the game of the system, but though sometimes compromise may be necessary, a revolutionary party cannot build its programme on bourgeois methods like horse-trading.[1] People's Democracy was a fine tight-rope to traverse.

At the national level the CPM and the CPI could be distinguished as pursuing in the post-1967 years the traditional tactics of the 'united front from below' and the 'united front from above' respectively. At the state level the distinction is blurred. The CPM in Kerala did not eschew 'from below' tactics, but increasingly used 'from above' tactics when expedient. To a greater degree than elsewhere in India the UF line had been a successful part of the repertoire of the undivided CPI in Kerala during the 1950s. Post-1967 experience, however, differed in two essentials: fronts now embraced communal, reactionary, and non-progressive elements; and they won power. In a highly fragmented political system the former was

242

virtually a condition of the latter, as the rival communist party leaderships recognized.

Both parties accepted electoral competition as one of the major arenas of mass action. Within the CPM, a minority (see below, p. 248) rejected the parliamentary path altogether. Few, though they included some important figures, pressed their opposition to the point of resignation or expulsion. A larger minority, generally known as the 'ultras', was critical of the alleged subjugation of mass action to ministerial constitutionalism but remained within the fold. Their continued presence intensified the ambiguity in Namboodiripad's own statement of the party's role in power as combining agitation and administration. Nevertheless, whatever the relative importance accorded to the two elements, there was no doubt that the Kerala CPM would remain committed to electoral competition as a major strategy in the medium term—and for at least three reasons.

First as the majority wing of the Kerala movement it inherited a tradition of exploiting representative institutions to wage the class struggle and strengthen the party. The split in Kerala did not separate revolutionaries from constitutionalists.[2] Second, CPM supporters, who included a disproportionate number of the underprivileged, saw little prospect of any improvement in their condition without a powerful presence in the Assembly, if not in government. The 1957-9 ministry had been uniquely 'their' government and similar hopes were entertained of the 1967 United Front. The emergence of leaders of low-caste origins tended, if anything, to strengthen the practical orientation of Kerala communism. O.P. Sangal argues that the mere fact of the CPM's emergence as the dominant political force in the state changed the psychology of the poor: 'the wages of agricultural workers increased far above the market rate just because of the changed political atmosphere' and 'it became possible for ordinary workers and peasant leaders to get any oppressive government official transferred.'[3] Third, given Kerala's high levels of literacy, newspaper readership, and political sophistication, a platform on the hustings and in the Assembly was a crucial means of communication for a mass communist party.

Apart from the attitude to Congress implicit in the distinction between the concepts of unity from above and from below, what differentiated the CPM and the CPI was their conception of the nature of state-level power and the relative importance of the uses to which it could be put. For the CPM leadership virtually all power lay with the central government and the forces which controlled it. Any possibility of independent action by provincial governments was minimal.

The purpose of participating in electoral competition therefore was primarily to publicize that reality, and secondarily to use administrative patronage to strengthen the party and administrative discretion to support class struggle. Though the CPI did not eschew the last, it argued that the CPM underestimated the autonomy of the state government, partly on the pragmatic grounds that there was more flexibility than the CPM's 'textbook revolutionaries'[4] admitted, but mainly because of their fundamentally different reading of the class character of India at the time. The bourgeoisie, who together with landlords and foreign imperialists, dominated the Indian state, were for the CPI differentiated into progressive 'national' and reactionary 'monopolist' elements. It was the party's task to unite with the former, whose historical mission was not yet fulfilled, and to struggle against the latter. In contrast the CPM discounted such a distinction and therefore saw its primary duty as outright opposition to the monopoly bourgeoisie and its landlord and imperialist allies. It was prepared to form tactical alliances with parties in some respects more reactionary than New Congress, but on no account to deal with Congress itself. The CPI on the other hand in principle (though not always in practice) excluded even tactical alliances with reactionary and communal parties but was ready to consider collaboration with New Congress.

Agitation and Administration

The CPM's policy towards participation in state governments and Namboodiripad's own account of that policy in 1967 were stamped with the marks of the experience of the 1957-9 ministry. The party's *Programme of People's Democracy* argued that People's Democratic governments gave the revolutionary movement a fillip and strengthened the mass movement but did nothing to solve the fundamental economic and political problems of the nation. All they could hope to achieve was 'immediate relief to the people' on the basis of consensual minimum programmes that would include agrarian reform and popular participation in state and lower-level administration.[5] Writing on the eve of the elections, Namboodiripad was optimistic that solid united fronts could inflict defeats on Congress and that non-Congress coalition governments 'combined with united action of the streets, fields and factories' would strengthen the opposition and facilitate the final displacement of Congress. However, he was pessimistic about the probability of Congress's accepting the verdict of the people. The Indian ruling classes might imitate their neighbours and establish 'a militaristic or other form of despotism.'[6]

In April 1967, after the installation of the UF governments in Kerala and West Bengal, the CPM Central Committee decided that the new governments should be seen as instruments of struggle rather than agents with real power to give substantial relief to the people. More equivocally, it added 'there is an ocean of difference between declaring them straight away as instruments of struggle and the direction to strive' so to utilize them.[7] Government as an instrument of struggle could be interpreted in three mutually reinforcing ways: the use of state patronage to strengthen the party; class struggle through direct action against propertied interests; and substantive conflict with the central (Congress) government.

The first needs little amplification. Within the limits of ministerial discretion it was a well-established convention of Indian political life. For the communists, long exposed to political verification, there was a fair case for redressing the balance. As Justice Mulla observed in rejecting charges against two former CPI UF Ministers, 'It is the duty of the politician to strengthen the hold of his group upon the electorate and if he looks after the interests of his supporters his conduct cannot be assailed' provided that his actions are within ministerial discretion.[8] Conflicts of interest inevitably arose between the partners, not least because the marxist control of the central departments enabled them to interfere in the working of non-marxist portfolios. Desirable though the energizing of a lethargic administration might be, class-based agitation to complement government action was possible only when one party, as in 1957-9, predominantly represented the lower class. Party policies and interests were often closely entwined, as in the case of industrial policy. T.V. Thomas, Industries Minister, was accused of anti-labour tendencies because he sought to commit the government to favouring recognition of trade unions 'having constitutions with adequate provisions for maintaining industrial peace', to arresting the further proliferation of trade unions, and, where possible, to reducing their number.[9] Clearly, foreign and domestic investment would be discouraged without some improvement in Kerala's labour relations and a check to the growth in the practice of subjecting managers to *gherao*. However, such a policy was also calculated to defend CPI-led interests on a union front increasingly threatened by CPM militancy. Though the CPM were not responsible for each and every labour dispute it is fair to say that their efforts to win ascendancy on the union front, coupled with the pro-labour sympathies of the KSP Labour Minister,[10] aggravated the industrial conflict which was inevitable given the structure of Kerala unionism and the general economic situation. 1968 was the state's worst year on record, with nearly 2.5 million man-days lost in strikes and lockouts in the industrial sector alone, which placed Kerala at the head of the All-India table of days lost per thousand industrial workers. Imbichi Bava's statement that Kerala would not be washed into the sea if the giant hydro-electric project at Idikki was not completed was the kind of comment which led to the UF's loss of support among the urban middle class, whose support in 1967 had been crucial to the defeat of Congress.[11] M.N. Govindan Nair's assertion that the CPM should choose between administration and agitation was sound advice if the UF was to survive.[12]

Similarly the CPM's line that the state government should administer Kerala but agitate against the Centre at every opportunity exacerbated divisions within the UF. The Muslim League was hostile to agitation as such on the ground that it undermined the rule of law. The CPI and the RSP suspected they were being used by the CPM for its own ends, which were to win over their supporters, to distract attention from the alleged failings of CPM ministers, and to counteract the influence of the ultras within the party.

The slogan 'agitation and administration', though implicit in the CPM's general line, actually originated in the Centre-State context as the CPM's response to an indiscreet statement by the Congress President, S. Nijalingappa, that the Namboodiripad ministry would be thrown out, if that became necessary. The appointment of V. Viswanathan as governor of Kerala, like that of Dharma Rao in West Bengal, indicated that the Centre was prepared for Presidential Rule. From Viswanathan's reputation—'the eyes and ears' of Delhi, his forthright statements such as *bandhs* do not produce rice, to which Gopalan replied that neither did elections—and his efforts to persuade Namboodiripad to resign in September 1968 it could also be inferred that the Congress President was expressing the sentiments of the Centre.[13]

The UF's minimum programme made no mention of any such dualism. In the section on Centre-State relations the partners merely expressed a determination to mobilize popular support to win more autonomy for the state government and an agreement to exert pressure on the Centre. There was no fiat for a generalized attack on the Centre *and* the Indian constitution along the lines of the CPM's post-1967 election document, *The New Situation and the Party's Tasks:* 'the crisis that has gripped the capitalist path of development in India has now projected itself into the political superstructure, the Federal Structure of the Indian Union.'[14] The Kerala High Court, in holding that action by the Chief Minister in accordance with the policy of agitation and administration was contrary to the law and had deliberately contributed to violence within the state,[15] expressed a view common inside the ministry and among the public that the

CPM's two-pronged strategy was a euphemism for the subversion of law and order. Much was made in the press nationally and locally of Ranadive's reported statement in London that the UF government's task was to 'unleash discontent' rather than 'give relief'.[16] A combination of agitation and administration was essential to a centrist strategy and implicit in the notions of people's democracy and the united front from below. Given adequate means of co-ordination between the UF partners, there was no reason in principle why agitation against the Centre and agitation designed to ensure effective implementation of government measures at local level need have undermined the front. Agitation designed to assert one party's hegemony in ministry and state alike, however, was a different matter.

Both the UF's Joint Declaration and the CPM's concept of people's democracy—with differing emphases—committed the 1967 ministry to something more than is implied in the generally accepted notion of administration. People's democracy allowed the possibility of agrarian reform and measures to increase popular participation in government at local as well as state levels. For all the delays and difficulties Mrs Gouri did take the fundamental land reform bill through all its stages and secure central approval short of formal presidential assent.

Progress on 'democratic de-centralisation' was much less impressive. The report of the three-man Vellodi Committee on administrative reorganisation *and* economy, appointed during Presidential Rule in October 1965, which reported in early 1967, was not discussed in the Assembly until July 1968.[17] Most of its recommendations were welcomed by the government and then pigeon-holed. A panchayati raj bill was introduced (to confer substantially greater powers on the Panchayat Boards). However, for two reasons it failed to reach the statute book before the ministry fell: the CPM's ambivalence about popular participation (its own organizational forms of 'democratic centralism' contained the same tension)[18] coupled with the shift in popular opinion by mid-1968 which rendered doubtful its capacity to retain control of existing CPM-dominated panchayats in any election for reconstituted panchayats.[19] The UF partners were little more enthusiastic. The second reason was that there were substantial administrative difficulties. The bill required the co-operation of the Panchayat Department and the Law and Revenue departments. In 1968 Ahmed Kurikkal of the Muslim League, the minister responsible, who was personally committed to rapid progress and whose party was the only UF member to perform well in the 1968 local elections, died at a time when the other concerned departments were preoccupied with the land reform measure for much of the relevant period.

The two significant steps made in respect of popular participation during the ministry underlined the degree to which the CPM's hegemonic aspirations could readily conflict with the theoretical premises of UFs and transitional peoples' democracies. In July 1967 the District Development Councils had been reconstituted and in September a state planning board had been created. After a seminar convened by the Board in October on 'Alternative Policies for the Fourth Five Year Plan', the new body published its framework in November. In principle the establishment of such a high-powered state organization to service the ministry in its arguments with the Centre on a wide variety of issues and to collect and collate information for improved planning within the state was an excellent one. However, it was headed by a CPM politician, disproportionately staffed by party sympathizers, and was seen by the UF partners as belonging to the CPM's agitprop machinery locally and nationally.[20] Similarly the advisory Civil Supplies Popular Committees, established in April 1967 to assist the Food Ministry in food procurement and distribution, had much to commend them but, fairly or not, they were criticized for partiality.[21] Subsequently the Centre declined to permit them to be placed on a regular footing through legislation.[22]

Centrists and Ultras

The change in the character of the CPM's approach to agitation—now to be combined with administration—and its assertion of hegemony over its UF partners, coupled with its failure to channel this into the speedy accomplishment of such structural reforms as its political line envisaged, was in part a function of attempts to reconcile internal party conflicts between Centrists and Leftists as well as a desire not to alienate the government of India prematurely.

There had been abundant evidence of inner party conflict in Kerala during 1966 and early 1967.[23] In December 1966 and January 1967 the Left had unsuccessfully sought to prevent fifteen well-known Centrists from standing as candidates in the forthcoming election—on a variety of counts, including criticism of China and the donation of blood to Indian troops. Wall posters signed by the so-called Kerala Red Guard appeared in the state capital in February, denouncing Namboodiripad as 'an agent of the bourgeoisie, rich peasants and decadent reactionaries' and listing the party's 'real revolutionaries'.[24] In May Imbichi Bava, the one Leftist CPM minister, replaced Namboodiripad as party secretary ostensibly on technical grounds. The post of party secretary is of key importance in any communist party but Imbichi Bava lacked the personal or party standing to capitalize on the position.[25] Parallel party centres began to appear in different parts of the state, a move which Namboodiripad and A.K. Gopalan countered with the full weight of their national and provincial stature by visiting all areas of doubtful loyalty. None the less the ultras, led by N.C. Sekhar and K.P.R. Gopalan, two of the oldest party members, gained control of both Cannanore, the largest district unit with over 5,000 members, and Trivandrum in the course of 1967. By the beginning of 1968 only Palghat, Kozhikode, and Ernakulam were securely under the control of the centrists.

The party leadership's difficulties were further increased by the intervention of the Chinese party. According to the CPC at the time of the 1967 elections 'revolutionary flames' were sweeping a country ripe for armed revolution.[26] By July the CPC was broadcasting and printing forthright condemnations of the revisionist ministries in Kerala and West Bengal and in August mounted a virulent personal attack on Namboodiripad that is said to have caused him great offence since he had twice earlier in the year privately and unsuccessfully sought to open a dialogue with the Chinese.[27] According to some reports, criticism from the ultras (nationally and locally), combined with the Chinese tirade, led Namboodiripad to contemplate resignation.[28] Shortly before the Central Committee meeting (Madurai) in August which reproved the Kerala party for subservience to its UF partners P. Sundarayya, the national secretary, announced that he had persuaded Namboodiripad to remain. But there is no convincing evidence that resignation was more than a tactical move on the Chief Minister's part.[29]

However, it is probable that the mounting attack on the party's Centrists forced Namboodiripad to compromise his original intentions. It was clear by mid-1967 that the price of defending a Centrist interpretation of a *state* democratic front could be a formal split in the party. The precise conception of the UF's role privately held by Namboodiripad is a matter of controversy. He had been instrumental (together with Jyoti Basu of West Bengal) in preventing the CPM from adopting a thorough-going Leftist line between 1964 and 1967, though this might be construed as designed to dissuade the party from suicidal conflict with powerful agencies of repression. The evidence of his actions early in the 1967-9 ministry, however, points in a Rightist direction: the offer of a joint legislative party to his partners in the front; the appointment of Mrs Gouri to handle land reform; the innovation of a co-ordination committee and the appointment of Azhikodan Raghavan as its CPM convenor; the 'social call' on Birla, head of one of India's leading 'monopoly' industrial houses in the wake of the highly critical Hazari report on licences granted to Birla business; his efforts to dissuade the party from adding Rs 8 crores to state expenditure by recommending central rates of dearness allowance;[30] his initial support for T.V. Thomas's arch-revisionist, development-oriented industrial policy; and the creation of a state planning board. There is a *prima facie* case to hypothesize that Namboodiripad was blown off course.

Events in Andhra and West Bengal had meanwhile made the continuance of the Kerala ministry and Namboodiripad's control of the Kerala party of crucial importance.[31] In Andhra the state plenum had overwhelmingly rejected the national leadership's draft ideological programme in preparatory party discussion for the national plenum at Burdwan in April 1968.[32] In West Bengal no state plenum took place.[33] Further evidence of the Centrists' uncertain hold there was the widespread allegations that the selection of delegates to Burdwan had been rigged. The Naxalbari peasant rising had led to the spread of naxalitism. Finally, the UF government, in which Basu was Deputy Chief Minister, had been ousted in November.[34]

Backed by the national leadership, Namboodiripad, A.K. Gopalan, and C.H. Kanaran drew up a package of measures designed to out-manoeuvre the opposition, central to which was the promotion of Gopalan himself as state secretary, and the reduction in size of the state committee from 52 to 24 members.[35] As Gopalan's unanimous election confirmed, he was acceptable to all factions. An old parliamentary hand, he had never held ministerial office. His organizational work for the party, particularly among the peasants had been invaluable. Impetuous and warm-hearted, he was never happier than in the thick of an agitation, leading from the front. Though from a Nambiar family, Gopalan was one of the handful of high-caste communist leaders to marry a low-caste party worker.[36] Highly intelligent, as his performance in the Lok Sabha witnessed, he never sought an intellectual status in the party. 'You do the thinking; I'll do the acting,' he once told Namboodiripad.[37] In a way which his leader was not, 'AKG' was universally loved within and without the party. On his death in 1975 the CPI-led ministry ordered the closure of all government offices as a mark of respect.[38]

The restructuring of the state committee was accomplished by the presentation of a 'slate' by the national leadership. Less popular and second-line Centrists such as Mrs Gouri and P. Govinda Pillai, the urbane and cultivated editor of *Deshabhimani*, were dropped at the same time as the first-rank ultras, such as K.P.R. Gopalan. Even so, the new committee included six known leftists, chiefly from Cannanore, as well as five 'waiverers'.[39] The state plenum accepted the draft ideological resolution by 213 to 25, though certain ultra amendments mustered up to 86 votes. As far as the Kerala ministry was concerned, the plenum went no further than calling for greater 'vigilance'. The leadership, however, had decided to step up its confrontation with the Centre, stopping just short of constitutional conflict, notably on September 19, when Namboodiripad after the despatch of Central Reserve Police to the state—which he likened to Soviet intervention in Czechoslovakia—reluctantly accepted Delhi's order to arrest central government employee pickets.[40]

By mid-1968 the pattern of a third communist party had emerged in Kerala, as elsewhere. Despite press reports of clandestine activities and Chinese contacts here and there[41] and growing signs of extremist parallel organization, both the terrorist and non-terrorist wings of the far left made only modest impact in the state.[42] The breakaway Communist Revolutionaries led by K.P.R. Gopalan and N.C. Sekhar were estimated to have 5 per cent of the CPM membership,[43] while the principal Naxalite grouping under Kunnikal Narayan, which organized the November 1968 attacks on the Tellicherry police and Pulpalli wireless stations in Malabar, scarcely warranted comparison in support or organization with Naxalites in West Bengal or Andhra. The reasons for their lack of popular support are discussed in the penultimate chapter (see below, p. 358).

In party terms Namboodiripad's position had been transformed by early 1969. Kerala was the one major CPM unit which the national leadership could be certain would pursue a Centrist line. The UF ministry had survived, though its premature obituary had appeared more than once in the press. What the Chief Minister now required was time for the much-delayed agrarian legislation (see below, p. 294) to complete its stages in the Assembly and receive presidential assent. The CPM might then claim credit for the most fundamental land reform in India, so legitimizing Namboodiripad's Centrism. To the degree that CPM supporters might differentially benefit from the act's implementation so long as the party remained in power Namboodiripad might secure the reprieve of his ministry. To this end he persuaded the State Committee in 1968 to agree to a Moplah-majority District in south Malabar on the mistaken assumption that League gratitude would be long lived.

It was not. In October the ministry fell. Though, as Hardgrave argues, it was the victim of its inherent contradictions, the timing still requires explanation.[44] First, it is significant that the land reform bill had recently completed its passage through the Assembly but awaited presidential assent. The CPM had already been charged with politically biased distribution of land to the landless.[45] Second, the League had secured the creation of Malappuram District for the Moplahs. According to the CPM, the League—elements of which were hostile to land reform—then took an opportunistic stance.[46] Mini Front sources claim that the League was now free to express its impatience with the CPM's 'big brother' behaviour. Both claims are credible.

The League's ideology—conservative, capitalist, and religious— and its interest in preventing communist erosion of its hold on the Moplah community made its participation in a CPM-led front as unnatural an alliance as it was for the CPM itself. It should be noted, however, that the united CPI had viewed Muslim sub-national and national aspirations with a sympathy influenced by Lenin's approach to the 'nationalities question'. Third, it was clear that a split in the Indian National Congress was imminent, and for the CPI (and the CPSU) that opened the possibility of consummating the party's commitment to the progressive national bourgeoisie by means of an alternative form of united front. Finally, Namboodiripad himself during the crucial months was in East Germany for urgent medical treatment. There is no reason to disbelieve his statement that 'for two months I was politically dead.'[47] Though Namboodiripad's subsequent tactics were criticized within the party, the fact that A.K. Gopalan —who sought to preserve the ministry in the Chief Minister's absence—was unable to reach an accommodation suggests that no compromise was possible.

The CPI and the National Democratic Front

Nationally the CPI's tactical line was the united front from above and its slogan the National Democratic Front, reflecting its reading of the course of post-independence Indian history, CPSU geo-political interest in friendly relations with India's ruling Congress party, and the reality of the CPI's mass base. Overall the strength of the CPI and the CPM is similar, but the CPI lacks the regional bases of the CPM in Kerala and West Bengal. Nor, given the (different) histories of the communist movement in these two states, the highly politicized and fragmented nature of the party systems, and the careful attention of rival party leaders to the maintenance of their following through patronage, was it likely that the CPI could sub-stantially expand its support at the expense of the CPM or other parties 'from below'. Although, as compared with the CPM bet-ween 1967 and 1970, the CPI was a united party, there were still pronounced differences both within state units and between them on party strategy, organization, and relations with the international communist movement, which led to considerable ambiguity in party doctrine and flexibility in interpretation. At a lengthy meeting of the CPI Central Executive at Patna in April 1968 it was agreed that no one tactical line was universally applicable and that the party's actions should be governed by the objective possibilities in each individual state. In Kerala this entailed recognizing the dangers inherent in economic stagnation, the divisions among both marxist and socialist parties, and in the UF's failure to satisfy the electorate. On the advice of Achutha Menon, who was simultaneously trans-lated to party headquarters to help in its revitalization, the CEC endorsed the efforts of Govindan Nair and T.V. Thomas to produce conspicuous ministerial efficiency, increased pressure on the CPM to speed legislation and executive action, and contingency plans in the event of the fall of the ministry. Given the relative autonomy of state units to pursue policies attuned to local conditions, it should be noted that the CPI's dependence on Soviet guidance can be exag-gerated. There is no evidence to indicate that the relationship bet-ween the CPSU and the Kerala CPI was other than consultative. The Soviet Ambassador and visiting dignitaries pay dutiful visits to the state but they are said to treat local party leaders with deference rather than expect it themselves.[48]

Thus the Kerala unit was able to pursue those policies which appeared to the State Committee, and in particular its leading mem-bers, Achutha Menon, Govindan Nair, T.V. Thomas, N.E. Balaram, and Sharma, as most appropriate to the local conditions. Whereas in West Bengal the CPI was inclined to a more militant stance, highlighting the 'non-peaceful possibilities of transition', in Kerala the party maximized the peaceful possibilities and minimized the role of agitation—in which the CPM was bound to win. At the same time it sought to isolate the CPM within the ministry, taking care, however, not to precipitate the UF's premature disintegration.[49]

Paradoxically the CPI in West Bengal was to show more en-thusiasm for leftist unity than the Kerala unit. In the latter the party reasonably presumed that the call of the CPI National Council in April 1969 (influenced by the formation of a UF Ministry in West Bengal) for closer working relationships with the CPM particularly in the legislatures would aggravate 'big brother' tendencies. It could lead to the CPM's cannibalizing the Kerala CPI as had happened with the SSP, KTP, and KSP. The CPI's experience of a common organizational framework in AITUC, which did not split until 1970, was a salutary one in Kerala as in West Bengal.[50]

The decision to form a Mini Front in 1969, though approved by the national leadership, was taken on the initiative of the Kerala CPI unit, despite the embarrassment it caused to the West Bengal unit which had joined with the CPM in the UF ministry formed after the February 1969 mid-term election there. However, it was set in the wider context of the Congress split.

In its 1964 programme the CPI had said that 'no National Democratic Front would be real unless the vast mass following of the
Congress and the progressive sections of the Congress at various
levels take their place in it' and it was the party's task to forge such a
unity.[51] Mrs Gandhi's support in the August 1969 presidential
campaign for the communist-backed V.V. Giri (sometime South
Indian railwaymen's leader, former Central Minister of Labour, and
from 1960 to 1965 popular Governor of Kerala) against her party's
official candidate, coupled with the nationalization of India's largest
banks, suggested that the National Democratic Front could now
become a reality. Events in Kerala afforded an opportunity to experiment with the practical implications of such a united front from
above without the final commitment of formally sharing power
with Congress. In November 1969 a now confident National
Council decided on a two-pronged strategy of unity and struggle,
unity with 'all progressive forces, including Congressmen' and
struggle against 'right reaction' on the one hand and the CPM on the
other, a policy not unlike the CPM's own 'agitation with administration'. K.M. George, the Kerala Congress leader, described the line
of unity and struggle as the biggest joke since the CPM's support for
agitation combined with administration.[52]

Two years later, in the wake of the Indo–Soviet Pact and the
Bangladesh War, Congress was finally persuaded to enter the CPI-
led Mini front ministry to ensure its survival. Shortly afterwards the
CPI held its 9th Congress at Cochin. According to *Link*, the CPI-
oriented weekly, the Kerala venue was fitting: it was at the 4th (1956)
Congress held in Palghat that Achutha Menon and Rajeshwar Rao
had 'led the struggle for recognition of the Congress democrats as
allies.' Menon now headed the first joint Congress–CPI ministry and
Rao was the party's general secretary.[53] However, sceptics inside and
outside the party argued that the new government was Congress in
all but name, that Mrs Gandhi's vaunted progressivism was little
more than window–dressing, and that the CPI lap dog would be
thrown to the Marxist wolves when it had served its turn. All of
which the platform admitted might well be true, but, it argued, if the
party did not take risks, it would be squeezed between Congress on
the one hand and the CPM on the other. No one present, and
certainly not the members of the Soviet delegation, who delivered a
warm encomium to their Malayali comrades, believed that the
road to New Delhi began in Trivandrum as some had done in
1956–7. However, given the party's limited options the gamble was
said to be worth taking. The CPI would swim with the nationalist
tide—the Indira Wave, *Garibi Hatao* (down with poverty), and the
victory in Bangladesh. Its agitation outside Kerala could be more

plausibly presented as principled if the CPI was perceived as genuinely seeking to collaborate in nation-building in Kerala. From the party's point of view Achutha Menon's somewhat ambiguous reputation in Congress circles, as the best Congress Chief Minister available, was not unwelcome. The combination of unity and struggle might gradually raise consciousness to the level where other like-minded ministries could emerge.

CPM, CPI, and the Political Crisis 1974-1977

As far as the CPM was concerned, the CPI line was self-delusion, if not a sign of continued subservience to the CPSU. The CPM interpreted India's growing economic difficulties in the late 1960s as being serious enough to precipitate a major political crisis. The Congress split was a manoeuvre to the left by the Indian ruling class, the benefits of which were exhausted by the time of the 1972 mid-term Assembly elections. Thereafter the decay of the system accelerated. Congress's security policies in West Bengal and Kerala reflected its political bankruptcy. The structural crisis overtaking India could be resolved only by 'a combination of parties and organisations of the left opposition . . . powerful and determined enough to reverse the economic and other policies pursued by the ruling party during the last 26 years', as outlined by the CPM's 9th Congress at Madurai in 1972.[54] The 'political demands' displayed a measure of clairvoyance in the light of the Emergency three years later: basic changes in the constitution to eliminate its misuse by the ruling party, the danger of one-party dictatorship, and a guarantee of all constitutional liberties as well as ensuring real and increasing autonomy for the states.[55]

These demands were influenced by the immediate situation in West Bengal, where the CPM had lost nearly 100 seats in the mid-term election, though its share of the vote fell only 4 per cent. The Party's allegations that Congress had rigged the polls were widely credited by impartial observers. Subsequently the incoming Congress ministry instituted a purge of CITU (CPM) union leaders. In reply the CPM boycotted the Assembly.

For Namboodiripad, who had been much criticized for his tactics in Kerala, it was an opportunity to defend the Centrist line. At the post-election Politbureau meeting he is reported to have urged self-criticism on the Bengali comrades.[56] Over-indulgence in extra-parliamentary methods merely provided the Centre with an excuse to persecute the party at the same time as it alienated the middle classes and middle peasants, without whom an Indian revolution was impossible. The CPM had lost, in his view, primarily because its tactics had not been based on the principle of fighting the real enemy: New Congress. The support of left-wing rag-bags was no substitute for the backing of right-wing money bags, the basis of his opportunistic arrangements with the Kerala right in 1970. If the West Bengal party carried on in this muddled way, his would be the only unit left for Congress to worry about. Clearly, Namboodiripad did not as yet intend to emulate the example of the West Bengal party by boycotting the Assembly.

Kerala required different tactics. The ministry was far from a seamless web, but it could expect to survive its full term. Though the CPM was the biggest party in the Assembly, it still constituted only half the total opposition. Some compromise was therefore inevitable wih Kerala Congress, Old (Organization) Congress, and the SSP if there was to be a strong and well-knit opposition. This was evidenced in an abandonment of the more destructive forms of mass action, which had alienated public opinion during the first Achutha Menon ministry, and the adoption of a 'responsible' and constructive approach to its role in the Assembly.[57] The change was facilitated by a reassertion of party discipline, which had been weak from 1968 onwards and had collapsed during the 1970 election campaign, and by a marked change in the composition of the CPM representation in the Assembly. Eight of the party's twenty-nine members sat for seats in the Palghat District, which had been noteworthy for its loyalty to the leadership during the ultra revolt, while Cannanore, the ultras' power base, was reduced to five MLAs, of whom three were Centrists.

By 1974 the CPM claimed that its 1972 reading of the course of the Indian crisis had been amply vindicated: the popular uprising in Gujarat, which forced the Congress ministry from office; the mini-general election in February; and the JP movement in Bihar. Mrs Gandhi's Congress, according to Namboodiripad, had gone back to the position of the undivided Congress in 1969.[58] Power was slipping away from Congress not in one state or even a group of states but at the Centre. There was, however, a crucial difference: the manoeuvre to the left had already been made and failed.

There was indeed an air of bewilderment in Delhi in early 1974. Unrest, even violence, was nothing new but Gujarat and Bihar were different in kind as well as degree. The agitation was not only widespread; it affected the Hindi heartland. Among its leaders was Jayprakash Narayan, who could claim the Gandhian mantle. The body of the movement was that very youth which had formed the shock troops of the Indira Wave; and, most damaging of all, the government found it could no longer rely with confidence on mobilizing the respectables of town and countryside to defuse agitation. If the consent of the governed had been withdrawn then recourse to the use of power rather than the exercise of authority to contain the agitation was inevitable.

The communists' special insights into the laws of historical development did not provide easy responses to the situation. The CPI was not altogether master in its own house since it had to bear in mind Soviet interests. Its policy of collaboration with Congress exposed it to the real danger of guilt by association; and it had to reconcile the views of several different state units: 'Congress was the same everywhere but the situations were different.'[59] Rajeshwar Rao conceded Congress's miserable failure but argued that anti-Congress feelings should not blind progressives to the fact that casteism, communalism, and linguistic chauvinism were greater dangers. Except that there was more of 'struggle against' and less of 'unity with' in 1974, the CPI's policy towards Congress remained fundamentally pragmatic: 'constructive co-operation in Kerala; limited electoral arrangements in UP and Orissa; 'critical support' to the ensuing fragile Congress ministries; the withdrawal of Biswanath Mukerjee, deputy leader of the ruling Progressive Democratic Alliance in West Bengal; and 'moral support' to the mass agitation in Gujarat.[60] For the moment there were no obvious costs: in January, Dange's daughter, Mrs Deshpande, won the prestigious Bombay Central Lok Sabha by-election from Congress in the wake of the Shiv Sena troubles there; and party membership continued to rise, not least in Kerala where membership now stood at 47,000, compared with 36,000 in 1972.[61]

The CPM's position appeared less problematic. On the basis of precedents the party would have been expected to respond by stepping up the level of agitation and adapting its form and intensity to the specific exigencies of the developing situation. There was, however, a marked note of caution in the CPM's relationship to the JP movement. Namboodiripad was unequivocal that he did not want a repetition of Gujarat and Bihar in the state. The leadership was doubtful about JP's backers, some of whom were 'right reactionaries', and fully alive to the dangers of operating outside its regional bases.[62]

Further, the CPM's involvement would invite the attentions of the 'repressive apparatus of the State', while in the improbable event of the movement's succeeding there was no doubt that its paymasters would swiftly dispense with the CPM's services. Finally, EMS was well aware of the need to gear party strategy to maintaining the party's grip on West Bengal and Kerala. Thus the CPM's strategy in Kerala was to make what capital it could out of Congress's problems elsewhere without over-commitment of resources and to concentrate its efforts on opening a front and mounting a campaign to win the Assembly election in 1975.

The key to formation of the front was Kerala Congress. Since the party was generally regarded as articulating the interests of the rich Christian and Nair landowners, bankers, and merchants of central Travancore and was indisputably to the right of the main body of the Congress movement, such an alliance encountered opposition both within the Kerala state unit and in the party Politbureau. At a PB meeting in October 1974, held near Trivandrum, Namboodiripad secured the party's clearance, having argued that the Kerala Congress was a substitute for the League. 'In spite of their subsequent treachery [this] did help the left movement for two years and we have no regrets. If the Kerala Congress would do the same why not?'[63] He also argued that its leader K.M. George had mellowed over the years. It is arguable that whatever the imperatives of electoralism—and they were strong for a majority party out of office for six years—the alliance with Kerala Congress excited more criticism than that with the League. The former was the party of the *Kayal Rajas*; the latter at worst a communally based pressure group working, in Malayali eyes, for a section of the poor.

When in May 1975 J.P. Narayan visited Kerala to solicit support the lack of response led him to conclude that Kerala was in the grip of election fever.[64] However, when the State of Emergency was declared, the CPM's arms' length relationship to the JP Movement did not save it from widespread detentions, especially of the middle-ranking cadre who were important in mass mobilization or election campaigning. For the CPM the Emergency presented a difficult choice; was it to go underground or was it to seek to remain an officially tolerated but emasculated opposition? So far as is known, the CPM had made no preparations for serious clandestine activity. Nothing need necessarily be inferred from the CPM's boycott of the Assembly in early 1975. This and similar gestures, though undoubtedly reflecting genuine disquiet in the party over the government's conduct, was none the less more of an opening shot in an election campaign than a rejection of democratic procedures *per se*.

Nationally the CPI was uneasy at the turn of events. While anything which made life difficult for the CPM was welcome, not all leaders believed in the party's line that the Emergency offered a further breakthrough in Congress–CPI co-operation. In Kerala although the State Council approved an extended lease of governmental power, Achutha Menon was aware that the assumption by Mrs Gandhi of plenipotentiary powers at the Centre would diminish the CPI's role in the Maxi Front. Karunakaran, said to be Mrs Gandhi's man, was likely to become the state's real Chief Minister but a demoted CPI would still sink if the Congress boat went down. It was also clear that conflict would develop on the mass front as Congress intensified its efforts to erode its rivals' hold on sections of organized labour. By 1976 the strains within the CPI were evident.[65] With the rise of Sanjay Gandhi as Mrs Gandhi's heir apparent and the pro-capitalist policy shift, the CPI began to engage in public criticism. A bitter riposte by the Prime Minister late in 1976 brought matters to a head. At the CEC meeting.in January 1977, S.A. Dange, party chairman, and N.K. Krishnan remained uncompromising in support of Mrs Gandhi while Rajeshwar Rao, party secretary, and Bhupesh Gupta argued for a reassessment.[66] The Kerala unit urged the continuance of the Congress alliance but West Bengal sought cooperation with the CPM. Mindful of Soviet endorsement of Mrs Gandhi, the CPI settled for the *status quo* as it faced the Lok Sabha and state elections: 'unity and struggle' and an alliance with Congress whenever possible. However—with the exception of Kerala—the result was disastrous as the Janata wave swept the north of the country: 7 seats instead of 23 in the Lok Sabha. By the 11th Congress in 1978 the CPI was beginning to re-evaluate a line that had failed to produce any shift to the left at national level and had assisted in the resurgence of anti-democratic, anti-labour, and reactionary forces.[67] Even in Kerala, the one apparent success of the alliance policy, it was Youth Congress—subsequently transformed into Congress (Urs)—not the CPI which had emerged to join the CPM as the dynamic 'progressive' forces of state politics. The 1977 split in Congress, the fall of Morarji Desai as Prime Minister (1979), and the break-up of Janata provided cover for the CPI's retreat from its alliance with Mrs Gandhi's Congress and its reversion to the leftist united front policies of 1967. In Kerala such a *volte face* was inevitable if the CPI was to avoid the political wilderness simply because Congress (U) was the dominant (and progressive) wing of the divided Congress. The CPM was thus able to state its own terms.

Notes

1   K. Mathew Kurian, Jan. 1970, quoted by Hardgrave, *Asian Survey* X (11), 1970, p. 1002.

2   Cf. Namboodiripad's comments on the bourgeois parliamentary mentality within the CPM (*IE*, 12 Nov. 1970) and remarks attributed to A.V. Aryan, a former CPM cadre and at the time leader of the Communist Unity Centre, describing Namboodiripad as 'a feudal socialist'. *Link*, 6 Feb. 1972.

     Citizen, 8 Nov, 1969, p. 24.

     C. Achutha Menon, 'Vindication of Faith', *Link*, 12 July 1970.
     New Situation and Party's Tasks (Calcutta, CPM, 1967), p.70;

Namboodiripad, 'Kerala and Bengal: Vanguard of Emerging Alternative', *People's Democracy*, 12 Mar. 1969.

6   *India Under Congress Rule* (1966), pp. 229-30.

7   *New Situation and Party's Tasks* (Calcutta, CPI (M), 1967, p. 70.

8   Govt of Kerala, *Report of the Commission of Inquiry in re: Shri M.N. Govindan Nair, Shri T.V. Thomas* (1971), p. 10.

9   *PKLA* XXIII (23), p. 2143.

10 Mathai Manjooran's views on this and related matters conflicted with those of his departmental officials. Interviews, senior civil servants, Tvm, Aug. 1973.

11 *SFP*, 4: *Industries and Infrastructure*, p. 4.

12 E.M.S. Namboodiripad, *Right Communist Betrayal of Kerala United Front and Government* (Calcutta, CPM, 1969), p. 7.

13 Interviews, IAS officer and political journalist, Tvm, Sept. 1973.

14 As n. 7 above, p. 49.

15 *Hindu*, 7 and 8 Aug. 1969; *IE*, 7 July 1969. See also *The Supreme Court Weekly Reporter* XVI 1970, pp. 336-57. Namboodiripad was found guilty of contempt of court in 1970 for asserting that 'Judges are guided by class hatred, class interests and class prejudices and where the evidence is balanced between a well dressed pot-bellied rich man and a poor ill-dressed and illiterate man the Judge instinctively favours the former.' The Supreme Court of India held that Namboodiripad's interpretation of Marx, Engels, and Lenin was erroneous. For Namboodiripad's reply see *The Kerala Law Reporter* XIX 1971, pp. 18-22.

16 *IE*, 22 and 27 June 1969. *Commerce*, 19 July 1969, p. 109.

17 Govt of Kerala, *Report of the Administrative Reorganization and Economy Committee* (1967).

18 V.V. Dakshinamoorthy, a CPM MLA, opposed the bill on the grounds that the measure would achieve little or nothing in the absence of changes in the Indian constitution and prior changes in social organization: *PKLA* XXV (4), pp. 248-50. K.M. Mani, the Kerala Congress leader, claimed that Mrs Gouri, the CPM Revenue Minister, opposed any decentralization of power: *PKLA* XXIV (24), p. 2185. For general statements of the lack of enthusiasm in all parties see E. Ahmed, *PKLA* XXII (7), p. 982 and Joseph Chazhikad, *PKLA* XXV (6), p.376.

19 In municipal elections held on 24 Apr. 1968 the UF won control of only of 24 authorities. From 1968 also student unions began to swing towards the Congress-led Kerala Students Union: *Hindustan Times*, Sept. 1970. The 1963 panchayat elections were contested on a non-party basis but one-third of the panchayats were thought to be controlled the CPM or CPI.

20 *PKLA* XXVI (22), p. 1668. The Mini Front abolished the Planning Board and replaced it with the State Planning Advisory Council, which excluded all CPM sympathizers. Subsequently the Planning Board was re-established. For the CPM view see Namboodiripad, *Planning Crisis* (1974), p. 104. The ideas of Dr K. Mathew Kurian, a key CPI member of the UF State Planning Board, can be sampled in K. Mathew Kurian, ed., *India—State and Society* (1972), pp. 1 and 85.

21 K.T. George, *PKLA* XXI (3), p. 307, XXI (16), pp. 1804-5.
22 *PKLA* XXII (21), p. 2553.
23 Fic, *Kerala*, pp. 388-9.
24 *Hindu*, 16 Feb. 1967. Joseph Lelyveld, 'Communism, Kerala Style', *New York Times Magazine*, 30 Apr. 1967, p. 59. The CPM publicly claimed that the poster was the work of the US Central Intelligence Agency.
25 E.K. Imbichi Bava (1917-) came from a poor family and was virtually the only Muslim in the party's senior ranks. His importance in helping to extend CPM influence among Muslims may have prevented him from establishing an alternative power base. For charges of corruption and misconduct while Imbichi Bava was UF Transport Minister see Govt of Kerala, *Report of the Commission of Inquiry in re: Smt. K.R. Gouri, Shri E.K. Imbichi Bava and Shri M.K. Krishnan* (1971). The charges against Imbichi Bava were not proved.
26 Mohan Ram, *Maoism in India* (1971), p. 52.
27 Interview, CPM leader, Tvm, Aug. 1973. Fic, *Kerala*, pp. 425-6.
28 *Hindu*, 7 Aug. and 23 Dec. 1967.
29 For an account of differences within the Politbureau at this time see Mohan Ram, *Indian Communism*, p. 238.
30 Namboodiripad had avoided any specific commitment to sanction Central rates of dearness allowance during the Jan. 1967 government employees' strike. *Kerala Kaumudi*, 8 and 9 Jan. 1967.
31 Fic, *Kerala*,p.435.
32 *The Ideological Resolution Adopted by the Central Plenum, Burdwan, 5-12 April 1968* records that inner-party discussions on the Central Committee's draft had revealed a fundamental disagreement among a section of the party: Franda, *Radical Politics in West Bengal*, p.210.
33 Mohan Ram, *Indian Communism*, p.244.
34 Franda, *Radical Politics in West Bengal*, p. 127. United News of India, Research Bureau, *India Today* (1970), pp. 62-71.
35 Hardgrave, in Brass and Franda, eds., p. 163.
36 It was his second marriage. The other well-known example of an inter-communal marriage in the senior ranks of the party was that between T.V. Thomas (Christian) and Smt. Gouri (Ezhava). Namboodiripad's children are married within the Brahmin caste.
37 Interview with a party worker assisting A.K. Gopalan, Tvm, Nov. 1977. Cf. Gopalan's own statement in his *In the Cause of the People* (p. 59): 'I am not at all sorry if people feel that I am a blind follower of E.M.S. I learned much from him . . . I have implicit faith in the strength of his political leadership and the purity of his character.'
38 *Hindu*, 23 Mar. 1977.
39 Political file, *Hindu* office, Tvm, n.d. [1968].
40 Interview, IAS officer, Tvm, Dec. 1974.
41 United News of India, Research Bureau, *India Today,* p. 517.
42 Interviews, a Deputy Inspector General of Police and senior operational police officers; Naxalite leaders.
43 K.P.R. Gopalan claimed that the extremists had the support of 25 to 35

per cent of CPM members. P. Sundarayya, the CPM national party secretary, estimated support at 15 per cent while the 1968 CPM *Political-Organization Report* put defections in Kerala at 5 per cent. Hardgrave, in Brass and Franda, eds., pp. 164–5.

44 Hardgrave, as preceding note, p. 156.
45 *PKLA* XXIi (2), p. 189, XXIV (21), p. 75. For Smt. Gouri's reply see *PKLA* XXIV (21), p. 104.
46 R.J. Herring, p. 325. Herring's research supports the CPM's allegations.
47 Political file, *Hindu* office, Tvm. 4 June 1970.
48 Interviews T.V. Krishnan (*Link*) and K.C. John (*Times of India*), Tvm, Sept. 1973.
49 For CPI tactics in West Bengal see Franda, *Radical Politics in West Bengal*, pp. 218 and 222.
50 Ibid., pp. 224–5 and 109–16.
51 *The Programme of the Communist Party of India, As Adopted by the Seventh Congress of the Communist Party of India, Bombay, 12-23 Dec. 1964* (New Delhi, CPI, 1965), p. 43.
52 Quoted in interview by K.C. John, Tvm, Sept. 1973.
53 *Link*, 3 Oct. 1971. Ouseph Varkey, however, argues that the CPI 'failed to see through the fog of ideological rhetoric with which Mrs Gandhi surrounded the [Congress] split': 'The CPI–Congress Alliance in India', *Asian Survey* XIX (29), 1979, p. 882.
54 Namboodiripad, *Conflicts and Crisis*, pp. 137 and 157.
55 Ibid., pp. 157–8.
56 Interview, CPM MLA, Tvm, Dec. 1970.
57 Interviews, political correspondent, Tvm, Aug. 1973 and public official, Tvm, Sept. 1973.
58 Interview, E.M.S. Namboodiripad, Tvm, Dec. 1974. Also his *Conflicts and Crisis*, p. 155.
59 Bhupesh Gupta, speaking at Tvm, quoted in *Hindu*, 29 Jan. 1974.
60 *IE,* 13 Feb. 1974.
61 *Hindu*, 10 Mar. 1974.
62 Interview, E.M.S. Namboodiripad, Tvm, Dec. 1974.
63 *Hindu*, 31 Oct. 1974.
64 *Hindu*, 13 May 1975.
65 N.E. Balaram, the CPI Kerala state secretary, described Namboodiripad's claim that there were differences over policy between him and Rajeshwara Rao, the party's national general secretary, as an 'absurd lie' Kuldip Nayar does not mention the Kerala CPI unit in an analysis of strains within the CPI during the Emergency (*IE*, 3 Mar. 1977), However, political correspondents interviewed in London (Nov. 1979) traced disagreements within the Kerala CPI leadership as to the wisdom of the alliance with the CPM, concluded in late 1979, back to the period of the Emergency.
66 *Hindu*, 12 Jan. 1977.
67 *Political Review Report* (Adopted by the Eleventh Congress), (New Delhi, CPI, 1978).

11

Front Politics, Economic Development, and Social Change 1967–1975

THIS third chapter on front politics assesses governmental performance from 1967 to 1975 and ends with a brief comment on the impact of the Emergency on Kerala's administration in 1975-7. It should be emphasized here that, although there were communist Chief Ministers, the communists never enjoyed a majority in the cabinet (Council of Ministers). The CPI and the CPM combined held six out of thirteen seats in the UF ministry. In the first Mini Front the CPI held three out of eight seats and in the second Mini Front four out of nine, while in the Maxi front it was reduced to three out of thirteen. Nor did the communists have a majority in the co-ordination committee, where the crucial inter-party bargaining took place (see below, p. 274). Whatever special influence the CPM's success in the 1967 election gave it in the UF ministry, or the CPI's key role in ministerial stability thereafter, one cannot equate the overall governmental performance of the four front ministries with communist hegemony, particularly after the entry of Congress into the Maxi Front in 1971. The detailed discussion that follows reflects not only the need to document the argument fully when the primary sources are not readily available outside Trivandrum itself but also the importance of the issue of the extent to which front governments contributed to economic development and social change.

At the most general level multi-party governments are an uncommon agency of change in developing countries. In India, which has sought to develop within a democratic framework that uneasily combines central direction with provincial autonomy, Kerala's experiment with coalitions of 'left and like-minded parties'—the somewhat evasive local characterization—is of sufficiently long standing to offer a fair test of their utility. For all their divergent conceptions of the role and significance of transitional front ministries, the CPM and the CPI shared a commitment to the minimum programme of 1967. After the collapse of the UF the CPM opposed the Mini and Maxi Fronts, using the alleged failures of the

CPI-led governments to implement this programme as the starting point for its far-reaching critique of the Indian polity as a whole. If neither the UF nor the Maxi Front ministries can be neatly categorized as state-level People's Democratic and National Democratic governments respectively, the record of the front administrations does shed light on the question of whether anything more than immediate relief is possible within the system. Finally, it is worth examining the effectiveness of communists in office. Besides the office of Chief Minister, the CPM's responsibilities between 1967 and 1969 included the key departments of Home, Revenue, and Law, while the CPI held the Electricity, Industries, and Commerce portfolios throughout the period under review as well as from time to time other 'nation-building' portfolios.[1] Did communist ministers generally discharge their ministerial responsibilities in any way differently from their non-communist colleagues as a result of a more advanced consciousness of their duties or greater exposure to party discipline? Did the CPM Ministers in practice try to achieve the minimum programme?

No definitive answers to these questions are possible. This analysis, which rests on a wider investigation than there is space to report, focuses on six topics closely related to the theme of economic development and social change: finance, the machinery of government, industrialization, public enterprise, land reform, and agricultural productivity. In these areas most, though not all, of the relevant facts can be established but what degree (and kind) of development and change could reasonably be expected, given national and provincial conditions, will remain a matter of opinion. Since in the present chapter the evidence often leads the author to adopt a critical tone it may be appropriate to anticipate the concluding summary (see below, Epilogue) by stating that in his opinion the achievements of the front ministries (and their official oppositions) were not insubstantial: the pioneering of new modes of political production, the restructuring of agrarian relations, the creation of the infrastructure of economic development, and the advancement of social welfare.

Finance for Development

Kerala, like other Indian states, has consistently demanded more control of 'its resources', laying the blame for India's slow growth rate and the continuance of regional disparities on Delhi's doorstep. Although the wickedness of 'stepmother'—the Centre—is part of the rhetoric of state politics, there are complicated issues at stake. Among the more significant contributors to the debate on centre-state relations Namboodiripad has emphasized the 'crisis of planning' which in his view has developed from the economic to the political level.[2] His writings synthesize several elements: the five-year plans as a focus of *national* aspiration; traces of Lenin's theory of nationalities in his support for states' rights—Kerala is 95 per cent Malayali; an 'anti-imperial' liberation struggle against Hindi Delhi; the feeling that government is remote, bureaucratic, and élitist; and a powerful critique of the course of Indian politics in the 1960s and 1970s which is firmly anchored in everyday discontents. India's economic progress had not, of course, kept pace with the optimistic plan targets or the expectations of the expanding population, though the achievements of planning are in the circumstances far from derisory. What is more difficult to accept is that progress would inevitably have been greater if the development agencies, namely the states themselves, had been financially more independent. It may be an illusion to assume that those who cannot spend one rupee properly would undergo a change of character when given one hundred rupees, and it is not impossible that greater states' autonomy might only have widened the gap between the Punjabs and the Keralas of India.

Finance for state development is dependent on central allocations—in the form of investment or assistance—and what the state is able to raise on its own account. Kerala has been among the most vociferous in alleging politically motivated discrimination in the distribution of Central resources for plan expenditure. Politicians of all parties have argued that not only has it not received a share proportionate to its population (3.9 per cent) but that no account has been taken of its contribution to Indian foreign exchange earnings or its 'backwardness'. The former has not been a criterion for allocation of resources between states nor is it clear why in a quasi-federal system it should be; while the validity of the latter claim turns on the relative importance of social and economic indices in a definition of backwardness.

In terms of Central Investment in All-India projects located in Kerala, the state's share was negligible during the First (1951-6) and Second Plan (1956-61) periods: Rs 1.9 crores in the Rare Earths and DDT factories at Alwaye. Thereafter Central Investment has steadily grown from 2.1 per cent of the total (Rs 49.2 crores) in the Third Plan period (1961-6) to 3.2 per cent (Rs 202.2 crores) by 1974-5. The most important projects have been the fertilizer and chemical combine, FACT, and the Cochin Oil Refinery. Schemes taken up during the 1970s include the Cochin Shipyard, Hindustan Latex, the manufacture of contraceptives, a bakery, and a newsprint factory.[3]

Prima facie are there real grounds for complaint? Other states have

received less favourable treatment in both absolute levels of investment and their relative share of investment.[4] Centrally financed and
controlled projects are part of the All-India economic infrastructure
and in general are necessarily sited on technical rather than social or
political grounds; where more than one site is available then speedy
and practical offers of state co-operation influence the outcome. In
its first fifteen years this was not always forthcoming in Kerala. Since
1969, however, the state government has shown a greater sense of
urgency—with visible results.[5] Significantly Kerala's governments
have generally followed the same principles in allocating major
investment resources between Districts. Noting the emphasis in the
Fifth Plan guidelines on reducing regional disparities within as well
as between states, the Maxi Front ministry admitted that 'all that can
be done...is to determine that part of the State Plan Outlay, (*excluding the requirements of projects of State-level importance*) which can be
earmarked for distribution among the regions...and to allocate this
...on the basis of a suitable formula.... The development departments...should be directed to locate their schemes, as far as possible, *subject to technical feasibility* in the relatively backward regions of
the State. This is good as far as it goes but then it does not go very
far.'[6]

Kerala's politicians, in common with those of other less favoured
states, sometimes argue that those who receive generous Central
Investment should be penalized by compensatory cuts in Central
Assistance. Although Central sector projects often turn out to be a
mixed financial blessing for the host state there is little economic logic
in the claim. In fact, Kerala's share of Central Assistance during the
Third, Annual, and Fourth Plan periods was consistent with its share
of the population and a dispassionate balancing of its needs as against
those of other states.[7] There is no clear evidence that Kerala has
suffered in this respect because of its communist and anti-Congress
proclivities. The Second Plan, to which the CPI gave a qualified
welcome, was already under way when the CPI took office in 1957.
The Third Plan was prepared after the ministry fell, at a time when
Delhi had every interest in easing the path of the prospective anti-
communist government. The first feasible opportunity for discrimination on political grounds did not occur until the third of the
Annual Plans (1968-9), but the two earlier annual plans had shaped
the third and by then the Deputy Chairman of the Planning Commission (the Prime Minister is *ex officio* Chairman) was Professor
Gadgil, a man not unsympathetic to the communist standpoint. It is
true that Kerala along with West Bengal did take the unprecedented
step of rejecting the draft outline of the Fourth Plan during the UF
period but this action was motivated by ideological rather than
substantive considerations.[8]

The scope of a state plan is considerably influenced by the finan- cial resources which the state government is able and willing to raise independently of the Centre. During the Second Plan Central Assist- ance as a percentage of Kerala's State Plan expenditure was 43 per cent, during the Third Plan 68 per cent, during the Annual Plans 68 per cent, and during the Fourth Plan an estimated 44 per cent, as against an originally envisaged 67 per cent. The scale of the state's own contribution to expenditure depends on five factors: the size of the Finance Commissions's award; the state's own taxation; its non- plan levels of spending; the profits, if any, of its public enterprises; and its ability to raise loans.

The Finance Commission effectively decides how just over one- third of all resources transferred from the Centre shall be distributed, 85 per cent accounted for by the state's share in central taxes and the rest in statutory grants-in-aid. In either case the transfer is uncondi- tional: the monthly cheque may be spent entirely as the state govern- ment sees fit. The size of grants-in-aid fluctuates according to the formulae adopted by the commissions and its exercise of discretion in their application. From the Third Finance Commission (1960-1), of which a prominent Congress ex-Chief Minister of Travancore- Cochin was a member, Kerala has done quite well, though the Fourth Commission (1968-9) was relatively less benevolent. This was one—but only one—factor in Kerala's growing financial em- barrassment during the 1970s. The Sixth Commission (1972-3), however, besides increasing the states' share of the overall award and recommending a major debt rescheduling exercise, took more ac- count of 'backwardness' in allocating resources between states. Kerala was assigned Rs 209 crores in grants-in-aid and was to receive 5.0 per cent of total transferred resources (population 3.9 per cent) compared with 4.4 per cent in 1969-74, and 5.6 per cent of the total debt relief. The commissioners, among them Dr Gulati, a member of the Centre for Development Studies, Trivandrum, prescribed a régime of vigorous collection of revenue and the unpalatable medicine of serious control of expenditure to restore Kerala to financial health.

The Commission's award was based on its downward revision of the state's own estimate of the total non-plan revenue gap over the next five years.[9] Kerala had forecast that it would be able to raise Rs 693 crores, mostly in taxes. The Commission increased this by Rs 28 crores. Its reassessment of the state's heady estimate of non-plan expenditure on *revenue* account was much more drastic. Rs 414 crores were deducted from the original estimate of Rs 894 crores, with major cuts all round: education (Rs 84 crores), health (Rs 44 crores), and civil service pay (Rs 32 crores). The hard-headed Commission declined even to provide for the commitments already entered into to revise employees' pay and dearness allowance. It also assumed much improved returns from state enterprises. That the Commission was surely right (see below, p. 286) offered no solace to a government eighteen months away from the polls.

Kerala's own taxation policy appears on the available evidence to have been little affected by communist or communist-led governments. The UF's Taxation Enquiry Committee, set up in December 1967 on Namboodiripad's initiative, claimed in its 1969 report that 'class politics is the essence of taxation.'[10] On that basis neither the 1957-9 nor the 1967-9 ministry (or indeed succeeding CPI-led fronts) escaped the pressures of 'entrenched economic interests' both in terms of fiscal policy and tax collection.[11]

Table 11.1   Kerala 1957-1969: Trends in State Taxes and Duties (percentage)

	1957-8 Accounts	1961-2 Accounts	1965-6 Accounts	1967-8 Revised estimate	1968-9 Budget estimate
Land revenue	9.1	6.9	6.9	4.0	3.2
Taxes on agri-cultural income	13.8	10.7	5.9	5.3	5.0
State excise	16.3	14.2	13.0	17.5*	16.7
Stamp duty	8.5	7.5	9.7	8.2	8.1
Registration fees	2.6	2.1	1.6	1.7	1.6
Vehicles	11.6	11.6	10.8	9.5	9.9
Sales tax	37.0	45.9	47.5	48.3	49.1
Other	1.1	1.2	4.7	5.4	6.3
Index	*100*	*173*	*290*	*397*	*421*

*Abolition of prohibition.
Source: Report of the Taxation Enquiry Committee, p. 539.

As the table shows, agricultural income tax—a progressive tax on the wealthy farmer—steadily declined as a percentage of all state taxes and duties while the regressive sales tax grew. It is true that sales tax had little effect on the very poor but it was hardly, as the Committee claimed, just a tax on the middle classes. By 1974 sales tax accounted for 55 per cent of the total tax offtake in the state and as a ratio of consumer expenditure (2.8) was the third highest in India. In the state government's view there was little scope for enhancement even on luxury items taxed at 12 to 15 per cent.[12] Land revenue income was also playing a smaller part, not least because of the sub-division of holdings to evade land reform.[13] In Kerala, as in India as a whole, the burden of taxation was increasingly shouldered by the urban areas and the agricultural sector was under-taxed.[14] Even if income tax is excluded the middle and working classes of the towns were far more heavily taxed than the rich and middle peasants, not to mention the 'feudal elements' of the countryside. It is true that Kerala tax effort, as measured by *per capita* taxation as a percentage of *per capita* income, at 5.56 (1974) was the fourth highest in India but it is hard to accept the ministry's contention in 1974 that the scope for further tapping of the instrument of taxation was limited in the light of the 1969 Taxation Committee's survey of evasion.[15] Its *conservative* conclusion was that only half the agricultural income tax due from farmers reached the exchequer, and only half the sales tax due on such important primary commodities as coconut, arecanut, and rubber.[16] Several businessmen admitted to the author that double book-keeping had for them a rather different meaning from that conventional in accountancy.[17] Inadvertently, the All-Kerala Hotel and Restaurant Owners' Association revealed to the Taxation Committee that only 6 per cent of its members paid tax.[18] Equivalent documentation is not available for the 1970s but it is noteworthy that the state government succeeded in collecting only four-fifths of its Fourth Plan target for additional taxation.[19] One other item of evidence contrasts the performance of Dr K.G.Adiyodi (Congress) and K.M.Mani (Kerala Congress) as Ministers of Finance during the Emergency. On assuming office the latter, who had the reputation of being the farmers' friend, is alleged to have summoned his staff to warn them of the dangers of 'over-assessment' and stayed his predecessor's order for the appointment of inspecting officers. It is also claimed that he was less enthusiastic about the transfer of incompetent or ineffectual officials.[20]

The third major source of finance for state development projects is borrowings from the market or financial institutions. Loans from the market are controlled by the Reserve Bank and up to and including the Fourth Plan have been disproportionately appropriated by credit-worthy advanced states.[21] Direct institutional loans from the Reserve Bank and the Life Insurance Corporation (LIC), the former for raising share capital for co-operative credit institutions and the latter for financing social services such as water supply and housing, are simply dependent on the viability of the proposed schemes and the urgency with which they are presented. Changes in central policy and the nationalization of the LIC opened up possibilities in the 1970s of which the Achutha Menon administration made significant use. It was credit from the LIC which rescued the one lakh housing scheme for the poor in 1973-4 (see below, p.298).

Private investment in Kerala has been limited. At the end of 1970 there were only three private companies with registered capital of more than Rs 1 crore: Aluminium Industries, Premier Tyres, and Travancore Rayons. Of Rs 10 crores invested in the ten biggest private companies, one-third was in companies whose early origin was indicated by the word 'Travancore' in the name. The first communist ministry has assured 'a safe, honourable, and permanent place' to private capital but met with little response.[22] Birla had concluded a tentative agreement to establish a rayon pulp factory but started production only after the ministry's departure. There were also infructuous contacts with Birla during the UF Ministry. On economic and political grounds the big business houses of India saw little reason to invest in the state. Kerala had no established industrial base. Its domestic market was modest and it was remote from the large markets of northern India. The militancy of labour was a further disincentive, as was the state's political instability—at least before 1970. Historically Kerala had no significant entrepreneurial class within its own Hindu community, while the Syrian Christians tended to invest in commercial agriculture, property, and banking, and latterly, as the political and fiscal climate has changed, to consume their surplus in high living. The number of industrial licenses issued for Kerala has been well below its proportion of the Indian population and far below what might be expected from a state with a leading position in college education.[23] The expansion of higher education has been associated with the pursuit of safe white-collar jobs whose increasing provision has led to powerful unionization and the appropriation of an ever-growing proportion of state resources to pay them.[24] Even the windfall of remittances—estimated at Rs 200 crores per year in November 1977 rising to an estimated 1,100 crores in early 1980—from oversea Malayalis employed as semi-skilled workers in the Gulf states has been primarily invested in the purchase of social status through property and marriage.[25]

It is significant that we could have gone so far in discussing the raising of development capital without reference to the co-operative movement. The successive Achutha Menon administrations exhibited renewed enthusiasm for co-operation as a means to economic development and social mobilization. Measures included an administrative upheaval in the department principally concerned, the appointment of one of the most able of the IAS officers as Registrar of Co-operatives,[26] the creation of co-operatives specifically designed to soak up educated unemployment, generate work in the modern industrial sector, and stimulate growth in the small-scale farming sector. Producers and workers' co-operatives should operate effectively on the basis of the pooling of small savings in the form of share capital; they provide the opportunity for direct involvement and that democratic participation constantly urged as both a means and an end by local politicians of all persuasions; their running costs should be modest; and they offer a vehicle for raising the consciousness of the masses.

The record of the co-operatives in Kerala, as in India as a whole, has, however, been far removed from these ideals. The three-tier system of organization—primary, district, and apex—has proved both unwieldy and exorbitantly expensive. Many societies have passed into the hands of local patrons, frequently protégés of the dominant local party. The conclusions of the All-India Rural Credit Review Committee of 1969 apply with particular force to many parts of Kerala. The intrusion of politics both at the state and the village level has vitiated the working of co-operatives, with the result that individuals who have not ingratiated themselves with particular parties or factions are virtually outside the scope of co-operative credit.[27] For several years co-operatives were bywords for corruption in Kerala, and their reputation was damaged still further during the first Communist ministry (see above, p. 163). It is fair to note, however, that the situation in some other states was often worse.

The unsatisfactory condition of co-operatives in Kerala is clearly evidenced in official reports: 43 per cent of agricultural credit societies in existence in 1970-1 were operating at a loss and more than one-fifth of outstanding loans was overdue.[28] By June 1975 45 per cent of the 1,700 societies were operating at a loss and 46 per cent of loans were overdue.[29] A similar pattern obtained in the coir industry, where in 1972 nearly two-fifths of the societies were under liquidation.[30] The Reserve Bank declined to finance coir co-operatives and it was not until 1974-5 that alternative institutional finance could be found.

One of the more bizarre examples of the difficulties in establishing the co-operative movement was the early history of the engineers' co-operative, ENCOS, formed from unemployed engineers (with some family capital at their disposal) to manufacture scooters under the presidency of the veteran CPI union leader P. Balachandran Menon. Each member was required to subscribe between Rs 2,000 and Rs 10,000 as share capital. For its part, the government arranged loans totalling Rs 2 crores. Before the factory had started full production the worker-shareholders had received three rises. None the less in January 1972, after only eighteen months, forty-five engineers struck work for more pay. When Balachandran Menon went to the factory he was subjected to *gherao* for the night and on his release the following morning retaliated by declaring a lock-out. ENCOS failed to fulfil the Chief Minister's expectations,[31] and was later wound up.

The report of the Committee on Public Accounts on the working of Kerala's 8,000 co-operatives in 1976-7 is highly critical of their operation. In some 10 per cent of cases the audit had been held up 'for want of records'.[32] Nearly 50 per cent of the societies had failed to complete their audits six months after the prescribed time limit. Information on the overall profit and loss position of co-operatives was furnished only for those societies controlled by the Co-operative Department. The departments concerned with Industries, Fisheries, and dairy products could not provide them. Noting that loss-making societies controlled by the Registrar of Co-operatives had accumulated deficits of Rs 11.35 lakhs in the four years from 1969-70 to 1972-3 as against the profitable societies' surplus of Rs 729 lakhs, the CPA found the steps taken to reduce the loss ineffective.[33] The Report of the High Level Committee presented in 1967 was still under consideration in 1976. The government was 'not making an earnest attempt to wipe out the difficulties' of the societies. 'The nerve centre of the economic life of the interior villages is the co-operative societies. As such if the affairs of the societies are allowed to deteriorate it would prove to be a disaster to the economic life of the village folk.'[34]

The Machinery of Government

Despite the constraints of the quasi-federal system (see above, pp. 6-9), Congress dominance at the Centre, and economic difficulties beyond provincial control, there was scope for coalition governments to undertake significant development initiatives at state level. But no ministry, be it capitalist, communist, or Rosicrucian, could provide any solution to Kerala's problems without fundamental changes in the means of political production, which, in 1967, were more obviously geared to the maintenance of various group and individual interests than to the attainment of any class-based objectives—much less the wider developmental aims presumed in the concept of either the National or the People's Democratic Front.

The character of interests had undoubtedly changed during the 1960s. The NSS, SNDP Yogam, and the churches no longer determined the fate of governments: Mannath (NSS) was dead; Sankar (SNDP), Kerala's former Chief Minister, failed to secure a Congress candidacy in either the 1970 Assembly or 1971 Lok Sabha elections; the churches was split between New Congress and Kerala Congress; and the Muslim League was held together only by the personal authority of Bafaki Thangal. Communal allegiance was, of course, still a factor in political calculations: in the selection of candidates in elections,[35] in the exercise of ministerial patronage, and in the evaluation of alternative courses of political action. However, it was no longer an overriding consideration. By 1970 only the Muslim League counted for much with government and by 1973 not even the League.

The decline of the communal element in Kerala politics may be attributed to economic and social differentiation within communities, the removal of many areas of communal rivalry from the political agenda by the routinization of job reservation, the rotation of discretionary appointments, the very success of the communal organization in raising educational levels, the rise of political parties as more efficacious intermediaries with government, and lastly the spread of unionization upwards into the middle and downwards into the labouring classes. Symbolic of the decline of the power of caste and communal organizations was the decision to form specifically Nair and Ezhava political parties in the 1970s and the ease with which the existing parties brushed aside their challenge.[36]

The articulation of interests had changed but the basis of political argument was still the division of existing resources rather than the creation of more. Whether the perspective is liberal democratic or marxist, Kerala was ill equipped for development. In the language of American political science the party system could not 'mobilize' for development because it did not aggregate demands. In marxist language 'fragmentation oppresses people'.[37] There was limited class-wide consciousness. Sectionalism expressed through the numerous parties and economism through countless unions, affiliated more or less loosely to the parties, predominated.[38] Party competition penetrated every corner of the economy and the society. Further, the individual parties themselves, including the CPM and the CPI, suffered from internal cleavages, commonly expressed in tensions between the ministerial and organizational wings, with the former embracing the majority of legislators and the latter the mass front including trade unions and student organizations. A first step in providing even immediate relief to the people was therefore the creation of machinery to co-ordinate decision-making within as well as between parties. In a more disciplined party system the operation of the cabinet system of government, coupled with joint parliamentary party meetings, might have ensured that the united front from above worked in reasonable harmony with the united front from below. In Kerala conditions more was required.

Namboodiripad's solution to the problem was the co-ordination committee. This was a multi-party liaison committee composed of one representative of each constituent party, normally a key organizational figure such as the party secretary. The Chief Minister presided *ex officio* and the committee was serviced by Azhikodan Raghavan of the CPM. The committee was designed to link mass party to cabinet, to agree broad lines of policy before individual ministers put forward detailed proposals to the council of ministers, and to facilitate private bargaining between the partners in the front. After the first few months, however, the committee tended to exacerbate conflict rather than reconcile it. Its frequently acrimonious proceedings were leaked to the press by the contending parties, decisions were flouted, and by mid-1969 it had ceased to meet. The failure of the committee stemmed from several factors: the bitterness of the rivalry between the two communist parties; the internal dissensions within the CPM; the sheer size of the UF's majority in the Assembly; and, arguably, the inability—partly dictated by circumstances beyond his control—of Namboodiripad to establish a Chief Ministerial role of honest broker. None the less the committee was an innovation of great importance, which Achutha Menon was to put to good use.

During Menon's first ministry the co-ordination committee was continued on the same principle of one representative from each constituent party in the ministry. The RSP, which supported the Mini Front but as a result of a decision of the party nationally did not join the ministry, also attended. This principle was then adapted after the 1970 election to incorporate Congress into the committee.[39] The new arrangement revealed the price the CPI and its partners had paid for power, but at the same time went far to securing a wide commitment from Congress. The committee was expanded to nine members, four of whom were nominated by the Congress Executive—the KPCC President, K.K. Viswanathan (who had opposed his party's participation in the committee), K. Karunakaran, leader of the Congress Legislative Party leader, A.K. Antony, the KPCC Secretary and Youth Congress chief, and C.M. Stephen, AITUC leader and associate of Sankar—and four by the Mini Front itself—Govindan Nair of the CPI, Bafaki Thangal of the League, Sreekantan Nair of the RSP, and Viswambharan of the PSP. Menon presided *ex officio* and Antony acted as convenor deputizing as chairman in the absence of the Chief Minister, thus minimizing the chances of 'misunderstandings' of the kind that had occurred in 1967-9 when both posts were held by the CPM. Antony's integrity was beyond dispute. Menon himself, capitalizing on his own reputation for political toughness and the ministry's uncertain majority in the Assembly, is said to have warned the committee at its first meeting that he was ready to resign if the proceedings degenerated a those of the UF had done. The warning was superfluous when the committee was a cabal of some of the most powerful figures from the medium-sized parties of Kerala politics, which may perhaps explain the absence of agenda and minutes. Later, after the incorporation of Congress into the ministry, its record was chequered and Congress was accused of hegemonic tendencies reminiscent of charges levelled at the CPM in 1967-9.

In addition to playing a key role in the survival of the ministry, the committee rather than the council of ministers was the locus of power.[40] Decision-making was a four-stage process. First came party meetings of varying degrees of formality and importance but basically of two types—central committees decided broad policies with all interests represented, and parliamentary caucuses discussed short-term tactics usually under the guidance of a minister and on important occasions with the party secretary present. Second, and interacting with the first stage, ministerial policy drafting, in which individual ministers, aided by private secretaries and in consultation with departmental officials, hammered out possible legislative or administrative initiatives. In the case of communist ministers they appear to have made their own choice as to whether their private office was staffed by a party man, a civil servant, or both. Third came the co-ordination committee which decided government policy in broad terms, sought to reconcile party conflicts of interest, and agreed the handling of the opposition. Under Menon and Antony discussions were frank but business-like and compromises were made, though from 1972 onwards with increasing difficulty. The Chief Minister was reported to have argued for the 'public interest', leaving his party's claim to be staked by his party colleagues.[41] Judged by attendance at the ensuing press conferences, in so far as power has concentrated anywhere in Kerala, this was where it lay.[42] Finally the cabinet met to thrash out the detailed implementation of what has been agreed in the co-ordination committee. Ministers distributed resources in detail but their strategic allocation was the task of the co-ordination committee. Once policy had been agreed the responsibility rested with the minister concerned and his department.

In Achutha Menon's view the single most important problem in the modernization of Kerala was the senior departmental officers, the Indian Administrative Service, the 'fifth wheel on the coach', acting as a brake.[43] After a series of incidents which strained relations between the Chief Minister and the IAS cadre Menon summoned a meeting of officers in 1971 to warn them against arrogance and aloofness and behaving like latter-day Namboodiri Brahmins, and to request more positive commitment to development objectives.[44]

Thereafter relations appear to have been more amicable. That some
IAS officers of the Kerala cadre, particularly of the older generation,
had difficulty in adjusting to the slow erosion of their status and
power is indisputable. K.K. Ramankutty, for example, appointed to
investigate allegations of CPI corruption in the procurement of land
for an agricultural university, in alleging that the Chief Minister had
sought to influence his findings by offering him a Vice-
Chancellorship on his retirement scornfully wrote in his report 'as if
the Vice-Chancellorship in this State is such a covetable thing for a
Member of the Board of Revenue.'[45] Another officer—formerly of
the ICS cadre—finally ran out of ministers prepared to accept him in
1973 and was dispatched as Special Commissioner to the remote and
inhospitable Wynad—an important post in itself but in the circumstances tantamount to internal exile.[46] It is also true that there were
individuals whose strict impartiality was doubted, notably the
group known as the 'class of '57', which had originally been
identified with the Christian Congress leader P.T. Chacko until his
death in 1964 and during the 1970s said to be close to the RSP leader,
Baby John.[47] However, Namboodiripad when Chief Minister, and
ministers generally did not share Achutha Menon's dissatisfaction
with the cadre at large. In any case the capacity of IAS officers to
contribute to the developmental process was limited by the fact that
on average (excluding promotions and training assignments) between 1957 and 1974 they spent only fourteen months in each
posting.

Senior officers for their part were critical of four aspects of
ministerial conduct: corruption and nepotism; politically motivated
breaches of rules and interference with orders; the lack of ministerial
interest in development plans once they had been inaugurated; and a
pusillanimous approach to discipline among the Non-Gazetted
Officers.[48] That corruption, nepotism, and the flouting of procedures were commonplace during the UF ministry is hardly in dispute. By 1974 a number of ministers in Menon's government had
also become notorious, including one CPI minister. Another non-
Congress minister privately boasted that he would need a convoy of
lorries to remove the proceeds of office from his official residence.[4]
One senior official (as well as political correspondents) was prepared
to describe the Maxi Front as the most corrupt Kerala had known.[5]
Whether or not this judgement was correct the author is not in
position to establish.

The more scandalous allegations of malpractice were almost
inevitably levelled at public corporations and *ad hoc* agencies (see
below, p. 287). One documented instance which embarrassed both
the CPI and the Chief Minister himself in so far as one of his nephew

was a beneficiary, concerned appointments to the government-owned Travancore-Cochin Chemicals Ltd (TCC). Despite a government order severely restricting recruitment to the public corporations in January 1970, TCC had created new posts with the intention, it was alleged, of providing jobs for relatives and friends of leaders of the ministry. The subsequent enquiry accepted that there had been some grounds for the decision to recruit but found that there had been 'gross malpractice' in the selection: marked answer papers had been unstapled and rearranged; many had been overvalued; and the best candidate, in the opinion both of the TCC and of the enquiry officer had not been appointed.[51] Despite these damning findings, on which the opposition turned the full glare of publicity, no action was taken.[52] The appointees remained undisturbed.

It is not difficult to understand why the Chief Minister of a multi-party administration would perforce tolerate corruption and nepotism. It is less clear why he should have failed to give more support to comprehensive anti-corruption legislation in the Assembly. Twice—in 1971 and 1973—a socialist lawyer MLA, Attingal Gopala Pillai, sought leave to introduce a Kerala Public Men (Inquiries) bill. On the first occasion the government promised its own bill in the following session; and on the second Menon objected: 'the issue was very complex and required careful scrutiny. Already there was a machinery existing to enquire into the allegations against Ministers' and a similar Bill was under the government's 'active consideration'.[53] No such measure appeared.

The civil service belief that ministers rapidly lost interest in projects that were originally launched in a blaze of publicity finds some confirmation in the inordinate delays in the completion of major as well as minor irrigation projects (see below, p. 281). However, there was more to this phenomenon than apathy. It was, for instance, the practice to continue to take up new irrigation projects for a variety of political and personal reasons rather than seek to complete existing projects. Just enough money was allocated to pay the staff and keep the work proceeding, however slowly. By this means more jobs were created, avenues of promotion opened up, and engineers and contractors pleased. Existing schemes were starved of funds; money was locked up; costs rose; and returns on investment were delayed.[54]

The final IAS charge against ministers of failing to support their efforts to control their staff reflected the impact of several factors. The combination of growing intervention in the economy as well as Kerala's far-reaching social policies had raised the proportion of the non-agricultural workforce in the public sector to two-fifths by 1970 and 47 per cent by 1975. Estimates of the cost in salaries vary but some put the figure as high as two-thirds of the state's revenue expenditure.[55] The largest group of public servants was the Non-Gazetted Officers (NGOs), numbering more than 150,000, concentrated in the state capital, and at this period chiefly organized by the CPM. Though discipline in government offices had been steadily eroded from at least 1957-9, most IAS officers discerned a marked deterioration during the 1967-9 ministry for which the CPM was not solely responsible. By the 1970s the NGO was the government's nightmare: a concentrated labour force gathered in grumbling offices, over-educated for its monotonous routine but under-educated for a role in nation-building, with its sense of relative deprivation accentuated by inflation. By one subterfuge or another the NGOs could strike with impunity since ministries in Kerala, as elsewhere in India, made up pay lost.

In 1967 the service rules had been amended to provide that employees would not be eligible for pay if they absented themselves without authority.[56] Such broken periods of service would not count towards leave or pension entitlements and could lead to the forfeiture of all past service and increments. In 1968 Namboodiripad had threatened to invoke the rule to deal with a strike of the Secretariat staff before staging a politic retreat. Menon pressed the matter further in 1972-3 by actually invoking the rule before settling for a modified form of sanction known as the *dies non* principle. The employee suffered an immediate loss of pay but was permitted to recoup this by working against his leave entitlement.[57]

Achutha Menon, whose party interest often coincided with the public interest in industrial disputes, was resourceful and determined in his efforts to bring the public sector labour aristocracy to heel, particularly by seeking to link bonus to productivity though his success was limited as strike statistics show. In December 1970 the government sought to end the chronic interruption of work on the major hydro-electric project at Idikki by a long-term agreement raising unskilled rates of pay by 50 per cent, coupled with the invocation of Defence of India rules to ban strikes and prohibit outside 'agitators' from entering the area. From time to time there was also recourse to the pre-emptive arrest of (opposition) troublemakers and in 1974 to the arrest of a group of strikers in their entirety, the State Electricity Board Chief Engineers. To the delight of the public these well-paid officials were unceremoniously transported to the discomforts of 'C' class prison accommodation, normally reserved for anti-social elements of the lowest class. However, the fact that the ministry after four years in office was driven to such extremities reflected its failure to restructure industrial relations.

In the process of development a vital part of government activity is the planning process. The broad shape of the plans is decided centrally but state governments have a direct impact on the outcome in three ways: they prepare the initial drafts and specify and cost priorities within the general framework; they implement the programmes as finally agreed; and decide what additional resources they are able and willing to raise to finance the desired plan (see above, pp. 7-8 and p. 268).

Prior to 1967 the Chief Minister, whose responsibilities include planning, co-ordinated the drafting of the state's submission through the Planning Department in association with the Bureau of Economic and Social Statistics. In September 1967 Namboodiripad took the important step of establishing a State Planning Board. Though initially the subject of much criticism as a CPM propaganda agency, it was to become an accepted and valuable part of the state's planning apparatus when reconstituted by Menon in 1970, as the Board's annual *Economic Review* illustrates. It, however, remained somewhat constricted by its limited establishment.[58] A further initiative was the creation in September 1970 of the Centre for Development Studies, jointly financed by the central and state governments and under the direction of the distinguished left-wing economist K.N. Raj. The Centre has gathered a nucleus of permanent members with established reputations and a complement of post-doctoral fellows. As a research unit, it has provided important policy-oriented studies of development based on Kerala data; but, whatever the intention may have been, the Centre has not become closely involved in the state's own planning or policy processes. Distrust between civil servants and Centre members is said to be mutual and strong, while ministers are apathetic.[59] The influence of the Centre has thus been marginal in Kerala itself—though not elsewhere.

The significance of the state's control over the implementation of plans is illustrated in Table 11.2, which compares the estimated expenditure as agreed between the central and state governments with the actual expenditure between 1951-2 and 1972-3. It is important to note that expenditure does not necessarily entail the achievement of the physical targets set (see below, p. 281). The figures show marked and consistent priorities in planned expenditure that are only partially explained by reference to nationally defined priorities. Even more striking are the considerable variations in the fulfilment of financial targets. Throughout, the biggest head was irrigation and power, accounting for two-fifths of the total from the Second Plan onwards. Of this, power generation took the major share. This is followed by social services, hovering just above one-fifth of the total, with education the largest element. Investment in

Table 11.2 Kerala 1951-74: Distribution of Plan Target Expenditure and Actual Achievement of Targets by Category (percentage)

	First Plan 1951-6		Second Plan 1956-61		Third Plan 1961-6		Annual Plans* 1966-9	Fourth Plan 1969-74	
	(1)	(2)	(1)	(2)	(1)	(2)	(1)	(1)	(2)†
Agriculture	10	(42)	10	(87)	14	(81)	23	15	(71)
Agricultural production & minor irrigation	9	(43)	6	(102)	9	(82)	9	9	(83)
Forests	neg.		1	(51)	1	(62)	1	1	(69)
Fisheries	neg.		1	(69)	2	(74)	5	3	(57)
Community development & co-operation	neg.		7	(81)	6	(98)	4	4	(114)
Irrigation & power	61	(89)	41	(96)	42	(129)	38	43	(91)
Irrigation	20	(88)	11	(103)	6	(90)	8	9	(82)
Power	41	(89)	27	(93)	33	(140)	29	32	(87)
Flood/erosion	neg.		2	(102)	3	(123)	1	2	(55)
Industry & mining	2	(45)	8	(88)	8	(84)	9	7	(79)
Large & medium	n.k.		2	(175)	4	(167)	5	4	(82)
Transport & communications	13	(126)	9	(129)	7	(110)	7	9	(103)
Social services	15	(128)	25	(85)	23	(109)	18	22	(105)
Education	1	(99)	14	(108)	11	(109)	10	8	(95)
Backward classes	3	(88)	3	(117)	1	(131)	neg.	2	(69)
Health	10	(135)	6	(55)	9	(118)	7	3	(59)
Housing	1	(361)	2	(67)	1	(61)	1	2	(178)
Actual expenditure (Rs. Crore)	26		80		182		144	233	

(1) Targeted expenditure.   * Outlay not available.   † Performance in terms of first 4 years' expenditure as percentage of 5 years' planned outlay.

(2) Actual outlay as percentage of (1)

Sources: Based on SFP, 8: Plan Expenditure in Kerala; FFYP 1974-9.

agricultural production and minor irrigation (9 per cent) was modest in a state chronically deficient in food grains, and the allocation to large and medium industry (5 per cent or less) even smaller. As the bracketed figures show, the achievement of financial targets varies significantly. The record is generally good on social services, transport and communications, and large and medium industry but disappointing in agricultural production and small-scale industry, and poor in forests and fisheries, two of Kerala's major natural resources. The range of variation is certainly greater than one would expect if practicalities were the only factor.[60]

Though some of the deviation from planned expenditure under different development heads was intentional, a major weakness of the process of planning in Kerala is the lack of any adequate machinery for its monitoring and evaluation. Some of the more wasteful consequences included the construction of a bridge over a canal that was itself cancelled, and of another bridge without a road to cross it.[61] Evaluation units existed in the State Planning Board and the Bureau of Economics and Statistics but their staffing was 'hardly sufficient for the laborious task' nor was their equipment: the evaluation officers did not even have a van and were acutely short of modern calculation machines.[62] No central monitoring agency existed at all in 1974. Such a body, with access to 'the highest authorities in administration', might have relieved bottle-necks and brought to notice some of the more alarming instances of incompetence, maladministration, and corruption revealed by the Committees on Public Accounts and Public Undertakings, some of which were the ministerial responsibility of communist politicians (see below, p. 286).

Industrialization

Kerala is an industrially backward state both absolutely and relative to a number of other Indian states. In 1957 there were 1,652 factories generating an average daily employment of nearly 108,000.[63] After a spurt during the first communist ministry (37 per cent increase in factories and 56 per cent in daily employment,[64] industrial growth was slow, as the accompanying tables show. When 1959 is taken as the base year (100), the index of working factories had reached 129 by 1966, 134 by 1969, and it remained at 134 when the Mini Front expanded into the Maxi Front in 1971.[65] Average daily employment rose slowly to 124 in 1966 and 128 in 1969 and 1971.[66] From 1972 to 1975 there was a striking 81 per cent rise in the number of working factories. The more modest 17 per cent growth in average daily employment has to be seen in the context of the economic difficulties

Table 11.3   Kerala 1959-71: Working Factories and Average Daily Employment by District

District*	% Population 1961	Factories 1959 % of total	Factories: index of growth (1959 = 100)			Average daily employment 1959 % of Total	Average daily employment: index of growth (1959 = 100)		
			1966	1969	1971		1966	1969	1971
Trivandrum	10.3	5.0	126	140	136	4.5	128	177	178
Quilon	11.5	14.9	121	133	133	41.0	128	136	138
Alleppey	10.7	10.8	116	111	107	7.6	108	94	99
Kottayam	10.3	10.0	117	127	128	4.8	119	111	114
Ernakulam	11.0	9.6	169	196	201	10.6	147	157	151
Trichur	9.7	11.7	185	209	201	9.3	117	122	126
Palghat	10.5	10.8	104	104	111	3.5	136	126	125
Kozhikode	15.5	12.0	126	131	134	10.7	112	107	103
Cannanore	10.5	15.2	106	86	79	7.9	110	93	91
State	100.0	100.0 (2,258)	129	134	134	99.9 (160,095)	124	128	128

* The nine-District system obtaining until 1969 is projected to 1971 for purposes of comparability.

Sources: SFP, 3: Labour; ER, 1969-76.

Table 11.4 Kerala 1972-5: Working Factories and Average Daily
Employment by District

District	% Population 1971	Factories 1972 % of Total	% Change 1972-5	Average daily employment 1972 % of Total	% Change 1972-5
Trivandrum	10.3	5.0	+43	6.4	+27
Quilon	11.3	13.3	+42	46.1	+11
Alleppey	10.0	10.6	+25	5.6	+11
Kottayam	7.1	6.5	+124	2.3	+45
Idikki	3.6	3.3	+7	1.9	+22
Ernakulam	10.1	15.1	+92	11.6	+25
Trichur	10.0	15.9	+50	8.9	+11
Palghat	7.9	8.6	+110	3.4	+33
Malappuram	8.7	1.8	+78	0.8	−15
Kozhikode	9.9	12.3	+126	8.2	+20
Cannanore	11.1	9.1	+141	5.7	+38
State	100.0	100 (3,487)	+81	99.8 (226,088)	+17

Source: ER, 1972-6.

of the period.[67] Even so, at the end of the Fourth Plan the industrial sector absorbed no more than one-fifth of the labour force but contributed only one-sixth of the state's income.[68] Capital employed per worker was about one-half of the Indian average. Some 30 per cent of industrial units use no power yet employed 50 per cent of the factory labour force. Levels of technology were simple and added value low.[69] Entrepreneurial initiative was lacking.[70] Agro-based industries predominated and 45 per cent of the industrial labour force was employed in cashew processing. Except in a few advanced industries daily and annual earnings were generally well below those in most other states, though the gap steadily narrowed as a result of a combination of union activity and state interventionism.[71]

Successive state plans have accorded a low priority to industrial development (see above, p. 280), which accounted for only some 8 per cent of total expenditure in the Third and Fourth Plans as compared to a national figure of between one-fifth and one-quarter.[72] Kerala governments have underspent their provision under this head whereas nationally it has been overspent.[73] Commenting on the small percentage earmarked in the Second Plan for Kerala's industrial development, Namboodiripad said that his Congress predecessors had been more interested in the construction of a street or school in their constituency than in planning a rational industrial policy.[74] No ministry had, however, been able to resist the socio-political pressures for improved social services, particularly education. Educational expenditure per head increased by 30 per cent between 1957-8 and 1959-60, by 31 per cent under the United Front ministry, by 20 per cent under the first two Achutha Menon governments, and by a further 86 per cent from 1971-2 to 1975-6.[75] One-third of the state's total expenditure in 1970-1 went on education, 10 per cent more than in its nearest rival, the Punjab.[76] Education and health are, of course, important elements of the industrial infrastructure but the argument would carry more weight if provision had not been so unequal, and showed so little sign of reduction. In 1974 those unfortunate enough to require hospitalization were ten times more likely to find a bed available in the state capital than in the rural areas of Malabar.[77]

If inequalities persisted in those areas of development in which Kerala has an outstanding record, the same was true of industrialization. As the tables show, with the exception of Trivandrum, regional disparties widened rather than narrowed between 1959 and 1971. Thereafter there was some improvement but only three of the seven industrially backward Districts recorded above-average increases in daily industrial employment over the period 1972-5.[78]

Given the absence of indigenous industrial enterprise, the low levels of capital formation in the state, and the failure to attract Indian private investment, the government has perforce assumed the role of industrial entrepreneur through wholly or partially owned state concerns and a variety of service agencies of which the State Industrial Development Corporation, and the State Financial Corporation are the most important.

Industrial development was chiefly the responsibility of CPI Industries ministers—and in fact, with one brief interruption, of T.V. Thomas from 1967 until his death in 1975. During the UF Ministry (see above, p. 215), Thomas's industrial policy, 'a clarion call to the private entrepreneurs to invest in Kerala,'[79] suffered from the coincidence of national economic difficulties and conflict within the government. In the public sector four wholly owned government companies were added to the existing twelve, and three partly owned government companies to the existing nine.[80] Only one of the seven—Chalakudy Potteries—was a manufacturing concern. The number of new private concerns was minimal.

During the 1970s the record improved considerably though the cumulative impact on employment opportunities was inevitably small. The Industrial Development Corporation had by 1976 given financial assistance to thirty-four companies to establish new projects—twenty-nine had begun production—and assisted thirteen others to expand or diversify. It had also set up twelve state sector companies, of which seven had begun production. Two important new development corporations were established—the Kerala Industrial and Technical Consultancy Organisation (1972) and the Kerala State Electronics Development Corporation (1973)—and a much-needed supervisory holding company, Kerala State Industrial Enterprises Ltd (1975), to improve the performance of the weakest state-owned concerns.[81] In the circumstances the ministry's performance was creditable.

It was a good deal less successful in the small-scale sector—industrial units with a maximum of Rs 5 lakhs of capital investment employing not more than 50 workers if power is used or 100 where it is not.[82] In the Indian context, and *a fortiori* in Kerala, small-scale industrialization has an important role in economic development and the relief of unemployment. In 1961 the contribution of this sector to Kerala's net output was 12 per cent, while the state accounted for 5.8 per cent of the total Indian small-scale workforce, a figure boosted by the traditional industries such as coir.[83] M.A. Oommen has provided a carefully researched case study of the small-scale sector in Kerala which obviates the need to examine the record in detail prior to 1967. Despite a renewed campaign to stimulate such industrialization in 1967 no significant changes took place until 1975.[84]

According to Oommen the objectives and programmes were sound enough but the actual performance of the sector was poor and compared unfavourably with the Punjab, West Bengal, Maharashtra, and Delhi.[85] There were widespread defects in design, strategy, and implementation as well as a failure to stimulate entrepreneurial talent latent in the state. On the evidence available there seems to have been little improvement in the 1970's. The State Small Industries Corporation continued to run at a loss, and the record of its eight production and service units was unimpressive. Between 1966-7 and 1969-70 four had consistently made profits; in 1970-1 one; in 1971-2 two; in 1972-3 none; in 1973-4 four; and 1974-5 two.[86] According to the government's *Economic Review 1976*, 'Financial and administration problems have all along bogged the working of the Corporation.'[87] Out of Kerala's 13,710 small-scale units 4,000 were closed or did not report and another 2,000 were classified as 'sick'.[88]

The ministry thereupon launched a 'massive new programme' for the creation of 10,000 new units and the revitalization of the existing ones over a four-year term, coupled with a reorganization of the Industries Department and a reconstruction of the corporation. The official description of the first stages does not inspire confidence. To begin with, 'district level conventions were held in all the districts, to enthuse the potential entrepreneurs and the public . . . and evolve specific plans of action.' Those 15,000 'entrepreneurs' who registered were then 'trained in a phased manner to set up selected industries' and in a record six weeks during August and September 1975 the first batch of eleven industrial estates—only eighteen estates had been established between 1961 and 1974—were provided with production units.[89] In July 1976 the second batch of twenty-two estates was 'to be commissioned shortly'.[90] Perhaps the commercial and institutional sources called upon to provide 80 per cent of the estimated overall cost of Rs 100 crores for the scheme were dragging their feet.

Public Undertakings

After agriculture the most important single element in Kerala's economic development is the operation of its public undertakings: utilities such as the Electricity Board, services such as the Road Transport Corporation, and commercial and industrial enterprises of a wide range. Here the record of the communist-led ministries has been poor and at times in the view of the Assembly's Committee on Public Undertakings (CPU) unacceptably bad.

Formally speaking, the government discharges its responsibilities in the public sector through departmental supervision and government nominees to the Boards of Directors. In practice the undertakings have been allowed to go their own way.[91] Senior officials nominated as directors seldom have time to attend Board meetings, have little or no knowledge of the industry concerned, and find themselves trapped between the vested interests of management and minister. The fact that seven members of the State Road Transport Corporation were government officials did nothing to ensure that the buses ran on time or profitably. Six years after the SRTC's formation in 1965 the corporation had still not completed the valuation of its assets and liabilities. By 1973–4 its accumulated losses had reached Rs 11 crores, two-thirds of its total capital investment.[92] 'The authorities are more interested,' the CPU reported, 'in promoting the interests of private parties than the welfare of the corporation.'[93]

Kerala State Electricity Board

The problems and defects of public sector undertakings can be well illustrated from the operations of the Electricity Board, the largest concern and the ministerial responsibility of the CPI throughout the period under review.[94] Reliable supplies of cheap power are of immense importance to industrialization and development in general. One of Kerala's most important assets is its hydro-electric potential, estimated at 6 per cent of India's total potential and of particular importance in view of the opportunities offered by the presence of high-value and rare metals such as titanium. The State Electricity Board (KSEB) is not only the largest but the most crucial of Kerala's public enterprises. On the evidence of report after report from the CPA and the CPU, as well as the findings of the Sankaran and Mulla Commissions, the KSEB had become a law unto itself. It had proved an overweening subject no Ministry could check.

The Board was formed in 1957 and its accumulated deficit had reached Rs. 14 crores by 1969-70.[95] It admitted that the servicing of its debt to the state government was the last claim on its finances and that, in contravention of the Electricity Supply Act, it was using the interest due on these loans for capital expenditure.[96] Its technical performance was on a par with its managerial record.[97] All its projects were years rather than months behind schedule. Only 72 per cent of the power generated could be transmitted because of the lack of sufficient transmission lines. One quarter of what was transmitted in Low Tension distribution was lost.[98] Interrruptions to supply were a regular occurrence and voltage was seldom within 10 per cent of the specified minimum.[99] Despite the progress with rural electrification the increase in consumption of electricity in Kerala was below that of India as a whole or neighbouring Tamil Nadu.[100]

The Board's establishment costs were half of its realization, the highest level of any State Electricity Board in India and double what they had been initially. None the less it was lethargic in sending out its invoices, incapable of checking its stock, and wont to pay its contractors without investigating whether the work had been done according to tender, or indeed at all.[101] Capital equipment was frequently under-utilized or left to rust and the system of purchase was lackadaisical when not actually corrupt.[102] Payments for overtime ran at two and a half times those of other state electricity boards and increased as staff numbers grew.[103] The tariff structure was virtually non-existent as far as the major industrial users were concerned, with the result that the more electricity was consumed the greater the loss to the Board. Even after the introduction of a tariff order for the High Tension customers in January 1970 'the charge for electricity supplied to them continued to be lower than the cost ... [104] **Perhaps the one thing to be said in favour of the Board** was that its industrial relations (outside of Idikki) were comparatively good—given the benefits of working for it, that is not surprising.

The Idikki project

The most expensive of the Board's ventures was the Idikki Hydro-Electric Project,[105] an Indo-Canadian collaboration. Work began in 1961 on a spectacular development of advanced design to generate 780 MW of electricity, utilizing one-third of the state's potential hydro-electric capacity and increasing its existing capacity by 150 per cent. According to the schedule of work settled in 1966-7, the first generation unit was to be completed in September 1970. Two years later the three dams were only 37 to 49 per cent complete.[106] Not until February 1976 did Idikki begin generating power. Meanwhile the estimated cost had more than doubled. The KSEB informed the Committee on Public Undertakings that the delays in the 1970s were caused by difficulties in clearing encroachers from the site, problems in the importation of equipment, labour troubles, and foundation problems with two of the dams, claims which the Committee firmly rejected. 'Board officials did not attend to this work with the right sense of urgency...there was no sufficient planning and foresight in the ordering and procurement of essential equipments.[107] 'It was amazing that the fault zone across the Kulamavu dam...was not detected initially.'[108] 'The committee are led to the conclusion that the investigation was done in a haphazard and unscientific manner.'[109] On the Board's relationship with the contractors the CPU commented that 'It seems that the...Board is allowing contractors to bungle, to desert work without any valid reason and fear of penalty contemplated in the agreement...a recurring and unhealthy feature which the Committee have come across year after year.'[110] The Committee went on to say that it had repeatedly come across instances where undue benefits which are not stipulated in the contract are given to contractors by the...Board without any valid reason.'[111] On the labour front, unions controlled by the ruling parties showed no more willingness to hasten the project's completion than those controlled by the CPM opposition; there was no certain prospect of alternative employment, and an understandable desire to exact the highest price for their labour in an environment riddled with corruption from top to bottom.[112] Neither the Idikki Review Board nor the High Level Committee was able to speed the work's completion. The timelessness of the project was reflected in the RSP Minister of Public Works' view in 1973 that there was no pressing need to plan industrial developments with Idikki power in mind.[113] In the event, energy surplus to Kerala's requirements is being sold and bartered to Tamil Nadu. In sum during the period under review, as well as earlier, the KSEB has been a public enterprise of which, on the official evidence, a Banana Republic might have been ashamed. As the Sankaran Commission reported, many of the highest officials of the Board were guilty of gross mismanagement yet 'they were allowed to go scot free and to retire in due course.'[114]

The performance of the KSEB and the Kerala State Road Transport Corporation, though exceptional in degree, reflected the malaise of public undertakings in the state generally—including a Soviet-assisted collective farm;[115] and since state intervention had become the norm, seriously inhibited economic growth. The return in 1967-8 on the state's Rs 137 crore investment in industrial concerns was negligible. Even excluding the KSEB and the KSRTC, the dividend was less than one per cent.[116] Loans went unrepaid— actual payments in 1966-7 were one-quarter and in 1967-8 were only one half of the budget estimate; and interest payments fell far short of what was due.[117] In 1970-1 all six government-owned companies were operating at a loss,[118] while Travancore Titanium Products was the only government-controlled company producing more than a nominal profit.[119] Though there was some improvement in 1975-6, four out of seven concerns still ran at a loss in the first year of the Emergency. Only one of the eight production and service units of the State Small Industries Corporation was working at a profit. In contrast three out of four major Central Sector Undertakings were running at a profit.[120] 'Instead of becoming an expanding source of additional resources . . .public sector enterprises in general,' according to the Taxation Enquiry Committee Report, 'have remained a drag on the State's resources.'[121] The Taxation Committee undertook twelve case studies of a cross-section of public undertakings. Only two had any sort of training programme for their staff; only two a proper sales organization; none had a research and development programme; and just three had either a clearly laid-down pricing policy or product planning. In the Committee's view, management was not simply 'conservative'; it was 'primitive'.[122] The situation was little different in 1974. Assembly Committee reports portray not 'state capitalism' but a degenerate form of feudalism in which managerial barons, their worker retainers, and marauding contractors pillaged the public treasury.

Social Relations and Land Reform

In anything but long-term developmental policies the direct opportunities available to state governments to modify socioeconomic relations and so the distribution of political power are limited—decentralization of decision-making and the democratization of administration, intervention in the stratification of educational and employment opportunities inherent in caste and communal structures, and agrarian reform. Of these three only agrarian reform, albeit the most fundamental, was attempted.

The leadership of the CPM and CPI alike remained ambivalent towards the concept of 'more power to the people', while front-wide apprehensions of electoral losses led to repeated postponements of panchayat elections after the initial contest in 1963. A panchayat raj bill was introduced on 3 August 1967 to devolve greater authority on the panchayats. Though the Select Committee submitted its report in August 1968 it was not considered until 26 March 1969. It was then pushed to one side to make time for the closing stages of the Land Reforms Bill and failed to reach its third reading before the fall of the ministry. As noted earlier (p. 247), circumstances contributed to the delay but Joseph Chazhikad, the then Father of the House, expressed a commonly held view when he told the Assembly that the UF government was simply not interested in handing over power to the people.[123] Two years later the Minister for Local Administration in the second Mini Front government promised the house a Panchayat Raj Bill in the next session, but instead a Kerala District Administration Bill was introduced. Discussion at the Report stage revealed the continuing ambivalence of both government and opposition MLAs on decentralization in principle and practice.[124]

A similar disinterest mixed with political caution was evident in successive governments' attitudes to the issue of communal reservation. In 1967 in response to a High Court direction (see above, p. 34) the UF Ministry had set up an inquiry under the former CPM MP, Nettur P. Damodaran, which initially included Achutha Menon among its members, to investigate whether or not the existing criteria for communal reservation and rotation in recruitment to government posts were still justifiable.[125] The system in use was essentially that drawn up in 1957 on the creation of the state of Kerala: half the appointments were reserved for the 'backward classes' according to a complex formula designed to ensure that 14 per cent of all entrants would be Ezhavas or Thiyas, 10 per cent Muslims, 10 per cent scheduled castes or tribes, 4 per cent Latin Catholics, and 11 per cent other listed backward classes or groups. Reservation did not preclude members of the backward communities from entry through open competition. After three years' work the Backward Classes Reservation Commission concluded that the only legally defensible way of determining backwardness by 1970 was an economic one, measured not by individual or family income or wealth but on the basis of the proportion of families in each community with aggregate incomes of Rs 8,000 or less, according to their sample survey (see above, p. 34). On this test 90 per cent of the population was backward, including most of the so-called forward communities. Ignoring the logic of their argument the Commission recommended that the economically-backward individual or family should benefit from reservation only if his *community* was 'inadequately represented' in the relevant category of public service, that is, if the percentage of posts held by his community was less than its proportion in the population as a whole.[126] However, those few families from backward communities earning more than Rs 8,000 would not be entitled to reservation. Of all government posts 38 per cent should be reserved for the backward communities so defined (and 8 per cent for the scheduled castes and 2 per cent for the tribes), allocated according to percentages weighted to counteract the degree of under-representation suffered by each backward group in specific categories of government service. Ironically a Marxist-led government had established an inquiry into the character and disadvantages of the backward *classes* which ended by defining them as backward *communities*, not classes at all.[127]

The commission admitted that socially balanced recruitment would not necessarily guarantee equal opportunities of promotion.[128] Although at all but the very highest levels of service the general principle was seniority-cum-merit, thinly veiled caste discrimination could still damage the career prospects of the backward in a service dominated from top to bottom by Nairs in particular and the forward communities in general. The Commission offered suggestions as to how the government could circumvent 'the procedural problems' involved in introducing a system of reservation for promotion,[129] but no general action was taken. Political considerations apart, there were those on both sides of the House who wondered whether the state could afford the extension of ascriptive criteria of selection from recruitment to promotion. This did not prevent the application of the principle of reservation to Kerala university staff, including professors and readers in 1974.[130] The Nettur report was officially buried in December 1978 when the new CPI Chief Minister, Vasudevan Nair, announced that it could no longer be acted upon as its survey was totally out of date.[131] Linked issues of the reform of student admission to private colleges and the appointment of staff have proved equally difficult of solution. Despite the passage of the Kerala University Bill, 1972, in 1974, and the establishment of a procedure for government influence on appointments in exchange for government payment of college teachers, many of the old abuses continue.[132]

Land Reform

The most important area in which a state government may restructure social relations is on the land. In India land reform has been slow and inefficient, frequently honoured in the breach rather than the observance. In a national context Kerala's land reform, begun by the 1957-9 ministry, brought to legislative fruition by the UF ministry, and implemented by the Mini and Maxi fronts has attracted attention as the most radical, comprehensive, and far-reaching in South Asia. As the following commentary attempts to show, it none the less highlights both the problems and the possibilities of fundamental reform.

As an act (with its subsequent amendments) it was painstakingly and thoroughly drafted. The consequential delays therefore enabled many landowners to avoid or evade its full impact. Further, the need to secure Central approval and to minimize the possibility of judicial rulings destructive of legislative attention inevitably led to compromises. Of these perhaps the most important was the absence of any provision for popular participation in the implementation of the act, especially as there was no adequate record of rights in land.

Implementation of the Act commenced on 1 January 1970 under the first CPI-led Mini Front ministry and continued under the successive Achutha Menon governments. In contrast to the enactment of the bill, the administrative record was unimpressive. Although some of the delays and difficulties were undoubtedly beyond the control of the ministries, and some implicit in earlier legislative compromises, the slow and imperfect implementation of key provisions also arose from the coalition governments' lack of political will and serious administrative failings. Not until the Emergency did the government and its machine show a real sense of urgency. It can be surmised that this poor executive performance had further reduced the number of landless labourers, hutment dwellers, and poor tenants who could have benefited from the act.

The 1959 Bill had been re-enacted in a modestly revised form by the Congress-PSP ministry and became law on 21 January 1961. However, many of its key provisions were struck down by the courts and in 1963 the Congress ministry introduced a replacement measure of a substantially different character.[133] Instead of the compulsory vesting of the rights of landlords and intermediaries in the government, the Kerala Land Reforms Act, 1963 placed the onus on the cultivator to apply to purchase those rights through the Land Tribunal. Although in many respects the 1963 act resembled its predecessor, the cumulative impact of the detailed changes was to shift the balance towards the existing vested interests and to halve the estimated amount of surplus land available for redistribution. Justifying its policy, the government maintained that agrarian reform should not set one section of rural society against another but should seek to maintain the natural harmony of interests in land.[134]

From the beginning the bill was bitterly opposed by the CPI, as also by the PSP; and after the ministry had declined to circulate it to elicit public opinion the CPI refused to participate in the Select Committee stage. The opposition's fears that there would be little transfer of rights from landlord to tenant and a further reduction in the potential surplus of land for redistribution to the landless proved well founded. The official *Land Reforms Survey in Kerala 1966-7* in fact showed that there was a sharp increase in new tenancies in 1965 as well as a growth in tenancies disguised as mortgages in the period after the passage of the act as well as immediately prior to it.[135] Only 3 per cent of the tenants in the sample had sought fixity of tenure under the act, no tenant had purchased the title to the land he cultivated through the Land Tribunal, and even those transfers which had taken place by mutual agreement covered less than one per cent of the plots leased. The ceiling provisions were not implemented but the *Survey* noted the hectic sales and transfers of land prompted by the introduction of the bill.[136] In any case the ceiling— 15 to 35 actual acres—applied to family units and unmarried adults, not to households. Since households averaged three family units or unmarried adults, more than 80 per cent of the 25,000 households with land in excess of 15 acres possessed no resumable land.[137] Taking account of this and the exemptions for plantations and spice gardens, the Survey estimated resumable excess land at 115,000 acres (2.5 per cent of the operated area), of which 86 per cent was in Malabar.[138]

In their 1966 Joint Declaration the UF partners committed themselves to an amendment of the 1963 act in favour of tenants, small landlords with no alternative means of subsistence, and *kudikidappukars* (hutment dwellers).[139] To all intents and purposes the result was virtually a new piece of legislation: 50 new sections were added to the existing 132; 60 sections were amended; 10 new definitions were introduced; and 20 others amended.[140] The key features of the legislation were the abolition of landlordism by the compulsory vesting of proprietorial rights in the government and their subsequent assignment to the cultivating tenants; the transfer of the onus of proof in disputes about the existence of tenancy from the tenant to the landlord; the broadening of the definition of tenant to include those without documentation, mortgages, several kinds of sharecroppers, the victims of various legal subterfuges aimed at evading land reform, and 'those honestly believing' they were tenants by simply 'deeming' them tenants. Hutment dwellers were granted security of tenure; arrears of rent, if any, were reduced to one year; and future annual rent was fixed at as little as two days' wages. The rights to resume land were heavily circumscribed and lapsed six months after the effective date of the act. Smallholders were allowed to resume up to half the land cultivated by a tenant to bring them up to five acres, even though the tenant's holding might be less than the ceiling. No land could be resumed at all from the hutment dwellers nor from tenants of the scheduled castes or tribes. The terms of compensation to the landlord were fixed at levels which were admittedly expropriatory: in general sixteen times the 'fair rent', on paddy land 50 per cent of the contract rent or 75 per cent of the pre-1961 contract rent whichever was the less, and 75 per cent of the contract rent on other lands. The compensation was to be paid in instalments to the government, who would then pay the landlord. Default did not, however, prejudice the tenant's right to land. Instalments would then be collected as arrears of land revenue. The *kudikidappukars* were granted the right to purchase their plot at 25 per cent of the plot's market value, half of which would be paid by the government, the remainder in twelve annual instalments.

The ceilings set by the act were the lowest in the sub continent, ranging from five 'standard acres' (6 to 7.5 acres) for a single adult to a maximum of 20 ordinary acres for a family with three minor children. In relation to the pressure on land the ceiling was quite high. In 1962 nearly 31 per cent of rural households were landless compared with the national figure of 12 per cent. In 1972 more than four-fifths of landholders operated less than one hectare (2.471 acres) and approaching half less than 0.25 hectares. The range of exemptions from the ceiling provisions was significantly reduced from those of the parent act. *Kayal* lands were now subject to the ceiling; while in the plantation sector land cropped with pepper, arecanut, cashew and coconut—previously exempt—was brought within the ceiling provisions relating to size of holdings.

The CPM had always insisted that land reforms should be evolved by the peasants themselves and though the bill emanated from Mrs Gouri and her Revenue Department the Minister herself was, of course, President of the *Kerala Karshaka Sangham* (Peasant union), and thus close to peasant thinking. The bill was also circulated to elicit public opinion. The implementation of the act was in official hands: the Land Board and Land Tribunals. It appears that this was a concession which the CPM was required to make by Central directive.[141]

The politics of the enactment and implementation of the legislation raise a number of significant issues. Although the bill was central to the programme of the CPM and the ministry as a whole it was not introduced into the Assembly until August 1968 and did not complete its legislative stages until October 1969. Among the factors which delayed the drafting of the bill were the immediacy of the food crisis in 1967 (food was part of Mrs Gouri's portfolio), the Minister's heart attack, a desire to see the results produced by the land reforms survey, and above all the determination to make legislation on a highly complex and politically contentious issue absolutely water-tight. The slow passage of the bill through its Assembly stages was attributed by the UF to the Centre's ambivalence about the radical character of the measure itself and reluctance to see non-Congress parties gain political capital from it, nationally as well as locally. The Congress and Kerala Congress opposition blamed the delay on the divisions within the UF. Other factors may have included the foot-dragging of the Muslim League, whose leadership included signific-ant landlord interests, and the gauntlet of central ministries which the measure had to run.[142]

The replacement of the UF ministry by the CPI-led Mini Front placed the CPM in a quandary. The members of the new govern-ment had not been significantly involved in the drafting of the legislation, yet they were now in a position to claim the credit for its implementation and appropriate the reform as their own. Further, where there was room for discretionary executive action, as in the distribution of land to the landless, the Mini Front parties might be expected to seek to strengthen their own support base. On the other hand the ministry included Kerala Congress, representing plantation and *kayal* interests, and enjoyed the support of Congress which had been hostile to the bill. The CPM had grounds for concern whether such a combination could be trusted to carry out a radical land reform with real commitment. However, opposition to the govern-ment might jeopardize the working of the measure. Co-operation meant supporting the CPI and collaboration with Kerala Congress and indirectly Mrs Gandhi's Congress. For a variety of reasons, including—after the collapse of the UF—inner-party criticisms of Namboodiripad, the party's leading centrist, the CPM chose milit-ant opposition.

Resting their case on events before as well as after the effective date of the act, 1 January 1970, the Mini Front argued that the CPM had urged the peasants and labourers to take direct action with the main aim of bringing down the ministry and in defiance of a law of the CPM's own making. Subsequent events, however, did much to vindicate the CPM's claim that the act would not be speedily and effectively implemented without pressure from below. One third of all applica-tions made to purchase *kudikidappukars* in the first three months of 1970 came from Alleppey District, where the tradition of militant organization was deep-rooted and CPM organization strongest.[143]

The challenge from the courts proved serious. In a series of judgments in 1970 the Kerala High Court invalidated important sections of the act and construed others in ways that undermined their impact.[144] As yet the act was not protected by incorporation into the 9th Schedule of the constitution, which precludes judicial review of state land reforms. Its sole protection under the constitution was Article 31A, whereby agrarian reforms cannot be challenged on the grounds that they interfere with the 'Fundamental Right' to property guaranteed by the constitution. The High Court, however, argued that this Article was intended to protect 'orderly and peaceable progress in accordance with the law...in the interests of the general public', not to protect a law which treated agrarian rights 'as it pleases'.[145] The 1969 act did not, therefore, merit protection.

In response to the courts' mutilation of the act the government enacted the Kerala Cultivators and Tenants (Temporary Protection) Bill, 1970; and in 1971, in the face of mounting protests from its own ranks and continuing opposition agitation, passed a further act designed to speed up the implementation of the 1969 measure. Among the more important provisions of this Kerala Land Reforms (Amendment) Bill, 1971 certain categories of land transfer and partition made since 1969 were voided and the rate of compensation was halved and fixed according to a scale, thus avoiding the delays and difficulties of fixing a market value.

The improvement was marginal. By the end of 1972 the surplus (according to the returns filed) was only 40,000 acres, of which 9,000 had been declared as excess lands by the Land Board, 4,500 acres taken over, and a mere 1,200 acres actually distributed to the landless. Of the estimated 343,000 *kudikidappukars*, 66 per cent had still not received a certificate of purchase.[146]

The administrative record was unimpressive. Though the absence of adequate records and shortages of staff caused problems there was widespread dissatisfaction with progress. The Committee on Estimates confirmed that many *kudikidappukars* were being deprived of their legislated rights by landlord coercion, noted that the government took 'a very lenient view' of landlords 'who wilfully abstain from filing returns', and was 'perturbed' to learn that after two and a half years the government had managed to take over only 538 acres of excess land.[147] During the first three years of the operation of the 1969 act the Land Tribunals were often composed of Block Development Officers who were 'young men with little practical experience or legal training, basically unequipped to do land reform work and simultaneously burdened with other responsibilities.'[148] The actual field investigation was the work of a poorly paid survey clerk who was inevitably susceptible to intimidation, influence, and corruption. The tribunals themselves were criticized by the Land Board for malpractice as well as lethargy. It was a system weighted against the poor except in areas where peasant and labour organization was strong.[149]

Stimulated by the CPM's launching of the 'Excess Land Agitation' and threats of militant action from Youth Congress and the CPI Karshaka Sangham, the government passed a further amending act in 1972. This provided for decentralization of the functions of the Land Board through taluk-level boards and advisory village committees (both to include representatives of the political parties). A cabinet-level Land Reforms Review Board with Mrs Gouri among its members, and a Task Force on Land Reforms, composed of officials, were established.[150]

The pace of implementation remained painfully slow. The Review Board took a year to begin operations; taluk boards were not established for six months; and village committees did not exist for at least two years after the passage of the Act. It is true that the absence of land records handicapped the expeditious processing of claims and returns, but the CPM had a fair case in arguing that notwithstanding these difficulties a total distribution of surplus land of 2,295 acres by September 1974 was poor by any standards.[151] Despite the evidence of evasion, malpractice, and corruption, not one person is known to have been prosecuted for the violation of any section of the 1969 act in its first four years of operation.[152] By 1974 the CPM (which, paradoxically in view of its pessimistic assessment of the possibility of working within the existing constitution, had taken great pains with the detail of the Land Reforms Act) had abandoned all co-operation with the government—which had shown such lack of political will and administrative capacity in implementing the measure but denied the CPM any credit for what was in conception the most radical agrarian reform in India. Mrs Gouri, who had supervised the drafting and had hitherto been 'the most active (and probably the most effective) member' of the Review Board, regarded her labours as utterly wasted: reform by constitutional means was impossible.[153]

One Lakh Houses Scheme

The contrast between the enthusiastic promotion of schemes and serious defects in their subsequent implementation is also illustrated by the programme to provide homes and land for those outside the purview of land reform, the One Lakh Houses Scheme. Though the immediate responsibility of the Muslim League Minister for Local Administration, the programme involved several other departments and both the Chief Minister and M.N. Govindan Nair, *inter alia* Minister for Housing, played a significant role. In October 1971 the government of India formulated a Central Sector plan to provide two cent house sites (one cent = .01 acre) free of cost for landless workers in the rural areas who had not benefited from land reforms legislation.[154] State governments were to be the agents. In December 1971 the Kerala Maxi Front decided to adopt and elaborate the scheme into a project to build 100 low-cost houses with four cents of land attached in each of the 960 panchayats, relying to a large extent on voluntary labour and raising additional monies from donations to the Chief Minister's Housing Fund. Half the houses and smallholdings were to be allotted to the scheduled castes and tribes. The project report was submitted to the government of India by 10 March 1972 and approved on 19 April 1972. The target date for the acquisition of the sites, development of the land, and allotment of sites was 1 May 1972, and for completion of the whole project an astonishing 1 November 1972. By July 1974 the ministry admitted that it was impossible to give any realistic date for completion.[155] Only 106 of the 960 panchayats had completed half or more of their quota, while 35 had not constructed a single house. At the end of 1976 57,000 houses had been completed and 33,000 actually distributed.[157]

Reviewing progress in 1975-6 the CPA praised it as 'a unique scheme . . . an example to show how major problems can be solved by active participation of the people in development if properly mobilised' which had housed one-sixth of Kerala's homeless despite the unprecedented inflation of 1973-5.[158] However, the same report, read in detail, presents a different picture. No estimate had been prepared of the total cost of the project before it was launched: 'it was a material oriented and not a financially oriented scheme.'[159] By 1975-6 public contributions amounted to Rs 1.13 crores against an expected Rs 10 crores and the scheme was saved only by a loan of Rs 1.5 crores from the Life Insurance Corporation. The financial records were seriously inadequate and the material orientation did not extend to proper supervision of such key inputs as cement or timber. Poor materials were supplied at inflated cost. There was little of the voluntary labour for which the government hoped, even from the beneficiaries of the scheme. What there was was un- or under-supervised and in many cases the work had to be completed by contractors, themselves no better supervised. Some of the architects initially employed to design the houses were incompetent. Many of the designs were ill-adapted to the climate and almost all were 50 to 100 per cent more expensive to construct than was necessary.[160] The choice of duplex plans was unpopular in a community with no tradition of semi-detached housing. Worse, some of the first generation collapsed as a result of poor design and construction. Only then did the ministry establish an expert technical committee to review the situation, and only then did it take advantage of the experience of the one local architect (whose truly low-cost constructions were already on view in Trivandrum) and of the studies in intermediate technology undertaken in K.N. Raj's Centre for Development Studies.[161] Finally there were serious doubts as to whether the beneficiaries of the scheme were those intended. The CPA's sample audit of Trivandrum District showed otherwise.[162] The application forms made no provision for evidence that the candidate was from the scheduled castes or tribes, who were supposed to constitute half the allotment, while in one-quarter of the panchayats the procedure for drawing lots from eligible applicants was not observed. Clearly the One Lakh Housing Scheme left much to be desired, the inevitable consequence of using 960 agencies simultaneously in contrast to the original Central policy of pilot projects in one or two Districts, presumably based on criteria of need rather than the standard apportionment of resources under the state government's scheme.

Two other initiatives to help provide for the landless are noteworthy: the Kanan Devan Hills (Resumption of Lands) Bill, 1971 and the Kerala Private Forests (Vesting and Assignment) Bill, 1971, and their respective anticipatory Ordinances. Kanan Devan was the largest British-owned tea estate (see above, p. 53) employing 30,000 workers on a permanent basis, and indirectly supporting a further 30,000. The vast majority were Tamils from the drought areas of Tamil Nadu. Foreign-owned plantations were an obvious target for communist-led governments but nationalization was precluded by Central policy. However, only about one-quarter of the total estate was planted with tea bushes. In the government's view the remainder was surplus land and it was unwilling to allow this to be taken over through encroachment organized by (opposition) political parties.[163] The company which had made an early return of 6,000 acres excess land under the 1969 Land Reforms Act argued that the remainder of the estate was either uncultivable or necessarily under forest to maintain the micro-climate required by tea or to provide fuel for the tea factory.[164] There was clearly force in both arguments. In the event Kanan Devan finally surrendered 29,000 acres in 1974, much of it marginal land, and all of it climatically unattractive to Malayali settlement. Interestingly only one MLA, a socialist, made the obvious point that the estate workers had earned preferential treatment in the distribution of the surplus land and government and opposition alike avoided the central fact that in simple justice it was the *Tamil* labourer who was the 'son of the soil' in the High Ranges.[165] A.K. Antony, the Youth Congress convenor of the co-ordination committee, suggested as a 'big leap towards socialism' that half the land should go to the educated unemployed youth of the state.[166] The bill as a whole was carried on 1 April 1971 by 78 votes to nil with 29 abstentions. In the oppositions's view the Bill was hastily and inadequately drafted, virtually conceded legal ownership to the company, and so opened the way to prolonged litigation and eventual compensation. The solution was to remit the bill to a Select Committee, and that procedure would also enable the House to take account of the outcome of the British company's challenge to the prior Ordinance in the Supreme Court.[167] However, the Mini Front was determined to pass the bill before the Ordinance ran out, to forestall, it claimed, the planters' circumventing the legislation and to minimize encroachment. The reasoned arguments on both sides of the House were mixed with partisan interests. The propaganda value of action against Kanan Devan, at a time when the ministry was under attack for its record on land reform and uncertain of its survival, was out of all proportion to the token effects of the measure.

The Kerala Private Forests Bill was introduced on 2 August 1971. These forests, mainly in Malabar, were a mixture of natural woodland and scrub, and were a consequence of the British presumption in the Malabar land settlement (see above, p. 16) that residual virgin land was *jenmi* land. Some 1,200 square miles in extent in 1946, it had been substantially depleted through purchase and encroachment by 1971.[168] Originally there had been 115 owners—families or temples—with rights extending over as much as 100,000 acres in some instances. Since the ministry could claim with justification that the absentee landlords had invested little or nothing in afforestation no compensation was offered, or in the event given. Though the bill's drafting was loose and the initial steps to take over the land clumsy,[169] the ministry's initiative was a *coup*. Once again, however, the administrative performance lacked vigour.[170]

The effects of the Kerala agrarian reforms are, as yet (1979), not entirely clear. Though landlordism has been largely eliminated and feudal and rentier relations abolished, the long drawn out process of legislation, the fine print of the acts, and the imperfections of its implementation inevitably enabled landlord families to spread their surplus through the extended kin network. None the less the transfer of proprietorial right has significantly benefited all classes of tenant. The vast majority, whose holdings were at or close to the ceiling, already enjoyed effective security of tenure but they have gained substantially in financial ways. On the whole—save for the dispossessed *kayal rajas*—the capitalist farmers, as was intended, have emerged strengthened.

Kerala's reforms have produced 'land to the tiller' only in a qualified sense. The 'tiller' is not here the field labourer but the tenant who 'cultivates', whether this means physically working the land or directing and supervising hired labour.[171] As the 1966-7 *Land Reforms Survey* showed, in Kerala 'cultivators' are often not even primarily agriculturalists but undertake full- or part-time employment outside the agrarian sector.[172] The tiller in the sense of 'agricultural labourer' gained the right to his hutment site and a few cents of adjacent land, but he did not always obtain the reality, for it is clear that where agricultural labour was not well organized some of those who were entitled to such rights were deprived of them. Nevertheless, relatively speaking, the change for those 243,000 *kudikidappukars* who obtained their rights was millennial.

As yet there is limited evidence as to the effect of the Kerala reforms on rural inequality. M.A. Oommen, for one, has argued, on the basis of a comparison of National Sample Survey data for 1959-60 and 1970-1, that although there has been a significant reduction in agrarian inequalities the gap still yawns wide. The long-run trend towards the proletarianization of the marginal peasant has been checked by land reforms, rural welfare measures and the unique socio-economic characteristics of the state. The dwarf cultivators are for the moment successfully resisting the tide of capitalist replacement of smaller by larger holdings but 'it is difficult to postpone the evil of proletarianization for long.'[173] P.K.B. Nair also emphasizes that the growth in the numbers of small marginal farmers was as much a function of the methods adopted by landlords to escape from the ceiling as of the direct provisions of the act itself.[174] Oommen's cautious assessment is reinforced by N. Krishnaji, who underlines the importance of commercial cropping-especially coconut and pepper-on very small holdings in arresting the process of class polarization in the countryside, paticularly during a period of rising farm prices.[175] Herring is equally sceptical of 'land to the tiller' on the Kerala model as a solution to the state's political and economic predicament or as a way to unleash productive forces.[176] The present writer does not dissent from the general thrust of these evaluations and would also emphasize the deradicalizing effect, at least in the short run, of Gulf moneys.

Agricultural Labour's 'Magna Carta'

Land reform did not address itself directly to the agricultural labourer's work situation: under-employment, insecurity of employment, and low wages. This coupled with field labour's increased unionization and politicization in a fiercely competitive party system, led to the introduction on 17 November 1972 by the Congress Agriculture and Labour Minister, Vakkom Purushothaman, of the Agricultural Workers Bill 1972.[177] In the care with which the bill was drafted and examined in committee the measure bore comparison with the 1969 Land Reforms Act. Entering its Select Committee stage on 17 November 1972 the bill did not re-emerge until 5 February 1974. The bill's objects were to 'maintain' (restore?) peace in the fields and to provide what the minister fairly described as the labourer's Magna Carta. Inquiry after inquiry had confirmed the pitiable condition of the two million agricultural workers. The Minimum Wages Act of 1948, under which the wages of field labour were fixed, was a dead letter and offered no hope to the un- or under-employed whose numbers had grown steadily with time. Though the daily rates of field labourers had risen during the 1960s and were now second to those of the Punjab, this did not necessarily entail a higher annual income.[178] The net worth of the agricultural labourer household on average (30 June 1971) was Rs 753 (£40), third lowest in the country; and the proportion of agricultural labourers with assets below Rs 500 at 66 per cent was the highest in India.[179]

The bare bones of the new bill were as follows: the legislation would cover every agricultural labourer except those already covered by the Plantation Labour Act and those working for dwarf owner tillers farming one acre or less (later increased to one hectare); from time to time the government would declare 'prescribed wages' for different regions in the light of the owners' economic position, and that would add a premium of up to 15 per cent on the 'minimum wages'. Higher rates were not precluded if agreed between the parties. The bill provided for some measure of security of employment. Those who had worked a holding the previous season would be given first preference and their names would be registered by the local authorities. Labour troubles were to be dealt with by Tribunals whose findings would be mandatory, as opposed to the existing voluntary conciliation procedures of the Industrial Relations Committees. 'Agricultural disputes' were redefined so as to recognize the union as the representative of the workers. Finally, there was to be a welfare fund—similar to that available to industrial workers—funded by contributions of 5 per cent of the daily wage from both employer and employee. Apart from Kerala Congress, all parties supported the measure, though the CPM and others expressed reservations on the effects of the exemption of smallholdings from the provisions.[180] With the exception of the Provident Fund Scheme, all parts of the act came into effect on 2 November 1975 and within six months one in twelve of the estimated total workforce had been registered.[181] Some two thirds of these so listed were in the rice-growing Districts of Alleppey and Palghat. In P.K.B. Nair's view, however, the act has conspired with falling agricultural prices and the fragmentation of holdings to harm rather than help farm labour.[182] It rigidified the wages structure at a time when the demand for labour was falling and naturally encouraged even those who were bound to employ field labour to reduce permanent labour to casual status. These forces had also reduced the bargaining power of the agricultural unions, further diminished by the outlawing of strikes under the Emergency.

Agricultural Performance

How far the process of proletarianization of the rural poor is irreversible depends on the state's agricultural performance: the farm sector is crucial to the state's economic advance as well as critical to its nutritional levels. Agriculture accounts for 55 per cent of the State Domestic Product and employs a similar percentage of the working population.[183] The room for increased output by extending the area under cultivation has been and is limited (see above, p. 47). In most parts of the state such growth could only be into marginal lands or at the expense of forest by encroachment. Increased productivity was essential. Yet in the fifteen years from 1956-7 to 1971-2 the cultivated area grew by 31.6 per cent while productivity increased only 11.9 per cent, giving an increase in production of 47.2 per cent.[184] Further, the increase in production was greatest in the plantation sector (95 per cent) and least in food grains (36 per cent). Among commercial crops as a whole, the increase in the cropped area was far more striking than the improvement in productivity and in a number of cases, including coconut, pepper, and cashew, yield declined significantly. The record in the food grain sector was better (30 per cent increase in yield and 24 per cent increase in area).[185] The accompanying table shows the percentage change in area, production and yield of selected crops from 1956-7 to 1975-6.

Among the important factors in agricultural development in Kerala are the high pressure of population on land, the extreme variations in physiography, the pre-eminence of valuable garden and plantation crops, the chronic food deficit, the symbolic significance of land (especially paddy) as a mark of social status, and the co-existence of a highly commercialized sector side by side with an under-developed small peasant field crop sector.

Clearly, the powers of state-level governments to stimulate growth are limited but it is indisputable that the record of Kerala ministries prior to 1970 compared poorly with that of other states. In 1968-9 agriculture accounted for only 9 per cent of Kerala's develop-

Table 11.5 Changes (percentage) in Selected Crops 1956/7-1975/6
by (1) Area (2) Productivity (3) Yield in kg/hectare

Crop	by 1967-8			by 1970-1			by 1974-5			by 1975-6		
	(1)	(2)	(3)	(1)	(2)	(3)	(1)	(2)	(3)	(1)	(2)	(3)
Rice	6	27	19	15	46	28	16	50	30	17	54	32
Pulses	-11	-10	1	-17	-25	-9	-22	-32	1	-30	-28	17
Coconut	31	14	-13	48	23	-14	63	17	-28	63	17	-28
Rubber	98	177	40	118	264	67	146	n.a.	174	150	n.a.	179
Pepper	15	-23	-32	30	-8	-29	36	0	-27	35	1	-25
Tapioca	43	68	18	41	85	31	52	288	155	52	258	135
Arecanut*	60	73	8	81	83	1	n.a.	n.a.	n.a.	n.a.	n.a.	n.a.
Cashewnut*	63	82	12	76	97	12	181	101	-28	183	103	-28

*Yield measured in nuts per tree.

Sources: ER 1959; FFYP 1974-9; SFP, 5: Prices, Table X.

ment expenditure—the lowest in India—and irrigation for 3 per cent—also one of the lowest. Under the UF ministry some progress was made (despite the conflicts between the CPI Agriculture Minister and his CPM colleagues), as the marked change in the area under rice and the paddy yield per hectare between 1967-8 and 1970-1 show: new high-yielding seeds were distributed; wasteland reclaimed; single crop land converted into double crop land; and the Agro Industries Corporation established to popularize agricultural machinery among the peasantry. There was also a noteworthy boost in the consumption of fertilizer.[186] None the less the administrative weaknesses so evident in the industrial arena were again manifest. The CPA was 'amazed to learn' that the Agriculture Department had gone ahead with a scheme to cultivate a new variety of rice (Tainan 3) on 900,000 acres on the basis of its experimental cultivation in the 1966-7 season on one acre at Pattambi. The variety turned out to be exceedingly unpopular with the farmers, and, since it cooked unsatisfactorily, also with their wives. After three years the scheme was abandoned. Worse still, the Director of Agriculture, the senior official in the department, admitted that no study of the reasons for the programme's failure had been made. The CPA concluded that the fact that such grandiose schemes were ending in disaster should serve as an eye-opener to those in charge of formulating plans and schemes.[187] It did not. In 1970 the State Cashew Development Corporation, founded in July 1969, acquired the right to collect Rs 35,000 worth of nuts from 5,000 acres of state-owned plantations. The venture returned a loss of Rs 25,000, which it attributed to disease and pilferage without offering figures for either, and the PCU to the company's 'inexperience'.[188] A Soviet-assisted State Farm was no exception: it ran into 'rough weather' and the PCU urged a high-level inquiry.[189] In 1980 Mrs Gouri, CPM Minister of Agriculture, wound up the two collective farms then in existence because of their continued and increasing losses.

During the 1970s the Achutha Menon ministries did take agricultural development far more seriously than their predecessors, encouraging the adaption of the technology of the green revolution to local agronomic conditions, establishing the Agricultural University (1971), organizing demonstrations at the local level, and creating co-operative style schemes such as the Small Farmer Development Programme.[190]

By 1976 Kerala had a sound infrastructure to bring about a breakthrough in the agricultural sector and had gone some way to creating the means of communication to take the new technology to the farmer, 82 per cent of whom (1976) are small (up to 2.5 acres) cultivators.[191] The returns were, however, still limited. In some

instances including cashew and coconut—Kerala's second most important crop—yield declined in the period under review, while the
per capita production of rice declined between 1971 and 1976, despite
the 5 per cent increase in production.[192] The impact of high-yielding
varieties of paddy is in Kerala, as elsewhere in India, positively
correlated with the size of holding.[193] The consumption of the
fertilizer so essential to the cultivation of the new paddy strains,
which had peaked in 1973-4 (79,000 tons), was actually less in 1975-6
(63,000 tons) than it had been in 1968-9 (70,000 tons).[194] As Achutha
Menon wrote in November 1976, the fragmentation of holdings in
Kerala requires some form of co-operative process suited to the
Kerala people and their stage of consciousness; but as T.N.
Jayachandran, a former private secretary to Menon, and at the time
Registrar of Co-operative Societies wrily put it, 'In Kerala where the
people are in general sharply individualistic . . . the fact that at least
four [out of eight] Joint Farming Societies could work on profit
during the year [1974-5]could be considered an achievement.'[195] Nor
did the eight Collective Farming Societies 'present a happy
picture'.[196] It might be argued that Kerala would be better advised to
look towards European models such as Denmark, rather than the
Soviet Union or China, and to consider intermediate agricultural
technology—one notes the progress of tapioca—to achieve higher
levels of output in the under-developed small-scale sector. For the
moment, claims that the combination of the new farming technology and Kerala's falling birth rate give grounds for optimism seem
premature.[197]

Note on the Impact of the Emergency

Though the Twenty-and the Five-Point Programmes offered little
to a state already generally in advance of their standards, the
Emergency did facilitate a much-needed improvement in the implementation of some major areas of development activity. Coupled
with the availability of food at fairly stable prices,[198] this helped to
account for the popularity of the Emergency as evidenced in the 1977
Assembly election results. In the sphere of land reform fear increased
the amount of surplus land notified to the authorities, while the
toning-up of the administrative process speeded its redistribution.[199]
By the end of 1976, 45, 516 ceiling returns had been filed declaring a
surplus of 106,000 acres, of which the government had taken posses-
sion of 52,000 acres and actually distributed 26,000 acres (8,600 in
1975). A further 8,000 acres had been reserved for public purposes.
Similarly there was a marked increase in the total number of applica-
tions by tenants for the assignment of the title to their holding; 10.8

lakh applications by the end of 1974, 20.2 in 1975, and 31.5 in 1976. Whereas in 1974 only half the cases had been disposed of, the figure at the end of 1976 was 83 per cent. Applications from hutment dwellers also rose from 3.3 lakhs in 1974 to 4 lakhs in 1976. Dramatic improvements were also seen in the progress of the One Lakh Housing scheme, though the recent injection of Life Insurance Corporation funds also assisted. Between 1974 and 1976 the number of completed houses virtually doubled from 30,000 to 57,000.[200] How effective the general improvement in administration was is difficult to tell. Absenteeism fell, as did the incidence of late arrivals and early departures from government offices. During the first year of the Emergency the Home Minister claimed that economic offences involving Rs 67 crores had been detected and he reported that seventy-seven civil servants had been compulsorily retired and action taken against another ninety-seven, chiefly in the police, revenue, and forest departments, on a variety of charges of corruption, favouritism, and abuse of authority.[201] At least at senior levels those forced to retire were generally officers whose integrity had long been doubted by their colleagues.[202] Nevertheless the purge was very modest. No ministers were indicted.

A striking feature of the Emergency in northern India was the improved performance of the public sector. Though Kerala enjoyed its respite from industrial strikes, which had cost 321,000 man days in the first half of 1975, there was no dramatic change among public undertakings in Kerala. The financial returns of the majority of public sector concerns were little different in 1975 and 1976 from those of 1974: unimpressive and often very poor.[203] At least the Idikki project was at last commissioned. On the whole the problems of public enterprises in Kerala were too deep-rooted to be quickly cured by a stiff dose of 'discipline'.

Notes

1 The principal portfolios held by the communists in this period were: *CPM 1967*: Namboodiripad—Chief Minister, General Administration, Integration, Planning, Home, Administration of Civil & Criminal Justice; Mrs Gouri—Revenue, Law & Legislation, Food & Civil Supplies, Social Welfare; Imbichi Bava—Transport and Communications; M.K. Krishnan—Forests, Harijan Welfare, Housing. *CPI 1967*: Govindan Nair—Agriculture, Electricity; T.V. Thomas—Industries and Commerce. *CPI 1969*: Achutha Menon—Chief Minister, General Administration, Integration, Planning, Law & Legislation, Electricity; P. Ravindran—Industries and Commerce, Labour, Forests; K.T. Jacob—Revenue, Food & Civil Supplies. *CPI 1970*: Achutha

Menon—Chief Minister, General Administration, Integration, Planning, Law & Legislation, Finance; N.E. Balaram—Industries and Commerce; P.S. Sreenivasan—Transport and Communications, Electricity, Forests; P.K. Raghavan—Harijan Welfare, Housing. *CPI 1971*: Achutha Menon—Chief Minister, General Administration, Integration, Planning; Govindan Nair—Transport and Communications, Electricity, Housing; T.V. Thomas—Industries and Commerce.

2   Namboodiripad, *Conflicts and Crisis*, pp. 150-60.
3   *FFYP 1974-9*, pp. 282-3 and 308-11.
4   *SFP*, 4: *Industries and Infrastructure*, pp. 57-61, Tables 7.11 and 7.12. *ER 1976*, p.118, Appendix 6.5.
5   Communication, IAS officer, New Delhi, Nov. 1977. Interview IAS officer, Tvm, Sept. 1974. *ER 1976*, p. 56.
6   *FFYP 1974-9*, p. 42 (present author's italic).
7   Kerala's share of Central Assistance in the Third and Fourth Plan periods was 4.8 and 5.0 per cent respectively. Criteria of need are in dispute: on many indicators of social development Kerala has been a relatively advanced state; on economic indicators it has been relatively backward but by no means the poorest. In 1960-1 *per capita* income in Kerala was estimated at Rs 259, Rs 47 below the All-India average of Rs 306. By 1974-5 (1960-1 prices) Kerala's *per capita* income had risen to Rs 307 and India's to Rs 343, narrowing the gap to Rs 36. *ER 1976* p. 99, Appendix 2.15. Calculations on different assumptions give Kerala an above average *per capita* income: Kerala Planning Board, *The Sixth Finance Commission's Award: a Summary* (1974), p. 48, quoting Central Statistical Organization figures. See also p. 65, Appendix III.
8   Morris-Jones, *The Government and Politics of India*, p. 155; Namboodiripad, *Planning in Crisis*, ch. IX.
9   *The Sixth Finance Commission's Award*, pp. 52-6.
10 Govt of Kerala, *Report of the Taxation Enquiry Committee* (1969), p. 6.
11 Ibid., p. 539, Table XXI. *Report of the Comptroller and Auditor General of India 1970-1; 1971-2; 1972-3; 1973-4.* (Tvm, Govt of Kerala).
12 *FFYP 1974-9*, pp. 33-4.
13 Holdings below 2 acres lost their exemption from land tax in 1971-2. *Report of the Comptroller and Auditor General of India 1971-2*, p. 3.
14 Kerala, *Report of the Taxation Enquiry Committee*, p. 536, Table XVIII, p. 537, Table XIX, and p.538, Table XX. The *per capita* tax burden (state taxes) on urban dwellers, if the *per capita* tax burden on rural dwellers is taken as unity, had grown from 5.88 in 1957-8 to 7.94 by 1964-5, while the *per capita* income of urban dwellers, if the *per capita* income of rural dwellers is taken as unity, had fallen over the same period from 5.45 to 4.72. The *per capita* rural income is noted as an under-estimate. For census purposes only 15 per cent of Kerala is classified as urban. For the Cttee's commentary see pp. 81-3 and 102 of the *Report*.
15 *FFYP 1974-9*, p. 33, Table 3.4 and pp. 34-5; Kerala, *Report of the*

Enquiry Committee, p. 499, Appendix IX and p. 506, Appendix X.

16 *Report of the Taxation Enquiry Committee,* pp. 117 and 509-10.

17 Interviews, businessmen, Tvm, Quilon, and Cochin. On evasion see *Report of the Taxation Enquiry Committee,* pp. 140-1.

18 Ibid.,pp. 150-1.

19 *FFYP 1974-9,* p. 34; Kerala, Planning Board, *The Sixth Finance Commission's Award* (1974), p. 51.

20 *Economic and Political Weekly,* 13 Mar. 1976.

21 Maharashtra, Gujarat, Tamil Nadu, and West Bengal, for example, have taken some 60 per cent of assistance given by India's three leading development banks. *FFYP 1974-9,* p. 38.

22 Lieten, *Economic and Political Weekly,* 6 Jan. 1979, p. 32.

23 In 1969 Kerala accounted for 0.9 per cent of all industrial licences issued, in 1970 2.8 per cent, and in 1971 (provisional) 1.2 per cent. On entrepreneurship in Kerala see M.A. Oommen, *Small Industry in Indian Economic Growth: a Case Study of Kerala* (1972), ch. VIII.

24 *FFYP 1974-9,* p. 607.

25 Interview. Member of Board of Revenue, Tvm, Nov. 1977; interview, Mar Gregorios, Archbishop of Trivandrum, London, June 1980.

26 T.N. Jayachandran.

27 *Manorama Year Book 1973,* pp. 432-3; *ER 1972,* p. 40.

28 Kerala Legislative Assembly, Cttee on Public Accounts (CPA) (1976-7), 29th Report, p. 16. Among societies in which the government had share capital investment of Rs 10,000 or more, the percentage was 53 per cent. The position was , however, improving. The CPA was highly critical. The fact that the Report of the High Level Cttee presented in 1967 was still under consideration in 1976 led it to conclude that 'the Government are not making an earnest attempt to wipe out the difficulties of the co-operative societies.'

29 *ER 1975,* p. 94.

30 CPA (1975-6), 25th Report, p. 29. More than one-fifth were 'dormant'. Nearly 60 per cent of all industrial co-operatives were dormant or under liquidation in 1971-2. Ibid.,p. 30.

31 *Manorama Year Book 1973,* p. 601.

32 CPA (1967-7), 29th Report, pp. 3 and 12-14.

33 Ibid., p. 19.

34 Ibid.

35 An interesting confirmation of this is found in Namboodiripad, *Social Scientist* (Tvm) 64, Nov. 1977. Logically the fact that party managers take account of the communal composition of constituencies in selecting candidates does not mean that the electorate as a whole thinks communally. It is, however, at the very least a factor in securing the marginal vote (see below, p. 321).

36 The [Nair] National Democratic Party (NDP) was formed on 22 July 1973, largely to act as a pressure group to lobby for an economic as opposed to a social definition of 'backwardness' in the reservation of government posts. *Malayala Manorama* (Kottayam), 23 July 1973. The

NDP supported the Ruling Front in the 1977 elections in exchange for the nomination of six candidates on the Congress ticket, of whom five were elected. The Ezhava SNDP yogam subsequently sponsored a rival party, the Socialist Republican Party (SRP), formed on 8 June 1975 as an organ for all (socially) backward classes. The SRP soon split, the non-Ezhava members leaving it. In the 1977 elections the SRP proved of no significance.

37 V.I. Lenin, *What is to be done?* (Oxford, OUP, 1963, p. 178.

38 Interviews, union leaders, CPM, CPI, RSP, and Congress, Tvm, Alleppey, and Quilon, 1973, 1974, and 1977.

39 The account of the working of the co-ordination committee in the Achutha Menon ministries is based on interviews with the political correspondents of *The Hindu* and *Times of India*, two IAS officers, and with ministers, including an extended discussion with an RSP minister.

40 Interview, RSP minister, Tvm, Sept.,1973 and a sometime private secretary to the then Chief Minister, Achutha Menon, Tvm, Sept. 1973.

41 Interview, political correspondent, *Hindu*, Aug. 1973 and a sometime private secretary to the then CM, Achutha Menon, Tvm, Sept. 1973.

42 Personal observation.

43 Taub, *Bureaucrats under Stress*, in chs. VI and VII documents the underlying tensions between politicians and administrators in a case study of Orissa. See also Kerala, *Report of the Administrative Reforms Committee*, vol. III, evidence of A.K. Gopalan MP and N.C. Sekhar MP, pp. 62 and 64. Achutha Menon's suspicion of IAS officers was of long standing and said to be rooted in a strong personal distaste for privilege. Interviews, political correspondents, *Link* and *Hindu*, Tvm, Aug. 1973 and IAS officers, Tvm, Aug. 1973 and Nov. 1974.

44 Interviews, IAS officers present at the meeting.

45 Kerala, *Statement on the Report of Enquiry by Shri K.K. Ramankutty, Member, Board of Revenue on Acquisition of land for the Agricultural University 1971* (1971), p. 15.

46 Dr C.R. Krishnamoorthy (a Tamil Brahmin).

47 Interviews, IAS officers, Tvm, 1973 and 1974.

48 These criticisms emanated from officers whose careers indicated that they had the confidence of the Chief Ministers.

49 Interview, Minister, Tvm, Sept. 1973.

50 Member, Board of Revenue, Dec. 1974.

51 Kerala, *Report of the Enquiry into Certain Appointments: Travancore–Cochin Chemicals Ltd.* (1971), para. 52.

52 Interview, Member, Board of Revenue, Aug. 1973.

53 *SPKLA*, 30 Mar. 1973, p. 114. Also interview, Attingal Gopala Pillai, Tvm, Nov. 1977.

54 Communication, IAS officer, 1974. The Cttee on Public Accounts (1975-6), 27th Report, provides illustrations: 'The Committee are distressed to note that out of the 19.5km. of the estimated canal work [at Badagara-Mahé], only 4 km. of the canal could be completed and made navigable till 1974 (after 13 years). They understood that cost of

the scheme has risen to Rs 240 lakhs . . .as against the original estimate of Rs 78 lakhs (and) might go up to Rs 300 lakhs' (p. 23). See also ch. IV, 'Works Expenditure', in *Report of the Comptroller and Auditor General of India 1970-1* and *1971-2*.

55   The *Sixth Finance Commission's Award*, p. 52, reports 'over 60 per cent.' Public sector employment figures are given in *ER 1976*, p. 13, Table 2.8.

56   *SPKLA*, 12 Oct. 1973, p. 14.

57   Ibid., 29 Mar. 1973, p. 108 and 22 June 1973, p. 86.

58   *FFYP 1974-9*, p. 596.

59   Ibid., p. 599. Interviews, Centre staff and IAS officers, 1973, 1974, and 1977.

60   The Reports of the Comptroller and Auditor General of India on Kerala give details of plan schemes, provision for which remained wholly or substantially unutilized and what was given as the 'reason for saving' by the responsible body.

61   CPA (1975-6), 27th Report, pp. 60-1.

62   *FFYP 1974-9*, pp. 595-6 and 611-15. Interviews, State Planning Board, Nov. 1974.

63   *ER 1959*, pp. 91-2. These figures are unreliable (p. 20).

64   Lieten, *Economic and Political Weekly*, 6 Jan. 1979. While these figures indicate the upward trend, they should be treated sceptically. *ER 1959*, pp. 20, 94, and 99.

65   Calculated from data in *SFP, 4: Industries and Infrastructure*, p. 7, Table 2.4.

66   *SFP, 3: Labour and Labour Force*, p. 6, Table 2.6.

67   *ER 1974*, p. 178, Appendix 5.1 and ibid., *1976*, p. 114, Appendix 6.1.

68   *FFYP 1974-9*, p. 277.

69   Ibid. *SFP, 4: Industries and Infrastructure*, pp. 8-17, Tables 2.6-2.16.

70   According to the *Kerala Labour and Industries Review*, Jan. 1964, p. 56, 'The dearth of entrepreneurial talent is perhaps the greatest limiting factor in the industrialisation of Kerala.' M.A. Oommen, *Small Industry in Indian Economic Growth*, pp. 186-7. See also *FFYP 1974-9*, p. 278.

71   *SFP, 4: Industries and Infrastructure*, pp. 4-5, Tables 1.9 and 1.11; ibid., 3: *Labour and Labour Force*, pp. 8-10, Tables 2.9-2.11; pp. 15-17, Tables 5.1-5.4; and pp. 18-20, Tables 7.1-7.8.

72   Ibid., 8: *Plan Expenditure in Kerala*, pp. 1-3, 25, and 53, Statements I, II, III, VII, and X.

73   Ibid., p. 53, Statement X.

74   Lieten, *Economic and Political Weekly*, 6 Jan. 1979.

75   *SFP, 6: Social Services*, p. 47, Table 131; *ER 1976*, p. 130, Appendix 9.21.

76   *SFP, 6: Social Services*, p. 48, Table 134.

77   *FFYP 1974-9*, pp. 44-6, Table 5.3.

78   *SFP, 4: Industries and Infrastructure*, p.7, Table 2.4. *ER 1972* (Appendix 5.1), *1974* (App. 5.1), *1975* (Apps. 5.1 and 5.2), *1976* (App. 6.1). *FFYP 1974-9*, p. 352.

79 *FFYP 1974-9*, p. 281.
80 Kerala Legislative Assembly, Cttee on Public Undertakings (CPU) (1973-4), 13th Report, p. 4; ibid. (1975-6), 24th Report, p. 46; ibid. (1976-7), 27th Report, p. 30. *FFYP 1974-9*, p. 284.
81 For a discussion of the work of the Kerala State Industrial Development Corporation see CPU (1976-7), 27th Report.
82 M.A. Oommen, *Small Industry in Indian Economic Growth*, p. 1.
83 Ibid., p. 11.
84 M.A. Oommen's study was not published until 1972. His preface notes that his basic conclusions would have been unaffected by the use of 1967-71 data. I am grateful for the help he gave in an interview in Trivandrum, Aug. 1973, as also that of civil servants who had been involved in the administration of this sector.
85 Oommen, as n. 82 above, p. 193.
86 *ER 1972*, p. 59, Table 5.3; *1974*, p. 111, Table 5.8; *1975*, p. 157, Table 5.12.
87 p.65
88 Ibid.
89 *ER 1975*, pp. 20 and 155-6.
90 Ibid., *1976*, pp. 64-5.
91 CPU (1971-2), 9th Report, p. 15, quoted again in CPU (1975-6), 24th Report, p. 27. *Report of the Taxation Enquiry Committee*, p. 279.
92 CPU (1975-6), 24th Report, p. 14.
93 Comment arising from the committee's displeasure at the indecision of successive governments in responding to a proposal in 1965 to transfer the printing of bus tickets from private agencies to the government press. CPU (1973-4), 15th Report, p. 27.
94 See n. 1 above.
95 CPU (1971-2), 4th Report, p. 1.
96 Ibid., p. 2.
97 Ibid. (1972-3), 10th Report, is replete with examples: see especially chs. 7,9 and 10. See also ibid. (1971-2), 4th Report, and ibid. (1976-7), 34th Report.
98 Ibid (1972-3), 10th Report, p. 88.
99 Ibid.
100 *SFP 4: Industries and Infrastructure*, pp. 66-7, Tables 8.10 and 8.11. CPU (1972-3), 10th Report, pp. 91-3.
101 CPU (1972-3), 10th Report, chs. 2,7, and 11.
102 Ibid., chs. 12 and 13.
103 Ibid. p. 135.
104 Ibid., p. 122.
105 The following account is based on: CPU (1971-2), 8th Report, and (1975-6), 25th Report; on interviews conducted at Idikki with project executives; and on interviews with ministers, senior civil servants, and trade union leaders.
106 CPU (1975-6), 25th Report, p. 2.
107 Ibid., p. 70.
108 Ibid., p. 3.

109   Ibid., p. 4.

110   Ibid., p. 73.

111   Ibid.,p. 78.

112   The wording of the CPU reports frequently indicates that the members presumed that corruption rather than incompetence was at the root of many of the Board's failings.

113   Interview, T.K. Divakaran, Tvm, Aug. 1973.

114   *SPKLA*, 16 Nov. 1972, p. 153.

115   T.N. Jayachandran, 'Farming Co-operatives in Kerala,' *Dharani*, Special no. Nov. 1976, p. 63.

116   *Report of the Taxation Enquiry Committee,* pp. 277-8.

117   Ibid., p. 278.

118   *SFP, 4: Industries and Infrastructure*, p. 34, Table 5.1.

119   Ibid., p. 35, Table 5.2.

120   *ER 1976*, pp. 48-60.

121   *Report of the Taxation Enquiry Committee*, p. 279.

122   Ibid., p. 282.

123   *PKLA* XXV (6), p. 376.

124   *SPKLA*, 29 Apr., 4 Aug., and 24 Nov. 1971. For an interesting discussion of the weakness of panchayats as development agencies see *Hindu*, 25 June 1976.

125   For the background to the appointment of the commision on 17 Oct. 1967 see above, p. 44, n. 85.

126   *BCRC*, vol. I, p. 108.

127   The discussion of the report was characteristically in terms of 'community'. See, for instance, Achutha Menon, the CPI Chief Minister, replying to a Calling Attention motion in 1972: 'Almost every community was agitating for concessions. He [Menon] warned that if such communal feelings were unchecked it would destroy peace and harmony.' *SPKLA*, 17 Nov. 1972, p. 164.

128   *BCRC*, vol. I, p. 228.

129   Ibid., p. 129.

130   Kerala University Bill, 1972: clause 6, sub-clause 2. *SPKLA*, 17 Apr. 1974, pp. 401-2.

131   *IE*, 7 Dec. 1978.

132   Interviews, senior university officials, IAS officers, and applicants for college teaching positions (from a range of communities), Tvm, Nov. 1975 and Nov. 1977.

133   The Congress-PSP coalition ministry had prepared a draft bill based on the defunct act. The succeeding Congress ministry, however, announced a new and comprehensive measure. Its broad (pro-landlord) shape was allegedly settled between R. Sankar, the Ezhava Chief Minister, and P.T. Chacko the Christian Revenue Minister, and Mannath, the NSS leader. In Chander's view Mannath was the key figure by reason of the ministry's dependence for survival on Nair Congressmen ('The Legislative Process in Kerala 1957-1969', pp. 325-6). The act is summarized in M.A. Oommen, *Land Reforms and Socio-Economic Change in Kerala*, pp. 44-53. A. Gangadharan, *Law of Land*

Reforms in Kerala (1974, 2nd edn) gives the full text of the original act, its amendments (to 1974), and legal commentary. The nuances of the argument between landlord and tenant interests are clear from the Report Stage in which the CPI participated: *SPKLA*, 2nd LA, 2nd Session-1963 (2nd Meeting).

134 Herrin, p. 280.
135 Bureau of Economic and Statistics, *Land Reforms Survey in Kerala 1966-7*, p. 73.
136 Ibid., p. 79.
137 Ibid., p. 104.
138 Ibid., p. 105.
139 *People's Democracy*, 9 Oct. 1966, pp. 6-8.
140 Herring, ch. 8, provides a valuable review of the main provisions. Gangadharan gives the complete legal documentation. M.A. Oommen, *Land Reforms and Socio-Economic Change in Kerala* is a short and helpful interpretation. I am grateful to R.J. Herring and M.A. Oommen for discussing Kerala land reforms and to Smt. Gouri, the CPM minister who supervised the drafting of the 1969 Act, for answering specific questions in an interview, Tvm, Aug. 1973.
141 *SPKLA*, 13 Oct. 1969. Speech of Smt. Gouri.
142 Five Central ministries were involved: Law, Planning, Agriculture, Commerce, and Home.
143 Govt of Kerala, *Administration Report: Land Board and Land Tribunals 1969-70*, p. lv; T.K. Oommen, 'Agrarian Legislations and Movements as Sources of Change: the Case of Kerala,' *Economic and Political Weekly*, 4 Oct. 1975, p. 1579; and his 'Agrarian Tension in a Kerala District: an Analysis', *Indian J. of Industrial Relations* 7 (2), Oct. 1971.
144 Govt of Kerala, *Kerala Land Reforms Act 1963 (1 of 1964): Judgments (Full Bench) of The High Court of Kerala*: Herring, p. 335.
145 *Kerala Land Reforms Act 1963 . . . Judgments*, p. 96.
146 *ER 1972*, p. 11.
147 Kerala Legislative Assembly, Cttee on Estimates (1972-3), 7th Report, p. 13.
148 Herring, p. 359.
149 Ibid. The administrative rules were not translated from English into Malayalam until mid-1973.
150 The Task Force was led by A.K.K. Nambiar, the civil servant who had worked on the drafting of the 1969 bill. It also included M.A. Oommen, an economist.
151 *ER 1974*, p. 84.
152 Herring, p. 358.
153 Ibid., p. 365; interview, Smt. Gouri, Tvm, Dec. 1974.
154 Cttee on Public Accounts (CPA) (1975-6), 26th Report, p. 1.
155 Ibid., p. 9.
156 Ibid., p. 10.
157 *ER 1976*, p. 7.
158 CPA (1975-6), 26th Report, p. 156.
159 Ibid., p. 5.
160 Interview, Mr. L.W. Baker, Tvm, Dec. 1974, an English architect

domiciled in Kerala who had himself designed low-cost housing. His view was widely shared among civil servants and economists.

161   In June 1973 a High Level Technical Cttee was appointed to investigate. The government had not felt that there was any necessity to appoint a Technical Cttee in advance since the 'design was simple' and 'much technical knowledge was not required'. CPA (1975-6), 26th Report, p. 55.

162   Ibid., pp. 51-4.

163   In this instance, the SSP.

164   Interview, General Manager, Kanan Devan Company, Munnar, Aug. 1973.

165   *SPKLA*, 1 Apr. 1971, p. 103.

166   Ibid., 30 Mar. 1971, p. 90.

167   Ibid., 31 Mar. 1971, p. 94 and 1 Apr, 1971, p. 102. Also ibid., 3 Nov. 1972.

168   Estimates of the loss vary. According to the Forest Dept the depletion was not less than one-quarter. Interview, senior forest officer, Tvm, Aug. 1973. M.P. Gangadharan stated that more than one-tenth had been turned into agricultural land. *SPKLA*, 3 Aug. 1971, p. 122.

169   The preceding Ordinance froze the movement of timber at a peak period for the timber processing industries. There was also concern when the act came into effect at the 'plight of the workers thrown out of employment' in the Gwalior Rayons forest plantations. *SPKLA*, 27 Aug. 1971, p. 312.

170   'The extent of land available for assignment is estimated to be about 1.5 lakh acres. Steps are under way for the assignment of these lands to indigent families' (*ER 1976*, p. 39). Forest officials expressed concern at the scale of illicit felling of valuable (and slow-growing) hardwoods by the erstwhile owners and others.

171   ' "Cultivate" with its grammatical variations means cultivate either solely by one's own labour or with the help of the members of his family or hired labourers or both, or personally direct or supervise cultivation by such members or hired labourers or both provided that such members or hired labourers have not agreed to pay or to take any fixed proportion of the produce of the land they cultivate as compensation for being allowed to cultivate it or as remuneration for cultivating it . . .' A. Gangadharan, p. 9. Some landlords (probably a majority) were undoubtedly capitalist managers rather than feudal rentiers. See also N.Krishnaji, 'Agrarian Relations and the Left movement in Kerala: a Note on Recent Trends', *Economic and Political Weekly*, 3 Mar. 1979.

172   Of 'landlords' in the 1966 *Survey*, 58 per cent (chiefly the smaller ones) received the major portion of their income from non-agricultural sources. Small owner-cultivators and small tenants were equally dependent on non-agricultural income. *Land Reforms Survey in Kerala 1966-7*, Appendix, Table 3. As Herring notes (p. 304), 'Ironically, the large holders, whether tenant, landlord, or owner-cultivator, the target of the ceiling legislation, were the most likely to be agriculturalists.'

173 'Inequalities in Kerala agriculture and land reforms', *Dharani*, Special no. Nov. 1976, pp. 41-8. Oommen holds the view that the reduction in inequality would have been much greater in Kerala but for the exemptions in favour of land under plantation crops and the malafide transactions to circumvent the ceiling provisions (p. 43).

174 'Some problems of the farm front in Kerala', *Dharani*, Special no. Nov. 1976, pp. 49-51.

175 N. Krishnaji, *Economic and Political Weekly*, 3 Mar. 1979, pp. 517-18.

176 Herring, p. 367. See also the comparative assessment of the economic argument for land reform based on studies of Sri Lanka, Pakistan, and Kerala in his ch. 12. Among other points he notes the disruption of agricultural production arising from higher levels of political consciousness and union organization among farm labourers in Kerala and the consequential tendency of agricultural entrepreneurs to avoid labour-intensive cultivation (p.647). See Mencher, *Economic and Political Weekly*, Annual no. Feb. 1978; also K.C. Alexander, 'Emerging Farmer-Labour Relations in Kuttanad', *Economic and Political Weekly*, 25 Aug. 1973, p. 1560: 'The co-operative and diffused relationship between farmers and labourers, structured by the norms of inter-caste relationship, has changed in Kuttanad into a specific contractual relationship within the framework of class struggle and mutual antagonism.'

177 The act was published in the *Kerala Gazette Extraordinary* (Govt of Kerala), 6 Aug. 1974.

178 M.A. Oommen, *Dharani*, Special no. Nov. 1976, pp. 44-5 and p. 47, Appendix B.

179 Ibid.,p. 46, Table V and p. 48, Table VI.

180 For Kerala Congress see E. John Jacob, Deputy Leader of the Kerala Congress MLAs and Chairman of the farm wing of the Kerala Congress party, the Kerala Karshaka Federation, *SPKLA*, 17 Nov. 1972, p. 172. In June 1974 the Federation resolved to pursue an 'independent political line' to safeguard farming interests which all parties, including Kerala Congress, were alleged to have betrayed. The Federation also opposed the growing alignment of Kerala Congress with the CPM and helped to form the breakaway Kerala Congress (Original) in Oct. 1974. By early 1977, however, the new party was in alliance with the CPM and the old party in the Ruling Front. For CPM attitudes see speech by Namboodiripad, *SPKLA*, 7 Feb. 1974, p. 33.

181 *ER 1976*, p. 39, Table 4.26.

182 P.K.B. Nair, *Dharani*, special no. Nov. 1976, p. 51.

183 *FFYP 1974-9*, p. 47.

184 Ibid., pp. 48-9.

185 Ibid., p. 49.

186 From 45,419 tonnes in 1966-7 to 70,330 and 72,010 tonnes in 1968-9 and 1969-70 resp. *ER 1976,* p. 108, Appendix 4.4.

187 CPA (1970-1), 3rd Report, pp. 3-4.

188 CPU (1973-4), 13th Report, pp. 42-3. Ibid. (1975-6), the 23rd Report, pp. 21-38, covering 1971-2 shows continuing acute concern: 'All the

difficulties which are mentioned by the Managing Director of the [Plantation] Corporation are faced by the private companies also. But in spite of these they are all making good profit' (p. 26).

189   According to T.N. Jayachandran, 'Farming Co-operatives in Kerala', *Dharani*, Special no. Nov. 1976, 'Due to initial teething troubles, absence of proper development of the land and deficiencies in management these societies [collective farming societies] do not generally present a happy picture' (p. 63).

190   For the Small Farmer programme see *ER 1976*, p. 26, *FFYP 1974-9*, pp. 92–4. On the Agricultural University *ER 1976*, p. 32.

191   C. Achutha Menon 'After Land Reforms What?' *Dharani*, Special no. Nov. 1976, p. 4. Sixty per cent of operational holdings are less than one acre.

192   *FFYP 1974-9*, p. 50; *SFP*, 5: *Prices*, Table X (Index of Area, Production and Productivity); *ER 1976*, p.22, Tables 4.6 and 4.7.

193   Herring, p. 606. P.K.B. Nair, *Dharani*, Special no. Nov. 1976, p. 51, and ibid., p. 5, C. Achutha Menon, 'After Land Reforms What?', quoting a study by the Evaluation Division of the State Planning Board on the performance of High Yielding Varieties in the Viruppu season of 1973–4.

194   *ER 1976*, p. 108, Appendix 4.4.

195   C. Achutha Menon, *Dharani*, Special no. Nov. 1976, p. 6 and T.N. Jayachandran, ibid., p. 63.

196   Jayachandran, ibid.

197   *The Economist* (London), 11 Feb. 1979.

198   *ER 1975*, p. 12, Table 1.8; p. 86, Table 3.21; p. 88, Table 3.23; and p. 89, Table 3.24. Ibid., *1976* p. 103, Appendix 3.6; and p. 105, Appendix 3.9. The 'toning up' of the administration had little effect on internal procurement of food grains, which fell from 4.25 per cent of production in 1973–4 to 2.93 in 1974–5 and 2.89 per cent in 1975–6.

199   'Land Reform Statistics as on 1st October 1976', *Dharani*, Special no. Nov. 1976, p.15, Table 3. *ER 1976*, p. 110, Tables 4.9–4.11.

200   *ER 1976*, p. 88.

201   Hindu, 11 July 1976,

202   Interviews, civil servants, Tvm, Nov. 1977.

203   *ER 1975*, pp. 129–42; ibid., *1976*, pp. 115–16, Appendix 6.2.

12

The Basis of Party Support 1965–1980

CHAPTER 4 above discussed the emergence of the communist movement as an electoral force from 1948 to 1960. The present chapter
examines the scale and nature of communist support in elections
from 1965 to 1980; and in its concluding section analyses the reasons
for the Naxalites' limited appeal in the state. A mass movement
cannot be measured simply by the ballot box. As Prakash Karat
notes, election results are merely partial reflections of more deep-
rooted changes.[1] However, it is undeniable that the comunist parties
compete vigorously for electoral support. In Namboodiripad's
words, 'every vote recorded in favour of the Communist Party [is]
the vote of a soldier fighting for the proletarian revolution.'[2] Not
every elector in practice sees his vote in this way, but it is reasonable
to presume that in such a highly politicized and literate society as
Kerala the votes cast for the dominant communist party, the CPM,
indicate the *broad* character of the mass movement.

Methodological Issues

The real problems are methodological: the isolation of the communist vote in a multi-party coalition system; and the treatment of
census data. In no election since the communist split of 1964 has
either party contested all constituencies. In 1965 the CPM put up 73
candidates (and supported 16 independents) for 133 seats; in 1967, 59
candidates; in 1970, 72; and in 1977, 68 for 140 seats. The CPI has,
except in 1965, fought fewer seats. As the allocation of constituencies among front partners varied with political exigencies the
CPM did not necessarily even contest those seats where it was the
strongest force in the coalition. Thus the CPM's 1967, 1970, and
1977 total polls of 23.5 per cent, 23 per cent, and 22 per cent
underestimated its potential. Conversely, the CPI's 9 to 10 per cent
of the vote in the 1967, 1970, and 1977 elections exaggerated its
support. Standing alone in 1965, it managed just 2.5 per cent of the
poll, and there is no reason to suppose that its position has improved
dramatically since that time.[3]

Any attempt to aggregate the two parties' votes would be misleading, though it is highly probable that the total communist vote has
fallen since 1960. It is also clear that the support of both communist
parties is geographically circumscribed. However, the CPM remains one of the two largest parties in the state, and so a pole of
alliance formation. Even its setback in 1977 does not invalidate this
proposition. In 68 contests the party won 46 per cent of the vote;
Congress, with more help from its allies, managed 52 per cent of the
poll from 54 contests. The fact that the CPM had been out of office
since 1969 merely underlines the strength of its mass base. However,
the fall in support in two hitherto key CPM areas, Alleppey and
Palghat Districts in 1970 and 1977 (see below, p. 326) is suggestive of
some erosion of its following consequent on the changes in agrarian
relations during the 1970s. (For the CPM's performance in the 1980
Assembly election see below, p. 330)

A further difficulty in the analysis of communist support is the
existence of three separate delimitations, covering 1957-60, 1965-70,
and 1977-80 respectively. Apart from the increase in the number of
constituencies and the abolition of the two-member constituencies
of 1957-60, substantial boundary changes render comparisons of
constituency voting impracticable for the period as a whole.[4]

A common device for circumventing the problem has been to use
the District rather than the constituency as the unit of analysis, on the
grounds that Districts normally contain exact numbers of
constituencies,[5] change slowly in character, and are ·important
benchmarks in censuses. On an All-India scale or in large states such
as Uttar Pradesh this is an admissible procedure, when suitably
qualified, but in Kerala it had decided disadavantages. The state has
only eleven Districts containing 11 to 20 constituencies each, within
which there is a good deal of social and economic variation. Yet
seven out of the nine 1961 Districts analysed by Dasgupta and
Morris-Jones fell into the highest of their four development
categories.[6] Further, as the following pages show, social, economic,
and political patterns do not conveniently accord with District
boundaries.

Two possibilities remain: to examine the pattern of seats held over
the three elections, 1965, 1967 and 1970, taking seats held by one
party in all three cases as 'safe seats' and two of the three elections as
'party-leaning', on the principle that this indicates which party if
any, is the leading political force; second, to treat the performance of
Congress and Kerala Congress standing alone and independent of
each other in 1967, and of the CPM in 1970, when it had no major
allies, as approximating to underlying bases of support. The following sections present and analyse this material.

The second methodological problem, of isolating socio-economic information, is easier to solve. Prior to 1971 the smallest unit for which data were published was the taluk, which would normally cover two to three Assembly constituencies. In their study of political preferences in Kerala, Krishna Murthy and Lakshmana Rao employed these taluk-level data to stratify constituencies according to town-size and agricultural labourer-cultivator ratio,[7] but in the absence of any clear exposition of the authors' procedure for allocating the 55 taluks to the 126 and 133 constituencies of their period, 1957-67, it would be wise to treat the method with caution.[8] In any case the occupational definitions used in the 1961 census are of doubtful validity.[9]

However, the publication of District census volumes for the 1971 census covering the lowest units of administration—panchayat and municipality—indirectly provides constituency-level data.[10] In Kerala the boundaries of Assembly constituencies—with trivial exceptions—follow panchayat and ward boundaries. Thus it has been possible to aggregate the census data to the constituency level, except in the case of Calicut I and II which are combined in the maps that follow and excluded in the statistical analysis. Independently, Lakshmana Rao and Leonard Cane have adopted a similar procedure in examining the support base on the Muslim League and Kerala Congress in 1965-70.[11] In succeeding sections these data are shown in map form for the more important census variables and subjected to multiple regression analysis in which the 1967 Congress vote and the 1970 CPM vote are taken as dependent variables.

Census data are not collected for the benefit of the student of politics. Some categories, for example 'cultivator' and 'agricultural labourer', are inevitably crude indicators of the reality of agrarian relations. Others, such as caste, are not collected on policy grounds. The bulk of agricultural labourers are still drawn from the 40 per cent of the population who belong to the backward castes and communities but the existence of a correlation with communist support would not show whether the vote was caste-based, class-based, or indeed both. Religious community is declared only at the taluk level. Lakshmana Rao and Cane include percentages of Christians, Hindus, and Muslims by constituency in their calculations but it is unclear whether this on the basis of taluk figures or by access to unpublished census information.[12] Here taluk data have been used to create 'dummy' categoric variables representing religious community by constituency for the purposes of the multiple regression analysis. The broad voting habits of the minority communities are not in dispute.[13] As Maps 21, 24, and 26 show, there is a pronounced spatial separation of ML and KC support in all elections from 1965 to

1980—reflecting the concentrations of Muslim and Christian settlement in Kerala. It would, of course, be of great interest to investigate the extent to which socio-economic differentiation within Muslim and Christian areas affects voting patterns, but the small number of cases (Assembly constituencies) precludes that.

The separation of Hindu majority consituencies in the data is, however, important in enabling us to investigate the contentious question of what influence caste exercises in the post-1967 period. Fic claims that the communists in Kerala soon cast aside a belief in 'economic forces as the inexorable propellants to Communism and began to direct [their] attention to the harnessing of the communal forces [i.e. caste and community] to the promotion of [their] aims.'[14] The 1967 victory in his view was 'due solely' to the CPM's skill in communal and party coalition-building and not to any significant mass shift towards the communists.[15] The major parties have maintained highly secret, detailed estimates of the caste composition of constituencies, and as Namboodiripad wrote in 1977 'it would, in fact, be totally unrealistic to close one's eyes to the fact that even those political parties which claim to be the most secular, above all considerations of castes and communities, have to consider, as one of the most important though not the sole factor the caste or communal composition of particular constituencies when they select their candidates for elections.' However, he adds, the caste factor 'is being steadily overshadowed by classes and parties which cut across the barriers of castes and communities.'[16] Logically, of course, the fact that party managers choose candidates with constituency communal balance in mind does not mean that the electorate is primarily moved by such factors, any more than does the fact that two-thirds of constituencies were represented by MLAs of the same community in 1965, 1967 and 1970 and only one-quarter by the same party.

One possible line of advance is a survey of individual elector's attitudes and background. The best-known study of Kerala by D.S. Zagoria does not include caste and community.[17] The present author, together with Dr. B. Dharmangadan therefore undertook a survey primarily to assess the precise significance of caste. A pilot adult survey in 1971 raised severe technical difficulties (see below, p. 364) and in 1974 the project was recast for a sample of nearly one thousand teenagers. The results are discussed in the section beginning at p. 349 below.

Electoral Geography

Map 21 shows the consistency of party support in the second half of the 1960s, distinguishing 'safe' (held three times) and 'party-

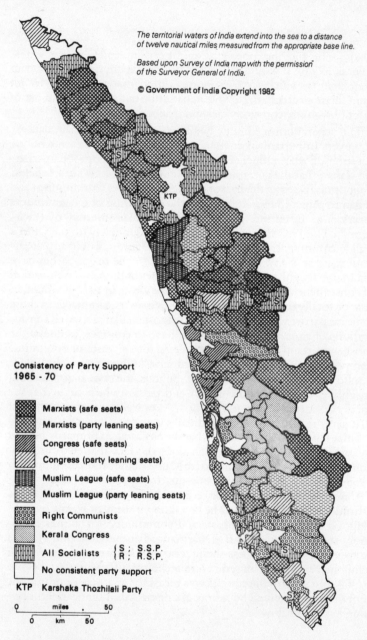

The territorial waters of India extend into the sea to a distance of twelve nautical miles measured from the appropriate base line.

Based upon Survey of India map with the permission of the Surveyor General of India.

© Government of India Copyright 1982

Consistency of Party Support 1965 - 70

- Marxists (safe seats)
- Marxists (party leaning seats)
- Congress (safe seats)
- Congress (party leaning seats)
- Muslim League (safe seats)
- Muslim League (party leaning seats)
- Right Communists
- Kerala Congress
- All Socialists $\begin{cases} S\ ;\ S.S.P. \\ R\ ;\ R.S.P. \end{cases}$
- No consistent party support

KTP   Karshaka Thozhilali Party

0   miles   50
0   km   50

Sources: Fic, *Kerala,* Tables XVII–XXV; verified list of results of Kerala Legislative Assembly election 1967 supplied by Dept of Politics, U. of Kerala; Election Commission, India, *Report on the General Election to the Kerala Legislative Assembly 1970.*

Map 21   Kerala 1965–70: Assembly Elections, Consistency of Party Support by Constituency

leaning' (held twice) seats. The reader may find it helpful to approach the pattern historically. The Muslim and Christian heartlands (see above, Maps 4 and 5) stand out as safe League and Kerala Congress territory. On the coast of Travancore and Cochin, where Ezhavas, fishermen, and low-caste Christian converts are numerous, the communists and RSP dominated as they did in 1952 and 1954 (see above, maps 9, 10 and 12) except in the urban area of Greater Ernakulam where three seats were safe Congress and one Congress-inclined. Further south the communists (more CPM than CPI) maintained their hold in Alleppey, the RSP in Quilon and its immediate hinterland, and the PSP in a few pockets in and around Trivandrum. In the interior of Travancore the plantation workers and scheduled castes of the foothills and High Ranges returned communists, CPI to the south (cashew factories) and CPM (plantations) to the north. CPM strength was greatest in Malabar where outside Moplah Malappuram, the CPM's hold on Cannanore and Palghat[18] was interrupted only by a crescent-shaped band of SSP seats, the odd personal seat (KTP), and Kasergod in the extreme north, historically part of the South Kanara District.

The complex spatial character of party support deserves comment, given the basic political cleavage between Congress and the CPM. First, though Kerala is small in area its communications are still poor. Ministers and officials cannot expect to reach Calicut from Trivandrum in less than a day and Tellicherry is effectively two days' journey. The fact that the seat of government is in the extreme south inevitably contributes to the preservation of local identities. Second, the basic traditional cleavages of religion and caste are still partially maintained through the twin nexuses of marriage and employment. Third, what share of scarce resources a constituency receives is strongly influenced by the individual or party connections with ministers in the Secretariat, where, despite the efforts of planners and administrators, the constituency's best friend is still its MLA and vice versa. Finally, both the strikingly localized character of voting patterns and the predominance of 'party leaning' as opposed to 'safe' seats probably reflect the continuing importance of communal differences in the constituency.

Map 22 shows the distribution of CPM support in 1970: its areas of strength were—with the exception of CPI-RSP dominated Quilon District—essentially those of the undivided party of 1960: central Cannanore, from which communism had spread in the 1930s, Palghat and the adjoining areas of Trichur and interior Malappuram, and the coastal and backwater parts of Alleppey and contiguous Kottayam, centred on Punnapra-Vayalar territory.

The CPM's showing was generally interpreted as a setback for the

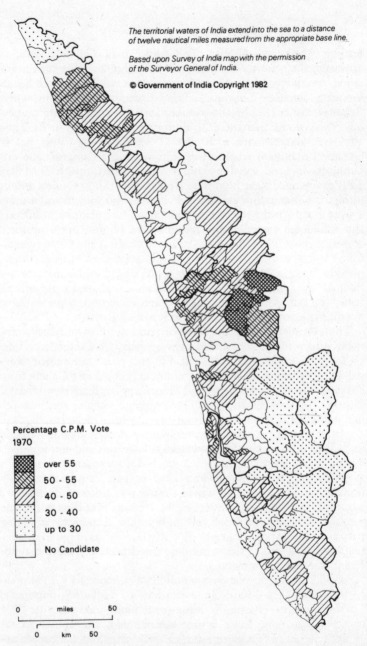

The territorial waters of India extend into the sea to a distance
of twelve nautical miles measured from the appropriate base line.

Based upon Survey of India map with the permission
of the Surveyor General of India.

© Government of India Copyright 1982

Percentage C.P.M. Vote
1970

- over 55
- 50 - 55
- 40 - 50
- 30 - 40
- up to 30
- No Candidate

0   miles   50

0   km   50

Source: Data from Election Commission, India, *Report on the General Election to the
Kerala Legislative Assembly 1970.*

Map 22 Kerala 1970: Percentage CPM Vote

party: though contesting 13 more constituencies than in 1967 it barely maintained its share of the poll and its representation was reduced from 52 to 28 seats. In 21 of these its proportion of the vote fell, in 8 cases by as much as 10 to 20 per cent. However, a major factor in this decline was the loss of Muslim League support in Malabar. Some Moplahs outside Malappuram did vote for the CPM but they were in a minority. In the longer term the CPI had some cause for alarm at the impact of Islam on its position in the north: economically, the Muslim community was 'coming up', a process accelerated in the mid-and late 1970s by the remittances of migrant Moplahs working in the Gulf states;[19] Muslim ministers in the cabinet were at pains to ensure that their community received its due share of resources; it could also be argued that the emergence in Malabar of Jana Sangh as an organized, albeit small, party together with the militant activities of the RSS was calculated to foster a *laager* mentality among Muslims; and finally the 1971 census confirmed that the Muslim population was increasing at a faster rate than the majority Hindu community. In the circumstances the CPM had held the line well. (Jana Sangh has grown in importance since this was written.)

It is in Travancore that the erosion of CPM support appears most obvious if comparison is made with the position of the undivided CPI in 1960 (see above, p. 127). In the south the CPM's chief rival was Youth Congress (YC). Some have argued that YC was to the late 1960s what the Communist Youth League had been to the late 1930s: a non-communal, youthful, radical movement reacting against the communalism, compromises, and corruption of the dominant party of the day.[20] In a sense Youth Congress in Kerala is also a synthesis of the Liberation Struggle and the communism it confronted. Several ranking leaders, most notably A.K. Antony, Chief Minister 1977-8, of the YC are Christians who participated in the events of 1959 but subsequently rejected the communalism and vested interests which partially informed the anti-communist movement in favour of the practical Congress Socialism which had permeated the CPI's 1957 manifesto. (Father Vadakkan's career illustrates a similar synthesis.) Youth Congress is not predominantly Christian but its attraction is understandable. For Latin Catholics it represented a political outlet acceptable to a backward class whose growing self-consciousness owed much to the educational facilities of the Roman Church. The formation of Kerala Congress appeared to have purged Congress of its more reactionary elements at a time when Congress nationally was seeking to renew its grass roots. One other force is of importance in assessing the development of Youth Congress—the growing numbers and articulateness of the college student. Above all else Youth

Congress and its junior wing, the Kerala Students Union, were committed to educational reform and the destruction of the power of the private college managements. It was probably this which accounted for the peculiar strength and independence of the YC movement in Kerala.[21]

The Elections of 1977 and 1980

Kerala's Assembly election in March 1977 was remarkable for the setback suffered by the CPM (see above, p.235): the party was reduced from 28 to 17 seats. In Palghat, in the past a marxist citadel, the CPM lost its existing Lok Sabha seat and surrendered seven Assembly seats. In another traditional stronghold, Alleppey District, it failed to win a single seat. Mrs Gouri, the party's deputy leader in the Assembly, led the list of notable casualties. The party's percentage poll, however, fell by only one per cent to 22 per cent.

Various explanations have been offered for the party's unimpressive showing in what had traditionally been a non-Congress state: the detention of the cadre; lack of funds; constituency gerrymandering; the impact of door-to-door canvassing by Youth Congress workers in the late stages of the campaign; and the opportunistic character of the CPM's electoral alliances as perceived by its traditional voters. Each is open to refutation.[22] The most convincing explanation turns on four factors: the uneven weight of the alliance structures; the impact on the CPM's rural support of the ministry's efforts to assist the landless labourer—the enfranchisement of the hutment dweller, the distribution of surplus land, the one lakh housing scheme, and the Agricultural Workers Act; the control of prices and the availability of food; the high female turnout, which is noteworthy; and, according to CPM leaders themselves, the negativism of their political tactics before and during the Emergency.[23]

It is very possible that the CPM had between 1967 and 1977 surrendered its hegemony in Kerala's political system. None the less it would have been wrong to conclude that it was therefore a spent force. It remained the largest party, polling nearly 2 million of the 8.8 million votes cast. In the 68 seats it contested it won a respectable 46 per cent of the poll, a figure set in context by the fact that Congress—which received many more cross votes from its allies than did the CPM—won 52 per cent of the poll in the 54 constituencies it contested. In the Lok Sabha election, where the electorate tended to vote on the larger national question of 'democracy versus dictatorship', the result was close in 7 of the 20 constituencies: less than 4 percentage points' difference in 4 constituencies. It is true that in the Assembly election a 2 per cent swing of votes would have

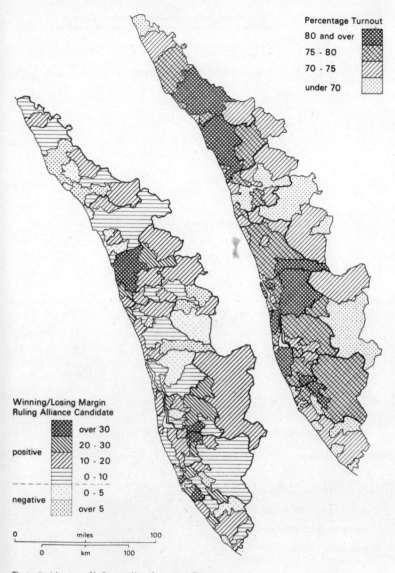

Percentage Turnout

80 and over
75 - 80
70 - 75
under 70

Winning/Losing Margin
Ruling Alliance Candidate

	over 30
positive	20 - 30
	10 - 20
	0 - 10
negative	0 - 5
	over 5

0   miles   100

0   km   100

The territorial waters of India extend into the sea to a distance
of twelve nautical miles measured from the appropriate base line.

Based upon Survey of India map with the permission   © Government of India Copyright 1982
of the Surveyor General of India.

Source: Data from *Hindu*, 21 and 23 Mar. 1977.

Map 23 Kerala 1977: Assembly Election, Turnout and Ruling Alliance
           Performance (Percentages)

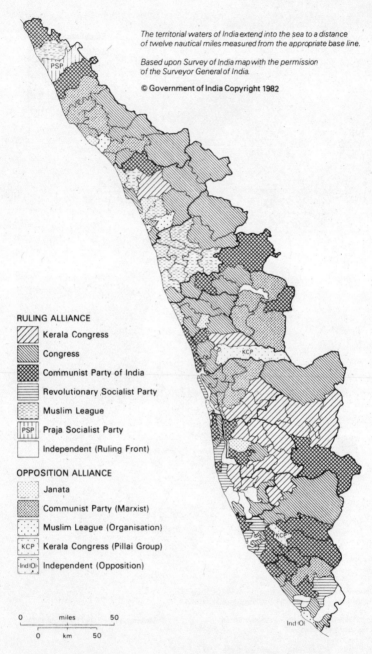

The territorial waters of India extend into the sea to a distance
of twelve nautical miles measured from the appropriate base line.

Based upon Survey of India map with the permission
of the Surveyor General of India.

© Government of India Copyright 1982

RULING ALLIANCE

- Kerala Congress
- Congress
- Communist Party of India
- Revolutionary Socialist Party
- Muslim League
- PSP Praja Socialist Party
- Independent (Ruling Front)

OPPOSITION ALLIANCE

- Janata
- Communist Party (Marxist)
- Muslim League (Organisation)
- KCP Kerala Congress (Pillai Group)
- Ind (O) Independent (Opposition)

0   miles   50

0   km   50

Source: As Map 23 above.

Map 24 Kerala 1977: Assembly Election, Winning Parties

given the CPM-led opposition only another 18 seats. However, outside Malappuram and central Travancore, as the margin of victory or defeat for Ruling Alliance candidates shows, there were few seats where a switch of allegiance by a caste, community, or group numbering no more than 10 per cent of the electorate would not have gained the opposition the seat.

The Elections of 1980

The degree to which victory at the polls had come to depend on the composition of electoral coalitions is further exemplified in the 1980 elections—as in 1977, Kerala voted within the space of a few days for its Lok Sabha and Assembly representatives.

Despite the Ruling Alliance's overwhelming victory in the March 1977 Assembly election Kerala came under Presidential Rule on 5 December 1979 as a result of the fragmentation and realignment of parties both nationally and locally. Thus when the Assembly poll took place on 21 January 1980 the rival fronts—the Left Democratic Front led by the CPM, and the United Democratic Front led by Congress-Indira or Convention Congress—were markedly different from those of 1977. However, between them the LDF and UDF accounted for 94 per cent of the votes cast. In the LDF were the three marxist parties (CPM, CPI, and RSP) as well as one wing of the erstwhile New or Ruling Congress (Congress-Urs), two wings of Kerala Congress (KC-Mani and KC-Pillai), and the 'rebel' All-India Muslim League. In the UDF were Congress-Indira, the 'official' Indian Union Muslim League, one wing of Kerala Congress, (KC-Joseph), the Praja Socialist Party, Janata, and two maverick communal parties, the (Nair) National Democratic Party and the (Ezhava) Socialist Revolutionary Party.

In terms of the number and distribution of potential votes, the LDF was the more powerful combination. For the first time since 1967 the marxist parties' support was combined, a factor that in several areas of Travancore and Cochin—particularly in Quilon District—made a victory for the left very likely or certain. The adherence of the Congress (Urs) wing of Congress, led by A.K. Antony, former Youth Congress Chief Minister (and named after Devaraj Urs, then Chief Minister of neighbouring Karnataka) was important not only because it divided the Congress vote but also because of the access it gave the LDF to the votes of the young and the less privileged particularly in Alleppey District, radicalized in the generation after the communist expansion of the1950s. Scarcely less important was the contribution of KC(M), articulating the interests of Christian and Nair farmers in northern Travancore and in Cochin.

The opposing UDF had the worst of the bargaining. Congress (I), though still a significant force throughout most of the state, was the end-product of three splits in the Congress movement. Apart from the IUML, dominant in the Moplah Malappuram District, all its allies enjoyed modest and localized support.

To emphasize the importance of coalition-building is not to deny that realignments took account of the inclinations of party members and the perceived opinions of target voters. There had been some shift, for example, from the Congress (I) pole of Kerala's political system to the CPM pole, notably in late 1978 and 1979. The results of Assembly by-elections and of local elections could be cited in evidence.[24]

Nevertheless, if there are suggestions of a left-right split in the pattern of alliances—to that extent vindicating Namboodiripad's consistent advocacy of isolating Congress, or its nationally dominant wing, even at the expense of short-run doctrinal purity—the case ought not to be overstated. In no two elections since Kerala was created have electoral alignments been the same. Only one trend seems beyond dispute: the progressive fragmentation of individual parties. The CPM's resistance to this trend is important to an appreciation of its continued role in state politics despite the party's apparent contraction as an electoral force.

Whereas in 1977 it was possible to isolate the CPM vote quite satisfactorily, in 1980 CPM performance is a matter of inference. Overall the LDF won 93 of the 140 seats in the Assembly and the UDF 46, one (rebel CPM) Independent completing the House. The CPM did not seek hegemony in terms of seats contested. The party's fight in 50 constituencies included some it could not hope to win, short of a landslide. In other cases the CPM as part of the price of maintaining the alliance agreed to stand down in favour of candidates put up by a partner even though it had claims to be the strongest force in that constituency. Its 35 victories therefore do not accurately reflect its relative standing any more than do the 17 victories of the CPI, a beneficiary of the CPM's electoral calculus. However, what may be revealing is the distribution of CPM seats as shown in Table 12.1 and in Map 26. Seven of the 35 victories were in Cannanore but only four in Palghat. Map 25 indicates that turnout was low (under 70 per cent) by Kerala standards in most of Palghat District and that the CPM margin of victory was small in what were effectively straight fights between rival fronts.

Taken together with the 1977 results in Palghat, the failure to win the Palghat Lok Sabha seat—keenly felt in the party—in 1980 and the generally diminished margins of CPM victory throughout the state, even with the backing of other LDF constituents, it seems probable

Table 12.1 Kerala 1980: Election Results by District

	No. of seats	LDF	UDF	Left Democratic Front							United Democratic Front							Mean % vote LDF
				CPM	CPI	Cong.U	AIML	KCM	KCP	RSP	Cong.	IUML	KCJ	Janata	PSP	NDP	Ind.	
Cannanore	16	13	3	7	2	3	1				1	1		1				54.66
Kozhikode	14	9	5	2	1	3	3				2	1		2				52.19
Malappuram	12	2	10	1		1					1	9						36.98
Palghat	11	5	6	4		1					3	1		1	1			49.47
Trichur	14	9	5	1	3	3		2			4	1						50.39
Ernakulam	14	11	3	6		4	1				1		2					51.11
Idikki	5	3	2	1	1			1			1		1					50.78
Kottayam	10	9	1	2	1	1		5					1					51.45
Alleppey	14	9	5	4	2	2				1	1		2	1		1		51.12
Quilon	16	15	0	4	5	1			1	4							1*	52.69†
Trivandrum	14	8	6	3	2	2				1	3	1				2		50.10
Seats won	140	93	46	35	17	21	5	8	1	6	17	14	6	5	1	3	1*	
Seats contested	140	140	140	50	22	30	11	17	2	8	53	21	17	29	6	9	n.a	

* K.K. Nair stood as an Independent in Pathanamthitta constituency and was opposed by both fronts. He was a 'rebel' CPM member.

† If K.K. Nair were included, the LDF percentage would be 54.88.

Note: Supported by the UDF, the SRP put up 7 candidates but won no seats.

Sources: Hindu and IE (Cochin), 23 Jan. 1980.

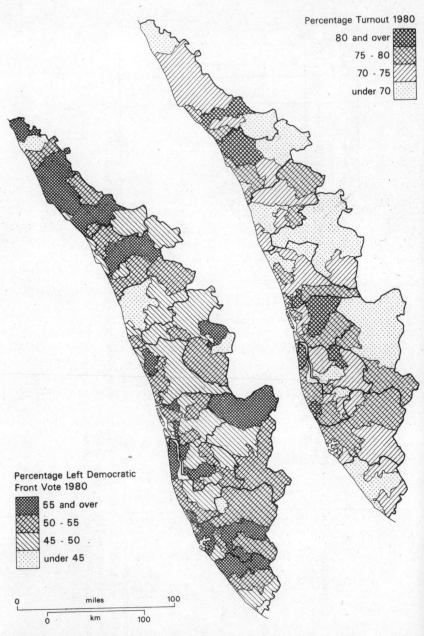

Percentage Turnout 1980

80 and over
75 - 80
70 - 75
under 70

Percentage Left Democratic
Front Vote 1980

55 and over
50 - 55
45 - 50
under 45

0   miles   100
0   km   100

*The territorial waters of India extend into the sea to a distance
of twelve nautical miles measured from the appropriate base line.*

© Government of India Copyright 1982

*Based upon Survey of India map with the permission
of the Surveyor General of India.*

Sources: Data from *Hindu* and *IE*, 23 Jan. 1980.

Map 25 Kerala 1980: Assembly Election, Turnout and Left Democratic
Front Performance

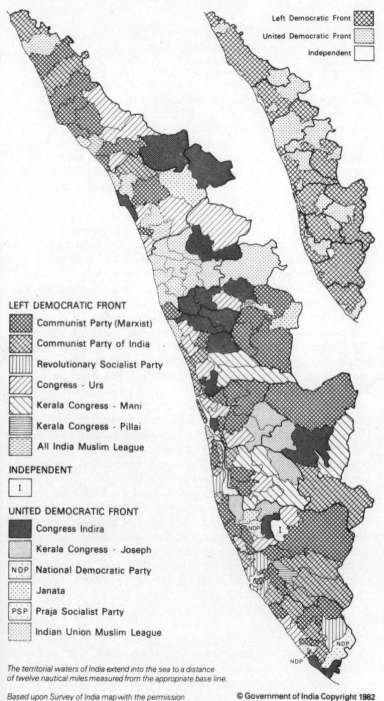

LEFT DEMOCRATIC FRONT

Left Democratic Front

United Democratic Front

Independent

LEFT DEMOCRATIC FRONT

Communist Party (Marxist)

Communist Party of India

Revolutionary Socialist Party

Congress - Urs

Kerala Congress - Mani

Kerala Congress - Pillai

All India Muslim League

INDEPENDENT

I

UNITED DEMOCRATIC FRONT

Congress Indira

Kerala Congress - Joseph

NDP National Democratic Party

Janata

PSP Praja Socialist Party

Indian Union Muslim League

*The territorial waters of India extend into the sea to a distance
of twelve nautical miles measured from the appropriate base line.*

*Based upon Survey of India map with the permission
of the Surveyor General of India.*

© Government of India Copyright 1982

Sources: As Map 25 above.

Map 26 Kerala 1980: Assembly Election, Winning Fronts and Parties.

that the CPM's support among the peasantry is being slowly eroded. Some observers have attributed this to the middle and rich peasants' alienation from the CPM as a consequence of the party's support for agricultural labourers in their fight for higher wages. Two other factors may also be important: first, the impact of the inflow of moneys from Malayalis working in the Gulf which has brought affluence to many hitherto underprivileged families in virtually every village and town in Kerala; and second a widespread concern at the CPM's failure to address itself in practical ways to the development of Kerala's economy.

If the Assembly election overall is taken as a reflection of the progress made by the marxist left in mobilizing a population at once both highly literate and poverty-stricken, it is hard to resist the conclusion that its advance has been checked. In Kerala terms turnout at 72 per cent was unimpressive. The LDF's total poll was just 50 per cent, compared with the UDF's 44 per cent; and there was still a pronounced geographical character to party support (Map 26) that bears no clear and consistent relationship to qualitative or quantitative measures of propertylessness (see below Map 27, p. 336).

Reference to the Lok Sabha poll held three weeks earlier may also be pertinent. On a lower turnout of 62 per cent the LDF won 12 of the 20 seats and the UDF 8. (Besides the CPM defeat in Palghat, M.N. Govindan Nair of the CPI and N. Sreekantan Nair of the RSP were notable leftist failures.) On the basis of the poll for each Assembly segment of the Lok Sabha constituencies the LDF would, if no change had occurred, have had a clear majority but not the sweeping victory in terms of seats it actually secured. First estimates suggest that the number of UDF voters increased only marginally while the number of LDF voters rose substantially. Two explanations may be offered: the sophistication of the Kerala electorate in distinguishing the criteria by which it selected its local and its national representatives;[25] and the poor quality of the UDF campaign—candidate selection was done at the last minute and there was an air of complacency which alienated an electorate that reacts against being taken for granted. But in either case we may infer that some LDF support—and within the front some marxist support—was conditional and contingent.

Census Data

Almost all analyses of communist support in India emphasize the importance of agrarian factors. Dasgupta and Morris-Jones characterize communist strongholds in rural India in terms of landlessness, smallness of agricultural operations, the preponderance of tenancies, and a relatively high rate of irrigation.[26] Krishna Murthy and Rao conclude that the communist appeal is more effective among the landless labourers than the poor peasant (owner cultivator). Zagoria reports that nearly half the total CPM and CPI base in Kerala comes from farm labourers, sharecroppers, the rural unemployed, and (here diverging from Krishna Murthy and Rao) cultivators of less than three acres.[27] Finally, from a marxist perspective Gough considers the distinction between Congress and communist to be substantially between the propertied and the propertyless with (small) tenant cultivators and the unskilled day labourer and unemployed providing the bulk of CPM support in the agrarian sector.[28]

Map 27 shows the distribution of four permutations of the agrarian data: the percentage of workers classed as cultivators and as agricultural labourers; labourers as a percentage of the total agricultural workforce; and the ratio of female to male agricultural labourers. Of these it is the last two which are of most political interest. Neither delineates the area of communist ascendancy perfectly but both are good approximations. The labourer-cultivator ratio underestimates CPM strength in Cannanore and the labourer-sex ratio in the Kuttanad, while both fail in Quilon, the CPI centre. One would expect the labourer-cultivator ratio to pick out communist strength, if any variable did, but the meaning of the labourer-sex ratio is less obvious. As we have noted earlier, there is a good deal of hearsay evidence that lower-caste women are radical in Kerala and it is possible that the use of group female labour in some stages of rice cultivation contributed to class consciousness.[29]

Two of the three areas where the communists were strongest—Palghat and the Kuttanad—are rice-growing areas. Since other paddy regions such as Tanjore and the Kistna-Godavari Delta have been identified with communism it is worth discussing Kerala's major paddy districts in a little more detail. Although both were characterized by a high incidence of landless labour, Palghat and the Kuttanad differed considerably in other respects. In Palghat (250,000 acres) the land was formerly owned by Namboodiris or Nairs and leased in by medium to small cultivators. Four-fifths of the sown area was double cropped; one-fifth was irrigated from reservoirs; the District is comparatively free from pests and diseases; and output comparatively reliable. Overall the cost of cultivation was moderate. Daily wages rates were low but the labourer was in a more favourable position than his counterpart in the Kuttanad since more days' work were available per year as a result of double cropping, and food was cheap. Generally speaking the relationship between the cultivator and labourer was co-operative and relatively traditional.[30] Trade unionism was not as strong as might have been expected from

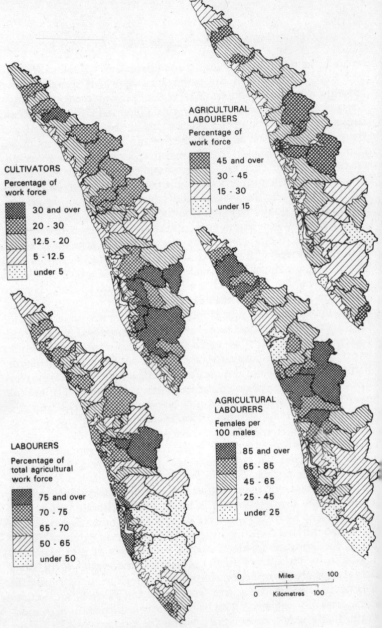

CULTIVATORS

Percentage of
work force

30 and over
20 - 30
12.5 - 20
5 - 12.5
under 5

AGRICULTURAL
LABOURERS

Percentage of
work force

45 and over
30 - 45
15 - 30
under 15

LABOURERS

Percentage of
total agricultural
work force

75 and over
70 - 75
65 - 70
50 - 65
under 50

AGRICULTURAL
LABOURERS

Females per
100 males

85 and over
65 - 85
45 - 65
25 - 45
under 25

0   Miles   100

0   Kilometres   100

The territorial waters of India extend into the sea to a distance
of twelve nautical miles measured from the appropriate base line.

© Government of India Copyright 1

Based upon Survey of India map with the permission
of the Surveyor General of India.

Source: Data from *Census of India 1971*, series 9: *Kerala*, pt X, *District Census
Handbooks*.

Map 27 Kerala 1971: Cultivators as % of Workforce; Agricultural
Labourers as % of Workforce; Agricultural Labourers as %
of Total Agricultural Workforce; Agricultural Labourers,
Females per 100 Males. All by Assembly Constituency

the District's communist leanings; and, as in Malabar generally, caste was far less divisive than in the south. Indeed Nair cultivators were often found to support the CPM: out of conviction, from hostility to the Namboodiri ruling class, or to minimize labour troubles.

The 110,000-acre Kuttanad consisting of seven taluks of Alleppey and three of Kottayam bordering on the largely reclaimed Vembanad Lake[31] is in complete contrast. Only 10 per cent of the land was double cropped though high-yielding varieties were the rule rather than the exception, as in Palghat. Four-fifths of the land was owned outright. Although the typical cultivator farms only one or two acres, the Kuttanad is dominated by the so called *Kayal* (backwater) *Rajas*, mainly Nairs by caste, and Kerala Congress in politics. No figures are available for the proportion of land held by the *Kayal Rajas* but one such who had declined to plant paddy in protest against the procurement price level and labour's demands, surrendered 2,000 acres to the state government under the Defence of India regulations.

Until the early 1940s bonded labour—usually scheduled caste—prevailed and wages were paid in kind. The traditional practices of the area are vividly described in *Two Measures of Rice*.[32] Soaring paddy prices led to the introduction of cash wages and in the aftermath of the war to the confrontation of organized labour and capital. However, unionization did little to stem the decline in real wages, the fall in days worked per year, or the growing insecurity of employment in the face of a labour surplus—exacerbated by the decline of the adjoining coir industry. Population density at 2,688 persons per square mile was nearly double the state average and 44 per cent of the total labour force were agricultural labourers. Finally literacy at 72 per cent was as high as anywhere in the state.

Thus communism has had somewhat different bases in Palghat and the Kuttanad. In both, the landless form the core of communist support, but the capitalist nature of the economy and the acute deprivation of the Kuttanad give the movement there a clear class character not present in Palghat. To that extent the movement's hold in the latter may be less secure, the more so as the CPM's organization has exhibited a certain complacency in Palghat.[33]

The rural economy is far from purely agrarian, as the coastal areas indicate (Map 27); and cottage and primitive manufacturing industry played an important part in the genesis of the communist and socialist movements in Kerala, particularly in Alleppey, Quilon, and Cannanore. Map 28 plots what the census calls 'domestic industry'—the information, of course, relates to 1971. On average only 4.5 percent of the workforce was engaged in cottage industries.

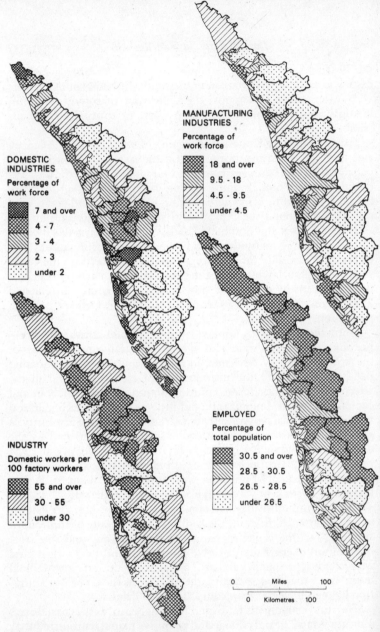

DOMESTIC
INDUSTRIES

Percentage of
work force

- 7 and over
- 4 - 7
- 3 - 4
- 2 - 3
- under 2

MANUFACTURING
INDUSTRIES

Percentage of
work force

- 18 and over
- 9.5 - 18
- 4.5 - 9.5
- under 4.5

INDUSTRY

Domestic workers per
100 factory workers

- 55 and over
- 30 - 55
- under 30

EMPLOYED

Percentage of
total population

- 30.5 and over
- 28.5 - 30.5
- 26.5 - 28.5
- under 26.5

0   Miles   100

0   Kilometres   100

The territorial waters of India extend into the sea to a distance
of twelve nautical miles measured from the appropriate base line.

Based upon Survey of India map with the permission
of the Surveyor General of India.

© Government of India Copyright 1982

Source: Data from *Census of India 1971*, series 9: *Kerala*, pt X, *District Census
Handbooks*.

Map 28 Kerala 1971: Workers in Domestic Industries as % of Work-
force; Workers in Manufacturing Industries as % of Workforce;
Domestic Workers per 100 Factory Workers; Employed % of
Population. All by Assembly Constituency

The highest category—above 7 per cent—is, as one would expect, found along the coast since the principal raw material of this sector is coconut. This distribution illuminates a number of coastal constituencies with communist or socialist records.

When we turn to the manufacturing sector proper there is no political pattern whatsoever, though the cashew and fish processing factories of Quilon do stand out. Nor has the ratio of domestic to manufacturing industry or the distribution of the employed percentage of the population any political significance. In the tertiary sector the residual 'other services'—urbanization by another name— shows that 'development' within Kerala is negatively related to communist support. (It does, however, highlight the involvement of both Muslim and Christian communities in business and the professions.) Similarly Map 29 brings into question the common belief that one reason for communist strength in Kerala is the state's high level of literacy: it is clear that there is no such relationship even if one considers only Hindu areas. The other negative conclusions should also be noted. Earlier maps (see above, p. 46) show population density and the percentage of irrigated rural land, both by taluk. Neither shows any association with the distribution of communist support.

Regression Analysis of Census Data on Voting

The maps show the census variables in isolation but we know that many of them are related and that some may act in conjunction. To take account of these probabilities it is necessary to turn to statistics. There are, in fact, several techniques which could be employed and it is very much a matter of judgement and opinion which is best in a particular instance. Each has its own assumptions and raises its own peculiar problems. In this case multiple regression has been adopted because we already know what to expect, our variables can be presented in standardized percentage form, and inspection shows there is no undue 'multi-collinearity'—in other words variables that are highly correlated with one another.[34]

In its most basic form of simple linear regression, this technique takes two variables, a dependent and an independent variable— crudely 'effect' and 'cause'—and tries to explain how changes in the value of the one are affected by changes in the value of the other, using two constants, *alpha* and *beta*. *Alpha*, the 'intercept', is the value of the 'effect' which is independent of changes in the value of the 'cause'; *beta*, the 'regression coefficient' is the rate at which the 'effect' changes for each unit of change in the 'cause'. Multiple regression is merely the extension of simple regression to more than

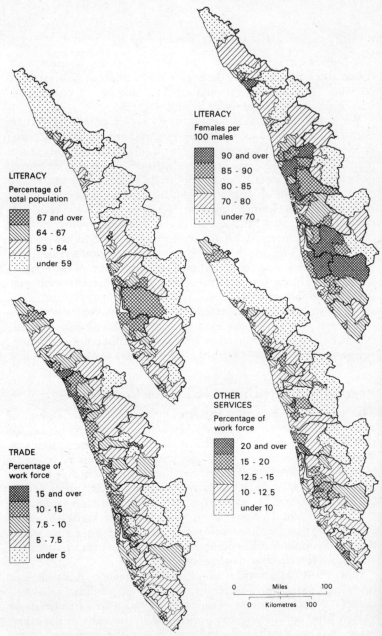

LITERACY

Percentage of
total population

- 67 and over
- 64 - 67
- 59 - 64
- under 59

LITERACY

Females per
100 males

- 90 and over
- 85 - 90
- 80 - 85
- 70 - 80
- under 70

TRADE

Percentage of
work force

- 15 and over
- 10 - 15
- 7.5 - 10
- 5 - 7.5
- under 5

OTHER
SERVICES

Percentage of
work force

- 20 and over
- 15 - 20
- 12.5 - 15
- 10 - 12.5
- under 10

0   Miles   100

0   Kilometres   100

*The territorial waters of India extend into the sea to a distance
of twelve nautical miles measured from the appropriate base line*

*Based upon Survey of India map with the permission
of the Surveyor General of India.*

© Government of India Copyright 1982

Source: As Map 28 above.

Map 29 Kerala 1971: Literacy; Literacy, Females per 100 Males; Workers
in Retail Trade as % of Workforce; Workers in Other Services as
% of Workforce. All by Assembly Constituency

one independent variable. Data in the real world are never simple and seldom strictly linear but the object of regression analysis in its fundamentals is to estimate the best possible straight line from observations of the two variables, or, in non-linear cases, the best possible alternative parameter. We try to fit our data to a straight line or curve. Regression produces a coefficient (of determination) called R^2 which tells us what the explanatory power of the equation is—how far the variables we have chosen account for change in the dependent variable. In this instance R^2, which varies between 0 and 1, would tell us how much of the variation in constituency voting behaviour can be attributed to those aspects of social and economic structure for which we have information. R^2 can be converted into a percentage directly so that 0.50 would mean that we had 'explained' 50 per cent of the total variance. Since in a democracy we do not assume that voting patterns are entirely determined by the structure of the society—certainly not in Kerala—this would be a very satisfactory result. In this example, if we hypothesized that in view of all we know about Kerala politics some 75 per cent of voting patterns might potentially be explicable in terms of social structure, then we could conclude that we had 'missed', or inaccurately measured, 25 per cent of the variation. Obviously, one should not abandon common sense when reading computer print-out; conclusions depend on qualitative factors including the reliability of the available measures of what judgement suggests are the key variables. Figures do not speak for themselves: they require interpretation. The exegesis of missing factors in the equation is, however, aided by one further facility of regression that is particularly useful when observations can be arranged geographically. It will estimate what the answer would have been if the equation had been applied to each case. The computer will calculate the election result according to the equation and give the difference between this and the actual result as a 're-sidual'. If these residuals are plotted on the map of constituencies we can then examine whether there are any patterned under- or over-estimates which could be accounted for by known, if not necessarily quantifiable, features of those areas.[35]

The analysis takes as its major dependent variables Congress performance in 1967 and CPM performance in 1970. Regressions were also conducted on the combined vote of all those parties—Congress, Kerala Congress, Jana Sangh, and Swatantra—which opposed the United Front in 1967 and on the combined vote of the CPM and SSP in 1970.

As 'explanatory' variables all those census measures so far considered were included, together with the percentage employed in plantations, fisheries and forestry, turnout (1967 or 1970 as appropriate), and a series of 'dummy variables' based on permutations of region (Malabar or Travancore-Cochin) and religion (Hindu, Christian or Muslim) which rested on the designation of constituencies as Muslim or Christian where taluk-level data indicated that over 40 per cent of the population belonged to one or other minority community and qualitative information supported the inference that the constituency was markedly Muslim or Christian in composition. Any constituencies about which there was doubt were classified as Hindu. The dummy variables are here intended to test two hypotheses: that the distinct historical development of Malabar still influences contemporary electoral behaviour and that religious community cross-cuts all other aspects of social and economic structure. (A list of the relevant variables is given at Table 12.2)

Regression analysis can be conducted in several different ways.

Table 12.2 Kerala 1967-1970: Key to Variables in Multiple Regressions on Voting Behaviour

Short label	Full variable	Form of variable
Hindu	Hindu majority constituency	Dummy
Hindu/Malabar	Hindu majority constituency in Malabar	Dummy
Labourer ratio	Agricultural labourers as % of total agricultural workforce	%
Female lab. ratio	Female agricultural labourers per 100 male agricultural labourers	%
Female lit. ratio	Female literates per 100 male literates	%
Labourer %	Agricultural labourers as % of total workforce	%
Manfg. wkr. %	Workers in manufacturing industry as % of total workforce	%
Cultivator %	Cultivators as % of total workforce	%
Other services %	Other service workers as % of total workforce	%
Christian	Christian majority constituency	Dummy
Plantns. & fishing %	Workers in live-stock, forestry, fishing, hunting and plantations, orchards and allied activities as % of total workforce	%
Literacy %	Total literates as % of total population	%
Turnout 1970	Turnout in 1970 election	%

Note: The addition of ^{2} to a variable indicates that this is a squared term (e.g. Cultivator $\%^2$ = Cultivator % × Cultivator %) to take account of curvilinear relationships in the data.

The most useful for the present work was found to be 'stepwise regression' with no pre-determined order of the entry of variables into the equation. The computer selects variables for inclusion in a sequence dictated by the extra contribution the new variable makes to the overall explanatory power of the equation, beginning with the most powerful single variable and working through to the least important. However, unless the F values are substantially different, there is no reason to place much reliance on this order, which may be contingent on precisely which variables are included or deleted. (F values constitute a test of significance of the variables and of the whole equation.) The order of steps may be revealing but it is far from constituting a causal chain.

The results are presented at Table 12.3 giving (a) the variables in order of their appearance in the step-wise regression; (b) the F-value and its level of significance; (c) R^2, which can be treated as the cumulative percentage of all the variations explained thus far; and (d) the change in R^2, the additional increment of explanation from the new variable. The smaller the F-value the less interesting the variable, but all the values given in the tables are above the conventional cut-off point of an F-value of 3.00. Two caveats are in order: first (unlike principal component analysis), once a variable has entered the equation, the variance it accounts for is excluded from further processing; and second, only two of the equations (Congress 1967 and Congress and 'right-wing parties' 1967) are based on data for virtually every constituency: 131 out of 133. In the other instances the analysis is based on 79 seats in the case of the CPM (1970) and 115 in the case of the combination of CPM and SSP (1970). For comparability a further regression is included of Congress support in 1967 based on the same 79 constituencies contested by the CPM in 1970.

A number of interesting observations can be made on Table 12.3. In every regression more than half the variance is 'explained'. Despite all the limitations of the information, voting appears quite closely related to the social and economic structure.[36] The actual percentage ranges from 53 per cent for Congress in 1967 (131 cases) to 67 per cent for the CPM in 1970 (79 cases). One could reasonably expect that the level of 'explanation' would be less for a party contesting every constituency especially when, like Congress, the party claims the status of a national rather than a 'class' party.

When we examine the individual equations there is a marked contrast between those for Congress and that for the CPM. The most important variable in the former is Hinduism, irrespective of whether we consider only the 79 constituencies the Marxists contested three years later (35 per cent), or 131 constituencies (33 per cent). For the CPM the first variable is the labourer-cultivator ratio

Communism in Kerala

Table 12.3 Kerala 1967-1970: Multiple Regressions on Voting Behaviour

Dependent variable	No. of cases	Stepwise order independent variables & sign	F value & significance level	R^2	Change in R^2
Congress 1967	131	+ Hindu	64.19···	.33	.33
		− Hindu/Malabar	23.28···	.43	.10
		+ Labourer ratio	20.23···	.51	.08
		+ Female lab. ratio^2	5.08·	.53	.02
Congress 1967	79	+ Hindu	41.53···	.35	.35
		− Hindu/Malabar	24.77···	.51	.16
		+ Labourer ratio	11.94···	.58	.07
		+ Female lit. ratio	8.94··	.62	.04
CPM 1970	79	+ Labourer ratio^2	36.94···	.32	.32
		+ Labourer %	20.32···	.46	.14
		− Manfg. wkr. %	5.15·	.50	.04
		− Cultivator %^{2}	6.90··	.54	.04
		− Manfg. wkr. %^{2}	7.17··	.58	.04
		− Other services %	8.29··	.62	.04
		− Christian	5.84·	.65	.03
		− Cultivator %	4.35·	.67	.02
CPM/SSP 1970	115	+ Labourer ratio^2	42.60···	.27	.27
		− Other services %	17.60···	.37	.10
		+ Female lab. ratio	10.23··	.42	.05
		− Plantns. & fishing %	7.87··	.46	.04
		− Christian	8.98··	.50	.04
		− Cultivator %^{2}	6.86··	.53	.03
Congress/ Kerala Congress/ Jana Sangh/ Swatantra 1967	131	− Hindu/Malabar	82.70···	.39	.39
		+ Christian	21.60···	.48	.09
		+ Literacy %^{2}	6.76··	.50	.02
		+ Literacy %	11.63···	.54	.04
		+ Turnout 1970	7.53··	.57	.03
		− Hindu	4.16·	.58	.01

··· Significance better than .001
·· Significance better than .01
· Significance better than .05

(32 per cent), the square sign indicating a curvilinear relationship. The impact of the variable increases as its value rises. There is the same contrast in the second variables to appear in the equations:

Congress performance is weak in the Hindu areas of Malabar; and the CPM is strong where the absolute percentage of agricultural labourers in the workforce is high. It is only at the third step that an agrarian variable shows up in the Congress equations, the labourer-cultivator ratio. Interestingly, however, this variable is positively related to Congress support just as it is to Marxist support, though it is linear not curvilinear in nature. Congress is *not* a cultivator's party, even though there are signs that CPM support is greater where cultivators are proportionately fewer in number. Whereas the Congress equations reach F levels in four steps, beyond which little additional variance is accounted for, the CPM equation suggests an array of factors at work: the party does not do well in constituencies where there are factory workers, Christians, or 'other service' workers. It is a rurally-based party.

When we extend the scope of the dependent variable to create a left alliance of SSP with CPM and a right alliance of Kerala Congress, Jana Sangh, Swatantra, and Congress the equations change in detail but the original contrast is maintained at the first step. The CPM/SSP total vote is best where the labourer-cultivator ratio is high and the Congress/Kerala Congress vote is worst in the Hindu areas of Malabar. As to be expected, the inclusion of Kerala Congress introduces Christian support and the high levels of literacy associated with the Christian belt around Kottayam. The inclusion of the SSP in the CPM equation increases the importance of 'other services' as a negative factor, while the labourer-sex ratio at last makes its appearance as an independent variable.

In sum, these findings are consistent with the previous historical account: Congress is weak in Malabar; the split in the party in 1964 was largely along the Hindu-Christian fault line; but within the Hindu areas of Travancore-Cochin Congress is the dominant party except where agrarian tension has been acute, as in the Kuttanad and in the depressed coir areas surrounding it. Conversely the CPM's strength is in those areas where agrarian relations have been worst: Malabar, much of Alleppey, and parts of Trichur. The regression equations cannot tell us whether caste as such is important but they do indicate that the variables which are its nearest approximations— the labourer-cultivator ratio and the percentage of agricultural labourers in the work force—are the most important correlates of CPM support in Kerala. If the backward castes or classes of the rural areas are the core of CPM support, the converse—that Congress is preponderantly the party of the cultivator and 'bourgeoisie'—is not on this evidence likely to be true. Congress is, outside Malabar, a party strong in Hindu areas just as Kerala Congress is strong in Christian areas. Support for Congress varies positively with the labourer-cultivator ratio which indicates that at least part of the backward classes finds shelter under its umbrella.

The apparently asymmetrical nature of the relationship between the two dominant parties of Kerala politics is not hard to explain. Even in the 79 constituencies where we have roughly comparable information—roughly because two different elections are involved—between one-third and two-fifths of the total vote might go to other parties if there were no electoral alliances. We know that several parties claim the disproportionate allegiance of the better-off in various communities: Kerala Congress of Christians and Nairs; the Muslim League of Muslims; and the ISP of Trivandrum Nairs. However, it is also true that Congress attracts the more successful Ezhavas. Finally, there is always the ecological fallacy to consider. That the CPM performs best in areas where the labourer-cultivator ratio is higher does not necessarily mean that all or only labourers support it. Certainly, in Palghat it is well known that many cultivating peasants are fervent Marxists. Indeed in much of the District whole villages support the CPM, as the Maoist line on revolution predicts.

The last stage in this analysis of aggregate constituency data is to examine the residuals as a check on the overall reliability of the equation and as an indication of possible 'missing' variables.

Maps 30 and 31 show the residuals for each constituency derived from the regression equations for CPM, CPM/SSP, Congress, and Congress/Kerala Congress votes, plotted in terms of the standard deviation, ranging from the very accurate estimates (which are correct to within half a standard deviation) to those few which are highly erroneous in over- or under-estimating the actual vote by more than two standard deviations. The standard deviation in each instance is: CPM 4.796; CPM/SSP 5.954; Congress 7.108; and Congress/Kerala Congress, Jana Sangh, and Swatantra 6.039. The unshaded areas of the maps represent a good prediction by the regression equation of the actual result, horizontal shading indicates underestimates, and screen (dots) over-estimates, both increasing in density as the error increases.

A study of these distributions suggests the following conclusions. The CPM/SSP and CPM equations both perform well but tend to under-estimate party strength in the three preponderantly CPM areas—central Cannanore, Palghat, and the part of Alleppey to the west of Vembanad Lake. Conversely the equation over-estimates CPM support in the far north of Cannanore, the Christian areas of the interior of Ernakulam and northern Kottayam, and, less markedly, Trivandrum, where the Nairs are comparatively numerous. In the Congress case the equation under-estimates the party's

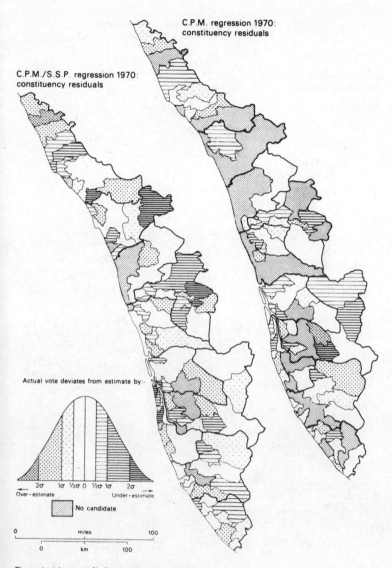

C.P.M. regression 1970:
constituency residuals

C.P.M./S.S.P. regression 1970:
constituency residuals

Actual vote deviates from estimate by:-

2σ 1σ ½σ 0 ½σ 1σ 2σ
Over-estimate   Under-estimate

No candidate

0   miles   100
0   km   100

The territorial waters of India extend into the sea to a distance
of twelve nautical miles measured from the appropriate base line.

Based upon Survey of India map with the permission
of the Surveyor General of India.

© Government of India Copyright 1982

Map 30 Kerala 1970: Assembly Election, CPM and CPM/SSP Regres-
          sions: Constituency Residuals

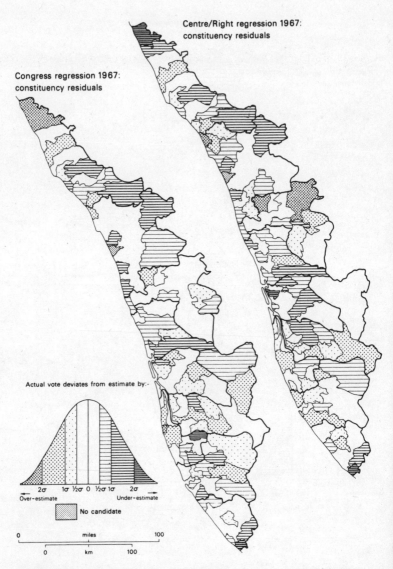

Centre/Right regression 1967:
constituency residuals

Congress regression 1967:
constituency residuals

Actual vote deviates from estimate by:-

2σ 1σ ½σ 0 ½σ 1σ   2σ
Over-estimate   Under-estimate

No candidate

0   miles   100
0   km   100

The territorial waters of India extend into the sea to a distance
of twelve nautical miles measured from the appropriate base line.

Based upon Survey of India map with the permission
of the Surveyor General of India.

© Government of India Copyright 1982

Map 31 Kerala 1967: Assembly Election, Centre/Right and Congress
Regressions: Constituency Residuals

support in much of the north except in the far north of Cannanore and over-estimates it in much of central and northern Travancore. The equation for the Centre/Right regression performs well generally, with some tendency to under-estimate in Christian areas and over-estimate in southern Travancore. Like all the other regressions, it too fails in the extreme north.

Two reasons might be suggested for the failure of the equations to do full justice to all areas of party strength: the independent contribution of party organization in mobilizing the vote; and the tendency of electors, irrespective of their place in the social structure, to support a clearly dominant party as a surer means of securing favours. Where the equations under-estimate the actual result it is possible that local caste and communal configurations are a factor, though this presumption must rest only on the claims of electoral managers.[37] Overall, however, the actual results in 1967 and 1970 are correctly estimated in half the constituencies to within half a standard deviation—plus or minus 2.5 to 3 per cent—which remains a very satisfactory result, given the imperfections of the data.

Politics and the Young

As explained earlier, Dr Dharmangadan and the author conducted a survey in 1974 on a sample of nearly one thousand teenagers (N=971) drawn from standards 8, 9 and 10 in twelve secondary schools in the Attingal and Trivandrum educational sub-districts within Trivandrum District. It was designed to elucidate the students' own political outlook and their parents' political loyalties in relation to the family social and economic background.[38] Teenagers are highly politically conscious in Kerala, certainly more so than in Britain. In a society where just over half the population is nineteen years of age or less, the attitudes of the young quickly affect the outlook of the electorate.

Ideally, the allegiance of the adult electorate should be tapped directly but a pilot study revealed major sampling problems.[39] Although children's reports·of their parents' political allegiance are of doubtful reliability in recent Western studies of political socialization, because of selective perception or ignorance,[40] the broad accuracy of such second-hand information in Kerala may be defended on the grounds of the high levels of politicization, the closeness of family relationships, and the regularity with which political affiliation is displayed in elections and political demonstrations. Since 45 per cent of the teenagers said their fathers had participated in some kind of political activity and one-third gave political affiliations different from those reported for their fathers, there are *prima facie* grounds for considering such evidence.

Trivandrum District is not a microcosm of the state. The investigation was concerned, however, with testing propositions rather than measuring the incidence of attitudes or opinions. Further, though the choice of area was determined by practical considerations, southern Travancore is a particularly suitable area in which to assess the relative importance of caste and community in political allegiance. It was here that caste was most obviously associated with political loyalties in the past. If caste is yielding to class or party in Attingal and Trivandrum, then it is very probable it has already succumbed elsewhere in Kerala.

By 1974 Congress's popularity was waning and Kerala had returned to its 'normal' pattern of fierce party competition. The Maxi Front made up of Congress, CPI, RSP, PSP, and the Muslim League had been in power since 1970 (Congress from 1971), but the opposition led by the CPM challenged the ministry strongly, capitalizing on national economic difficulties, dissension within the government, and the ministry's mixed record. Student politics in Kerala—and here this applies to the later standards of secondary schools, considered here, as well as to colleges—usually anticipates adult trends by anything between a year and eighteen months; and a swing away from Congress and its allies in the Kerala government is evident in the hypothetical voting preferences of the youth sample shown in Table 12.4.

These figures do not indicate the state-wide allegiance of students. Nevertheless, the numbers involved are large enough to justify examination of the basis of support in this area for all major parties except the Muslim League.

The survey was designed to maximize the possibilities of effective analysis by focusing on the last compulsory school standard—standard 10—and aiming at an equal number of boys and girls and of

Table 12.4 *Trivandrum District 1974:*
Youth Voting Preferences (percentage)

None	Ruling Coalition					Opposition			
	Cong (N)	CPI	RSP	PSP	ML	CPM	KC	Cong.(O)	Others
1.4	20.2	9.4	3.7	4.2	1.1	22.6	33.5	1.5	2.4
	................38.6....................					........57.6............			

Cong. (N): New Congress.
Cong. (O): Old Congress.

pupils living in urban and rural areas. Of the sample, 83 per cent
were in the last standard, 13 per cent in standard 9, and 4 per cent in
standard 8. By age 95 per cent were 14 years or older and three-
quarters between 14 and 16. Boys made up 52 per cent of the sample.
Compared with Kerala as a whole, there was an urban bias: 52 per
cent of the sample lived in rural areas, with boys and girls evenly
distributed between rural and urban homes.

The distribution of the sample on most sociological variables is
consistent with what we know of this part of Trivandrum District.
As the summary tables show, one in eight fathers was unemployed
and another one in eight was a 'coolie'.[41] The biggest occupational
groups were white collar (clerical, 37 per cent) and semi-skilled
workers (34 per cent). Almost all students answered the question on
family income: 10 per cent returned none (the unemployed), 35 per
cent between Rs 100 and 299 per month, one-fifth Rs 300 to 499,
and a further one-fifth more than Rs 500. Only 4 per cent failed to
give their caste or community. The high-caste Nairs (46 per cent)
were the largest group, followed by 'Other Hindus' (21 per cent)
mainly lower caste in the traditional hierarchy, Ezhavas (11 per cent)
and Christians (8 per cent).

As Table 12.5 confirms, caste and community interrelate with the
family's occupational and financial standing. The summary
percentages for those earning Rs 300 or more per month show that
the Nairs, Forward Christians, Catholics, and Muslims are still far
better placed economically than Ezhavas, other low-caste Hindus,
and Backward Christians. Brahmins, however, appear to be losing
ground.

The persistence of differences in the objective circumstances of the
forward and backward communities does not inhibit the educational
and occupational *aspirations* of the latter. Four-fifths of the sample
aspired to post-secondary education, varying little by community;
and virtually the whole sample hoped for professional or white-
collar jobs.

Forwardness and backwardness has been a major source of
twentieth-century political conflict in Kerala. Changing aspirations
may betoken the breakdown of these alignments, or alternatively
strengthen them, since the gulf between aspiration and achievement
remains wide. Two questions then arise. Is the association between
caste and community and party declining? And, if it is, what is
replacing it—'class', as crudely measured in terms of income and
occupation and more subtly as 'political consciousness' or simply
some 'secularized' form of party loyalty? The survey offers three
indicators of political allegiance: the respondent's hypothetical vote;
his/her rank ordering of the parties as first, second, or third choice;

Table 12.5 Trivandrum District 1974: Family Income per month
by Caste and Community (% of sample)

Community	None	Under Rs 100	Rs 100-299	Rs 300-499	Rs 500 +	% With Rs 300 +	Mean Rs	N =
Brahmin	19.5	12.2	29.3	17.1	22.0	39.1	287	41
Nair	6.3	13.5	34.6	21.3	23.8	45.1	328	445
Ezhava	9.5	23.8	32.4	19.0	15.2	34.2	260	105
'Other Hindus'	8.3	21.6	40.2	17.2	12.3	29.5	246	204
Backward Christian*	16.3	14.3	42.9	18.4	8.2	26.6	223	49
Catholic	27.8	nil	22.2	5.6	44.4	44.4	415†	18
Forward Christian*	nil	nil	22.2	33.3	44.4	59.3†	415†	9
ALL CHRISTIANS	17.1	9.2	35.5	17.1	21.1	38.2	291	76
Muslim	8.8	21.1	28.1	15.8	26.3	42.1	289	57

* 'Backward' and 'Forward', following Kerala practice, are used to designate those Christian communities which are socially and economically disadvantaged and those which are advanced.

† Catholic and Forward Christians combined.

and his/her report on how his or her father votes. But if we cross-tabulate these by community, income, and occupation then it appears that community matters most. For reasons of space, only four tables (12.6-9) are presented, but all other tabulations (not reproduced here) point in the same direction.

Table 12.6 shows those fathers reported as voting for a marxist party (CPM, CPI, or RSP) statistically controlled by the family's caste, income, and occupation.

Table 12.6 Trivandrum District 1974: Caste, Income, and Occupation by Father's Reported Vote for CPM/CPI/RSP

Income	Occupation	Community	% CPM/CPI/RSP	N=
Rs 100–299	White collar	Nair	19	47
Rs 300–499	White collar	Nair	21	52
Rs 100–299	Semi-skilled	Nair	25	69
Rs 300–499	Semi-skilled	Nair	32	22
Rs 100–299	Coolie	Nair	27	11
Rs 100–299	White collar	Low caste	35	17
Rs 300–499	White collar	Low caste	71	21
Rs 100–299	Semi-skilled	Low caste	53	55
Rs 300–499	Semi-skilled	Low caste	62	21
Rs 100–299	Coolie	Low caste	59	27

Note: Low caste = Ezhava and Other Hindus.

No sub-group of Nairs gives as much support to a marxist party as the least enthusiastic sub-group from the lower castes. Occupation and income are better indicators of how lower-caste electors will vote than high-caste electors, though as Nairs lose status by taking semi-skilled jobs, especially if these are not better paid, their readiness to vote communist (actually CPI not CPM in this area) increases. On the other hand low-caste workers of higher occupational status and income show a greater not a smaller disposition to support the left on the perfectly rational grounds that the communists have championed the Non-Gazetted Officer, the typical white-collar worker of Kerala and India, and assiduously attended in particular to the needs of the lower-caste civil servant.

Tables 12.7 and 12.8 show that this pattern remains essentially the same among the younger generation. There is some growth of support for the marxist parties among young people from those

*Table 12.7   Trivandrum District 1974: Youth Support
for CPM by Caste, Community, and Income (percentage)*

Community	Income				
	None	− Rs 100	Rs 100–299	Rs 300–499	Rs 500+
Nair	18	16	17	18	17
Ezhava	20	16	32	50	27
Other Hindus	29	30	30	53	24
All Christians	15	14	7	8	13
Muslims	40	25	25	22	0

*Table 12.8   Trivandrum District 1974: Youth Support for
CPM/CPI/RSP by Caste, Community, and Income (percentage)*

Community	Income				
	None	− Rs 100	Rs 100–299	Rs 300–499	Rs 500+
Nair	43	29	27	28	29
Ezhava	50	28	47	75	47
Other Hindus	53	49	47	62	48
All Christians	23	29	26	15	13
Muslims	40	25	50	22	7

communities—Nairs, Christians, and Muslims—where the fathers
were most hostile—a trend slightly more obvious among the poorer
than the better-off. Nevertheless, caste differences still remain very
pronounced. Nairs and Christians remain consistently low in their
support for the marxist parties, except among the poorest of Nairs
who turn to the (Nair-led) CPI. Among the Ezhavas and Other
Hindus the CPI (in particular) and the RSP also appeal to the very
poor and to the most prosperous among Ezhavas. Even so, the
appeal of the CPM, CPI, and RSP is still greatest among teenagers
from moderately well-off white-collar homes.

If we examine the actual movement between generations, as
shown in Table 12.9, two conclusions may be drawn: only the CPM
(80 per cent), Kerala Congress (79 per cent), and Congress (70 per
cent), the major parties in the District, retained the majority support
of children from homes which supported those parties. On the other
hand nearly half the children from CPI homes and more than half
from RSP homes abandoned those parties. Second, though there

Table 12.9 Trivandrum District 1974: Inter-generational Party Allegiance

Father's reported vote Party	N=	% of children reporting same party as father	No. of 'rebels' who went to:						Number lost to major parties	Net change in vote between generations: N=
			RSP	CPI	CPM	KC	PSP	Cong.		
None	61	15	4	8	11	17	1	8	49	+8
RSP	29	41		4	7	2	3	0	16	+2
CPI	88	55	4		11	13	3	7	38	+44
CPM	169	80	4	9		12	2	4	31	+34
KC	323	79	7	7	19		2	26	61	
PSP	43	61	2	3	4	2		2	13	−2
Cong.	201	70	3	9	23	19	0		54	−7
Totals	914	67%	24	40	75	65	11	47		

was a great deal of (and varied) inter-generational movement, the
CPM and Kerala Congress were the principal net beneficiaries. In
percentage terms the CPM did best, gaining 26 per cent more
support.

The continuing importance of community in voting preferences is
consistent with the answers to a number of questions on caste. The
sample, irrespective of party allegiance, overwhelmingly rejected
the idea of inter-caste marriage for a member of their family. Se-
venty per cent disapproved; 15 per cent approved; and 15 per cent
had no opinion. Only one in five dismissed communalism as unim-
portant in Kerala politics and half thought communalism influenced
government under the control of either Congress (53 per cent) or
CPM (48 per cent), proportions which again varied little with party
allegiance. The one exception was the priority which respondents
gave to different factors in deciding how to vote. Personal qualities
prevailed over both party and community, a finding which might be
seen in the context of the fact that little more than one-third believed
that politicians had the people's interest at heart, a cynicism matched
only by the teenagers' attitude to government servants. One-quarter
thought of them as 'servants of the people' but three-fifths as engaged in their own aggrandizement. Despite this disenchantment
four-fifths, including CPM supporters, believed in the citizen's duty
to vote and in democracy as the best form of government.

Such highly-generalized questions may invite scepticism. More
specific questions about social and political beliefs are also revealing.
As Table 12.10 shows, CPM and Congress supporters are at or near
opposite poles on every issue except astrology: 16 points apart on
'law and order', 13 on the Naxalites, 16 on the police as agents of the
ruling class, and 15 on strikes as labour's 'only way' forward. Even

*Table 12.10 Trivandrum District 1974: Selected Socio-Political Beliefs
by Party (percentage deviation from sample mean)*

				Belief in		
	Astrology	Prohibition	Law & order	Naxalites	Police as ruling class agents	Strikes as 'Only way'
CPI	+10	+5	+1	+5	− 1	−3
CPM	− 6	−9	−9	+5	+10	+8
KC	+ 4	0	+1	−1	− 6	0
Cong.	− 7	+4	+7	−8	− 6	−7
Mean %	44	45	76	20	23	51

so, the results indicate that ideological differences among the young are relatively modest. The limited degree to which party support is related to young people's attitudes is also evident in answers to an open-ended question which foreign country was most admired. There was general enthusiasm for the Soviet Union (35 per cent) which was strongest among CPM supporters (44 per cent) and weakest among Kerala Congress followers (28 per cent), and a universal disinterest in China (2 per cent). The US (15 per cent) and the UK (10 per cent) were admired by small minorities of the sample. Again, it is true to say that there was little difference on the basis of party allegiance.

Respect for the USSR does not appear to affect their conception of political priorities—the political agenda—any more than does the existence of two communist parties. Both open-and closed-ended questioning elicited the same order of business; jobs, food supplies, and prices—with communalism as an also-ran. Nationalization was rarely mentioned and not one of the 219 CPM supporters in the sample raised in any form the issue of Centre-State relations which has always been a key item in CPM campaigning; perhaps this is not surprising as many CPM supporters inherit their political allegiance, are no more keenly interested in politics than the sample overall, and on average less politically knowledgeable.

In 1974 we may say that party preferences in southern Kerala were still strongly influenced by caste and community and that young people recognized that communalism was a central fact of political life. Irrespective of occupation or income, Christians, Nairs, and Muslims were resistant to any variety of communism but the CPI had some attraction to those whose families were without regular income. Among the low-caste Ezhava and 'other Hindus' there was much greater support for the communists which actually rose with income until the family was quite prosperous by Kerala standards. The most typical communist in the area sampled was, in fact, a white-collar Ezhava employee earning between Rs 300 and Rs 499 per month (1974 income levels). Among the teenagers voting is regarded as a duty (and a right). Though a minority dissented, competitive democracy was seen as the best form of government despite a widespread admiration for the Soviet Union. However, there was a widespread cynicism about politicians and civil servants and little deep attachment to political parties. In deciding how to vote, the sample is clear that the key consideration was the candidate, not the party, so we may safely assume that all forms of local and political power and influence, legitimate or otherwise, entered the electoral calculus. While there were some ideological differences between supporters of the CPM and Congress, these could be exaggerated. Young CPM supporters were only moderately politically conscious. Each party had its bedrock but except in the case of the Kerala Congress—perhaps because of its communal overtones—a substantial minority of a party's poll is fluctuating and unreliable. In fine, one might observe that our analysis does not suggest that this part of Travancore has the makings of the Yenan of India.

These conclusions are not to be seen as detracting from the findings of studies by such scholars as Gough and Mencher, who have chiefly worked in Alleppey and areas of CPM strength in Malabar. Nevertheless it is important to underline that the District studied here is equally a part of Kerala.

The Weakness of the Naxalites

One distinctive feature of Kerala's experience as a state with a strong communist movement in the late 1960s was the relative weakness of the extreme left. In examining this it is worth distinguishing between the so-called Naxalites and ultras. 'Naxalite' was (and is) a term used loosely in India to describe a wide variety of Maoist or marxist-leninist political groupings who rejected 'working within the system'. Some but by no means all, were committed to armed uprising, terrorism, or other forms of violence in pursuit of their cause. For others—often styling themselves Communist Revolutionaries—there were no such immediate plans. Instead the objective was to build a dedicated cadre who would eschew any participation (tactical or otherwise) in the existing party or political system and would proselytize as true believers among the masses. The term 'ultra' was commonly used in Kerala to describe those on the far left of the CPM—some of whom were expelled from, or resigned, party membership—who suspected the party leadership of a centrist compromise whereby administration featured no less significantly than agitation in party thinking. The ultras' attitude to representative institutions was unequivocally leninist: participation in the Assembly (and *a fortiori* the government) must be predicated on an overriding determination to expose the contradictions inherent in liberal democracy and so hasten its destruction.

In Kerala the ultras and Communist Revolutionaries were far. more important than the Naxalites, as they are generally understood. With the exceptions of the small groups around Kosala Ramdas and Kunnikal Narayan, the extreme left generally regarded violence in any form as futile and at least in the existing circumstances as contrary to marxist-leninist principles.[42] The failure of the extreme left in Kerala can best be approached from two perspectives: the ultras' attempts to capture control of the CPM from within the party organization; and the nature of the Naxalites' potential basis of popular support.

The reasons for the centrists' defeat of the ultras have already been considered in detail (see above, p. 248). Namboodiripad and A.K. Gopalan enjoyed a commanding personal ascendancy within the party. The centrists deployed their control of the CPM machine with considerable skill. The party's mass base rested on a tradition of electoralism and the party led the existing UF ministry. Recognition of this latter fact is evident in the ultras' ambivalence towards the contesting of elections and the tenure of representative positions. Ramdas, for example, announced in September 1968 that the Kerala Communist Revolutionaries 'would take a firm decision as to when the MLAs and representatives in the local self-government bodies who had joined [them] should give up these elected posts.'[43] Two of the three Communist Revolutionary MLAs, K.P.R. Gopalan and K.K. Annan, continued to attend the Assembly until its dissolution in 1970, and also supported the CPI-led Mini Front ministry against the CPM in 1969-70.

From the second perspective it appears that the Naxalites lacked a socio-economic constituency of one or other of the kinds associated with the movement elsewhere in India. The percentage of tribals was low. Apart from North and South Wynad—in which the Naxalites were active—there were no taluks where tribals constituted more than 5 per cent of the population.[44] There was no urban proletariat such as was found in Calcutta while the rural poor, though more numerous than in any other Indian state, were not available for Naxalite mobilization for several reasons. The hutment dwellers were relatively well protected from eviction; a major land reform giving them at least the title to their minuscule plot was slowly moving through its legislative stages; all parties had connived since Independence in forest encroachment; and in their different ways the communist party, Catholic Church, Muslim community, and S.N.D.P. Yogam had given the under-privileged a semblance of self-respect and hope in this world or the next.

More puzzling is the failure of the Naxalites to establish a major base among the student population. College campuses were fertile grounds for the movement in West Bengal and Bombay. Kerala had the highest percentage of college-educated youth and an unenviable record of graduate unemployment. Further, the student body was highly politicized. Yet, though the CPM-led student wing was at one point threatened with a split and there was a good deal of Naxalite talk on the campuses, few followed the young idealist Philip M. Prasad, a politics graduate and former CPM student leader, into the revolutionary underground.[45] In Kerala those who took that path tended to be the less able students found in private tutorial colleges. Those factors which limited the appeal of the movement in the population at large affected young people, but there were particular explanations also. Colleges in the state are dispersed and frequently in the management of caste and communal organizations.

The majority of students did eventually succeed in securing employment but their chances of success both in the job and marriage markets—and of their brothers and sisters—was heavily conditional on an unblemished 'reputation'. There were clear if unwritten limits to student militancy and politics. Those from the lower castes were under the additional pressure that their family had often scraped and saved to secure their child a hold on the education ladder. In any case caste and community still divided one student from another at table and in friendship.[46] It should also be noted that, compared to the major cities of India, even the state capital is provincial and its students' minds more exercised by their immediate problems than by the thoughts of distant Chairman Mao. No Naxalite funds were available to sustain an independent student organization; but in fact students at this period turned towards the Congress-supported Kerala Students Union. The CPM Students Federation of India was tarnished by its association with an increasingly unhappy government. College elections in 1968 and 1969 demonstrated that not only did the Naxalites make little headway among the student body but also that the CPM was losing support to Youth Congress.

It should also be said that the Naxalites—in the loose sense of the term—lacked leadership of the calibre found elsewhere. The most prominent figure, Kunnikal Narayan, was formerly a second-rank CPM leader in Calicut who in circumstances that remain obscure had withdrawn from active participation. Together with his wife he had run a tutorial college before emerging as a known Naxalite sympathizer. Old friends in the CPM and CPI who sought to dissuade him from terrorism attributed his activities to a personality disorder. Other claimed that he was acting as an *agent provocateur* on behalf of the American CIA or the Central authorities anxious to find an excuse to depose the UF ministry. Both theories appear unlikely. Of his followers only A. Varghese, who subsequently formed his own group, was of the stuff of revolutionaries. From a poor Catholic family which had migrated from central Travancore to Wynad, he wielded some influence among the tribals. When captured, his determined interrogation produced no information and he was eventually shot in suspicious circumstances.[47] The Naxalites' small numbers in Kerala meant that they could even less afford the factionalism which afflicted the movement everywhere.

In all not more than 16 deaths were at this time attributed to the Naxalites—twelve well established—including that of the CPM organizer Azhikodan Raghavan, the one public figure to be assassinated.[48] That so little terrorist activity took place reflects much about the nature of Kerala society and its structure: premeditation is unusual; violence is rare; traditional social controls are still powerful; and in the rural areas, which constitute 85 per cent of the state, virtually every man, woman, and child is accounted for by his neighbours. The settlement pattern is arguably inimical to the kind of revolutionary take-over that temporarily occurred in Naxalbari (West Bengal) at this time or had occurred in Telengana earlier. For all the absence of modern technology (so long as the people oppose 'anti-social elements') it is a policemen's paradise: circumscribed means of communication—the track between the rice fields; a population divided socially but not physically by caste and community; habitations at the corner of every field; and the curfew of the subtropical night. Only in the forests, and especially in the tribal areas, could the Naxalites survive; and even there significant movements could be monitored from the compounds of forest officer and planter: once Achutha Menon, the Chief Minister after intensive lobbying by one District Collector and senior police officers—gave the order, it was only a matter of months before the ringleaders were in custody and their followers scattered, although Naxalite activity continued intermittently throughout the 1970s and into the 1980s.

Notes

1 Book review of Victor M. Fic, *Kerala: Yenan of India* in *Social Scientist* (Tvm) 7, Aug. 1972, p. 72.
2 *Hindu,* 30 Nov. 1970.
3 CPI membership grew during the period but local commentators did not perceive any significant growth in mass support. Political journalists and academic students of politics in Trivandrum considered that the CPI was unlikely to win more than three or four seats on the strength of its own vote alone. This weakness was one factor in the party's decision to form a front with the CPM in 1979 for the 1980 Assembly election.
4 K.G. Krishna Murthy and G. Lakshmana Rao, *Political Preferences in Kerala* (1968) attempt an analysis of the 1957 to 1967 elections after noting the difficulties (p. 33). Thirty-five constituencies underwent boundary changes 'of more than 50 per cent' at the 1965 delimitation (p.40.)
5 The most stimulating example of this approach is B. Dasgupta and W.H. Morris-Jones, *Patterns and Trends in Indian Politics: an Ecological Analysis of Aggregate Data on Society and Elections* (1976).

6   Ibid., p. 69, Table 3.8.
7   As n.4 above, pp.34–8.
8   See especially p.42: 'So it can safely be said that about two to three Assembly constituencies fall into each taluk . . . .if a taluk stands very high in respect of labour-cultivator ratio, the constituency belonging to this taluk is classified as high.'
9   In the 1971 Census a worker was defined as a person whose *main* activity was participation in any economically productive work whereas in the 1961 Census a worker was taken to mean a person who engaged in any economically productive work without regard to his or her main activity. Thus in 1961 a housewife would be categorized as an economically productive worker if she worked on non-domestic tasks as a secondary activity. The 1961 Census concerned itself with any employment in the previous 15 days while the 1971 census confined itself to employment in the preceding week.
10 *Census of India 1971,* Series 9: *Kerala,* pt X, *District Census Handbooks— Alleppey,* p.49. I am grateful to K. Narayanan, Director of Census Operations in Kerala, for guidance on census data. *District Census Handbooks* also give data by village and ward that normally enable Assembly constituency boundaries to be identified when they do not precisely follow panchayat or municipal limits. I am grateful to S. Varadachary for obtaining volumes not available in the India Office Library, London.
11 'Religious Parties in Kerala: a Multiple Regression Analysis', *Political Scientist* (Ranchi) VIII–XI (Jan–June 1972 to July–Dec. 1974).
12 Ibid., p. 79.
13 p. 88
14 *Kerala,* p. 5; see also Richard Wigg, *The Times,* 20 Dec 1979.
15 *Kerala,* p. 406.
16 *Social Scientist* (Tvm) 64, Nov. 1977, p.3.
17 Zagoria, *Problems of Communism* XXII (1), 1973.
18 Malappuram District, formed on 16 June 1969, was created out of part of Palghat District and part of Kozhikode District.
19 *Washington Post,* 12 Mar. 1980. Of remittances from abroad, especially from the Gulf states, estimated for India at Rs 1,800 crores, Kerala's share was as much as Rs 400 crores. 'A good part of these money inflows is being utilised by the recipients for investment in real estate and houses. Consequently, land values even in rural areas have shown a tendency to escalate substantially in recent years.' *ER 1978,* p. 5.
20 Interview, K.C. John, *Times of India* correspondent, Tvm, Sept. 1973.
21 The Youth Congress movement in Kerala was hostile to Sanjay Gandhi during the Emergency, despite his identification with the Youth Congress of the north of India.
22 Points made in explanation by Dr. T.V. Sathyamurthy, U. of York, in a paper given to a seminar at the School of Oriental and African Studies, London, July 1977. For CPM allegations that there was rigging of votes see *IE* (Cochin), 23 Mar. 1977. See also James Manor, 'Where Congress Survived: Five States in the Indian General Election of 1977', *Asian*

Survey XVIII (8), 1978. The detention of CPM cadres had not seriously damaged the party's performance in the 1965 Kerala Assembly election. A source close to the CPM leadership denied in a private communication to me that there was any serious shortage of funds. In any case the CPM's mass base ensured that it was much less dependent on cash for an effective campaign. Constituency boundaries in 1977 were essentially those published in 1974, well before the Emergency, and not criticized at the time. The fact of intensified activity by Youth Congress workers late in the campaign does not necessarily indicate that it swung voting preference. Finally, it is not clear why the CPM's traditional voters, used (even inured) to some opportunism in the party's electoral understandings over elections since 1965, should have reacted more strongly on this occasion, particularly in view of the obvious difficulties of building a strong left-wing alliance in early 1977. See also T.J. Nossiter, *J. of Commonwealth & Comparative Politics* XVI (1), 1978.

23 Written communications, May 1977.

24 For the results of the mini general election of 17 May 1979 in which Ruling Alliance candidates were defeated in Parassala, Thiruvalla, Tellicherry, and Kasergod Assembly constituencies see *Hindu*, 18 May 1979. For commentary see K.T. Zacharias 'By-Election Politics,' *Economic and Political Weekly*, 5 May 1979, 'Divided Ruling Front', ibid., 9 June 1979, 'New Alignments,' ibid., 25 Aug. 1979; also Tvm Staff Reporter, 'A Forerunner to New Alignments', *Hindu*, 17 May 1979.

25 The choice in the Lok Sabha poll may have been conditioned for some electors by the effective alternatives nationally. Mrs Gandhi was contrite, India's one world figure, and promised at least positive government, in contrast with the feeble record of the various warring factions of the erstwhile Janata. In contrast in Kerala the selection of a state government was influenced by different considerations: the political appeal and record of the rival chief contenders; and the desire to ensure that class and communal interests were pressed in the Assembly and Council of Ministers. It seems that A.K. Antony, the Congress (U) leader, was preferred by some who voted for the UDF in the Lok Sabha poll over K. Karunakaran, the Congress (I) leader on grounds of the degree to which the former was seen as a man of principle and programme and the latter still lived under the cloud of suspicion generated by the Rajan episode and was identified with the machinery rather than the issues of politics. It is also possible that some Kerala Congress supporters who had voted for the UDF in the parliamentary poll chose to back the KC (M) wing in the Assembly poll as the representative of those farming and communal interests articulated by Kerala Congress as a whole because it was a member of what was clearly to be the winning team.

26 *Patterns and Trends in Indian Politics*, p. 292.

27 *Political Preferences in Kerala*, pp. 69-72.

28 *International J. of Comparative Sociology* VIII (1), 1967, pp. 86-7.

29 It is also possible that this variable acts as a surrogate for community

membership, since, with the exception of Moplah Malappuram and parts of the adjoining Kozhikode and Palghat Districts, Hindu womenfolk are more likely to be found working in the fields than Muslim or Christian women.

30 Govt of Kerala, *Report of the Kuttanad Enquiry Commission*, p. 22.

31 V.R. Pillai and P.G.K. Panikar, *Land Reclamation in Kerala* (1963); *Report of the Kuttanad Enquiry Commission*, p. 5.

32 Thakazhi Sivasankara Pillai, *Two Measures of Rice; Report of the Kuttanad Enquiry Commission*, p. 22; K.C. Alexander, 'Emerging Farmer-Labour Relations in Kuttanad', *Economic and Political Weekly*, 25 Aug. 1973; Mencher, *Economic and Political Weekly*, Annual no. Feb. 1978.

33 Interviews, CPM activists, Tvm, Nov. 1977.

34 For an outline of the method and its problems see Dasgupta and Morris-Jones, p. 324.

35 I am most grateful to D.J. Sinclair of the London School of Economics for drawing my attention to the relevance of this technique.

36 Dasgupta and Morris-Jones (p.222) report R^2 values of 50 to 60 per cent for state-level regression equations based on socio-economic data whereas at the national level (on large numbers of observations) the equivalent R^2 is less than 30 per cent except for the communists (after the split, the CPM) which ranges between 41 per cent (1962) and 51 per cent (1967).

37 Logically the fact that election agents (and candidates) believed caste to be an important factor (usually in explaining their defeats) does not demonstrate that caste is important.

38 A fuller account of the findings is given in the Proceedings of the 1st World Conference on Malayalam (U. of Kerala, forthcoming). The questionnaire was administered in Malayalam. Copies of this and its English translation can be obtaind from Dr B. Dharmangadan, Dept of Psychology, Kariavattom Campus, University of Kerala or the author.

39 A significant number of potential respondents in a random sample of the electoral register of the Trivandrum II constituency declined to be interviewed. In other cases it proved impossible to trace addresses given in the register.

40 David Marsh, 'Political Socialisation: a Political Review' (unpublished Ph. D. thesis, U. of Exeter, 1973).

41 'Coolies' was the English word used in Trivandrum to describe labourers generally.

42 Written communications, N.C. Sekhar and K.P.R. Gopalan, Dec. 1974. See also K.C. John, 'Naxalites split in Kerala,' *Times of India*, 12 Dec. 1970.

43 *Hindu*, 19 Sept. 1968.

44 The 1971 percentages of scheduled castes and tribes in North Wynad was 21.7 and South Wynad 19.1. *FFYP 1974-9*, p. 44.

45 Interview, P.M. Prasad, Tvm, Dec. 1970.

46 Interviews, students and academics, colleges, central and southern Kerala.

47 Police sources interviewed stated that the physical results of his interrogation were such that his production in court would have been embarrassing.

48 **Suspicion fell first on a former CPM MLA, A.V. Aryan, then leader of** the Communist Unity Centre, and an important trade union figure in Trichur: *SPKLA*, 25 Sept. 1972. Another version blamed Youth Congress supporters, while a story circulating in Trichur town claimed that he was killed to secure a document compromising a prominent political figure. It is indicative of the near-universal revulsion in Kerala at violence against persons in pursuit of politial objectives that the CPM spokesman moving the Adjournment Motion regarding Raghavan's murder, V.S. Achuthanandan, expressed satisfaction at the response of the leaders of 'all shades of opinion' and of the government: ibid., p. 3.

13

Epilogue

THE communist movement in India has often been criticized for an excessive dependence on the direction of foreign communist parties. This apparent subservience to Soviet, British, or Chinese guidance may be, of course, a symptom rather than a cause of the alleged failure of Indian communists to develop an indigenous strategy; and to that extent there is an element of circularity in such reasoning.[1] In the present study of one of the two Indian states where communism has established itself as an integral part of the political system, the author has argued that the sources, roots, character, and course of the movement are primarily regional. On two occasions it may be contended that the Kerala communists responded to explicit foreign guidance: the swift implementation of the peaceful transition line with the formation of the 1957 ministry and in the CPI's collaboration with New or Ruling Congress from 1969 to 1979. Neither case is clear cut. In the former the Kerala unit of the CPI was prepared to govern at provincial level as early as 1953, either alone or in partnership with other left-wing parties. In the latter there is something to be said for the view that the alliance with Congress was the Kerala party's only chance of survival as a significant entity and for the reasoning of the CPI Chief Minister, Achutha Menon, that the common people could not afford to wait for a textbook revolution. The post-1964 CPI, however, is not the dominant communist party in Kerala as measured by the strength of the mass movement, whether expressed through the ballot box or on the streets. The state unit of the CPM, guided ideologically by E.M.S. Namboodiripad, has certainly been independent of external communist direction.

Franda has argued that in West Bengal communism is intimately related to the decline of Bengal and to the Bengali search for a new regional identity and political power.[2] Though Malayali communism is also connected with a sub-national search for identity, the appeals of communism have been strong for several other reasons: the break up of the joint family system, the intensity of caste discrimination, the agrarian situation, the scale and character of traditional industry, and the diffuse effects of high levels of education. Congress was weak: in the northern part of the state because of the

366

identification of the older generation with the *kanomdars* and Congress's failure to meet the ideological or organizational challenge of the Congress Socialists; in the south because of caste and communalism and Sir C.P. Ramaswami Aiyar's obdurate refusal to grant responsible government. The 'freedom struggle' in its conventional sense was secondary to the agrarian struggle in Malabar and to the struggle for responsible government in Travancore and Cochin. By 1940 the communist movement had taken root in several parts of Kerala. The party's immersion in the popular movements of the region enabled it to survive isolation from the mainstream of national political life in the 1940s better than units in most other provinces. Thereafter during the 1950s the communist party was well placed to capitalize on popular disenchantment with the provincial Congress and the PSP, to harness the *Aikya Kerala* movement, and to offer the promise of a government earnestly committed to a minimum programme of a Congress Socialist character. In the process it was to create a distinctive 'Kerala Communism' committed to both representative democracy and active socialism and adapted to the peculiar structures of Malayali society and culture: not an Asian analogue of Eurocommunism but a unique synthesis of popular mobilization through the ballot box and the *bandh* to use semi-autonomous government as an instrument of struggle in social and economic reconstruction.[3]

Contingent factors such as the creation of the state of Kerala and shifting communal loyalties may have made the communist victory certain in 1957 but District Board elections in Malabar and Assembly elections in Travancore-Cochin in 1954 show that the communist party had already marshalled the poor to its side—the majority of the Hindu community and minorities of the Muslim and Christian communities. It had also won over a significant following among the high-caste Hindus. Class position was, of course, closely linked to caste and community at the time; and inter-communal rivalries— chiefly among the gentry and bourgeoisie or the rising élite of the major backward community, the Ezhavas—had featured prominently in the politics of twentieth century Travancore and Cochin. However, the communist party by no means articulated communal interests *per se*. Inevitably the CPI sometimes found itself entramelled by the demands of its Ezhava following but its leadership was predominantly high caste and its policies and propaganda entirely secular. It is true that the cadre like its followers was overwhelmingly Hindu but this was more a function of the ideological and social control of the Church and the Mosque over their sections of the population than any derogation from the concept of class mobilization. Community remains a factor in political calculations. That it is no longer the dominant consideration in any commentator's view is in part a result of the efforts of the 1957-9 government. The communist parties have also contributed to the modification of the basis of patron-client relationships in the direction of specifically political bondings as well as to their diminution in importance as a linkage between élites and citizenry.

Except for a small group of communist revolutionaries and Naxalites, all communists have accepted the inevitability, and indeed in most cases the propriety of electoral politics. In this respect Kerala contrasts with West Bengal where electoralism has commanded variable degrees of support within the communist movement. The dominant tradition of Malayali communism, after as well as before the split, has been centrist in the sense that the seeking and exercise of power at local and state levels has been seen as an important instrument of struggle. Among the factors which explain this are the pressures arising from the parties' grass roots; the democratic predilections of the Nair and Namboodiri leaders who shaped the movement's traditions in the state; the absence of viable alternatives; the weakness of (and divisions within) the rival Congress movement; and indeed the tangible progress made through the exercise of political power. Electoralism has not, however, been divorced from other forms of struggle though at times there have been strains. Office is a doubly frustrating experience: high expectations are even less capable of satisfaction than in some other open political systems, for in two respects Kerala is not master in its own house—because of relative subordination to Delhi and the sheer scale and intensity of its socio-economic problems; and office necessarily entails some subordination of agitation to ministerialism as a result of the differentiation of roles in opposition and government. (Successful revolutionaries are no strangers to this dilemma.) Further the remarkable levels of basic literacy and the universality of press readership in a context of group pluralism ensure that the smallest failing is magnified.

Three times the dominant centrist line of the Kerala movement has been exposed to serious criticism: in 1958 from the organizational 'radicals'; in 1967-8 from the disenchanted ultras within the State Council of the CPM; and in 1974 at the time of the CPM boycott of the assembly when there was, according to well-informed party and non-party sources the possibility that the leadership might itself reject constitutionalism.[4] In the event the Emergency supervened. This and subsequent developments at the All-India level have led the CPM to reaffirm its Centrism first because of a heightened awareness of the painful consequences of a reactionary or communal backlash and second because of a feeling that India's electoral volatility offers opportunities for an opening to the left.

While there is no reason to doubt the communist legislators's general ideological beliefs, in a provincial assembly like that of Kerala 'parliamentary work' is difficult to subsume under such theoretical heads as the struggle between 'bourgeois state power' and 'proletarian hegemony'. The major debates are concerned primarily with questions of priorities within a minimum 'practical' programme that is common to both government and opposition in the state, and with issues of maladministration, inefficiency, and corruption. Calling Attention motions and Question Hour are used as they would be in any legislative body to raise particular matters of sectional or local concern. Second readings of bills are debated in general terms but not in specifically marxist ones. In fact the three overriding impressions left by a perusal of the proceedings of the Assembly are the serious attention to the practicalities of change, the ordinary backbencher's desire to call the government to account, and his wish to let his constituents know that he is looking after their special interests. In Assembly committees MLAs of all parties have shown considerable capacity to take up issues raised by the Accountant General's audit and established a role as a scourge of the administration. Early in 1980 the Assembly decided (echoing developments in the UK parliament) to introduce 'shadow' committees to monitor the work of individual government departments. Out of the House and into the corridors of power in the Secretariat, the CPM and CPI MLAs, no less than others, seek the thousand and one favours and considerations—transfers, jobs, promotions— which strengthen their respective parties' power base. Class enemies and political opponents are as readily approached as friends and comrades within a community of little more than 130 'political and social workers' who share a common culture.[5] However, the communist parties are not immune from the combined effects of selective recruitment to legislative positions and parliamentary socialization. A Harijan CPM MLA explained his past refusal to accept the 'boon from the party' of a safe seat in the Assembly in terms of his fear that, like others before him, he would 'lose the affection of the common man.'[6] None the less Kerala's politicians are remarkably accessible, committing two or three hours a day to seeing a stream of callers, often without appointment, on matters grave or trivial. No political figure could survive in Kerala—or India for that matter— without this contact.

The Kerala communist movement has more readily accepted the united front as a premise of communist advance in India and more whole-heartedly sought to implement it over the years than the CPI and CPM in other states. Both in Kerala have been pragmatic in their choice of allies, including the mutual alliance of 1967. The CPI manoeuvred an unenthusiastic KPCC into a ruling front under its own Chief Ministership, so establishing a precedent of Congress-CPI collaboration in line with the aim of 'national democracy'. The CPM has not always been so successful. Its courtship of the Muslim League between 1967 and 1969 came to naught and enabled the CPI to break up the UF and form the first of the CPI-led ministries that were to erode CPM hegemony. However, Namboodiripad's tactics of exploiting differences within other parties and his steadfast attempt to construct alliances on the principle of isolating the main enemy ultimately created the electorally strong and comparatively homogeneous Left Democratic Front of 1980. On the other hand it is clear that even without the complicating factor of the Emergency the CPI has not been able to capitalize on its tactical successes in terms of popular support. Its membership has grown,[7] as have party funds, but there is little evidence that it has expanded its mass support base. The CPM, however, has more or less maintained its individual electoral support.

The achievement of ministerial stability within the framework of a front of parties owes much to the innovation of the co-ordination committee initiated by Namboodiripad, and more firmly established by Achutha Menon, a device which assists cohesion within parties as well as between them and circumvents the problem of how to co-ordinate united front policy and action without a joint legislative party.

Despite some of the more extravagant utterances of CPM ultras between 1967 and 1969, it is clear that the CPM no less than the CPI was—and is—prepared to use the existing constitutional machinery to bring about socio-economic change. The three most senior leaders of the CPM, E.M.S. Namboodiripad, A.K. Gopalan, and Mrs Gouri, differed from their equivalents in the CPI, Achutha Menon, Govindan Nair, and T.V. Thomas more in emphasis than substance: the former were pessimistic; the latter were optimistic. In practice the CPM has taken its ministerial and parliamentary responsibilities no less seriously than the CPI, and its criticisms of the record of the Mini and Maxi fronts were reasoned and by no means unjustified. Further, though the CPI-led ministries habitually sought to represent the CPM as a factious and irresponsible opposition, the CPM on occasion in the public interest withdrew agitations (for example in the Kuttanad) or gave the government (for example over land reform) the benefit of its expertise.

In government the record of the united CPI and its successor parties was a mixed one. At state level the scope for legislative initiative to restructure basic social relations is limited. Land reform is unquestionably the movement's most solid achievement even though its impact has been diminished by the time span involved in enacting a definitive measure and by the slow pace of implementation under the Mini and Maxi fronts. Successive communist or communist-led administrations have not, however, accomplished the decentralization of decision-making and executive control implicit in *panchayati raj*. Given that successive ministries habitually postponed new elections to the bodies established in 1963—finally held in 1979—it is reasonable to infer that the CPM and the CPI are as lukewarm as other parties on the subject of 'more power to the people'. One final area of significance is education. In Kerala the dominance of community-run colleges and schools presents a unique problem. The 1957-9 ministry's efforts to bring the private managements under some measure of supervision contributed to its downfall. Communist-led ministries have since proceeded more cautiously but without a great deal of success. The Kerala University Bill, 1967, which became law on 21 January 1969, tackled only some of the issues and in any case a number of its provisions were subsequently struck down in the courts as abusing the rights of minority communities under the constitution. Despite the Kerala University Bill, 1972, which became law in April 1974, government has generally failed to subject the private colleges to effective supervision.

At the executive level communist ministers have varied considerably in their efficiency, and, it is alleged, in their integrity. Two conclusions may, however, be drawn: first, communist and communist-led ministries have taken up many schemes—often, it could be argued, too many; but second the overall quality of communist administration has not been significantly different from that of non-communist administration. In part this is a function of the common constraints and pressures under which all ministers operate, in part of the nature of the administrative machine itself, and in part of the shared background, experience, and culture of communist and non-communist élites. None the less only a few communist ministers have earned a reputation inside or outside the Secretariat for drive, effectiveness, and incorruptibility.

Probably the most lasting contribution made by the communist movement in Kerala is its politicization and mobilization of the propertyless and underprivileged. The 1957-9 government in particular did much to liberate the poor and free the society from the tyranny of caste and communalism. The subsequent fragmentation of the political system has inhibited the development of the true class consciousness implicit in the concept of the united front from below. Despite and because of the competition between the different parties seeking to organize the agricultural and industrial workforces substantial gains have been made. At the same time it must be conceded that the chief beneficiaries of communist rule have been the peasants (in part by design) not the labourers and (unintentionally) the government employees not the workers in the traditional cottage industry sector such as coir, whose condition has changed little since 1945.

At the All-India level the pro-peasant bias of the CPM is evident in its agrarian resolutions, which have been centrally concerned with the abolition of landlordism.[8] The party has used a patently unreal criterion to distinguish 'landlord' from 'rich peasant'—the former relying wholly on wage labour while the latter performs (some) manual labour himself. The definitional problem is particularly clear in Kerala, where, according to one study, one-third of peasants with holdings of only 1.25 to 2.5 acres employ wage labour.[9] The CPM's anxiety to draw rich peasants and *a fortiori* 'middle peasants' into the struggle is in its own view a reflection of the very class origins of the party's *kisan* activists. Inevitably once landlordism is abolished and tenants emancipated, as in Kerala, the 'contradictions' which flow from the conflict between labour's demands for higher wages and the peasants' reluctance to concede them become obvious. Further, the peasants join in the demands of commercial farmers for 'fair prices'. In the Indian context such fair prices invariably strengthen the rich peasant and commercial farmers and work against the interests of the poor. It may be argued then that the CPM's line on agrarian reform is soft towards the interests of rich and middle peasants and inappropriate to the particular circumstances of Kerala. According to Krishnaji the state unit of the CPM, for all its real contribution to the raising of labourer and poor peasant consciousness, has succumbed to political expediency. It is, he argues, the party's attitude towards rich peasants and those landowners who derive much of their income outside agriculture that 'obstructs the growth of the left movement and if unchanged can make the movement progressively less and less proletarian in character.'[10] A similar view is taken by K.N. Raj, who sees the colonization of the left movement by rich peasants and the bureaucratic and commercial middle classes as a serious danger to the evolution of 'a genuinely more broad-based political and economic system'.[11] Some go further and contend that embourgeoisement has proceded apace. 'J.M.', for example, writing in the marxist-leninist *Frontier*, believes that 'one of the major reasons why the Marxists are in trouble in Kerala is that many of the local-level leaders are now landowners . . . . Those who are leaders of the labourers are also employers of labour.'[12] Joan Mencher also sees little hope for the poor of Kerala 'unless and until they develop a new leadership from their own ranks'.[13]

Such informed pessimism commands respect even though the

potential shape of such an alternative left movement or politico-economic system is not indicated. What raises more difficulty, however, is the feasibility of such a class purification in Kerala, where educational aspiration is universal, where educational attainment is tangible among the poor, and where the class struggle itself is increasingly bureaucratized. Such communist leaders as send their own children to private Christian schools and colleges do indeed confer advantages on them in the competition for qualifications and jobs but the children of their followers none the less have opportunity sufficient to legitimize the system. A related stimulus to the deradicalization of all but the very poorest strata has been the availability in recent years of semi-skilled and skilled work in the Gulf. It is not an exaggeration to assert that scarcely a village in the state has been untouched by 'Gulf money' and the refrigerators, cars, houses, and marriage alliances it can buy.

The bureaucratization of the class struggle is implicit in the concept of peaceful transition and is arguably compounded by many features of the social structure and culture of Kerala society. It is still possible to observe a measure of apparently spontaneous action by the poor, though some of its forms in fact undermine class consciousness: in Kerala the theft of sacred objects from rival places of worship; in northeast India the violent agitation by the 'sons of the soil' against migrants hungry for jobs and land; and throughout the country an epidemic of crime involving the degradation of women (hitherto extremely rare) through rape and the theft of personal ornaments—of deep symbolic significance as well as financial value. However, in Kerala it is inevitable that the 'political and social worker' of the future must learn his skills as much in the colleges as at the factory gates—given the complexity of the laws germane to virtually all areas of social conflict, the sophistication of rival tribunes of the people, and the ultimate recourse in practice to government, Assembly, and courts.

One may readily grant that 'bourgeois attitudes' as well as leninist calculation and marxist ideology have played their part in communist practice in Kerala but it is the author's contention that the key figures, particularly E.M.S. Namboodiripad, Achutha Menon, and Mrs Gouri, have been principally guided by what, from a communist perspective, was possible within the system, due account being taken of Kerala traditions and provincial and national constraints. The redistribution of poverty may in some abstract sense be just, but even if such an exercise were politically possible it would clearly be futile, and particularly so in Kerala.

A more serious charge may be that the communist movement—and here the dominant CPM is the first accused—has failed to complement its perennial concern about problems of distribution and welfare with an equivalent and persistent commitment to problems of production, vital both from a humanitarian point of view ('the immediate needs of the people') and from a strategic one when there is intense party competition and no sign of revolutionary change round the corner. The inflow of funds from the Gulf expatriates, approaching £2 million per day, offers a unique opportunity for economic development on the basis of the existing social infrastructure of education, health, and mass mobilization to which communism has contributed much. (There are also individual entrepreneurs, consultants, engineers, and technologists of Malayali origin active in India and the Middle East.) It is true that in the early 1970s—after T.V. Thomas's abortive Industrial Policy during the 1967-9 UF ministry—the CPI-led administrations under Achutha Menon had pushed the development of the Kerala economy to the forefront, but although the record was imaginative in terms of initiatives subsequent performance left much to be desired. The CPM has, however, often taken an indifferent and sometimes even a negative stance on developmental issues. During the 1970s it could fairly claim that its role in opposition was to criticize rather than to initiate; but neither interviews with party leaders nor the contributions of party intellectuals to academic conferences afford grounds for supposing that the CPM was sufficiently seriously addressing itself to a changing agenda for Kerala politics away from the rhetorical platforms of public debate. The ablest figures, Namboodiripad and Mrs Gouri, have been in poor health for some time; the present CPM Chief Minister, E.K. Nayanar, had not in his first six months in office made much mark; while scrutiny of the records of the party's rising generation offers little encouragement in this area. If we note the contrast with the situation in West Bengal where the CPM Chief Minister, Jyoti Basu, has effectively begun the rejuvenation of the economy, it seems possible that the explanation for the CPM's comparative disregard of economic growth in Kerala may lie in the very traditions of Malayali society and culture. It is these same traditions, mediated through communism, socialism, and religious social movements, which have made the state a model for the uplift of the underprivileged through political competition within a democratic framework.

India's problem state has been one of the country's most important political laboratories. In a recent work on India a Fabian socialist concludes that what is needed is the extension to the whole country of the approach of the communist-led Kerala and Congress-led Karnataka governments if India is to achieve social justice and avoid an authoritarian future—almost certainly of the right not the left[14] although Joan Mencher in emphasising the limited gains made by agricultural labourers rightly cautions against over enthusiam for the Kerala 'model'.[15] In the short and medium term at least, the significance of the communist movement in Kerala seems more likely to rest on the export of its socio-political technology to other states in India than on the export of communism as such. (The product may be marketed elsewhere, without regard to the patent rights of the communist multinational.) Short of some unforeseeable and cataclysmic development at the All-India level it is hard to see communism spreading far from its regional bases in Kerala and West Bengal precisely because its roots are, and are perceived by the rest of India to be, distinctively Malayali and Bengali respectively. The communist movements of these two states are, despite their best endeavours, seen more as being analogous to such regional parties as the DMK and its successors of Tamil Nadu and the Akali Dal of the Punjab than as national parties with a class-based appeal and potential.

The volatile course of events in India as a whole since the 'JP Movement' of 1973-4—the Emergency, the Janata victory, the disintegration of the Janata government and party, Mrs Gandhi's sweeping return to power in January 1980, the death of her son Sanjay Gandhi, widely predicted as her successor—is leading to modifications in communist positions. The CPI and CPM have responded by forging some measure of agreement on common political action. This new-found amity has been helped on the CPI side by reappraisal of the party's support for the Emergency, the resignation of S.A. Dange as party chairman, and his subsequent expulsion; and fostered on the CPM side by growing concern over the party's sluggish growth,[16] fears as to the consequences of Mrs Gandhi's return to power, and an improvement in the CPM's relationship with the CPSU.

The resultant left and democratic front has paid dividends for both parties, greater, as measured by the Lok Sabha and Kerala Assembly polls, for the CPM than the CPI. Some commentators have discerned signs of important ideological innovation in this but such claims seem premature.[17] No significant initiatives have yet emerged from the CPI, which in any case is still recovering from a period of serious inner party conflict. The CPM is clearly dominated by Centrism.[18] Namboodiripad, probably the Indian communist movement's most original mind, became the party's general secretary in 1978 in succession to P. Sundarayya, who had found himself increasingly out of touch with party thinking. E.K. Nayanar, state secretary of the CPM in Kerala from 1971 and from January 1980 to October 1981 Chief Minister, appears committed—like Jyoti Basu in West

Bengal—to the political line historically associated with Namboodiripad: co-operation with left and democratic parties on minimum programmes and the constant reiteration of the important theme of states' autonomy vis-a-vis Delhi. Conceivably, of course, the states' rights movement could become the equivalent in federal politics of the united front in state politics but such a development appears increasingly remote with the growth of chauvinist, separatist and minority forces.

While this book was in the press, in October 1981 the LDF Ministry fell as a result of defections by anti-Indira Congress parties. On 28 December 1981 a Congress (I)-led coalition took office. Since its survival depends on the Speaker of the Assembly's casting vote, a mid-term election seems imminent, but whatever the outcome of the polls — dependent as much on bargaining over alliances as on the appeal to the poor of the LDF'S pro-labour policies—the place of the CPM in any democratic political system in Kerala is secure, just as it is in West Bengal. What, however, the communist movement has not been able to achieve is any real breakthrough into the Hindi heartland of India where it is the Bharatya Janata Party, with its aggressive and disciplined Hindu chauvinist RSS cadre, which is making strides as the alternative to Indira Congressism. It is difficult to be sanguine about the prospects for the Left in India.

Notes

1 Franda, *Radical Politics in West Bengal,* p. 242.
2 Ibid., pp. 7-20 and 268.
3 B.T. Ranadive, 'Carrillo's "Eurocommunism and the State"', *Social Scientist* (Tvm) 75 (1978); Bhupesh Gupta, 'Communists in Parliament', *World Marxist Rev.* 21 (9), 1978.
4 Interviews, Mrs K.R. Gouri, Tvm, Nov. 1974; public official, Tvm, Nov. 1974 and Nov. 1977.
5 'Political and social worker' is the commonest self-description of full-time politicians and party workers, irrespective of party. Of those 95 MLAs reporting a specific occupation in 1971, the largest group was lawyers (24) followed by agriculturalists (22). Lawyers, teachers, and journalists combined, made up 58 of the number. Businessmen (4) and industrial workers (2) were rare. Kerala Legislative Assembly, *Who's Who 1971* (1972)
6 Interview data kindly supplied by Professor R. Ramakrishnan Nair, U. of Kerala.

7   In part this may well be a function of its 'liberalised policy' of recruitment. In Kerala the CPI membership is reported as 65,346. M.H.J.,
'Party Matters', *Economic and Political Weekly*, 24 Nov. 1979.
8   N. Krishnaj, 'Agrarian Relations and the Left Movement in Kerala:
a Note on Recent Trends', *Economic and Political Weekly*, 3 Mar. 1979,
pp. 518-19.
9   Data from *The Third Decennial World Agricultural Census 1970-1* (report
for Kerala Bureau of Economics and Statistics), quoted by Krishnaji, as
preceding note, p. 519.
10 Krishnaji, p. 520.
11 K.N. Raj, *The Politics and Economics of 'Intermediate Regimes'* (Bombay,
Orient Longman for Gokhale Inst. of Politics and Economics [? 1973]).
12 'The Left in Kerala', 30 Sept. 1978.
13 'The Lessons and Non-Lessons of Kerala: Agricultural Labourers and
Poverty', *Economic and Political Weekly*, Special no. Oct. 1980.
14 David Taylor, *India: the Politics of Change* (London, Fabian Society,
1980, Research Series 345), p. 23.
15 As note 12 above.
16 *Hindu*, 2 Dec. 1979.
17 Gautam Adhikari, 'Towards a National Alternative', ibid., 20 Jan.
1979. See also K.K. Katyal, 'Towards Communist Reconciliation',
ibid., 10 Apr. 1978; Ajit Roy, 'Blinkered by Parliamentarism', *Economic
and Political Weekly*, 18 Aug. 1979; Darryl D'Monte, 'CPM Comes into
Its Own', *IE*, 25 Jan. 1980; and Conrad Wood, 'India—Rethinking the
Alternative', *Morning Star* (London), 26 July 1978. Bhupesh Gupta,
'Communists in Parliament', *World Marxist Rev.* 21(9) 1978 is an
orthodox statement of the CPI's view of work on the parliamentary
front which hints at change (p. 50).
18 The CPM's objective as restated in the Draft Political Resolution for the
January 1982 Eleventh Congress is firmly set 'in the context of the immediate situation, with the authoritarian challenge as the main danger'.
Although 'the Party does not forget its revolutionary objective'...'in the
present struggle'...'for the building of the Left and Democratic Front [the
CPM aims] by popularising its programme [among] all bourgeois parties,
by changing the correlation of political forces through broader mobilisation
and, above all, by leading mass struggles [to] bring into the arena precisely
those classes that must take a prominent part in building the People's
Democratic Front' which presages 'a People's Democratic Revolution to
open the way to Socialism'. *Draft Political Resolution for Eleventh Congress of
the Communist Party of India [Marxist] (January, 1982)*, (New Delhi, Central
Committee of the Communist Party of India, Marxist, 25 November
1981), p.70.

Appendices

Appendix 1: Assembly Elections 1951–1980

TRAVANCORE-COCHIN
  10 Dec. 1951—5 Jan. 1952   15–26 Feb. 1954

KERALA (created 1 Nov. 1956)
  28 Feb.-11 Mar. 1957   17 Sept. 1970
  1 Feb. 1960   19 Mar. 1977
  4 Mar. 1965   21 Jan. 1980
  20 Feb. 1967

Appendix 2: Governments 1949–1980

(Short periods when no government apparently exists are explained by the difference between the date on which a Chief Minister's resignation is accepted and the point at which it takes effect, i.e. on the formation of a new government.)

TRAVANCORE—COCHIN

1	T.K. Narayana Pillai (Congress) (Congress)	1 July 1949 — 26 Jan. 1950
2	T.K. Narayana Pillai (Congress) (Congress)	26 Jan. 1950 — 3 Mar. 1951
3	C. Kesavan (Congress) (Congress)	3 Mar. 1951 — 6 Sept. 1951
4	C. Kesavan (Congress) (Congress)	6 Sept. 1951 — 12 Mar. 1952
5	A.J. John (Congress) (Congress)	12 Mar. 1952 — 16 Mar. 1954
6	Pattom Thanu Pillai (PSP) (PSP)	16 Mar. 1954 — 14 Feb. 1955

7 P. Govinda Menon (Congress)   14 Feb. 1955 — 23 Mar. 1956
   (Congress)
8 President's Rule   23 Mar. 1956 — 5 Apr. 1957

KERALA (created 1 Nov. 1956)

1 E.M.S. Namboodiripad (CPI)   5 Apr. 1957 — 31 July 1959
   (CPI with Independents)
2 President's Rule   1 Aug. 1959 — 22 Feb. 1960
3 Pattom Thanu Pillai (PSP)   22 Feb. 1960 — 26 Sept. 1962
   (Congress-PSP)
4 R. Sankar (Congress)   26 Sept. 1962 — 10 Sept. 1964
   (Congress-PSP)
5 President's Rule   10 Sept. 1964 — 6 Mar. 1967
6 E.M.S. Namboodiripad (CPM)   6 Mar. 1967 — 24 Oct. 1969
   (United Front: CPM, CPI, SSP, ML,
   RSP, KTP, KSP)
7 C. Achutha Menon (CPI)   1 Nov. 1969 — 1 Aug. 1970
   (Mini Front: CPI, ML, KC, ISP)
8 President's Rule   4 Aug. 1970 — 4 Oct. 1970
9 C. Achutha Menon (CPI)   4 Oct. 1970 — 25 Sept. 1971
   (Mini Front: CPI, ML, RSP, PSP)
10 C. Achutha Menon (CPI)   25 Sept. 1971 — 22 Mar. 1977
   (Maxi Front: New Congress, CPI, ML,
   RSP, PSP; on 26 Dec. 1975 KC joined
   the ministry)
11 K. Karunakaran (Congress)   25 Mar. 1977 — 25 Apr. 1977
   (Ruling Front: Congress, CPI,
   KC, ML, RSP)
12 A.K. Antony (Congress)   27 Apr. 1977 — 27 Oct. 1978
   (Ruling Front: Congress,
   CPI, KC, ML, RSP)
13 P.K. Vasudevan Nair (CPI)   29 Oct. 1978—7 Oct. 1979
   (Ruling Front: Congress, CPI, KC,
   ML, RSP)
14 C.H. Mohammed Koya (IUML)   12 Oct. 1979 — 1 Dec. 1979
   (IUML, NDP, PSP)
15 President's Rule   5 Dec. 1979 — 24 Jan. 1980
16 E.K. Nayanar (CPM)   24 Jan. 1980 — 26 Oct. 1981
   (Left Democratic Front: CPM,
   Congress U, CPI, KCM, RSP, AIML)

Appendix 3: Biographical Notes

The party affiliation given in brackets immediately after a name is that applicable at the time of going to press.

Antony, A.K. (Congress (U)) 1940- . Graduated 1963; BL 1965; active in student and labour movements; pres. KSU and Kerala Pradesh YC and gen. sec. KPCC; later pres. KPCC; MLA 1970; Ruling Congress Chief Minister 1977-8; subsequently aligned with Congress (Urs) and pres. KPCC (U).

Balaram, N.E. (CPI) 1919- . Ed. to 8th Standard; teacher; worked in Ramakrishna Mission before entry into politics as INC activist 1934; CSP 1936; CPI 1939; various arrests; underground 1947-52; MLA 1957, 1960; Industries Minister 1970-1; many party posts, including sec. CPI State Council; *kisan* and trade union worker; author.

Bava, E.K. Imbichi (CPM) 1917-, . B. poor Moplah family, Malappuram Dist. No formal ed. INC 1936; sec. Kerala Students' Federation 1939; CSP; CPI 1940; various arrests early 1940s, including during Quit India movement. Rajya Sabha 1952-4; MLA 1957; MP 1962; CPM Minister of Transport 1967-9.

Chacko, P.T. (INC) 1915-64. Catholic from Kottayam Dist; BA, BL; TSC 1938; various arrests; advocate Travancore High Court 1941; pres. Catholic Youth Congress; MLA Travancore 1948 and Congress Chief Whip 1948; Mem. Indian Constituent Assembly 1949; MP 1952-3; MLA 1957-64; Home Minister 1960-4.

Divakaran, T.K. (RSP) 1920-76. B. Quilon Dist; Secondary School Leaving Certificate; TSC; active in trade unions Quilon; various arrests including 1940, 1945, 1946 & 1949; founder member KSP; RSP 1947; MLA Travancore-Cochin & Deputy Leader of Opposition 1952; Chairman Estimates Cttee Travancore-Cochin Assembly; pres. Kerala unit UTUC; RSP Minister of Works 1967-9; Leader of House, KLA, 1969-70.

George, K.C. (CPI) 1903- MA, LLB (Lucknow); sec. All-Travancore Youth League; mem. TSC and KPCC in 1930s; various arrests; CPI 1940; MLA 1957; Food Minister 1957-9; party intellectual and organizer.

George, K.M. (KC) 1919-76. BL. INC 1941; editor *Deepika* 1945-8; gen. sec. KPCC 1953-5; MLA Travancore-Cochin 1954; MLA 1957-76; founder chairman KC 1964; Minister of Transport & Health 1969-70; briefly Transport Minister in 1976.

Gopalan, A.K. (CPM) 1904-77. B. prestigious Nambiar family, Cannanore; ed. Mission High School and Brennan Coll., Tellicherry; teacher; INC 1927; CSP 1934; mem. AICC; pres. & sec. KPCC; CPI 1940; MP 1952-77; many arrests; pres. *All-India Kisan Sabha;* CPM PB; ill health in later years.

Gouri (Gowri), K.R. (CPM) 1919- .B. Shertallai, Alleppey Dist; BL. Lawyer; active in trade union and peasant work; pres. *Kerala Karshaka* (peasant)*Sangham*; MLA Travancore–Cochin 1952 & 1954; MLA 1952-77 & 1980; Revenue Minister 1957-9 & 1967-9; Agriculture Minister 1980-1. One of few women prominent in Kerala politics; married T.V. Thomas (*q.v*).

John, Baby (RSP) 1922- . BA; TSC 1938; Congress 1939-48; founder member of KSP and then RSP in Kerala; active trade union worker; excommunicated from Catholic Church for political activities; MLA Travancore–Cochin 1952 & 1954; KLA 1960, 1967-; gen. sec. Kerala unit UTUC; Revenue Minister 1971-9 and Education Minister 1980-1 .

Karunakaran, K. (Congress-Indira) 1918- . Student and trade union activist; founder member Kerala unit of INTUC; member Indian delegation to International Labour Office 1957; member Trichur municipality 1945-7; MLA Cochin 1948-9 and Travancore–Cochin 1952 & 1954; MLA 1965-; leader Congress Legislature Party 1967-70; Chairman PAC 1968-9 & 1969-70; mem. Congress Working Cttee 1969; Home Minister 1971-7; Chief Minister for three weeks 1977 until resigned as result of allegations arising from the death of a student during the Emergency; supporter of Mrs Gandhi's wing of Congress. Leader of Opposition, KLA 1980-1 .

Kesavan, C. (INC) 1891-1969. B. Ezhava family nr Quilon; BA, BL; active in Abstention movement and sec. SNDP; sec. JPC and a founder of TSC; various arrests; Minister in first Travancore government 1948; pres. KPCC; Chief Minister Travancore–Cochin 1951-2.

Koya, C.H. Mohammed (IUML) 1928- . B. nr Calicut; ed. to Intermediate Standard; journalist; chief editor *Chandrika;* one of founders of Malabar Students' Federation; Municipal Councillor, Calicut 1952-9; gen. sec. Kerala State ML 1955-67; MLA 1957-62 & 1967-73 & 1977- ; MP 1962-7 & 1973-7; Education Minister 1967-9; Education & Home Minister 1969-70; Home Minister 1970-1; Education Minister 1971-3 & 1977-9; Chief Min. 1979.

Kunju. P.K. (ISP) 1906 or 1908- . B. Alleppey Dist, Muslim family; ed. to Intermediate level. Chief Whip of Samyuktha Party (1937) and of TSC (1938) in Srimulam Assembly of Travancore; resigned from Congress in 1940; jt sec. Kerala State ML; pres. Travancore–Cochin ML 1952; joined PSP 1953; PSP Minister of Labour Travancore–Cochin 1954; MLA 1960; SSP (and then ISP) Finance Minister 1967-9 until resignation to face judicial inquiry.

Mani, K.M. (KC-M) 1933- . Graduated 1953 & in law 1955; practising lawyer; entered politics as active mem. of INC; mem. KPCC; founder mem. KC. MLA 1967- ; Finance Minister 1975-7; Home Minister 1977-9 & Finance Minister 1980-1 .

Menon, C. Achutha (CPI) 1913- . B. Trichur; BA, BL; distinguished academic career culminating in gold medal for Hindu Law at Madras U.; set up legal practice Trichur but turned to politics 1936-7; sec. Cochin Dist. Congress Cttee and mem. KPCC; joined CPI 1942 after considering becoming a Christian; various arrests; underground 1948-52; MLA Travancore–

Cochin 1952; KLA 1957; Finance Minister 1957-9; Chief Minister 1970-7 when retired from active politics; many party posts; a film enthusiast.

Nair, M.N. Govindan (CPI) 1910- . B. Pandalam, Alleppey Dist, into well-known Nair family; BA; teacher; NSS and Harijan uplift worker; spent a year in Gandhi's ashram at Warda; TSC; said to have organized anti-Japanese activities in 1940; CPI 1940; prominent trade unionist around Quilon; MLA Travancore-Cochin1952-4; *Rajya Sabha* 1962-7; KLA 1967 & 1970; MP 1977; Minister for Agriculture and Electricity 1967-9 & 1971-7; leading party organizer; party secretary Kerala 1957.

Nair, N. Sreekantan (RSP) 1915- . MA; INC 1936; gen sec. All-Travancore Youth League 1937; TSC 1938; Coir Factory Worker Union strike, Alleppey, 1938; All-Travancore Congress Cttee 1939; TSC working cttee 1942-6; various arrests; member KPCC 1945; resigned from TSC working cttee over nationalization of education 1946; CSP 1946; organized KSP 1947; RSP 1948; MP 1952, 1962, 1967, 1971; prominent trade unionist.

Nair, P.K. Vasudevan (CPI) 1926- . Law graduate; student and youth politics; pres. All-India Students' Federation & All-India Youth Federation; CPI 1942; member CPI CEC; MP 1957, 1962 & 1967; KLA 1977; Industries Minister 1977-8; Chief Minister 1978-9.

Namboodiripad, E.M. Sankaran (CPM) 1909- . Gave up BA studies at St Thomas College, Trichur, to join Civil Disobedience Movement; founder member CSP in Kerala 1934; sec. KPCC 1934 & 1938-40; elected Madras Legislative Assembly 1939; founder member CPI in Kerala; member Central Secretariat CPI from 1941; PB CPI from 1950; acting gen. sec. June-Dec. 1953, July-Dec. 1954 & 1955-6; MLA 1957-9; Chief Minister 1957-9 & 1967-9; gen. sec. CPI 1962-3; various terms of imprisonment from 1933 to 1966; CPM's leading theoretician. CPM gen. sec.

Nayanar, E.K. (CPM) 1920- . B. Cannanore Dist; primary ed.; became full-time communist worker in his teens; one of chief accused in the Kayyur incident 1942 but went underground; MP 1967; elected MLA in a by-election; after death of C.H. Kanaran, elected sec. of State Cttee of CPM; chief editor CPM organ, *Deshabhimani*; MLA 1980 and Chief Minister 1980-1 .

Pillai, Mannath Padmanabhan (INC) 1878-1970. Began as teacher 1894, later qualifying in law and setting up practice; active in Harijan uplift; organized the NSS 1914 and gen. sec. for 31 years; prominent in Vaikom *Satyagraha* 1924 and Guruvayur Temple Entry *Satyagraha* 1931; TSC 1938; leading figure in Liberation Struggle and important force in Kerala politics 1960-5; most remembered for contribution to social reform, education, and Nair community.

Pillai, A. Pattom Thanu (PSP) 1885-1970. BA. Worked as chemist in Travancore Dept of Agriculture but resigned to become a teacher; BL 1914; practised as lawyer in Trivandrum; elected to Srimulam Assembly of

Travancore 1927 and represented Trivandrum constituencies for next 35 years; most prominent leader of TSC, and its pres. 1938–48; Chief Minister Travancore (Congress) 1948, of Travancore-Cochin (PSP) 1954, of Kerala (PSP) 1960; Governor of Punjab 1962, later of Andhra Pradesh.

Pillai, P. Krishna (CPI) 1906-48. B. Vaikom, Kottayam Dist; studied to Fifth Standard; later taught Hindi; gave up teaching to participate in 1930 salt *satyagraha* at Calicut; sec. CSP 1934; founder of Kerala communist movement; died from snake-bite while underground.

Raghavan, Azhikodan (CPM) 1920-72. INC 1937; labour movement in Malabar 1939; imprisoned 1945 for speech made during railway strike; CPM organizer; assassinated Trichur, 23 Sept. 1972.

Sankar, R. (INC) 1909-72. BA 1928; headmaster; BL 1937; practised as lawyer at Quilon; TSC 1938; various arrests; gen. sec. TSC 1940–4; gen. sec. SNDP *yogam* 1944–54; MLA Travancore 1948; Mem. Indian Constituent Assembly 1949; pres. KPCC 1959 and leading figure in Liberation Struggle; Deputy Chief Minister Kerala 1960; Chief Minister 1962; vehement anticommunist.

Thomas, T.V. (CPI) 1910-77. B. into Thaiparambil family, Factory Ward, Alleppey; BA, BL; started practice as lawyer at Alleppey; TSC 1939 and formed Radical Group within TSC 1939; active trade union front; pres. All-Travancore Trade Union Congress, Estate Workers' Union and Coir Factory Workers' Union, Alleppey, 1939; various imprisonments including one as result of involvement in Punnapra-Vayalar Rising; MLA Travancore-Cochin 1952 & 1954; MLA 1957 & 1967-77; Minister for Labour and Transport 1957-9; Industries Minister 1967-9 & 1970-7; married K.R. Gouri (*q.v.*).

Appendix 4: Glossary

Abkari Government revenue from the sale of liquor, drugs, etc.
Aikya Kerala United Kerala
Bandh A form of strike action
Cent One-hundredth of an acre
Chitties (Kuries) An indigenous savings and credit system prevalent in Kerala
Crore Unit of 10 million
Devaswom Lit. belonging to the deity; pertaining to the Hindu temple
Dewan Chief Minister of a princely state
Gherao Lit. encirclement; the coercion of an individual by surrounding him/her, usually accompanied by the chanting of slogans but without the use of actual physical violence
Goonda A ruffian, usually with reference to one hired by a person or party to intimidate or molest rivals.

Hartal A form of strike action

Illam A palace, usually the ancestral home of a lineage of Namboodiri Brahmins

Jatha A political procession

Jenmi (janmi) Hereditary owner of land in Kerala

Kanomdar (kanumdar) In the Malabar system of land tenure an intermediary who leased land from the hereditary owner and in turn sub-leased all or part of it to tenants-at-will

Karanavar The eldest male member of a Hindu joint-family unit in Kerala, who managed the property and affairs of the family

Kayal Low-lying land reclaimed from the Vembanad Lake in the Kuttanad area of Alleppey and Kottayam Districts; paddy land in this region

Kayal Raja A wealthy farmer cultivating *kayals* in the Kuttanad

Khadi White, hand-loom cloth associated with Gandhi; the customary dress of Congressmen

Khilafat The office of the Khalifa, the Caliphate; in India, the movement to restore the Caliph (1919-21)

Kisan North Indian word for peasant, also used in the south

Kudikidappukar A hutment dweller; a squatter on another's land

Kuzhikanomdar A tenant who leased land, either waste or in need of improvement, in exchange for making improvements

Lakh Unit of 100,000

Lathi A bamboo stick some six feet in length used by Indian police in riot and crowd control

Moplah (Mappila) Muslim from Malabar

Muthalalee Rich man or fig. 'boss'

Mylapore A suburb of Madras City which gave its name to an influential connection of Madras politicians and dignitaries in the late nineteenth and early twentieth centuries

Panchayat Orig. a caste or village council of five wise men. Now the bottom tier of rural local government. A panchayat is composed of a small number of villages

Pradesh Province or state

Praja Tenant; subject

Ryot Cultivator or farmer

Ryotwari Land revenue system under which assessments are made on individual landholdings

Sambandham The alliance of a Namboodiri Brahmin and a Nair woman; sometimes translated as 'an arrangement for sleeping in the night.'

Sangham An association or society

Sarvodaya A Gandhian social service movement

Satyagraha Lit. truth- or soul-force. The Gandhian technique of passive resistance or non-cooperation; the application of moral pressure for political objectives

Shahīd A witness or martyr

Sanyasi A Hindu holy man who has renounced his worldly possessions and
family

Sircar (sirkar) The court or palace of a native ruler; the state or government

Sudra The bottom caste (service) in the four-fold Hindu caste system

Taluk A revenue sub-division of a district; a local administrative unit

Tarawad The joint family in the matrilineal systems of Kerala

Thampuran A general term for lord or master

Thangal (Tangal) Lit. 'They'. An honorific applied in the Moplah community to those claiming descent from the Prophet Muhammad

Toddy A country liquor fermented from the sap of the coconut palm

Vakil An agent, legal representative, or lawyer

Verumpattomdar A tenant-at-will

Yogam A religious association

Zamindar A landholder paying permanently settled revenue directly to the
government; a landlord

Appendix 5: General Abbreviations

AICC	All-India Congress Committee
AIML	All-India Muslim League
AITUC	All-India Trade Union Congress
CEC	Central Executive Committee
Commn	Commission
Congress (I)	Congress (Indira)
Congress (U)	Congress (Urs)
C.P.	Sir C.P. Ramaswami Aiyar
CPA	Committee on Public Accounts
CPC	Chinese Communist Party
CPI	Communist Party of India
CPM	Communist Party of India (Marxist)
CPSU	Communist Party of the Soviet Union
CPU	Committee on Public Undertakings
CSP	Congress Socialist Party
Cttee	Committee
DF	Democratic Front
DMK	Dravida Munnetra Kazhagam
FACT	Fertilisers and Chemicals of Travancore, Ltd.
Hist.	Historical
IAS	Indian Administrative Service
ICS	Indian Civil Service
INC	Indian National Congress

Inst.	Institute
INTUC	Indian National Trade Union Congress
IOL	India Office Library, London
ISP	Indian Socialist Party
IUML	Indian Union Muslim League
JPC	Joint Political Congress
KC	Kerala Congress
KC (J)	Kerala Congress (Joseph)
KC (M)	Kerala Congress (Mani)
KC (Pillai)	Kerala Congress (Pillai group)
KLA	Kerala Legislative Assembly
KMPP	Kisan (or Karshaka) Mazdoor Praja Party
KPCC	Kerala Pradesh Congress Committee
KSEB	Kerala State Electricity Board
KSP	Kerala Socialist Party
KSRTC	Kerala State Road Transport Corporation
KSSP	Kerala Samyuktha Socialist Party
KSU	Kerala Students Union
KTP	Karshaka Thozhilali Party
LDF	Left Democratic Front
MES	Muslim Education Society
MKU	Malanad Karshaka Union
ML	Muslim League
MLA	Member of a State Legislative Assembly
MP	Member of the Lok Sabha
NDF	National Democratic Front
NDP	National Democratic Party
NSS	Nair Service Society
PB	Politbureau
PDF	People's Democratic Front
PEPSU	Patiala and East Punjab States Union
PSP	Praja Socialist Party
RSP	Revolutionary Socialist Party
RSS	Rashtriya Swayam Sevak Sangh
SNDP	Sree Narayana Dharma Paripalana Yogam
SP	Socialist Party
SRP	Socialist Republican Party
SSLC	Secondary School Leaving Certificate
SSP	Samyuktha Socialist Party
TSC	Travancore State Congress
TTNC	Travancore Tamil Nad Congress
Tvm	Trivandrum
U.	University
UDF	United Democratic Front

UFL	United Front of Leftists
UTUC	United Trade Union Congress
YC	Youth Congress

Appendix 6: Bibliographical Abbreviations

B.	*Bulletin*
BCRC	Govt of Kerala, *Report of the Backward Classes Reservation Commission*, 2 vols. (1970)
CDS, *Poverty*	Centre for Development Studies (Trivandrum, Kerala), *Poverty, Unemployment and Development Policy* (New York, 1975; Bombay, 1977)
DRS, *ICPD*	Democratic Research Service (Bombay), *Indian Communist Party Documents 1930-1956* (1957)
DRS, *KUC*	Democratic Research Service (Bombay), *Kerala Under Communism: a Report* (1959)
ER	Govt of Kerala, *Economic Review* (annually)
FFYP 1974-9	Govt of Kerala, State Planning Board, *Fifth Five Year Plan 1974-9: a Draft Outline* (1973)
Fic, *Kerala*	Victor M. Fic, *Kerala: Yenan of India* (1970)
IE	*Indian Express*
J.	*Journal*
LRSK	Govt of Kerala, Bureau of Economics and Statistics, *Land Reforms Survey in Kerala 1966-7* (1968, mimeo)
Namboodiripad, *Kerala*	E.M.S. Namboodiripad, *Kerala, Yesterday, Today and Tomorrow*, 2nd edn (1968)
PKLA	Legislative Assembly, *Proceedings of the Kerala Legislative Assembly* (Malayalam)
R.	*Review*
SFP (followed by series number and title)	Govt of Kerala, State Planning Board and Bureau of Economics and Statistics, *Statistics for Planning*, 1:*Agriculture* (1972); 2: *Manpower* (1972); 3:*Labour and Labour Force* (1972); 4:*Industries and Infrastructure* (1972); 5: *Prices* (1972); 6: *Social Services* (1972); 7: *Income and Consumption* (1972); 8: *Plan Expenditure in Kerala* (1972); 9: *Rates and Ratios* (1974); 10: *Export and Import Statistics* (1972)
SPKLA	Legislative Assembly, Synopsis of the Proceedings of the Kerala Legislative Assembly (English)

Bibliography

1. Unpublished Records
2. Official Publications
3. Communist Party Publications
4. Books and Articles
5. Newspapers and Periodicals

1. Unpublished Records

Centre for the Study of Developing Societies, New Delhi; Communist Party of India, Trivandrum; Department of Politics, University of Kerala; English Archives, Trivandrum; India Office Library, London; the Secretariat, Trivandrum.

2. Official Publications

CENSUSES

1875 *Report on the Census of Native Cochin*. Madras, 1877.
1875 *Report on the Census of Travancore*. Trivandrum, 1876.
1881 *Imperial Census: Operations and Results in the Presidency of Madras*, vol. IV: *Final Census Tables*. Madras, 1883.
1891 *Report on the Census of Cochin*, pt 1. Cochin, 1893.
1891 *Census of India, Madras*, vol. XIII: *Report*; vol. XIV: *Tables*; vol. XV: *Tables*. Madras, 1893.
1901 *Census of India*, vol. XX: *Cochin*, pt I. Ernakulam, 1903.
1901 *Census of India*, vol. XXVI: *Travancore*, pt I. Trivandrum, 1903.
1911 *Census of India*, vol. I: *India*, pt I. Calcutta, 1913.
1911 *Census of India*, vol. XXIII: *Travancore*, pt I. Trivandrum, 1912.
1921 *Census of India*, vol. XIII: *Madras*, pts. I, II. Madras, 1922.
1921 *Census of India*, vol. XXV: *Travancore*, pt I. Trivandrum, 1922.
1921 *Census of India*, vol. XXI: *Cochin*, pts. I, II. Ernakulam, 1923.
1931 *Census of India*, vol. XIV: *Madras*, pts. I, II. Madras, 1932.

1931   *Census of India*, vol. XXVIII: *Travancore*, pts. I, II. Trivandrum, 1932.
1941   *Census of India*, vol. XIX: *Cochin*, pt II. Ernakulam, 1944.
1941   *Census of India*, vol. XXV: *Travancore*, pt I. Trivandrum, 1942.
1961   *Census of India*, vol. VII: *Kerala*, pt IA (i) and pt IX, *Census Atlas*. New Delhi, 1965.
1971   *Census of India*, Series 9: *Kerala*, pt II-A, *General Population Figures*. New Delhi, 1972. *Kerala*, pt X, *District Census Handbooks—Alleppey, Cannanore, Ernakulam, Idikki, Kottayam, Kozhikode, Malappuram, Palghat, Quilon, Trichur, Trivandrum*. New Delhi, 1972-4.

GOVERNMENT OF COCHIN

Reports of the following bodies:
    Landlord and Tenant Commn of Cochin. 1909.
    Agrarian Problems Enquiry Cttee of Cochin. 1949.
Memorandum describing the Agricultural Conditions in the Cochin State and indicating the General Lines on which Improvement of Agriculture should proceed. 1908.
Menon, C. Achyuta. *The Cochin State Manual*. 1911.
Iyer, L.A. Krishna. *The Cochin Tribes and Castes*. 1912. 2 vols.
Administration Reports. The government's annual *Administration Report* is a digest of administration reports from individual departments.

GOVERNMENT OF INDIA

Reports of the following bodies:
    Labour Investigation Cttee (*Report on Labour Conditions in Coir Mats and Matting Industry, by Ahmad Muktar*). 1945.
    —(Enquiry into Conditions of Labour in Plantations in India, by D.V. Rege, ICS). 1946.
    Election Commission (*Report on the First General Elections in India 1951-2*). 1955. 2 vols.
    Ministry of Home Affairs (*Report of the States Reorganization Commn 1953*). 1955.
    Ministry of Labour and Employment, Labour Bureau. (*Report of the Second Enquiry on Agricultural Labour in India*, vol. I: *All-India*, 1960; vol. VII: *Kerala, 1961*.
Returns showing the Results of Elections to Central Legislative Assembly and the Provincial Legislatures in 1945-6. 1948.
Ministry of Home Affairs. *Communist Violence in India*. 1949.
Survey of Labour Conditions in Tea Plantations and Tea Factories in India 1961-1962. 1962.

GOVERNMENT OF KERALA

Reports of the following bodies/officials:
    Administrative Reforms Cttee. Vol. I, 1961; vols. II and III, 1960.
    Rice Deal Inquiry Commn. 1959.
    Commn for Reservation of Seats in Educational Institutions. 1966.
    Administrative Reorganisation and Economy Cttee. 1967.
    Enquiry Commn on Transmission and Distribution of the Kerala Electricity Board. 1967.
    Bureau of Economics and Statistics (*Land Reforms Survey in Kerala 1966-7*). 1968 (mimeo).
    Coir Board, Cochin (*Report on Labour Conditions in the Coir Manufacturing Industry*). 1969.
    Taxation Enquiry Cttee. 1969.
    Backward Classes Reservation Commn. 1970. 2 vols.
    Coir Board, Cochin, Study Team (*Possibilities of Coir Development*). 1970.
    Commn of Inquiry in re: Shri M.N. Govindan Nair, Shri T.V. Thomas. 1971.
    Commn of Inquiry in re: Smt. K.R. Gouri, Shri E.K. Imbichi Bava and Shri M.K. Krishnan. 1971. 4 parts.
    Commn of Inquiry on Allegations regarding Acquisition of Land for Kerala Agricultural University. 1971.
    Cttee on Unemployment. 1971.
    Enquiry into Certain Appointments: Travancore–Cochin Chemicals Ltd. 1971.
    Kuttanad Enquiry Commn. 1971.
    Commn of Inquiry against B. Wellingdon Former Minister of Health. 1972.
    Commn of Inquiry in re: Shri P.R. Kurup. 1972.
    High Level Cttee on Electronics Industry. 1972.
    Planning Board (*Report of the Study Group on Mechanisation in Coir Industry in Kerala*). 1973.
    Justice Shri V. Balakrishna Eradi (*On the Allegations made against Dr. K.G. Adiyodi, Finance Minister of Kerala in the Issue of* Kerala Kaumudi *dated 13th September 1974*). 1975.
Third Five Year Plan: Draft Outline. 1960.
Kerala in Maps. 1964.
Kerala Panchayat Raj Bill. 1967.
Kerala Panchayats (Amendment) Act. 1969.
Planning Board. *Alternate Policies for the Fourth Five Year Plan.* 1969.
—*Kerala and the Award of the Fifth Finance Commission.* 1969.
Coir Board, Cochin. *Coir Industry in India.* 1970.
Fourth Five Year Plan (1969-74). 1970.
Kerala Panchayats (Amendment) Bill. 1970.

Kerala Private Forests (Vesting and Assignment)Bill. 1971.

Story of the Ernakulam Experiment in Family Planning. 1971.

Kerala Agricultural Workers' Bill. 1972.

State Planning Board and Bureau of Economics and Statistics. *Statistics for Planning.* Nos. 1-8 and 10, 1972; No. 9, 1974. (For individual titles, see Appendix 6 above.)

State Planning Board. *Fifth Five Year Plan 1974-9: a Draft Outline.* 1973.

Indian Administrative Service Graduation List. 1974.

Legislature Secretariat. *Digest of Kerala Laws.* 1974.

New Deal to Farm Labour: Salient Features of the Kerala Agricultural Workers' Bill. 1974.

Planning Board. *The Sixth Finance Commission's Award: a Summary.* 1974.

Bureau of Economics and Statistics. *Basic Statistics relating to Kerala Economy 1956-7 to 1973-4.* 1975.

Kerala Forges Ahead: UF Ministry Five Years in Retrospect. 1975.

Dept of Planning and Economic Affairs. *Twenty Point Programme: Progress of Implementation in Kerala.* 1976.

Dept of Public Relations. *The Press in Kerala.* 1977.

Kerala Election Reportage 1977. 1977.

Administration Reports. The government's annual *Administration Report* is a digest of administration reports from individual departments.

Annual Plan (annually).

Civil List.

District Gazetteers (A. Sreedhara Menon, ed.): *Alleppey* (1975), *Cannanore* (1972), *Ernakulam* (1965), *Kottayam* (1975), *Kozhikode* (1962), *Palghat* (1976), *Quilon* (1964), *Trichur* (1962), *Trivandrum* (1962).

Economic Review (annually). The first volume in this series was entitled *Kerala 1959: an Economic Review* and was published in 1960.

Legislative Assembly. *Gleanings from the Question Hour* (serially).

—*Proceedings of the Kerala Legislative Assembly* (in Malayalam).

—Reports of the Committee on Public Undertakings.

—Reports of the Estimates Committee.

—Reports of the Committee on Public Accounts.

—*Synopsis of the Proceedings of the Kerala Legislative Assembly* (in English).

—*Who's Who.*

Press Digest (daily).

GOVERNMENT OF MADRAS

Reports of the following bodies/officials:

Malabar Special Commissioner [W Logan] (*Report on Malabar Land Tenures*). 1882. 2 vols.

Commn on Malabar Land Tenures in 1884. 1885.

Malabar Land-Tenures Cttee of 1885. 1887.

Malabar Tenancy Cttee of 1927–8. 1928. 2 vols.

Rao, D. Narayana, *Survey of Cottage Industries in the Madras Presidency*. 1929.

Madras Provincial Banking Enquiry Commn. 1930. 5 vols.

Economic Enquiry Cttee. 1931. 3 vols.

Sathyanathan, W.R.S. *Report on Agricultural Indebtedness*. 1935.

Malabar Tenancy Cttee. 1940. 2 vols.

Correspondence on Moplah Outrages in Malabar for the years 1849-53. 1863. 2 vols.

Correspondence on Moplah Outbreaks of Malabar, 1853-59. 1863. 2 vols.

Correspondence regarding the Relation of Landlord and Tenant in Malabar 1852-6. 1881.

Turner, Sir Charles. *Minutes on the Draft Bill relating to Malabar Land-Tenures*. 1885.

Moberly, M. *The Report of the Settlement of the Malabar District*. 1900.

Innes, C.A. *Malabar District Gazetteer*. 1908.

Macewen, A.R. *Settlement Scheme Report of the Eight Plain Taluks of the Malabar District*. 1929.

Logan, W, *Malabar District Manual*. 1951. 2 vols.

Criminal Court Statistics.

Statistical Atlas of Malabar (quinquennial series).

GOVERNMENT OF TRAVANCORE

Reports of the following bodies/officials:

Unemployment Enquiry Cttee. 1928.

Banking Enquiry Cttee. 1930. 2 vols.

Economic Depression Enquiry Cttee. 1931.

Enquiry on Co-operative Societies. 1934.

Pillai, P. Parameswaran (*Report on the Scheme for Introduction of Basic Land-Tax and the Revision of Agricultural Income Tax*). 1946.

Unemployment Enquiry Cttee 1948, 1952.

Aiya, V. Nagam. *Travancore State Mannual*. 1906. 3 vols.

Iyer, L.A. Krishna. *The Travancore Tribes and Castes*. 1937 and 1939. 2 vols.

Pillai, T.K. Velu. *Travancore State Mannual*. 1940. 4 vols.

Tampi, A.N. *Economic Survey of Travancore*. 1941.

—*Enquiry into the Sub-division and Fragmentation of Agricultural Holdings in Travancore*. 1941.

Defence of Travancore Manual, as on 2-10-1945. 1945.

Consolidated General Index and Reference Guide to the Acts and Proclamations of Travancore, Ed.II. 1946.

Acts and Proclamations (annually).

Administration Report (annually).

Statistics of Travancore (annually).

Travancore Government Gazette. (serially).

GOVERNMENT OF TRAVANCORE-COCHIN

Reports of the following bodies:

Travancore-Cochin Land Policy Cttee. 1950.

Election Commission (*Report on the First General Elections in the Travancore-Cochin State held under the Constitution of India 1951-2*). 1953.

Minimum Wages Advisory Cttee for Plantations 1953. 1954.

Survey of Unemployment. 1954.

Coir Advisory Cttee. 1955.

Cttee on Coir Mats and Matting and Manufacturing Industry. 1955.

Minimum Wages Cttee for Plantations 1952. 1955.

Travancore-Cochin Banking Enquiry Commn. 1956 (mimeo), published by Govt of India.

Travancore-Cochin Expert Cttee on Agricultural Income-Tax and Sales Tax. 1956.

Prohibition Survey. 1957.

Second Five Year Plan (1956-61): First Year's Programme. 1956.

Acts and Ordinances.

Administration Reports. The government's annual *Administration Report* is a digest of administration reports from individual departments.

Proceedings of the Legislative Assembly.

Statistics of Travancore-Cochin (annually).

3. Communist Party Publications

Communist Statement of Policy. For the Struggle for Full Independence and People's Democracy. Resolution passed by the Central Executive Committee of the CPI, held in Bombay on December 7-16, 1947. Bombay, People's Publishing House, 1947.

Police Terror against Malabar Kisan. Memorandum of the Malabar District Committee of the CPI to the Congress Working Committee. Bombay, People's Publishing House, 1947.

Down with Autocracy. Tasks before the States' People's Movements. Bombay, People's Publishing House, n.d., *ca.* 1948.

Political Thesis of the Communist Party of India. Adopted at the Second Congress, held in Calcutta from February 2 to March 6, 1948. Bombay, M.V. Kaul for CPI, 1948.

On People's Democracy. Bombay, People's Publishing House, 1949.

Draft Programme of the Communist Party of India. Issued by the CPI Politbureau in April 1951. Bombay, People's Publishing House, 1951.

Programme of the Communist Party of India. Adopted at the All-India Party Conference, held in October 1951. Bombay, People's Publishing House, 1951.

Statement of Policy by the Communist Party of India. Issued by the Politbureau in May 1951. Bombay, People's Publishing House, 1951.

Build Broadest United Front. Declaration of the All-India Conference of the CPI, held in Bombay on October 23, 1951. *Crossroads,* 26 Oct. 1951.

Minimum Programme for UDF Issued by Communist MPs and MCs. New Delhi, 25 April 1952 (mimeo).

A Programme to Meet People's Demands. Draft Programme of the Democratic Front in the Malabar District Board. *New Age,* 28 Nov. 1954.

Communique of the Meeting of the Central Executive of the CPI. Held in New Delhi from June 14 to 26, 1955. *New Age,* 3 July 1955.

Political Bureau Statement. Government for a Kerala State. *New Age,* 20 Nov. 1955.

Political Resolution. Adopted at the Fourth Congress of the Communist Party of India, held in Palghat from April 19 to 29, 1956. New Delhi, CPI, 1956.

The CEC of the CPI Resolution on the XX Congress of the Communist Party of the Soviet Union, March 26-31, 1956. *New Age,* 8 Apr. 1956.

Resolution: Communist Proposal for Building a Democratic and Prosperous Kerala. Adopted by the Kerala Provincial Conference of the Communist Party, held in Trichur from June 22 to 24, 1956. *New Age,* 22 July 1956.

Kerala Committee of the CPI. Unity on Programme and Formation of Alternative Government. Adopted at the conference held in Ernakulam on October 9, 1956. *New Age,* 21 Oct. 1956.

Report on the Plenary Meeting of the Kerala Committee of the CPI, held in Alwaye on January 1-3, 1957. *New Age,* 13 Jan. 1957.

Communist Party Explains Why No Electoral Agreement in Kerala, Resolution of the Kerala Committee of the CPI, adopted at Alwaye on January 1-3, 1957. *New Age,* 20 Jan. 1957.

Political Bureau Resolution on Kerala Victory. Adopted at a meeting in Ernakulam from March 22 to 24, 1957. *New Age,* 31 Mar. 1957.

Constitution of the Communist Party of India. Adopted at the Extraordinary Party Congress, Amritsar, April 1958. New Delhi, CPI, 1958.

On the Decisions of the National Council. Report of A. Ghosh on the results of the National Council's meeting held in Madras from October 8 to 13, 1958. New Delhi, CPI, 1958.

Resolutions of the Communist Party of India. Adopted at the Extraordinary Party Congress, held in Amritsar in April 1958. New Delhi, CPI, 1958.

Kerala's Answer to KPCC Charges. New Delhi, CPI, 1959.

Rule of Terror in Central Travancore, Memorandum submitted by A.K. Gopalan to the Government of Kerala on February 14, 1960. New Delhi, CPI, n.d., *ca.* 1960.

Draft Programme of the Communist Party of India. Prepared by S.A. Dange, P.C. Joshi, and G. Adikhari, presented to the VI Congress of the CPI in April 1961. *New Age* (monthly), Apr. 1961.

Draft Programme of the Communist Party of India. Prepared by B. Gupta and P. Ramamurthy, and presented to the VI Congress of the CPI in April 1961. *New Age* (monthly), Apr. 1961.

Fight Against Revisionism. Political-Organisational Report adopted at the Seventh Congress of the Communist Party of India, Calcutta, October 31-November 7, 1964. Calcutta, [CPI-M], 1964.

Resolution Adopted at the Seventh Congress October 31 to November 7, 1964 [CPM]. Calcutta, National Book Agency, n.d.

Constitution of the Communist Party of India. Adopted at the Seventh Congress, October 31 to November 7, 1964. Calcutta, Communist Party of India-Marxist, 1965.

Resolutions of the Central Committee of the Communist Party of India, Tenali, June 12-19, 1966. Calcutta, CPI-M, 1966.

Election Manifesto. Tvm, CPI, 1967.

Election Review and Party's Task. Adopted by the Central Committee of the Communist Party of India-Marxist, Calcutta, April 10-16, 1967. Calcutta, CPI-M, 1967.

Ideological Debate Summed Up by the Polit Bureau. Calcutta, CPI-M, 1968.

Our Tasks on Party Organisation. Adopted by the Central Committee of the Communist Party of India-Marxist, Calcutta, October 28-November 2, 1968. Calcutta, CPI-M, n.d.

Political Resolution Adopted by The Eighth Congress. Cochin, CPM, 1968.

[CPM] *Politbureau's Resolution on Kerala's Political, Economic and Food Situation* [Malayalam]. Tvm, Minerva Press, 1968.

Political-Organizational Report of the Eighth Congress of the CPI (M). Calcutta, CPI (M), 1969.

Right Communist Betrayal of Kerala UF and Government. A Collection of Documents. Calcutta, CPM, 1969.

Keralavum Kendra Governmentum (Malayalam). Tvm, CPM, 1971.

Our Approach to J.P.'s Slogans—E.M.S. Namboodiripad. *People's Democracy*, 22 June 1975.

Communists and Work in Parliament. *People's Democracy,* 27 July 1975.

Central Committee Statement, New Delhi, March 26-27, 1977. *People's Democracy*, 3 Apr. 1977.

Manifesto of the Communist Party of India (Marxist) on the Election to the Lok Sabha, 1977. *People's Democracy*, 6 Feb. 1977.

Political Review Report (Adopted by the Eleventh Congress), New Delhi CPI, 1978.

4. Books and Articles

Adhikari, G. *The Communist Party and India's Path to National Regeneration and Socialism.* New Delhi, New Age Press, 1964.

—and Mohit Sen, eds. *Lenin and India.* New Delhi, People's Publishing House, 1970.

Ahmad, Muzaffar. *S.A. Dange and the National Archives.* Calcutta, n.p., 1964.

Ahmed, Bashiruddin. Communist and Congress Prospects in Kerala\. *Asian Survey* VI, July 1966.

Aiyappan, A. *Social Revolution in a Kerala Village.* Bombay, Asia Publishing House, 1965.

Aiyar [Sir], C.P. Ramaswami. Introductory Essay (Accent on Kerala-1), *Illustrated Weekly of India,* 12 Sept. 1965.

Aiyer, Sir C.P. Ramaswami. Speeches. Tvm, Govt Press, 1936-9. 3 vols.

Alexander, K.C. Changing Status of Pulaya Harijans of Kerala. *Economic and Political Weekly,* Special no. July 1968.

—Emergence of Peasant Organisations in South India. *Economic and Political Weekly,* 28, June 1980.

Arnold, David. The Police and Colonial Control in South India. *Social Scientist* (Tvm) 48, July 1976.

Asher, R.E. 'Three Novelists of Kerala', in T.W. Clark, ed., *The Novel in India.* London, Allen & Unwin, 1970.

Austin, H. *Anatomy of the Kerala Coup.* New Delhi, People's Publishing House, 1959.

Ayyar, K.V. Krishna. *The Zamorins of Calicut.* Calicut, Norman Printing Bureau, 1938.

—*A Short History of Kerala.* Ernakulam, Pai, 1966.

Baker, C.J. *The Politics of South India 1920-1937.* Cambridge, CUP, 1976.

—'Debt and the Depression in Madras, 1929-1936', in Clive Dewey and A.G. Hopkins, eds., *The Imperial Impact: Studies in the Economic History of Africa and India.* London, Athlone Press. 1978.

Balaram, N.E. *A Short History of the Communist Party of India.* Tvm, Prabhatham Publishing, 1967.

Basavanapunniah, M. *Our Views on E.M.S. Namboodiripad's Critique of Draft Programme.* New Delhi, n.p., 1964.

Bayley, D.H. *The Police and Political Development in India.* Princeton, NJ, Princeton UP, 1969.

Baxter, Craig, comp. *District Voting Trends in India: a Research Tool.* New York, Southern Asian Inst., School of International Affairs, Columbia UP, 1969.

Benn, D.M. 'The Theory of Plantation Economy and Society: a Methodological Critique'. *J. of Commonwealth & Comparative Politics* XII (3), 1974.

Bhagat, K.P, *The Kerala Mid-Term Election of 1960: the Communist Party's Conquest of New Positions.* Bombay, Popular Book Depot, 1962.

Bhalla, R.P. Economic Aspects of Elections in India. *India Political Science R.* II (1 & 2), Oct, 1967-Mar. 1968.

Bhattacharya, N.C. 'Leadership in the Communist Party of India', in Iqbal Narain, ed., *State Politics in India.* Meerut, Saipur, 1967.

Bhattacharya, Sachidananda. *A Dictionary of Indian History*. New York, George Braziller, 1967.

Blackburn, Robin, ed. *Explosion in a Subcontinent*. Harmondsworth, Penguin Books, 1975.

Blackton, Charles S. Sri Lanka's Marxists. *Problems of Communism* XXII, Jan.–Feb. 1973.

Bristow, Sir Robert. *Cochin Saga*. London, Cassell, 1959.

Brown, L.W. *The Indian Christians of St. Thomas: an Account of the Ancient Syrian Church of Malabar*. Cambridge, CUP, 1956.

Busteed, M.A. *Geography and Voting Behaviour*. London, OUP, 1975.

Centre for Development Studies (Tvm, Kerala). *Poverty, Unemployment and Development Policy: a Case Study of Selected Issues with Reference to Kerala*. New York, UN, Dept of Economic and Social Affairs, 1975; Bombay, Orient Longman, 1977.

Chaitanya, Krishna. *A History of Malayalam Literature*. New Delhi, Orient Longman, 1971.

Chander, N. Jose. 'The Legislative Process in Kerala, 1957-1969'. Unpublished Ph.D. thesis, University of Kerala, Tvm, 1973.

Chandrasekharan, K. The Constitutional (Thirteenth) Amendment Bill. *News and Views* (Tvm, Kerala Law Academy) II (5), 1972.

Chatterji, Saral K. ed. *The Coalition Government*. Madras, Christian Literature Society for Christian Inst. for the Study of Religion and Society, Bangalore, 1974.

Cheriyan, C.V. *History of Christianity in Kerala*. Tvm, Kerala Hist. Society, 1973.

Chettur, Usha. Nayars. *Illustrated Weekly of India*, 20 Dec. 1970.

Crouch, Harold. *Trade Unions and Politics in India*. Bombay, Manaktalas, 1966.

Dale, Stephen F. *Islamic Society on the South Asian Frontier: the Māppilas of Malabar 1498-1922*. Oxford, Clarendon Press, 1980.

—'The Mappilla Outbreaks: Ideology and Social Conflict in Nineteenth Century Kerala'. *J. of Asian Studies* XXXV (1), 1975.

—The Islamic Frontier in Southwest India: the Shahid as a Cultural Ideal among the Mappillas of Malabar. *Modern Asian Studies* II (1), 1977.

—A Reply to Wood. *J. of Asian Studies* XXXVI (2), 1977.

Dalwai, Hamid. *Muslim Politics in Secular India*. New Delhi, Nachiketa Publications, 1968.

Damodaran, K. The Past. *Seminar* 178, June 1974.

—Memoir of an Indian Communist. *New Left Review* 93, Sept.–Oct. 1975.

Das Gupta, Ashin. *Malabar in Asian Trade 1740-1800*. Cambridge, CUP, 1967.

Dasgupta, Biplab. *The Naxalite Movement*. Bombay, Allied Publishers, 1974.

—and W.H. Morris-Jones. *Patterns and Trends in Indian Politics: an Ecological Analysis of Aggregate Data on Society and Elections*. Bombay, Allied Publishers, 1976.

Davies, Christie. The Relative Fertility of Hindus and Muslims. *Quest* 99, Jan.-Feb. 1976.

Dean, V.M. *New Patterns of Democracy in India*. Cambridge, Mass., Harvard UP, 1959.

Democratic Research Service (Bombay). *Indian Communist Party Documents 1930-1956*. Bombay, Democratic Research Service and Institute of Pacific Relations, 1957.

—*Kerala Under Communism: a Report*. Bombay, Democratic Research Service, 1959.

Dhanagare, D.N. Agrarian Conflict, Religion and Politics: the Moplah Rebellions in Malabar in the Nineteenth and Early Twentieth Centuries. *Past and Present* 74, 1976, pp. 113-41.

Dougal, Sonia. *The Nun-runners*. London, Hodder & Stoughton, 1971.

Druke, D.N. *Soviet Russia and Indian Communism*. New York, Bookman, 1959.

Edwards, Michael. *British India 1772-1947*. London, Sidgwick & Jackson, 1967

Eldersveld, S.J. Party Identification in India in Comparative Perspective. *Comparative Political Studies* 6 (3), 1973.

Elliott, Carolyn M. Decline of a Patrimonial Regime: the Telengana Rebellion in India 1946-51. *J. of Asian Studies,* 34(1), 1974.

Etienne, G. *Patterns of Indian Agriculture*. Berkeley, U. of California P., 1968.

Fic, Victor M. *Peaceful Transition to Communism in India: Strategy of the Communist Party*. Bombay, Nachiketa Publications, 1969.

—*Kerala: Yenan of India*. Bombay, Nachiketa Publications, 1970.

Fischer, Ruth. The Indian Communist Party. *Far Eastern Survey* XXII (7), 1953.

Forrester, Duncan B. Electoral Politics and Social Change. *Economic and Political Weekly,* Special no. July 1968.

Franda, Marcus F. India's Third Communist Party. *Asian Survey* IX (6), 1969.

—*Radical Politics in West Bengal*. Cambridge, Mass., MIT Press, 1971.

Frankel, Francine R. *India's Green Revolution: Economic Gains and Political Costs*. Princeton, NJ, Princeton UP, 1971.

—*India's Political Economy 1947-1977: the Gradual Revolution*. Princeton, NJ, Princeton UP, 1978.

Fuller, C.J. *The Nayars Today*. Cambridge, CUP, 1976.

Gangadharan, A. *Law of Land Reforms in Kerala*. Cochin, Travancore Law House, 1974. 2nd edn.

Gelman, H. 'The Communist Party of India—Sino-Soviet Battleground', in A. Doak Barnett, ed., *Communist Strategies in Asia*. New York, Praeger, 1963.

George, K.C. *Immortal Punnapra-Vayalar*. New Delhi, CPI, 1975.

George, K.M. *A Survey of Malayalam Literature*. Bombay, P.S. Jayasinghe, Asia Publishing House, 1968.

George, V.C. *Christianity in India through the Ages*. Kottayam, Fr Joseph Vadakkekara, 1972.

Giri, V.V. *My Life and Times*. London, Macmillan, 1976.

Goldstein, Carol. *Kerala: a Unique Experiment*. Englewood Cliffs, NJ, Carol Goldstein, 1963.

Gopal, Ram. *British Rule in India*. New York, Asia Publishing House, 1963.

Gopal, S. *British Policy in India 1858-1905*. Cambridge, CUP, 1965.

Gopalan, A.K. *Kerala — Past and Present*. London, Lawrence & Wishart, 1959.

—*Harijanam* (Malayalam). Kottayam, SPCS, 1972.

—*In the Cause of the People*. New Delhi, Orient Longmans, 1973.

Gough, Kathleen. Changing Kinship Usages in the Setting of Political and Economic Change among the Nayars of Malabar. *J. of the Royal Anthropological Inst*. 82, (1) 1952.

—The Nayars and the Definition of Marriage. *J. of the Royal Anthropological Inst*. LXXXIX (1 & 2), 1959.

—'Indian Nationalism and Ethnic Freedom', in P. Bidney, ed., *Concepts of Freedom in Anthropology*. The Hague, Mouton, 1963.

—Social Change in South India. *Economic Development and Cultural Change* XIII (3), 1965.

—Village Politics in Kerala-I and II. *Economic Weekly*, 20 and 27 Feb. 1965.

—Kerala Politics and the 1965 Elections. *International J. of Comparative Sociology* VIII (1), 1967.

—'Literacy in Kerala', in J. Goody, ed., *Literacy in Traditional Societies*. Cambridge, CUP, 1968.

—Communist Rural Councillors in Kerala. *J. of Asian and African Studies*, III (3-4), 1968.

—Peasant Resistance and Revolt in South India. *Pacific Affairs* XLI (4), 1968-9.

—'Political Party Conflict in a Kerala Village', in M.C. Pradhan, ed., *Anthropology and Archaeology*. London, OUP, 1969.

—'Palakkara: Social and Religious Change in Central Kerala', in K. Ishwaran, ed., *Change and Continuity in India's Villages*. New York, Columbia UP, 1970.

—Indian Peasant Uprisings. *Economic and Political Weekly*, Special no. Aug. 1974.

—and Hari P. Sharma, eds. *Imperialism and Revolution in South Asia*. New York, Monthly Review Press, 1973.

Griffith, W.E. *The Sino-Soviet Rift*. Cambridge, Mass., MIT Press, 1964.

Gupta, Bhabani Sen. *The Fulcrum of Asia: Relations Among China, India, Pakistan and the USSR*. New York, Pegasus, 1970.

—'S.A. Dange, E.M.S. Namboodiripad and Jyoti Basu, Divergent Leaders of Communism in India', in R. Swearingen, ed., *Leaders of the Communist World*. New York, Free Press, 1971.

—*Communism in Indian Politics*. New York, Columbia UP, 1972.
—India's Rival Communist Models. *Problems of Communism* XXII, Jan.-Feb. 1973.
Gupta, Bhupesh. Communists in Parliament. *World Marxist Rev.* 21 (9), Sept. 1978.
Hanson, A.H. *The Process of Planning: a Study of India's Five-Year Plans 1950-1964*. London, OUP for Royal Inst. of International Affairs, 1966.
—*Planning and the Politicians*. London, Routledge & Kegan Paul, 1969.
—and Janet Douglas. *India's Democracy*. London, Weidenfeld & Nicolson, 1972.
Hardgrave, Robert L., Jr. Caste, Class and Politics in Kerala. *Political Science R*. 3 (1) 1964.
—Caste in Kerala: a Preface to the Elections. *Economic Weekly*, 21 Nov. 1964.
—Caste and the Kerala Elections. *Economic Weekly*, 17 Apr. 1965.
—Caste: Fission and Fusion. *Economic and Political Weekly*, Special no. July 1968.
—The Marxist Dilemma in Kerala: Administration and/or Struggle. *Asian Survey* X (11), 1970.
—'The Kerala Communists: Contradictions of Power', in Paul Brass and Marcus F. Franda, eds., *Radical Politics in South Asia*. Cambridge, Mass., MIT Press, 1973.
—*India: Government and Politics in a Developing Nation*. 2nd edn. New York, Harcourt, Brace, 1975.
—'The Communist Parties of Kerala: an Electoral Profile', in M. Weiner and J.O. Field, eds., *Electoral Politics in the Indian States*, vol. iv. New Delhi, Manohar Book Service, 1975.
—'The Mappilla Rebellion, 1921: Peasant Revolt in Malabar. *Modern Asian Studies* II (1), 1977.
—'Peasant Mobilisation in Malabar: the Mappilla Rebellion, 1921', in Robert I. Crane, ed., *Aspects of Political Mobilisation in South Asia*. Syracuse, NY, Syracuse University, Maxwell School of Citizenship and Public Affairs, 1976. (South Asia series, no. 1)
Hardy, Peter. *The Muslims of British India*. Cambridge, CUP, 1972.
Harrison, Selig S. Caste and the Andhra Communists. *American Political Science R*. L (2), 1956.
—Communism in India: the Dilemma of the CPI. *Problems of Communism* VIII (2), 1959.
—*India: the Most Dangerous Decades*. Princeton, NJ, Princeton UP, 1960.
Hart, Henry C. and Ronald J. Herring. 'Political Conditions of Land Reform: Kerala and Maharashtra', in R.E. Frykenberg, ed., *Land Tenure and Peasant in South Asia*. New Delhi, Orient Longman, 1976.
Hartman, H. Changing Political Behaviour in Kerala: a Preface to Elections. *Economic Weekly*, Annual no. Jan. 1964.
Hatch, Emily G. *Travancore; a Guide Book for the Visitor*. Lodon, OUP, 1933.

Herring, Ronald J. 'Redistributive Agrarian Policy: Land and Credit in South Asia'. Unpublished Ph.D thesis, U. of Wisconsin, Madison, 1976.

—Abolition of Landlordism in Kerala: a Redistribution of Privilege. *Economic and Political Weekly*, 28 June 1980.

Hicks, Lady Ursula Kathleen. *Federalism: Failure and Success: a Comparative Study*. London, Macmillan, 1978.

Houtart, Francois and Genevieve Lemercinier. Socio-Religious Movements in Kerala: a Reaction to the Capitalist Mode of Production, *Social Scientist* (Tvm) 71 & 72, June and July 1978.

Hunter, Thelma. Indian Communism and the Kerala Experience of Coalition Government 1967-69. *J. of Commonwealth Political Studies* X (1), 1972.

Irani, C.R. *Bengal: the Communist Challenge*. Bombay, Lalvani Publishing House, 1971.

Ittiavira, Varghese. *Social Novels in Malayalam*. Bangalore, Christian Inst. for the Study of Religion and Society, 1968.

Iyer, V.R. Krishna. *The Social Mission of Law*. New Delhi, Orient Longman, 1976.

Jacob, K.T. *Tiller Gets Land in Kerala*. New Delhi, CPI, 1970.

Jadeja, Y.D. Structural Pattern and Modes of Election in Panchavati Raj. *Indian J. of Public Administration* XVI (1), 1970.

Jayaraj, D. 'Democratic Governments in Kerala, 1957-1970'. Unpublished Ph. D. thesis, University of Kerala, Tvm, 1977.

Jeffrey, Robin. The Social Origins of a Caste Association, 1875-1905: the Founding of the S.N.D.P. Yogam. *South Asia* I (4), 1974.

— *The Decline of Nayar Dominance: Society and Politics in Travancore, 1847-1908*. London, Chatto & Windus for Sussex UP, 1976.

—Temple-entry Movement in Travancore, 1860-1940. *Social Scientist* (Tvm) 44, Mar. 1976.

—'A Sanctified Label: "Congress" in Travancore Politics', in D.A. Low, ed., *Congress and the Raj*. London, Heinemann, 1977.

—Matriliny, Marxism, and the Birth of the Communist Party in Kerala, 1930-1940. *J. of Asian Studies* XXXVIII (1), 1978.

—'Peasant Movements and the Communist Party in Kerala 1937-57', in D.B. Miller, ed., *Peasants and Politics: Grass Roots Reactions to Change in Asia*. Melbourne, Edward Arnold, 1978.

—'Travancore, Status, Class and the Growth of Radical Politics', in Robin Jeffrey, ed., *People, Princes and Paramount Power: Society and Politics in the Indian Princely States*. Delhi, OUP, 1978.

Johari, J.C. *Naxalite Politics in India*. Delhi, Inst. of Constitutional and Parliamentary Studies, 1972.

John, K.C. Naxalites Split in Kerala: Make no Headway. *Times of India*, 12 Dec. 1970.

— *The Melting Pot: Kerala 1950s-1970s*. Tvm, Prasanthi Printers, 1975.

John, P. John. 'Coalition Governments in Kerala, 1957-70'. Unpublished Ph.D. thesis, U. of Kerala, Tvm, 1978.

John, P.K. Fundamental Rights and Constitutional Checks. *News and Views* (Tvm, Kerala Law Academy) 4 (1), 1974.

Jose, A.V. Origins of Trade Unionism Among the Agricultural Labourers in Kerala. *Social Scientist* (Tvm) 60, July 1977.

Joshi, P.C. *Land Reforms in India: Trends and Perspectives.* New Delhi, Allied Publishers, 1975.

Julien, F. Stratégies Communistes au Kerala. *France-Asie* no. 1, 1968.

Karat, Prakash. Book Review of Fic, Victor M., *Kerala: Yenan of India. Social Scientist* (Tvm) 7, Aug. 1972.

—Agrarian Relations in Malabar 1925-1948. *Social Scientist* (Tvm) 14 & 15, 1973.

—The Peasant Movement in Malabar 1934-40. *Social Scientist* (Tvm) 50, 1976.

—Organised Struggles of Malabar Peasantry 1934-40. *Social Scientist* (Tvm) 56, 1977.

Kareem, C.K. *Kerala Under Haider Ali and Tipu Sultan.* Cochin, Paico for Kerala History Association, 1973.

Karnik, V.B. *Communist Ministry and Trade Unions in Kerala.* New Delhi, International Confederation of Free Trade Unions, Subdivision Asian Regional Organisation, 1959.

—*Indian Trade Unions: a Survey.* Bombay, Manaktala, 1966.

Katrak, Savak, India Communist Party Split. *China Quarterly*, July-Sept. 1963.

Kaul, J.M. The Split in the C.P.I. *India Quarterly* XX (4), 1964.

Kautsky, John H. *Moscow and the Communist Party of India.* New York, Wiley, 1956.

—*Communism and the Politics of Development, Persistent Myths and Changing Behaviour.* New York, Wiley, 1968.

Kerala Pradesh Congress Cttee. *Memorandum Submitted to President, Indian Republic.* Tvm, 1958.

—*The Kerala Situation.* New Delhi, 1959.

[Kerala Pradesh Congress Cttee]. *True Picture of the Situation in Kerala (a Rejoinder).* Ernakulam, 1959.

Klatt, Werner. Caste, Class and Communism in Kerala. *Asian Affairs,*Oct. 1972.

Kochanek, Stanley A. *The Congress Party of India.* Princeton, NJ, Princeton UP, 1968.

—*Business and Politics in India.* Berkeley, U. of California P., 1974.

Koshy, M.J. *Constitutionalism in Travancore and Cochin.* Tvm, Kerala Hist Society, 1972.

—*Genesis of Political Consciousness in Kerala.* Tvm, Kerala Hist. Society, 1972.

—*Last Days of Monarchy in Kerala.* Tvm, Kerala Hist. Society, 1973.

Kothari, Rajni. Continuity and Change in India's Party System. *Asian Survey* X (11), 1970.

Krishnaji, N. Agrarian Relations and the Left Movement in Kerala: a Note on Recent Trends. *Economic and Political Weekly,* 3 Mar. 1979.

Krishnan, T.V. *Kerala's First Communist: Life of 'Sakhavu' Krishna Pillai.* New Delhi, CPI, 1971.

Kumar, Dharma. *Land and Caste in South India.* Cambridge, CUP, 1965.

Kurian, K. Mathew, ed. *India—State and Society.* New Delhi, Orient Longman, 1972.

Kurian, Raju. Patterns of Emigration from Kerala. *Social Scientist* (Tvm) 78, Jan. 1979.

Kurup, K.K.N. The Peasant Movement in Kasaragod Taluk 1935-1942. *J. of Kerala Studies* II (1), 1975.

Kusuman, K.K. Punnapra-Vayalar Rising 1946. *J. of Kerala Studies* III (1),1976.

Kuttapan, M. Kerala's Economic Development to 1969. *Mainstream,* 15 Mar. 1969.

Labedz, Leopold. *Revisionism. Essays on the History of Marxist Ideas.* New York, Praeger, 1962.

Langley, W.K.M. ed. *Century in Malabar: the History of Peirce, Leslie & Co. Ltd. 1862-1962.* Madras, Madras Advertising Co., 1962.

Laqueur, W. and L. Labedz, eds. *Polycentrism: the New Factor in International Communism.* New York, Praeger, 1962.

Lieten, Georges Kristoffel. China and the Undivided Communist Party of India. *Social Scientist* (Tvm) 36, July 1975.

—The Economic Structure of Kerala in the mid-50s. *J. of Kerala Studies* II (4), 1975.

—Indian Communists Look at Indian Communism. *Economic and Political Weekly,* 10 Sept. 1977.

—Education, Ideology and Politics in Kerala 1957-59. *Social Scientist* (Tvm) 62, Sept. 1977.

—Progressive State Governments: an Assessment of the First Communist Ministry in Kerala. *Economic and Political Weekly,* 6 Jan. 1979.

Lèmercinier, Geneviève and Francois Houtart. *Church and Development in Kerala.* Cochin, Pastoral Orientation Centre, 1974. Mimeo.

Malaviya, H.D. *Kerala: a Report to the Nation.* New Delhi, People's Publishing House, 1958.

MacKay, W.S.S. *Kanan Devan Planters' Association, 93rd A.G.M. Speech by Chairman.* Coonoor, Information Service of United Planters' Association, 1952.

McInnes, Neil. *The Communist Parties of Western Europe.* London, OUP for Royal Inst. of International Affairs, 1975.

Mankekar, D.R. *The Red Riddle of Kerala.* Bombay, Manaktala, 1965.

Manor, James. Where Congress Survived: Five States in the Indian General Election of 1977. *Asian Survey* XVIII (8), 1978.

Markose, A.T. 'Public Corporations in Kerala'. Colombo, unpublished Ms., 1974.

Marx, Karl. *Letters on India*, eds. B.P.L. and Freda Bedi. Lahore, Contemporary India Publication, 1936.

Masani, M.R. *Communist Party of India: a Short History*. London, D. Verschoyle, 1954.

Mathur, P.R.G. Socio-Economic Changes among the Weaker Sections of the Population of Kerala. *J. of Kerala Studies* IV (1), 1977.

Mathew, E.T. Power Development in Kerala. *Social Scientist* (Tvm) 62, Sept. 1977.

— and P.R. Gopinathan Nair. Socio-Economic Characteristics of Emigrants and Emigrants' Households: a Case Study of Two Villages in Kerala. *Economic and Political Weekly*, 15 July 1978.

May, Christopher. 'Some Lesser Leaders of the Communist Movement in Kerala', in W.H. Morris-Jones, ed., *The Making of Politicians: Studies from Africa and Asia*. London, Athlone Press, 1976.

Mayer, Adrian C. *Land and Society in Malabar*. London, OUP, 1952.

Mencher, Joan P. Changing Familial Roles Among South Malabar Nayars. *Southwestern J. of Anthropology* 18 (3), 1962.

— 'The Nayars of South Malabar', in M.F. Nimkoff, ed., *Comparative Family Systems*. Boston, Mass., Houghton, 1965.

— Namboodiri Brahmins: an Analysis of a Traditional Elite in Kerala. *J. of Asian and African Studies* I, 1966. pp. 183–96.

— Kerala and Madras: a Comparative Study of Ecology and Social Structure. *Ethnology* V (2), 1966.

— 'Agricultural Labour Unions: Some Socioeconomic and Political Considerations', in Kenneth David, ed., *The New Wind: Changing Identities in South Asia*. The Hague, Mouton, 1977.

— Agrarian Relations in Two Rice Regions of Kerala. *Economic and Political Weekly* Annual no. Feb. 1978.

— The Lessons and Non-Lessons of Kerala: Agricultural Labourers and Poverty. *Economic and Political Weekly*, Special no. Oct. 1980.

Mendelsohn, Oliver. The Collapse of the Indian National Congress. *Pacific Affairs* 51(1), 1978.

Menon, A. Sreedhara. *A Survey of Kerala History*. Kottayam, National Book Stall, 1967.

Menon, C. Achutha. *What Happened in Kerala: Review of the 30 Months of Namboodiripad Government*. New Delhi, CPI, 1969.

— After Land Reforms, What? *Dharani,* Special no. Nov. 1976.

Menon, K.P. Padmanabha. *A History of Kerala*. Ernakulam, Cochin Govt Press, 1924–37. 4 vols.

—*C. Sankaran Nair.* New Delhi, Ministry of Information and Broadcasting, Publications Division, 1971.

Menon, K.R. Class Character of State Power in India. *Social Scientist* (Tvm) 23, Oct, 1973.

Menon, P.K.K. *History of the Freedom Movement in Kerala.* Tvm, Govt of Kerala, 1972.

Menon, V.P. *The Story of the Integration of the Indian States.* London, Longman, 1956.

Miller, Eric J. Caste and Territory in Malabar. *American Anthropologist* LVI, 1954, pp. 410–20.

—'Village Structure in North Kerala', in M.N. Srinivas, ed., *India's Villages.* 2nd rev. edn. New Delhi, Asia Publishing House, 1961.

Miller, Roland E. *Mappila Muslims of Kerala.* New Delhi, Orient Longman, 1976.

Mitra, Ashok. The Kerala Elections: a Statistical Analysis. *Economic Weekly,* Special no. June 1960.

Moraes, Frank. *India Today.* New York, Macmillan, 1960.

Morris-Jones, W.H. *The Government and Politics of India.* 3rd rev. edn. London, Hutchinson, 1971.

—ed. *The Making of Politicians: Studies from Africa and Asia.* London, Athlone Press, 1976.

Moynihan, Daniel P. with Suzanne Weaver. *A Dangerous Place.* London, Secker & Warburg, 1979.

Muggeridge, Malcolm. *Chronicles of Wasted Time,* vol. II. London, Collins, 1973.

Mukherjee, Sadhan. *Who Really Aids India, USA or USSR? A Study in Contrast of Economic Assistance.* New Delhi, CPI, 1972.

Mullik, B.N. *My Years with Nehru 1948-64.* New Delhi, Allied Publishers, 1972.

Murthy, K.G. Krishna and G. Lakshmana Rao. *Political Preferences in Kerala.* New Delhi, Radha Krishna, 1968.

—and—'Muslim League and Communal Voting'. *Mainstream,* 27 Apr. 1968.

Nair, Balakrishnan. *Parliamentary Control over Administration.*Tvm, Kerala Academy of Political Science, 1973.

Nair, C. Gopalan. *The Moplah Rebellion 1921.* Calicut, n.p., 1923.

Nair, K. Karunakaran, ed. *Who is Who of Freedom Fighters in Kerala.* Tvm, Govt Press, 1975.

Nair, K. Ramachandran. *Industrial Relations in Kerala.* New Delhi, Sterling Publishers, 1973.

Nair, K. Sukumaran. *Administrative Co-ordination at State Level in India: a Study of the Government Secretariat and the Board of Revenue in Kerala.* Tvm, Kerala Academy of Political Science, 1975.

—*Rural Politics and Government in Kerala.* Tvm, Kerala Academy of Political Science, 1976.

Nair, P.R. Gopinathan. Education and Socio-economic Change in Kerala, 1793-1947. *Social Scientist* (Tvm) 44, Mar. 1976.

Nair, R. Ramakrishnan. *Constitutional Experiments in Kerala.* Tvm, Kerala Academy of Political Science, 1964.

—*How Communists Came to Power in Kerala.* Tvm, Kerala Academy of Political Science, 1965.

— *The Middle Class in Kerala.* Tvm, Kerala Academy of Political Science, 1974.

—and T.J. Nossiter. 'The Rules of the Electoral Game: Kerala 1970'. *South Asian Review* IV (3), 1971.

Namboodiripad, E.M.S. *A Short History of the Peasant Movement in Kerala.* Bombay, People's Publishing House, 1943.

—*Food in Kerala.* Bombay, People's Publishing House, 1944.

—*On The Agrarian Question in India.* Bombay, People's Publishing House, 1952.

— *The National Question in Kerala.* Bombay, People's Publishing House, 1952.

—Questions and Answers: Nationalities and the Right of Secession. *Crossroads*, 6 Sept. 1953.

—Stalin and Mao on the National Liberation Movement. *New Age* (monthly), Nov. 1953.

—Why no Socialism Now in India. *New Age* (monthly), Nov. 1953.

— *The Peasant in National Economic Reconstruction.* Delhi, People's Publishing House, 1954.

— *The Economic Problems of Kerala* (Malayalam). Tvm, Prabhat Book House, 1956.

—On Inner Party Struggle — Mao's Contribution. *New Age* (monthly), Mar. 1956.

— *The Mahatma and the Ism.* New Delhi, People's Publishing House, 1958.

—Six Main Reasons for Devicolam Victory. *New Age*, 1 June 1958.

— *Twenty-Eight Months in Kerala: a Retrospect.* New Delhi, People's Publishing House, Dec. 1959.

—The Way of a Revolutionary. *World Marxist R.* 6 (3), 1963.

—*Note for the Programme of the CPI.* New Delhi, 4 Windsor Place, 1964.

—*Revisionism and Dogmatism in the C.P.I.* New Delhi, New Age Press, 1965.

—*Economics and Politics of India's Socialist Pattern.* New Delhi, People's Publishing House, 1966.

—*Problems of National Integration.* Calcutta, National Book Agency, 1966.

—*What Really Happened in Kerala.* New Delhi, National Book Agency, 1966.

—*India under Congress Rule.* Calcutta, National Book Agency, 1967.

—*Kerala, Yesterday, Today and Tomorrow.* 2nd edn. Calcutta, National Book Agency, 1968.

—*Atmakatha* (Malayalam). Tvm, Deshabhimani Book House, 1970.

—The Long Revolution. *Social Scientist* (Tvm) 24, Sept. 1973.

— *Indian Planning in Crisis*. Tvm, Chintha, 1974.

— *Conflicts and Crisis, Political India: 1974*. New Delhi, Sangam Books Orient Longman, 1974.

— Class Character of the Nationalist Movement. *Social Scientist* (Tvm) 37, Aug. 1975.

— Marxism and India. *Sunday Standard* (Madras), 4 Apr. 1976.

— Economic Backwardness of Harijans in Kerala. *Social Scientist* (Tvm) 48, July 1976.

— Mao Tse-tung's Contribution to Theory and Tactics of Revolution. *Social Scientist* (Tvm) 50, Sept. 1976.

— 'Castes, Classes and Parties in Modern Political Development with Special Reference to Kerala', in *1st World Conference on Malayalam, Kerala Culture and Development, Abstracts of Papers,* Section III: 'History'. Tvm, Kerala University, 1977; reprinted in *Social Scientist* (Tvm) 64, Nov: 1977.

— New Phase of Political Development in India. *Social Scientist* (Tvm) 86, Sept. 1979.

Narain, Iqbal, ed. *State Politics in India*. Meerut, Saipur, 1967.

Narayan [Nambudiripad], Kattumadam. Nambudiris. *Illustrated Weekly of India*, 5 Mar. 1972.

Nayar, P.K.B. *Development of Kerala: Problems and Promises*. Tvm, U. of Kerala, Dept of Sociology, 1972.

Nayar, V.K.S. 'Communal Interest Groups in Kerala', in D.E. Smith, ed., *South Asian Politics and Religion*. Princeton, NJ, Princeton UP, 1966.

— *Governmental Instability in Kerala*. *Indian J. of Political Science* XXVII (1-2), Mar.-Apr. 1966.

— 'Kerala Politics since 1947: Community Attitudes', in Iqbal Narain, ed., *State Politics in India*. Meerut, Saipur, 1967.

— 'Parties and Instability in Kerala', in Iqbal Narain, ed., *State Politics in India*. Meerut, Saipur, 1967.

Noble, William A., ed. *Kerala State, India: Bibliography* [European languages]. Columbus, Mo., U. of Missouri, Geography Dept, 1970.

Nossiter, Bernard D. *Soft State: a Newspaperman's Chronicle of India*. New York, Harper & Row, 1970.

Nossiter, T.J. 'Communist Leadership in Kerala: the Business of the Many, the Art of the Few', in B.N. Pandey, ed., *Leadership in South Asia*. New Delhi, Vikas, 1977.

— State-Level Politics in India, 1975-1977: the Emergency and its Aftermath in Kerala. *J. of Commonwealth & Comparative Politics* XVI (1), 1978.

— Coalition Governments, Kerala 1969-75 (Parts 1-3). *Focus* (Tvm, Legislative Assembly) VII, 1977-8.

— with R. Ramakrishnan Nair, 'The Rules of the Electoral Game: Kerala 1970'. *South Asian R*. IV (3), 1971.

Omvedt, Gail. 'Non-Brahmans and Communists in Bombay.' *Economic and Political Weekly*, 21 & 28 Apr. 1972.

Oommen, M.A. *Land Reforms and Socio-Economic Change in Kerala*. Madras, Christian Literature Society, 1971.

—*Small Industry in Indian Economic Growth: a Case Study of Kerala*. Tvm, Research Publications, 1972.

—*Study on Land Reforms*. New Delhi, OUP/IBA, 1973.

—Rise and Growth of Banking in Kerala. *Social Scientist* (Tvm) 51, Oct. 1976.

Oommen, T.K. Agrarian Tension in a Kerala District: an Analysis. *Indian J. of Industrial Relations* 7 (2), 1971.

— Agrarian Legislations and Movements as Sources of Change: the Case of Kerala. *Economic and Political Weekly*, 4 Oct. 1975.

Overstreet, Gene D. Soviet and Communist Policy. *J. of Politics* 20 (1), 1958.

—The Communists and India. *Foreign Policy B.* 39 (4), 1959.

—and Marshall Windmiller. *Communism in India*. Berkeley, U. of California P., 1960.

Pachaur, R.K. *Energy and Economic Development in India*. New York, Praeger, 1977.

Palmer, Norman D. India in 1976: the Politics of Depoliticisation. *Asian Survey* XVII (2), 1977.

Panikkar, K.M. *Malabar and the Portuguese*. Bombay, D.B. Taraporevala 1929.

—*Malabar and the Dutch*. Bombay, D.B. Taraporevala, 1931.

The Foundations of New India. London, Allen & Unwin, 1963.

Panikkar, K.N. Agrarian Legislation and Social Classes: a Case Study of Malabar. *Economic and Political Weekly*, 27 May 1978.

Panikkar, P. Sukumara. 'The Muslim League in Kerala'. Unpublished Ph.D. thesis, U. of Kerala, Tvm, 1977.

Parakal, Pauly V. *CIA Dagger Against India*. New Delhi, CPI, 1973.

Paranjape, H.K. Centre-State Relations in Planning. *Indian J. of Public Administration* XVI (1), 1970.

Park, R.L. Indian Election Results. *Far Eastern Survey* 7, May 1952.

Pathun, S.G. *The Syrian Christian Churches of Kerala*. London, Asia Publishing House, 1963.

Phadnis, Urmila. *Towards the Integration of Indian States 1919-1947*. London, Asia Publishing House, 1968.

Pillai, K. Padmanabha. *Red Interlude in Kerala*. Tvm, Kerala Pradesh Congress Committee, 1959.

Pillai, Thakazhi Sivasankara (trans. M.A. Shakoor). *Two Measures of Rice*. Bombay, Jaico, 1967.

Pillai, V. Gangadharan. *State Enterprises in Kerala*. Tvm, Kerala Academy of Political Science, 1970.

Pillai, V.R. and P.G.K. Panikar. *Land Reclamation in Kerala*. London, Asia Publishing House, 1965.

Podipara, Placid J. *The Thomas Christians*. London, Darton, Longman & Todd, 1970.

Poplai, S.L., ed. *1962 General Elections in India*. New Delhi, Allied Publishers, 1962.

Prakash, B.A. 'Impact of Foreign Remittances: a Case Study of Chavakkad Village in Kerala'. *Economic and Political Weekly*, 8 July 1978.

Pullapilly, Cyriac K. The Izhavas of Kerala and their Historic Struggle for Acceptance in the Hindu Society. *J. of Asian and African Studies* XI (1 & 2), 1976.

Pye, Lucian W., ed. *Communications and Political Development*. Princeton, NJ, Princeton UP, 1963.

Pylee, M.V. and N.C. John. Fourth General Elections in Kerala. *Political Science R.* (Jaipur) VI (3 & 4) and VII (1 & 2), 1967 and 1968.

Rajendran, G. *The Ezhava Community and Kerala Politics*. Tvm, Kerala Academy of Political Science, 1974.

Ram, Mohan. *Indian Communism: Split within a Split*. New Delhi, Vikas, 1969.
—*Maoism in India*. New Delhi, Vikas, 1971.

Ranadive, B.T. Lessons of Kerala, *New Age* (monthly), Sept. 1959.
—Eurocommunism and the State. *Social Scientist* (Tvm) 75, Oct. 1978.

Rao, G. Lakshmana and R. Seethalakshmi. Socio-Economic Support Bases of Communists in Kerala. *Indian J. of Political Science* XXIX (4), 1968.

Rao, G. Lakshmana and Leonard Cane. Religious Parties in Kerala: a Multiple Regression Analysis. *Political Scientist* (Ranchi) VIII-XI, Jan.-June 1972 to July-Dec. 1974.

Rao, K.V. *Parliamentary Democracy of India*. Calcutta, World Press, 1961.

Rao, M.B., ed. *Documents of the History of the Communist Party of India*, vol. VII (1948-50). New Delhi, CPI, 1976.

Rao, M.S.A. *Social Change in Malabar*. Bombay, Allied Publishers, 1957.

Rasul, M.A. *A History of the All India Kisan Sabha*. Calcutta, National Book Agency, 1974.

Ravindran, T.K. *Vaikkam Satyagraha and Gandhi*. Trichur, Sri Narayana Inst. of Social and Cultural Development, 1975.

Ray, K.N., P.G.K. Panikar, and T.N. Krishan. *Some Perspectives on Planning and Development with Particular Reference to Kerala*. Tvm, Centre for Development Studies, 1972.

Retzlaff, Ralph. 'Revisionism and Dogmatism in the Communist Party of India', in R.A. Scalapino, ed., *The Communist Revolution in Asia*. Berkeley, Calif., Prentice Hall, 1965.

Riley, Parkes. 'Poverty, Literacy, and the Communist Vote in India'. *Asian Survey*, XV (6), 1975.

Rose, Saul. *Socialism in Southern Asia*. London, OUP for Royal Inst. of International Affairs, 1959.

Roy, Subodh, ed. *Communism in India: Unpublished Documents, 1925-1934*. Calcutta, CPI, 1972.
—*Communism in India: Unpublished Documents, 1934-1945*. Calcutta, CPI, 1976.

Rudra, Ashok. The Left Front Government. *Economic and Political Weekly*, 3 Sept. 1977.

Rumbold, Sir Algernon. *Watershed in India 1914-1922*. London, Athlone Press, 1979.

Saradamoni, K. Land Reforms: Next Step in Kerala. *Mainstream,* 30 Apr. 1977.

Sen, Bhowani and Mohit Sen. *National Democracy and People's Democracy: Essays in Honour of Ninetieth Birthday of Comrade Georgi Dimitrov*. New Delhi, CPI, 1972.

Sen, Mohit. Kerala and Amritsar. *New Age* (monthly), July 1959.

Shea, T.W. Barriers to Economic Development in Traditional Societies: Malabar, a Case Study. *J. of Economic History* XIX (4), 1959.

Shivakumar, J. Union-State Financial Relations. *Indian J. of Public Administration* XVI (2), 1970.

Singh, Hari Kishore. *A History of the Praja Socialist Party 1934-59*. Lucknow, Narendra Prakashan, 1959.

Singh, Jitendra. *Communist Rule in Kerala*. New Delhi, Diwan Chand Information Centre, 1959.

Sinha, K.C. Communist-led Ministries in West Bengal and Kerala. *Current History* 54 (320), 1968.

Somjee, A.H. *Democracy and Political Change in Village India*. New Delhi, Orient Longman, 1971.

Spate, O.H.K. *India and Pakistan: a General and Regional Geography*. London, Methuen, 1954.

Stokes, Eric. *The Peasant and the Raj*. Cambridge, CUP, 1978.

Swai, Bonaventura. Notes on the Colonial State with Reference to Malabar in the Eighteenth and Nineteenth Centuries. *Social Scientist* (Tvm) 72, 1978.

Swearingen, R., ed. *Leaders of the Communist World*. New York, Free Press, 1971.

Swee, Goh Keng. 'Nature and Appeals of Communism in Non-Communist Countries', in John Wilkes, ed., *Communism in Asia*. Sydney, Angus & Robertson, 1967.

Taub, Richard P. *Bureaucrats Under Stress, Administrators and Administration in an Indian State*. Berkeley, U. of California P., 1969.

Thomas, Cyriac. 'The Church and Politics in Kerala'. Unpublished Ph. D. thesis, U. of Kerala, Tvm, 1975.

Thomas, P.T. *Sabarimalai and its Sastha*. Madras, Christian Literature Society, 1973.

Tissérant, Eugène. *Eastern Christianity in India: a History of the Syro-Malabar Church from the Earliest Times to the Present Day*. London, Longman, Green, 1957.

Turlach, Manfred. *Kerala: Politisch-Soziale Struktur und Entwicklung eines Indischen Bundeslandes*. Wiesbaden, Otto Harrasowitz, 1970.

United News of India, Research Bureau. *India Today*. New Delhi, Ranjit, 1970.

Unniraja, C. Fifth Kerala Communist Conference. *New Age* (monthly), Jan. 1960.

Vadakkan, Joseph. *A Priest's Encounter with Revolution*. Madras, Christian Literature Society for Christian Inst. for the Study of Religion and Society, Bangalore, 1974.

Varghese, T.C. *Agrarian Change and Economic Consequences: Land Tenures in Kerala 1850-1960*. Calcutta, Allied Publishers, 1970.

Varughese, K.V. 'The Seven Party United Front Government in Kerala', in Saral K. Chatterji, ed., *The Coalition Government*. Madras, Christian Literature Society for Christian Inst. for the Study of Religion and Society, Bangalore, 1974.

Varkey, Ouseph. The CPI-Congress Alliance in India. *Asian Survey* XIX (9), Sept. 1979.

Velayudhan, R. *Kerala: the Red Rain Land*. New Delhi, Indian Inst. of Social Affairs, 1958.

Visalakshi, N.R. President's Rule in Kerala. *Indian J. of Political Science* XXVII (1-2), 1966.

—*Administration of Village Panchayats in Kerala*. Tvm, Educational Supplies Depot, 1967.

Warriner, D. *Land Reform in Principle and Practice*. Oxford, Clarendon Press, 1969.

Washbrook, David. *The Emergence of Provincial Politics: the Madras Presidency 1870-1920*. Cambridge, CUP, 1976.

Wavell, Archibald Percival, Ist Earl. *Wavell: the Viceroy's Journal,* ed. Penderel Moon. London, OUP, 1973.

Weiner, Myron. *Party Politics in India*. Princeton, NJ, Princeton UP, 1957.

—The 1977 Parliamentary Elections in India. *Asian Survey* 17 (7), 1977.

Wood, Conrad. Historical Background of the Moplah Rebellion. *Social Scientist* (Tvm) 25, Aug. 1974.

—The First Moplah Rebellion against British Rule in Malabar. *Modern Asian Studies* 10 (4), 1976.

—Moplah Outbreaks: a Discussion Contribution. *J. of Asian Studies* XXXVI (2), 1977.

—'Peasant Revolt: an Interpretation of Moplah Violence in the Nineteenth and Twentieth Centuries', in Clive Dewey and A.G. Hopkins, eds., *The Imperial Impact: Studies in the Economic History of Africa and India*. London, Athlone Press, 1978.

Wood, John B. Observations on the Indian Communist Party Split. *Pacific Affairs* 38 (1), 1965.

Woodcock, George. *Kerala: a Portrait of the Malabar Coast*. London, Faber & Faber, 1967.

Wright, Theodore P., Jr. The Muslim League in South India since Independence: a Study in Minority Group Political Strategies. *American Political Science R.* LX (3), 1966.

— 'The Effectiveness of Muslim Representation in India', in D.E. Smith, ed., *South Asian Religion and Politics*. Princeton, NJ, Princeton UP, 1966.

Yesudas, R.N. *People's Revolt in Travancore: a Backward Class Movement for Social Freedom*. Tvm, Kerala Hist. Society, 1975.

Zagoria, D.S. The Ecology of Peasant Communism in India. *American Political Science R.* LXV (1), 1971.

— A Note on Landlessness, Literacy and Agrarian Communism in India. *Archives européennes de sociologie* 13 (2), 1972.

— The Social Bases of Communism in Kerala and West Bengal: a Study in Contrast. *Problems of Communism* XXII (1), 1973.

Zinkin, Taya. *Reporting India*. London, Chatto & Windus, 1962.

5. Newspapers and Periodical Literature

Blitz; *Chandrika* (Malayalam); *Chintha* (Malayalam); *Commerce*; *Crossroads*; *Deccan Herald*; *Deepika* (Malayalam); *Deshabhimani* (Malayalam); *Dharani*; *Eastern Economist*; *Economic and Political Weekly* (until 1965, *Economic Weekly*); *Hindu*; *Hindustan Times*; *Illustrated Weekly of India*; *Indian Express* (Madurai edition to 1974; Cochin edition from 1974); *Janayugam* (Malayalam); *Kerala Kaumudi* (Malayalam); *Kerala Mail*; *Liberation*; *Link*; *Madras Mail*; *Mainstream*; *Malayala Manorama* (Malayalam); *Mass Line* (Cochin); *Mathrubhumi* (Malayalam); *New Age* (weekly and monthly); *New Kerala*; *People's Democracy*; *Quest*; *Seminar*; *Social Scientist* (Tvm); *The Statesman*; *Thought*; *Times of India*; *World Marxist Review*.

Index

Adikhari, G., 185

Adiyodi, Dr K.G., 231 n.53, 269

Administrative Reforms Committee, Kerala (1957), 166-7

Agrarian relations, 47-8; bill to reform (1957-61), 149-53, 292; and Congress growth in Malabar, 67-8; courts and land reform, 151, 292, 296; and Congress Socialist Party, 72-3; Kuttanad, 337; land ceilings, 294; Land Reforms Act (1963), 192, 292-3, 292 n.133; Land Reforms (Amendment) Act (1969), 218, 220, 222, 247, 290-7, 300-1, 306-7; Land Tribunals, 296-7; Palghat District, 335-7; and tenures, 51; *see also* Agricultural labour; *Kudikidappukars*

Agricultural labour, 30, 32, 47, 52; and Agricultural Workers' Act (1974), 301-3; in censuses, 320; CPI Ministry and, 150-1; position of, 301; voting patterns, 335; wages of, 150 n.53, 302

Agriculture, 14, 52-5, 303-6; and plans, 280-1; State and collective farms, 305

Aiyar, Sir C.P. Ramaswami: attempt to assassinate, 92; career, 79-80; character, 119 n.40; and education policy, 154; and Punnapra-Vayalar Rising, 90-2; and Travancore, 80-2, 89, 92

Alleppey District: agricultural labour in, 302; coir workers' strike (1937), 81-2, (1946), 90; and CPI split, 186; and CPM, 319, 326;

and land reform, 295; voting in 1980, 329

All-India Trade Union Congress, 59-60, 159-62, 229, 253, 274; and CPI split in Kerala, 185

All-Malabar Peasants' Union, 74, 84

All-Travancore Trades Union Congress, 85

Andhra Pradesh 119, 202-3, 250; communism in, 9, 86-8; elections and CPI (1955), 116

Antony, A.K., 229, 233, 235, 274, 299-300, 325, 329

Aryan, A.V. 365 n.48

Backward Classes Reservation Commission, Kerala (1967), 29, 33-7, 290-1

Balaram, N.E., 253, 259 n.65

Bangla Congress, 203

Bava, E.K. Imbichi, 216, 220, 246, 248-9

Cannanore District: and CPM Ultras, 249; and feudalism, 72; and pepper, 54, 57; voting pattern in (1957-60), 134; (1965-70) 323, 335, 346-9

Cashew: Development Corporation, 305; exports, 55; factories, 58, 233; industry and workers' political leanings, 55, 194, 323, 339; strike in factories (1963), 194; yield, 303

Centre for Development Studies (Trivandrum), 37, 267, 279, 299

Centre of Indian Trade Unions, 60, 255

Centre-State relations, 6-9, 246; financial, 264-8; and land reform, 294, 299

Chacko, P.T., 163, 196, 276, 292 n.133; and Indian Administrative Service, 166

Chander, Jose, 152

Chandrika, 70

Chetty, Sir R.K. Shanmughom, 82

Chirakkal Taluk, 73, 97 n.23, 93 n.107

Civil Disobedience Movement: first (1930), 70; second (1932), 71

Cochin Congress, 83, 148

Cochin State: agrarian relations in, 15, 17, 83; early political movement, 77-8, 82-3; elections (1948), 108, 111, 113; and Indian independence, 92-3; model state, 15; and United Kerala, 94

Coir manufacturing. communism and socialism, 90, 337-8; exports, 55; unionism and, 60, 90; working conditions, 58-9, 160-1

Commission for Reservation of Seats in Education Institutions, Kerala (1965), 37

Communalism: and Moplah Rising, 69; Tellicherry (1971), 227; and toleration in Kerala, 21

Communist League (Trivandrum, 1931), 65, 75, 82

Communist Ministry, 1957-9: administration and reform, 162-7; agrarian reform, 149-53; amnesty, 158; Andhra Rice Deal, 163; assessment, 167-70; Catholic-Nair alliance against, 156; cell courts, 157; and churches, 144; and co-operatives, 163-4; alleged corruption, 163; educational reform, 153-6; formation of, 147-9, and Indian Administrative Service, 164-5; and industry, 281; Labour Contract Societies, 163-4; law and order under, 146-7, 158-9; and Liberation Struggle, 147; local govern-

ment and panchayats, 167; and mass party 143; MLAs as legislators and representatives, 167-9; and Nehru, 146-7; and party discipline, 157; party differences concerning, 142, 145-7; police policy of, 157; party and state apparatus, 145; trade unions and strikes, 159-62

Communist Revolutionary Party, 222, 251, 358-9

Congress (I), 236, 329; and agrarian classes, 335, 345-6; and community, 343-5; inter-generational political movement, 356; trends in support (1977-80), 330

Congress Radicals, 233

Congress Socialist Party in Kerala: Cochin, 83; development of, 72-7; and elections, *KPCC, 1940,* 66-8, *Madras, 1937,* 74; and Gandhian Congressmen, 66-7, 71-2; and marxism, 75-6; and Muslims, 70, 74; and office, 76-7; organization, 74; and peasants, 72-3

Congress (Urs), 259, 329

Co-operative societies, 163-4; and agriculture, 306; record in Kerala, 270-2,

Co-ordination Committee, 217, 219, 224, 227, 229, 249, 263; and decision-making, 273-5

Corruption: 216, 231 n.53, 307; and co-operatives, 271; and CPI Ministry, 163; and Indian Administrative Service, 276; and Maxi Front, 220 n.25, 230; and Ministers, 276-7; and tax evasion, 269; and UF Ministry, 216-18, 220

CPI before split: (1) All-India: Amritsar Congress (1958), 105, 143-4; Calcutta Theses, 87; and CPSU, 105-6, 181, 366; Congresses of: *1948,* 87; *1953,* 88, 107, 118, 120; *1956,* 88, 120-1; *1958,* 105; *1961,* 181-2; and

District, 55-6; and CPC, 248-9; Centrists in, 248 ff., 358-9; and communal reservation, 290-1; community in selection of election candidates, 273; Congresses of: *1964*, 183-4; *1972*, 255; and CPSU, 202; discipline in, 256; and elections, *1965*, 187 ff., *1967*, 206-11, *1970*, 221 ff., *1977*, 235, 319, 326; electoral support for, 318, 323, 325-7, 330-4; and Emergency, 258; Excess Land agitation, 297; free of foreign guidance, 366; government portfolios, 264; 'immediate relief to the people', 244, 247-8; Indian 'crisis' of 1972-5, 255-8; and JP Movement, 230; and Kerala Congress, 256-8; and land reform implementation, 295; and LDF, 236-7; 'liberation struggle', (1974), 230, 256-7; Maxi Front Ministry, 227-31, 255-6; Mini Front Ministries, 219-20, 219 n.21, 225-6; MLAs suspended, 220; and Muslim League 187; peasantry, 334-5, 372; political line, 201; and representative democracy, 242-3, 370; Sino-Indian conflict, 192; and State-level power, 243-5; UF, formation of, 204-6; UFL, (1964), 187; Ultras in, 243 ff., united front from below, 242; and voting intentions of youth, 353-5; *see also* United Front Ministry
CPSU, 105-6, 110, 121, 145-6, 179, 180-1, 200-1, 252-3, 254, 259, 366
Cranganore, 78, 111

Damodaran, K., 72, 75, 108, 118, 142, 153, 162, 166
Damodaran, Nettur P, 290
Dange, S.A., 75, 109, 145, 162, 200, 201 n.4, 259, 372; *Letters*, 183-4
Dasgupta, Biplab, 319, 334-5

Decentralization, 247
Deepika, 144, 155-6
Democratic Front (1970), 221-2
Des(h)abhimani, 85, 93, 108, 250
Dharmangadan, B., 321, 349
District Development Councils (Kerala), 167, 248
Divakaran, T.K., 220, 288

Elections: *Cochin, 1948*, 108, 111, 113; *India, 1934 and 1945*, 70, *1951-2*, 107, *1971*, 225-6, *1977*, 233, 326, 334, *1980*, 330, 334; *Kerala, 1957*, 122 ff., *1960*, 122 ff. *1965*, 186, 188-94, *1967*, 206-11, *1970*, 220-4, 323-4, *1972-3*, 228, *1975*, 231, *1977*, 233-5, 273 n.36, 319, 326-7, 334, *1980*, 236-7, 329-30, 334; *Malabar, 1946*, 93, *1951-2, 116-17, 1954*, 93, *1951-2*, 116-17, *1954*, 118; *Travancore, 1948*, 110-13; *Travancore-Cochin, 1951-2*, 109, 111-15, *1954*, 109, 115; candidate selection for Assembly elections, 273 n. 35; and coalition-building, 329-30; correlates of voting in Kerala, 339-49; District analysis, 319; geography of, 323; municipal, 187; Namboodiripad elected to Madras legislature (1939), 76; to student union executives, 130, 247 n. 19, 360
Emergency, State of, 286; and communists 258-9; effects in Kerala 231-4; and state elections, 326
Eurocommunism, 5, 367
Ezhavas, 30-2, 77, 290; and communism, 78, 133-4; and Congress split, 186, 195; education, 154; and land, 48; and Travancore politics, 80-81

Fertilisers and Chemicals of Travancore, Ltd, 265
Fic, Victor M., 124-6, 140, 144, 187, 321

422 *Index*

Menon, Dr Konnanath Balakrishna, 85, 101 n.67

Menon, P. Balachandra, 271

Menon, Panampilly Govinda, 120, 154, 157

Menon, V.K.N., 166

Menon, V.R. Krishna, 225-6

Mini Front, First Ministry: and by-elections, 220; confidence motion, 220; and Congress, 219-21; and CPM, 219-20; dissolution, 221; formation of, 217-19; and land reform, 295-6

Mini Front, Second Ministry: election performance, 222; formation of, 221; ministry, 224-6; and panchayats, 290

Ministries in Kerala *see* Communist Ministry; United Front Ministry; Mini Front, First Ministry; Mini Front, Second Ministry; Maxi Front Ministry

Mitra, Ashok, 130

Moplahs: 14-15, 23-58, 228; communalist attack on (1971), 227; and communism, 25, 204, 325; and Kerala election (1965), 189, 195; in government service, 205; job reservation, 290; and Malappuram, 217; 'Outrages', 24; Rising of, 24, 68-70, 227; social change and politics, 228; voting of, 325

Morris-Jones, Prof. W.H., 8, 319, 334-5

Mulla, Justice Anand Narain, 245, 287

Mundassery, Joseph, 34, 95, 228 n.38; and Kerala education, 154-6

Murthy, Krishna, K.G., 320, 335

Muslim Education Society, 228

Muslim League, 25, 116, 123, 127, 187-9, 194, 218, 320; and CPM, 229; and Congress 226-9; dissension in, 228-9; and Mrs Gandhi, 221; ideology of, 252, 272; and Inner Front (1967), 215; and land reform, 251-2, 295; and Malap-puram, 217, 251-2; Opposition Muslim League, 233-4, 246; split in, 229; and United Front (1966), 204; and voting, 323

Nairs: elections, *1957*, 126-7, 134; *1965*, 194-5; and job reservation, 273; in Kuttanad, 53; and land, 22, 48; and Malabar politics, 29, 67; and Nair Service Society, 28-9; occupation and income, 28-9; and Socialist Party, 113; social organisation, 22, 27-8; Travancore politics, 80-1; and voting intentions of youth, 353

Nair, Chandrashekhar, 157

Nair, C.K. Govindan, 71, 84, 196

Nair, K. Kelappan, 71, 75, 116, 118

Nair K.P. Madhavan, 83

Nair, M.N. Govindan, 126, 180, 194, 215, 219, 237, 246, 274, 297, 334; and CPI Ministry, 141, 143-6, 166; and Nair Service Society, 147, 153, 157

Nair, N. Sreekantan, 85, 90-1, 161, 164, 274, 334

Nair, P.K.B., 301-2

Nair, P.K. Vasudevan, 235-6, 291

Nair, R. Ramakrishnan, 124

Nair, Sardar Chandroth Kunhiraman, 99 n, 36

Nair Service Society, 28-9, 34, 88, 92, 126-7, 195, 272; and educational reform, 156; elections, *1957*, 126-7, *1967*, 211, 272; and land reform, 152-3, 292 n.133

Namboodiri Brahmins, 26-7, 48

Namboodiripad, E.M.S., 71-2, 74-6, 84, 167, 191, 202, 230-1, 235-6; allegations against, 217, 248; character, 147-8; and CPC, 110, 249; and communal factor, 321; and co-ordination committee, 273; and CPI Ministry, 140-1, 144-7; and Czechoslovakia, 251; detention of, 182; and election (*1965*), 189; and *gherao*, 237 n.2; as ideologist and thinker, 88,